1704

TENTH EDITION

PUBLIC ADMINISTRATION AND PUBLIC AFFAIRS

Nicholas Henry

Georgia Southern University

PEARSON

Prentice
Hall

Upper Saddle River, New Jersey 07458

Library of Congress Cataloging-in-Publication Data

Henry, Nicholas
   Public administration and public affairs / Nicholas Henry.—10th ed.
      p.   cm.
   Includes bibliographical references and index.
   ISBN 0-13-222297-3
   1. Public administration.   I. Title.
JF1351.H45 2006
351.73—dc22

2006023640

Editorial Director: Charlyce Jones Owen
Executive Editor: Dickson Musslewhite
Editorial Assistant: Jennifer Murphy
Associate Editor: Rob DeGeorge
Marketing Manager: Emily Cleary
Marketing Assistant: Jennifer Lang
Director of Production and Manufacturing: Barbara Kittle
Managing Editor: Lisa Iarkowski
Production Liaison: Joe Scordato
Production Assistant: Marlene Gassler
Prepress and Manufacturing Manager: Nick Sklitsis
Prepress and Manufacturing Buyer: Mary Ann Gloriande
Manager, Cover Visual Research and Permissions: Karen Sanatar
Cover Art Director: Jayne Conte
Cover Design: Bruce Kenselaar
Composition/Full Service Project Management:
      Integra/Sowmya Balaraman
Printer/Binder: R. R. Donnelley & Sons, Inc.
Cover Printer: Phoenix Color Corp.

Credits and acknowledgments borrowed from other sources and reproduced, with permission, in this textbook appear on appropriate page within text.

Pearson Education LTD.
Pearson Education Singapore, Pte. Ltd
Pearson Education, Canada, Ltd
Pearson Education–Japan
Pearson Education Australia PTY, Limited

Pearson Education North Asia Ltd
Pearson Educación de Mexico, S.A. de C.V.
Pearson Education Malaysia, Pte. Ltd
Pearson Education, Upper Saddle River, New Jersey

10 9 8 7 6 5 4 3 2 1
ISBN: 0-13-222297-3

*To my late father, Samuel Houston Henry,
whose elegance, integrity, and love
lit my life.*

Contents

Preface

Public administration. The words conjure nightmares of green eyeshades; faceless, pitiless, and powerful bureaucrats; and a misdirected, perhaps misanthropic, governmental juggernaut crushing all who question it.

Public affairs. The phrase connotes visions of fearless and free debate; ennobling social missions; and the surging sweep of civic life.

For both public administration and public affairs, the reality lies somewhere in between. Public administration always has been and always will be the grubbing, tedious execution of public policies, but it also always has been and always will be an endeavor of high drama and colossal consequences. Public affairs always has been and always will be the ultimate and finest expression of democracy, but it also always has been and always will be a demeaning chore of cutting sleazy deals and micromanaging corrupt and rapacious special interests.

We entitle this book *Public Administration and Public Affairs*, because it examines the realities underlying the stereotypes that are brought out by both phrases. *Public Administration and Public Affairs* is, at root, about the public interest. It explains both the means used to fulfill the public interest and the human panoply that is the public interest.

The tenth edition of a book is always worthy of note, if, for no other reason, because its editions have entered into the double digits. With this edition, *Public Administration and Public Affairs* enters that happy realm. We think that it has done so principally because it simply keeps up with the tumultuous world of public administration and public affairs (a variation, perhaps, of Woody Allen's observation that much of success is due to simply showing up), and it reports that tumult in a reasonably engaging manner.

Over the preceding three decades or so, *Public Administration and Public Affairs*, despite its clear orientation toward U.S. readers, has been translated and published in Chinese, Japanese, Romanian, and portions of it in Spanish. There is also an Indian edition and other national editions in English.

We relate this polyglot publishing history to demonstrate that, with accelerating appreciation, public administration is seen around the globe as central to "good government," and good government is seen by the world's people as central to the good life. As with its preceding editions, the tenth edition of *Public Administration and Public Affairs* portrays a discipline and a profession that are increasingly recognized by all citizens in all nations as vital to their lives, their liberty, and their pursuit of happiness.

Readers of past editions of this book will notice far more heads and subheads in the tenth edition. We think that they help clarify discussions and organize concepts more crisply.

Past users will also find a trove of new material. In fact, the tenth edition is the most thoroughly revised edition yet. Some of the new, seriously revised, or significantly expanded discussions in this edition are listed in rough order of their appearance, as follows:

- The resurrection of the "Good Government" movement.
- Vernon, California: A case of unconstrained public administration.
- Americans' experiences with their public administrators.
- Knowledge management, and the importance of the bureaucrat in assuring that public policy is made with full and accurate information.
- The introduction of a new paradigm of public administration: Paradigm 6, Governance. After more than three decades of new editions, this is the first time that a new paradigm has been added.
- The decline of government as the employer of choice for public administrators, and the rise of the independent sector.
- The rise of networked public administration.
- Motivator factors in organizations.
- The moral significance of organizations in society.
- "Who Must Be Sacrificed?" in organizations.
- "Social Tests" for organizations.
- An expanded treatment of organizational intelligence.
- New case studies of organizational dynamics, including examples drawn from the American experience in Iraq.
- New case studies of "groupthink" in organizational decision making.
- How public organizations change and adapt.
- Dramatic new figures illustrating the splintered accountability, bureaucratization, and red tape that are endemic to the public sector.
- A new section on the "stopping power" of the bureaucrat.
- The irony and the failure of governmental reorganization.
- The differing behavior of boards of directors in the public, private, and nonprofit sectors.
- The penetrating impact of the environment on the public agency.
- Why governments resist change.

- The unique behavior of nonprofit organizations.
- Differences in leadership behavior, and the different meanings of successful leadership, in the public and private sectors,
- New insights and examples on the problems of privacy *versus* policy in public information systems.
- What happens when data matching fails? The case of a child predator.
- The USA Patriot Act of 2002, the Real ID Act of 2005, and privacy officers.
- New trends in computer hacking and databank security.
- Governments' progress and failure in the management of information technology.
- The pervasive and beneficial impact of electronic government.
- A significantly expanded treatment of political corruption, including new examples drawn from the New York City schools, Alabama local government, the Pentagon, and school districts.
- The useful role that performance measures and program evaluations play in detecting corruption, and their limited usefulness in eradicating corruption.
- The New Public Management as public administration's latest iteration of the historic public productivity movement.
- Governments' response to Hurricane Katrina as a compelling example of why the New Public Management is needed and relevant.
- Performance measurement and public program evaluation.
- A major and important addition is that of public finance, which provides wholly new and extensive material on the price that Americans are willing to pay for their governments; governments' use of general and special funds; the income, sales, property, and other taxes; other sources of governmental revenues; what policy areas that each level of government spends its money on; tax reform; Social Security and Medicare; the future of Social Security; intergovernmental revenue and own source revenue; the role of the federal government in the national economy; supply side economics; fiscal and monetary policies; and federal tax cuts, borrowing, deficits, debt, and surpluses.
- New examples of how agencies acquire budgets from legislatures.
- The deepening crisis in the traditional merit system, and governments' slow abandonment of the merit principle.
- The reform of public human resource management.

- Public pay and job security in comparison to the private sector.
- Political executives and the newly understood and vital role that governmental experience plays in agency performance.
- The politicization of the Federal Emergency Management Agency, and its collapse during Hurricane Katrina.
- Governments' move toward pay for performance.
- The latest Supreme Court rulings on affirmative action.
- Facts about cultural and sexual bias in testing.
- The progress of public employees of color, women, and older or disabled Americans in securing jobs and promotions in governments.
- Strategic planning and scenario planning in governments.
- The selling of public assets.
- Trends in federal privatization, including new directions set by the Federal Activities Inventory Act, the rise of competitive sourcing and federal service contracts, and new information about federal privatization personnel.
- Lobbyland: The rise of lobbying, special interests, revolving doors, and big money.
- New cases in federal contracting incompetence, including contractors in Iraq, among other examples.
- New privatization developments in the states.
- Twenty-year trends of local governments contracting with private companies, nonprofit organizations, and other governments to implement public policy.
- Characteristics of local governments that privatize services.
- Business is not necessarily better: The case for competition in improving governmental performance.
- Public authorities and special districts, their differences and similarities.
- Public enterprises, government corporations, government-sponsored enterprises, and other quasi governments.
- Financial fears and government-sponsored enterprises
- The independent sector and its role in governance.
- The ups and downs of federal fiscal support for states and communities.
- The flypaper effect of intergovernmental grants.
- Interstate compacts, multistate legal action, and uniform state laws.

- Characteristics of local governments that enter into intergovernmental agreements.
- An expansion, due to popular demand, of the box, entitled "A Load of Local Governments" in Chapter 12, providing even more figures and factoids about counties, municipalities, townships, school districts, and special districts.
- The rise of ethics in the public sector.
- Ethics and the effective organization.
- The affects of philosophy on public policy.

Also revised in the tenth edition are the five extensive appendices that have made *Public Administration and Public Affairs* a useful reference work for students, professors, and professionals alike.

Appendix A lists information sources, journals, and organizations by subfield. It is designed to facilitate the reader's ability to identify resources that are available in his or her particular area of interest and draws its listing of information sources, journals, and organizations from the three more extensive appendices (that is, Appendices B, C, and D) that follow.

Appendix B lists and annotates bibliographies, encyclopedias, dictionaries, and directories in public administration and related fields. Library of Congress call numbers are included for the user's convenience.

Appendix C is an expanded list of selected journals and periodicals that are relevant to public administration. As with Appendix B, Appendix C features Library of Congress call numbers, as well as brief explanations of the publications listed.

Appendix D lists selected academic, professional, and public interest organizations. It includes their Web sites and descriptions of what they do.

Appendix E explains what kinds of jobs are available in the public and nonprofit sectors, how to get them, and the salaries that one might expect. Appendix E is significantly expanded and lists numerous new Web sites for tracking down scholarships, internships, and positions in public administration and independent associations. Advice on acquiring an M.P.A., how to network and interview, and writing one's résumé is also provided, along with a sample résumé.

Nicholas Henry
Savannah, Georgia

Acknowledgments

In the first edition of this book, I stated that I owed an intellectual debt to at least three of my teachers, Lynton Keith Caldwell, Jack T. Johnson, and York Y. Wilbern. I still owe my teachers an intellectual debt. Although it has been some time since I sat in their classrooms, their impact has waxed, not waned, over the years.

The earliest of these unique teachers, Jack Johnson, passed away some time ago. His impact on me was formative, and his advice and friendship are deeply missed.

I have since added a fourth person to this small circle: Frank J. Sackton. Professor Sackton (also Lieutenant General Sackton, retired) introduced me to the classroom of the practical world during the dozen years that I spent at Arizona State University. It was a rare education indeed, and one that I shall always treasure.

I am indebted to my editor at Prentice Hall, Rob DeGeorge, for his insightful advice and unflagging help I am indebted to my editor at Prentice Hall, Rob DeGeorge, for his insightful advice and unnflagging help, and to my production editor, Sowmya Balaraman, for her sharp eyes.

I also am indebted to my colleagues, students, and the book's reviewers who have had such a constructive influence on the continuing evolution of *Public Administration and Public Affairs*.

The following reviewers provided valuable suggestions: Mary Ellen Balchunis-Harris, LaSalle University; and Naim Kapucu, University of Central Florida.

As always, my wife, Muriel, and my children, Adrienne and Miles, and their spouses, Kevin and Anna, provided the deepest level of support. The book is for them, my mother and departed father, and, much to my gratification, my grandchildren, Callum, Margaret, and Charlotte, but this edition is dedicated my late father. This one's for you, Pop.

Nicholas Henry

Part I

Paradigms of Public Administration

Bureaucracy is in our bones. Prehistoric evidence unearthed at archeological digs suggests that the rudiments of a bureaucratic social order were in place 19,000 years ago.[1] Bureaucracy predates, by many millennia, *Homo sapiens*'s earliest experiments with democracy, the emergence of the globe's great religions, and the dawn of civilization itself. Bureaucracy may not be basic to the human condition, but it is basic to human society.

Not everyone agrees that bureaucracy and government are basic to society. The primary critique of government and its bureaucrats amounts to a distortion of Thomas Jefferson's famous dictum that the best government is the least government. This criticism holds that the very best government is no government at all, and that the worst government is any government whatsoever. Government, in sum, is inherently bad. As one prominent and powerful antigovernment ideologue put it, "I don't want to abolish government. I want to reduce it to the size where I can drag it into the bathroom and drown it in the bathtub."[2]

Certainly, there are some bad governments that do bad things, and the examples of pervasive governmental corruption and callousness are countless. Consider the Cameroonian cops who stopped a traveler forty-seven times during a 300-mile journey to demand bribes.[3] Or, in India, farmers who must pay baksheesh to their local governments' accountants to gain a clear title to their farms, or the rickshaw drivers who routinely sacrifice a sixth of their meager earnings to extortionist police.[4] Or the 15 percent of Americans who sometimes go hungry because they cannot afford food,[5] a proportion that is—in the richest economy on earth, one that controls over a third of the world's wealth[6]—larger than those in Canada, Japan, and Western Europe.[7]

But it is inescapable that there are also some good governments that do good things. Moreover, those good things that good governments do are fundamental to human dignity, security, and happiness.

The planet's people have long been united in their view that "good government" (an admittedly musty notion, but one that warrants renewal) is crucial to a good life. A massive and ongoing study, begun in the late 1970s, of citizens in seventy-two countries on six continents finds that "the basic ideas of democracy are virtually universally accepted around the world," regardless of culture, and that these ideas are "viewed as the only game in town," even by the residents of dictatorships.[8]

There is more, however, to the universal longing for good government than just a desire for democracy. Clean, open, and honest government is equally longed for. Global polls find that political corruption ranks third in people's minds, after crime and AIDS, as a "very big" problem in their countries.[9]

The stirring, prodemocracy revolutions that began with the fall of the Berlin Wall in 1989,[10] and that continue today, dramatically demonstrate this "very big" problem. These revolutions consistently have sounded a leitmotif of anticorruption that matches in intensity the demand for democracy. We have heard this omnipresent cry to crush corruption from Kiev to Kyrghistan, from Beirut to Budapest, from Tblisi to Tiananmen.

And with reason. For one, healthy democracy—defined as large numbers of citizens voting repeatedly in competitive elections—associates with the relatively successful control of corruption, and this correlation holds on a global scale.[11] There is, in brief, a pleasing link between robust democracy and governmental honesty. The widening wave of worldwide demonstrations for democracy and against corruption would seem to indicate that people viscerally understand this connection.

For another, corruption costs. The World Bank tells us that global corruption costs an estimated $2.3 trillion per year,[12] or approximately the same amount as the annual budget of the government of the United States. Political corruption appears to inflate the prices for goods by as much as 15 percent to 20 percent, and corrupt public officials who skim tax payments may cost their governments as much as 50 percent of their tax revenue.[13] ("Skim," in these instances, may not be the precisely accurate verb; perhaps "pour" is more to the point.)

Those benighted citizens who are saddled with pervasively corrupt governments must bribe officials to the tune of an additional 3 percent to 10 percent of the cost of government services as the price for assuring the reasonably prompt delivery of those services.[14] Of course, they have already paid for these government services, at least ostensibly, with their taxes.

But wait. There's more. Corruption and poverty walk hand in hand. Countries seen as corrupt have lower levels of foreign investment, whereas countries that reduce corruption experience improved child mortality rates, higher per capita income, and greater literacy, among other benefits.[15] Not one of the nineteen impoverished nations that have been granted debt service relief through the Heavily Indebted Poor Countries Initiative is rated as anything better than having "serious to severe" governmental corruption.[16]

In contrast to the globe's people, and despite corruption's colossal cost, much of the globe's officialdom has been slow, even recalcitrant, in recognizing the overweening importance of good government in bettering people's lives. The World Bank asserts, accurately, that corruption has been "treated as a taboo subject" by the international development community for decades.[17]

Fortunately, this ostrichlike view is changing, and this change parallels the democratic changes coursing through the globe's governments. Thirty-five countries, including the United States, have agreed to the Organisation for Economic Cooperation and Development's Anti-Bribery Convention, which was activated in 1999. In 2003, ninety-five nations, including the United States, signed the United Nations Treaty to Combat Corruption. The World Bank, whose mission is to assist in the economic development of poorer countries, has recognized that "corruption is one of the most serious obstacles to development," and has made fighting corruption "a central institutional priority."[18] The United Nations Development Program, the world's largest aid agency, has made "good government" its "top priority in poverty fighting" on the grounds that "without good government, reliance on trickle-down economic development and a host of other strategies will not work.[19]

Finally, good government rests on competency. As with democratic and uncorrupted government, well-managed government clearly enhances the daily lives of people. A study of the states found that there was a solid and positive relationship between a high level of "state management capacity" and a high quality of life for state citizens.[20]

We have witnessed the consequences of incompetent government when Hurricane Katrina devastated the Gulf Coast on August 29, 2005 (an episode that we recount in the box in Chapter 7), and we have seen the consequences of competent government when terrorists murdered some 3,000 people on September 11, 2001.

After 9/11, government was the core institution that responded to the horror. In contrast to the Katrina catastrophe, in 9/11 credit was given to government, and properly so, for courageous rescues and the restoration of order. Surveys indicated that Americans' trust in their government essentially doubled immediately following the attacks.[21] As an astute observer noted, until that fateful day, "one idea took hold all along the political spectrum: Government was rapidly losing its relevance, its reach, and its right to make demands on the purses and practices of private citizens." Following September 11, that relevance, reach, and right were accorded renewed legitimacy.

Good government, then, rests on three pillars: democracy, honesty, and competency. Public administrators are essential to each of these pillars.

The place of public administrators in ensuring the values of democracy is perhaps the most nuanced, but nonetheless crucial. Introducing bureaucracies to democracies is a delicate business, for bureaucracy and democracy are antithetical systems. The former is hierarchical, elitist, specializing, and informed; the latter is communal, pluralist, generalizing, and ill informed if not ignorant.

Reconciling these realities is not a task for the timorous. Yet such a reconciliation is vital if advanced industrial democracies are to continue to be advanced, industrial, and democratic. The nexus of where noetic elite and democratic mass meet—where this reconciliation occurs (or fails to occur) in the most central and deepest terms—is in the public bureaucracy.

Public administration is the device used to reconcile bureaucracy with democracy. *Public administration* is a broad-ranging and amorphous combination of theory and practice; its purpose is to promote a superior understanding of government and its relationship with the society it governs, as well as to encourage public policies more responsive to social needs and to institute managerial practices attuned to effectiveness, efficiency, and the deeper human requisites of the citizenry. Admittedly, the preceding sentence is itself rather broad ranging and amorphous (although one reviewer of this book described our definition as "a classic"[22]), but for our purposes it will suffice.

Whereas the role of public administrators in protecting and advancing democratic values can be as subtle and sophisticated as it is central, the criticality of bureaucrats to our remaining two pillars of good government, those of honesty and competency, is straightforward. It is primarily the public bureaucracy that investigates and roots out political corruption; it is the bureaucracy that researches and recommends what new or revised benefits, or policies, society needs; it is the bureaucracy that delivers those public benefits; and it is the bureaucracy that assesses the effects of government policies and adjusts them accordingly.

In Part I, we begin our book's discussion of the place of public administrators in assuring good government by offering two histories of public administration. The first is cultural, and the second intellectual.

In Chapter 1, we review the longstanding and everlasting tension between bureaucracy and democracy in the United States. We find that American culture constrains administrative action in the public sector, and, while most Americans cheer this constraint, there is a downside.

In Chapter 2, we review the intellectual evolution of public administration. How public administrators see themselves and their proper field of action in a democracy deeply affects the health of democracy itself. This perspective is formed more in the halls of academe than in the corridors of power, so we devote some pages to the history of ideas in public administration. So welcome to *Public Administration and Public Affairs*, welcome to Part I, and welcome to one of the most exciting and rewarding career possibilities on earth.

Notes

1. Scott Van Nystrom and Luella C. Nystrom, "Bureaucracy in Prehistory: Case Evidence from Mammoth Bone Dwellers on the Russian Steppes," *International Journal of Public Administration* 21 (Winter 1998), pp. 7–23. Archeological evidence found near Kiev, Ukraine, leads these scholars to conclude that "rudiments of bureaucracy, as an organizing principle, likely existed at least 12,000 to 19,000 years ago" (p. 7).
2. Grover Norquist, as quoted in Thomas L. Friedman, "Osama and Katrina," *New York Times* (September 7, 2005). Norquist, who, among other innovations, invented the "no new tax" pledge to be signed by newly elected officials, and who has been described by Newt Gingrich, the former Speaker of the House, as "the single most effective conservative activist in the country," has also said that conservatives "have a lot in common . . . . They want the government to go away. That is what holds together the conservative movement." See John Cassidy, "The Ringleader," *The New Yorker* (August 1, 2005), pp. 42, 46.
3. These extortions were experienced by Robert Guest and are recounted in his "Africa Earned Its Debt," *New York Times* (October 6, 2004).
4. Gurcharan Das, former head of Procter & Gamble in India, writing in the *Times of India*, as cited in Thomas L. Friedman, "Think Global, Act Local," *New York Times* (June 6, 2004).
5. The Pew Global Attitudes Project, *Most of the World Still Does Without*. Pew Research Center Report. (Washington, DC: Pew Research Center for the People and the Press, 2003). This survey involved more than 38,000 interviews in forty-four countries.
6. As derived from data in U.S. Bureau of the Census, *Statistical Abstract of United States, 2004–2005* (Washington, DC: U.S. Government Printing Office, 2005), Table 1336. Figure 34 percent is for 2002 and refers to the gross national incomes of seventy-seven reporting countries.
7. Pew Global Attitudes Project, *Most of World Still Does Without*.
8. Pippa Norris, as quoted in Richard Morin, "Islam and Democracy," *Washington Post* (April 28, 2002). Norris and Ron Inglehart examined data from more than 100,000 interviews conducted between 1995 and 2001 as part of Harvard's *World Values Study*.
9. Pew Global Attitudes Project, *What the World Thinks in 2002* (Washington, DC: Pew Research Center for the People and the Press, 2002). Respondents in nineteen countries ranked crime as their top national concern; AIDS was ranked as the top concern in thirteen, and political corruption in eleven. Political corruption tracks crime quite closely, in that citizens in those countries who are highly concerned about crime also are highly concerned about corruption.
10. Actually, the origins of this worldwide series of prodemocracy and anticorruption revolutions, which accelerated mightily after 1989 and gained even more speed in the 2000s, could, perhaps more properly, be traced to the Portuguese people's overthrow of their Fascist government in 1974.
11. Alok K. Bohara, Neil J. Mitchell, and Carl F. Mittendorff, "Compound Democracy and the Control of Corruption: A Cross-Country Investigation," *Policy Studies Journal* 32 (Winter 2004), pp. 481–499. This was a global study based on the World Bank Institute's corruption data for 1996, 1998, and 2000, and the corruption perception surveys coordinated by Transparency International.
12. World Bank calculation as cited in John Ashcroft, *Prepared Remarks of Attorney General John Ashcroft at the World Economic Forum*, Davos, Switzerland, January 22, 2004 (Washington, DC: U.S. Department of Justice, 2004), p. 2.
13. Rick Stapenhurst and Sahr Kpundeh, eds., *Curbing Corruption: Toward a Model for Building National Integrity* (Washington, DC: World Bank, 1999). http://publications.worldbank.org/ecommerce/catalog/product-detail?product_id=208301&.
14. Ibid.

15. World Bank Institute, as cited in Transparency International, *Perceived Corruption Index 2005* (Berlin: Author, 2005).
16. Ibid. None of the nineteen countries scored above 4 out of 10 possible points in 2005.
17. Stapenhurst and Kpundeh, *Curbing Corruption.*
18. James Anderson, Joel Hellman, Geraint Jones et al., *Anticorruption in Transition: A Contribution to the Policy Debate* (Washington, DC: World Bank, 2000), p. xiv.
19. Barbara Crosette, "U.N. Says Bad Government Is Often Cause of Poverty," *New York Times* (April 5, 2000). See also United Nations Development Program, *Overcoming Human Poverty: UNDP Poverty Report 2000* (New York: Author, 2000).
20. Jerrell D. Coggburn and Saundra K. Schneider, "The Relationship between State Government Performance and State Quality of Life," *International Journal of Public Administration* 26 (December 2003), pp. 1337–1358. This research involved correlating data on state management capacity derived from the 1999 Government Performance Project's grades, and various measures of state quality of life. Economic conditions and public policies in the states also have significant, and predictable, effects, but "our results clearly indicate that the management capacity of state governments also contributes directly to improving the overall quality of life for state citizens" (p. 1337).
21. Jim Hoagland, "Government's Comeback," *Washington Post* (September 26, 2001).
22. William H. Harader, "Whither Public Administration?" *Public Administration Review* 37 (January/February 1977), p. 98.

CHAPTER 1

Big Democracy, Big Bureaucracy

Culture counts. Milieu matters. Environment affects.

These realities pertain to all human activities, and public administration—faceless, impersonal, and even dehumanizing though it may seem—is no exception. More than most of society's activities, in fact, public administration is intensely human and thus deeply embedded in its local culture.

Constraint: The Context and Tradition of Public Administration in the United States

The social context in which the tradition (in contrast to the profession) of public administration in the United States has been nurtured is a unique amalgam of forces, both cultural and intellectual. These forces have birthed a *tradition* (which *Webster's* defines as the "belief, habit, practice, principle handed down verbally from one generation to another, or acquired to each successive generation from the example preceding it") of American public administration. That tradition may be reduced to a word: constraint.

By contrast, the private sector's watchword is quite the opposite of constraint; business's buzzword is aggression. It is difficult, after all, to conceive of the shrewd, daring, and rapacious "robber barons"—the flamboyant tycoons of the nineteenth century who founded the American corporate state—as being associated with any administrative tradition of constraint. Ted Turner, the spectacularly innovative and candid entrepreneur who founded CNN and other cable networks put it this way: "You play to win. And you know you've won when the government stops you."[1]

At least three early and highly influential articulations of core American values placed them squarely in the tradition of American public administration that was beginning to gel in the eighteenth century: the Articles of Confederation, the first state constitutions, and the debates and writings of the nation's founders, especially Alexander Hamilton and Thomas Jefferson. All of these manifestations were strongly shaped by the Native American and English legacies of government and its administration.[2]

Administration by Ambassadors: The Articles of Confederation

The Articles of Confederation and Perpetual Union—which, from 1781 to 1789, provided the first framework for the new nation—were as emblematic of the early Americans' fondness for managerial mishmash as they were evidentiary of Americans' insistence on administrative constraint.

The state governments reigned supreme under the Articles. Congress was essentially powerless and was really a convention of ambassadors from the states rather than an assembly of legislators. Members of Congress were chosen by state legislatures, which could recall them at will. The Articles of Confederation did set up a rudimentary national civil service, but it was a bizarre bureaucratic beast that had no authority to act on its own or enforce much of anything. The national civil service reported directly to committees of the Continental Congress.

There was no chief executive. In fact, the first draft of the Articles of Confederation, written in 1776, was rejected by the Second Continental Congress on the specific grounds that it had proposed an overly empowered executive, and this bias against executive authority extended to *every* national officeholder; under the Articles, every continental official had a one-year term, and each one was subject to term limits.[3]

When Daniel Shays ignited his ill-conceived Rebellion in 1786 (the country's first tax revolt), the nation's political leaders discovered that no arm of "American government," such as it was, had been authorized or organized to put down the disturbance, and eventually that chore fell to the Massachusetts state militia. At least one petulant English observer foresaw the impossibility, as demonstrated by Shays' Rebellion, of his former colonies to ever found a government worthy of the name, and he attributed this failure to Americans' fixation on a weak executive: "As to the future grandeur of America, and its being a rising empire under one head, whether Republican or Monarchial, it is one of the idlest and most visionary notions that was ever conceived even by writers of romance."[4]

Administration by Legislators: The First State Constitutions

At about the same time that the Articles of Confederation were being written, the states were busily drafting their own constitutions. Eleven of the thirteen states adopted constitutions between 1776 and 1780. Connecticut and Rhode Island did not write their constitutions until well into the

next century and instead retained their charters, which had been granted to them by Britain in the 1600s.

The eleven states that adopted constitutions were notably aggressive in limiting the powers of the chief executive. Only New York's constitution (with that of Massachusetts running a distant second) provided a reasonably strong executive, and the remaining constitutions severely restricted their chief executives' appointment and veto powers. The governor in these nine states amounted to little more than a military commander, and all executive and most judicial powers—as well as legislative authority—were placed firmly within the legislatures.

It might appear to some that the absence of authority granted by the Articles of Confederation to the national government, and the virtual absence of authority provided by the great majority of the original state constitutions to elected or appointed state administrators, were pioneering testaments to true, populist, and "natural" democracy. Hardly. Passing few people (an average of about 6 percent) were allowed to vote on anything or anyone in any of the states, and only three states (Massachusetts, New Hampshire, and New York) permitted their chief executives to even be elected independently by those few people who were qualified to vote; in the remaining ten states, governors were named by the legislature or judiciary. In only one state, Massachusetts, were the people permitted to ratify their own state's constitution by popular vote. Democracy was not only new—it was also distrusted. Constrained public administrators, in other words, do not necessarily equate with healthy democracy.

Administration by Enfeebled Executives: Jefferson Prevails

Layering and striating all of this early American activity in drafting confederations and constitutions was the massive brilliance of the early American political elite, but particularly that of Hamilton and Jefferson.

Hamilton's approach to public administration was paramountly practical. Hamilton extolled a strong chief executive, equating a strong executive with the "energy" needed to make a government function: "A feeble executive [by contrast] implies a feeble execution of government. A feeble execution is but another phrase for a bad execution; and a government ill executed . . . must be, in practice, a bad government."[5] Things, in sum, had to get done.

But even more than a strong chief executive, Hamilton advocated a *very* strong bureaucracy. Hamilton urged that department heads be paid exceptionally well, that they possess substantial powers, and that their tenure in office should extend beyond that of the chief executive who appointed them.[6]

Hamilton's notions on how public administration ought to work were in direct contradiction to the ideas and ideals of Jefferson, whose influence on the American administrative tradition was far more pervasive than was Hamilton's. In stark contrast to Hamilton, who embraced a dynamic government, Jefferson disdained the very idea of it. Jefferson wrote to his friend and soul mate, James Madison (who could, as legitimately as Jefferson, represent the tradition of administrative constraint), "I am not a friend to a very energetic government. It is always oppressive. It places the government more at their ease, at the expense of the people."[7] Perhaps it is this perspective that explains why the word "administration" is nowhere to be found in the Constitution that Madison largely wrote.[8]

The tradition of administrative constraint may have stalemated federal action more effectively in domestic affairs than in foreign ones.

Infernal Vernon: A Case of Unconstrained Public Administration

We have been suggesting that local public administrators are constrained especially tightly in their actions. But there are exceptions. Here is one.

The City of Vernon, California, has an official population of ninety-one, mostly very economically secure, souls. Sixty of these residents have been registered voters for many years, and almost all them are city employees or are related to a city official. Most live in heavily-subsidized housing provided by the city, which owns almost all the residences in Vernon, with some houses renting for less than $150 per month—this, in the hot Los Angeles real estate market.

The city, which bills itself as "Exclusively Industrial," supplies electricity and gas to firms—and to their 44,000 employees—doing business in Vernon with remarkably lucrative results. Vernon has more than $100 million in cash and investments, an amount more than double its general operating budget. From the 1970s to the present, the city clerk typically has been the highest-paid municipal employee in California. In 2005, the retiring city administrator walked away with nearly $600,000 in salary, bonuses, and payments for unused vacation time.

In 1978, Vernon's city clerk disqualified enough challenger ballots to assure that the grandson of the city's founder was elected mayor. In 1980, he did it again. For the next quarter-century, the city canceled all elections. The next election was scheduled, ostensibly, for April 2006.

Then, in January 2006, eight newcomers moved into a building in town, and promptly registered to vote in Vernon's municipal elections. Three of them filed petitions to run for city council. Their apparent leaders were a disbarred lawyer who had been convicted on charges of embezzlement and forgery, and a disgraced and deposed city treasurer of nearby South Gate, who was facing a federal prison sentence after being convicted a year earlier for corruption that had almost bankrupted that city.

More newbies followed, and, in a matter of weeks, Vernon's electorate burgeoned by more than two-fifths to eighty-six registered voters. Vernon's five city council members, each of whom

One distinguished scholar contends that Jefferson's "profound distrust of bureaucracy" is in part responsible for the "presidential tendency" to be "proactive in relation to foreign affairs and reactive in relation to domestic issues where power must be shared with Congress".[9]

Certainly these generalizations would seem to apply to Jefferson himself. As an indicator of his reservations over an energetic chief executive and his preference for a passive one (at least when it came to domestic matters), Jefferson (1801–1809) is one of only seven presidents, and the only two-term president, who never vetoed an act of Congress. Yet in foreign affairs Jefferson acted with stunning boldness. For example, Jefferson executed, virtually unilaterally, the Louisiana Purchase, which doubled the size of the nation—

hardly a dilettantish dabble in diplomacy. So controversial, in fact, was the purchase that a respected U.S. Senator from Massachusetts tried to organize a secession of *Northern* states![10] A more recent example of this strange duality is the surreal spectacle that occurred in 1998, when the House of Representatives voted to impeach the president (for only the second time in history) on charges pertaining entirely to domestic affairs, while the president simultaneously launched a major and sustained air war on Iraq because it refused to cooperate with weapons inspectors from the United Nations.

The federal legacy of constrained public administration may be one that pertains far more to national matters than to international ones. It is, uniquely, a legacy of administrative

---

had served in office from thirty to fifty years, were not pleased. The council rescinded the voting registrations of the eight new residents, including the three council candidates, and, for good measure, cut off their power, condemned their building, and evicted them. Private investigators, cruising in cars with tinted windows and no license plates, were dispatched. They followed and videotaped suspected "ringer residents," and not only in Vernon, but in other communities as well. In one incident, a pistol was drawn.

True to tradition, the city cancelled its election for 2006. Charges were duly filed, and the Superior Court ruled that Vernon reinstate the voters' registrations and actually hold an election. These it did. At the end of election day, however, the city clerk (who, coincidentally, was also the son of the recently-retired city administrator) confiscated the ballots and locked them away in City Hall, an unprecedented act that, at the very least, was questionable under state law.

The clerk's justification was that the ballots should not be tallied until Vernon's swelling court docket was decided. And Vernon did indeed have large lump of lawsuits. The three challengers had brought suit to disenfranchise more than eight out of ten Vernon's voters on the grounds of conflict of interest. Moreover, a dozen voters, including the mayor, claimed residence in Vernon, but allegedly lived elsewhere, thereby disqualifying them as voters. The District Attorney for Los Angeles County was investigating corruption charges that centered on the city clerk. Vernon, in turn, was embroiled in its own suit to seal its records from review by prosecutors.

An administrator in the county's registrar's office mused, "You know, Vernon kind of keeps falling into this category you just don't find legal citations for. . . . It's very, very strange . . . They're one the most unusual little jurisdictions I've ever encountered."

Or, as another seasoned observer put it, "Vernon acts more like a for-profit company or . . . a private club than a city (White)."

Sources: The following articles were published in 2006 by the *Los Angeles Times* and written by Hector Becerra: "Vernon Shoo-Ins Shoo Outsiders" (February 12): "In Tiny Vernon, a Surge in Voters" (April 7): "Judge Is to Have Key Role As Vernon Casts Votes" (April 11): "Vernon's Inaction on Vote Stumps Experts" (April 13): "S. Pasadena Is Tired of Vernon Politics" (April 15): and "Vernon Fights to Keep Records Private" (April 26). "Infernal Vernon," *Los Angeles Times* (April 14, 2006); "Otis White's Urban Notebook," *Governing* (April 2006), p. 19.

and political schizophrenia—an enfeebled executive for the country, but an energetic one for the globe.

The Governors of Constraint

In the states, governors have gained a modicum of executive power over the last two centuries, although the evidence supporting their power is mixed.

A series of national surveys of state agency heads found that, in 1964, only a third of these respondents thought that the governor had more control and oversight over their agencies than the legislature, but today almost half, 49 percent, say this.[11] Another study of all the states confirmed this legislative influence. The governors and the legislatures were almost dead even when it came to controlling executive agencies in four key areas dealing with budgets and policies.[12]

Despite the governors' gains in power over time, however, by any normal criterion of management their authority still remains tightly constrained and fragmented. In eighteen of the forty-two states with lieutenant governors, the governor and lieutenant governor are elected independently, and, presumably, have political agendas that differ. (The nation, in contrast to the states, recognized quite early the potential destructiveness of its own version of this managerial malfunction, and in 1804 the country relieved the federal government of this strange arrangement, as it applied to the president and vice president, by ratifying the Twelfth Amendment to the Constitution.) Of the almost 2,000 major administrative officers in the fifty states, nearly 300 are elected directly by the people, and an additional 750 are appointed by someone or somebody other than the governor. More than half of the key public administrators in the states, in other words, administer from power bases that are independent from their state's chief executive officer.[13]

Almost all of these state administrators may be reelected without limit. Not so the governors, two-thirds of whom have some sort of term limitation imposed on them. One consequence, of course, is that not only do these key administrators have their own electoral bases, but they also

may play in the political game for considerably more innings than the governors, which is, in itself, an additional power source.

The consequences of these conditions are predictable. An ongoing study of more than 1,000 state agencies concluded that "the degree of executive control in the American states is modest at best."[14]

The Limits of Local Administration

At the local level, public administration is characterized by unusually weak elected executives (even by American standards).

Certain themes emerge in the ways that local elected chief executives are constrained. Almost three-fourths of county commission chairs,[15] roughly half of the elected chief executives of towns and townships, and nearly a fourth of municipal mayors,[16] are not elected to office by popular vote, thereby denying them their own electoral power bases. By contrast, legislators and legions of other local officials, such as sheriffs, treasurers, tax collectors, coroners, and clerks, are voted into office.[17]

Well over four-fifths of local elected chief executives are part-timers, a condition that hardly enhances their executive powers. Large majorities serve as both elected chief executives *and* voting legislators, a confusing combination that melds the executive and legislative branches in ways that undermine executive authority. Terms of office are brief, and only a minority has terms as long as four years. Large majorities of local elected chief executives are denied the normal powers of the president and the governors, notably the veto, preparation of the budget, and appointment powers.[18] Details concerning the constraints that limit the power of local elected chief executives are provided in the box in Chapter 12.

In all American governments, but especially local ones, the eighteenth-century's values of constrained public administration still flourish verdantly. One overweening irony of limiting local leaders is that research indicates that weaker local chief executives and administrators seem to associate with less efficient and more expensive governments![19]

Government, Public Leaders, and Public Trust

From the tradition of constrained public management has emerged a deterioration in the relationship between citizens, their governments, and their public leaders.

Americans' trust in government is in decline. As Figure 1-1 shows, only 37 percent of Americans may be categorized as trusting government, compared to a high point of nearly twice that percentage, 61 percent, thirty-eight years earlier.

Clusters of Contempt

Distrust of the public sector takes two forms that are difficult to separate.

Distrust of Elected Leaders. One form is that of popular distrust of the nation's political leadership. Distrust of elected political leaders arrays along generational lines, with younger and middle-aged people being less trustful of leaders than older Americans.[20]

Only 16 percent of Americans trust elected officials to do the right thing.[21] Nearly half of Americans say elected officials (24 percent) or political parties (24 percent) are responsible for "what is wrong with government."[22]

Another survey found that 31 percent of Americans believed that public decisions are best left to "successful business people," and another 31 percent thought that they should be left to "nonelected experts." "People's most intense desire for the political process is that it not take advantage of them by allowing certain entities, such as special interests and elected officials, to reap personal gains at the expense of ordinary people like themselves. . . . And rank-and-file Americans are convinced the existing structures of American politics allow ordinary people to be played for suckers."[23]

Distrust of Government. The second dimension is that of popular distrust of the institution of government itself. Distrust of government's size, direction, performance, and power arrays along gender, racial, and partisan lines. Through the late 1990s, men, white people, and Republicans were

Figure 1-1   Trust in Government Index 1958–2004

Source: *The National Election Studies*, University of Michigan. *The NES Guide to Public Opinion and Behavior* (Ann Arbor, MI: Author. 2005).

Note: Index comstructed using data from the following questions:

"How much of the time do you think you can trust the government in Washingon to do what is right—just about always, most of the time or only some of the time?"

"Would you say the government is pretty much run by a few big interests looking out for themsleves or that it is run for the benefit of all the people?"

"Do you think that people in the government waste a lot of money we pay in taxes, waste some of it, or don't waste very much of it?"

"Do you think that quite a few of the people running the government are (1958–1972: a little) crooked, not very many are, or do you think hardly any of them are crooked (1958–1972: at all)?"

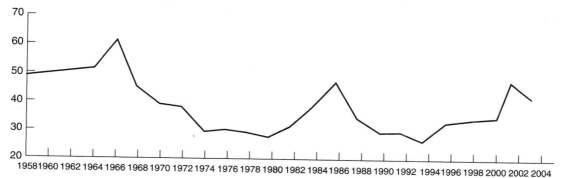

more critical of government than were women, people of color, and Democrats.[24]

In the 2000s, however, shifts became evident. Men by and large expressed "a fair amount" or "a great deal" of trust in government, with women, for the most part, indicating less trust. Whites generally demonstrated higher levels of trust in government than did people of color, with African Americans holding the least trusting views of government. And, perhaps most surprising, Republicans responded that they had a more trust in government than did Democrats, and Republicans' trust was greater for each governmental level—federal, state, and local—than was Democrats' trust in government.[25]

Bureaucrats: Image and Reality

Americans have been losing confidence in their governments and their political leaders. American culture seems to have accelerated this decline in confidence but, paradoxically, Americans' personal experiences with their public administrators seem to have slowed that decline.

The Bureaucratic Image

Reputedly, Americans disdain the bureaucrat. If, indeed, they do (and the evidence belies this), their disdain has been sustained by elected officials, intellectuals, and the media.

Bashing Bureaucrats: Politicians' Pandering. Politicians routinely run against the bureaucracy in their ceaseless grubbing for votes. The election campaign chant of bureaucratic "waste, fraud, and abuse" has been a rhetorical standard of office-seekers for more than a generation.[26] Once elected to office, politicians are measurably and radically more contemptuous of public administrators than are the voters whose support they sought.[27] An analysis of the 104th Congress found that representatives used the word, "bureaucrat," on more than 70 percent of the occasions when they referred to public administrators, and

that in nearly 84 percent of these congressional references to "bureaucrats," the term was used pejoratively.[28]

Demonizing Bureaucrats: Academia's Undermining. Intellectuals foster an image of bureaucracy that ranges from its being merely unresponsive to dangerously antidemocratic. An analysis of introductory college textbooks on American government found that over three-fourths of them portray public administrators as "government employees who stay on forever," and two-thirds depict government bureaucracy as "all powerful and out of control."[29] Another analyst concluded that "the most deeply rooted and persistent misconception" of these texts is that federal administrators "are not accountable" to Congress.[30]

This anti-public-administration propaganda begins at an early age. A content analysis of British and American children's literature found that British public servants were portrayed as measurably more benevolent and competent than were American public servants.[31]

Trashing Bureaucrats: Media's Message. The media reflect these views. A study of how local newspapers treated the governments of their own cities found a tilt toward the negative and the trivial.[32] A review of a spate of movies released over several years concluded that federal administrators were "the baddest villains in Hollywood films."[33]

That dominant American medium, television, is complicit, too. A unique analysis of prime-time television programs broadcast from 1955 through 1998 found that portrayals of civil servants and public officials shifted from highly positive to highly negative over the forty-three years, displacing businesspeople as "television's least likeable occupational group." Prior to 1975, three-fourths of entertainment episodes reaffirmed the integrity of the political system, but since then three-fourths have portrayed the system as corrupt, and not a single episode on prime-time television during the 1990s showed government serving the public.[34]

Do Americans really believe that their public administrators are against them?

The Bureaucratic Reality

Evidently not. Two-thirds of Americans say they trust federal workers to do the right thing.[35] Almost seven out of ten Americans, 69 percent, say that they have a favorable opinion of government workers, up from 55 percent sixteen years earlier.[36] Only 6 percent of Americans blame government employees for "what is wrong with government," compared to four times that number who say elected officeholders are responsible for government's failures.[37] These favorable ratings appear to be attributable to a high level of personal service to citizens that public administrators provide.

Experiencing Bureaucrats. A national poll asked Americans if they had ever gone to a federal, state, or local agency to get "the government" to do something that was not related to routine matters, such as applying for a driver's license. Some two-thirds stated that they had found their civil servants to be helpful and that they were satisfied with the special services that they received, with a plurality stating that they were highly satisfied.[38] Another national survey found that nearly three-quarters of the respondents said that "the people at the [government] office" were very efficient (43 percent) or fairly efficient (31 percent) in handling their problems, and more than three-fourths said that they were treated fairly; indeed, only 12 percent said that they were treated unfairly.[39]

When we poll by each level of government, comparable results emerge. A survey of people, mostly professionals, who had personally used the services of five federal agencies found that, on average, approximately seven out of ten respondents held a favorable view of the agency and felt that they had been shown courtesy by its employees.[40] The public's ratings of state governments' services typically range from three-fifths to over four-fifths of citizens reporting satisfactory or highly satisfactory experiences with state bureaucrats.[41] A "meta-analysis" of 261 citizen surveys and covering more than 200,000 respondents in forty states found "generally favorable assessments" by citizens of their local governments' services.[42] There are additional surveys of citizens' experiences with bureaucrats that have found results quite similar to these.[43]

Is Business Better? We have fewer data regarding how services provided by governments compare with services delivered by private companies in the view of citizens who use both, and it is important to know this; after all, citizens might be "satisfied" or "very satisfied" with public services, as polls indicate, but ecstatic with joy over corporate ones, indicating a relative failure by government. Government, however, holds its own. What surveys there are on this issue indicate that there is "no systematic difference in attitudes toward public and private services among respondents,"[44] and that the federal government closely rivals, and occasionally surpasses, the private sector in terms of "customer satisfaction" with its services.[45]

In sum, as one reviewer of surveys on the subject concluded, "the American public does not appear as disdainful of bureaucrats as the projected media image would indicate."[46]

The Bureaucrat: Government's Savior? In fact, the evidence also suggests that government bureaucrats are leading the way in restoring Americans' trust in government.

In the analysis of the users of the services offered by five federal agencies, cited earlier, almost seven out of ten of these respondents had a favorable view of the particular agency, but slightly more than only four out of ten held a favorable view of government in general.[47] A poll that distinguished between "general respondents" and "recent customers" of nine representative services provided by the federal, state, and local governments found that fewer than seven out of ten of the general respondents ranked these services as good or very good, but nearly three-fourths of recent customers ranked these services as good or very good.[48] A survey of citizens' experiences with six services provided by local governments found that, on average, well over four-fifths of the respondents rated the provision of these services as good or excellent, but less than three-fifths of these same respondents rated local government itself as good or excellent.[49]

Bureaucrats, battered and bruised by elected officials, intellectuals, and the media, are nonetheless valued and respected by the people.

Revolt and Resistance: Americans and Governmental Growth

It is, perhaps, comforting to know that Americans by and large get along with their governments' bureaucrats and think well of the way that they deliver services. It was, in part, this benign popular perspective that facilitated, over the course of the twentieth century, the dramatic growth of American governments.

Consider some facts. By the close of the 1800s, government workers at all levels accounted for less than 2 percent of the American population (which was itself a near tripling from only thirty years earlier), and government revenues at all levels amounted to about 8 percent of the economy.[50] Today, by contrast, the proportion of all government workers has more than tripled, accounting for more than 7 percent of the resident population, and total government revenues have nearly quadrupled their share of the economy and amount to nearly 32 percent of the gross domestic product (GDP). At all levels, annual government revenues exceed $3 trillion and exceed $10,300 per American.[51]

Let us place the relative powers of government over the last hundred or so years in a more human perspective. By the beginning of the twentieth century, John D. Rockefeller of Standard Oil was the wealthiest person in America, with about $25 billion.[52] By the beginning of the twenty-first century, Bill Gates of Microsoft was the wealthiest person in America, with about $51 billion.[53] Rockefeller could have paid off the entire national debt (less than $3 billion) with 10 percent to 15 percent of his wealth.[54] But with the national debt surpassing $8 *trillion* today,[55] Gates could not even come close to paying it off.

Although the growth of American governments is impressive, we should place it in context, and it is clear that governments in the United States loom less large in the economic lives of their citizens than do governments in other developed nations. As we noted, the revenues collected by all American governments amount to 32 percent of the gross domestic product. But the tax revenues collected at all levels by the governments of nineteen Western and Central European democracies, Australia, Canada, Japan, New Zealand, and South Korea amount to nearly 45 percent of their respective GDPs, on average—almost a third higher take than in the United States.[56] So it appears that American governments are not, in relative terms, the economic powerhouses that governments are in almost all other roughly comparable industrialized democracies.

Nevertheless, American governments have grown and continue to grow. But in the 1970s, things changed.

California's notorious Proposition 13 of 1978, voted in by a two-to-one popular margin, slashed property taxes in the state and became the symbol of the revolt against government and taxes. The revolt continues. Since 1978, twenty-seven states have inflicted taxation or expenditure limitations upon themselves.[57] Thirteen states require legislative "supermajorities," ranging from 60 percent to 75 percent of legislators' votes, to raise taxes.[58] Almost all states (forty-six) have imposed tax or expenditure limits of some sort on their local governments.[59] How effective these efforts have been is debatable but, overall, something slowed the growth of government.

Between 1946 (the year following the end of World War II) and 1978 (the year of California's Proposition 13, which most observers peg as the year of the tax revolt's first shot heard around the nation), the revenues collected by the federal government as a percentage of personal income grew by about one-half of 1 percent per year (17 percent over thirty-two years), and the revenues of state and local governments as a percentage of personal income grew by 4 percent per year, nearly doubling over the same period. But *after* 1978, federal revenues as a percentage of personal income essentially held flat, and after 2001, as a consequence of unprecedented federal tax cuts, it actually declined.[60] Similarly, after 1978, the growth of state and local revenues as a percentage of personal income was slashed by three-fourths to a growth rate of about 1 percent per year.[61]

It is clear that the tax revolt has not reversed the growth of government. But it is also clear that, relative to the economy as a whole, the rate of governmental growth has been radically slowed.

Power: The Gray Eminence of the Public Administrator

Because powerful political, social, economic, and technological forces underlie bureaucracy, it follows that a bureaucracy has power. But the power of bureaucracy comes clothed in clouds, curtained in fog, and cloaked in mist.

We try here to clear away some of those clouds, fog, and mist.

Staying Power

One major form of power that the bureaucracy has is simply its staying power. Perhaps the most infamous example of the staying power of public bureaucracies is the International Screwthread Commission (formed in 1918, with a sixty-day life span), which one observer called the "commission that will not die."[62]

Herbert Kaufman completed the first empirical research on the staying power of public bureaucracies and concluded, reluctantly, that it was awesome. Of 175 identifiably separate agencies within the federal government, only 15 percent had disappeared a half century later. When Kaufman compared the "death rate" of government agencies with the rate of business failures over the same period, he found that in any given year the rate of business failure exceeded the rate of agency death.[63]

Although subsequent research has questioned Kaufman's methodology,[64] it is a reasonable conclusion that most Americans believe, regardless of what evidence may be provided to them, that government organizations are indeed "immortal."

Bureaucratic Political Power

It is increasingly obvious that bureaucracy is now a major policymaking arm of government—perhaps *the* major policymaker. One careful analysis of the American states found that the states' public "managerial capacity" itself should be placed "alongside other more commonly studied state characteristics as an important influence" on public policy formation. In other words, the ability and professionalism of public administrators rank with such powerful political forces as interest groups and ideology in the making of state policies.[65]

Limiting Legislatures: The Loss of the Legislative Veto. At least some of the basis of public administrators' power to make public policies is found in the Constitution—or, at least, in the courts' interpretation of it. In 1983, the Supreme Court decided that it is unconstitutional for Congress (and, presumably, any legislature) to overturn or forbid an act taken by an executive agency in the course of administering a law enacted by Congress, *even if Congress itself tries to overrule that agency's act by majority vote!* To do so, the Court held, would violate the Constitution's separation of powers. Instead, if Congress does not like the way that public administrators in the executive branch are interpreting or managing a law that Congress has already passed, Congress must actually rewrite and revote on its own legislation.[66] Of course, the president would have the power to veto this rewritten legislation, so it is highly unlikely that Congress would undertake the considerable effort required by the judiciary of legislatively vetoing (that is, overruling) acts by public administrators.

This judicial stance accords the bureaucracy considerable discretionary power. For example, public administrators in the U.S. Department of Education have enacted rules (being contested by several states) that prohibit schools from expelling special education students who have discipline problems (including those who bring guns and drugs to school), despite the absence of any specific legislation requiring such policies. Public administrators in the Army Corps of Engineers have enacted highly controversial limitations on the use of privately owned wetlands based on a law (the 1972 amendments to the Federal Water Pollution Control Act of 1956) that never mentions the word "wetlands"; the law addresses only "navigable waters," which the

Corps has interpreted to include wetlands, which, of course, are neither navigable nor waters.[67]

Policymaking Power.   Research substantiates the policymaking power of public administrators, but with some interesting twists. Appointed public executives and staffers who are not necessarily in the career civil service possess considerable power in suggesting new policies and setting policymaking agendas, and career civil servants flex large political muscles in conceiving, shaping, and structuring multiple solutions to public problems.

In a careful, empirical, and original analysis of the federal policymaking process, it was found that, while "no one set of actors dominates the process" of agenda setting and policymaking, "elected politicians and their appointees come closer than any other."[68] The researcher, in fact, concluded from his study that the president and members of Congress were quite important in the initiation of new ideas and the formation of the policy agenda for the nation. "With respect to agenda setting, then, a top-down model of the executive branch seems to be surprisingly accurate."[69]

Almost equally important, however, in proposing new policies and agenda setting were top presidential appointees (who actually were ranked higher than the president), White House staffers, and congressional staffs. Career civil servants were considerably less important in originating new ideas for public policy and setting the national agenda, but they were extremely significant in structuring the alternative solutions that could be applied to recognized public problems.

What this scholar found in the federal government appears to be replicated, by and large, in state governments, too.[70] One study concluded that legislative budget analysts in four representative states "establish the basic foundation for legislative decision-making . . . are agenda setters . . . [who develop] policy options, and . . . budget recommendations."[71]

Stopping Power.   Bureaucrats, in brief, have the power to do things. They also possess the power to not do things. It is always easier to wreck rather than erect, to immobilize rather than

mobilize, to stop rather than go. Entropy trumps energy. When this fact of physics is applied to bureaucracy, the power of the bureaucrat, however negative, waxes truly remarkable.

Consider the case of John R. Bolton in his capacity as arms-control chief in the State Department during the first term of President George W. Bush. During that period, Bolton allegedly stymied for two years the disposal of sixty-eight tons of Russian plutonium capable of fueling 8,000 nuclear bombs (a task that he was charged with facilitating, not undermining); staved off attempts to communicate with North Korea about its nuclear weapons program; fought the reappointment of the respected and Nobel-Peace-Prize-winning director of the International Atomic Energy Agency, despite significant disagreement within the State Department about his doing so; withheld American support of the European initiative to offer Iran incentives as a means of terminating its suspected development of nuclear weapons; and blocked a new strategic opening to India concerning the sharing of civilian nuclear technology.

In 2005, the president appointed a new secretary of state and nominated Bolton as ambassador to the United Nations, moves that effectively cut him out from these and other policymaking loops. Almost immediately, Russia agreed to eliminate its plutonium; a U.S. meeting was scheduled with North Korea; the chief of the International Atomic Energy Agency was cleared for reappointment; the United States joined the Europeans in a common approach to Iran (but only after American diplomats initiated a secret meeting with their European counterparts that excluded Bolton); and plans to share civilian nuclear technology with India moved forward. As a former official at Foggy Bottom put it, "throughout his career in the first Bush administration, he was always playing the stopper role for a lot of different issues and even when there was an obvious interest by the president to move things forward, Bolton often found ways of stopping things by tying the interagency process in knots."[72]

True, it is always easier to block rather than build, but that reality does not detract from the power of the bureaucrat. If anything, it enhances it.

Bureaucrats and Legislators

Bureaucrats' power has led to a growing intimacy between administrators and legislators—an intimacy that has deepened at all levels of government.

Bureaucratizing Congress. There are more than 40,000 congressional staffers, and they have significant levels of influence in the policymaking process.[73] One especially thorough examination observed that "staffers exert a strong influence on material with which they deal because of their position astride the office communications process, their control of factual data, and the expertise and professional judgment which they bring to their jobs. . . . On occasion, they argue vigorously for or against a certain policy position."[74]

Bureaucratizing State Legislatures. A parallel pattern is evident in the states. Currently, the nation's more than 7,400 state legislators employ more than 36,000 legislative staffers, or nearly five staffers per legislator, and the number of legislative staffers is growing by about 2 percent to 3 percent annually.[75]

As with Congress, the role of staffs at the state level, particularly in such heavily staffed legislatures as those in California, Illinois, and New York, is a powerful one. As a former staffer in one highly professionalized legislature put it, "The most remarkable discovery that I made during my tenure as a staff member was the amount of power I had over bills on which I worked. The members relied almost entirely on staff to accurately summarize the legislation and also to develop compromises among the many interests which were brought into conflict by these bills."[76]

Bureaucratizing Local Legislatures. At the local level, appointed bureaucrats largely run the show. Even though nearly a fifth of American municipalities have no chief appointed official (normally a city manager), in almost two-thirds of *all* cities and towns the city manager has overall responsibility for developing the budget (57 percent), or shares this responsibility with the mayor (7 percent); in another 10 percent of municipalities, the budget is developed by the chief financial officer.[77] In well over half of all cities and towns, the city manager has sole authority to appoint department heads (39 percent), or shares that power with the mayor (17 percent); the city managers' responsibility for appointing department heads is growing over time, and at the expense of the mayors' authority to do so.[78]

There is a small raft of research indicating that city managers view themselves as legitimate, appropriately powerful policymakers in their cities.[79] These studies have found, quite consistently, that (to quote one review of this literature) "virtually all managers always or nearly always participate in the formulation of policy and set the council agenda."[80] Ninety-six percent of city managers initiate policy proposals.[81] In fact, most city council members in large council-manager cities not only perceive their city managers to be more involved in policymaking and mission development than are they, but they also *approve* of their managers' involvement in these areas,[82] and their approval waxes with time and experience.

An analysis of city council members in council-manager cities found that those members who had served for eight or more years showed a greater respect for staff, and understood the own roles better measurably more than did their newly-elected colleagues.[83]

Studies of other local legislative bodies also tend to validate the hypothesis that public administrators are policymakers. For example, studies of policymaking in school boards found that the professional school superintendent was the major formulator of board policy,[84] and that boards adopted the policies recommended by their superintendents an astonishing 99 percent of the time.[85] Without question, the trend at all levels of government is one of lawmaking bodies bureaucratizing, and of bureaucrats becoming increasingly influential in the making of laws.

Bureaucrats and the Elected Executive: The Presidential Experience

Just as the public bureaucrats have gained and are gaining autonomy as policymakers at the expense of legislators, public administrators also have encroached on the political independence of elected chief executives. Elected chief executives, notably presidents, are deeply aware of this encroachment. Consider the following comments made by presidents of the United States about "their" bureaucracy.

- Harry Truman: "I thought I was the president, but when it comes to these bureaucrats, I can't do a damn thing."[86]
- Richard Nixon: "We have no discipline in this bureaucracy! We never fire anybody! We never reprimand anybody! We never demote anybody!"[87]
- Jimmy Carter, in the final year of his presidency: "Before I became president, I realized and was warned that dealing with the federal bureaucracy would be one of worst problems I would have to face. It has been worse than I had anticipated."[88]

Why do presidents feel this way? We offer a couple of small but revealing examples:

More than four decades ago, President John F. Kennedy was pestered by his brother, Attorney General Robert Kennedy, over the fact that there was a large sign directing drivers to the Central Intelligence Agency's Langley, Virginia, headquarters. The attorney general saw this sign every day that he commuted to work and grew increasingly irked; he believed that its presence violated federal policy by advertising the address of the supersecret spy agency. After listening to intensifying complaints of his brother, President Kennedy ordered an aide to have the sign removed; the aide, in turn, directed the Interior Department to remove it. Nothing happened. A few days later, the president repeated his order. Again, nothing happened. Aggravated by both the bureaucracy and his brother's persistence, the president personally called the official in charge of signs: "This is Jack Kennedy. It's eleven o'clock in the morning. I want that sign down by the time the attorney general goes home tonight, and I'm holding you personally responsible." The sign was removed and the president had learned a lesson: "I now understand that for a president to get something done in this country, he's got to say it three times."[89]

Such an understanding of supposed bureaucratic inertia is held, in fact, by most presidents. But quite the opposite can occur. Consider the experience of President Jimmy Carter. President Carter's daughter Amy was having difficulty one Friday afternoon on a homework problem about the industrial Revolution. Amy asked her mother for help, who asked an aide if she knew the answer. The aide called the Labor Department for assistance. Labor was pleased to oblige. On Sunday, a truck pulled up to the White House with Amy's answer: a massive computer printout, costing an estimated $300,000 and requiring a special team of analysts to work overtime. The department thought it was responding to an order from the president. Amy received a "C" for her homework assignment.[90]

Presidential frustrations with "their" bureaucracy are legion. Fortunately (at least to some degree), their frustrations seem to be primarily a product of the immensity, complexity, and publicness of the federal service, and not of willful bureaucrats bent on attaining personal policy agendas. Although there are some isolated examples of agencies that have intentionally sabotaged presidential policies,[91] research consistently reveals that top administrators are extraordinarily responsive to executive directives.[92]

Noetic Authority and Knowledge Management: The Bases of Bureaucratic Power

How has the bureaucracy grown so in political importance?

Knowledge Is Power

The fundamental response must be that in a highly complex and technologically oriented society such as the United States, those who control and manipulate information gain power. The old saw that "knowledge is power" has never been more true than it is today.

Although the executive branch typically commands a near-monopoly of public knowledge, and this monopoly grants it great power, the other branches are capable of creating their own bureaucracies to gather knowledge, too. When they do, power follows.

One study found that when the legislative branch established its own bureaucratic base of knowledge, as Congress and the larger state and local legislatures have done, the legislature becomes more powerful, and at the direct expense of executive agencies. This research found that the more highly professionalized the legislature was, and the larger its staff, the lower the influence of the agencies *in their own policy areas.*[93]

In short, knowledge, regardless of its institutional locale, is power. "Administration is knowledge. Knowledge is power. Administration is power"; this "simplistic syllogism" is a dominating reality of our post-industrial age.[94]

The idea that knowledge is power has been refined over time and reduced to the phrase, *noetic, authority*, or the power that derives from knowledge.[95] Public administrators, increasingly, are literally defined by noetic authority. They implement their noetic authority through *knowledge management*, or the collection, organization, and use of social and organizational data for the purpose of developing and delivering public policy.[96]

Knowledge, Complexity, and Control

In a more empirical mode, investigators have noted the web of relationships among knowledge, organizational complexity, and political control.

Knowledge and Complexity. The larger and more complex the public agency and the polity it inhabits, the more political control appointed administrators appear to gain. In a study of school boards, it was found that the professional school superintendent had far more power relative to members of the school board in big cities, substantially less power in the suburbs, and even less power in small towns.[97] Similarly, a national survey of city managers found that the larger the city, the likelier the manager would be intensely involved in municipal policymaking.[98]

These and other analyses indicate that, as the public organization and the political system become more complex, public administrators gain more power. This power derives from their much readier access to critical information.

Knowledge and Control. Public administrators are quick to defend their unique knowledge base. A national survey of city managers found that more than 60 percent voiced strong opposition to a full-time, professionally paid city council: "This item evoked the strongest expression of opinion in the entire series of questions."[99] Moreover, a majority of managers opposed the provision of a full-time separate staff for the mayor and 77 percent reported that they always or nearly always resisted council involvement in "management issues." These strongly held opinions on the part of city managers indicate that the appointed urban chief executive is well aware that his or her foundation of political power is the control of information. Hence, a full-time professional staff for the mayor and a full-time, hard-working city council that is interested in "management issues" are anathema to the typical city manager.

Public executives also have been known to not merely discourage the dissemination of information as a means of preserving their power, but also to actively suppress it. Consider some examples.

- In 1971, President Richard M. Nixon grew concerned about monthly unemployment figures and ordered his commissioner of labor statistics to stop holding news conferences in which the data were released and interpreted.[100]
- During the administration of President Bill Clinton, Vice President Al Gore "drove some environmental researchers out of government positions because their views on global warming and ozone depletion clashed with his own."[101]
- In 2003, the chief actuary of the Medicare program concluded that the proposed new benefit of adding prescription drugs would cost about $150 billion more than the White House said it would cost. The actuary reported that his politically appointed boss, the head of Medicare, had threatened to fire him if he released his analysis, an act that has been illegal since 1912.[102]
- In 2004, more than sixty distinguished scientists signed a statement stating that the administration had "misrepresented scientific knowledge and misled the public about the implications of its policies."[103]

- In 2005, the highly respected top administrator for women's health in the U.S. Food and Drug Administration resigned in protest because "higher levels in the administration" disregarded the agency's own panel of experts' recommendation that a politically controversial contraceptive be made more widely available to women. In her resignation letter, she wrote: "I can no longer serve . . . when scientific and clinical evidence, fully evaluated and recommended for approval by the professional staff here, has been overruled."[104]

- Also in 2005, the Government Accountability Office reported that the administration's program to study climate change failed to address a crucial component—how rising temperatures could affect people and the environment—as required by law.[105] The White House squelched its own Agriculture Department's report that found a link between potentially dangerous bacteria and animal waste in large farms; its own Environmental Protection Agency's conclusions about global warming; its own Centers for Disease Control and Prevention's statement on its Web page that education about birth control does not lead to increased sexual activity; its own National Cancer Institute's finding that abortion does not increase a woman's likelihood of getting breast cancer; and its own Health and Human Services Department's discovery of racial bias among health care providers.[106] The White House also scotched the 9/11 Commission's conclusion that officials of the Federal Aviation Administration ignored numerous advanced warnings concerning possible airline hijackings and suicide missions by Al Qaeda terrorists;[107] the Pentagon declined to provide Congress with cost estimates for the wars in Afghanistan and Iraq; and the Bureau of Labor Statistics was ordered to stop reporting mass layoffs.[108]

Knowledge and the Public Interest.   Fortunately, these incidents are the exception, not the rule. One observer summed up these political efforts to quash public information this way: "Politics as usual? Not really. Hard as it may be to believe . . . the executive branch has traditionally succeeded at hewing to the ideals of objectivity and nonpartisanship . . . [Government agencies] have produced reliable numbers, even when those numbers have made sitting Presidents look worse . . . The people who have made this possible are among the most heavily scorned figures in American life—George Wallace's 'pointy-headed bureaucrats.' . . . [Yet, these bureaucrats are] the only professionals in government—the only ones to say what they think instead of what they believe their bosses and voters want them to. Would we trust the unemployment numbers if, every time a new President came along, he replaced the entire Bureau of Labor Statistics with a new crop of cronies and campaign aides?"[109]

Therein lies the power—and the honor—of the public administrator.

Notes

1. Quoted in Ken Auletta, "The Lost Tycoon," *The New Yorker* (April 23 and 30, 2001), p. 154.
2. It can be plausibly argued that the American tradition of constrained public administration stems from America's first settlers. The Iroquois Confederation, an alliance of several tribes that stretched from Kentucky to the Great Lakes, as well as the tribes of the Eastern seaboard, were notably averse to authority. The Great Law of Peace, which was the governing code of the Iroquois Confederation, was "concerned as much with constraining the [ruling] Great Council [of the Confederation] as with granting it authority," and the "framers of the Constitution . . . were pervaded by Indian images of liberty." One ethnographer of the Iroquois writes that "their whole civil policy was averse to the concentration of power in any single individual." See Charles C. Mann, "The Founding Sachems," *New York Times* (July 4, 2005). Lewis Henry Morgan is quoted.

   For arguments on the influence of English public administration on its American counterpart, see, for example, Woodrow Wilson, "The Study of Administration," *Political Science Quarterly* 2 (June/July 1887), pp. 197–222, especially pp. 206–219, Lynton K. Caldwell, "Novus Ordo Seclorum: The Heritage of American Public Administration," *Public Administration Review* 36 (September/October 1976), pp. 476–488. Michael W. Spicer, *The Founders, The Constitution, and Public Administration* (Washington, DC: Georgetown University Press, 1995). As Wilson wrote: "The English race long and successfully studied the art of curbing executive power to the constant neglect of the art of perfecting executive methods" (p. 206).
3. Garry Wills, *A Necessary Evil* (New York: Simon & Schuster, 2000).
4. Josiah Tucker, as quoted in Page Smith, *The Constitution: A Documentary and Narrative History* (New York: Morrow Quill, 1980), p. 82.
5. Alexander Hamilton, "No. 70," in Clinton Rossiter, ed., *The Federalist Papers* (New York: New American Library, 1961), p. 423.

6. Of the globe's nations, the city-state of Singapore seems to have adopted Hamilton's ideas the most thoroughly. Its prime minister, cabinet ministers, and supreme court justices are paid approximately $1 million per year, with comparable salaries down the line. In a country of four million people, there are reserves of $100 billion. For a pointed review, see Thomas L. Friedman, "Singapore and Katrina," *New York Times* (September 15, 2005).

7. Quoted in Catherine Drinker Bowen, *Miracle at Philadelphia* (Boston: Little, Brown, 1966), p. 105.

8. To be fair, however, the word "administration" does appear in *The Federalist Papers* 124 times. See Jerry Mitchell, *The American Experiment with Government Corporations* (Armonk, NY: Sharpe, 1998), p. 6.

9. Lynton K Caldwell, "The Administrative Republic: The Contrasting Legacies of Hamilton and Jefferson," *Public Administration Quarterly* 13 (Winter 1990), pp. 483–484.

10. For a revealing exposition of this episode, we suggest, Stephanie P. Newbold, "Statesmanship and Ethics: The Case of Thomas Jefferson's Dirty Hands," *Public Administration Review* 65 (November/December 2005), pp. 669–677.

11. Deil Wright, "Public Administration Revolutions in the American States: A Half-Century of Evolving Roles and Responsibilities Among State Agencies and Administrators in the Federal System," Third Annual Lent D. Upson Lecture, Graduate Program in Public Administration, Wayne State University, Detroit, MI, March 20, 2002. Current figures are for 1999.

12. F. Ted Hebert, "Governors as Chief Administrators and Managers," in *Handbook of State Government Administration*, John J. Gargan, ed. (New York: Marcel Dekker, 2000). The research was conducted in 1994.

13. National Commission on the State and Local Public Service, *Hard Truths/Tough Choices: An Agenda for State and Local Government Reform*. First Report (Albany, NY: The Nelson A. Rockefeller Institute of Government, State University of New York, 1993), p. 16.

14. Yoo-Sung Choi, Chung-Lee Cho, and Deil S. Wright, "Administrative Autonomy among American State Agencies: An Empirical Analysis of Fragmentation and Functionalism," *International Journal of Public Administration* 27 (January 2004), pp. 373–398. The quotations are on pp. 382 and 394.

15. Tanis J. Salant,"Trends in County Government Structures," *Municipal Year Book, 2004* (Washington, DC: International City/County Management Association, 2004), p. 40. Figures are for 2002.

16. Susan A. MacManus and Charles S. Bullock III, "The Form, Structure, and Composition of America's Municipalities in the New Millennium," *Municipal Year Book, 2003* (Washington, DC: International City/County Management Association, 2003), pp. 9,17. Figures are for 2001.

17. U.S. Bureau of Census, *Census of Governments, 1992*, Vol. 1, No. 2 (Washington, DC: U.S. Government Printing Office, 1995), pp. 9–19.

18. Salant, "Trends in County Government Structure," pp. 35–41, and MacManus and Bullock, "Form, Structure, and Composition of America's Municipalities in New Millennium," pp. 3–18.

19. See, for example, J. Edward Benton, "County Government Structure and County Revenue Policy: What's the Connection?" *State and Local Government Review* 35 (Spring 2003), pp. 78–89; Victor De Santis and Tari Renner, "The Impact of Political Structures on Public Policies in American Counties," *Public Administration Review* 54 (May/June 1994), pp. 291–295; William E. Lyons, "Reform and Response in American Cities: Structure and Policy Reconsidered," *Social Science Quarterly* 59 (June 1978), pp. 118–132; and Robert J. Lineberry and Edmund P. Fowler, "Reformism and Public Policies in American Cities," *American Political Science Review* 61 (September 1967), pp. 701–716. However, one examination of twenty counties found that when counties moved to a strong chief executive, there was "virtually no effect on rates of change in county fiscal behavior" (p. 315). See David R. Morgan and Kenneth Kickham, "Changing the Form of County Government: Effects of Revenue and Expenditure Policy," *Public Administration Review* 59 (July/August 1999), pp. 315–324.

20. Pew Research Center for the People and the Press, *Deconstructing Distrust: How Americans View Government* (Washington, DC: Author, 1998), p. 2. Data are for 1997.

21. Ibid.

22. Hart-Teeter Poll, *America Unplugged: Citizens and Their Government* (Washington, DC: Council for Excellence in Government, 1999), p. 4. Data are for 1999.

23. John R. Hibbing and Elizabeth Theiss-Morse, "Americans' Desire for Stealth Democracy: How Declining Trust Boosts Political Participation," Paper Presented at the Annual Meeting of the Midwest Political Science Association (Chicago, April 2001), Table 1 and pp. 2–3. Data are for 1998. See also John R. Hibbing and Elizabeth Theiss-Morse, *Stealth Democracy: Americans' Beliefs about How Government Should Work* (New Delhi: Cambridge University Press, 2002).

24. Pew Research Center for the People and the Press, *Deconstructing Distrust*, p. 2. Data are for 1997.

25. Richard L. Cole, John Kincaid, and Alejandro Rodriguez, "Public Opinion on Federalism and Federal Political Culture in Canada, Mexico, and the United States, 2004," *Publius* 34 (Summer 2004), p. 210. Figures are for 2004. Surveys also indicate that top public executives and administrators have no more confidence in government and the people running it than the average citizen. See: Gregory B. Lewis, "In Search of Machiavellian Milquetoasts: Comparing Attitudes of Bureaucrats and Ordinary People," *Public Administration Review* 50 (March/April 1990), pp. 220–227; and National Academy of Public Administration, *Key Issues of Governance, Public Management and Public Administration* (Washington, DC: Author, 1999).

26. Annenberg Campaign Data Base, as cited in Paul C. Light, *The True Size of Government* (Washington, DC: Brookings, 1999), p. 88.

27. Subcommittee on Intergovernmental Relations. Committee on Government Operations, U.S. Senate, *Confidence and Concern: Citizens View Government, A Survey of Public Attitudes. Part 2.* 93rd Congress, 1st Session (Washington, DC: U.S. Government Printing Office, 1973), p. 310. This was national Harris poll. Consider some representative findings from this unique survey: 60 percent of elected officials said civil servants did things "by the book" compared to 23 percent of the public; 48 percent of politicians said civil servants "play it safe" compared to 21 percent of the citizenry; 58 percent said they were "bureaucratic" versus 14 percent; 25 percent said they "make red tape" versus 12 percent; and 14 percent of elected officials said public administrators were "dull," compared to 6 percent of the public. Only in questions that concerned the honesty of public administrators did elected officials express more favorable opinions of their bureaucrats than did the public, possibly because these officials realize that they can be held accountable for bureaucratic corruption.

28. Thad E. Hall, "Live Bureaucrats and Dead Public Servants: How People in Government Are Discussed on the Floor of the House," *Public Administration Review* 62 (March 2002), pp. 242–251. The terms "public servant" and "civil servant" are associated with positive connotations about 95 percent of the time, and even "government workers" garners over 60 percent positives when it is used. But, relative to the use of "bureaucrat," these terms are not used much. Republicans call public administrators "bureaucrats" more frequently than do Democrats, and its use is increasing over time.

29. Beverly A. Cigler and Heidi L. Neiswender, "Bureaucracy in the Introductory American Government Textbook," *Public Administration Review* 51 (September/October 1991), p. 444.

30. David J. Lorenzo, "Countering Popular Misconceptions of Federal Bureaucracies in American Government Classes," *Political Science and Politics* (December 1999) p. 744.

31. Marc Schwerdt, "Stories of Service: Public Service in the Children's Literature of United States and Great Britain," *Politics and Policy* 31 (June 2002), pp. 195–214.

32. C. Artwick and Margaret T. Gordon, "Daily Newspapers and Portrayals of US Cities," *Newspaper Research Journal* 19 (1,1998), pp. 54–63.

33. Carrie Rickey, "Hollywood Movies Cast Government as Bad Guy," *Philadelphia Inquirer* (July 7, 1996). The review covered the first half of the 1990s.

34. Partnership for Trust in Government, Council for Excellence in Government, *Images of Government in TV Entertainment* (Washington, DC: Center for Media and Public Affairs, 1999), pp. 1–2. The analysis encompassed 1,234 series episodes and 9,588 characters, of whom 2,664 (28 percent) were public sector employees: teachers, law enforcers, public officials, and civil servants. Teachers and law enforcers fared better than civil servants and public officials (with civil servants portrayed slightly more favorably than public officials) and were positively portrayed but also slipped over time. Seventy percent of the episodes that dealt with governmental performance portrayed government as a poor performer. It is noteworthy that 29 percent of the American public hold the media responsible for "what's wrong with government." Only special interest groups score higher, at 38 percent. See Hart-Teeter Poll, *America Unplugged*, p. 3. Data are for 1999.

35. Pew Research Center for the People and the Press, *Deconstructing Distrust*, p. 2.

36. Ibid. Figures are for 1997 and 1981.

37. Hart-Teeter Poll, *America Unplugged*, p. 4. Figures are for 1999. Twenty-four percent of respondents blame elected politicians for government's problems.

38. Subcommittee on Intergovernmental Relations, Committee on Government Operations, U.S. Senate, *Confidence and Concern, Part 1*, pp. 173–175, and *Part 2*, pp. 301, 303, 305, 311, 313, 315, 319, and 321. Data are for 1973.

39. Daniel Katz, Barbara A. Gutek Robert L. Kahn, and Eugenia Barton, *Bureaucratic Encounters* (Ann Arbor: Institute for Social Research, University of Michigan, 1975), pp. 64, 68, 69, and 221. Data are for 1973.

40. Pew Research Center for the People and the Press, *Performance and Purpose: Constituents Rate Government Agencies* (Washington, DC: Author, 2000). Data are for 2000.

41. As derived from data in Theodore H. Poister and Gary T. Henry, "Citizen Ratings of Public and Private Service Quality: A Comparative Perspective," *Public Administration Review* 54 (March/April 1994), p. 158; Subcommittee on Intergovernmental Relations, Committee on Government Operations, U.S. Senate, *Confidence and Concern, Part 1*, pp. 173–175 and *Part 2*, pp. 301, 303, 305, 311, 313, 315, 319, and 321; Barbara J. Nelson, "Clients and Bureaucracies: Applicant Evaluations of Public Human Service and Benefit Programs," paper presented at the American Political Science Association, Washington DC, 1979, pp. 6–8; and Stuart M. Schmidt, "Client-Oriented Evaluation of Public Agency Effectiveness," *Administration & Society* 8 (February 1977), pp. 412, 421–422.

The Poister and Henry article is based on a poll of Georgians conducted in 1993. The congressional data are from a national Harris poll conducted in 1973. The Nelson paper reflects a 1978 survey of applicants for Ohio's government services. The Schmidt article is based on a questionnaire administered in 1976 concerning the Wisconsin State Employment Service.

42. Thomas I. Miller and Michelle A. Miller, "Standards of Excellence: U.S. Residents' Evaluations of Local Government Services," *Public Administration Review* 51 (November/December 1991), p. 503.

43. See Steven A. Peterson, "Sources of Citizens' Bureaucratic Contacts: A Multivariate Analysis," *Administration and Society* 20 (August 1988),

pp. 152–165, and any of the editions of Charles Goodsell's *Case for Bureaucracy*, Chapter 2.

44. Poister and Henry, "Citizen Ratings of Public and Private Service Quality," p. 155.

45. American Customer Satisfaction Index, *ACSI Overall Federal Government Scores with Historic Scores of Agencies Measured, 1999–2004* and as derived from data in *National Quarterly Scores: ACSI 1994 to Q4 2004* at http://www.customerservice.gov. Fifty-three "customer groups" served by thirty-nine federal agencies, accounting for essentially all customer services provided by the federal government, are surveyed. The private sector has surpassed the federal government on customer satisfaction in five out of six years, but the scores are close, ranging from 68.6 percent to 72.1 percent for the federal government, and from 70 percent to 74.2 percent for industry.

46. Charles T. Goodsell, *The Case for Bureaucracy: A Public Administration Polemic,* 2nd ed. (Chatham, NJ: Chatham House, 1985), p. 106.

47. As derived from data in Pew Research Center for the People and the Press, *Performance and Purpose.*

48. Poister and Henry, "Citizen Ratings of Public and Private Service Quality," p. 158.

49. Susan M. Willis-Walton and Alan E. Bayer, *Quality of Life in Virginia: 2003* (Blacksburg: Center for Survey Research, Virginia Polytechnic Institute and State University, 2003), pp. D9–D10. This was a 2002 survey of Virginians.

50. U.S. Advisory Commission on Intergovernmental Relations, *The Federal Role in the Federal System: The Dynamics of Growth, A Crisis of Confidence and Competence,* A-77 (Washington, DC: U.S. Government Printing Office, 1980), pp. 111, 131. In 1900, the total government labor force (1.4 million workers) amounted to 1.8 percent of the population (in 1870 it was only 0.7 percent but had attained 2.8 percent by 1920), and in 1902 all government revenues ($1.7 billion) amounted to 8.2 percent of the gross national product. Even by 1913, this figure was still 8.1 percent, but by 1922 (following World War I), it had hit 12.8 percent.

51. As derived from data in U.S. Bureau of the Census, *Statistical Abstract of the United States, 2006* 125th ed. (Washington, DC: U.S. Government Printing Office), Tables 418, 451, and 1335. The government employment-to-population ratio is for 2003. Government receipts as a percentage of GDP, total receipts, and receipts per person are for 2003.

52. Ron Chernow, *Titan: The Life of John D. Rockefeller, Sr.* (New York: Random House, 1998).

53. "Forbes Four Hundred," Forbes Magazine, http://www.forbes.com. Figures are for 2005.

54. The national debt was $2.8 billion in 1912, the year when Rockefeller's Standard Oil Corporation was shattered by federal antitrust litigation.

55. For readers wishing to know the current federal debt precisely, check U.S. Bureau of the Public Debt, The Federal Debt to the Penny, http://www.publicdebt.treas.gov/opdpenny.htm.

56. As derived from data in U.S. Bureau of the Census, *Statistical Abstract of the United States, 2006,* Table 1335. Figures are for 2004. This percentage is very stable over time. In 1970, American taxes as a percentage of GDP were 29 percent. It appears that the United States not only has a very low tax rate overall, but also that each kind of its taxes—that is, income, Social Security, sales, and property taxes—is lower than the same tax in its counterpart countries. See Sven Steinmo, "Why Is Government So Small in America?" *Governance* 8 (July 1995), pp. 303–334.

57. Mandy Rafool, "The Fiscal Perspective: State Tax and Expenditure Limits," *The Fiscal Letter* 5 (Fall 1996), all. Figure is for 1996.

58. American Association of State Colleges and Universities, *State Issues Digest* (Washington, DC: Author, 1998), pp. 8–9. Figure is for 1998.

59. As derived from the data in U.S. Advisory Commission on Intergovernmental Relations, *Tax and Expenditures Limits on Local Governments,* M-194 (Washington, DC: U.S. Government Printing Office, 1995), pp. 5–10.

60. As derived from data in American Council on Intergovernmental Relations, *Significant Features of Fiscal Federalism, 1995,* Vol. 2 (Washington, DC: Author, 1998), p. 54, for 1978–1994 growth rates, and David Osborne and Peter Hutchinson, *The Price of Government: Getting the Results We Need in an Age of Permanent Fiscal Crisis* (New York: Basic Books, 2004), pp. 44–47, for subsequent growth rates.

61. As derived from American Council on Intergovernmental Relations, *Significant Features of Fiscal Federalism, 1995,* Vol. 2, p. 54. Current growth rates are for 1978–1994. State and local revenue growth refers to revenue derived from these governments' own revenue sources and does not includes intergovernmental revenue transferred to them by other governments. For some related analyses, see Tyson King-Meadows and David Lowry, "The Impact of the Tax Revolt on State Fiscal Caps: A Research Update," *Public Budgeting and Finance* 16 (Spring 1996), pp. 95–112; Paul G. Lewis, "Durability of Local Government Structure: Evidence from California," *State and Local Government Review* 32 (Winter 2000), pp. 34–48; and Tom Rown, "Constitutional Tax Expenditure Limitations in Colorado: The Impact on Municipal Governments," *Public Budgeting and Finance* 20 (August 2000), pp. 29–50.

62. Jim Clark, "The International Screwthread Commission," *Washington Monthly,* as reprinted in *Doing Public Administration: Exercises, Essays, and Cases,* Nicholas Henry, ed. (Boston: Allyn and Bacon, 1978), pp. 41–42.

63. Herbert Kaufman, *Are Government Organizations Immortal?* (Washington, DC: Brookings Institution, 1976). The years covered were 1923–1973.

64. B. Guy Peters and Bryan W. Hogwood, "The Death of Immortality: Births, Deaths, and Metamorphoses in the U.S. Federal Bureaucracy, 1933–1983," *American Review of Public Administration* 18 (June 1988), p. 131.

65. Jerrell D. Coggburn and Saundra K. Schneider, "The Quality of Management and Government Performance: An Empirical Analysis of the American States," *Public Administration Review* 63 (March/April 2003), pp. 206–213. The quotation is on p. 206.

66. The judiciary has ruled only rarely that the constitutional principle of separation of powers is an adequate reason for legislators to negate a policy made by an executive agency, rather than by the legislature. The last time that the Supreme Court ruled in any major way that agency rule making violated separation of powers was in 1935, in the cases of *Schechter Poutry Crop. v. United States and Pamamá Refining Co. v. Ryan.* In both, the Court held that the National Industrial Recovery Act was unconstitutional. The 1983 case, in which the Court ruled that the legislative veto was unconstitutional, was U.S. Immigration and Naturalization Wervice v. Chada.

67. Robert Kasten, "It's a Tough Competition for the Werst Regulation," *Washington Times* (July 23, 1996).

68. John W. Kingdon, *Agendas, Alternatives, and Public Policies* (Boston: Little, Brown, 1984), p. 47.

69. Ibid., p. 34.

70. For a good review of this research, as well as some original findings, see Virginia Gray and David Lowery, "Where Do Policy Ideas Come From? A Study of Minnesota Legislators and Staffers," *Journal of Public Administration Research and Theory* 10 (July 2000), pp. 573–597.

71. Kim U. Hoffman, "Legislative Fiscal Analysts: Influence in State Budget Development," *State and Local Government Review* 38 (1, 2006), p. 49.

72. Peter Baker and Dafnia Linzer, "Policy Shifts Felt after Bolton's Departure from State Dept.," *Washington Post* (June 20, 2005). Rose Gottemoeller, a Clinton administration official who worked on nonproliferation issues, is quoted.

73. Kingdon, *Agendas, Alternatives, and Public Policies,* p. 34.

74. Harrison W. Fox, Jr. and Susan Webb Hammond, *Congressional Staffs: The Invisible Force in American Law Making* (New York: The Free Press, 1977), p. 144. See also: Barbara S. Romzek, "Accountability for Congressional Staff," *Journal of Public Administration Research and Theory* 10 (August 2000), pp. 413–446.

75. Julia Lays, "Then and Now," *State Legislatures* (July/August 1999), pp. 50–56. Figures are for 1999.

76. Michael J. BeVier, *Politics Backstage: Inside the California Legislature* (Philadelphia: Temple University Press, 1979), p. 229.

77. MacManus and Bullock, "Form, Structure, and Composition of America's Municipalities in New Millennium," p. 11. Figures are for 2001. Nineteen percent of municipalities have no chief appointed official.

78. Tari Renner and Victor S. DeSantis, "Municipal Form of Government: Issues and Trends," *Municipal Year Book, 1998* (Washington, DC: International City/County Management Association, 1998), pp. 34, 36. Figures are for 1996.

79. See, for example, Ronald A. Loveridge, *The City Manager and Legislative Policy* (Indianapolis: Bobbs-Merrill, 1971); Robert J. Huntley and Robert J. McDonald, "Urban Managers: Managerial Style and Social Roles," *Municipal Year Book, 1975* (Washington, DC: International City Management Association, 1975), pp. 149–159; Betty A. Zisk, *Local Interest Politics: A One-Way Street* (Indianapolis: Bobbs-Merrill, 1973), p. 58; R. E. Green, "Local Government Managers: Styles and Challenges," *Baseline Data Report* 19 (March 1987), pp. 1–11; and James H. Svara, *Official Relationships in the City* (New York: Oxford University Press, 1990).

80. James H. Svara, "Council and Administrator Perspectives on the City Manager's Role: Conflict, Divergence, or Congruence?" *Administration and Society* 23 (August 1991), p. 231.

81. Robert T. Golembiewski and Gerald Gabris, "Today's City Managers: A Legacy of Success-Becoming- Failure," *Public Administration Review* 54 (November/December 1994), p. 525.

82. James H. Svara, "The Shifting Boundary between Elected Officials and City Managers in Large Council-Manager Cities," *Public Administration Review* 59 (January/ February 1999), pp. 47–48.

83. John Nalbandian, "Politics and Administration in Council-Manager Government: Differences between Newly Elected and Senior Council Members," *Public Administration Review* 64 (March/April 2004), pp. 200–209. This was an analysis of council members in the greater Kansas City area.

84. Harmon Ziegler and M. Kent Jennings, with the assistance of G. Wayne Peak, *Governing American Schools: Political Interaction in Local School Districts* (North Scituate, MA: Duxbury, 1974).

85. Harvey J. Tucker and L. Harmon Ziegler, *Professionals versus the Public: Attitudes, Communication, and Response in School District* (New York: Longman, 1980), p. 143.

86. Quoted in Clinton Rossister, *The American Presidency* (Ney York: American Library, 1956), p. 42.

87. Richard Nixon, as quoted in Richard P. Nathan, *The Plot That Falled: Nixon and the Administrative Presidency* (New York: John Wiley and Sons, 1975), p. 69.

88. Jimmy Carter, as quoted by Haynes Johnson, "Tests," *Washington Post* (April 30, 1978).

89. John F. Kennedy, as quoted in Peter Goldman et al., "The Presidency: Can Anyone Do the Job?" *Newsweek* (January 26, 1981), p. 41.

90. United Press International, "Amy's Homework Aid Likely Costs Thousands," *Arizona Republic* (February 9, 1981).

91. See, for example, Hugh Heclo, *A Government of Strangers: Executive Politics in Washington* (Washington, DC: Brookings, 1977); B. Dan Wood, *Bureaucratic Dynamics: The Role of Bureaucracy in Democracy* (Westview, CN: Westview, 1994); and Marissa Martino Golden, *What Motivates Bureaucrats? Politics and Administration during the Reagan Years* (New York: Columbia University Press, 2000).

92. For a good, brief review of this, see George C. Edwards, III, "Why Not the Best? The Loyalty-Competent Trade-Off in Presidential Appointments," *Brookings Review* 19 (Spring 2001), pp. 12–16.

93. Matthew Potoski and Neal Woods, "Designing State Clean Air Agencies: Administrative Procedures and Bureaucratic Autonomy," *Journal of Public Administration Research and Theory* 11 (April 2001), pp. 203–221.

94. James D. Carroll, "Service, Knowledge, and Choice: The Future as Post-Industrial Administration," *Public Administration Review* 35 (November/December 1975), p. 578.

95. James D. Carroll, "Noetic Authority," *Public Administration Review* 29 (September/October 1969), pp. 492–500.

96. The notion of "knowledge management" first appeared in Nicholas Henry, "Knowledge Management: A New Concern for Public Administration," *Public Administration Review* 34 (May/June 1974), pp. 189–196. A symposium on knowledge management soon followed. See James D. Carroll and Nicholas Henry, symposium editors, "Symposium on Knowledge Management," *Public Administration Review* 35 (November/ December 1975), pp. 567–602. The term and the concept continue to be salient. See, for example, Ramón C. Barquin, Alex Bennet, and Shereen G. Remez, eds., *Knowledge Management: The Catalyst for Electronic Government* (Vienna, VA: Management Concepts, 2001), and Ramón C. Barquin, Alex Bennet, and Shereen G. Remez, eds., *Building Knowledge Management: Environments for Electronic Government* (Vienna, VA: Management Concepts, 2001).

97. Ziegler and Jennings, *Governing American Schools*, pp. 177–178.

98. Huntley and McDonald, "Urban Managers," p. 153.

99. Ibid., p. 150.

100. David E. Rosenbaum, "Politics as Usual, and Then Some," *New York Times* (September 20, 2005).

101. Ibid.

102. Robert Pear, "Agency Sees Withholding of Medicare Data from Congress as Illegal," *New York Times* (May 4, 2004). The actuary was Richard S. Foster. The head of Medicare said he was just kidding when he threatened to fire Foster.

103. Quoted in Rosenbaum, "Politics as Usual, and Then Some."

104. Marc Kaufman, "FDA Official Quits Over Delay on Plan B." *Washington Post* (September 1, 2005). Susan F. Wood was the assistant commissioner for women's health and director of the Office of Women's Health in the FDA. The contraceptive the question was known as Plan B.

105. U.S. Government Accountability Office, *Climate Change Assessment: Administration Did Not Meet Reporting Deadline*, GAO–05–338 Climate Change Assessment (Washington, DC: U.S. Government Printing Office, 2005). None of the planned twenty-one studies met this requirement of the Global Change Research Act of 1990.

106. Leonard Pitts Jr., "A Political- Free Zone in D.C.? Ridge Must Be Kidding," *Savannah Morning News* (August 9, 2004).

107. Eric Lichtblau, "9/11 Report Cites Many Warnings about Hijackings," *New York Times* (February 10, 2005).

108. James Surowiecki, "Hail to the Geek," *The New Yorker* (April 19 and 26, 2004), p. 70.

109. Ibid.

CHAPTER **2**

Public Administration's Century in a Quandary

All professions are intimately aligned with intellectuals whose role is one of defining what the profession is. Public administration is no exception.

In this chapter we review the successive definitional crises of public administration—that is, how the field has "seen itself" in the past.[1] These paradigms of public administration are worth knowing because one must appreciate where the field has been to understand where it is. We suggest that public administration is unique, that it differs significantly from both political science (public administration's "mother discipline") and management (public administration's traditional alter ego).

Public administration has developed as an academic field through a succession of six paradigms. Each phase may be characterized according to whether it has "locus" or "focus."[2]

Locus is the institutional "where" of the field. A recurring locus of public administration is the government bureaucracy, but this has not always been the case and often this traditional locus has been blurred.

Focus is the specialized "what" of the field, its body of knowledge and expertise. One focus of public administration has been the study of certain "principles of administration," but again, the foci of the discipline have altered with the changing paradigms of public administration.

The paradigms of public administration may be understood in terms of locus or focus; when one has been relatively sharply defined in academic circles, the other has been ignored and vice versa.

The Beginning

Woodrow Wilson largely set the tone for the early study of public administration in an essay entitled, "The Study of Administration," published in the *Political Science Quarterly* in 1887. In it, Wilson observed that it "is getting harder to *run* a constitution than to frame one," and called for the bringing of more intellectual resources to bear in the management of the state.[3]

Wilson's seminal article has been variously interpreted by later scholars. In reality Wilson himself seems ambivalent about what public administration really was. Wilson failed "to amplify what the study of administration actually entails, what the proper relationship should be between the administrative and political realms, and whether or not administrative study could ever become an abstract science skin to the natural sciences."[4]

Nevertheless, Wilson unquestionably posited one unambiguous thesis in his article that has had a lasting impact on the field: Public administration was worth studying. Political scientists would later create the first identifiable paradigm of public administration around Wilson's contention.

Paradigm 1: The Politics/Administration Dichotomy, 1900–1926

Our benchmark dates for the Paradigm 1 period correspond to the publication of books written by Frank J. Goodnow and Leonard D. White; these dates, like the years chosen as marking the later periods of the field, are only rough indicators. In *Politics and Administration* (1900), Goodnow contended that there were "two distinct functions of government," which he identified with the title of his book. "Politics," said Goodnow, "has to do with policies or expressions of the state will," while administration "has to do with the execution of these policies."[5] Separation of powers provided the basis of the distinction. The legislative branch, aided by the interpretive abilities of the judicial branch, expressed the will of the state and formed policy; the executive branch administered those policies impartially and nonpartisanly.

The emphasis of Paradigm 1 was on locus—where public administration should be. Clearly, in the view of Goodnow and his fellow public administrationists, public administration should center in the government's bureaucracy. The justification of this locus became known as the *politics/administration dichotomy.*

This somewhat naive distinction between politics and administration would plague the field and the practice of public administration for years to come.

American Public Administration: Origins

Public administration received its first serious attention from scholars during this period largely as a result of the reformist "public service movement" that was sweeping the American political landscape in the early twentieth century.

Think Tanks for Public Service. One of the first concrete developments that reflected the public service movement was the founding, and funding, of the New York Bureau of Municipal Research in 1906 by John D. Rockefeller. The bureau was a prototype of what we now know as "think tanks," and it was extraordinarily influential in laying the intellectual groundwork of what public administration should be, producing some of the early guides for a wide variety of public administrative tasks. Its research was targeted specifically at improving the governing of New York City.

These activities, mundane though they may seem to us, were revolutionary at the time. Tammany Hall, the corrupt political machine that ran the city, felt directly threatened by the bureau, referring to it as "The Bureau of Municipal Besmirch," and initiated a smear campaign designed to emasculate it. The campaign backfired, and encouraged reformers in other cities to emulate the bureau's success. By 1928, seventy-four cities had independently funded research bureaus, and they continued to multiply, both domestically and abroad, through the early 1940s.[6]

Public Administration and the Universities. In 1912, the New York Bureau of Municipal Research and its counterparts across the country were featured in an edition of *Annals of the American Academy of Political and Social Science,*[7] and this academic publicity may have tweaked further the already accelerating interest of the professoriate, particularly political scientists, in the nascent notion of public administration.

In that same year, a Committee on Practical Training for Public Service was established by the American Political Science Association and, in 1914, its report recommended with unusual foresight that special "professional schools" were needed to train public administrators, and that new technical degrees might also be necessary for this purpose.[8] This committee formed the nucleus of the Society for the Promotion of Training for the Public Service, founded in 1914—the forerunner of the American Society for Public Administration (ASPA), which was established in 1939.

Public administration soon emerged as a building block of political science. A report issued in 1914 by the American Political Science Association stated that the field of political science was concerned with training for citizenship; professional preparations such as law and journalism; educating researchers; and training "experts and to prepare specialists for governmental positions."[9]

The relations between the "public administrationists" (that is, the academics) and the public administrators (that is, the practitioners) were at this time quite close—indeed, little distinction was made between the two. In 1911, the New York Bureau of Municipal Research established (and ran) the nation's first school of public administration, the Training School for Public Service. In 1924, the school, which had produced the nation's first trained corps of public administrators, was transferred lock, stock, and students to Syracuse University, where it became the nation's first public administration program to be associated with a university—the Maxwell School of Citizenship and Public Affairs.[10]

Public administration began picking up academic legitimacy in the 1920s; notable in this regard was the publication of Leonard D. White's *Introduction to the Study of Public Administration* in 1926, the first textbook entirely devoted to the field. White's text was quintessentially American Progressive in character and, in its quintessence, reflected the general thrust of the field: Partisan politics should not intrude on administration; management lends itself to scientific study; public administration is capable of becoming a "value-free" science in its own right; the mission of administration is economy and efficiency, period.[11]

The Uses of the Dichotomy

There were two long-term effects of Paradigm 1, one practical and the other intellectual.

The Dichotomy and the Professionals. As a practical matter, the politics/administration dichotomy offered some protection for a fledgling profession.[12] Public administration in general was still new when the Depression struck in 1929, and there was good reason to believe that a corps of professional government administrators would be seen as a disposable luxury by elected officeholders, especially in hard-pressed smaller governments. The politics/administration dichotomy, which held that what public administrators did was entirely different from what elected officeholders did, provided an ideological shield behind which public administrators could lower their political profile and justify their costs.

The conscious or not-so-conscious decision by early public administrators to embrace the contention that they were different—and starkly so—from politicos may well have been shrewd and prudent in protecting their young profession, but it did have regrettable consequences. Most notably, it reduced in the public eye the prospect of public administrators as real or potential public leaders. Ironically, creating a corps of unusually well educated public leaders, who were also public administrators, had been the hope of those scholars who first posited the idea that administration differed from politics.

The Dichotomy and the Intellectuals. Intellectually, the net result of Paradigm 1 was to strengthen the notion of a distinct politics/administration dichotomy by relating it to a corresponding value/fact dichotomy. Thus, everything that public administrationists scrutinized in the executive branch was imbued with the colorings and legitimacy of being somehow "factual" and "scientific," while the study of public policymaking and related matters was left to the political scientists. Largely because of the emphasis on "science" and "facts" in public administration, a foundation was laid for the later "discovery" of certain scientific "principles" of administration.

Paradigm 2: The Principles of Administration, 1927–1937

In 1927, W. F. Willoughby's book *Principles of Public Administration* appeared as the second fully fledged text in the field, and we have selected its publication as the beginning of the field's second paradigm. Although Willoughby's *Principles* was as entirely American Progressive in tone as White's *Introduction*, its title alone indicated the new thrust of public administration: That certain scientific principles of administration existed; they could be discovered; and administrators would be expert in their work if they learned how to apply these principles.

A Reputational Zenith

The principles of administration period saw a flowering of public administration, both professionally and academically. "Professional associations for government employees had grown with 'unexampled rapidity' . . . Research in the field of public administration had also expanded dramatically. . . . University and college programs in public administration were proliferating [in fact, they quadrupled in about a decade], and governments were calling on the public administration community to provide advice on administrative problems more and more frequently."[13]

Critical to the establishment of public administration's rising legitimacy was the role of "the Rockefeller philanthropies," which transferred millions of dollars to municipal bureaus and universities. Between 1927 and 1937 "No important part of the public administration community was untouched by these philanthropies."[14]

It was during the phase represented by Paradigm 2 that public administration reached its reputational zenith. The focus of the field—its essential expertise in the form of administrative principles—waxed, while no one thought too seriously about its locus. Indeed, the locus of public administration was everywhere, since principles were principles and administration was administration, at least according to the perceptions of Paradigm 2. By the very fact that the principles of administration were indeed *principles*—that is, by definition, they "worked" in any administrative setting, regardless of sector, culture, function, environment, mission, or institutional framework and without exception—it therefore followed that they could be applied successfully anywhere.

In 1935, the Public Administration Clearing House held a conference at Princeton University, and the conference's report was radically different from the report issued in 1914. Suddenly political scientists had great difficulties with the idea of founding separate schools of public administration and believed instead that existing courses in political science departments and in other relevant disciplines, provided an education that was entirely adequate for budding bureaucrats. The conference, therefore, found itself "unable to find any single formula which warrants the establishment of an isolated college or university program which alone will emphasize preparation exclusively for the public service." Only a "university-wide approach" would be satisfactory, since the problem of public administration education exceeded the "confines of any single department or special institute or school."[15]

As a more modern scholar has since observed, "A logical consequence of this reasoning" as expressed by the Princeton Conference of 1935, "could have been the elimination of public administration as a discrete field of study within the universities."[16] Such were the dangers of not having a firm and stationary intellectual focus on which to build a curriculum.

Rebels with a Cause

Despite these difficulties, however, scholars who identified with the study of public administration nonetheless found it useful to establish, four years after the publication of the Princeton report, the American Society for Public Administration, which continues to function as the nation's primary association of scholars and practitioners of public administration. It is clear that ASPA represented "above all an attempt to loosen public administration from the restraints of political science."[17]

But the founding of ASPA was more than that: It was also an attempt to promote public administration as an identifiable profession.

The rebels of the thirties expressed public administration's conscious need to become both a discipline and a profession. But disciplines and professions have their own orthodoxies, and the "high-noon of orthodoxy,"[18] as it often has been called, of public administration was marked by the publication in 1937 of Luther H. Gulick and Lyndall Urwick's *Papers on the Science of Administration.* This landmark study also marked the high noon of prestige for public administration. Gulick and Urwick were confidantes of President Franklin D. Roosevelt and advised him on a variety of matters managerial; their *Papers* were a report to the President's Committee on Administrative Science.

Principles were important to Gulick and Urwick, but where those principles were applied was not; focus was favored over locus, and no bones were made about it. As they said in the *Papers*, "These principles can be studied as a technical question, irrespective of the purpose of the enterprise, the personnel comprising it, or any constitutional, political, or social theory underlying its creation."[19]

Gulick and Urwick promoted seven "principles" of administration and, in so doing, gave students of public administration that snappy anagram, POSDCORB. POSDCORB was the final expression of administrative principles. It stood for

P lanning
O rganizing
S taffing
D irecting
CO ordinating
R eporting
B udgeting

The Uses of the Principles

POSDCORB was public administration in 1937. To be fair, Gulick and Urwick (although perhaps more so in Gulick's case) clearly understood that their "principles" were not immutable facts of nature but were simply helpful touch points in conveying an understanding of how organizations worked and what public administrators did.[20] Nevertheless, over time, they became rigid "scientific principles" in the minds of the many readers of their work—a process encouraged, no doubt, by the predilections of later scholars to prop up straw men that they then could merrily demolish.

The Challenge, 1938–1950

In the year following the publication of Gulick and Urwick's defining opus, mainstream public administration received its first real hint of intellectual challenge. In 1938, Chester I. Barnard's *The Functions of the Executive* appeared. Its impact on public administration was not overwhelming at the time, but it later had considerable

influence on Herbert A. Simon when he was writing *Administrative Behavior*, his devastating critique of the field.

Dissent from mainstream public administration accelerated in the 1940s in two mutually reinforcing directions. One objection was that politics and administration could never be separated in any remotely sensible fashion. The other was that the principles of administration were something less than the final expression of managerial rationality.

Demurring to the Dichotomy

Although inklings of dissent began in the 1930s, a book of readings in the field, *Elements of Public Administration*, edited in 1946 by Fritz Morstein Marx, was one of the first major volumes to question the assumption that politics and administration could be dichotomized. All fourteen chapters in the book were written by practitioners and indicated a new awareness that what often appeared to be neutral "administrative" decisions often were heavily laden with political preferences and paybacks.

The Demise of the Dichotomy.   The abandonment of the politics/administration dichotomy culminated in 1950 when a leading scholar wrote in public administration's leading journal that, "A theory of public administration means in our time a theory of politics also."[21] With this declaration, the dichotomy died.

As a consequence, the nature of the field was fundamentally altered, and also, regrettably, diminished. The field's founders had harbored no qualms about the wisdom of differentiating public administration from the hoi polloi of politics because they firmly believed that only a knowledgeable, noble elite (that is, public administrators) could pull the people from their pestilent cistern of civic suffering, and into the light of prosperity and progress. Consider what Wilson wrote in this regard: "the many, the people. . . . are selfish, ignorant, timid, stubborn. . . . they are not the children of reason. . . . [Hence] bureaucracy can exist only where [it is entirely] . . . removed from the common political lives of the people. . . ."[22]

Wow. We forget, perhaps mercifully, just how arrogant the field's first thinkers could be. But it was an arrogance that, whatever its drawbacks, did imbue the public administration pioneers with a sense of mission, leadership, superiority, and elan that was largely lost when public administration became as "common" as politics. With time, the revisionist ideology that politics and administration were inseparable—indeed, indistinguishable—took root and rigidified.

The Dichotomy Resurgent? Today, this immoderate view has mellowed.[23] Yes, politics and administration do co-exist on the same continuum, but, at the far ends of that continuum, political acts (such as appointing to government jobs unqualified nephews) can be distinguished from administrative acts (such as appointing to government jobs the most qualified applicants drawn from a competitive pool), and easily so. True, it may be less easy to separate the political from the administrative in the middle reaches of that continuum, but we nonetheless understand that politics' values relate more to community, pluralism, personality, loyalty, passion, and ideology, whereas public administration's values relate more to hierarchy, elitism, impersonality, professionalism, dispassion, and neutrality. Politics and administration are differing "constellations of logic."[24]

Of even greater interest, and irony, new research suggests that the early public administrationists who first enunciated the politics/administration dichotomy may have got it at least partially right. An analysis of economic development activities in 516 cities in the United States found that "the Progressive ideology of the separation of politics from administration, institutionalized in the council-manager plan, allows administrators and elected officers to more easily resist opportunistic behavior. Economic and political forces have significant effects that are different for mayor-council communities than for council-manager communities."[25]

Things change so that they may remain the same.

Puncturing the Principles

Arising simultaneously with the challenge to the traditional politics/administration dichotomy

of the field was an even more basic contention: That there could be no such thing as a "principle" of administration. Although several scholars contributed to this view,[26] the most formidable dissection of the principles notion appeared in 1947: Simon's *Administrative Behavior: A Study of Decision-Making Processes in Administration Organization*, a volume of such intellectual force that it led to Simon's receiving the Nobel Prize in 1978.

Simon showed that for every "principle" of administration there was a counter principle, thus rendering the whole idea of principles moot. For example, the traditional administrative literature argued that bureaucracies must have a narrow "span of control" if orders were to be communicated and carried out effectively. Span of control means that a manager can properly "control" only a limited number of subordinates; after a certain number is exceeded (authorities differed on just what the number was), communication of commands grows increasingly garbled and control becomes increasingly ineffective and "loose." An organization that followed the principle of narrow span of control would have a "tall" organization chart (see Figure 2-1).

Span of control makes sense up to a point.[27] Yet, as Simon observed, the literature on administration argued with equal vigor for another principle: If organizations were to maximize effective communication and to reduce distortion (thereby enhancing responsiveness and control), then there should be as few hierarchical layers as possible—that is, a "flat" hierarchical structure. The logic behind this principle is that the fewer people who must pass a message up or down the hierarchy, the more likely it is that the message will arrive at its appointed destination relatively intact and undistorted. This, too, makes sense up to a point. The "flat" hierarchy required to bring the bureaucracy in accord with this principle of administration would have an organization chart like that in Figure 2-2.

Obviously to Simon and now to us, the two "principles" are mutually contradictory and therefore by definition could not be principles. This dilemma encompassed the whole of the traditional public administration literature, but it was never more than suspected of being so stark a case until Simon published his book.[28]

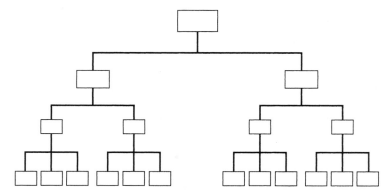

Figure 2-1   The "Principle" of Narrow Span of Control

By midcentury the two defining pillars of public administration—the politics/administration dichotomy and the principles of administration—had been abandoned by creative intellects in the field. This abandonment left public administration bereft of a distinct epistemological and intellectual identity.

Reaction to The Challenge, 1947–1950

In the same year that Simon decimated the traditional foundations of public administration in *Administrative Behavior*, he offered an alternative to the old paradigms. For Simon, a new paradigm for public administration meant that there ought to be two kinds of public administrationists working in harmony and reciprocal intellectual stimulation: those scholars concerned with developing "a pure science of administration" based on "a thorough grounding in social psychology," and a larger group concerned with "prescribing for public policy."[29]

Despite a proposal that was both rigorous and normative in its emphasis, Simon's call for a "pure science" put off many scholars in public administration. Simon's urging that social psychology provide the basis for understanding administrative behavior struck many public administrationists as foreign and even worrying; most of them had no training in social psychology.

But if, for whatever reason, the postwar public administrationists were reluctant to depart political science, political scientists were reluctant to let them do so. The American Political Science Association was in financially tight straits. Political scientists were aware that not only had public administrationists threatened secession in the past, but also now other subfields, such as international relations, were restive. In 1952, an article was published in the *American Political Science Review*, the field's leading journal, that put the matter plainly, and called for the continued "dominion of political science over public administration . . . [its] strange and unnatural child."[30]

Figure 2-2   The "Principle" of Maximized Communications

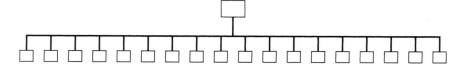

Paradigm 3: Public Administration as Political Science, 1950–1970

As a result of these essentially political concerns and the icy intellectual critiques of the field, public administrationists leaped back with some alacrity into the warm and engulfing sea of political science. The result was a renewed definition of locus—the governmental bureaucracy—but a corresponding loss of focus.

In brief, this third phase of definition was largely an exercise in reestablishing the linkages between public administration and political science. But the consequence of this exercise was to "define away" the field, at least in terms of its analytical focus, its essential "expertise." Thus, writings on public administration in the 1950s spoke of the field as an "emphasis," an "area of interest," or even as a "synonym" of political science.[31]

A survey of graduate education in public administration found such enormous diversity of forms and emphases in university programs[32] that one observer could accurately state, "The study of public administration in the United States is characterized by the absence of any fully comprehensive intellectual framework."[33] Public administration, as an identifiable field of study, began a long, downhill spiral.

Things got relatively nasty by the end of the decade and, for that matter, well into the 1970s. In 1962, public administration was not included as a subfield of political science in the report of the Committee on Political Science as a Discipline of the American Political Science Association. In 1964, a major survey of political scientists indicated a decline in faculty interest in public administration generally.[34] In 1967, public administration disappeared as an organizing category in the program of the annual meeting of the American Political Science Association. A leading scholar wrote in 1968 that "many political scientists not identified with Public Administration are indifferent or even hostile; they would sooner be free of it," and added that the public administrationist has an "uncomfortable . . . second-class citizenship."[35] Between 1960 and 1970, only 4 percent of all the articles published in the five major political science journals dealt with public administration,[36] and, even in the late 1970s, the president of the American Political Science Association dismissed public administration as an "intellectual wasteland."[37]

The Impact of Political Science: Bureaucracy in the Service of Democracy

Political science—the biological parent, the "mother discipline" of public administration—clearly has had a profound effect on the character of the field. Public administration was born in the house of political science, and its early rearing occurred in its backyard. The fundamental precepts of American political science—the self-evident worth of democracy, a pluralistic polity, political participation, equality under law, and due process are examples of these precepts—continue to hold sway among even the most independently minded public administrationists. While it can be convincingly argued that the American civic culture inculcates these values among all its intellectuals, and that American public administrationists would cherish democratic values regardless of their roots in political science, it nonetheless seems valid that the environment of political science sharpened and deepened the commitment of public administrationists to the country's core constitutional concepts. If, to indulge in speculation, public administration had been born and bred in the nation's business schools, would we have the same kind of academic field that we have today? Perhaps not. In any case, one can argue that, despite the disdain with which political science often treated public administration, political science was a salutary former of the field in laying its philosophic and normative foundations. Bureaucracy in a democracy existed not to serve the rulers, but the ruled.

Beyond providing a base of democratic values, however, political science seems to have less utility in the education of public administrators. Asks a scholar: "What can political science contribute to the improvement of practitioner skill?

An overview of the major intellectual approaches within political science suggests the answer is 'not much.'"[38] Or, to put the matter plainly, political science educates for (to quote one particularly lucid synopsis) "intellectualized understanding" of public administration, whereas the field itself educates for "knowledgeable action,"[39] and these epistemologies—academic *versus* professional—have fundamental differences.

Paradigm 4: Public Administration as Management, 1956–1970

Partly because of their second-class citizenship in a number of political science departments, some public administrationists began searching for an alternative. Although Paradigm 4 occurred roughly concurrently with Paradigm 3, it never received the broadly based favor that political science garnered from public administrationists. Nonetheless, the management option (which sometimes is called "administrative science" or "generic management") was a viable alternative for a significant number of scholars in public administration and, for some, it still is. But in both the political science and management paradigms, the essential thrust was one of public administration losing its identity and its uniqueness within the confines of some "larger" concept.

As a paradigm, management provides a focus but not a locus. It offers techniques, often highly sophisticated techniques, that require expertise and specialization, but in what institutional setting that expertise should be applied is undefined. As in Paradigm 2, administration is administration wherever it is found.

The Groundswell of Management

A number of developments, mostly stemming from the country's business schools, fostered the alternative paradigm of management. From the mid-fifties through the mid-sixties, a spate of scholars writing in a variety of journals accelerated the drumbeat of generic management as the logical successor to more "parochial" paradigms, such as public administration and business

administration.[40] In 1956, the important journal *Administrative Science Quarterly* was founded by a public administrationist on the premise that public, private, and nonprofit administration were false distinctions, that administration was administration, and we have selected this journal's debut as our benchmark for Paradigm 4.

These intellectual currents had a genuine impact on the curricula of universities. A 1961 survey of graduate study in public administration in the United States concluded that there was "a groundswell development that tends to pervade all others," and this was the idea that generic management constituted a unifying epistemology in the study of institutions and organizations, whether public, nonprofit, or private.[41] By the early 1960s, as many as a fifth of the business administration programs joined the study of business administration with public administration, economics, or other social sciences.[42]

Fundamentally Alike in All Unimportant Respects

Is public administration a subfield of management? Does public administration, at root, amount to little more than an understanding of civil service regulations, while the core managerial functions—such as budgeting, planning, and managing human resources, among other activities—remain essentially the same, whether they are practiced in businesses, nonprofits, or governments?

The Role of Organizational Research.   To some degree, of course, the determination of whether public administration and management are one and the same or separate and distinct depends upon the perspective of the viewer. Those theorists who concentrate on organizations that have instrumental missions (such as profits), whose approach to the organization is fragmented and characterized by case studies, and who analyze the organization in terms of its separate components and processes, usually argue that that the supposed differences between the public administration and management are artificial: Management is management is management. By contrast, those analysts who focus on organizations that have societal missions, and who treat the organization in holistic, systemic terms, generally hold that public administration is quite different from management.[43]

Just as individual scholars can have differing viewpoints on the question of where public administration fits, so can the larger literature that they both write and read. In the case of the management literature, and despite occasional protestations by management scholars to the contrary, the administrative phenomenon is typically cast in terms of the business world. A glance at virtually any introductory text in management brings this point home; government, when it is mentioned at all, often is treated as a "constraint" in the "task environment" of the corporation.

Of greater importance than the biases of individual researchers, however, is that the growing compendium of objective scholarship on this topic finds that public administration and private management are indeed distinct. As we shall see in Part II, a burgeoning spate of research that empirically compares public and private organizations casts grave doubt that the public and private administrative sectors can be fruitfully approached as a single entity except in the broadest strokes conceivable.

It follows that if public and private management are indeed separate, then those disciplines that attempt to understand these separate managerial sectors must rely to a significant degree on different sets of knowledge. And research indicates this to be the case. A careful study of eight major representative schools of generic management found that there were a total of no fewer than thirty different courses comprising the "common" core of courses for a masters degree! There was a "substantial amount of disagreement about the commonality of administrative tools and techniques."[44]

The Reality of the Real World. Experiential, as well as empirical, data support the contention that public administration is unique. As we review in Part II, the data indicate that the real-world skills needed by public administrators and business managers differ markedly. Those successful businesspeople who have become public managers are among the first to deny that there are significant similarities between the public and private sectors;[45] public administrators who enter the corporate world experience comparable difficulties of transition.[46]

Some seminally important research on federal bureau chiefs confirms that career public administrators are measurably better government managers than are those managers who are brought into government from other sectors, such as business and academe. Even though these new-to-government managers have higher levels of education and more varied professional experiences, on average, than do career public administrators, these bureau chiefs "get systematically lower management grades than bureau chiefs drawn from the civil service." It is the governmental careerists who are, by far, the more effective agency heads. In fact, educational and multi-experiential variables "are uncorrelated with management performance."[47] Sector counts.

The emerging consensus of both scholars and practitioners increasingly appears to be that public and private management are, to cite Wallace Sayre's old saw, "fundamentally alike in all unimportant respects."[48]

The Impact of Management: Understanding the "Public" in Public Administration

If political science was profoundly influential on the evolution and underlying values of public administration, management was less so. But, in many ways, the impact of management on public administration was also more positive. This is not to say that the household environment created by the field of management for public administration was one of warmth and succor. It was not. But instead of treating public administration like an abusive parent, as political science occasionally did, management let public administration stay in its house like an absent-minded aunt who was never quite sure who was living in which room and who often forgot to serve meals.

Management had some distinct and beneficial influences on public administration. Among them was its pressure on public administrationists to develop new methodologies of management that worked where traditional, private-sector methods did not,[49] and we review some of these techniques in Part III. But an unambiguously clear impact of the management paradigm was that it pushed public administrationists into rethinking what the "public" in public administration really meant.

"Publicness" and "Privateness"

Defining the "public" in public administration has long been a knotty problem for academics. In part, this is because western culture has yet to sort out the "complex-structured concept" of *publicness* and *privateness* in society.[50]

Publicness and privateness in society are comprised of three dimensions: agency, interest, and access.

Agency, in this sense, refers to the basic distinction between an agent acting on his or her own behalf (that is, privately), or as a government official whose actions affect others (that is, publicly).[51]

Interest is concerned with who benefits and who suffers. Hence, it is the interest of the private firm to benefit only the people in it or own it. By contrast, it is the interest of a government to serve every member of the community.

Access refers to the degree of openness that distinguishes publicness from privateness. Access encompasses access to *activities*, *space*, *information*, and *resources*.

The Institutional Definition of "Public"

Traditionally, when public administrationists thought about what the "public" in public administration meant at all, they thought about it in *institutional*, or *agency*, terms, in other words, the management of tax-supported agencies that appeared on government organization charts. The bureaucracy—the agencies—constituted the "locus" of public administration that held sway over the field's focus during the periods of Paradigms 1 (the politics/administration dichotomy) and 3 (public administration as political science). The institutional definition of "public" still dominates thinking in the field. One review of some of the more important literature on public organizations concluded that the vast majority of writers (70 percent of the books reviewed) took an "agency" perspective, as opposed to an "interest" or "access" view in analyzing public organizations.[52]

Nevertheless, there are real problems with an agency definition, and public administration's experience with Paradigm 4 helped tease these out. The most notable problem is that of the real world. Privatization, the rise of nongovernmental organizations, and many other developments all have conspired to make *public* administration an elusive entity, at least when attempts are made to define it in empirical terms that are based on an institutional construct. Alternatives were needed.

The Philosophic Definition of "Public"

During the 1970s, the alternative that emerged was a normative, philosophic one. The normative definition of public administration focused not on government agencies as such, but on those more dynamic phenomena that affected the public interest. Thus, rather than concentrating on the Department of Defense, for example, as its proper public locus, and leaving, say, Boeing Corporation to students of business management, public administrationists began to understand that the Department's contractual and political relationships with Boeing should now be their central object of study, since these relationships clearly involved the public interest.

The Organizational Definition of "Public"

The philosophic definition of public administration clearly had advantages over the institutional one, but there were problems with it, too. It was, after all, not terribly precise; one person's idea of the public interest might not be shared by another. Hence, a third option for defining the "public" in public administration presented itself: the organization.

Public administrationists had muddled around for years with the notion that public and private organizations were distinctly different, but many of them drew this conclusion more from ideological beliefs than from empirical research.

Beginning in the late 1970s, however, a spate of new research appeared that focused on the public organization. As we explain in Part II, this research is relatively unambiguous in concluding that there is at least one, absolutely critical difference between the public organization and its private counterpart, and from which many other important differences derive: the impact of the organization's outside environment on its inner workings and general behavior. What the new (and, for that matter, the old) literature on organizations is contending is that the influence of the environment is far more crucial to the behavior of public organizations than to private ones.

Private citizens, legislators, special interests, public boards, and other organizations significantly shape the public organization's resources, processes, decisions, and mission infinitely more minutely and authoritatively because they have vastly greater access to the meetings, offices, information, and resources of public organizations than to private organizations.

Our definitions of *public* administration—institutional, normative, and organizational—are in no way mutually exclusive; rather, they are mutually reinforcing. Together, they form the "public" in public administration, the locus of both the field and the profession.

The Working Differences between Public Administration and Private Management

Researchers have identified numerous distinctions between the worlds of public administration and private management. These differences pertain to four broad aspects of executive work: the task environment of the organization, organizational missions, structural constraints, and personal values.

More specifically, relative to private managers, public administrators must deal with more complex, less stable, and less competitive organizational environments and more organizationally penetrating environmental forces. Organizationally, the public sector's goals are more distinctive, more numerous, and less defined. Decision making in the public sector is more constrained by bureaucracy, red tape, and less autonomy. Finally, public administrators themselves are less materialistic, less loyal to their

organizations, and more committed to serving the public interest in facilitating social change.[53]

Scholars may dispute the validity of these distinctions,[54] but they are widely accepted as likely. We review them in various guises throughout this book.

The Forces of Separatism, 1965–1970

Even at its nadir during the period of Paradigms 3 and 4, public administration was sowing the seeds of its own renaissance. This process—quite an unconscious one at the time—took at least three distinct but complementary forms. Two were academic, and the third was professional.

Separatism in the Halls of Academe: Nuanced Notions

Two intellectual developments occurred in universities that had the unanticipated effect of encouraging public administration scholars to reconsider their linkages with political science.

"Science, Technology, and Public Policy." One was the emergence of "science, technology, and public policy" curricula in universities, largely during the 1960s. These programs, although broadly interdisciplinary, often were dominated by public administrationists located in political science departments. By the late 1960s, there were about fifty such curricula and they were situated for the most part in the top academic institutions of the country.

It was largely this new focus of science, technology, and public policy that gave those public administrationists connected with political science departments any claim to intellectual distinction during the 1960s. This renewed identity came in part because the focus of science, technology, and public policy did not (and does not) rely conceptually on the pluralist thesis favored by political science. Instead, the focus is elitist rather than pluralist, synthesizing rather than specializing, and hierarchical rather than communal.

"The New Public Administration." The second academic development was that of "the new public administration." In 1968, a conference of young public administrationists on the new public administration was held, and its proceedings revealed a growing disinclination to examine such traditional phenomena as efficiency, effectiveness, budgeting, and administrative techniques. Conversely, the new public administration was very much aware of normative theory, philosophy, and activism. If there was an overriding tone to the new public administration, it was a moral tone.[55] Nevertheless, with hindsight the "new P.A." can be viewed as a call for independence from both political science (it was not, after all, ever called the "new politics

---

Public Administration as Neither Management Nor Political Science

Luther Gulick, public administrationist and confidante of President Franklin D. Roosevelt, suggests that the "politico-administrative system" is unique and warrants a unique treatment.

My point is best illustrated by a lesson I learned from President Franklin D. Roosevelt. In January 1937, Brownlow, Merriam and I finished our report to the President on the administrative management of the government.

As you will remember, both the old age pension and the unemployment laws provided for contributions by the employer and the employee and the setting up of individual accounts under the name of each man and women covered. Millions of personal accounts were involved.

When it comes to making payments to those who retired or were unemployed, however, payments were to be made on the basis of legally defined amounts, which had little or no relation to the cash balances in the individual accounts. Thus, the individual cash accounts were quite superfluous for the administration of the system.

The technical experts thus reached the conclusion that individual accounts were totally unnecessary, and were a great administrative waste. I presented the idea to the President. He asked a number of questions, and said to come back. Something apparently troubled him about the suggestion.

Some days later he had me up to his room where he generally had breakfast in bed. He asked me to restate the proposition, and then said: "I don't see any hole in the argument, but the conclusion is dead wrong. The purpose of the accounts for Tom, Dick, and Harry is not to figure what we collect or pay. It is to make it impossible when I am gone for the ... Republicans to abolish the system. They would never dare wipe out the personal savings accounts of millions. You can't do that in America!"

Immediately I knew he was right. His reasoning rested not solely on the dramatic political insight stated so simply, but also on the psychological impact of personal accounts on the recipients and on those who paid into the social security account.

The error we technical management and accounting experts almost fell into was the inadequate definition of the system which we were analyzing. We did a good job on the law, on the bookkeeping, on administrative mechanics, and the fiscal and cost analysis. But we missed two dimensions of the problem, the political and the psychological, and we overlooked the problem of strategy which was always so important in the mind of the President.

Luther Gulick
Public Administration Review

of bureaucracy") and management (since management always had been emphatically technical rather than normative in approach).

A Bright but Brief Interlude. The science-technology-and-public-policy and the new-public-administration movements were short-lived. Science, technology, and public policy programs eventually devolved into specialized courses dealing with information systems and environmental management, while the new public administration never lived up to its ambitions of revolutionizing the discipline. Nevertheless, both movements had a lasting impact on public administration in that they nudged public administrationists into reconsidering their traditional intellectual ties with both political science and management and contemplating the prospects of academic autonomy.

Separatism in the Corridors of Power: Pride to the Practitioners!

While these intellectual currents were coursing through the halls of academe, an entirely separate wave was roiling in the corridors of power. For want of a better term, we will call it "practitioner pride," and it, too, fostered the rise of an independent field of public administration.

The symbol of this rising pride in the professionalism of public administration was the founding in 1967 of the National Academy of Public Administration.

Its founders wanted to create an association of the nation's most distinguished public administrators and academics who could serve as a resource in the solution of public problems—much like the National Academy of Sciences serves as the nation's single most authoritative advisor to government on scientific matters. Like the National Academy of Sciences, in fact, the National Academy of Public Administration is chartered by Congress, and it is the only other academy in the country that holds a congressional charter.

Membership is determined by vote of some 500 Fellows of the academy, and it is functioning much in the manner that its founders anticipated.

In sum, both the academic and practitioner communities of public administration were, in the last years of the sixties, moving toward an enhanced self-awareness. By 1970, the separatist movement was underway.

Paradigm 5: Public Administration as Public Administration: 1970–Present

"Public administration as public administration" refers to public administration's successful field of study and practice.

Public administration's fifth paradigm is, in some ways, a return to the locus of the governmental bureaucracy. The bonds linking pupils, professors, and public administrators could be unabashedly strengthened in a nurturing atmosphere, free from snide asides by political scientists about public administration's predilection for "nuts and bolts," and absent condescending comments by business faculties about the "sinecures" of gutless government bureaucrats.

NASPAA's Nascency

In 1970, the National Association of Schools of Public Affairs and Administration (NASPAA) was founded, and we have chosen that event as marking the beginning of Paradigm 5, a paradigm that continues to this day. The association is composed of some 250 colleges and universities that offer the country's Master of Public Administration (M.P.A.) programs, and its formation represented not only an act of secession by public administrationists, but also a rise of self-confidence as well. In 1983, its members decided to become the accrediting agency for the M.P.A. degree, and today more than a hundred M.P.A. programs have been accredited by NASPAA.

Surveys indicate that administrators of master of public administration degree programs find that accreditation by NASPAA brings with it a higher prestige for the M.P.A. program, a more effective program, and an enhanced ability to recruit higher quality faculty and students.[56]

An analysis of all NASPAA-accredited programs concluded that "the NASPAA standards appear to work well; students across the set of NASPAA-accredited schools appear to receive largely the same training in the core curriculum . . . [and M.P.A.] programs are generally more focused on professional skills" than they likely would be without those standards.[57]

The Statistics of Secession

Surveys of NASPAA's member institutions (which comprise the most definitive list of M.P.A. programs in the United States) that have been taken since 1973 indicate that public administration's secession from the fields of political science and management is real. Between them, freestanding schools, departments, and institutes of public administration, public policy, and urban studies consistently have amounted to about half of all university public administration programs, and this percentage is rising.[58]

For the last three decades or so, from less than a third to almost two-fifths of M.P.A. programs have remained housed in political science departments, and their proportion is declining over time.[59] The number of public administration programs that are housed within other kinds of schools or departments—typically, schools of business administration or departments of management—has fallen over the years, declining from 17 percent in 1973 to 12 percent currently.[60]

This move toward an autonomous academic field appears to have been good for public administration. Research indicates that the most effective M.P.A. programs are those that are administered by freestanding schools and departments of public administration,[61] and these units are experiencing the fastest rates of student growth of all organizational types.[62]

There are over 26,000 students enrolled in masters degree programs in public administration and public affairs, up from fewer than 11,000 in 1973. More than half of M.P.A. students are women, and over a fourth are students of color.[63]

Paradigm 6: Governance, 1990–Present

Beginning in the 1980s, a number of trends accelerated that connote fundamental change in how we perceive government and its administration.

We group these trends under the rubrics of globalization, redefinition, and devolution,[64] and these developments are causing enormous change within and among the three sectors—public, private, and nonprofit—that are the pillars of the American institutional construct.[65]

- *Globalization.* Multinational corporations, the Internet, worldwide environmental issues, freer and faster international trade and travel, among other developments, are challenging the traditional place and powers of governments in the United States and other countries.
- *Redefinition.* Increasingly, governments are "reinventing" themselves less in terms of power and hierarchy and more in terms of partnership and collaboration. Empowering government workers and citizens, working with nongovernmental organizations to deliver services, introducing competition, measuring performance, satisfying "customers," and related developments all reflect this definitional shift.
- *Devolution.* American governments are relinquishing, by design or default, their traditional powers to individual citizens (often through information technologies); groups of citizens; public–private partnerships; the nonprofit sector, the private sector; public authorities; associations of governments; and other governments.

The Future of Government

We consider these developments in greater detail in upcoming chapters, but what, in their totality, do these accelerating trends mean?

Blurring, Flattening, and Withering.   We think that these developments will alter governments in the following ways:

- *Boundaries will blur.* The institutional distinctions between the public, nonprofit, and private sectors, and between federal, state, and local governments, already are fuzzy, muddy, and gray and will grow fuzzier, muddier, and grayer.
- *Governments will flatten and spread.* Governments have always been hierarchies and likely always will be. Nevertheless, just as private corporations are flattening and spreading,[66] governments are adapting and restructuring their largely vertical organization to accommodate

and exploit burgeoning horizontal networks that encompass information technologies, other governments, and other sectors. This restructuring will accelerate.

- *Governments will reduce their capacity and scale.* Globalization pressures governments to reduce their sovereignty so that earth may be governed as a planet. International cooperation in the areas of climate, commerce, and violence (including violence within nations, not just between them) all point to this outcome. Redefinition and devolution persuade governments to reduce their responsibilities so that other entities in all three sectors may take them over and deliver public services. As one scholarly wit winsomely asked, "Wither the state?"[67]

The Emergence of Governance. In other words, we are moving away from *government,* or the control over citizens and the delivery of public benefits by institutions of the state, and we are moving toward *governance,* or configurations, of laws, policies, organizations, institutions, cooperative arrangements, and agreements that control citizens and deliver public benefits. Government is institutional; governance is institutional *and networked.*

The emergence of governance is amply documented. A unique analysis of more than 800 empirical studies, covering a range of disciplines, found a general shifting away from "hierarchical government" and a distinct movement toward "horizontal governing." Over the past decades, there has been "a gradual addition of new administrative forms that facilitate governance."[68]

"Governing by network,"[69] as governance has been called, is "one of the central policy and management issues of our time: It must be recognized that involving partners to produce government services places more—not less—responsibility on public officials."[70]

The Practice of Governance. What, in practice, does governance mean? Consider some examples.

The federal government spends 53 percent *more* on contracts with private companies to implement national policies than it spends to pay its own civil service.[71] Washington hires through contracts, grants, and intergovernmental agreements more

than *eight times* the number of civilian employees who are on its payroll.[72]

All fifty states privatize some public services.[73] States spend about a fifth of their budgets on contracting with the private and nonprofit sectors.[74] Wisconsin, for instance, has reduced its welfare rolls by 90 percent by coordinating a network of agencies, businesses, and non profit organizations,[75] and in parts of the state, "a welfare recipient can use most of the social service system without encountering a single public employee."[76]

For at least two decades, barely half of all city and county services have been delivered solely by those governments' own employees; the other half of local services are delivered by public-private partnerships, profit-seeking companies, nonprofit organizations, other governments, subsidies, franchises, volunteers, vouchers, and other means.[77] Every city and county has used at least one of these alternative methods of providing services, and at one time or another, every service, from parks to police, operated by local governments has been contracted out.[78]

An extensive study of public administrators charged with economic development responsibilities in 237 American cities found that these managers spent the equivalent of one full working day out of five on "handling the interdependencies between their organizations and others." The typical city government linked its efforts with some sixty other governments, nonprofit organizations, and companies over the course of just two years as it tried to develop its urban economy.[79]

Understanding and managing these complex intergovernmental and intersectoral interdependencies is the new face of public administration.

The Results of Governance. More than a half-century ago, the distinguished scholar Paul Appleby described the process of public administration in terms that foretold governing by network. Public administration, Appleby said, is "making a mesh of things."[80]

Making a mesh of things seems to work reasonably well. A study of 500 Texan school districts conducted over five years concluded that, "at a minimum, managerial networking boosts educational performance," and "for the most salient performance indicator," that of student pass rates on standardized tests, "managerial networking contributes to positive results."[81]

What indicators we have suggest that governance works, and that it may work better than government.

The Future of Public Administration

Not much more than a third, 36 percent, of the graduates of the twenty elite schools of public administration started and then stayed with government. Far fewer started work in the nonprofit or private sectors and then switched to government.[82] These graduates of the top M.P.A. programs are not leaving government for greener pastures; only 27 percent say that they departed government for a better salary, but almost three times that number, 73 percent, say that they left for "more challenging work."[83]

We are not in the business of knocking government. We do want to illustrate, however, that the institutions that capture the imaginations and loyalty of those Americans who are among the most passionately committed to the public service are increasingly less likely to be the institutions of government.

A Paradigmatic Balance? or, Public Administration, Happy at Last

We think that government will remain the central institution of public administration, even in its current Governance Paradigm. Nevertheless, in what institutional setting—public, nonprofit, or private—public administration will be done is more open to alternatives than ever before. As with Paradigms 2 and 4, the field's institutional locus is lessened in Paradigm 6. But its focus—implementing social change—may never have been sharper.

Nevertheless, locus is retained in public administration's current paradigm because the locus-centered Paradigm 5 — public administration as public administration—continues unaltered. As in Paradigm 5, public administration will remain an autonomous profession, regardless of where it is practiced.

By becoming its own freestanding field, which is the core and continuing reality of Paradigm 5, public administration laid the foundation needed to prepare, as Harvard's president put it, "a profession of public servants" for the nation.[84] Paradigm 5 has not been replaced by Paradigm 6, and likely never will be. Instead, Paradigms 5 and 6 overlap in time. Uniquely, both paradigms work in tandem with each other.

Perhaps public administration has achieved, at last, a beneficent balance between its locus and its focus.

Notes

1. We do not go too far down the past, however, and confine ourselves to the last hundred years or so in the United States. For those who would like to explore deeper and wider, we suggest Mark R. Rutgers, "Beyond Woodrow Wilson: The Identity of the Study of Public Administration in Historical Perspective," *Administration & Society* 29 (July 1997), pp. 276–300.
2. Robert T. Golembiewski, *Public Administration as a Developing Discipline*, Part I, *Perspectives on Past and Present* (New York: Marcel Dekker, 1977).
3. Woodrow Wilson, "The Study of Administration," *Political Science Quarterly* 2 (June/July 1887), pp. 197–222; reprinted 50 (December 1941), pp. 481–506.
4. Richard J. Stillman II, Woodrow Wilson and the Study of Administration: A New Look at an Old Essay," *American Political Science Review* 67 (June 1973), p. 587. More accurately, in formulating his politics/administration dichotomy, Wilson apparently misinterpreted some of the German literature that he read on public administration. In any event, the politics/administration dichotomy clearly has had an impact on the evolution of public administration. See, for example, Paul Van Riper, "The American Administrative State: Wilson and the Founders—An Unorthodox View," *Public Administration Review* 43 (November/December 1983) pp. 447–490, and Daniel W. Martin, "The Fading Legacy of Woodrow Wilson," *Public Administration Review* 48 (March/April 1988), pp. 631–636.
5. Frank J. Goodnow, *Politics and Administration* (New York: Macmillan, 1900), pp. 10–11.
6. This discussion was drawn from Daniel W. Williams's two enlightening articles: "Evolution of Performance Measurement until 1930," *Administration & Society* 36 (May 2004), pp. 131–165, and "Measuring Government in the Early Twentieth Century," *Public Administration Review* 63 (November/December 2003), pp. 643–659. The New York Bureau of Municipal

Research continues to this day as the Institute of Public Administration (it was renamed in 1931), and it still is located in New York City, where it consults locally, nationally, and internationally.

7. *Annals of the American Academy of Political and Social Science* 41 (May 12, 1912), entire issue.

8. Committee on Practical Training for Public Service, American Political Science Association, *Proposed Plan for Training Schools for Public Service* (Madison, WI: American Political Science Association, 1914), p. 3.

9. *Proceedings of the American Political Science Association, 1913–1914*, p. 264, as cited in Lynton K. Caldwell, "Public Administration and the Universities: A Half Century of Development," *Public Administration Review* 25 (March 1965), p. 54.

10. The financier of the Bureau's Training School for Public Service was Ms. E. H. Harriman, who raised some $250,000 and turned it over to the Bureau of Municipal Research for a school. Ms. Harriman had preferred that her school be in a university in the first place but could find no takers; the presidents of Harvard, Yale, and Columbia were approached by her, but she found them to be "polite but amused" by her proposal. See Luther Gulick, "George Maxwell Had a Dream," *American Public Administration: Past, Present, Future*, Frederick C. Mosher, ed. (Syracuse: Maxwell School of Citizenship and Public Affairs and the National Association of Schools of Public Affairs and Administration, 1975), p. 257.

11. Dwight Waldo, "Public Administration," *Political Science: Advance of the Discipline*, in Marian D. Irish, ed. (Englewood Cliffs, NJ: Prentice Hall, 1968), pp. 153–189.

12. Much of this discussion is based on Svara, "The Politics/Administration Model as Aberration."

13. Alisdair Roberts, "Demonstrating Neutrality: The Rockefeller Philanthropies and the Evolution of Public Administration, 1927–1936," *Public Administration Review* 54 (May/June 1994), p. 222.

14. Ibid.

15. Morris B. Lambie, ed. *Training for the Public Service: The Report and Recommendations of a Conference Sponsored by the Public Administration Clearing House* (Chicago: Public Administration Clearing House, 1935).

16. Caldwell, "Public Administration and the Universities," p. 57.

17. Dwight Waldo, "Introduction: Trends and Issues in Education for Public Administration," in *Education for Public Service: 1979*, Guthrie S. Birkhead and James D. Carroll, eds. (Syracuse: Maxwell School of Citizenship and Public Affairs, Syracuse University, 1979).

18. The famous phrase was first written by Wallace Sayre in "Premises of Public Administration: Past and Emerging," *Public Administration Review* 18 (March/April 1958), pp. 102–105. The quotation is on p. 104.

19. Lyndall Urwick, "Organization as a Technical Problem," in *Papers on the Science of Administration*, Luther Gulick and L. Urwick, eds. (New York: Institute of Public Administration, 1937), p. 49.

20. For a good analysis of this point, see Thomas H. Hammond, "In Defense of Luther Gulick's 'Notes on the Theory of Organization,'" *Public Administration* 68 (Summer 1990), pp. 143–173.

21. John Merriman Gaus, "Trends in the Theory of Public Administration," *Public Administration Review* 10 (Summer 1950), p. 188.

22. Wilson, "The Study of Administration," pp. 501, 504.

23. For an enlightening example see Robert S. Montjoy and Douglas J. Watson, "A Case for a Reinterpreted Dichotomy of Politics and Administration as a Professional Standard in Council-Manager Government," *Public Administration Review* 55 (May/June 1995), pp. 231–239.

24. John Nalbandian, "Reflections of a 'Pracademic' on the Logic of Politics and Administration," *Public Administration Review* 54 (November/December 1994), pp. 531–536. For a similar approach to this point, see also James E. Skok, "Policy Issue Networks and the Public Policy Cycle: A Structural–Functional Framework for Public Administration," *Public Administration Review* 55 (July/August 1995), pp. 325–332.

25. Richard C. Feiock and Jaehoon Kim, "Credible Commitment and Council-Manager Government: Implications for Policy Instrument Choices," *Public Administration Review* 63 (September/October 2003), pp. 616–625. The quotation is on p. 616.

26. See, for example, Robert A. Dahl, "The Science of Public Administration: Three Problems," *Public Administration Review* 7 (Winter 1947), pp. 1–11, and Dwight Waldo, *The Administrative State: A Study of the Political Theory of American Public Administration* (New York: Ronald, 1948). Simon himself granted a foreshadowing of his *Administrative Behavior* with his aptly titled, "The Proverbs of Administration," *Public Administration Review* 6 (Winter 1946), pp. 53–67.

27. Span of control is a venerable block in the theory of organizations, and Luther Gulick, an early advocate of span of control in public organizations, lamented the lack of empirical research concerning it. Happily, the objective study of the concept of span of control is emerging. See, for example, Kenneth J. Meier and John Bohte, "Span of Control and Public Organizations: Implementing Luther Gulick's Research Design," *Public Administration Review* 63 (January/February 2003), pp. 61–70, and Nick A. Theobald and Sean Nicholson-Crotty. "The Many Faces of Span of Control: Organizational Structure across Multiple Goals," *Administration & Society* 36 (Winter 2005), pp. 648–660.

28. Ironically, the notion of "principles" of public administration has been quashed so thoroughly that there is some scholarly activity underway to bring principles back. As one writer in the field has contended, "The utility of tested administrative principles . . . is as great as it was in 1939." However, this author, as well as other, argues that we should define the concept of administrative principle considerably more flexibly than does the dictionary and has suggested that, "A principle is a generalized normative statement based on experience and does not

purport the universality of a theory of law." See Ronald C. Moe, "Traditional Organizational Principles and the Managerial Presidency: From Phoenix to Ashes," *Public Administration Review* 50 (March/April), p. 136.

A principle as a "generalized normative statement" seems to be what Luther Gulick had in mind when he wrote "Notes on the Theory of Organization," in his and Urwick's *Papers on the Science of Administration* of 1937 (pp. 1–45). And while we agree that there are some general precepts that public administrators would be well advised to follow (e.g., authority should match accountability), and that it is the responsibility of the academics to, in conjunction with the practitioners, develop these precepts, we do not believe that changing the definition of the word "principle" is the way to do it. Its somewhat casual use by Gulick and Urwick in 1937 not only set them up for scholarly attack later, but also the attacks themselves probably deflected needed research on how public organizations work, and this was a disservice. Nevertheless, the first condition in any field of academic and professional endeavor should be retaining clarity and precision of language; hence, redefining or fogging up what "principle" means is not a particularly fruitful way of advancing the discipline.

Moe also has stated that principles of public administration should be resurrected in the form of a renewed recognition of public law as the foundation of the field, and this is a more straightforward argument. See Ronald C. Moe and Robert S. Gilmore, "Rediscovering Principles of Public Administration: The Neglected Foundation of Public Law," *Public Administration Review* 55 (March/April 1995), pp. 135–146.

29. Herbert A. Simon, "A Comment on 'The Science of Public Administration,'" *Public Administration Review* 7 (Summer 1947), p. 202.

30. Roscoe Martin, "Political Science and Public Administration—A Note on the State of the Union", *American Political Science Review* 46 (September 1952), pp. 660, 665.

31. Martin Landau reviews this aspect of the field's development cogently in "The Concept of Decision-Making in the 'Field' of Public Administration," *Concepts and Issues in Administrative Behavior*, Sidney Mailick and Edward H. Van Ness, eds. (Englewood Cliffs, NJ: Prentice Hall, 1962), pp. 1–29. Landau writes, "Public administration is neither a subfield of political science, nor does it comprehend it; it simply becomes a synonym" (p. 9).

32. Ward Stewart, *Graduate Study in Public Administration* (Washington, DC: U.S. Office of Education, 1961).

33. William J. Siffin, "The New Public Administration: Its Study in the United States," *Public Administration* 24 (Winter 1956), p. 357.

34. Albert Somit and Joseph Tanenhaus, *American Political Science: A Profile of a Discipline* (New York: Atherton, 1964), especially pp. 49–62 and 86–98.

35. Dwight Waldo, "Scope of the Theory of Public Administration," in *Theory and Practice of Public Administration: Scope, Objectives, and Methods,* James C. Charlesworth, ed. (Philadelphia: American Academy of Political and Social Science, 1968), p. 8.

36. Contrast this figure with the percentage of articles in other categories published during the 1960–1970 period: "political parties," 13 percent; "public opinion," 12 percent; "legislature," 12 percent; and "elections/voting," 11 percent. Even these categories dealing peripherally with "bureaucratic politics" and public administration evidently received short shrift among the editors of the major political science journals. "Region/federal government" received 4 percent, "chief executives" won 3 percent, and "urban/metropolitan government" received 2 percent. The percentages are in Jack L. Walker, "Brother, Can You Paradigm?" *PS* 5 (Fall 1972), pp. 419–422. The journals surveyed were *American Political Science Review, Journal of Politics, Western Political Quarterly, Midwest Political Science Journal,* and *Polity.*

37. Heinz Eulau (1977) as quoted in Krishna K. Tummala, "Comparative Study and the Section on International and Comparative Administration (SICA)," *Public Administration Review* 58 (January/February 1998), p. 21.

38. David L. Weiner, "Political Science, Practitioner Skill, and Public Management," *Public Administration Review* 52 (May/June 1992), p. 241. Opposite views, of course, exist. See, for example, Marcia Lynn Whicker, Ruth Ann Strickland, and Dorothy Olshfski, "The Troublesome Cleft: Public Administration and Political Science," *Public Administration Review* 53 (November/December 1993), pp. 531–541.

39. Caldwell, "Public Administration and the Universities," p. 57.

40. See, for example, Edward H. Litchfield, "Notes on a General Theory of Administration," *Administrative Science Quarterly* 1 (June 1956), pp. 3–29; John D. Millett, "A Critical Appraisal of the Study of Public Administration," *Administration Science Quarterly* 1 (September 1956), pp. 177–188; William A. Robson, "The Present Stage of Teaching and Research in Public Administration Towards the Future," *Public Administration* 39 (Autumn 1961), pp. 217–222; Andre Molitor, "Public Administration Towards the Future," *International Review of Administration Sciences* 27 (No. 4, 1961), pp. 375–384; Ivan Hinderaker, "The Study of Administration: Interdisciplinary Dimensions," *Summary of Proceedings of the Western Political Science Association,* Supplement to *Western Political Quarterly* 16 (September 1963), pp. 5–12; Paul J. Gordon, "Transcend the Current Debate in Administration Theory," *Journal of the Academy of Management* 6 (December 1963), pp. 209–312; Lynton K. Caldwell, "The Study of Administration in the Organization of the University," *Chinese Journal of Administration* (July 1965), pp. 8–16, 70; and Keith M. Henderson, *Emerging Synthesis in American Public Administration* (New York: Asia Publishing House, 1966).

41. Stewart, *Graduate Education in Public Administration,* p. 39.

42. Delta Sigma Pi, *Eighteenth Biennial Survey of Universities Offering an Organized Curriculum in Commerce and Business Administration* (Oxford, OH: Educational Foundation of Delta Sigma Pi, 1962).

43. James L. Perry and Kenneth L. Kraemer, "Part Three: Is Public Management Similar of Different from Private Management?" in *Public Management: Public and Private Perspectives*, James L. Perry and Kenneth L. Kraemer, eds. (Palo Alto, CA: Mayfield, 1983), p. 56.

44. Kenneth L. Kraemer and James L. Perry, "Camelot Revisited: Public Administration Education in a Generic School", *Education for Public Service, 1980*, Guthrie S. Birkhead and James D. Carroll, eds. (Syracuse: Maxwell School of Citizenship and Public Affairs, Syracuse University, 1980), p. 92.

45. See, for example, Michael Blumenthal, "Candid Reflections of a Businessman in Washington," *Fortune* (January 29, 1979); A. J. Cervantes, "Memoirs of a Businessman-Mayor," *Business Week* (December 8, 1973); and James M. Kouzes, "Why Businessmen Fail in Government," *New York Times* (March 8, 1987).

46. Donald Rumsfeld, "A Politician Turned Executive," *Fortune* (September 10, 1979).

47. David E. Lewis, *Political Appointments, Bureau Chiefs, and Federal Management Performance* (Princeton, NJ: Princeton University, Woodrow Wilson School of Public and International Affairs, 2005). The quotations are on pp. 2 and 4, respectively. Prior to the advent of the administration of George W. Bush in 2001, it essentially was impossible to objectively and comparatively grade agency performance. Under Bush, the Office of Management and Budget, in cooperation with the President's Management Council, the National Academy of Public Administration, Congress, and others, developed a management grading system for all agencies. Once this system was in place, objectively determined agency performance could be correlated with the backgrounds of agency heads.

48. The original expression of this mythic and enduring *pronunciemento* by Sayre is unclear. Graham T. Allison Jr. reports that, after being a formative figure in the planning of the nation's first generic school of management at Cornell University, Sayre departed for Columbia University and, evidently as a parting shot, issued his famous aphorism. See Graham T. Allison Jr., "Public and Private Management: Are They Fundamentally Alike in All Unimportant Respects?" in Perry and Kramer, eds., *Public Management*, pp. 72–92.

49. Five good example of this literature are Susan Welch and John C. Comer, *Quantitative Methods for Public Administration: Techniques and Applications,* 2nd ed. (Homewood, IL: Dorsey, 1988); E. S. Quade, *Analysis for Public Decisions*, 2nd ed. (New York: North Holland, 1982); David N. Ammons, *Tools for Decisions Making: A Practical Guide for Local Government* (Washington, DC: CQ Press, 2002); Richard D. Bingham and Marcus E. Etheridge, eds, *Reaching Decisions in Public Policy and Administration: Methods and Applications* (New York: Longman,

1982); and John Kenneth Gohagan, *Quantitative Analysis for Public Policy* (New York: McGraw-Hill, 1980). For an applied version of some of these techniques, see Nicholas Henry, ed., *Doing Public Administration: Exercises in Public Management*, 3rd ed. (Dubuque, IA: William C. Brown, 1991).

50. Stanley I. Benn and Gerald F. Gaus, "The Public and the Private: Concepts and Action," in *Public and Private Social Life*, S. I. Benn and G. F. Gaus, eds. (New York: St. Martin's, 1983), p. 5. Much of the following discussion is drawn from this source.

51. Ibid., p. 9

52. James L. Perry, Hal G. Rainey, and Barry Bozeman, "The Public–Private Distinction in Organization Theory: A Critique and Research Strategy," Paper presented by the 1985 Annual Meeting of the American Political Science Association, New Orleans, August 29–September 1, 1985, Table 1.

53. This list is based on one provided by George A. Boyne, "Public and Private Management: What's the Difference?" *Journal of Management Studies* 39 (January 2002), pp. 97–122. The author identified thirteen "distinctions," and all are covered in the paragraph, if in abbreviated form.

54. Boyne, in ibid., analyzed thirty-four studies published in Britain and the United States (twenty-eight were American) on distinctions alleged in the literature between public and private management. He found them to be "methodogically crude" in some significant respects (p. 104). Five of the thirteen distinctions identified by Boyne had not been tested empirically, and he found that only three of the remaining eight were possibly valid: Public organization are more bureaucratic, and public administrators are less materialistic and less organizationally loyal than are their counterparts in business.

55. The key work in this tradition remains the papers presented at the 1968 conference, which are published in Frank Marini, ed., *Toward a New Public Administration: The Minnowbrook Perspective* (Scranton, PA: Chandler, 1971).

56. Mark R. Daniels, "Public Administration as an Emergent Profession: A Survey of Attitudes About the Review and Accreditation of Programs," Paper presented at the National Conference of the American Society for Public Administration, New York, April 1983, and J. Norman Baldwin, "Comparison of Perceived Effectiveness of MPA Programs Administered Under Different Institutional Arrangements," *Public Administration Review* 48 (September/October 1988), pp. 876–884.

57. David A. Breaux, Edward J. Clynch, and John C. Morris "The Core Curriculum Content of NASPAA-Accredited Programs: Fundamentally Alike or Different?" *Journal of Public Affairs Education* 9 (October 2003), pp. 259, 271.

58. National Association of Schools of Public Affairs and Administration, *Almanac of Public Affairs, Administration, and Policy Education Data* (Washington, DC: Author, 2005). http://www.naspaa.org/principals/

almanac/Survey2003/. In 2003, 59 percent of these programs were in separate schools, colleges, departments, institutes, centers, or some "other organizational location." The survey was conducted in 2004, and the response rate was 80 percent. In 1973, public policy and urban studies programs were not specifically identified in the survey, but 48 percent of public administration and public affairs programs were in separate professional schools or departments that reported to the central university administration or a dean. See National Association of Public Affairs and Administration, *1986 Directory: Programs in Public Affairs and Administration* (Washington, DC: Author, 1986), p. xix.

59. Ibid (both citations). In 2003, 29 percent of public administration programs were in political science departments, and in 1973, 36 percent were. The current 2003, figure is the lowest proportion of political science departments yet recorded in these surveys; the highest, 38 percent, occurred in 1983.

60. H. George Frederickson, "The Respositioning of American Public Administration," *PS* 32 (December 1999), pp. 701–711.

61. Baldwin, "Comparison of Perceived Effectiveness of MPA. Programs Administered Under Different Institutional Arrangements," p. 876. Baldwin surveyed 207 M.P.A. program directors, and received responses from 158, over a 76 percent response rate.

62. Robert Cleary, "Masters Programs in PA Continue to Expand," *PATimes* 19 (December 1, 1996), p. 2.

63. National Association of Schools of Public Affairs and Administration, *Almanac of Public Affairs, Administration, and Policy Education Data.* Current figures are for 2003. Figure for 1973 is from National Association of Schools of Public Affairs and Administration, *1986 Directory*, p. xix.

64. Some of the following discussion has been drawn from Frederickson, "The Repositioning of American Public Administration," and Donald F. Kettl, "The Transformation of Governance: Globalization, Devolution, and the Role of Government," *Public Administration Review* 60 (November/December), pp. 488–497.

65. As one prestigious report written by leaders in all three sectors put it: "Sea changes in technology, communication, the global economy, and the power and role of government are causing self-assessments within the business, nonprofit, and government sectors. The roles of the sectors are changing. . . . " See the Three Sector Collaborative Project of the Conference Board, Council on Foundations, Independent Sector, National Academy of Public Administration, National Alliance of Business, and National Governors' Association, *Changing Roles, Changing Relationships: The New Challenge for Business, Nonprofit Organizations and Government* (Authors: ND), p. iii.

66. Raghuram Rajan and Julie Wulf, *The Flattening Firm: Evidence from Panel Data on the Changing Nature of Corporate Hierarchies*, NBER Working Paper 9633 (Washington, DC: National Bureau of Economic Research, 2003). This study of more than 300 large U.S. firms found that the number of corporate officers who reported directly to the CEO had almost doubled from an average of four in 1986 to seven in 2003; that the number of levels in the management hierarchy between division heads and CEOs had declined by a fourth; and that there had been a reduction in the ranks of middle managers.

67. Ira Sharkansky, *Wither the State? Politics and Public Enterprise in Three Countries* (Chatham, NJ: Chatham House, 1979).

68. Carolyn J. Hill, "Is Hierarchical Government in Decline? Evidence from Empirical Research," *Journal of Public Administration Research and Theory* 15 (Spring 2005), pp. 173–196. The quotations are on p. 173. For a succinct placement of governance in a historical context, see Eran Vigoda, "From Responsiveness to Collaboration: Governance, Citizens, and the Next Generation of Public Administration," *Public Administration Review* 62 (September/October 2002), pp. 527–540.

69. Stephen Goldsmith and William D. Eggers, *Governing by Network: The New Shape of the Public Sector* (Washington, DC: Brookings, 2004).

70. Stephen Goldsmith and William D. Eggers, "Government for Hire," *New York Times* (February 21, 2005).

71. Federal Procurement Data System, *Federal Procurement Report* (Washington, DC: Author, 2004), p. 2, and U.S. Bureau of the Census, *Statistical Abstract of the United States, 2004–2005*, 124th ed. (Washington, DC: U.S. Government Printing Office, 2005), Table 483. In 2003, the federal government spent more than $305 billion in contracts and $143 billion in federal civilian payrolls.

72 Paul C. Light, *Fact Sheet on the New True Size of Government* (Washington, DC: Brookings, 2003), p. 4. In 2002, there were 14,434,000 federal civilian employees, including 1,756,000 who were on the federal payroll. The rest were paid indirectly via federal contracts, grants, and mandates.

73. Keon S. Chi, Kelley A. Arnold, and Heather M. Perkins, "Privatization in State Government Trends and Issues," *Spectrum: The Journal of State Government* 76 (Fall 2003), pp. 12–21.

74. John R. Bartle and Ronnie LaCourse Korosec, *Procurement and Contracting in State Government, 2000* (Syracuse, NY: Syracuse University Government Performance Project, 2001), p. iv. Figure is for 2001 and refers to state operating budgets. Medicaid contracts are not included.

75. Goldsmith and Eggers, "Government for Hire."

76. Goldsmith and Eggers, *Governing by Network*, p. 14.

77. In 1982, 51 percent of all city and county services were delivered by those governments' own employees; in 1988, 49 percent were; in 1992, 48 percent; in 1997, 49 percent; and in 2002, 52 percent. See Elaine Morley, "Patterns in the Use of Alternative Service Delivery Approaches," *Municipal Year Book, 1989* (Washington, DC: International City Management Association, 1989), p. 37, for data from which were derived the 1982 and 1988 figures, and Mildred Warner and Amir Hefetz, "Pragmatism over Politics: Alternative Service

Delivery in Local Government, 1992–2002," *Municipal Year Book, 2004* (Washington, DC: International City/County Management Association, 2004), p. 10, for the 1992–2002 figures.

78. Rowan Miranda and Karlyn Andersen, "Alternative Service Delivery in Local Governments, 1982–1992," *Municipal Year Book, 1994* (Washington, DC: International City/County Management Association, 1994), p. 28. All counties and municipalities contract out services to the private and nonprofit sectors, and half contract with other governments to deliver services.

79. Robert Agranoff and McGuire, "American Federalism and the Search for Models of Management," *Public Administration Review* 61 (November/December 2001), pp. 671–681. The quotation is on p. 677.

80. Paul H. Appleby, *Policy and Administration* (Tuscaloosa: University of Alabama Press, 1949), p. 15.

81. Laurence J. O'Toole., Jr. and Kenneth J. Meier, "Desperately Seeking Selznick: Cooptation and the Dark Side of Public Management in Networks," *Public Administration Review* 64 (November/December 2004), pp. 688, 690. A downside of networking was that most of its benefits went to "privileged" students, but not "marginalized" ones.

82. "On the Move," *Government Executive* (January 2000), p. 10.

83. Paul C. Light, *The New Public Service* (Washington, DC: Brookings, 1999), p. 89.

84 Derek Bok, "President's Report, 1973–1974," *Harvard Today* 18 (Winter 1975), p. 10.

Part II

Public Organizations

In the following chapters, we explain organizations—their threads of theory, fabric of forces, and fibers of people.

We focus, of course, on *public organizations*, which are collectivities of people whose mission emphasizes the delivery of goods and services that benefit people outside, rather than people inside, the organization. This definition is realistic (and even relatively succinct) because it implicitly recognizes that public organizations are not necessarily peopled by would-be saints; hence, the purpose of public organizations only "emphasizes" benefiting others, a nuance which accepts that public organizations, like private ones, can legitimately benefit their own employees, too. Still, the emphasis on serving others is real, and it associates with some very real differences between public and private organizations.

All organizations, regardless of sector, have some basic similarities, and we shall review these, but our real interest lies in revealing behavioral differences among organizations by sector. The *private sector* includes profit-seeking companies; the *nonprofit sector* covers private associations that have purposes other than seeking profits; and the *public sector* is composed of governments, government agencies, government corporations, and sometimes nonprofit organizations. (At the risk of getting ahead of ourselves, we refer to the reader to Figure 11-1, in Chapter 11, for a breakdown of the characteristics of the public, independent, and private sectors.)

Part II may be that portion of this book that will have the most lasting value for you as you enter the world of organizations. It covers the intellectual evolution of organization theory and organizational behavior, the major theoretical and behavioral concepts in the field, discusses why bureaucrats behave in the ways they do, and attempts to help you gain a bit of insight about what to expect should you find yourself working in the public sector.

CHAPTER 3

The Threads of Organization: Theories

In this chapter, we examine various perspectives on organizations and trace the intellectual evolution of organization theory.

Models, Definitions, and Organizations

The notion of "models," a useful epistemological device in the social sciences, has considerable utility in discussing what an organization is. A *model* is a tentative definition that fits the data available about a particular object. Unlike a definition, a model does not represent an attempt to express the basic, irreducible nature of the object and is a freer approach that can be adapted to situations as needed. Thus, physicists treat electrons in one theoretical situation as infinitesimal particles and in another as invisible waves. The theoretical model of electrons permits both treatments, chiefly because no one knows exactly what an electron is (that is, no one knows its definition).

So it is with organizations. Organizations are different creatures to different people, and this phenomenon is unavoidable. Thus, organizations are "defined" according to the contexts and perspectives peculiar to the person doing the defining.

It is not enough, however, to "define" organizations, as two famous organization theorists once did, with the phrase, "organizations are more earthworm than ape."[1] As an indication of their simplicity, these scholars are correct, to be sure, but it is possible to ascertain additional characteristics of organizations that will be useful in our model for the remainder of this book. Organizations

- are purposeful, complex human collectivities.
- are characterized by secondary (or impersonal) relationships.
- have specialized and limited goals.
- are characterized by sustained cooperative activity.
- are integrated within a larger social system.
- provide services and products to their environment.
- are dependent upon exchanges with their environment.

These features make up our working model of organizations, both public and private.

Organization theorists, using essentially this list of characteristics but stressing different features of it, have produced a vast body of literature on the nature of organizations. The literature can be trisected into these major streams: the closed model, the open model, and "the newer tradition," which attempts to synthesize both models.[2] These three streams, each with its own "schools" and substreams, constitute the threads of organization theory. Table 3-1 summarizes these literatures by theoretical school.

Table 3-1   The Models of Organization Theory

The Closed Model	The Literature of Model Synthesis: Uncertainty Reduction	The Open Model
1. Bureaucratic theory (Weber)	(Barnard, Simon, March and Simon, Cyert and March, Thompson)	1. Human relations (Roethisberger and Dickson, Maslow, Mayo, Herzberg)
2. Scientific management (Taylor, the Gilbreths)		2. Organization development (Lewin, McGregor, Bennis, Beckhard, French and Bell, Lippitt, Shepard, Blake Benne, Bradford, Argyris, Golembiewski)
3. Administrative, or generic management (Mooney and Reiley, Gulick and Urwick, Fayol, Follett)		3. The organization as a unit in its environment (Barnard, Selznick, Clark, Downs, Warwick, Meyer)

The Closed Model of Organizations

The closed model of organizations goes by many names. Bureaucratic, hierarchical, formal, rational, and mechanistic are some of them, and there are at least three permutations, or schools, that have thrived within its framework: bureaucratic theory, scientific management, and administrative management (sometimes called generic management).

Characteristics of the Closed Model of Organizations

We rely on a classic analysis[3] in listing the principal features of the closed model of organizations.

- Routine tasks occur in stable conditions.
- Task specialization (i.e., a division of labor) is central.
- Means (or the proper way to do a job) are emphasized.
- Conflict within the organization is adjudicated from the top.
- "Responsibility" (or what one is supposed to do, one's formal job description) is emphasized.
- One's primary sense of responsibility and loyalty is to the bureaucratic subunit to which one is assigned (such as the accounting department).
- The organization is perceived as a hierarchic structure (that is, the structure "looks" like a pyramid).

- Knowledge is inclusive only at the top of the hierarchy (in other words, only the chief executive knows everything).
- Interaction between people in the organization tends to be vertical (that is, one takes orders from above and transmits orders below), but not horizontal.
- The style of interaction is directed toward obedience, command, and clear superordinate/subordinate relationships.
- Loyalty and obedience to one's superior and the organization generally are emphasized, sometimes at the expense of performance.
- Prestige is "internalized," that is, personal status in the organization is determined largely by one's formal office and rank.

So runs our closed model of organizations. One should recall that, like any model, it is an "ideal type."[4] An *ideal type* is what an organization (or any other phenomenon) tries to be. Once we know what something wants to become (such as a little girl who wants to become a firefighter), we can predict with some accuracy how it will behave (the same little girl probably will want a toy fire engine for her birthday). In this logic, closed-model organizations behave in such a way as to fulfill the twelve characteristics just posited, although this is not to say that any actual organization meets all twelve features in practice. Of organizations that are widely known, the Pentagon likely comes closest to accomplishing the requisites of the closed model.

Bureaucratic Theory

The earliest school of the closed model is that of bureaucratic theory. Its best known representative is Max Weber, a remarkable German sociologist who also gave us the sociology of religion, a theory of leadership and, with them, those phrases familiar to scholars and practitioners in public administration: "the Protestant work ethic" and "charisma." In what is perhaps a too succinct summary of Weber's model of bureaucracy, the features of bureaucracy amounted to

- hierarchy.
- promotion based on professional merit and skill.
- the development of a career service.
- reliance on and use of rules and regulations.
- impersonality of relationships among career-professionals in the bureaucracy and with their clientele.

Open-model theorists dislike the rigidity, the inflexibility, the emphasis on means rather than ends, and the manipulative and antihumanist overtones of Weberian bureaucratic theory.

But, in Weber's defense, these criticisms often have been overdrawn and certainly have not been leveled with Weber's own social context in mind. Weber was writing at a time when positions of public trust still were assigned on the basis of class rather than ability. To Weber, an impersonal, rule-abiding, efficient, merit-based career service provided the surest way of fulfilling the public interest in the face of a politically fragmented Germany and an arrogant, powerful, yet somewhat silly *Junker* class, and this was to the good of society. In short, Weber, in a large sense, was not antihumanist in his thinking, but the effects of the bureaucracy that he so loudly touted could be, both to the citizens who were governed by the bureaucracy and to the bureaucrats themselves.

Scientific Management

Another major literary stream encompassed by the closed model is represented by the theories of scientific management. Scientific management refers to what is more popularly known as time-motion studies; it flourished at the beginning of the twentieth century and remains very much in use today in industry.

Scientific management's overriding concern was to improve organizational efficiency and economy for the sake of increased production. Human beings were perceived as being adjuncts of the machine, and the primary objective of scientific management was to make them as efficient as the machines they operated. This view of humanity applied solely to workers on the assembly line and in the lower organizational echelons; it did not apply to upper-echelon managers—it was to them that the scientific management literature was addressed.

Key representatives of the scientific management school include Frederick Taylor (who gave scientific management its name with his 1911 volume, *Principles of Scientific Management*) and Frank and Lillian Gilbreth.[5] The person-as-machine conception, replete with all its discomfiting moral overtones, are on clear display in the writings of Taylor and the Gilbreths. A notorious example occurs in Taylor's (likely fictional[6]) story of Schmidt, the pig-iron hauler, whom Taylor unabashedly declared to be "stupid . . . phlegmatic . . . [and] more nearly resembles in his mental make-up the ox than any other type."[7] After Taylor analyzed Schmidt's physical movements, he ordered him to change how he moved his body and, as a result of these "scientific" alterations in Schmidt's physical behaviors, Schmidt's production went up from twelve and a half tons of pig-iron hauled per day to forty-seven tons. Taylor is obviously proud of his feat in rendering Schmidt a more efficient, machinelike man, and because of such feats he was eminently successful as a time-motion expert in his day. Similarly, Frank and Lillian Gilbreth developed the concept of the "therblig," each one of which represented a category of eighteen basic human motions—all physical activity fell into a therblig class of one type or another. (The scientific management experts rarely were constrained by modesty, false or otherwise; try reading therblig backwards.)

The person-as-machine model of scientific management doubtless has a distasteful aura. People are not machines. This distaste, however, has often been extended by some critics to include a distaste for the notion of efficiency. Outside the realms of theory, few are against efficiency in government, least of all the governed. So one must be wary of dismissing the value of efficiency along with "Taylorism" (as scientific management also is called), as occasionally has been done by humanist critics of the school.

Administrative Management

The final literature based on the closed model is administrative management. Luther Gulick and Lyndall Urwick's *Papers on the Science of Administration* (noted in Chapter 2) is an outstanding example of administrative management addressed to the public administrator, but most of this literature was aimed at the business manager.

The odd term (odd, at least, by today's standards), *administrative management*, surfaced in the 1930s as an effort to distinguish it from its predecessor, scientific management. Administrative management is broader in concept and more concerned with leading and changing the organization, and less concerned with measuring how efficiently the organization's workers are working.

Administrative management is also called *generic management* because its fundamental assumption is that management is management, wherever it is found, and therefore this school devoted its energies to the discovery of "scientific principles" of administration that worked in any and all institutional settings—from corporations and clubs, to governments and gulags—and in any and all cultural contexts—from Boston and Botswana, to Paris and Paraguay. Writers in this stream usually offered up very specific principles of administration: Gulick and Urwick listed seven principles (recall POSDCORB); James D. Money and Alan C. Reiley, in their aptly entitled and influential *Principles of Organization*, found four; another major researcher, Henri Fayol, unearthed fourteen. Among the premier scholars in the administrative management tradition, Mary Parker

Follett was one of the few who fudged when it come to enumerating principles of administration, but then she was unusually ahead of her time.[8]

Administrative management is closer in concept to Weberian bureaucratic theory than to Taylorian scientific management. The major reason for this is that bureaucracies are less concerned with time-motion economies than are assembly lines, and both bureaucratic theorists and administrative management analysts primarily were concerned with the optimal organization of administrators rather than production workers.

Despite this similarity, however, there was a subtle difference between bureaucratic theory and administrative management, and one that provides a linkage between the closed and open models of organizations. Weber, like Taylor, did not think much about underlings and toilers in organizations beyond their capacities for obedience (in Weber's case) and production (in Taylor's case), and both capacities were regarded as being almost limitless, provided that managers took their respective writings to heart. But with the emergence of the theorists of administrative management, a hint surfaced that underlings and toilers in organizations conceivably might have minds of their own.

Such a grudging concession to the thinking powers of subordinates represented a recognition that subordinates were people (like managers) and could think (almost like managers). It was left for certain writers using the open model to assert that underlings and toilers could indeed think, feel, and behave on their own, and often differently from the ways they were supposed to. Some of these writers would argue that subordinates could outthink, outsmart, and outfox their superordinates— and did—with both ease and frequency.

The Open Model of Organizations

Like the closed model, the open model goes by many names. Collegial, competitive, free market, informal, natural, and organic are some of them.

The historical origins of the open model actually precede the intellectual roots of the closed model by more than a century and a half. The beginnings of the open model can be traced to

Count Louis de Rouvroy Saint-Simon, the brilliant French social thinker, and to his protégée Auguste Comte, the "father of sociology."[9]

Partly as a reaction to the stultification of the last days of the French kings and the explosiveness of the French Revolution, Saint-Simon, and later Comte, speculated on what the administration of the future would be like. They thought that it would be predicated on skill rather than heredity, "cosmopolitanism" (by which Saint-Simon meant the development of new professions based on technology) would be the order of the day, and organizations themselves would be a liberating force for humanity. Throughout, Saint-Simon and Comte stressed the value of spontaneously created organizations that developed "naturally" as they were needed.[10]

Characteristics of the Open Model of Organizations

The principal features of the open model of organizations[11] are

- Nonroutine tasks occur in unstable conditions.
- Specialized knowledge contributes to common tasks (thus differing from the closed model's specialized *task* notion in that the specialized *knowledge* possessed by any one member of the organization may be applied profitably to a variety of tasks undertaken by various other members of the organization).
- Ends (or getting the job done), rather than means, are emphasized.
- Conflict within the organization is adjusted by interaction with peers, rather than adjudicated from the top.
- "Shedding of responsibility" is emphasized (in other words, formal job descriptions are discarded in favor of all organization members contributing to all organizational problems).
- One's sense of responsibility and loyalty is to the organization as a whole.
- The organization is perceived as a fluidic network structure (that is, the organization "looks" like an amoeba).

- Knowledge can be located anywhere in the organization (in other words, everybody knows something relevant about the organization, but no one, including the chief executive, knows everything).
- Interaction between people in the organization tends to be horizontal (that is, peers interact with peers), as well as vertical.
- The style of interaction is directed toward accomplishment, "advice" (rather than commands), and is characterized by a "myth of peerage," which envelops even the most obvious superordinate/subordinate relationships.
- Task achievement and excellence of performance in accomplishing a task are emphasized, sometimes at the expense of obedience to one's superiors.
- Prestige is "externalized" (i.e., personal status in the organization is determined largely by one's professional ability and reputation, rather than by office and rank).

So runs our open model of organizations, which, like the closed model, is an ideal type. It seldom if ever exists in actuality, although a major university might come close (which is why the open model occasionally is called the "collegial" model).

Human Relations

Human relations, the first of three schools of the open model, focuses on organizational variables never considered in the closed model: cliques, informal norms, emotions, and personal motivations, among others. Paradoxically, this focus resulted from what originally was intended to be a research undertaking in scientific management, a literature at the opposite end of the continuum in terms of the views held by its theorists.

The Hawthorne Experiments. In 1924 Elton Mayo and Fritz J. Roethlisberger began a series of studies (later known as the Hawthorne studies, for the location of the plant) of working conditions and worker behavior at a Western Electric factory.[12] Their experiment was predicated on the then-plausible Taylorian hypothesis that workers would respond like machines to changes in working conditions. To test their hypothesis they intended to alter the intensity of light available to a group of randomly selected workers. The idea—that when the light became brighter, production would increase, and when the light became dimmer, production would decrease—is all very commonsensical, of course. The workers were told they would be observed as an experimental group. The lights were turned up and production went up. The lights were turned down and production went up. Mayo and Roethlisberger were disconcerted. They dimmed the lights to near darkness, and production kept climbing.

Among the explanations of this phenomenon that later came forth were

- Human workers probably are not entirely like machines.
- The Western Electric workers were responding to some motivating variable other than the lighting, or despite the lack of it.
- They likely kept producing more in spite of poor working conditions because they knew they were being watched.

Mayo and his colleagues were so impressed by these initial findings that they ultimately conducted a total of six interrelated experiments over an eight-year period. In part because of the massive size of the undertaking, the Hawthorne studies number among the most influential empirical researches ever conducted by social scientists. Most notably they produced the famous term, "Hawthorne effect," or the tendency of people to change their behavior when they know that they are being observed. But even more important, the studies were interpreted by succeeding generations of management scientists as validating the idea that unquantifiable relationships (or "human relations") between workers and managers, and among workers themselves, were significant determinants of workers' efficiency.

A reinterpretation of the Hawthorne data, using statistical techniques that were unavailable to Mayo and Roethlisberger, has undermined the original "human relations" interpretation. An important analysis of the data concluded that human relations were *not* the reasons behind worker efficiency, but rather such traditional motivators as "managerial discipline," fear (in the form of the Depression), reduction of fatigue (the experimental groups were given rest periods), and money (the groups also were given group pay incentives) were the real

reasons underlying increased productivity.[13] Nevertheless, the Hawthorne studies marked the continuation of the Saint-Simonian tradition after a century-long gap, and the beginning of human relations as we know it.[14]

A Hierarchy of Human Needs. Notable in terms of the impact of the human relationists is their research on motivation and job satisfaction. Much of this research centers around the "hierarchy of human needs" developed by A. H. Maslow. Maslow perceived human desires to be based first on (1) physiological needs (such as eating), which provided the foundation for the human's next greatest need, (2) economic security, then (3) love or belongingness, (4) self-esteem, and finally, (5) self-actualization.

Self-actualization refers to the individual growing, maturing, and achieving a deep inner sense of self-worth as he or she relates to his or her job and organization. In terms of the person and the organization, Maslow wrote that these "highly evolved" self-actualized individuals assimilated "their work into the identity, into the self, that is, work actually becomes part of the self, part of the individual's definition of himself."[15]

Hygienic Factors and Motivator Factors. Frederick Herzberg stimulated much of the empirical research that related to Maslow's hierarchy of needs.[16] Herzberg developed the concept that there were two basic classes of phenomena that made people feel bad or good about their jobs. One class related to the *context* of the job and included such factors as working conditions, organizational policies and procedures, and salary; Herzberg called these "extrinsic" dimensions *hygienic factors*, and they correspond more or less with the base of Maslow's pyramid of human needs, where physiological and security needs are found.

Herzberg's second category related to the *content* of the job and included such factors as professional and personal challenge and growth in the position, appreciation of a job well done by supervisors and peers, and a sense of being responsible for important matters; Herzberg called these "intrinsic" aspects *motivator factors*, and they relate by and large with the upper reaches of Maslow's pyramid: belongingness, self-esteem, and self-actualization.

Motivating   Organizational   Excellence.
Herzberg's framework and various modifications
of it have produced a voluminous body of literature that attempts to answer such questions as: Do
workers who feel good about their jobs make organizations more viable? If so, what makes workers
feel good? Do hygienic factors make workers feel
better than motivator factors, or vice versa?
Reviews of this literature usually conclude that
there is not a clear-cut body of empirical results
that relates organizational effectiveness to "the
humanistic model of organizational motivation,"[17]
and empirical tests of the "happy-productive
worker thesis" yield mixed results.[18]

Perhaps the principal limitation of studies that
have attempted to test the hypotheses of human
relations is that they largely are confined to examining these linkages *within* a particular organization,
but not *across* organizations. Recently, however,
researchers are conducting large-scale analyses
across many companies and organizations, an
approach that moots the dilemma of different
organizations yielding different conclusions.

Perks, Pay, and the Productive Organization.
First, what do we know about the impact of
hygienic factors on organizational productivity?
Do perks, pay, and other benefits of this sort boost
organizational productivity?

No. A large metanalysis examined this question,
and researchers sorted through data concerning
policies on work hours, vacations, flextime, child
care, and similar hygienic factors in 732 manufacturing firms in the United States and Europe. They
found no relationship—none—between progressive hygienic policies (such as shorter hours, generous vacations, and so forth) and more
productive, competitive companies. Nor did the
analysts find any correlation between curmudgeonly and stingy benefits and less, or more, competitive corporations.[19] People, of course, do work
for perks, pay, and other hygienic factors, but
something else makes them productive workers.

In fact, other large-scale research indicates that
hygienic factors are only marginally present in
employees' thinking about their jobs. In a study of
more than 6,000 managers and employees of
twenty-six organizations in the United States and
Canada, three-fifths of supervisors and workers

had almost no clue about what they needed to do
to get a raise or a bonus, even though, in most
instances, they were not terribly satisfied with
their pay.[20]

If hygienic factors do not affect an organization's productivity one way or the other, then do
motivator factors influence it?

**Kindness,   Caring,   and   the   Competitive
Organization.**   Yes. This same study also found
that when employees did have knowledge about
how to improve their compensation—that is,
when someone had communicated what was
expected of them, shown that they cared for them,
and encouraged their development—their satisfaction with their pay rose considerably.[21]

A particularly huge metanalysis conducted
over twenty-five years focused on what made
companies the best relative to four crucial measures of organizational strength: productivity,
profit, employee retention, and customer satisfaction. The researchers found that when employees
felt that they knew what was expected of them at
work, had what they needed to do their jobs right,
had the opportunity "to do what I did best every
day," believed that someone at work cared about
them as a person, had received recognition for
work well done over the last seven days, and
thought there was someone at work who encouraged their development, then the business unit
scored markedly high on all four measures of
workplace strength.[22]

These dimensions, as well as other important
ones unearthed in the metanalysis, are motivator
factors, not hygienic ones. "Bringing your pay
and benefits package up to market levels while a
sensible first step, will not take you very far. These
kinds of issues are like tickets to the ballpark—
they can get you into the game, but they can't help
you win."[23]

**Rude, Crude, and Lewd: The Impact of Negative
Motivators.**   To place the importance of motivator factors in perspective, consider what happens
to organizations when *negative* motivators
predominate. That is, what are the effects on an
organization when its members are not mutually
supportive and caring; but instead are rude,
sarcastic, and uncivil with each other?

Incivility in organizational life is extensive. A series of studies conducted over eight years involving more than 2,400 employees representing organizations "in all industrial classifications" in the United States and Canada found that from a tenth of these workers and executives witnessed incivility daily in their workplaces, and from a fifth to half reported that they, personally, were the direct targets of uncivil behavior at least once a week.

The organizational costs of incivility are considerable. Resolving conflicts in a typical Fortune 1000 firm involves, on average, 13 percent of an executive's time, or almost seven weeks per year. One out of eight victims of uncivil behavior in the workplace leaves for other jobs to escape the situation. These departures tote up when we realize that turnover costs from 1.5 to 2.5 times the salary of each employee who leaves, amounting to an average of $50,000 per exiting employee in all jobs in the United States. "Even members of the power elite do not get away with incivility scot-free", and about a third of the less powerful targets of incivility retaliate by avoiding, or by spreading unflattering rumors about, the instigator; a fifth purposely dilly-dally in responding to the requests of uncivil instigators.

"The results are clear: incivility is costly to organizations and their members in subtle but pervasive ways that can include decline in job satisfaction, fading of organizational loyalty, and of leadership's impact."[24]

So, to answer our questions: Yes, there is a positive correlation between employees who like their work and competitive, successful, and productive organizations. Hygienic factors furnish the base, but motivator factors are more important in helping employees like their work.

Do Public Organizations Motivate Public Managers? Does government furnish its employees with motivator factors, or those workplace qualities that most help employees enjoy their work? When compared to the private sector, the evidence tilts favorably toward the public sector.

Over the years, large majorities of federal employees—typically, almost nine out of every ten—consistently state that, "the work I do on my job is meaningful to me," and this response handily surpasses every other measure of job satisfaction, such as satisfaction with supervisors and pay.[25] In an analysis of a matched set of more than 1,000 federal and 500 corporate managers, it was found that federal managers were much more likely to "come to work" because of the "nature of their jobs" (nearly a third of federal managers *versus* a fifth of business managers), and they were much less likely to do so because of compensation (less than a third of federal manager *versus* nearly half of business managers), despite the fact that government managers were significantly more satisfied with their salaries than were managers in business. Federal administrators were much likelier than were business managers to believe that they "accomplished something worthwhile at work" (six out of ten *versus* less than half).[26]

Do Nonprofit Organizations Motivate Nonprofit Managers? Organizations in the nonprofit sector appear to provide even more motivators to their employees than do those in the public sector, not to mention those in the private sector. A unique survey of 1,140 employees in the nonprofit sector that compared its results with comparable surveys of federal and private-sector workers, concluded that "the nonprofit sector has the healthiest workforce in America," and that its health centers on motivator factors.[27]

For example, more than two-thirds, 68 percent, of nonprofit employees strongly believe that they are given the chance to do the things that they do best, compared to about half of federal and corporate employees. And more than two-fifths, 44 percent, of nonprofit workers said that they trust their organizations to do the right thing "just about always," compared to only a fourth of federal employees and 37 percent of business employees.[28]

In sum, the evidence by and large implies that both government and nonprofit administrators receive more motivator factors in their workplaces than do business managers, and nonprofit managers may garner more motivators than do public administrators. In theory, at least, these features should render the public sector more productive than the private one.

Organization Development

An important subfield of the open model is called *organization development* (OD). OD is a planned, organization-wide attempt directed from the top that is designed to increase organizational effectiveness and viability through calculated interventions in the active workings of the organization using knowledge from the behavioral sciences.[29]

OD: Mission and Methods. The mission of organization development is to

- improve the individual member's ability to get along with other members;
- legitimate human emotions in the organization;
- increase mutual understanding among members;
- reduce tensions;
- enhance "team management" and intergroup cooperation;
- develop more effective techniques for conflict resolution through nonauthoritarian and interactive methods;
- evolve less structured and more "organic" organizations.

Organization development owes its origins to the social psychologist Kurt Lewin and his colleagues' groundbreaking experiments of the 1940s.[30] These and later researchers developed therapy group and sensitivity training, techniques that encourage people to be candid about their views of challenges facing the company and their co-workers' ability to meet those challenges. These small groups are then joined with other small groups for purposes of exchanging perspectives (a process known as "interlocking group conferences" or "intergroup development"), and surveys of employees are undertaken and the results widely circulated, until the corporate structure has become a "managerial grid"[31] that facilitates better communication and organizational responsiveness.

OD: The Public Experience. In a study of 47 percent of all known public-sector applications, it was found that organization development, for the most part, were both far-reaching and successful. "Public-sector OD interventions tend to hunt the bigger game: racial tension; conflict . . . ;

basic reorganization," and 84 percent of the respondents in this survey reported that organization development had had positive and intended effects on their agencies, only 9 percent reported negative effects.[32] These rates were quite comparable to the private sector's experience with OD.[33]

"Public sector interventions seem to be equally effective [with private sector interventions] at enhancing both individual development and organizational performance."[34]

OD: Crises and Caveats. Despite some real success, as organization development matures, its practitioners seem to grow less confident in their mission. The field seems, in the view of some, to have moved from a "faddish rise in the 1960s, its downturn while under attack in the 1970s, and its subsequent morphing into many forms during the 1980s and 1990s," transforming itself to the point that "it is hardly recognizable in most organizations" and may end up as "a historical artifact."[35] A survey of more than 6,000 OD practitioners found that most felt that the field lacked a clear definition and was muddled about its return on investment and perceived value of the work performed.[36]

In sum, we seem to have a crisis of confidence in organization development. Not only do the field's practitioners speculate that applying OD may be counterproductive in rendering organizations more effective, but some worry that the very idea of using OD to boost organizational performance is a sellout of the field's central value of improving human lives in the workplace. The bottom line and "the mind-set of management" have perverted the power, presence, and perspective of organization development; as a consequence, employees trapped in "the grubby realities of worklife soon figure out whose side [these] breezy, self-assured, and excessively articulate" OD consultants are truly on, and they are not on the employees' side.[37] They are, contemptibility (in this viewpoint), on management's side.

All of this is, of course, fine. It is admirable that organization development exists as a profession to help people open up in their organizations. Executives who hire OD consultants to improve their organizations' performance, however, should be aware that their priority may not be shared by the consultants they hire.

The Organization as a Unit in Its Environment

A third school of the open model is less bulky as a literature but nonetheless is separate and identifiable. Notable writers among its early contributors can be traced at least as far back as the 1930s,[38] although this literary stream is currently undergoing a significant revitalization. It is characterized by use of the organization as a whole as its analytical unit (in contrast to the other schools' preference for the small group), its theme of the organizational pressures and constraints emanating from the environment, and organizational strategies designed to cope with environmentally-spawned problems.

Adapting to the Environment. Organization theorists often refer to this literary stream as *adaptive systems* or *contingency theory*, terms that emphasize the idea that organizations change because of their exchanges with their task environments.

Because this literary stream emphasizes so heavily the organization's relations with its task environment, a word of explanation about what the term *environment* means in the context of organization theory may be helpful. "Speaking metaphorically, you might liken the [organization's task] environment to a reticular pattern of incessant waves constituting a perpetually varying net or screen continuously through . . . organizations. . . . The openings in the ever-changing screen constantly assume different shapes and sizes. At the same time, the organizations themselves are always changing as they try to avoid being swept away. If the two sets of changes are such that an organization can 'fit' through the 'holes' when the screen passes, the organization survives; if not, it is carried off."[39]

It is with this appreciation of the relationship between an organization and its task environment in mind that the idea of "co-optation" was originated by Phillip Selznick in his classic study of the Tennessee Valley Authority (TVA).[40] *Co-optation* referred to the strategy employed by

the TVA's board of directors in gaining the acceptance, and ultimately the strong support, of initially hostile local interests by granting their representatives membership on the board. TVA, as a result, influenced and cajoled the local interests far more profoundly than the local interests influenced the TVA; in short, TVA co-opted the local interests but was required to modify slightly its own purposes in so doing.

There may have been a "sleeper effect" in the TVA's co-optation of local interests. In a more recent analysis, it was found that those local interests which had been co-opted by the top administrators of the Tennessee Valley Authority had, nearly forty years later, become considerably more powerful, and, in fact, were able to develop a sufficient level of power that they could "foster new operative goals for TVA and to prevent TVA initiated modifications of those goals."[41]

The Environment of the Public Organization. As the studies of the Tennessee Valley Authority imply, the task environment has an unusually heavy and distorting impact on the public organization, We contrast the differences between how public and private organizations react to their environments along several dimensions in the next two chapters, but we should note here that, if the literature on the differences between public and private organizations agrees on anything, it is that *public organizations must deal with far more constraints and controls emanating from the environment than private organizations.* This reality deeply affects every aspect of the public organization: processes, structure, decision making, administration—everything.

The Closed and Open Models: The Essential Differences

We have reviewed two eminently disparate models of organizations and their respective literary emphases. In essence, their fundamental differences may be reduced to four: assumptions about the organizational environment, assumptions about the nature of human beings, assumptions about the role and legitimacy of manipulation in organizations, and assumptions about the moral significance of organizations in society.

Assumptions about the Organizational Environment

The closed model is predicated on the belief that organizations exist in a stable, routine environment, and the open model is predicated on the belief that organizations must function in an unstable environment, replete with surprises. Both models, however, assume that organizations will act in order to survive and, ultimately, to thrive.

The beauty in these two differing perceptions of organizations is that both models work in the respective environments posited for them. That is, an open-model organization likely would "die" in a stable environment, and a closed-model organization probably would wither in an unstable environment. To recall our earlier description of the task environment, one way or the other, an organization must adapt so that it can "fit" through the "holes" of the environmental screening equipment that sweeps incessantly through it if it is to survive.

To elaborate, when an organization that is superbureaucratic, rigid, and routinized around long-standing patterns of well-ordered and predictable stimuli that have emanated from a habitually

---

Closed or Open Organizations?

Sometimes it is difficult to distinguish the difference between a closed or open organization, at least when it pertains to the plight of the person in the organization.

Every audience contains the "direct action" manager who shouts, "Kick him!" And this type of manager is right. The surest and least circumlocuted way of getting someone to do something is to kick him in the pants—give him what might be called the KITA.

There are various forms of KITA, and here are some of them.

Negative physical KITA

This is a literal application of the term and was frequently used in the past. It has, however, three major drawbacks: (1) It is inelegant; (2) it contradicts the precious image of benevolence that most organizations cherish; and (3) since it is a physical attack, it directly stimulates the autonomic nervous system, and this often results in negative feedback—the employee may just kick you in return. These factors give rise to certain taboos against negative physical KITA.

The psychologist has come to the rescue of those who are no longer permitted to use negative physical KITA. He has uncovered infinite sources of psychological vulnerabilities and the appropriate methods to play tunes on them. "He took my rug away"; "I wonder what he meant by that"; "The boss is always going around me"—these symptomatic expressions of ego sores that have been rubbed raw are the result of application of:

Negative Psychological KITA

This has several advantages over negative physical KITA. First, the cruelty is not visible; the bleeding is internal and comes much later. Second, since it affects the higher cortical centers of the brain with its inhibitory powers, it reduces the possibility of physical backlash. Third, since the number of psychological pains that a person can feel is almost infinite, the direction and site possibilities of the KITA are increased many times. Fourth, the person administering the kick can

stable environment suddenly is confronted with a "new," unstable environment, the organization either must "loosen up" and adapt or die. Conversely, when an organization is superfluidic and tackles each challenge emanating from its environment as something unique, new, and fresh (which indeed may be the case), with no attempt to discover commonalities among tasks and to categorize and routinize them along "rational" lines, is confronted over time with a highly stable and structured environment, the organization either must adapt or die from its own inefficiency and absence of structure and routine relative to its environment.

So, in terms of their matching with environmental stability, or the lack of it, both the closed and open models make sense. As environments change, so must the organizations in it.

Assumptions about the Nature of Human Beings

The second basic difference between the closed and open models parallels the first, in that their respective models of human beings match the models of organization. Douglas McGregor called these two models "Theory X" and "Theory Y."[42]

Theory X applies to the closed model. Its underlying belief structure assumes that work is not liked by most people, most people prefer close and unrelenting supervision, most people

---

manage to be above it all and let the system accomplish the dirty work. Fifth, those who practice it receive some ego satisfaction (one-upmanship), whereas they would find drawing blood abhorrent. Finally, if the employee does complain, he can always be accused of being paranoid, since there is no tangible evidence of an actual attack.

Now, what does negative KITA accomplish? If I kick you in the rear (physically or psychologically), who is motivated? I am motivated; you move! Negative KITA does not lead to motivation, but to movement. So:

Positive KITA

Let us consider motivation. If I say to you, "Do this for me or the company, and in return I will give you a reward, an incentive, more status, a promotion, all the quid pro quos that exist in the industrial organization," am I motivating you? The overwhelming opinion I receive from management people is, "Yes, this is motivation."

I have a year-old Schnauzer. When it was a small puppy and I wanted it to move, I kicked it in the rear and it moved. Now that I have finished its obedience training, I hold up a dog biscuit when I want the Schnauzer to move. In this instance, who is motivated—the dog came? The dog wants the biscuit, but it is I who want it to move. Again, I am the one who is motivated, and the dog is the one who moves. In this instance all I did was apply KITA frontally: I exerted a pull instead of a push. When industry wishes to use such positive KITAs, it has available an incredible number and variety of dog biscuits (jelly beans for humans) to wave in front of the employee to get him to jump.

Why is it that managerial audiences are quick to see that negative KITA is not motivation, while they are almost unanimous in their judgment that positive KITA is motivation? It is because negative KITA is rape, and positive KITA is seduction. But it is infinitely worse to be seduced than it is to be raped; the latter is an unfortunate occurrence, while the former signifies that you were a party to your own downfall. This is why positive KITA is so popular; it is in the American way. The organization does not have to kick you; you kick yourself.

Frederick Herzberg
Harvard Business Review

cannot contribute creatively to the solution of organizational problems, motivation to work is an individual matter, and most people are motivated by the direct application of threat or punishment. It is apparent that organizations exemplifying the closed model not only would fit but also possibly might be appealing to Theory *X* people.

Theory Y, which goes by other titles as well, such as System 4, self-actualization, intrinsic motivation, and Eupsychian management, has quite another underlying belief structure. Theory *Y* assumes that, given the right conditions, most people can enjoy work as much as play, most people can exercise self-control and prefer doing jobs in their own way, most people can solve organizational problems creatively, motivation to work is a group matter, and most people often are motivated by social and ego rewards. It is apparent that organizations predicated on the open model likely would attract Theory *Y* people.

Assumptions about the Role and Legitimacy of Manipulation

Manipulation in an organizational context simply means getting people to do what you want them to do. The closed model, particularly its bureaucratic theory school, has no qualms about employing manipulative methods. It advocates "using" people for the sake of the organization's ends. Moreover, the callous use of authoritarian coercion in manipulating people is seen as entirely legitimate. The open model, most notably its organization development school, occasionally appears to argue against the practice of manipulation of people by other people. Manipulation is seen as dehumanizing, "dematurizing,"[43] and generally nasty.

There is, however, a fundamental dilemma in the value set of those who advocate the open model: The ends of the individual member of the organization and the ends of the organization are not invariably one and the same. "The reconciliation of man and his organization has proved to be an essential but perhaps hopeless task. Either the individual is autonomous or the organization is dominant, for the very notion of individualism wars against even benevolent organization."[44]

In sum, manipulation is necessary in the open model as well as in the closed model of organizations. Only the styles of manipulation differ. The closed-model theorists, in the tradition of Weber, believed in orders and obedience, rules and regulations, punctuality and punctiliousness. The human dysfunctions of these manipulative techniques are obvious; rigidity, impersonality, alienation, narrowness, and stultification number among the human and organizational liabilities of authoritarian manipulation. But there are also human advantages to the crudities of the closed model's manipulative techniques: People in closed model organizations "know where they stand." The authoritarianism of the closed model is for people who like things straightforward and clear-cut.

Just as the disadvantages of the closed model's manipulative techniques are apparent, so the advantages of the open model's methods of manipulation are clear; humanism, openness, communication, teamwork, and innovation are enhanced by the use of open-model concepts. But there are also liabilities to the social–psychological brand of manipulation employed by the open model. The more refined manipulative methods stemming from small group theory, supportive relationships, myths of peerage tend to camouflage the unavoidable exercise of power in organizations. As a result, people in open model organizations may never be sure "where they stand."

More significantly, if they think that they do know where they stand, their knowledge may be the end-product of a manipulation of their psyches so subtle as to render them analogous to the "conditioned" human shell of the protagonist in George Orwell's *Nineteen Eighty-four*, who uncontrollably shrieked "Long Live Big Brother!" even as he despised him. Eric Fromm expresses this idea more succinctly with his concept of *willing submissiveness*; that is, although organizational subordinates may appear to have "team spirit" (and actually may have been so successfully manipulated as to believe they have it), the psychological techniques used to create their willing submissiveness induces in reality a subliminal and deep internal resentment toward their superiors bordering on hatred.[45] There is, in fact, empirical research suggesting that this is precisely what happens in organizations that use the open model's techniques of manipulation.[46]

Assumptions about the Moral Significance of Organizations in Society

The fourth principal difference between the closed and open models is particularly germane to the study of public administration and centers on how their respective theorists have viewed the organization and its moral relationship with the larger society.

The Moral View of the Closed Model.   Weber provides an especially solid example of a closed model theorist who makes his values explicit in this regard. Bureaucracy, Weber held, replete with its own internal injustices, dehumanizing rules, and monocratic arbitrariness, was vital in its very rigidity and rationalism in mitigating the unorganized societal lunacy that it confronted. If Weber's notion of the bureaucracy's station in society could be illustrated, it would look something like Figure 3-1.

Weber was not unsympathetic to the plight of the individual bureaucrat. Indeed, he bemoaned that the passion for bureaucracy among his German students "is enough to drive one to despair."[47] But, when all was said and done, Weber could accept the dehumanization of society's social servants, who were somehow apart from the other citizens, on the grounds that the bureaucracy was essential to social progress and the elimination of injustice.

The Moral View of the Open Model.   In contrast to Weber, the open model theorists have a com-pletely different idea of the organization's role in society. To them, every citizen is encased in some sort of bureaucratic organization, and this imprisonment is not good: "Bureaucracy gives birth to a new species of inhuman beings. People's social relations are being converted into control relations. . . . Psychologically, the personality type is that of the rationalistic expert, incapable of emotion and devoid of will."[48]

Thus, for the public bureaucracy to manipulate and dehumanize its own bureaucrats in order to further society's goals and establish rational social justice is self-defeating because the bureaucrat and the citizen are one and the same. Hence, what is good for the individual is equally good for society. The open model perceives society as a series of overlapping, interlocking, and interacting organizations, and there is no unorganized, irrational society "out there," roiling beyond the organizations' boundaries. The open model's concept of society and the bureaucracy looks like Figure 3-2.

Who Must Be Sacrificed?   This difference between the closed and open models leads to quite different ethical conclusions and justifications by those who tout them. When push comes to shove, someone must pay the price of advancing society, and a fundamental distinction between the two models pivots on just who must pay that price.

Those who advocate the closed model state that the organization's clerks and laborers must be sacrificed for the larger good of revolutionizing society. This social revolution, which only bureaucratic organizations can achieve, is the creation of a more fair, honest, equitable, and

Figure 3-2   The Open Model's View: Organizations *as* Society

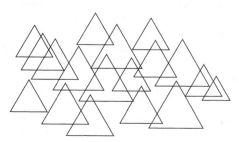

Figure 3-1   The Closed Model's View: Organizations *and* Society

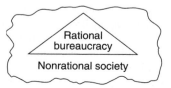

transparent society. Because only organizations can bring us that just society, and because organizations must struggle to bring it to us, underlings are the logical members of the organization to perish at the front lines of that struggle. The organization's executives, by contrast, must be protected because these leaders are at the core of changing society for the better, whereas the organizations' clerks and laborers are merely the tools used by the executives to accomplish far-reaching and beneficial social change.

Those who advocate the open model state that the organization itself must be sacrificed for the larger good of revolutionizing society. The creation of a more just society (which is cast in precisely the same terms as in the closed model) is not facilitated by organizations, as the closed model contends but is obstructed by them. If destroying this blocking infrastructure of bureaucratic organizations is impractical (as it likely is), then at least indoctrinating, transforming, and, if necessary, replacing the organization's leadership will suffice. Optimally, these top executives should be replaced not by new executives, but by nonhierarchical, democratic, self-actualized teams of clerks and laborers; at the very least, however, they will be replaced by leaders who understand and are committed to eliminating the stultifying, dematurizing, and dehumanizing bureaucratic and organizational forces that permeate society.

The Literature of Model Synthesis

Students of organizations may be initially puzzled by the fundamentally different paradigms of organization theory represented by the closed and open models. The closed model assumes that people hate work, organizations are rational, their environments are stable, coercion is basic, bureaucrats are different from citizens, and bureaucracies are the saviors of society. The open model assumes that people love work, organizations are irrational, their environments are unstable, coercion is unacceptable, bureaucrats and citizens are one and the same, and bureaucracies are the bane of society. These are basic differences. Can they be reconciled and, if so, how?

The answer to the first part of the question is a qualified "yes," and the attempt to do so is represented by the "newer tradition" of organization theory as exemplified by Barnard's *Functions of the Executive*, Herbert A. Simon's *Administrative Behavior*, James G. March and Simon's *Organizations*, Richard Cyert and March's *A Behavioral Theory of the Firm*, James D. Thompson's *Organizations in Action*, and Paul R. Lawrence and Jay W. Lorsch's *Organization and Environment*.

The essence of the literature of model synthesis is that it starts with the open model (that is, it assumes that organizations are spontaneous collectivities of people with their own goals and drives, who are operating in an uncertain environment) but explains organizational behavior as being motivated by a need to routinize and rationalize the organization's internal workings and its relationships with its environment whenever and wherever possible. This is essentially a Darwinian notion (adapt or die).

To adapt, organizations try to reduce uncertainty.

Are Public Organizations Different?

As this chapter has implied, whatever their context and mission, all organizations share certain similarities. Still, the environment and purpose of an organization can change its behavior, and public-sector organizations differ from their private-sector and independent-sector counterparts on both dimensions.

To emphasize the behavioral differences between public and private organizations is not orthodox. Historically, organization theorists have done just the opposite (the profoundly influential sociologist, Talcott Parsons, likely set the standard in this regard)[49] and have minimized, ignored, or denied such differences: "Virtually all the major contributions to the field [of organization theory] were conceived to apply broadly across all types of organizations. . . . the distinction between public and private organizations received short shrift. . . . Public organizations as a distinctive category receive sporadic, speculative attention, with the clear implication that their distinctiveness plays a minor role compared to other influences."[50]

And there is some reason to believe that, in terms of distinguishing organizational behavior, the public/private distinction sometimes cloaks other kinds of organizational differences that function at a deeper level than society's convenient but shallow categories of "government" and "business." For example, one study of how federal, state-and-local, and private sector managers implemented policy found that the state and local administrators and the private managers approached implementation in a fashion that was far more similar to each other, and that only the federal administrators who differed![51] The public/private distinction obviously did not explain these differences.

Okay. But when all is said and done, the public/private distinction works a lot—in fact, most—of the time in understanding many kinds of organizational dynamics. Admittedly, it is sometimes used as a "first-pass" distinction that may not always apply in every analysis; it may well veneer more profound and important realities; it is not perfect. But it works pretty well, and we like it.

So, as we shall learn in the following two chapters, yes, public organizations are different.

Notes

1. James G. March and Herbert A. Simon, *Organizations* (New York: John Wiley, 1958), p. 4.
2. James D. Thompson, *Organizations in Action* (New York: McGraw-Hill, 1967).
3. Tom Burns and G. M. Stalker, *The Management of Innovation* (London: Tavistock, 1961).
4. Max Weber, *From Max Weber*, in H. H. Gerth and C. Wright Mills, eds. (New York: Oxford University Press, 1946).
5. See especially Frederick W. Taylor, *Principles of Scientific Management* (New York: Harper & Row, 1911); and Frank G. Gilbreth, *Primer of Scientific Management* (New York: Van Nostrand, 1912).
6. Charles D. Wrege and Amedeo G. Perroni, "Taylor's Pig-Tale: A Historical Analysis of Frederick W. Taylor's Pig-Iron Experiment," *Academy of Management Journal* 17 (March 1974), pp. 6–27.
7. Taylor, *Principles of Scientific Management*, p. 59.
8. See especially Luther Gulick and L. Urwick, eds., *Papers on the Science of Administration* (New York:

Institute of Public Administration, 1937); James D. Mooney and Alan C. Reiley, *The Principles of Organization* (New York: Harper & Row, 1939); M. P. Follett, *Creative Experience* (New York: P. Smith Company, 1924); and Henri Fayol, *General and Industrial Management* (London: Pittman, 1930).

9. Alvin W. Gouldner, "Organizational Analysis," in *Sociology Today*, Robert K. Merton, Leonard Broom, and Leonard S. Cottrell, Jr., eds. (New York: Basic Books, 1959), pp. 400–428.
10. More recently, this idea has been called "ad hocracy." See Alvin Toffler, *Future Shock* (New York: Random House, 1970).
11. Burns and Stalker, *The Management of Innovation.*
12. Fritz J. Roethlisberger and William J. Dickson, *Management and the Worker* (Cambridge, MH: Harvard University Press, 1939).
13. Richard Herbert Franke and James D. Kaul, "The Hawthorne Experiments: First Statistical Interpretation," *American Sociological Review* 43 (October 1978), pp. 623–643.
14. For a fascinating explication of the origins of human relations in the twentieth century, we commend: J. H. Smith, "The Enduring Legacy of Elton Mayo," *Human Relations* 51 (March 1998), pp. 221–240.
15. Abraham Maslow, *Eupsychian Management: A Journal* (Homewood, IL: Dorsey, 1965), p. 1.
16. See, for example, Frederick Herzberg, *Work and the Nature of Man* (Cleveland: World Publishing, 1966).
17. Frank K. Gibson and Clyde E. Teasley, "The Humanistic Model of Organizational Motivation: A Review of Research Support," *Public Administration Review* 33 (January/February 1973), pp. 89–96.
18. T. A. Wright and B. M. Staw, "Affect and Favorable Work Outcomes: Two Longitudinal Tests of the Happy-Productive Worker Thesis," *Journal of Organizational Behavior* 20 (January 1999), pp. 1–23.
19. Nick Bloom, Tobias Kretschmer, and John Van Reenen, *Work-Life Balance, Management Practices and Productivity* (London: Centre for Economic Performance, 2006). The authors use the term, "work-life balance" to encompass a number of hygienic factors used by organizations.
20. Paul W. Mulvey, Peter V. LeBlanc, Robert L. Heneman et al., *The Knowledge of Pay Study: E-Mails from the Front Line* (Scottsdale, AZ: WorldWork and The LeBlanc Group, 2002).
21. Ibid.
22. Marcus Buckingham and Curt Coffman, *First, Break All the Rules: What Do the World's Greatest Managers Do Differently?* (New York: Simon and Schuster, 1999). The six items listed in the text were the most critical of twelve that the authors indicated as extremely significant. The remaining six items related purely to motivators factors, and included, Do my opinions count? Does the mission of my company make me feel that my work is important? Are my co-workers committed to quality work? Do I have a best friend at work? Have I talked to someone about my progress? And have I had opportunities to learn and grow? The 2,500 "business units" were

in two dozen companies spanning a dozen industries. Supporting evidence from a different, but equally massive, angle comes from a review of national opinion polls conducted from 1973 through 1994. In almost every year, more than half of Americans said that "a feeling of accomplishment" is the "most important." See: Karlyn Bowman, *Attitudes About Work and Leisure in America* (Washington, DC: American Leadership Institute, 2001), Table W-9.

23. Buckingham and Coffman, *First, Break all the Rules*, p. 29.

24. Christine M. Pearson and Christine L. Porath, "On the Nature, Consequences and Remedies of Workplace Incivility: No Time for 'Nice'? Think Again," *Academy of Management Executive* 19 (February 2005), pp. 7–18. The quotations are on pp. 8 and 11.

25. U.S. Merit Systems Protection Board, *The Federal Workforce for the 21st Century: Results of the Merit Principles Survey 2000* (Washington, DC: U.S. Government Printing Office, 2003), p. 11. In the four surveys conducted between 1989 and 2000, from 78 percent to 88 percent of federal workers said that their job was meaningful to them, and in three of the four surveys, from 87 percent to 88 percent said so. By contrast, satisfaction with supervisors came in at around six out of ten employees, and satisfaction with pay ranged from 28 percent to 50 percent.

26. Princeton Survey Research Associates and the Brookings Institution, *Health of the Public Service* (Washington, DC: Authors, 2001) http://www.brook.edu. Data are for 2001. Details, in order of presentation in the text are: 30 percent of federal managers come to work because of the nature of their jobs, compared to 22 percent of private managers; 32 percent of federal managers do so because of compensation compared to 47 percent of private managers; 42 percent of federal managers are "very satisfied" with their salaries compared to 33 percent of private managers; and 59 percent of feds say that they "accomplish something worthwhile at work" compared to 45 percent of business managers. Fifty-six percent of federal managers and 57 percent of private managers strongly agree that they are given a chance to what they do best, and 77 percent of federal and 79 percent of private managers strongly agree that they can make decisions on their own. Resource questions had several dimensions, but, for example, only 37 percent of federal managers said they had the technological equipment needed to do their jobs well, compared to 47 percent of business managers.

27. Paul C. Light, as quoted in Brookings Institution, *Winning the Talent War: Brookings Survey Finds the Nonprofit Sector Has the Most Dedicated Workforce* (Washington, DC: Author, 2002), p. 2. See also Paul C. Light, "The Content of Their Character: The State of the Nonprofit Workforce," *Nonprofit Quarterly* 9 (Fall 2002), pp. 7–16.

28. Ibid., both sources. The survey of nonprofit workers was compared with two other surveys of 1,051 federal employees and 1,005 private-sector employees that were conducted under the direction of the Brookings Institution.

29. Richard Beckhard, *Organizational Development: Strategies and Models* (Reading, MA: Addison-Wesley, 1969), pp. 20–24.

30. Wendell L. French and Cecil H. Bell, Jr., *Organization Development: Behavioral Science Interventions for Organization Improvement* (Englewood Cliffs, NJ: Prentice Hall, 1973).

31. Douglas McGregor, *The Professional Manager* (New York: McGraw-Hill, 1967); and Robert R. Blake and J. S. Mouton, *The Managerial Grid* (Houston: Gulf Publishing, 1964).

32. Robert T. Golembiewski, Carl W. Proehl, Jr., and David Sink, "Success of OD Applications in the Public Sector: Toting Up the Score for a Decade, More or Less," *Public Administration Review* 4 (November/December 1981), p. 681. The authors counted 574 OD applications in the public sector conducted between 1945 and 1980.

33. Peggy Morrison, "Evaluation in OD: A Review and an Assessment," *Group and Organization Studies* 3 (March, 1978), pp. 42–70; and Jerry Porras, "The Comparative Impact of Different OD Techniques and Intervention Intensities," *Journal of Applied Behavioral Science* 15 (April, 1979), pp. 156–178.

34. Peter J. Robertson and Sonal J. Seneviratne, "Outcomes of Planned Organizational Change in the Public Sector: A Meta-Analytic Comparison to the Private Sector." *Public Administration Review* 55 (November/December 1995), p. 554.

35. Larry E. Greiner and Thomas G. Cummings, "Wanted: OD More Alive Than Dead!" *Journal of Applied Behavioral Science* 40 (Winter 2004), p. 374.

36. Jeana Wirtenberg, Lillian Abrams, and Carolyn Ott, "Assessing the Field of Organization Development," *Journal of Applied Behavioral Science* 40 (Winter 2004), pp. 465–480. The survey was sent to members of the Organization Development Network, the Organization Development Institute, and the International Organization Development Association.

37. Thomas H. Fitzgerald, "The O.D. Practitioner in the Business World: Theory vs. Reality," *Organizational Dynamics* 16 (Summer 1987), pp. 25, 27.

38. See, for example, Chester I. Barnard, *The Functions of the Executive* (Cambridge: Harvard University Press, 1938); Philip Selznick, *TVA and the Grass Roots* (Berkeley, University of California Press, 1949); and Burton R. Clark, *Adult Education in Transition* (Berkeley: University of California Press, 1956).

39. Herbert Kaufman, *Time, Chance, and Organizations: Natural Selection in a Perilous Environment* (Chatham, NJ: Chatham House, 1985), p. 67.

40. Selznick, *TVA and the Grass Roots.*

41. Richard A. Couto, "Co-optation in TVA: Selznick Updated," Paper delivered at the 1981 Annual Meeting of the American Political Science Association, New York, September 3–6, 1981, abstract page. See also: Richard A. Cuoto, "TVA's Old and New Grass Roots: A Reexamination of Cooptation," *Administration and Society* 19 (February 1988), pp. 443–455.

42. Douglas McGregor, *The Theory of Human Enterprise* (New York: McGraw-Hill, 1960).

43. Chris Argyris, *Organization and Innovation* (Homewood, IL: Richard D. Irwin, 1965).

44. Allen Schick, "The Trauma of Politics: Public Administration in the Sixties," in *American Public Administration: Past, Present, Future*, Frederick C. Mosher, ed. (Tuscaloosa, AL: University of Alabama Press, 1975), p. 170.

45. Eric Fromm, *The Art of Loving* (New York: Harper & Row, 1956).

46. See, for example, C. Casey, "'Come, Join Our Family': Discipline and Integration in Corporate Organizational Culture," *Human Relations* 52 (February 1999), pp. 155–178.

47. Max Weber, quoted in Elizabeth Kolbert, "Why Work? A Hundred Years of the Protestant Work Ethic," *The New Yorker* (November 29, 2004), pp. 157, 160.

48. Ralph P. Hummel, *The Bureaucratic Experience: A Critique of Life in the Modern Organization*, 4th ed. (New York: St. Martin's, 1994), p. 3.

49. See, for just one example, Talcott Parsons, *The Social System* (Glencoe, IL: Free Press, 1951).

50. Hal G. Rainey, *Understanding and Managing Public Organizations*, 2nd ed. (San Francisco: Jossey-Bass, 1997), p. 55.

51. Robert McGowan, Robert Spagnola, and Roger Brannan, "The Role of Sector in Determining Organizational Effectiveness: A Comparative Assessment," *Public Productivity and Management Review* 17 (Fall 1993), pp. 15–27.

CHAPTER **4**

The Fabric of Organizations: Forces

In this chapter, we move from our overview of the intellectual evolution of organization theory—its "threads"—to a consideration of its "fabric"; that is, how organization theorists explain the ways in which organizations weave those threads into a fabric—sometimes they weave a tapestry, other times a drop cloth. Or, to put it another way, Chapter 4 addresses how organizations, especially public and nonprofit organizations, adapt and relate to the manifold forces that roil in them and in the society surrounding them.

Society and the Assessment of Organizations

Organizations may be evaluated by society according to one of three "tests," and the appropriateness of any one of these tests depends on the nature of the organization.[1] Table 4-1 arrays the kinds of tests that societies use to assess their organizations by types of organizations. (The table also shows the decision-making strategies that these organizations use, and we discuss these strategies in greater detail later in the chapter.) We review these tests in turn.

Testing for Efficiency. The *efficiency*, or *economic*, *test* assesses an organization's ability

to fully and satisfactorily complete its tasks using the fewest resources possible. It is applicable to organizations that have "crystallized standards of desirability," and whose members believe they fully comprehend the relationships between causes and effects.

The efficiency test is nearly always appropriately applied to for-profit companies. For example, executives in our hypothetical corporation of International Widget have a solid notion of what they want to do and how to do it: Maximize profits (that is, their standards of desirability are quite firm and clear, or "crystallized") and manufacture widgets as cheaply as possible (that is, there is a clear causal connection between high profits and cheap production). Thus, assessing the performance of International Widget as an organization is both objective and easy because efficiency tests are applicable.

Testing for Effectiveness. The *effectiveness*, or *instrumental*, *test* assesses an organization's ability to fully and satisfactorily complete its tasks—period. Unlike the efficiency test, no judgments are made about how many resources the organization consumes (or wastes) in achieving it mission. The effectiveness test is less objective, less easy to apply, and less optimal in evaluating organizational performance than the efficiency test.

Table 4-1   Societal Assessment and Organizational Decision-Making Strategies by Causation and Outcome

		Standards of Desirability and Preferred Outcomes	
		Crystallized Standards and Agreement about Outcomes	Ambiguous Standards and Disagreement about Outcomes
Beliefs about cause and effect	Agreement	*Efficiency*, or *economic*, tests are used by society to assess the organization.	*Social tests* are used by society to assess the organization.
		Computational, or *analytical*, *decision making* is used by the organization.	*Compromise*, or *bargaining*, *decision making* is used by the organization.
		Example: a research lab	*Example*: Congress
	Disagreement	*Effectiveness*, or *instrumental tests* are used by society to assess the organization.	*Social tests* are used by society to assess the organization.
		Judgmental decision making is used by the organization.	*Inspirational and/or authoritarian decision making* is used by the organization.
		Example: Department of Defense	*Example*: Charles DeGaulle's Fifth Republic in France

Effectiveness tests often are applicable to public agencies. Like International Widget, public agencies may have crystallized standards of desirability but, unlike International Widget, the agencies' members are uncertain about what causes what. As a result of this situation, the efficiency test no longer is a suitable evaluative tool because, when no one is sure about causality, there is no way of assessing the efficiency of what the organization is doing.

The Department of Defense, for instance, has a crystallized standard of desirability (adequate deterrent), but its officers are unsure about whether their programs actually are establishing that deterrent. None of them knows if their defense policies are sufficient to deter a nuclear attack (until and unless, of course, one comes). Thus, unlike the officials of International Widget, the Pentagon brass always will be uneasy about whether its programs are maximizing its mission achievement. Hence, we see Defense spending as much money as it can muster as a means of maximizing its standard of desirability (that is, its unproven deterrent capacity), but International Widget spending as *little* money as possible as a means of maximizing *its* standard of desirability (that is, its profits).

Testing for Society. The *social test* assesses an organization's ability to appear relevant and useful in achieving a social mission. It is applicable to those organizations that have ambiguous, rather than crystallized, standards of desirability. In other words, members in such an organization are not merely uncertain about whether or not they achieving their goals; they are even uncertain about what goals they *want* to achieve. Such an organization might be a social service agency; often, no one in these organizations can express, except in the most general and vague terms, just what it is that they do, much less the best way of doing it.

Both social and effectiveness tests of organizational worth are the kinds of evaluational tools that societies usually use to assess their public and nonprofit organizations. Both tests are problematic, but at least the reasons for their problems are fairly clear: Public and nonprofit organizations, like the polity they serve, often are saddled with grandiose, but unspecific, missions and are usually left to their own devices when it comes to operationally defining and achieving those missions.

An investigation of 389 newly founded, nonprofit social service organizations in metropolitan Toronto concluded that the acquisition of "external legitimacy" by these new social service organizations far outweighed the use of internal management changes within these organizations in predicting their long-term survival. Conversely, changes in the "internal coordination" of these organizations (a term encompassing changes in the organizations' chief executives, service areas, goals, client groups, and structure) bore no relationship (with one exception, that of changing the chief executive) to the survival rates of these non-profit organizations.[2] Social tests then, while oftentimes less than measurable, appear to be vitally important to the success of nonprofit- and public-sector organizations.

Information and Intelligence in Organizations

How information, intelligence, and knowledge are used, distorted, and transmitted has considerable significance for what we have just considered: how society assesses its organizations. What is striking is how limited society's knowledge is. Similarly, the knowledge used by organizations themselves is strikingly limited.

Limited or not, how knowledge is acquired and used by organizations is being recognized as a critical component in the success of organizations, and the emergence of the "knowledge executive," (or managers whose job is to handle large volumes of information) in local governments,[3] and the creation of the "chief knowledge officer," "chief information officer," or "chief learning officer," among other titles, in corporations as large as Coca-Cola and General Motors, give proof to this recognition.[4] Herbert A. Simon observed that "how to process information" will emerge as the core challenge for executives,[5] and studies of top-level public executives have confirmed his prediction: they do indeed spend most of their time seeking and analyzing information.[6]

Information, in sum, is important. *Knowledge* has been defined, in fact, as "what changes us."[7] Knowledge is superior to *data* ("a meaningless point in time when not considered in context")

and *information* ("data, passed through a person's mind, that becomes meaningful"), but falls a bit short of *wisdom* (or profound understanding of one's place in the universe).[8] In an organizational context, the acquisition of knowledge, or at least information, as opposed to data or wisdom, is the more sensible and appropriate objective.

Hierarchy and Information

If knowledge changes us, it is discomfiting to know that organizations can change knowledge. Organizational hierarchies can and do distort, impede, and channel information for their own purposes. These pathologies occur in both centralized and decentralized organizations, and in closed and open organizations.

Centralization and the Fate of Intelligence. Organizational conflict, personal power, and informational control are inextricably intertwined, and this seems to be especially true in closed-model, centralized organizations. Consider a case drawn from the regime of Iraq's Saddam Hussein. For a full year prior to the American invasion of that country in 2003, the research director in Iraq's secret police and intelligence agency, the *Mukhabarat*, wrote for Saddam "three assessments saying that the Americans would attack Iraq and that we had no chance to resist them." The director provided these reports to one General Abed, Saddam's most trusted aide, personal secretary, and bodyguard (he was so trusted that he was allowed, uniquely, to wear a pistol in Saddam's presence). Abed "refused to give these [assessments] to the president, however. Like everyone else, he was afraid to tell him the truth."[9]

Decentralization and the Fate of Intelligence. Even when people trust each other and are working as a team, both of which are emblematic of the open-model, decentralized organization, information still may be distorted and prevented from reaching the people who need it and can act on it. In these organizations, the pathology appears to be less one of fear, and more one of fumbling.[10]

The classic example of what happens to knowledge in a decentralized organization is the surprise of American troops at Pearl Harbor during the Japanese attack in 1941. The Japanese secret code had been broken, and there is substantial evidence showing that various elements in the military and foreign services knew approximately when and where the Japanese would attack. But the information failed to reach the forces at Pearl Harbor in time.[11]

Information and the Irony of Organizational Reform. In sum, the arrangement of organizational relationships seems not to be a panacea for curing problems of organizational information. We do know, however, that the more layers of hierarchy, the more organizations and organizational subunits that are charged with similar responsibilities, and the more that information is "handled" as it is passed up, down, and around the bureaucracy, the more likely it is that the information will be delayed and distorted, and the less likely that it will reach someone who can intelligently act on it.[12]

Ironically, governments rarely "reform" their information functions in ways that mitigate these pathologies. Indeed, just the opposite. In response to the terrorist attacks of September 11, 2001, Congress created a "superstructure" organization, the Department of Homeland Security that surmounted twenty-two existing agencies that have remained largely intact and unaltered. The 9/11 Commission recommended,[13] and Congress and the president enacted, a National Intelligence Directorate that has thirty-four subunits (including two counterterrorism centers in different agencies); an intelligence-management budget that is five times more than what was previously spent; and twice the number of staffers than expected.[14] Among the seventy-four recommendations of the Commission on the Intelligence Capabilities of the United States Regarding Weapons of Mass Destruction (which was established to determine why there were no weapons of mass destruction in Iraq after the United States had invaded that country because federal officials believed that there were such armaments) were proposals for a new National Security Service,

a new Human Intelligence Directorate, a new National Counterterrorism Center, a new National Clandestine Service, a new Counter Proliferation Center, a new Innovation Center, a new National Intelligence Council, and a new Deputy Director of National Intelligence for Integrated Intelligence Strategies.[15] Many of these and other recommendations have been implemented, but the old intelligence bureaus remain, resulting in an overlayered bureaucracy of old and new agencies with overlapping jurisdictions and missions that seems, according to "several" foreign intelligence services, to have resulted in decline in the performance of the Central Intelligence Agency (CIA).[16]

We render no judgments about the efficacy of these and other actions and suggestions for federal intelligence reform. But some of them do not seem wholly consistent with what we know about information and bureaucracy.

Absorbing Uncertainty. One of the more intriguing ways in which hierarchy distorts information is called *uncertainty absorption,*[17] whereby data that initially are regarded as tentative, uncertain, and "soft" by the persons who collect them become increasingly final, certain, and "hard" as they are sent up through the decision-making hierarchy.

Consider, for example, the Central Intelligence Agency's efforts to detect the presence of Iraqi weapons of mass instruction prior to the American invasion of that country in 2003. For the previous five years, the agency had had no spies of its own in Iraq who could provide information about these weapons. And, even if the CIA had had agents in Iraq, it is doubtful that they could have uncovered any information about the weapons because Iraq's president, Saddam Hussein, went to considerable lengths to conceal from United Nations inspectors and even his own military that, in reality, he no longer had such weapons. The CIA's analysts "did the best they could with what they had . . . [but] the agency failed to make clear to American policymakers that their assessments were increasingly based on very limited information." Moreover, analysts were denied the option of stating in their reports that they did not have enough information to

Information, Intelligence, Organizations, and Four Dead Horses

Information and intelligence in organizations often exist only in the eye of the beholder. In the eyes of a number of beholders in Arizona, neither information nor intelligence characterized a senseless incident involving the Internal Revenue Service (IRS), the Arizona Livestock and Sanitary Board, and a herd of horses.

Carl J. Jatho was a freewheeling entrepreneur from Kingman, Arizona, a small town in the northern part of the state, who headed a tax-preparation business called The Bookkeeper. For various reasons, Jatho and his bookkeeping ran into legal troubles. For example, he admitted in court to signing up customers for fictitious mining partnerships as part of his tax shelter scheme. Ultimately, Jatho pleaded guilty to five counts of tax fraud that cheated the federal government out of an estimated $45 million in taxes owed by some 3,800 taxpayers. So many of these bilked taxpayers appeared in federal court en masse during Jatho's trial that the press took to calling them "The Jatho People." Ultimately Jatho was sentenced to three years in prison, fined $150,000, and ordered to pay $1.2 million for preparing fraudulent tax returns. Jatho was imprisoned in September 1986.

Among Jatho's remaining assets were thirty-five to forty horses that he kept fenced on his ranch in Kingman. Apparently no one thought too seriously about the fate of Jatho's horses until early January 1987, when officials from the Arizona Livestock and Sanitary Board, the Internal Revenue Service (IRS), and some local agencies met to discuss what to do with them. What precisely occurred at this meeting is unclear. The IRS had the legal authorization to seize the horses as part of its civil case but decided not to do so because its officials believed that only seventeen of the horses belonged to Jatho, and no one was sure which of the beasts were his. The Mohave County Animal Control Board and the Mohave County Sheriff's Office thought that the animals fell under the jurisdiction of the State Livestock Board, but the Livestock Board decided not to act

make a judgment—so they made judgments anyway. Although the analysts included caveats in their reports, those passages, according to the chief American weapons inspector, "tended to drop off as the reports would go up the food chain" of the government. "As a result, virtually everyone in the United States intelligence community during both the Clinton and the . . . Bush administrations thought Iraq still had the illicit weapons. . . . And the government became a victim of its own certainty."[18]

Information and Decision Making

As the preceding case study implies, information and knowledge are more important than ever before in organizational decision making.

And therein lies the problem: All of us are inundated by data, and using data to make decisions while drowning in data seems futile. The economist Friedrich von Hayek famously extended this idea to large and complex organizations, and even to societies, arguing that no one person could ever have enough information to make rational economic decisions. Von Hayek held that market forces provided the best information for decision making, and there can be little question that his critique has merit, as a perusal of the experiences of those nations that have implemented centralized state economic planning indicate.[19]

Know-Nothing Decision Making. Hence, it should not be too surprising that decision makers on the grounds that it believed the IRS had jurisdiction. It did appear from subsequent press reports, however, that neither the IRS nor the Livestock Board had plans to take care of the horses, and that each agency knew that the other was not going to assume responsibility for them either.

Five days after the meeting, the press reported that four of Jatho's horses had died from starvation. When questioned by the press about how and why this had occurred, IRS agent William Bronson stated that the horses were in such poor condition that they could not be sold, adding, "We are a tax collecting agency, not a humane society." At this point, the State Livestock Board acted and seized the horses, noting in the process that hay and other feed had been in the storage shed behind the Jatho house during the entire five months that had passed since Jatho entered prison. In an apparent effort to show that it was on top of the problem, the Livestock Board filed charges of willful neglect and cruelty to animals against Jatho, who had, of course, been in prison during the preceding four months. Meanwhile, the Phoenix office of the Internal Revenue Service was besieged with phone calls from irate citizens.

The senior Senator from Arizona, Dennis DeConcini, soon got into the act by writing the Commissioner of the IRS that the incident in Kingman was the "result of either a severely flawed policy by the agency or negligent actions taken by IRS personnel," and launched his own inquiry. As an aide to Senator DeConcini noted, "The word 'insane' is used rather frequently in news stories because news stories cover unusual and unexpected things, but I don't ever recall seeing a news story where the word 'insane' was more applicable. . . . You don't just leave forty horses there to die. It's crazy. There's nothing rational about it."

Mohave County Supervisor Becky Foster, after noting that a number of citizens had offered to donate food or money for the benefit of the horses, stated, "This restores your faith in humanity." Then, as she watched workers dump the dead horses into a truck, she burst into tears.

Sources: Steve Daniels, "Outraged Arizonans Rally to Rescue Starving Horses," *The Arizona Republic*, January 14, 1987; Andy Hall and Steve Daniels, "Agencies Trade Blame for Abandoned Horses," *The Arizona Republic*, January 15, 1987; and "The Cold Hands of the IRS," *The Arizona Republic*, January 16, 1987.

in organizations "gather information and do not use it. They ask for reports and do not read them. They act first and receive requested information later and do not seem to be concerned about the order."[20]

Nevertheless, it is startling to learn that four-fifths of organizational information, according to one study, is filed away but never used,[21] and the literature is rife with examples of information being generated so that managers might make better decisions and yet bearing no apparent relationship to those decisions.[22] Why is this so?

Organization theorists and decision scientists have provided two explanations for these pathologies. One is that "information overload" can occur, and organizations and the people in them simply are unable to process the information they have because of organizational and human limitations.[23] A second explanation often offered is that the information itself is poor or the wrong kind of information, and while there may be a great deal of information (that is, data), it is not information that we can use (that is, knowledge).[24]

These explanations imply that organizations are not too bright. But another explanation is that the apparent absence of a match between information and decisions in organizations is a reflection of organizational sophistication.[25]

Those who gather data in organizations and those who make decisions in them live in very separate worlds. Although more than seven out of ten workers say that their main job is "tracking down information,"[26] and more than four out of ten managers believe that the cost of collecting information exceeds its value,[27] the actual costs of gathering knowledge, while high, are largely hidden.[28]

Information as Symbol. "Individuals and organizations will consistently over invest in information . . . because the acts of seeking and using information in decisions have important symbolic value to them and to the society. . . . Since legitimacy is a necessary property of effective decisions, conspicuous consumption of information is a sensible strategy for decision makers. The strategy need not be chosen deliberately. It will characterize processes that work."[29]

The public sector seems especially adroit in its use of information as a legitimizing symbol. One investigation of management control systems in ninety-nine defense contracts found "no empirical evidence . . . that information was used for controlling project cost, schedule, or quality," but that "most managers still believed that collecting and reporting information led to project control." The "perceived value among managers" of information's symbolic use was the study's "most remarkable" finding.[30]

Making Decisions Better and Faster. By this logic, then, decisions that are information intensive have a greater legitimacy in organizations, and as a result it is ultimately easier to gain organizational acceptance of decisions and their smoother implementation. Because decision makers implicitly recognize this utility of information, it follows that better decision makers would invest more in gathering information than would poor decision makers, even if the information had nothing in particular to do with making the decision itself. Thus, "organizations that exhibit an elaborate information system and conspicuous consumption of information will . . . be more effective decision makers than those who do not."[31]

Organizations that are information-sensitive also will make their decisions more rapidly. A careful study of eight microcomputer manufacturing firms found that fast decision makers used more information in making their decisions than did slower decision makers. Fast decision makers also developed more alternatives in deciding how to deal with problems and seemed to rely on counseling with respected colleagues more than did slower decision makers. The study found that a pattern of information reliant, advice seeking, and rapid decision making led to "superior performance" by executives.[32]

In sum, research on how information is used in decision-making by organizations leads us to the conclusion that a process which purports to be rational shows only intermittent and weak connections between information gathered and the decision that results. This seems odd. When we learn more about how decisions really are made in organizations, however, this oddity becomes more understandable; we look at decision-making in organizations next.

Decision Making in Organizations

The one finding unearthed by social scientists about how decisions are made in organizations that seems irrefutable is that the process is only minimally rational. The principal reason for this nonrationality is that decisions are made by people, and people are less than logical. Herbert Simon, perhaps more than any other social scientist, enlightened the world about this darker side of decision making.

The Decision Premise

First, Simon held that all human beings make decisions on the basis of a worldview that reflects past experiences and perceptions, but not necessarily the realities at hand. Simon called this phenomenon the *decision premise*, or the values and viewpoints held by each member of the organization, on which he or she bases every decision he or she makes regarding the organization.[33]

These individual values and viewpoints are unique to the individual, but many can be altered and influenced through the use of organizational means and sanctions available to those in positions of control, the division of labor in the organization and how it affects the individual, standard operating procedures used in the organizations, the socialization and training of new members of the organization, and the kinds of people who are selected to join the organization. Together, these techniques can mold each individual's decision premise in a way that reduces organizational uncertainty by making the individual's decisions predictable. When uncertainty is low (e.g., "I trust Mary to do the right thing . . ."), authority and control often are relinquished or "decentralized" (". . . so I've made her responsible for the job").

The Bounds of Individual Rationality

Even if the organization has done an admirable job in adjusting the decision premises of its members to match more closely its culture, it still does not follow that its people are making more rational and informed decisions. Human decision makers, after all, are still human, and hence limited.

Bounded Rationality.   Simon called this condition of the human species *bounded rationality*, or the idea that the reasoning powers of the human mind are bound to a small and simple plot compared to the vastness and complexity of the territory spanned by the problems that human minds are expected (expected, at least, by traditional theorists in economics and management) to comprehend and solve.[34]

What does bounded rationality mean in practice? Consider the first statistically significant study of traffic forecasting in transportation—an area in which decision makers use relatively expansive and precise information to make decisions, and thus is a field in which fairly accurate decision making can be reasonably anticipated. The analysts researched 210 projects in fourteen countries, and found that there was a "very high statistical significance that forecasters generally do a poor job of estimating the demand for transportation infrastructure projects." Passenger forecasts were overestimated, on average, by 106 percent in nine out of ten railroad projects, and for half of all road projects, the variation between actual and forecasted traffic was more than 20 percent.[35]

This is bounded rationality. It is universal.

Researchers have amplified for us the limitations of our species when it comes to making decisions. The psychologist George Miller, for example, determined that the mind can distinguish a maximum of seven categories of phenomena at a time, but beyond that number loses track.[36] (This finding reputedly convinced telephone executives to give us seven-digit telephone numbers.) People tend to use heuristic thinking (or "rules of thumb") in making decisions, which is invariably flawed, and base their decisions on their perception of the *status quo*, rather than on an objective comparison of known variables; people also are biased in favor of protecting against losses relative to planning for gains in making decisions, so stability is favored over change.[37] Empirical research suggests, in fact, that decision makers prefer information that protects them against anticipated losses over information that they can use to make gains.[38] Emotion plays a fulsome part in decision making, and a decision seems to be an emotional, or affective, response to one's environment, which is overlain by a later, more rational response.[39] Solutions that provide quick results are preferred to those which result in delayed returns.[40] Environment generally plays a large role in how a person makes decisions.[41]

Victims of Groupthink.   Stress accompanies decision making, and, as a consequence, avoidance and denial are frequently the handmaidens of the decision process.[42] Making decisions within the context of a tightly knit group seems to narrow the options considered by decision makers even further. *Groupthink* can occur when in-group decision makers share common values, and are under pressure; this combination can produce an overconformity among decision makers that displaces critical thinking, and "is likely to result in irrational and dehumanizing actions directed against out-groups."[43]

Groupthink is not merely a group making decisions. As we explain later, decisions that are made consultatively usually are superior decisions. Groupthink happens when conformity supplants genuine consultation—that is, the seeking out of new views.

The United States' decision to invade Iraq appears to provide an example of how groupthink works in practice. Here is the official assessment by the Commission on Intelligence Capabilities of the origins of "the Intelligence Community's erroneous National Intelligence Estimate of October 2002," which concluded that Iraq did indeed possess weapons of mass destruction, a conclusion that furnished a principal justification for the invasion: "At some point . . . [the intelligence community's] premises stopped being working hypotheses and became more or less unrebuttable conclusions; worse, the intelligence system became too willing to find confirmations of them in evidence that should have been recognized at the time to be of dubious reliability. Collectors and analysts too readily accepted any evidence that supported their theory that Iraq had stockpiles and was developing weapons programs, and they explained away or simply disregarded evidence that pointed in other directions."[44]

"Satisficing" Decisions.   Because the rationality of decision makers is so limited by the human brain and organizational culture, decisions are rarely, if ever, optimal. If not optimal, then, what are they?

Simon answered this question by calling the decisions made by people in organizations "satisficing" decisions—that is, they *satisfied* the makers of decisions and *sufficed* enough for the organization to get by, or combined, *satisficed*.[45] This was a radical assertion in its day, when chief executive officers were assumed to be omniscient and infallible—as long as the organizations that they headed were still managing to lurch along. Simon was suggesting that, even if the organization thrived, it would thrive infinitely more if its decision makers' rational capacities were not so limited.

The Bounds of Organizational Rationality

The decision maker's own organization constitutes most of his or her decision-making environment, and this organizational environment can itself exude bounded rationality, and even irrationality. Sometimes members of the same organization are in stark disagreement about how the world works and the direction that their organization should be taking.

Types of Organizational Decision Making. Two noted organization theorists developed an influential "typology of decision issues," in which they matched decision-making strategies with whether organizational members agreed or disagreed about what causes what, and whether members agreed or disagreed about what the organization should do.[46] (Recall our earlier review of these variables in terms of how societies assess their organizations.) For example, in a bureaucracy of specialists, in theory, everyone would agree about causation ("If you fill out the form, then you will get your Social Security check"), and they would agree about decision outcomes ("Social Security is worthwhile to society"). In such a bureaucracy, decisions would be made *computationally*, or *analytically*, that is, with little or no internal debate about values and with decisions made on the basis of shared technical perceptions (although even computational decision making still is characterized by bounded rationality). Other kinds of bounds on organizational rationality necessitate other kinds of decision-making strategies, all of them more political in nature and based more on power than on analysis. Table 4-1, which we referred to earlier in our discussion of what sorts of tests that societies use to assess various kinds of organizations, also shows the decision-making strategies used by these organizations.

Mismatching Organizations and Decision Making. Or, at least, Table 4-1 illustrates which decision-making strategy *ought* to be used by each type of organization if successful and effective decisions are to be made. A decision maker in an organization that is characterized by high levels of agreement among stakeholders on standards, goals, and causality (such as a research lab) would ill-serve his or her organization by making decisions inspirationally, which is a decision-making strategy much more suited to an organization in which there are high levels of *dis*agreement among stakeholders. Rather, the appropriate decision-making strategy in this instance would be an analytical one.

Research indicates, however, that most makers of important decisions do precisely this—that is, they *typically* select a decision-making strategy that is *inappropriate* to the kinds of bounds that constrain their organization. An analysis of 315 strategic decisions in U.S. and Canadian organizations found that this happened in nearly six out of ten decisions, and as a result, these major decisions "were much less successful" than those that were made in conjunction with the decision strategy that matched (as shown in Table 4-1) their type of organization.[47]

Decision Making in Public Organizations: A Different Dynamic

This analysis leads us to some research on how decision making in the public and private sectors differ from each other. And decision making in the two sectors does differ, and markedly so. As one empirical analysis concluded, whether the sector is public or private "creates substantive differences" in decision making.[48]

An Attenuated Autonomy. Decision making in public organizations is less autonomous than in the private sector,[49] and procedures are more constricting.[50] Practitioners who have served in both the public and private sectors at high levels note that legislators (who are the equivalent of board directors in the business world) are less likely to agree with public administrators on organizational goals, are less expert and less informed on substantive issues, and are less likely to be consistent in dealing with government executives and external constituents than are board members.[51] Compared to the private sector, government is driven more by process than by results, is less transparent, and, despite what they perceive to be talented and dedicated public employees, there remains a stubborn resistance to change.[52]

An analysis of 210 "upper managers" in both sectors was more explicit: "The image of public organizations that emerges is one of little organizational coherence in the identification of strategic decisions. In addition, the ability of top-level managers to control the decisions and actions of their organizations is called into question."[53]

An attenuated autonomy in public decision making does not seem to be limited by national boundaries. A comparison of public and private organizations in Denmark found that publicness correlated strongly with "low managerial autonomy."[54]

A Complex Process. Such phenomena have a distinct impact on the decision-making process of public organizations and require that decision makers be more aware of their symbolic leadership role and "image management," deal with vastly more decision criteria and decision-making participants, and have a broader scope and greater complexity of decision.[55] Typically, for example, decision makers in the private sector are measurably more likely to focus on the relatively straightforward and unambiguous datum of financial performance when making decisions than are their counterparts in the public sector.[56]

Conversation and Consultation. Adding to its complexity, decision making in the public sector is a much more participative affair than it is in the private one, and this wide participation associates with a more disjointed decision-making process. "Publicness is associated with greater decision participation but not smoothness." Decision makers in public organizations tend to swirl sporadically through a series of intense meetings and conversations with each other when making decisions and are much more likely than those in private organizations to engage in both formal and informal interaction with other members of the organization when making decisions.[57] In fact, both the public and nonprofit sectors have been pushing the boundaries of participatory decision making through their use of "large-group interaction methods," which can involve as many as 2,000 people at one time, in making decisions.[58]

Taking It Slowly and Cautiously. This and other research[59] suggests that decision making in public organizations may be slower than in private ones, and slower decision making may be a product of a culture of caution in public agencies. One thorough

- slow
+ participatory

study that compared public and private executives and managers found that public organizations were less likely to take risks (or, to quote the research, had lower levels of "managerial entrepreneurship") than were private ones, regardless of the organizational mission.[60] Another study based on the same extensive data set concluded that what does associate with courageous decision making is not sector as such, but rather certain characteristics, notably high levels of trust among top managers in their employees, a clear organizational mission (these two qualities seem to be especially important), little red tape, strong linkages between promotion and performance, and low involvement with elected officials.[61]

These organizational characteristics can (at least in theory) be found in either sector, although, to be candid, most of them are much more likely to be found in the private sector than in the public one. It follows that nonprofit and for-profit organizations may tend to be less risk-aversive than government agencies.

Deciding to Innovate.   On the other hand, there is evidence that public administrators and business managers, all things being equal, are equally unafraid to tackle change. An experiment to test for sectoral differences in implementing reform found that "managers in the civil service are as willing as their counterparts in business to engage in . . . reform activity."[62] Another analysis found that "Despite controls . . . career public administrators [at all levels of government] do innovate," and do so far more frequently than do elected office holders and nonprofit public-interest groups.[63]

The Quality Question.   Decision making in the public sector, in sum, seems marked by higher levels of constraint, complexity, consultation, disjointedness, and intensity than in the private sector. Goals are murkier, and the decision process may be slower.

Do these features associate with decisions of higher or lower quality? There is little research that clearly links each of these characteristics with objectively defined poorer or better decisions, although there are some analyses which conclude that the restricted freedom[64] of decision makers and the slowness[65] of decision making (which characterize the public sector) do correlate with poorer decisions. On the other hand, consultation with others (but not groupthink) associates with better decisions,[66] and consultation is notably present in public decision making.

In one of the few attempts to match the decision-making techniques used by each sector with the quality and successful implementation of the decisions made, it was determined that government managers who relied primarily on soliciting the views of experts and used hard data made the highest quality decisions and enjoyed the highest rates of implementation. Public administrators who relied more on analyzing issues or bargaining with stakeholders were less successful.[67]

Changing the Public Organization

Public agencies are not associated in the public mind with swift-paced change. But they do change.

Why Public Agencies Change

One theoretician usefully categorizes public organizations and matches these categories to propositions about why they change. Public agencies that are dominated by professionals change when there is a perceived loss of professional competence and capacity in the agency; public agencies that are protected by patrons, such as legislators, change when they lose their patrons; and "routinized" public organizations, or those that have churned the same old rut for many years, demonstrating little capacity and scant responsiveness in the process, change when expectations about what they should be doing increase in a sustained way over time.

Even if these events should occur, however, change is by no means assured. For the public organization to actually change in significant ways still requires that its members come to grips with the forces surrounding them, notably demands for greater responsiveness; that their leaders succeed in creating a proactive organization; and then only when the agency's leaders have "the support of oversight bodies" and "are *allowed* to be responsive" to environmental demands is organizational change feasible.[68]

This construct is insightful in that it apportions the relative roles that technology, people, and the environment play in altering public organizations. We consider these factors in greater detail next.

The Likely Limited Role of Technology

The technology (recall that *technology* in this sense refers to what the organization does and how it does it) of the organization seems to be less of a factor in inducing organizational change in the public sector than it is in the private and nonprofit sectors. There are at least two reasons for this: What public organizations do rarely if ever changes, and the technology of public organizations is itself resistant to change.

Constraining What Public Agencies Do. What public organizations do tends not to change because legislatures and other elements of the task environment generally inhibit technological change; the Social Security Administration, for example, is not likely to diversify and start manufacturing widgets, in addition to mailing Social Security checks. But this does not hold for private and nonprofit organizations, which can diversify with relative ease into wholly new technologies, markets, and even missions. Because the technologies of public organizations seldom, if ever, change, it follows that relatively little organizational change will occur because of technological change.

This is not to say that public organizations are immune to the changes that accompany technological developments. The computer, for example, is a new technology that has altered virtually every other technology used by organizations, including public organizations, and, as we describe in Chapter 6, significant organizational and behavioral change has accompanied this new technology. Nevertheless, the simple reality of public organizations is that they cannot branch out into new missions and methods with anything like the freedom of private and nonprofit organizations.

Process Technologies **versus** *Product Technologies.* Equally elemental is the fact that public organizations produce *processes,* such as policies, programs, and services; rarely do they produce *products,* such as pickles, planes, and widgets. Processes change much more slowly than products. Challenges of coordinating, convincing, and collaborating are considerably more complex and time consuming for changing a process than they are for producing a product.

This reality of organizational technology slows organizational change in organizations that are process-intensive, such as governments. For example, a study of 101 banks found that, over eleven years, "product innovations" were "adopted at a greater rate and speed than process innovations."[69] Hence, even within the same type of organization, and even within the *same organization,* processes change much more slowly than do products. So there is some reason to conclude that the public sector *necessarily* changes less rapidly than do the private and nonprofit sectors, simply because of the nature of its work.

People Changing Their Public Organization

If technology does not seem to be hugely influential in causing organizational change in the public sector, what about the people in the public organization? Does their behavior account for the bulk of organizational change?

Paladins of Public Change. As we discuss in Chapter 5, people are important in changing public organizations. Leaders, though more constrained in public agencies than in corporations and independent organizations,[70] can and do make a mark.[71]

In the public sector, however, it appears that, in contrast to the corporate world, top executives are less important than are middle- and even lower-level employees. These organizational members cause more organizational change and innovation than do any other sort of stakeholder, including organizational leaders. "A surprising result" of a study of significant innovation in governments "is that the most frequent initiators of innovations were not politicians [who accounted for 18 percent of innovations] . . . or even agency heads [23 percent] . . . but middle managers and front-line staff," who were responsible for nearly half, 48 percent, of all governmental change.[72]

Another analysis of the twenty-two largest federal agencies, using a massive data set supplied by the U.S. Merit Systems Protection Board, supports these findings and found that "front-line supervisors" played a critical role in making their agencies more effective performers.[73] Young professionals, in sum, may have more opportunities to make a mark in the public sector than in the private one.

Still, when all is said and done, are the public organization's members more responsible for changing their organization than are the riptides of the public organization's tumultuous task environment?

Human Choice or Environmental Determinism? One of the major debates in organization theory, perhaps the dominant debate, is called *human choice* (that is, human decision makers in the organization choose organizational destiny) *versus environmental determinism* (that is, powerful forces in the task environment determine organizational destiny). One exhaustive review of the literature identified the questions of whether the people inside the organization or the environment outside the organization had the greater influence on an organization's destiny as two of the four "central perspectives" constituting the "debates in organization theory,"[74] and other analysts have described the issue as "one of the most pervasive and central arguments" in the field.[75]

It does not behoove the reader for us to review at length this professorial dispute.[76] In a nutshell, however, the advocates of human choice hold that leadership is significant, perhaps paramount, in achieving organizational success. More often than not, the literatures of business administration and strategic planning implicitly express this view.

Others have a more pantheistic perspective: "The Tolstoyan view of leaders as chips tossed about by the tides of history rather than masters of events cannot be rejected a priori. . . . even if leaders *do* appear to be as important as conventional opinions hold them to be, the quality of leadership will nevertheless prove to be randomly rather than systematically distributed among organizations, and chance will therefore remain the main factor in organizational survival."[77]

What, in brief, this and many other leading organization theorists are saying is that people do not count for much in shaping organizations.[78] We do not subscribe to the view that the organization's people are merely the pathetic pawns of omnipotent environmental forces. People can and do make a difference in determining their organizations' destiny. We do believe, however, that, when it comes to *public* organizations, a strong case can be made that the task environment is a major, and perhaps the primary, agent of organizational change. People in public organizations still make a difference, but making that difference is harder to do than it is in private and nonprofit organizations.

Deep Change: The Impact of the Environment on the Public Organization

So heavy is the impact of the task environment that it results in polar opposites in defining just what effective administration is in each sector. One study of executive work behavior compared forty managers in city governments with forty managers in industry and concluded that the public managers believed—and, in fact, accurately so—that they had little control over how they used their time, and thus accorded scant effort to "time management," relative to the corporate managers. Urban managers were considerably more victimized by forces in their organizations' task environment than were their counterparts in the private sector; they spent less time alone in their offices; less time on planning; were more "rushed" to get things done; and spent nearly twice as much time on the telephone than did private managers.[79] Similarly, research found that the public executives devoted far more time to crisis management than did private managers.[80]

More significantly, *effective* managers displayed quite different work behaviors depending on whether they worked in the public or private sectors. In the study of urban and industrial managers, it was found that *more effective public administrators* were more flexible, planned less, and had less control over their time than did industrial managers. In fact, the *less effective public administrators* spent more time on planning their time than did the more effective public managers, while quite the reverse held true in the private sector: less effective industrial managers spent less time planning their time than did more effective industrial managers.[81]

Public administration, it appears, is different.

The Environment's Impact: From Orders to Osmosis

The task environment's influence on the public organization assumes many forms, ranging from the statutory and official to the subtle and osmotic. The former includes laws, court decisions, contracts, and agreements; the latter includes lobbyists, special interests, polls, media, and citizens. Neither of these lists is remotely comprehensive.

Consider some examples of both extremes of environmental determinism.

Impact by Orders. All legislatures pass laws affecting their governments' agencies, and these laws, while often needed and appropriate, nonetheless are instances of the agencies' task environment changing the agencies. The extreme version of this sort of environmental impact by legislation, however, occurs when legislatures order their agencies to open themselves wide to all manner of penetration by innumerable environmental sources, and to an extent that is unheard of in the other sectors.

An example of this kind of opening up is provided by the Freedom of Information Act of 1966.

Under the act, any member of the public may demand information from federal agencies. Public administrators have performed conscientiously and effectively in complying with the act, and 92 percent of some *four million* requests for information that are made each year are granted in full (information pertaining to national security and citizen privacy is exempt under the act), but responding to these demands is onerous. To meet a request for information, agencies must execute no fewer than fifteen distinct tasks, and federal administrators work from one to as many as 916 median days to fulfill a request. The public's demand for information under the act is growing by about a fourth each year.[82]

All state agencies must cope with what are known as *state administrative procedure acts* that insert citizens deeply into the administrative and decision-making processes of state government. (The federal government and virtually all local governments also have administrative procedure acts or their equivalents.) Forty-seven state legislatures require their agencies' administrators to read the letters of any citizens who might wish to write about their proposed rules (that is, the decisions that the agencies' managers wish to make), forty of which also require that their agencies listen to citizens' opinions during agency hearings. Citizens in thirty-four states may petition the agency proposing a rule to hold a hearing; nineteen states permit the public to petition the agency to postpone the date that the rule goes into effect; and in a dozen states citizens may petition state agencies to demand that it prepare a detailed economic analysis for any proposed rule. In forty-five states, citizens may go over the agency's head and appeal to entities that review any new rules proposed (*proposed*, not enacted) by an agency.[83] It is, perhaps, small wonder that public administrators sometimes complain of tread marks left on their foreheads by citizens appealing their decisions to a higher authority.

As these examples demonstrate, not only are public administrators far more exposed to demands emanating from outside their organizations, but they also must fulfill these demands or be punished by law. Meeting these demands is vexing, enervating, distracting, and peripheral to the central missions of their agencies.

Impact by Osmosis.   Official edicts are by no means the only way that the task environment affects public organizations. Perhaps of even greater impact on the inner workings of government agencies are environmental forces that are not even directed at influencing them or, at most, influence them only with exquisite indirection.

Consider this: A study of the federal Food and Drug Administration's (FDA) process for approving newly developed drugs found that, if a disease was merely *mentioned* in the *Washington Post* twelve times over twelve months, then one full month, on average, was knocked off the time that it took the FDA to approve the drug. If the ailment was mentioned two-dozen times over a year, then the approval time declined by two months, and so on. This was the case regardless of the severity of the disease, its frequency, its cost, and the availability of other drugs. Similarly, the better financed advocacy groups got their drugs approved faster than did the less well-financed groups.[84]

Or this: Another analysis found that for every story in the *New York Times* concerning a natural disaster abroad, the federal government allocated, on average, almost $600,000 more in additional U.S. aid to the afflicted country. This was the case even after controlling for the wealth of the nation affected and the number of people left homeless or killed by the disaster. Indeed, one article in the *Times* was worth more in American disaster relief than 1,500 deaths. A large portion of the globe's disasters, about a third, generate no aid from the United States, but stories about a particular disaster in the *Times* also increased the likelihood that the United States would decide to send assistance to the country that had experienced it.[85]

Environmental Determinism and the Public Organization.   These instances bespeak an environmental determinism of a rare order. The pubic organization is so attuned to nuances in its task environment—subtleties that only it, apparently, can sense—that it readily and even radically responds to them. The environment need not be comprised only of obvious and brutish forces to change the public organization; osmosis works, too.

Whether they are rough or refined, environmental forces affect public organizations in at least five unique, and uniquely profound, ways that distinguish them from organizations in the private and nonprofit sectors. To wit, the task environment of the public organization renders any reorganization of the government extremely difficult and not terribly productive; splinters agency accountability; bureaucratizes the public organization; adds red tape; and lowers organizational performance and the quality of organizational decision making.

We consider these sad syndromes next.

The Iron Triangle: Resisting Reorganization

Governments rarely reorganize, and the reason they resist reorganization pertains directly to the environment in which they find themselves.

Reorganizational Resistance.   The resistance to governmental restructuring is known as the *iron triangle,* or the exceptionally strong bonds that exist among the executive agency, its legislative oversight committees, and the affected special interests, all of which are threatened by any proposed rearrangement of their relationships. Of these three points of the iron triangle, the legislature often reigns supreme. In the federal government, "Congress must agree with any restructuring proposals submitted for consideration by the president for them to become a reality."[86]

Usually, Congress does not agree.[87] In 1938, for example, Franklin Delano Roosevelt (FDR), at the apex of his presidential power, was roundly crushed in the House of Representatives when he attempted to reorganize his own executive branch. Historians state that this stunning "defeat was the worst that President Roosevelt would suffer in three terms as President"[88]—stark testimony indeed to the power of pressure groups. More recently, the on-again, off-again efforts by special interests and ideologues to dismantle the Departments of Commerce and Education have been successfully resisted for decades by countervailing special interests and ideologues.

The states display a somewhat different reorganizational dynamic. States had not seriously undertaken reorganization—or, for that matter, organization—of their governments until the 1960s. "By the middle of the twentieth century state bureaucracies often contained one hundred to two hundred units,"[89] all ostensibly reporting to the governor, the legislature, or an independent board. Governors and legislators undertook to correct the resultant lack of coordination by consolidating their governments, and between 1965 and 1990, twenty-six states reduced the number of their agencies and replaced them, for the most part, with a broader, cabinet form of structure.[90] How sweeping these reorganizations were is open to debate, and those few agencies that were eliminated typically "had minuscule budgets," or "their functions continue to be performed by other agencies."[91]

Since 1990, however, a pattern that parallels the federal experience has emerged. Despite fiscal crises that likely could be alleviated by reorganizing state governments for greater efficiency, legislative and gubernatorial attempts to do so comprise a litany of failure.[92]

Reorganizational Futility. On a rare occasion, governments do restructure, but, whatever the reason for the reorganization might have been, it is almost never fulfilled. An example of the apparent futility of restructuring government is the founding in 2002 of the Department of Homeland Security. This was the largest reorganization of the federal government in more than fifty years, involving twenty-two agencies and 171,000 employees. Nevertheless, despite the fact that its creation was inspired by the terrorist massacres of September 11, 2001, it took more than a year to create the department, and the two largest (and perhaps most critical) agencies charged with homeland security, the Central Intelligence Agency and the Federal Bureau of Investigation, were excluded from the reorganization. And, even after the Department of Homeland Security's founding, there were *still* 123 federal agencies and offices scattered among sixteen departments with responsibility for counterterrorism.[93]

This situation is not unique. Though scarce, those few reorganizations of the federal government that have occurred, "virtually never [are] . . . combined to eliminate program duplication. Missions are not realigned or even rationalized. Program laps upon program. Responsibilities are not coordinated."[94]

Our point is that governmental reorganization, for whatever purpose and regardless of the public good that it might bring, is a tough task. Not only are reorganization attempts stymied by internal resistance to change in the agencies, but, more profoundly, powerful external forces, notably legislatures and special interests that flourish in the public organization's task environment, have vested stakes in how public agencies are organized; typically, these environmental forces have the power to keep governments organized as they are.

Who's in Charge Here? The Fragmentation of Agency Accountability

Government agencies suffer from at least two kinds of environmental penetration that fragments their administrative coherence and, with it, their accountability to the public. One is that the responsibility for managing a single policy often is scattered among multiple agencies, and the other is that a single agency often must report to multiple bosses.

A Parsing of Policies. Coherence of policy execution is not a hallmark of government. In part, this condition exists because legislatures scatter the public programs comprising a public policy like seeds to the wind among executive agencies. Most federal agencies, in fact, implement three or more major, and quite different, public policies. The U.S. Department of Agriculture, for instance, spends only about two-fifths of its appropriated funds on agriculture; another two-fifths of its funding goes to income security programs.[95]

Consider some other examples of this legislative parsing of public policy.[96] Although our examples are national ones, comparable cases exist in state and local governments as well.

- Four different federal agencies are responsible for land management.
- Seven agencies manage forty programs involving job training.
- Eight federal agencies operate fifty programs to aid the homeless.
- Nine agencies run twenty-seven teen pregnancy programs.
- Nine agencies manage "at least" eighty-six teacher-training programs.
- Eleven federal agencies and twenty offices administer more than ninety early-childhood programs, including nine agencies that manage sixty-nine programs aimed exclusively at children under the age of five.
- Twelve federal agencies implement more than thirty-five food safety laws.
- Thirteen of the fourteen cabinet departments administer 342 economic development programs.
- Twenty-three agencies operate more than 200 foreign aid programs to nations that were formerly part of the Soviet Union.
- Twenty-nine agencies execute 541 clean air, water, and waste programs.
- More than fifty federal agencies are charged with planning and executing drug control strategies.
- And, as we have noted, 123 federal offices and agencies in sixteen departments "coordinate" federal antiterrorism efforts.

A Bevy of Bosses.   It follows that, just as the responsibility for implementing policies is parsed with legislative abandon among a passel of public agencies, there also is a bevy of bosses to whom these agencies must report.

In contrast to the chief executive officers of companies and nonprofit organizations, who report to a single board of directors, the heads of government agencies often report to dozens of their equivalents in the form of legislative oversight committees. The Department of Defense, for instance, reports to no fewer than thirty-six congressional committees and subcommittees, a number that is considered to be commendably lean in federal administrative circles,[97] but not, perhaps, in others.

As part of the process of reporting to these oversight committees, federal agencies must adhere to an astounding 3,627 congressional reporting requirements—not reports, we should emphasize, but *requirements* for at least one, and likely many, reports. These reporting requirements are burgeoning by about a fifth per year.[98]

The quantity of committees to which agencies report is determined to some degree by the visibility of the agency's policy area. Terrorism, for instance, is hot; public administration is not. For purposes of publicity and reelection, it behooves legislators to be somehow connected with those policies that are unusually salient; hence, the higher the policy's profile, the more legislators clamor to be on committees that oversee those agencies that implement it.

We see this phenomenon play out in national security issues. Consider the case of the federal Department of Homeland Security. Seventy-nine congressional committees, every U.S. Senator, and at least 412 of the 435 members of the House of Representatives, or 95 percent, have some degree of responsibility for homeland security.[99]

Figure 4-1 illustrates the "system" of congressional oversight for the department. It is not a diagram that one would associate with anything resembling an organization chart. It is a diagram, however, that one might associate with The Mind of God.

An Undercutting of Accountability.   To some degree, this scatteration of accountability for the management of a single public policy among many agencies, and its oversight among many legislative committees, is unavoidable. As we have frequently noted, public policies typically are characterized by vaguely stated goals, and as a consequence they meander among executive agencies and legislative committees alike, tightening turf tensions that fester in both branches. Reigning in these tendencies is difficult. Nevertheless, legislatures' parsing of a single policy among many executive agencies, and their penchant for assigning many legislative overseers to the administration of a single policy, undermines the effective management of that policy, wastes resources, and checkmates the achievement of governments' goals. These are serious impairments to accountability in government. And the origin of

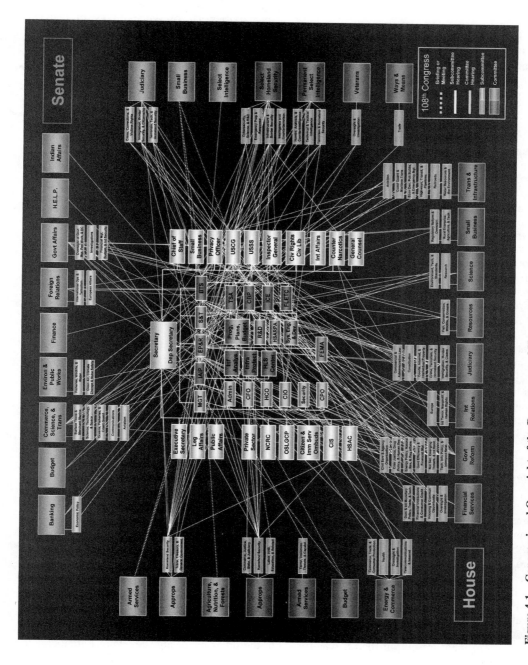

Figure 4-1 Congressional Oversight of the Department of Homeland Security

Source: Center for Strategic and International Studies and Business Executives for National Security, *Untangling the Web: Congressional Oversight and the Department of Homeland Security* (Washington, DC: Authors, December 10, 2004).

these impediments is the environment of the public organization.

The Bureaucratization of the Public Organization

Governments are notoriously bureaucratic. Government workers themselves think that their agencies are overly bureaucratic: Forty percent of federal employees at all ranks say that there are "too many layers of supervisors and managers" between them and top management in their organizations, compared to only 24 percent of business employees who say this.[100]

Bureaucratization of government is burgeoning. At the federal level, government's organization chart heightened as the number of different executive titles grew, nearly quadrupling over forty-four years. The number of these federal executive titles now stands at sixty-four. As a result, innovative, but odd, administrative titles are increasingly common. A brief sampling: Deputy Assistant Deputy Administrator, Principal Deputy Deputy Assistant Secretary, Deputy Associate Assistant Secretary, Assistant Deputy Assistant Secretary, and, last but not least, Principal Assistant Assistant Secretary.[101] We are not making these up.

Government's girth grew, too. Over the same forty-four years, the total number of senior title holders in the federal government widened by a factor of almost six, from 451 to 2,592.[102]

Explaining Bureaucratic Accretion. Why is this?

Anthony Downs was among the first to assess the impact of the public organization's task environment on its internal structure. Downs argued that organizations deprived of free market conditions in their environments, such as government agencies, were more pressured to *bureaucratize*—that is, to accrete thick and multiple layers of administrative hierarchy—than were organizations that functioned in the marketplace. Because it was so much more difficult for public organizations to measure output than it was for private organizations (which had an "automatic" measure of output called the profit margin), more

methods were needed to control spending, assure fair treatment of clients, and coordinate large-scale activities. The presence of these procedures, in turn, demanded extensive monitoring to ensure compliance, and such monitoring meant more reports, more effort spent on internal communications, and more managers to do it. Thus, Downs's "law of hierarchy" is a function of an organization's task environment, and whether or not that environment provides market mechanisms.[103]

A somewhat different interpretation of the role that environmental factors play in adding to the hierarchy of public organizations also has surfaced. This view concurs that the task environment has an unusually salient impact on public organizations, and that public organizations react to environmental influences by adding on increasingly complex mechanisms. However, this perspective contends, such bureaucratization is not a sign of resistance to new demands from the environment, as Downs implies, but is instead one of eagerness to accommodate those demands; "additional layers of hierarchy result in part from their openness to their environments."[104]

The Dysfunctions—and Functions—of Bureaucratization. Whatever the way that the task environment induces hierarchical accretion in public agencies, the dysfunctions of bureaucratization are legion. They include the loss by the chief executive of direct access to, and control of, the lower reaches of the administrative hierarchy; consequently, accountability disperses and deteriorates; information is distorted and delayed as it passes up and down the hierarchy; authority to act diminishes, and in public agencies, "demosclerosis," sets in.[105]

Bureaucracy does affect organizational performance, too, but, oddly, research suggests that bureaucracy can both improve and undercut performance, depending on the goals in question. At least two analyses of school bureaucracies found that more bureaucracy led to lower academic performance by students.[106] This was true across grade levels, and regardless of whether the bureaucracy was at the district or school level.[107] On the other hand, high levels of bureaucratization associated with better attendance and lower dropout rates.[108]

Another study of more than a thousand school districts in Texas supported these mixed discoveries and found that "the extent of bureaucracy is not related to failures." Instead, "the only consistent results" are that organizational failures correlate with a large number of organizational goals and a high level of difficulty involved in achieving those goals.[109]

In brief, bureaucracy, that bane of politicians, public administrators, and the public, can work well—or not.

Reams of Red Tape: The Processes of the Public Organization

One of the clearer signs of bureaucratization is the presence of *red tape*, or the proliferation of rigid rules, complex procedures, and convoluted processes. Government agencies are wrapped in ribbons of red tape; the annual compilation of federal regulations, the *Federal Register*, typically exceeds 4,000 rules and 70,000 pages. Research indicates that not only do public organizations have more rules than private ones,[110] but that the sources of rules in public organizations are almost entirely external and essentially unlimited: legislatures, auditors, accounting departments, budget bureaus, purchasing offices, human resources agencies, unions, and the minions of outside special interests are examples.[111]

Fortunately, the propensity of public-sector organizations to add more rules is not endless and eventually diminishes over time. The more rules that accrete, the less likely that more rules will be added because the trove of accumulated rules actually does enable these organizations to "increasingly respond to environmental challenges in a programmed way."[112]

Rue the Rules!   It is heartening to learn that enough good rules can help rationalize, over time, an organization's relations with its task environment (at least if that environment's reasonably stable and predictable), and, in this sense, can boost long-term efficiencies. Nevertheless, we normally do not associate red tape with responsiveness. This is because red tape, by and large, can cause a public organization to perform less

effectively with both its internal stakeholders and its external clients.

Internally, red tape correlates positively with less entrepreneurial and less innovative organizations.[113] Indeed, when public administrators perceive relatively little red tape, they also report higher levels of motivation and commitment to constructive social change.[114]

Regrettably, "public organizations tend to have a higher level of perceived red tape than private organizations,"[115] and when public managers sense reams of red tape in their agencies, they become discouraged, demoralized, and alienated. A survey of top state administrators found that roughly three out of ten cited "less red tape" as a primary reason for privatizing their agencies' programs, and less red tape ranked third out of eight possible reasons.[116]

Red tape is often seen as the prime culprit responsible for a bevy of bureaucratic injustices. A study of top public and private managers found that both sets of executives agreed in roughly equal measure on the need to enforce rules, but that public administrators were much more likely to believe that their agency's rules resulted in their professional performance being inadequately recognized and rewarded in terms of pay and promotion.[117] An intensive survey of public managers in state health and human services agencies concluded that organizational red tape evidenced a strong association with employee alienation: "Red tape is a consistently negative and statistically significant influence in all alienation models."[118]

Externally, red tape associates with poor organizational performance. An experiment on the role of red tape in dealing with clients found that high levels of red tape led to clients receiving fewer fully justified benefits.[119] Another study found that the more regulations and procedures imposed in the intergovernmental grants-in-aid system, the more administrators would be generated by school districts.[120]

The Meaning and Mapping of Red Tape.   The public schools of New York City provide a splendid example of the profound effects that red tape can have on the in-house processes of a public agency. There are sixty-four separate sources of law governing the city's schools: 850 pages of state law, another 720 pages of state regulations, 15,000 formal decisions by the state commissioner of education, hundreds of pages of collective bargaining agreements, thousands of pages of federal law affecting schools, and more thousands of pages of regulations promulgated by the chancellor of the New York City schools.[121]

These laws, rules, and regulations entangle themselves into a Gordian's knot of red tape that complicates every administrative process extant in the city's schools, no matter how mundane. Want to replace a school's faulty furnace? Then be prepared for a long and heavy haul. Figure 4-2 shows the steps that the city's school administrators must take to replace a furnace. Imagine what it takes to fire a teacher.

Reconsidering Red Tape: A Modest Defense of the Indefensible.   Red tape, in brief, brings reams of dysfunction to all organizations, regardless of sector. But, in the public sector, the reasons for the presence of disproportionate levels of red tape are at least comprehensible, and perhaps even defensible.

If red tape can result in inefficiency and ineffectiveness, it also represents impartiality and fairness to those both inside and outside the public bureaucracy. With rigid rules and inflexible procedures in place, the chances of everyone being treated equally are enhanced. Nothing provides those rules and procedures like red tape; indeed, they are the defining elements of red tape.

In a word, red tape can provide *justice*, an idea that is central to democratic government.

Administrative Autonomy and the Performance of Public Organizations

Just as the task environment spawns a debilitating resistance to reorganization, an undercutting of accountability, an accretion of bureaucracy, and roundelays of red tape within public organizations, it also weakens their overall performance. This weakening seems to be largely the result of the constrained autonomy imposed by external environmental forces on public administrators.

A growing number of empirical investigations all point to this conclusion. Greater organizational autonomy and independence, at least up to a point, associate with a higher quality of administration. To cite some of the studies in this regard:

• A study of nine citizen advisory boards in Michigan concluded that a high level of autonomy of those boards had a direct and beneficial impact on their effectiveness: "Some of the citizen advisory boards were more effective than others in gaining their objectives and this was found to be related to the degree of independence which they attained."[122]

• A study of the impact of the Government in the Sunshine Act of 1976, which opened to public scrutiny the meeting procedures of more than fifty federal agencies headed by boards of directors or similar bodies, found that most agency officials felt "that the strictures of the law weakened them in executing their responsibilities and weakened agency performance, especially in policy development."[123]

• National surveys of local public works directors in the United States conclude that working in a "political environment" constitutes the primary set of "impediments to effective management."[124]

• A ten-year study of the experiences of 20,000 students, teachers, and principals in some 500 public and private schools in the United States concluded that "the best determinate of the school's effectiveness was the degree of autonomy it enjoyed from bureaucracies and other outside interference. None of the other factors that usually preoccupied reformers, including class size, faculty salaries and spending per pupil, mattered as much."[125]

• Later research on schools, in this case, of 534 public school districts in Texas, also found that "the best agencies are affected by far fewer forces in their environments."[126]

• An analysis of the safety records of twenty-four nuclear power plants in the United States found that the administrative autonomy of a nuclear plant correlated with a high safety record. "If poor performers are given more autonomy, this analysis suggests, their safety record is likely to improve. . . ."[127]

• Sixty percent of federal civilian employees say that Congress "acts in ways to worsen the management" of their agencies, and 41 percent say that the president does.[128]

• A four-year study of American governments concluded that much of the perceived unresponsiveness, inefficiency, and ineffectiveness of government is attributable to its lack of autonomy: public administrators are "trapped in archaic systems that frustrate their creativity and sap their energy."[129]

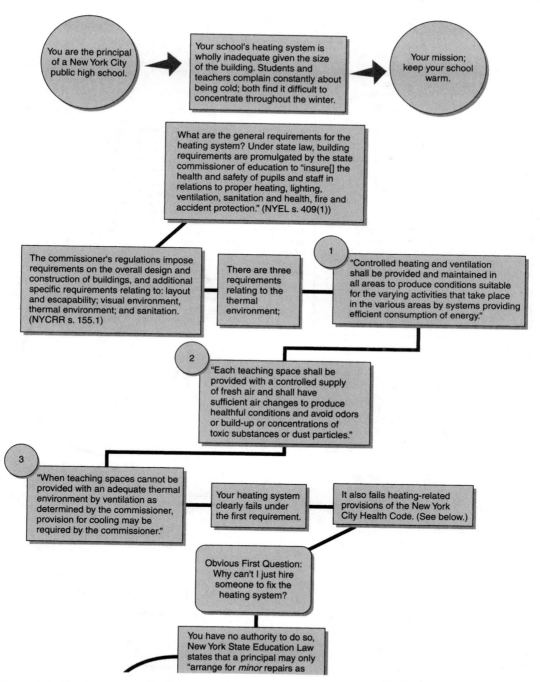

Figure 4-2 Reams of Red Tape: Steps that Must Be Taken to Replace a Heating System in a New York City Public School

Source: Common Good, "How Do I Replace a Heating System?" *Over Ruled: The Burden of Law on America's Public Schools.* (ND), http://cgood.org/burden-of-law.html

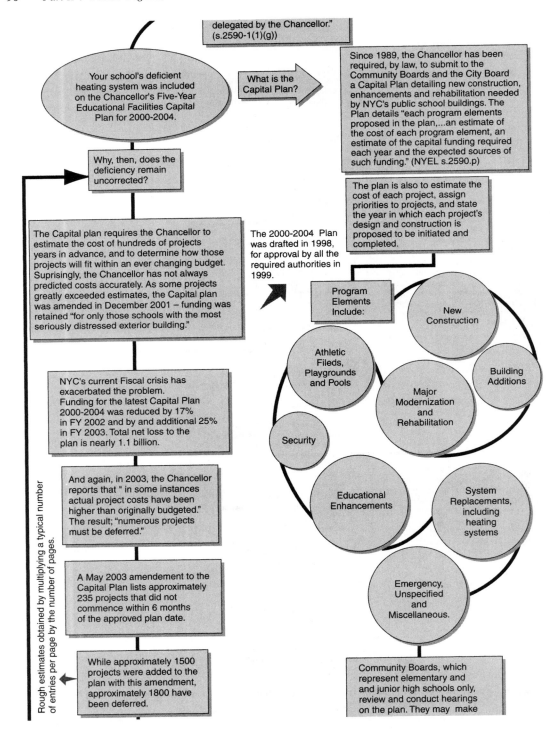

delegated by the Chancellor."
(s.2590-1(1)(g))

Your school's deficient heating system was included on the Chancellor's Five-Year Educational Facilities Capital Plan for 2000-2004.

What is the Capital Plan?

Since 1989, the Chancellor has been required, by law, to submit to the Community Boards and the City Board a Capital Plan detailing new construction, enhancements and rehabilitation needed by NYC's public school buildings. The Plan details "each program elements proposed in the plan,...an estimate of the cost of each program element, an estimate of the capital funding required each year and the expected sources of such funding." (NYEL s.2590.p)

Why, then, does the deficiency remain uncorrected?

The plan is also to estimate the cost of each project, assign priorities to projects, and state the year in which each project's design and construction is proposed to be initiated and completed.

The Capital plan requires the Chancellor to estimate the cost of hundreds of projects years in advance, and to determine how those projects will fit within an ever changing budget. Suprisingly, the Chancellor has not always predicted costs accurately. As some projects greatly exceeded estimates, the Capital plan was amended in December 2001 – funding was retained "for only those schools with the most seriously distressed exterior building."

The 2000-2004 Plan was drafted in 1998, for approval by all the required authorities in 1999.

Program Elements Include:

New Construction

Athletic Fileds, Playgrounds and Pools

Building Additions

Major Modernization and Rehabilitation

NYC's current Fiscal crisis has exacerbated the problem. Funding for the latest Capital Plan 2000-2004 was reduced by 17% in FY 2002 and by and additional 25% in FY 2003. Total net loss to the plan is nearly 1.1 billion.

Security

And again, in 2003, the Chancellor reports that " in some instances actual project costs have been higher than originally budgeted." The result; "numerous projects must be deferred."

Educational Enhancements

System Replacements, including heating systems

A May 2003 amendment to the Capital Plan lists approximately 235 projects that did not commence within 6 months of the approved plan date.

Emergency, Unspecified and Miscellaneous.

Rough estimates obtained by multiplying a typical number of entries per page by the number of pages.

While approximately 1500 projects were added to the plan with this amendment, approximately 1800 have been deferred.

Community Boards, which represent elementary and and junior high schools only, review and conduct hearings on the plan. They may make

Figure 4-2   Continued

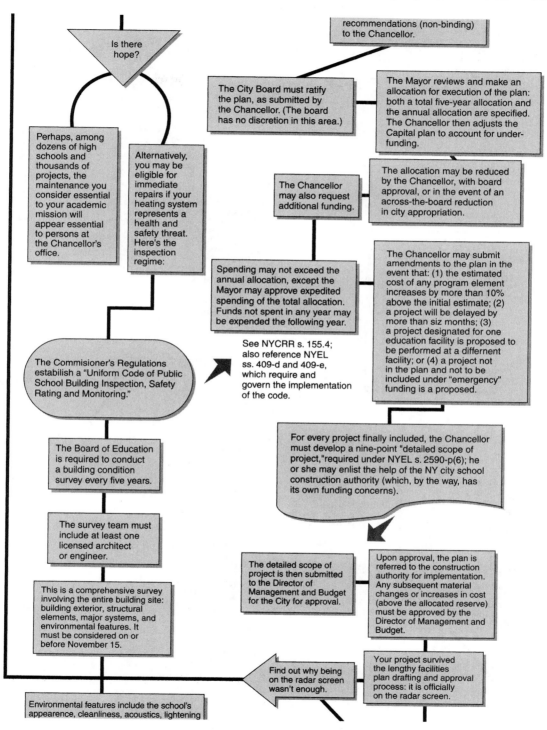

Is there hope?

recommendations (non-binding) to the Chancellor.

The City Board must ratify the plan, as submitted by the Chancellor. (The board has no discretion in this area.)

The Mayor reviews and make an allocation for execution of the plan: both a total five-year allocation and the annual allocation are specified. The Chancellor then adjusts the Capital plan to account for under-funding.

Perhaps, among dozens of high schools and thousands of projects, the maintenance you consider essential to your academic mission will appear essential to persons at the Chancellor's office.

Alternatively, you may be eligible for immediate repairs if your heating system represents a health and safety threat. Here's the inspection regime:

The Chancellor may also request additional funding.

The allocation may be reduced by the Chancellor, with board approval, or in the event of an across-the-board reduction in city appropriation.

Spending may not exceed the annual allocation, except the Mayor may approve expedited spending of the total allocation. Funds not spent in any year may be expended the following year.

The Chancellor may submit amendments to the plan in the event that: (1) the estimated cost of any program element increases by more than 10% above the initial estimate; (2) a project will be delayed by more than siz months; (3) a project designated for one education facility is proposed to be performed at a differnent facility; or (4) a project not in the plan and not to be included under "emergency" funding is a proposed.

The Commisioner's Regulations estabilish a "Uniform Code of Public School Building Inspection, Safety Rating and Monitoring."

See NYCRR s. 155.4; also reference NYEL ss. 409-d and 409-e, which require and govern the implementation of the code.

For every project finally included, the Chancellor must develop a nine-point "detailed scope of project,"required under NYEL s. 2590-p(6); he or she may enlist the help of the NY city school construction authority (which, by the way, has its own funding concerns).

The Board of Education is required to conduct a building condition survey every five years.

The survey team must include at least one licensed architect or engineer.

The detailed scope of project is then submitted to the Director of Management and Budget for the City for approval.

Upon approval, the plan is referred to the construction authority for implementation. Any subsequent material changes or increases in cost (above the allocated reserve) must be approved by the Director of Management and Budget.

This is a comprehensive survey involving the entire building site: building exterior, structural elements, major systems, and environmental features. It must be considered on or before November 15.

Find out why being on the radar screen wasn't enough.

Your project survived the lengthy facilities plan drafting and approval process: it is officially on the radar screen.

Environmental features include the school's appearance, cleanliness, acoustics, lightening

Figure 4-2   Continued

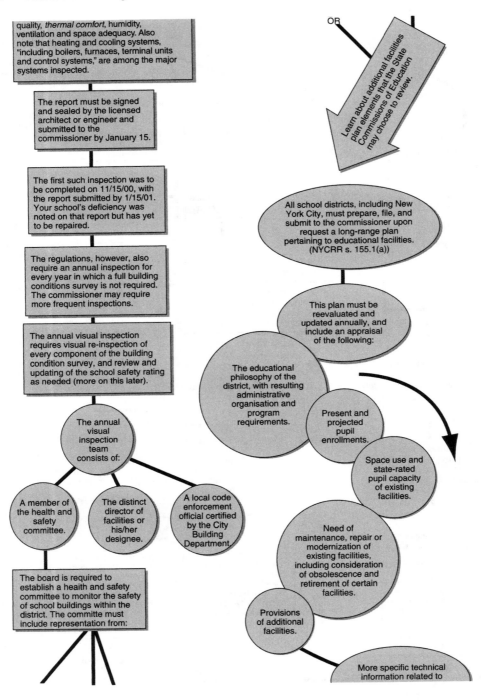

quality, *thermal comfort*, humidity, ventilation and space adequacy. Also note that heating and cooling systems, "including boilers, furnaces, terminal units and control systems," are among the major systems inspected.

The report must be signed and sealed by the licensed architect or engineer and submitted to the commissioner by January 15.

The first such inspection was to be completed on 11/15/00, with the report submitted by 1/15/01. Your school's deficiency was noted on that report but has yet to be repaired.

The regulations, however, also require an annual inspection for every year in which a full building conditions survey is not required. The commissioner may require more frequent inspections.

The annual visual inspection requires visual re-inspection of every component of the building condition survey, and review and updating of the school safety rating as needed (more on this later).

The annual visual inspection team consists of:

A member of the health and safety committee.

The distinct director of facilities or his/her designee.

A local code enforcement official certified by the City Building Department.

The board is required to establish a health and safety committee to monitor the safety of school buildings within the district. The committe must include representation from:

OR

Learn about additional facilities plan elements that the State Commissions of Education may choose to review.

All school districts, including New York City, must prepare, file, and submit to the commissioner upon request a long-range plan pertaining to educational facilities. (NYCRR s. 155.1(a))

This plan must be reevaluated and updated annually, and include an appraisal of the following:

The educational philosophy of the district, with resulting administrative organisation and program requirements.

Present and projected pupil enrollments.

Space use and state-rated pupil capacity of existing facilities.

Need of maintenance, repair or modernization of existing facilities, including consideration of obsolescence and retirement of certain facilities.

Provisions of additional facilities.

More specific technical information related to

Figure 4-2   Continued

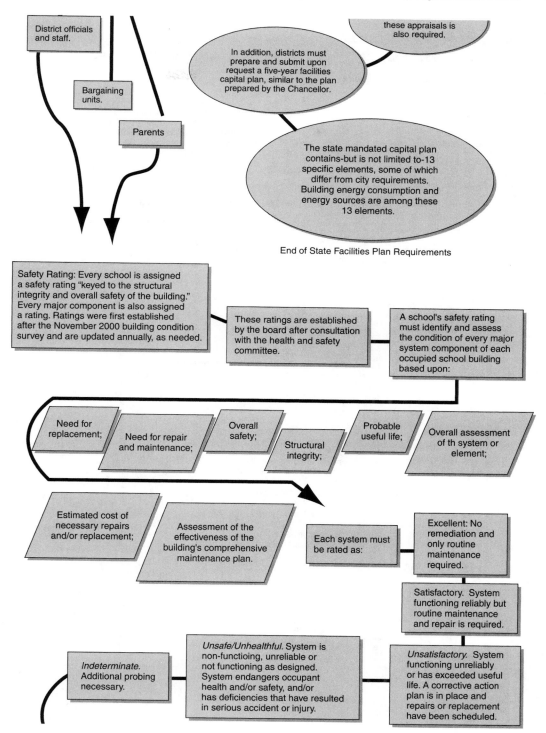

District officials and staff.

Bargaining units.

Parents

these appraisals is also required.

In addition, districts must prepare and submit upon request a five-year facilities capital plan, similar to the plan prepared by the Chancellor.

The state mandated capital plan contains-but is not limited to-13 specific elements, some of which differ from city requirements. Building energy consumption and energy sources are among these 13 elements.

End of State Facilities Plan Requirements

Safety Rating: Every school is assigned a safety rating "keyed to the structural integrity and overall safety of the building." Every major component is also assigned a rating. Ratings were first established after the November 2000 building condition survey and are updated annually, as needed.

These ratings are established by the board after consultation with the health and safety committee.

A school's safety rating must identify and assess the condition of every major system component of each occupied school building based upon:

Need for replacement;

Need for repair and maintenance;

Overall safety;

Structural integrity;

Probable useful life;

Overall assessment of th system or element;

Estimated cost of necessary repairs and/or replacement;

Assessment of the effectiveness of the building's comprehensive maintenance plan.

Each system must be rated as:

Excellent: No remediation and only routine maintenance required.

Satisfactory. System functioning reliably but routine maintenance and repair is required.

Indeterminate. Additional probing necessary.

Unsafe/Unhealthful. System is non-functioing, unreliable or not functioning as designed. System endangers occupant health and/or safety, and/or has deficiencies that have resulted in serious accident or injury.

Unsatisfactory. System functioning unreliably or has exceeded useful life. A corrective action plan is in place and repairs or replacement have been scheduled.

Figure 4-2   Continued

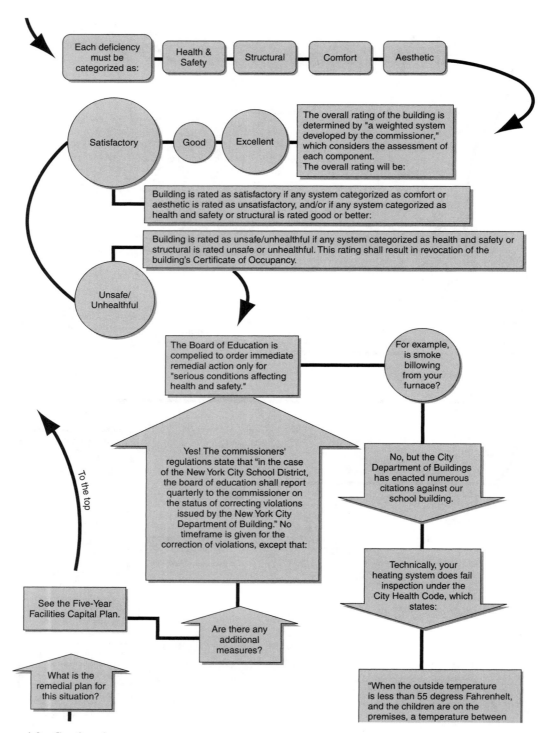

Figure 4-2   Continued

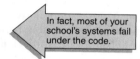

68 and 72 degress Farenhelt shall be maintained in all parts of the building used by the children."

Figure 4-2   Continued

What the research by and large indicates, in short, is that, within the American context of extreme openness, some enhancement of public agencies' administrative independence and organizational autonomy likely will result in more efficient and effective government, with little or no new resources being required.[130]

Freezing and Flexibility: The Environment of the Nonprofit Organization

As we have been discussing, public sector organizations are far more battered by forces in their environments than are organizations in the private sector, but this pummeling seems to be at least as severe in the nonprofit sector. However, third-sector organizations have greater flexibility than government agencies, and even, to some degree, corporate organizations, to deal with those pressures.

Environmental Forces and Organizational Freezing. An intriguing study of a university library that was in the process of administratively breaking down because of too many demands and not enough resources sheds some light on how independent organizations deal with increasingly harsh environmental realities. The researcher examined how institutions without the benefits of functioning in a free-market environment, where pressures could be adjusted through

market mechanisms, responded to environmental overload.[131] He delineated fourteen strategies used by such organizations to cope with rising levels of environmental stress, including queuing (e.g., keeping library patrons in waiting rooms "outside" the organization); the creation of branch facilities; creation of a mobile reserve (such as teams of personnel transferable to units as needed); the evolvement of specific performance standards, followed immediately by a reduction of those standards; a "brainstorming" search for a "magic formula"; promotion of self-service (for example, letting patrons into the stacks, which is a radical strategy because it represents a deliberate reduction of organizational sovereignty); the limitation of work to capacity as determined by rigid, ritualistic rules and characterized by the denial of error and the refusal of challenge; and, ultimately, the dissolution of the organization.

The library, in a very real sense, had no choice but to play out this scenario. It did not have the control over demands from its environment that, say, International Widget would have had. International Widget could simply boost the price of widgets, and thereby reduce demand, or overload. But the library—and, presumably, any nonprofit or public organization— did not have this option. It had to adjust internally.

One can infer from this case study that, as a declining environment forces public organizations to change, the organization's response grows less rational, more "bureaucratic," and more negative as its environmental conditions worsen. More systematic research supports this conclusion. A survey of 1,312 administrators and board chairs of small, independent colleges found "that as a college moved from moderate to severe decline it experienced a significant increase in five organizational responses: (1) centralization of decision making, (2) no long-term planning, (3) high employee turnover, (4) resistance to change, and (5) loss of excess resources." Even slow growth, no growth, or moderate decline produces "the politicizing of the college's climate" and an acceleration of "special-interest group activity."[132] This is "the cesspool syndrome"; as the organization downsizes to accommodate decline, "dreck" rather than "cream" rises to top (because the best talent flees to better jobs), thereby accelerating the decline.[133]

Freedom and Flexibility.   Nevertheless, it does appear that independent organizations do find ways of dealing with a declining environment that private organizations, and, to a lesser degree, public organizations, seem unable to undertake. In a fifteen-year study of the ten highly autonomous "provinces" of the largest religious order in the United States (the Jesuits), it was found that this nonprofit organization dealt with an increasingly difficult environment by increasing cooperation among its provinces (or subunits) and placing a priority on the internal exchange of information. "There is little reason to believe that this would have happened without the trigger of decline."[134]

This kind of interorganizational coordination does not appear to occur among private-sector organizations. At least one study has concluded, for example, that cooperative, interorganizational "strategic capacity" in a hostile environment is essentially unobtainable to private firms.[135]

But this possible advantage is not without its costs. The intensifying cooperation and expanding linkages among organizational units renders the administrator's role more complex and his or her power weaker: "The administrator's role changes from autocrat to facilitator."[136]

So, just as the college library experienced a loss of organizational sovereignty when environmental overload swamped it, so the individual nonprofit administrator loses managerial flexibility and freedom when interorganizational cooperation and information sharing are used as a strategy to cope with an environment that is growing more difficult for the organization to thrive in. It is yet another instance of the attenuated autonomy of the independent administrator.

In this chapter, we have reviewed a few of the forces affecting organizations. One of those forces is people and how they behave, especially people inside organizations. We consider this unpredictable force next.

Notes

1. James D. Thompson, *Organization in Action: Social Science Bases of Administrative Theory* (New York: McGraw-Hill, 1967), pp. 83–98. We should note that in discussing what we call the "effectiveness test," Thompson employs the term, "instrumental test," exclusively. We think that his terminology is unnecessarily obscure and have substituted it with the term, "effectiveness test."

2. Jitendra V. Singh, David J. Tucker, and Robert J. House, "Organizational Legitimacy and the Liability of Newness," *Administrative Science Quarterly* 31 (June 1986), pp. 171–193. "External legitimacy" was measured by the organization's acquisition of a listing in Toronto's *Community Directory*, a charitable registration number, and a large and distinguished board, among other factors.

3. Harland Cleveland, *The Knowledge Executive: Leadership in the Information Society* (New York: Dutton, 1985); and Harland Cleveland et al., "In Search of the Knowledge Executive: Managers, Microcomputers, and Information Technology," *State of Local Government Review* 24 (Spring 1992), pp. 48–57.

4. Joan S. Lublin, "More Corporate Fiefdoms Become Chiefdoms," *Wall Street Journal* (July 8, 1996). For more on corporate "knowledge management," see Chris Marshall, Larry Prusak, and David Shpilberg, "Financial Risk and the Need for Superior Knowledge Management," *California Management Review* 38 (Spring 1996), pp. 77–101; and Martha M. Hamilton, "Managing the Company Mind," *Washington Post* (August 18, 1996).

5. Herbert A. Simon, *Administrative Behavior: A Study of Decision-Making Process in Administrative Organizations*, 3rd ed. (New York: Free Press, 1976), p. 292.

6. See, for example, Marc A. Levin, "The Information-Seeking Behavior of Local Government Officials," *American Review of Public Administration* 21 (December 1991), p. 283; David N. Ammons and Charldean Newell, *City Executives: Leadership Roles, Work Characteristics, and Time Management* (Albany: State University of New York Press, 1989); and Herbert A. Kaufman, *The Administrative Behavior of Federal Bureau Chiefs* (Washington, DC: Johns Hopkins, 1981).

7. Stafford Beer, "Managing Modern Complexity," *The Management of Information and Knowledge. Panel on Science and Technology* (11th meeting). Proceedings before the Committee on Science and Astronautics. U.S. House of Representatives, 91st Congress, Second Session, January 27, 1970, No. 15 (Washington, DC: U.S. Government Printing Office, 1970).

8. Timothy L. Cannon, "Harnessing Customer Knowledge: Merging Customer Relationship Management with Knowledge of Management," in Ramón C. Barquin, Alex Bennet, and Shreen G. Remez, eds., *Knowledge Management: The Catalyst for Electronic Government* (Vienna, VA: Management Concepts, 2001), pp. 416–417. In our discussion, we tend to use the terms *information* and *knowledge* interchangeably.

9. Samir Khairi Tawfik, former director of the Center of the Department of Research in the Presidential Institute of Iraq, as quoted in Jon Lee Anderson, "Saddam's Ear," *The New Yorker* (May 4, 2003), p. 68.

10. Although we provide a couple of examples of this fumbling in the text, we refer the reader to Michael Elliott's superb analysis, "They Had a Plan," in *Time* (August 12, 2002), pp. 28–43. This is an account of the federal government's efforts to prepare for a terrorist attack on the United States, specifically by Al Qaeda, 1999–2001. This episode is too complex to recount here, but it exemplifies the problem of acting on information in a highly decentralized (or what Elliott calls, with reason, "shambolic") organization.

11. John Toland, *Infamy: Pearl Harbor and Its Aftermath* (New York: Berkley, 1982).

12. See, for example, Gordon Tullock, *The Politics of Bureaucracy* (Washington, DC: Public Affairs Press, 1965); Harold L. Wilensky, *Organizational Intelligence: Knowledge and Policy in Government and Industry* (New York: Basic Books, 1967), pp. 43–58; and Beer, "Managing Modern Complexity."

13. National Commission on Terrorist Attacks Upon the United States, *The 9/11 Commission Report*. Final Report (Washington, DC: U.S. Government Printing Office, 2005).

14. David Ignatius, "Fix the Intelligence Mess," *Washington Post* (April 21, 2006).

15. The Commission on the Intelligence Capabilities of the United States Regarding Weapons of Mass Destruction, *Report to the President of the United States* (Washington, DC: U.S. Government Printing Office, 2005).

16. Ignatius, "Fix the Intelligence Mess."

17. James G. March and Herbert A. Simon, *Organizations* (New York: John Wiley, 1958), p. 165.

18. James Risen, "Ex-Inspector Says CIA Missed Disarray in Iraqi Arms Program," *New York Times* (January 26, 2004). The chief weapons inspector was David A. Kay.

19. See, for example, Friedrich von Hayek's "Economics and Knowledge," *Economica* 4 (Fall 1937), pp. 33–54, and "The Use of Knowledge in Society," *American Economic Review* 35 (Fall 1945), pp. 519–530.

20. Martha S. Feldman and James G. March, "Information in Organizations as Signal and Symbol," Paper presented at the Western Political Science Association in San Francisco, California, March 27–29, 1980. See also Feldman and March, "Information in Organizations as Signal and Symbol," *Administrative Science Quarterly* 26 (June 1981), pp. 171–186. The following quotations are drawn from the paper first cited.

21. Hemphill and Associates, as cited in "Data Data," *Inc. Magazine* (January 1999), p. 70.

22. See, for example, Thomas D. Clark, Jr., and William A. Shrode, "Public Sector Decision Structures: An Empirically Based Description," *Public Administration Review* 39 (July/August 1979), pp. 343–354; Charles E. Lindblom, "The Science of Muddling Through," *Public Administration Review* 19 (Spring 1959), pp. 79–88; Morton H. Halperin, *Bureaucratic Politics in Foreign Policy* (Washington, DC: Brookings Institution, 1974); and Michael D. Cohen and James G. March, *Leadership and Ambiguity: The American College President* (New York: McGraw-Hill, 1974).

23. See, for example, Steven Chan, "The Intelligence of Stupidity: Understanding Failures and Strategic Warning," *American Political Science Review* 73 (1979), pp. 171–180.

24. See, for example, Irving L. Janis and Leon Mann, *Decision Making: A Psychological Analysis of Conflict, Choice, and Commitment* (New York: Free Press, 1977).

25. Feldman and March, "Information in Organizations as Signal and Symbol."

26. Pitney Bowes, *Workplace Communications in the 21st Century*, as cited in "Data Data." Seventy-one percent of workers said this.

27. Reuters Business Information Survey, as cited in ibid. Forty-four percent of managers said this.

28. Feldman and March, "Information in Organizations as Signal and Symbol."

29. Ibid., pp. 23–24.

30. E. Sam Overman and Donna T. Lorraine, "Information for Control: Another Management Proverb?" *Public Administration Review* 54 (March/April 1994), pp. 193–195.

31. Feldman and March, "Information in Organizations as Signal and Symbol," p. 25.

32. Kathleen M. Eisenhardt, "Making Fast Strategic Decisions in High-Velocity Environments," *Academy of Management Journal* 32 (September 1989), pp. 543–576.

33. Simon, *Administrative Behavior*, pp. 48–52. For an interesting discussion of the decision premise in the context of ethical choice in the public sector, see

Debra W. Stewart, "The Decision Premise: A Basic Tool for Analyzing the Ethical Content of Organizational Behavior," *Public Administration Quarterly* 8 (Fall 1988), pp. 315–328.

34. Simon, *Administrative Behavior.*

35. Bent Flyvberg, Mette K. Skamris Holm, and Soren L. Buhl, "How (In)accurate Are Demand Forecasts in Public Works Projects?" *Journal of the American Planning Association* 71 (Spring 2005), pp. 131–136. The quotation is on p. 131.

36. George Miller, "The Magic Number Seven, Plus or Minus Two," *Psychological Review* 63 (March 1956), pp. 81–97. For an excellent review of this literature, see George Keller and Ann McCreery, "Making Difficult Educational Decisions: Findings from Research and Experience," Paper presented at the 25th Annual Conference of the Society for College and University Planning, Atlanta, Georgia, July 31, 1990.

37. Daniel Kahneman and Amos Tversky, "Choices, Values, Frames," *American Psychologist* 39 (June 1984), pp. 341–350.

38. James Brown and Zi-Lei Qiu, "Satisficing When Buying Information," *Organizational Behavior and Human Decision Processes* 51 (June 1992), pp. 471–482.

39. Suzanne Langer, *Mind: An Essay on Feeling* (Baltimore MD: Johns Hopkins University Press, 1988).

40. Robert Frank, "Shrewdly Irrational," *Sociological Forum* 2 (September 1987), pp. 21–41.

41. For an excellent review of decision theory, see James G. March, *A Primer on Decision Making: How Decisions Happen* (New York: Free Press, 1994).

42. Janis and Mann, *Decision-Making.*

43. Irving Janis, *Victims of Groupthink* (Boston: Houghton-Mifflin, 1972), p. 13.

44. The Commission on the Intelligence Capabilities of the United States Regarding Weapons of Mass Destruction, *Report to the President of the United States*, p. 10.

45. Simon, *Administrative Behavior.*

46. James D. Thompson and Arthur Tuden, "Strategies, Structures, and Process of Organizational Decision," *Comparative Studies in Administration*, James D. Thompson et al., eds. (Pittsburgh: University of Pittsburgh Press, 1959), pp. 195–216.

47. Paul C. Nutt, "Making Strategic Choices," *Journal of Management Studies* 39 (January 2002), pp. 57–96. The quotation is on p. 67. See also Nutt's "Selecting Decision Rules for Crucial Choices: An Investigation of the Thompson Framework," *Journal of Applied Behavioral Science* 38 (March 2002), pp. 99–131.

48. Gordon Kingsley and Pamela Norton Reed, "Decision Process Models and Organizational Context: Level and Sector Make a Difference," *Public Productivity and Management Review* 14 (September 1991), p. 409.

49. Bruce Buchanan II, "Government Managers, Business Executives, and Organizational Commitment," *Public Administration Review* 35 (July/August 1975), pp. 339–347; Louis G. Gawthrop, *Administrative*

Politics and Social Change (New York: St. Martin's, 1971); and Lewis C. Mainzer, *Political Bureaucracy* (Glenview, IL: Scott, Foresman, 1973).

50. Mainzer, *Political Bureaucracy*; John D. Millett, *Organization for the Public Service* (Princeton, NJ: Van Nostrand, 1966); and Edward A. Holdaway, et al., "Dimensions of Organizations in Complex Societies: The Educational Sector," *Administrative Science Quarterly* 20 (March 1975), pp. 37–58.

51. W. Michael Blumenthal, "Candid Reflections of a Businessman in Washington," *Fortune* (January 29, 1979), pp. 2, 6, 49; Donald Rumsfeld, "A Politician-Turned-Executive Surveys Both Worlds," *Fortune* (September 10, 1979), pp. 88, 94; and Herman L. Weiss, "Why Business and Government Exchange Executives," *Harvard Business Review* (July/August 1974), pp. 129–140.

52. Thomas R. Davies, "The Inside Story," *Governing* (December 2003), p. 64. This was an interview with seven top information technology officials in state governments who had also served in the private sector.

53. Kinglsey and Reed, "Decision Process Models and Organizational Context," p. 409.

54. M. Antonsen and T. B. Jorgensen, "The Publicness of Public Organizations," *Public Administration* 75 (Summer 1997), pp. 327–357.

55. Robert A. Dahl and Chester E. Lindblom, *Politics, Economics, and Welfare* (New York: Harper & Row, 1953); and Robert T. Golembiewski, *Humanizing Public Organizations* (Mt. Airy, MD: Lomond, 1985).

56. E. E. Solomon, "Private and Public Sector Managers: An Empirical Investigation of Job Characteristics and Organizational Climate," *Journal of Applied Psychology* 71 (June 1986), pp. 247–259; and Charles R. Schwenk, "Conflict in Organizational Decision-Making: An Exploratory Study of Its Effects in For-Profit and Not-for-Profit Organizations," *Management Science* 36 (January 1990), pp. 436–448.

57. D. J. Hickson, R. J. Butler et al., *Top Decisions: Strategic Decision Making in Organizations* (San Francisco: Jossey-Bass, 1986).

58. John M. Bryson and Sharon R. Anderson, "Applying Large-Group Interaction Methods in the Planning and Implementation of Major Change Efforts," *Public Administration Review* 60 (March/April 2000), pp. 143–162. Large-group interaction methods got their start in the 1960s and "will soon become standard practice in the public and nonprofit sectors" (p. 152).

59. Dahl and Lindblom, *Politics, Economics, and Welfare*; Golembiewski, *Humanizing Public Organizations.*

60. Myung Jae Moon, "The Pursuit of Managerial Innovation: Does Organization Matter?" *Public Administration Review* 59 (January/February 1999), pp. 31–43.

61. Barry Bozeman and Gordon Kingsley, "Risk Culture in Public and Private Organizations," *Public Administration Review* 58 (March/April 1998), pp. 109–118.

62. Lois Recascino Wise, "The Use of Innovative Practices in the Public and Private Sectors: The Role of

Organization and Individual Factors," *Public Productivity and Management Review* 23 (December 1999), p. 150. The research was done in Sweden.

63. Sandford Borins, "Loose Cannons and Rule Breakers, or Enterprising Leaders? Some Evidence About Innovative Public Managers," *Public Administration Review* 60 (November/December 2000), pp. 498–507.

64. See the discussion and citations on this topic which appear next in this chapter, under "Administration in Organizations," most notably in the portion on the impact of the task environment on the quality of public administration.

65. Eisenhardt, "Making Fast Strategic Decisions in High-Velocity Environments," and Steve Molloy and Charles R. Shwenk, "The Effects of Information Technology on Strategic Decision-Making," *Journal of Management Studies* 32 (May 1995), pp. 288–304.

66. See, for example, James Surowiecki, *The Wisdom of Crowds* (New York: Little, Brown, 2004); Eisenhardt, "Making Fast Strategic Decisions in High-Velocity Environments"; and David M. Welborn, William Lyons, and Larry W. Thomas, "The Federal Government in the Sunshine Act and Agency Decision-Making," *Administration and Society* 20 (February 1989), pp. 480–492.

67. Paul C. Nutt, "Public–Private Differences and the Assessment of Alternatives for Decision-Making," *Journal of Public Administration Research and Theory* 9 (April 1999), pp. 305–349.

68. Paul C. Nutt, "Prompting the Transformation of Public Organizations," *Public Performance and Management Review* 27 (June 2004), pp. 9–33. Emphasis added. We suggest reading the four "Comments" following Nutt's article.

69. Fariborz Damanpour and Shanthi Gopalakrishnan, "The Dynamics of the Adoption of Product and Process Innovations in Organizations," *Journal of Management Studies* 38 (January 2001), pp. 45–66. The years covered were 1982–1993.

70. Mark A. Abramson, "The Leadership Factor," *Public Administration Review* 40 (November/December 1989), pp. 562–565.

71. James N. Doig and Erwin C. Hargroves, eds., *Leadership and Innovation: A Biographical Perspective on Entrepreneurs in Government* (Baltimore, MD: Johns Hopkins University Press, 1987).

72. Borins, "Loose Cannons and Rule Breakers, or Enterprising Leaders?", p. 506.

73. Gene A. Brewer, "In the Eye of the Storm: Front-Line Supervisors and Federal Agency Performance," *Journal of Public Administration Research and Theory* 15 (October 2005), pp. 505–523.

74. W. Graham Astley and Andrew H. Van de Ven, "Central Perspectives and Debates in Organization Theory," *Administrative Science Quarterly* 28 (June 1983), p. 245.

75. Lawrence G. Hrebeniak and William F. Joyce, "Organizational Adaptation: Strategic Choice and Environmental Determinism," *Administrative Science Quarterly* 28 (June 1983), p. 245.

76. We have changed our mind. In earlier editions of this book, we held a different view and discoursed at length on the academic disputations involving organizational determinism and choice. The reader may wish to consult: the eighth edition (2001), pp. 101–105; the seventh edition (1999), pp. 107–111; the sixth edition (1995), pp. 91–97; the fifth edition (1992), pp. 86–91; or the fourth edition (1989); pp. 86–92.

77. Herbert Kaufman, *Time, Chance, and Organizations: Natural Selection in a Perilous Environment* (Chatham, NJ: Chatham House), pp. 69, 150. Emphasis is original.

78. For other examples, see Howard E. Aldrich, *Organizations and Environments* (Englewood Cliffs, NJ: Prentice-Hall, 1979); and John Child, "Organization, Structure, Environment, and Performance: The Role of Strategic Choice," *Sociology* 6 (January 1972), p. 1.

79. Lyman W. Porter and John Van Maanen, "Task Accomplishment and the Management of Time," in *Managing for Accomplishment,* Bernard Bass ed. (Lexington, MA: Lexington Books, 1970), pp. 180–192.

80. Alan W. Lau, Cynthia W. Pavett, and Arthur R. Newman, "The Nature of Managerial Work: A Comparison of Public and Private Sector Jobs," *Academy of Management Proceedings* (August 1980), pp. 339–343.

81. Porter and Van Maanen, "Task Accomplishment and the Management of Time."

82. U.S. Government Accountability Office, *Information Management: Implementation of the Freedom of Information Act,* GAO–05–648T (Washington, DC: U.S. Government Printing Office, 2005). Figures are for 2002–2004, except the task and time figures, which are for 2004. The GAO surveyed twenty-five agencies that handled over 97 percent of all Freedom of Information Act requests.

83. Dennis O. Grady and Kathleen M. Simon, "Political Constraints and Bureaucratic Discretion: The Case of State Government Rule Making," *Politics and Policy* 30 (December 2002), pp. 650–655. Figures are for 1997.

84. Daniel P. Carpenter, "Groups, the Media, Agency Waiting Costs, and FDA Drug Approval," *American Journal of Political Science* 46 (July 2003), pp. 490–505. Carpenter examined the cases of 450 new drugs reviewed by the FDA between 1977 and 2000.

85. A. Cooper Drury, Richard Stuart Olson, and Douglas A. Van Belle, "The Politics of Humanitarian Aid: US Foreign Disaster Assistance, 1964–1995," *Journal of Politics* 67 (May 2005), pp. 454–473. The authors analyzed 2,337 natural disasters. Each story in the *New York Times* resulted in an additional $594,057, on average, in U.S. aid for the disaster's victims. Ten stories in the *Times* lifted the probability of the afflicted country receiving aid from 47 percent to 50 percent. The United States sends no assistance to the victims in 34 percent, on average, of natural disasters, and, of the assistance that it does send, the average amount is about $5 million. The other major variable that

affected aid was strategic: If the afflicted nation was a U.S. ally, it received, on average, about seven times more assistance.

86. U.S. General Accounting Office, *Executive Reorganization Authority: Balancing Executive and Congressional Roles in Shaping the Federal Government's Structure*, GAO–03–624T (Washington, DC: U.S. Government Printing Office, 2003), p. 7.

87. There are exceptions. Most observers think that the first Hoover Commission, which lasted from 1947 to 1949, was quite successful, with 70 percent of its recommendations accepted by Congress and implemented, including twenty-six out of thirty-five proposed reorganization plans. The willingness of the Truman administration to work with Congress was instrumental in its success. See ibid., p. 9.

88. Alisdair Roberts, "Why the Brownlow Committee Failed: Neutrality and Partisanship in the Early Years of Public Administration," *Administration and Society* 28 (May 1996), p. 3. As the title of this source implies, FDR hardly was asking Congress to approve a reorganization of federal agencies that was politicized or idiosyncratic; rather, he was asking Congress to implement the 1937 recommendations of the prestigious Committee on Administrative Management.

89. Richard C. Elling, "Administering State Programs: Performance and Politics," in *Politics in the American States: A Comparative Analysis,* 8th ed., Virginia Gray and Russell L. Hanson, eds. (Washington, DC: CQ Press, 2004), p. 267.

90. James Conant, "Management Consequences of the 1960–1990 'Modernization' of State Government," in *Handbook of State Government Administration*, John J. Gargan, ed. (New York: Marcel Dekker, 2000).

91. Elling, "Administering State Programs," p. 267.

92. Alan Greenblatt, "A Little Bit of Reform," *Governing* (August 2003), pp. 40–41.

93. National Commission on the Public Service, *Urgent Business for America: Revitalizing the Federal Government for the 21st Century.* Report of the National Commission on the Public Service (Washington, DC: U.S. Government Printing Office, 2003), p. 16.

94. Ibid., p. 36. As with any generalization, there are exceptions, and in this case it is the reforms recommended by the first Hoover Commission in 1949. Because the commission's members had taken great pains to work with Congress as they formulated their suggestions, the great majority of them were implemented.

95. U.S. General Accounting Office, *Federal Budget: Agency Obligations by Budget Function and Object Classification for Fiscal Year 2003*, GAO–04–834 (Washington, DC: U.S. Government Printing Office, 2004), highlights page. Figures are for 2003. By major policy, we mean the federal government's fifteen official budget functions, such as National Defense, International Affairs, and General Science, Space, and Technology.

96. The following examples are drawn from National Commission on the Public Service, *Urgent Business for America*, pp. 15–16, 36–37.

97. Center for Strategic and International Studies and Business Executives for National Security, *Untangling the Web: Congressional Oversight and the Department of Homeland Security* (Washington, DC: Authors, 2004), p. 2. Figure is for 2004.

98. Joint Committee on the Organization of Congress, *Organization of the Congress.* Final Report (Washington, DC: U.S. Government Printing Office, 1993). http://www.house.gov/rules/jcoc2ar.htm. Figure is for 1992 and represents a 242 percent growth rate in congressional reporting requirements over twelve years.

99. Center for Strategic and International Studies and Business Executives for National Security, *Untangling the Web*, p. 2. Figure is for 2002.

100. Princeton Survey Research Associates and the Brookings Institution, *Health of the Public Service* (Washington, DC: Authors, 2001). http://www.brook.edu. Figures are for 2001.

101. Paul C. Light, *Fact Sheet on the Continued Thickening of Government* (Washington, DC: Brookings, 2004). The years covered are 1960–2004.

102. Ibid.

103. Anthony Downs, *Inside Bureaucracy* (Boston: Little, Brown, 1967), pp. 52–59, 145–146.

104. Marshall W. Meyer, *Change in Public Bureaucracies* (London: Cambridge University Press, 1979), p. 5.

105. Jonathan Rauch, *Demosclerosis: The Silent Killer of American Government* (New York: Times Books, 1994). See also Rauch's, *Government's End: Why Washington Stopped Working* (Washington, DC: Public Affairs Press, 1999).

106. Kevin B. Smith and Christopher W. Larimer, "A Mixed Relationship: Bureaucracy and School Performance," *Public Administration Review* 64 (November/December 2004), pp. 728–736; and John Bohite, "School Bureaucracy and Student Performance at the Local Level," *Public Administration Review* 61 (January/February 2001), pp. 92–99.

107. Bohte, "School Bureaucracy and Student Performance at the Local Level."

108. Simth and Larimer, "A Mixed Relationship."

109. Kenneth J. Meier and John Bohte, "Not with a Bang, but a Whimper: Explaining Organizational Failures," *Administration & Society* 35 (March 2003), pp. 104–121. The quotations are on p. 104.

110. See, for example, Stuart Bretschneider, "Management Information Systems in Public and Private Organizations: An Empirical Test," *Public Administration Review* 50 (September/October 1990), pp. 536–545; Antonsen and Jorgensen, "The Publicness of Public Organizations," pp. 327–357; and Moon, "The Pursuit of Managerial Innovation."

111. Donald P. Warwick, *A Theory of Public Bureaucracy* (Cambridge, MA: Harvard University Press, 1975), pp. 72–80, 188–191.

112. Hal G. Rainey, Sanjay Pandey, and Barry Bozeman, "Research Note: Public and Private Managers' Perception of Red Tape," *Public Administration Review* 55 (November/December 1995), pp. 567–574.

113. Bozeman and Kingsley, "Risk Culture in Public and Private Organizations."

114. Patrick G. Scott and Sanjay K. Pandey, "Red Tape and Public Service Motivation Findings from a National Survey of Managers in State Health and Human Services Agencies," *Review of Public Personnel Administration 25* (Summer 2005), pp. 155–180.

115. Moon, "The Pursuit of Managerial Innovation," p. 38.

116. Keon S. Chi, Kelley A. Arnold, and Heather M. Perkins, "Privatization in State Government: Trends and Issues," *Spectrum: The Journal of State Government* 76 (Fall 2003), p. 14. Figure is for 2002.

117. Rainey, Pandey, and Bozeman, "Research Note," pp. 567–574.

118. Leisha De Hart-Davis, "Red Tape and Public Employees: Does Perceived Rule Dysfunction Alienate Managers?" *Journal of Public Administration Research and Theory* 15 (January 2005), pp. 133–149.

119. Patrick G. Scott and Sanjay K. Pandey, "The Influence of Red Tape on Bureaucratic Behavior: An Experimental Simulation," *Journal of Policy Analysis and Management* 19 (Autumn 2000), pp. 615–653.

120. John Meyer, W. Richard Scott, and David Strang, "Centralization, Fragmentation, and School District Complexity," *Administrative Science Quarterly* 32 (June 1987), pp. 188–201.

121. Diane Ravitch, "Burden of Rules, Regulations is Eroding School Discipline," *Savannah Morning News* (January 3, 2005).

122. David G. Houghton, "Citizen Advisory Boards: Autonomy and Effectiveness," *American Review of Public Administration* 18 (September 1988), p. 293.

123. Welborn, Lyons, and Thomas, "The Federal Government in the Sunshine Act and Agency Decision-Making," p. 483.

124. Claire L. Felbinger, "Impediments to Effective Management in Bureaucracies: The Perceptions of Public Works Directors," *Public Productivity and Management Review* 14 (Fall 1990), pp. 12, 15.

125. John E. Chubb and Terry M. Moe, *Politics, Markets, and America's Schools* (Washington, DC: Brooking, 1990).

126. Jeff Gill and Kenneth J. Meier, "Ralph's Pretty-Good Grocery versus Ralph's Super Market: Separating Excellent Agencies from the Good Ones," *Public Administration Review* 61 (January/February 2001), p. 14.

127. Alfred A. Marcus, "Implementing Externally Induced Innovations: A Comparison of Rule-Bound and Autonomous Approaches," *Academy of Management Journal* 31 (June 1988), p. 249.

128. Paul C. Light, "To Restore and Renew: Now Is the Time to Rebuild the Federal Public Service," *Government Executive* (November 2001). http://www.brook.edu.

129. David Osborne and Ted Gaebler, *Reinventing Government: How Entrepreneurial Skill Is Transforming the Public Sector* (Reading, MA: Addison-Wesley, 1992), p. xviii.

130. In a remarkable feature article in *Fortune*, one of the nation's foremost business magazines, precisely this point was argued, and strongly so. See David Kirkpatrick, "It's Simply Not Working," *Fortune* (November 19, 1990), pp. 20–21. To be fair, however, not all the research agrees that more autonomy will result in more effective public agencies. See Diane Vaughan, "Autonomy, Interdependence, and Social Control: NASA and the Space Shuttle *Challenger*," *Administrative Science Quarterly* 35 (June 1990), pp. 225–257.

131. Richard L. Meier, "Communications Overload," *Administrative Science Quarterly* 7 (March 1963), pp. 529–544.

132. John D. Sellars, "The Warnings Signs of Institutional Decline," *Trusteeship* 2 (November/December 1994), p. 13.

133. Arthur G. Bedeian and Achilles A. Armenakis, "The Cesspool Syndrome: How Dreck Floats to the Top of Declining Organizations," *Academy of Management Executive* 12 (February 1998), pp. 58–67.

134. Dean C. Ludwig, "Adapting to a Declining Environment: Lesson from a Religious Order," *Organization Science* 4 (February 1993), p. 54.

135. Kathryn R. Harrigan, "Strategic Formulation in Declining Industries," *Academy of Management Review* 4 (June 1980), pp. 599–604. See also James E. Austin, "Strategic Collaboration between Nonprofits and Business," *Nonprofit and Voluntary Sector Quarterly* 29 (March 2000), pp. 69–97.

136. Ludwig, "Adapting to a Declining Environment," p. 54.

CHAPTER **5**

The Fibers of Organizations: People

"Threads" served as our metaphor for theories of organizations, and "fabric" was our metaphor for the interwoven forces that form organizations. In this chapter, "fibers"—the woof, weft, and tensile strength of organizations—constitute our metaphor for the people in organizations and how they behave in them.

The Motives of Public and Nonprofit Administrators

Why do some people choose to work in the public or nonprofit sectors, but not the private one? Money? Security? A chance to make a difference?

An Overview

Much of the research seems to agree that the following factors play a greater role in drawing people to work in public and nonprofit organizations, in contrast to inducing people to enter into business careers:[1]

- People who enter public service likely have lower needs for wealth than people who enter the corporate sphere,[2] and this seems to be especially true for those entering the nonprofit sector.[3]

- There may be a higher need among people entering government service for job security relative to people in the private sector, although this seems to be much less the case for those joining nonprofit associations, who may have an even lower need for job security than those entering business organizations.[4]

- Those who enter public service—but especially those who enter the nonprofit sector—appear to be considerably more driven to "make a difference" and achieve public and social goals than do those who enter the private sector.[5]

- "Public service motivation" is more pronounced in women than men; higher among people with more education than people with less education; and more present among public employees who are managers than among those who are not managers. In fact, managerial status associates more strongly with public service motivation than even "the personal characteristics of the respondents."[6]

The Motives of Public Managers

It appears that even though the nation's young adults are motivated primarily to do work that will change society for the better, those who actually enter government service may be motivated primarily by job security.

On the one hand, national surveys find that, whereas "a good salary and job security" are major motivations among young people to enter government employment, "doing good wins over doing well." Almost half, 47 percent, of young adults are far more attracted to government service by opportunities to help people and make a difference in society (with women the clear leaders in this regard), and this proportion is growing dramatically over time. By contrast, only about a fourth, 26 percent, say that that would enter government because of pay and benefits, and a slim 11 percent would do so for job security.[7]

On the other hand, a survey of public administrators revealed that "job security" was the main reason why 59 percent actually took a job in government, whereas "the chance to make a difference" was the principal motivation for only 41 percent.[8] Young Americans want to make a difference, but, as we discussed in Chapter 1, it may be that fewer of those who do are entering government.

Still, even this conclusion must be tentative. A massive study of public employees in the United States found that "public employment is a substantively important and highly significant predictor of civic participation. Overall, public servants are far more active in civic affairs than are other citizens," and appear to be "catalysts" in improving society at large.[9] Public administrators clearly want to make a difference, both in and out of government.

The Motives of Nonprofit Managers

Americans who *really* want to make a difference appear to join the nonprofit sector more readily than any other. More than six out of ten nonprofit workers state that they joined their organization to help the public and for a chance to make a difference, and not for the job security or benefits. By contrast, roughly three out of ten federal employees and about two out of ten private-sector workers say this.[10] A mere 16 percent of nonprofit employees state that their paycheck is the reason they come to work, in contrast to 31 percent of federal workers and 44 percent of business employees.[11]

The research on job motivation is only one inlet in the ocean of literature on organizational behavior, and there are at least three other bays that are uniquely useful in understanding bureaucrats.

They are the literatures of adult development, cultural behavior, and political behavior, which we review next.

Models of Adult Development

People change. How people change, and what effects those changes might have on the organizations in which they work, have been the subjects of psychological and social-psychological research since the 1930s.[12]

Turning Points

The adult development psychologists, taken together, have identified a series of psychological tasks that everyone must confront as a means of interpreting how people approach each stage of their lives, and with what attitudes. Erik Erikson, for example, posits a progressive mastery of psychological tasks that hinges on a series of critical turning points. From birth to year one, trust or mistrust can be inculcated into the psyche of the individual as a result of his or her early experiences with others; from one to six, the turning point becomes one of developing autonomy as an individual versus shame; from six to ten, initiative or guilt; from ten to fourteen, industry as opposed to inferiority; from fourteen to twenty, identity versus role confusion; from twenty to forty, intimacy or isolation; from forty to sixty-five, generativity or creativity, as opposed to stagnation; and from sixty-five until death, a strong sense of ego and integrity as opposed to overwhelming despair.[13]

Different analysts have developed variations on this theme, but the theory is essentially the same: A person is faced with critical turning points in his or her life, and these occur at specific ages. Importantly, one can become mired in the negative option of any given phase and fail to move beyond that phase.

The adult psychologists agree that when people are in their twenties and thirties, the most overriding psychological task is that of achieving personal intimacy. It is during this phase that a person shifts from his or her dependency on parents to an intimacy with (or isolation from) mates and peers.

The next major phase is what is known popularly as the "midlife crisis." How intense that crisis is varies from individual to individual, but people experience at least a "midlife transition," if not a dramatic crisis. Midlife transition is a period occurring from as early as the late thirties, through as late as the early sixties, and women may experience more of a crisis during this phase than men.[14]

It is during midlife that the individual chooses between such deeply set alternatives as looking at career options, resigning oneself to having attained all that one can attain professionally or personally, and accepting, or becoming embittered, over one's condition. This period is one of determining whether an individual can "keep the meaning" of what his or her life or career has signified in reality, or, instead, becoming rigid and inflexible over a personal set of principles that may have grown hollow over time.[15]

Finally, an individual enters late adulthood, a period in which one reflects on what one's life has meant. These reflections focus on the development of a sense of integrity about what he or she stands for, as opposed to a sense of despair over what one has failed to accomplish.[16] One can, in sum, close one's life with serenity and contentment, or sadness and self-contempt.

Adult Development and the Public Organization

Research that related the experience of Canadian executives in both the public and private sectors to adult life-span development found a strong correlation between high and low levels of satisfaction with the organization and one's work and specific phases of adult development.[17]

Reality Shock.   The first phase, which the researchers call "reality shock," and which occurs during the twenties when one enters one's first "real job," is characterized by bottom-scraping disillusion, and this is particularly true in the public sector. Comparisons of students who had internships in government with those who had not worked in public agencies found measurably higher levels of cynicism about government,

lower levels of trust in government, and a stronger belief that public employees were incompetent, dishonest, and lazy among the interns.[18]

Overcoming reality shock and dissatisfaction with the job is followed by a period of socialization in the organization and personal growth, which occurs in the thirties. It is during this phase that the manager invests a sense of self in the organization and in his or her career. This is a period of "settling down,"[19] and "career consolidation."[20]

Not everyone, however, settles down. In one examination, a tenth of the sample remained "perpetual boys," and never matured, while a larger group simply stagnated.[21] Another researcher found that almost half of his sample "had major difficulties" during the career-consolidation phase and could not create the basis for "an even moderately satisfactory mid-life."[22]

Developing Adults and Satisfying Work.   If one is capable of consolidating one's career and enters the late thirties through the mid-forties, job satisfaction takes a steep downward spiral. This is the infamous "midlife crisis," and one researcher found that this period could be so traumatic that some executives psychically withdraw from life and become "organizational sleepwalkers."[23] It appears that if one has less egocentrism and narcissism, and more tolerance, flexibility, and openness, one improves one's chances of weathering the midlife crisis,[24] but, in any event, the prospects loom larger during this period of engaging new careers, new lifestyles, and new spouses.

Job satisfaction typically rebounds during the late forties and fifties. This is a period of "acceptance,"[25] or "keeping the meaning" of one's life and personal principles.[26]

The roller coaster of job satisfaction takes yet another dip in the mid-to-late fifties, and continues to decline, although not as rapidly, through the early sixties as the individual nears retirement. Oddly, it appears that, while job satisfaction continues to decline, the individual's satisfaction with his or her organization appears to bounce back toward the end of his or her career.[27] "As individuals enter midlife, extrinsic rewards for higher levels of performance and achievement lose their lustre, as interest in affirming one's identity and concerns for protecting the self-concept increase."[28]

Models of Cultural Behavior

Relatively few theorists have considered the specific impact of *national cultures* (or "the collective mental programming of people in an environment"[29]) on organizational behavior, but some who have deserve mention. We deal with two aspects of national culture and organizations: organizational behavior and managerial behavior.

National culture has a large impact on not only how organizations behave, but also on how managers manage. What has become increasingly clear is that the American lens of management theory, which focused most of the international thinking about management in the twentieth century, may obscure more than it reveals about managerial behavior in countries other than the United States. "Cultural values of the United States underlie and have fundamentally framed management research, [and] thus organizational science, with inappropriate universalism."[30]

Dimensions of National Culture.

Certainly the most systematic and massive attempt to categorize national cultures in ways that are potentially useful to managers is by Geert Hofstede. Hofstede has identified five fundamental dimensions of national culture: power distance, uncertainty avoidance, individualism–collectivism, masculinity–femininity, and long-term–short-term orientation. Specific national cultures can be any combination of these.[31]

Power Distance.

Power distance refers to "the extent to which a society accepts the fact that power in institutions and organizations is distributed unequally."[32] Societies characterized by "small" power distance believe, among other things, that inequality should be minimized, superiors should be accessible, all should have equal rights, and that a latent harmony exists between the powerful and the powerless; cultures with a "large" power distance believe that a social order rightly assures proper inequalities in society, superiors should be inaccessible, power should have privileges, and that latent conflict exists between the powerful and the powerless.

Uncertainty Avoidance.

Uncertainty avoidance is the extent to which a culture feels threatened by ambiguity. Cultures with "weak" uncertainty avoidance are more accepting of uncertainty, live from day to day, have lower stress levels, believe time is free, accept dissent, are unthreatened by social deviations, are more risk prone, are not too nationalistic, are youth oriented, and are not enamored by a lot of rules. "Strong" uncertainty avoidance cultures perceive uncertainty to be a continuous threat, experience greater stress, believe time is money, promote consensus over dissent, consider deviance to be dangerous, are security conscious, are highly nationalistic, are distrustful of the young, and like a lot of rules.

Individualism–Collectivism.

Individualism–collectivism refers to a continuum of cultures; at one extreme (individualism), society is seen as a loose grouping of people whose primary concern is in caring for themselves, while the opposite extreme (collectivism) reflects a tight social framework in which in-groups are distinguished from out-groups, and the in-group is expected to take care of the individual member in exchange for his or her total allegiance to it. In the individualist culture, identity is based on the individual, leadership is the ideal, and decisions are made by the individual. In collectivist cultures, personal identity is based on the social system, membership in the organization or in-group is the ideal, and decisions are made by the group.

Masculinity–Femininity.

The *masculinity–femininity* dimension, like individualism–collectivism, is a continuum ranging from a masculine pole in which assertiveness, performance, money, independence, ambition, machismo, and indifference to others are characteristic, to a feminine extreme in which nurturing, quality of life, people, the environment, interdependence, service, androgyny, and caring for others are the dominant values.

Long-Term–Short-Term Orientation. Finally, *long-term–short-term orientation* refers to a cultural direction relative to time. Nations with a long-term orientation are directed toward the future and value thrift and persistence. Countries with a short-term orientation are more poised toward the past and present, and place premiums on respect for tradition and fulfilling social obligations.

Patterns of Geography and Language. Although there are numerous exceptions, countries tend to group along the foregoing cultural dimensions by geography and language. For example, the seven Latin American countries that Hofstede surveyed are all cultures that accept large inequalities of power relationships, strongly avoid uncertainty, and are collectivist. All the Asian countries that Hofstede studied are large power-distance countries, collectivist, and have a long-term orientation.

Common language plays a part, too. All ten English-speaking countries, including those in Africa and Asia, are accepting of uncertainty and are masculine, and, except for those in Asia, all English-speaking countries are individualistic.

The Uniqueness of the United States. The United States is a small power-distance country (that is, its citizens value equality); a weak uncertainty-avoidance nation (in fact, it is well below average, indicating high risk taking propensities and tolerance for dissent, among other characteristics); is exceptionally individualistic as a society; is well above average as a masculine culture; and has a short-term orientation.

Other research confirms much of Hofstede's findings and has also found that, in comparison to Europeans, Americans are considerably more patriotic, more religious, and more conservative. Americans are much more likely than Europeans to believe that the primary role of government is to ensure the freedom needed for people to pursue their own goals and much less likely to think that government's main purpose is to guarantee that no one is in need.[33] These dimensions have fashioned a national culture that is uniquely American.

Organization Theory and the American Bias. Because the United States is unique, its uniqueness should dampen the enthusiasm of Americans for interpreting managerial behavior in other countries by relying only on their own cultural perspective. Consider, for example, A. H. Maslow's "hierarchy of human needs," described in Chapter 3, and which is absolutely central to mainstream organization theory, especially human relations and organization development. Maslow's theory, which culminates in the ultimate personal achievement, self-actualization, is predicated on the idea that certain basic needs must be satisfied first, such as the need for security.

Achievement Motivation Cultures. Hofstede's research indicates that Maslow's theory of motivation is less than universal and, in fact, is bound in the American cultural context. Self-actualization is a concept that can be supported only in a society that places a high premium on performance and achievement (or a society that is strongly individualistic and masculine, as is the United States), and on a willingness to take risks so that achievements may be made (or a culture that has weak uncertainty avoidance—again like the United States). But not all societies have these features. In fact, only the English-speaking cultures in Hofstede's study were identified as both masculine and weak uncertainty-avoidance countries. Even more revealing, according to Hofstede, the "striking thing about the concept of achievement is that word itself is hardly translatable into any language other than English"![34]

The United States and the other English-speaking nations, in sum, are *achievement motivation* cultures and thus can relate to a hierarchy of human needs that places achievement near the top and security near the bottom.

Security Motivation Cultures. But other cultures have different motivations. Some cultures, for example, may be masculine (like the United States) but also have strong needs to avoid uncertainty (such as Italy, Japan, and Mexico). These nations are *security motivated* (a combination of achievement and security) that places security near the top of the pyramid of human needs and personal achievement (i.e., self-actualization) near the bottom.

Social Motivation Cultures. Other nations may, like the United States, have weak uncertainty-avoidance qualities but are feminine cultures (a combination found in all the Scandinavian nations), and still others may be cultural polar opposites of the United States, being feminine societies that have strong needs to avoid uncertainty (a combination found in Israel and Thailand). In both these instances, *social motivation* explains individual behavior in organizations: quality of life plus risk taking in Scandanavia, and quality of life plus security in Israel and Thailand.

In sum, a theory of human motivation that presupposes achievement to the exclusion of other possibilities (as Maslow's hierarchy does) "is not the description of a universal human motivation process—it is the description of a value system, the value system of the U.S. middle class to which the author [Maslow] belonged."[35]

Organizational Behavior and the American Bias. Cultural variables seem to call into question the whole open model of organizations (recall Chapter 3), at least when that model is cast into cultures which differ from that of the United States.

Culture and Power. For instance, although the United States is a small power-distance country, and equality and accessibility are valued, it does not score terribly high on this dimension, and a number of nations, such as Israel, Norway, and Sweden, have power distances that are even smaller. In these countries, organizational subordinates are much more likely to participate in decision making. In fact, in those cultures with the smallest power distances "the very idea of management prerogatives is not accepted."[36]

On the other hand, nations with large power distances, such as France and Italy, show little interest in participative decision making in the American style. "This suggests that subordinates in a large power distance culture feel even more comfortable with superiors who are real autocrats,"[37] although one major study, based on Hofstede's model, of twenty-one nations found that a high level of stress at work associated positively with large power distances in the national culture.[38]

France places a particularly high premium on large power distance. "In spite of all attempts to introduce Anglo-Saxon management methods, French superiors do not easily decentralize . . . nor do French subordinates expect them to."[39] When one multinational corporation issued a directive to all its worldwide subsidiaries that salary adjustment proposals should be initiated by each employee's immediate supervisor, the corporation's French managers interpreted this to mean that the supervisor *three levels above* should initiate salary adjustments![40]

Culture and Uncertainty. Power distance relates to organizational decentralization and centralization, but another cultural feature bears on the use of formal rules—on "bureaucracy." That feature is uncertainty avoidance.

Cultures with strong needs to avoid uncertainty are much more prone to rely on written regulations and procedures than are weak uncertainty-avoidance countries. Confronted with the same problem, management students from France, what was then West Germany, and Britain recommended three different ways of solving it. The French students recommended referring the problem to a higher level; the Germans, from a culture with very strong uncertainty-avoidance needs but (unlike France) relatively small power distances, blamed the lack of written rules as causing the problem and recommended that they be drafted; the British, from a small power distance and strongly individualistic culture, ascribed the problem to poor communication and proposed some sort of training program. For the French, the organization is a pyramid (it is both centralized and formal), for the Germans it is a well-oiled machine (formal, but not centralized), and for the British it is a village market (neither centralized nor formal).[41]

American culture seems to be relatively free of these particular mind-sets, and this may account for the comparative success of American corporations in other countries. Like the British students, American managers do not believe in hierarchy for its own sake (as in France) or in rules for their own sake (as in Germany), but only in using (or not using) hierarchy and rules to achieve results. This orientation reflects the highly individualistic and masculine aspects of the United States. But the extreme individualism of American culture is fundamentally at odds with the collectivist traditions of other cultures, such as all of the nations surveyed in Latin America and Asia. These cultures believe in loyalty to the organization, and individuals are less likely to calculate their behavior on the basis of what the organization can do for them.

Models of Political Behavior

A third theme on the nature of the administrative human being that falls within the social-psychological framework deals with how administrators behave politically in organizations. The findings and speculations extant in this field of research have particular relevance to public administration, for politics influences the public administrative sector as no other.

Locals *versus* Cosmopolitans and the Vexing Question of Loyalty

Alvin Gouldner, in a classic essay,[42] itemized organizational roles along a political dimension. In an empirical analysis of a small college's faculty and administration, Gouldner distinguished between "locals" and "cosmopolitans." *Locals* derive their power and sense of personal identity (their self-actualization, if you will) from *internal* organizational factors. Locals were loyal to the organization as a whole; well satisfied with everything in the organization; deployable to many parts of the organization when needed; suspicious of outsiders; and often oriented toward the past.

Culture and the Bureaucrat

The following selection discusses how national culture affects public bureaucrats. Its author is an Englishman and professor of English literature who is also Assistant Director-General of the United Nations Educational, Scientific, and Cultural Organization.

People, we assume, are much the same everywhere; personality will out, and the ups-and-downs of life are much the same everywhere, too. Sure, but the ways these qualities and experiences express themselves differ in different societies. Each society has several ranges of typical face, and the distinctions between them become finer and finer as you look at them. There is a lean, quizzical, face one finds among clever men on the Eastern seaboard of the United States, the face of an intelligent man in a wide-open, mass-persuasive society who is not to be taken in, who has kept his cool and his irony. Such a face is not so likely to be found among its counterparts in Eastern Europe; the winds which beat on these men are different. Their faces are graver, more direct, and yet more reserved.

Because I have met them at some crossroads in my own life, I am particularly interested in a range of faces which cluster round the idea of a public man in Britain. At his most characteristic, this man is in his middle-fifties. His appearance is what the whisky advertisements, giving it more of a gloss than it really has, call distinguished. His face is well shaven but not scraped; it has a healthy bloom, but not an outdoor roughness; it is smooth, but not waxy. What is by now quite a full face is as solid as leather club-armchairs, and as decently groomed; it smells as good as the public rooms of those clubs. The hair is often marked by the appearance of Cabinet Minister's wings, that is, it is brushed straight back above the ears to plump out at the sides; it has a silvery sheen. The teeth are strong, one sees when the lips, as they readily do, curl back into a full, firm smile. They suggest someone who is used to talking in public and to deciding, to biting firmly into

Conversely, *cosmopolitans* related to factors *external* to the organization, such as their professional associations. In contrast to the locals, cosmopolitans were more loyal to a part of the organization than to the organization as a whole (i.e., the department rather than the college); dissatisfied with many aspects of the organization; and were more highly educated, specialized, and alienated from their colleagues than the locals.

The Uses of Locals and Cosmopolitans. Gouldner's creative thinking about cosmopolitans and locals has spawned numerous replications, many of them useful. Later research has linked cosmopolitanism with heightened professionalism, greater innovation, and the earlier adoption of innovation by organizations.[43] Much of this research suggests that cosmopolitans are of greater utility to organizations facing an increasingly fast-paced and challenging task environment than are locals. Conversely, locals are perceived as having a unique claim as organizational stabilizers in this same task environment, and that this stabilizing quality derives directly from their greater loyalty to the organization.

This traditional distinction leads some writers to extol the worth of locals in terms of assuring organizational loyalty, and emphasizing that individual commitment to the organization is good. Hence, it is argued that the "localistic co-optation" (based on some ruthless manipulative techniques) of employees by top management is necessary because it assures the organizational loyalty of employees, and, thereby, organizational stability.[44] But an organizational loyalty that is redolent of, "My bureaucracy, right or wrong!" is not necessarily conducive to the longer term health, success, or even survival of the organization which commands

---

problems. They are wonderfully communicative teeth, and remarkable evidence that from all the possible ways of using teeth, the ways we smile or grimace, we select only some: we select from the codebook of tooth-signals in our society . . .

Among the most striking in the line of public figures is the old-young man; and they are most often found in the higher reaches of education. These men are slim, with little trace of a paunch even at fifty-five; their faces still show the outlines formed when they were Head boys at their public schools or good day-schools. There is a French public type of about the same age who is in some ways similar; but the differences are interesting and, to me, unexpected. The French type is even leaner; he is also more elegant, better groomed, and more professional-looking than the Englishman. He is likely to have close-cropped hair and glasses with the thin gold rims. It all fits with being called a "haut fonctionnaire." The English type is more casual, looser in the limb. . . .

Not long ago I was lost before a new kind of face. Or rather, I mistrusted my own reading of it; it was too easy and dismissive. This was a politician from the United States, a man who had been successful in oil or insurance well before he was forty and who now, in his middle forties, had an assured, thrusting, mercantile, tanned, smoothly smiling but tough look. To me the face, the whole manner, was two-dimensional, unmarked. It was like the face of a well-groomed dog. It said only: "Public acquaintance . . . manipulation . . . action"; not: "Friendliness . . . thought . . . feeling." Had such a man, you wondered, ever felt shabby or insecure? Oddly, it was easier to imagine him crying. There was probably within the rhetorics available to him a form of crying that would do. But I was probably wrong, unable to read the signals in a way which got me near his character, which made him three-dimensional, capable of real grief and joy, unpublic. I couldn't easily imagine him in his underwear, and when I did he looked like an advertisement in *Esquire.*

Richard Hoggart
On Culture and Communication

it. No organization can succeed in the longer haul if it is populated by the organizational equivalents of Kamikaze pilots, just as no organization can long succeed if it is peopled by budding Benedict Arnolds.

Although a low level of employee commitment to the organization brings with it problems of an unstable workforce and hampered career opportunities for members, extreme levels of commitment among members, such as one occasionally finds in military units or athletic teams, can result in an organization losing its "flexibility and finding itself burdened with overzealous employees, and it may become vulnerable to a variety of unethical and illegal behavior. In brief, the commonly assumed linear relationship between commitment and desirable consequences should be questioned."[45]

Joined at the Hip: Locals, Cosmopolitans, and Organizational Success.

This digression on localistic co-optation, organizational commitment, and the organizational utility of employee loyalty reflects the traditional, if implicit, view of the literature on cosmopolitanism and localism that the (disloyal) cosmopolitans are the exclusive agents of change, while the (loyal) locals are the last bastions of stability. Increasingly, however, the research indicates that *organizational adaptability can be enhanced by locals*, as well as by cosmopolitans, and that *organizational stability can be enhanced by cosmopolitans*, as well as by locals. This is new.

Gouldner and many of his intellectual progeny implicitly assumed that an employee ultimately had to choose (consciously or not-so-consciously) between cosmopolitanism and localism, and that the strategically managed organization balanced these personality types as its chief means of balancing the need to adapt with the need to routinize. Now the research is suggesting that *both* types are needed to maximize the attainment of *each* objective.

Locals, for example, working with cosmopolitans, increase the chances of successful organizational innovation. A study of hospitals found that those hospitals demonstrating the greatest flair for innovation were characterized by a cosmopolitan professional, such as a physician, *and* a local administrator working together. Less

effective was a combination of two cosmopolitans; their outer-directed needs and ignorance of the local organization resulted in less innovative organizations. The least innovative hospitals were those characterized by a local professional and a local administrator. The researchers concluded that, to maximize organizational innovation, "it is necessary to include the bureaucratic [i.e., local] and professional [i.e., cosmopolitan] perspectives within an organization."[46]

Just as locals can help enhance organizational innovation, cosmopolitans can help develop organizational stability. A study of intercollegiate sports programs in the United States concluded that the inculcation of "intense loyalty" among members of the organization was useful if that loyalty were held by members who also reflected cosmopolitan traits—who were, in short, not only intensely loyal, but also highly sensitive to the task environment, the need to adapt, and professional values. "To the extent that an organization is able to engineer the alignment of individuals' professional goals with those of the organization," it is likelier to enhance *both* organizational stability and innovation.[47] A study of lawyers drew a similar conclusion.[48]

In other words, the best of both worlds is possible: Deep personal commitment to the organization can equate with great personal success, both within the organization and in the marketplace, and deep personal commitment to professionalism and an understanding of the marketplace can equate with great organizational success.

The notion of cosmopolitanism and localism is significant to public administration because of the field's reliance on professionals from many fields. We consider the implications of this development more thoroughly in Chapter 9.

Career Types and Their Political Motivations

A more refined study of the roles bureaucrats play in public organizations was undertaken by Dwaine Marvick.[49] Marvick asked, "what must management do in order to cope with persons having different career perspectives?" and then studied federal administrators to find an answer.

Marvick trisected public bureaucrats by how they perceived their careers, and the style in which they conducted themselves in their agencies. He dubbed these roles institutionalists, specialists, and hybrids.

Institutionalist Perspectives. *Institutionalists* corresponded roughly to Gouldner's locals. As a group, institutionalists believed in their organization, and were relatively high in their demands for organizational advancement and unqualifiedly high in their quest for organizational prestige. They tended not to stress the task-oriented features of their jobs but preferred to emphasize its benefits and had spent most of their careers in government, often in the military. Institutionalists generally were found to be midlevel bureaucrats, encumbered by few family ties, had relatively low educational attainments, and had short job histories—that is, they had changed positions (though had not necessarily advanced) within the government frequently. Institutionalists were very sociable people within the organization and were extremely loyal to it and to their co-workers, optimistic, and complacent.

Specialist Perspectives. *Specialists* were at the opposite end of the spectrum from institutionalists and were similar to Gouldner's cosmopolitans. Unlike institutionalists, who occupied generalized managerial slots, specialists tended to be highly educated professionals. Specialists were not particularly concerned about personal advancement in the organization and had virtually no interest in organizational status rewards and executive positions. What they did want very badly, however, was the freedom to do their own thing, to be in jobs that allowed them to use their professional skills on a daily basis. In terms of career histories, specialists tended to have experience both in public and private bureaucracies and had less military experience than institutionalists. Although they favored working alone and were less likely to be involved in group decisions than institutionalists, specialists had more influence within the organization than did institutionalists. Specialists were by far the most critical of the agency's performance and of bureaucratic methods generally; in this sense, specialists were "manifestly maladjusted" in their working relationships.

Hybrid Perspectives. *Hybrids,* or *politicized experts*, drew their characteristics from both institutionalists and specialists. Like specialists, hybrids were highly educated professionals, were advanced in organizational rank, had experience in both the public and private sectors, and were disinterested in organizational prestige. Like institutionalists, hybrids were very concerned with acquiring executive positions and moving up to higher paying jobs. Interestingly, in this light, hybrids tended to have far heavier family responsibilities than either institutionalists or specialists. Hybrids, like institutionalists, were not especially critical of meetings and similar bureaucratic paraphernalia and were well adjusted to their jobs; like specialists, they were likely to be disgruntled when they felt that they were being distracted from their work. Most importantly, hybrids had no sublimated goals, unlike either of the other two types. Hybrids' goals were explicit and personal, and they were quite amenable to using either place or skill criteria to advance their goals.

Career Types: Perils and Potentialities. All three groups possess perils and potentialities for public organizations. Institutionalists can become rule-oriented and inflexible; their sociability can degenerate into cliquishness, their loyalty into recalcitrance to change, and they resist performance evaluation along quantitative, measurable scales. Yet, institutionalists provide the bureaucracy with genuine organizational stability and furnish the needed lubrication among interpersonal relationships in the agency.

Specialists tend to displace the agency's goals because their individual, professional projects are more important to them than the organization's welfare, and this propensity can diminish organizational performance. Moreover, their highly critical cast and lack of place commitment can cause sinking morale, disharmony, and high rates of turnover. Yet, when properly placed, specialists can get things done in a most effective way, and they are not inclined to compete politically with other members of the bureaucracy.

Hybrids bring the most dangers and benefits to the organization. Their chief danger lies in their instability. Hybrids are fair-weather friends, "superficial and showy performers." Their lack of both place and skill commitments render them unpredictable. Yet, hybrids are the most likely people to assess accurately and holistically the dynamics and problems of the organization. Unlike the other two groups, they possess no sublimated personal needs that might interfere with their realistic evaluation of the organization and where it is going. Nevertheless, hybrids must be watched, for they are prone to change the organization purely for their own self-betterment.

What is notable about Marvick's typology is that his classifications associate with variables that can be found in any personnel file—educational attainments, job histories, family responsibilities, and so on. This is useful administrative knowledge.

Darwinism and the Organizational Personality

There is, at least, one other item that, if not commonly found in the typical personnel file, is information that could be easily obtained and which yields genuine predictability about how a person is likely to behave in an organizational setting. That item is the order of the person's birth relative to his or her siblings.

In an important book,[50] Frank Sulloway provides massive statistical evidence that birth order is the primary factor in determining a person's propensity to rebel—or, to phrase it another way, to engage in revolutionary creativity. To come to this conclusion, Sulloway applied multivariate analysis to more than 7,000 historical figures, including those at the center of nearly 4,000 scientific revolutions; the almost 900 members of the National Convention that governed France at the height of the French Revolution; some 700 people who led the Protestant Reformation; and the men and women who took part in sixty-one American reform movements. All this resulted over a million "biographical data points" covering some 500 years of history.

Those who are "firstborns" in a family identify with power and strength, and, when "laterborns" enter into the family picture, use their power, strength (and size), to defend their position in the family structure. Firstborns tend to be more jealous, aggressive, defensive, and confident than laterborns and are overrepresented among Nobel laureates and political leaders. Winston Churchill, Ayn Rand, George Washington, and Rush Limbaugh are firstborns.

Laterborns (and firstborns who had deep conflicts with their parents), by contrast, tend to identify with fellow underdogs, question authority and the status quo, be more open, imaginative, independent, generous, and liberal than their firstborn siblings. Laterborns are disproportionately represented among explorers, rebels, and heretics. Joan of Arc, Karl Marx, Vladimir Lenin, Thomas Jefferson, Jean Jacques Rousseau, and Bill Gates are laterborns.

Why is this? The answer is biological and Darwinian: Childhood is the search for a stable niche in the family structure, just as evolution is the result of the cell's search for a stable niche in nature. Both processes pertain to Charles Darwin's "principle of divergence," which holds that diversification (whether in the family or in nature) is a tactic that helps the individual minimize competition with other individuals for scarce resources. Therefore, it "pays" firstborns to be conservers and protective of all the love and rewards that they (once) were receiving on an exclusive basis in their families, just as it "pays" laterborns to seek new ways of gaining entry to that love and those rewards. The less that firstborns and laterborns compete in this process (in other words, the less "like" firstborns that laterborns are), the greater the probability that laterborns will gain love and rewards in the family; "successful" laterborns are those who have found and occupied a niche (that is, a place which is noncompetitive with and unthreatening to firstborns) in the family structure.

Of course, birth order is not an infallible method of detecting rebellious tendencies in a person. Shy firstborns, for example, are more likely than are extroverted firstborns to be open to new experiences (shy firstborns are more reflective than are extroverts), whereas shy laterborns are more likely to be less confident about their rebellious views than are extroverted laterborns. Nevertheless, birth order is the major determining factor in explaining why some people protect the establishment and other rebel against it: later-borns are, literally, "born to rebel."

And both those who conserve the status quo and those who revolt creatively against it often are leaders, a type of organizational actor that we consider next.

Leadership in Organizations

Leadership "is an influence relationship among leaders and followers who intend real change that reflect their mutual purposes."[51] We begin our discussion of organizational leadership by explaining the differences between administration and leadership.

Administration or Leadership?

The dilemma of discerning the differences between leadership and administration has been around for some time.

Increasingly, it is becoming recognized that leadership and administration are of equal importance to the success of organizations. And—again increasingly—*leadership* is seen as *dealing with change*, whereas *administration* is viewed as *coping with complexity*.

One leadership researcher who does a particularly good job in this regard argues that leadership and management are of equal importance to the organization because "each system of action involves deciding what needs to be done, . . . and then trying to insure that those people actually do the job. But each accomplishes these three tasks in different ways."[52] *Leadership's* way of accomplishing these tasks is *to set a direction*—create a vision—for the organization; *align people* in a way that they can implement leadership's vision and *communicate* that vision to them; and *motivate* and *inspire* people to attain the vision—in other words, *keep them moving in the right direction.* It is the responsibility of *management* to *plan* and *budget* for the direction set by leadership; *organize* and *staff*—create the organizational structure—to implement the plan; and *control activities* and *solve problems* in achieving the plan.

The relative importance of these functions of leadership and administration to the organization depends on the conditions of the time. In periods of slow change and a placid environment, management is of greater significance; in times of rapid change and a turbulent environment, leadership is. "A peace time army can usually survive with good . . . management up and down the hierarchy. . . . A war time army, however, needs competent leadership at all levels. No one yet has figured out how to manage people effectively into battle; they must be led."[53]

Another leadership scholar sums up the role of administration and management in leadership theory rather well: "If we cannot manage effectively without leading, then certainly there is no fundamental distinction between leadership and management. . . . Management, pure and simple, is necessary and essential to the good life as we have come to experience it, and as such it has as much going for it as leadership does."[54]

Leaders at the Top: Boards of Directors

Almost all organizations are controlled by small groups of people who make policy and set their organization's direction. These groups are known generically as *boards of directors*, and the more able board members are, the more likely that the organization that they head will exhibit high performance.[55] Boards are, or at least can be, crucial to organization success or failure.

Depending on the sector, boards exhibits quite different characteristics and accord significantly different degrees of power to the chief executive officers (CEO) who report to them. We consider these traits in turn.

The Private-Sector Board. We should note up front that there is big and bodacious fact about private-sector boards that is rarely, if ever, present in public- and nonprofit-sector boards. Corporate board directors get paid for their service. For the largest corporations, this pay is significant and is nearing, on average, $200,000 annually.[56] This compensation likely accounts for a number of behaviors among board directors that are unique to the private sector.

Without questions, corporate boards of directors accord wide powers to their chief executive officers. In fact, careful, multiyear studies have found that CEOs often exercise formidable power over their boards. The practice of chief executive officers chairing their own boards of directors is "widespread,"[57] and perhaps as many as four-fifths of corporate CEOs chair their own boards.[58] Many CEOs are empowered to appoint some or all of their board's members; not infrequently, chief executive officers will appoint themselves and their own employees to the boards to which they ostensibly report.[59] Diversity rarely is a factor in these appointments, perhaps because those boards whose members are "demographically similar to the firm's CEO" are more likely to be dominated by the chief executive officer and to "result in more generous CEO compensation contracts."[60]

Should a director move to limit the power of the company's chief executive officer, no matter how appropriately, ostracism is the consequence. One study of more than a thousand board directors found that when directors pushed to implement one of four actions (all of which are recommended by the Securities and Exchange Commission as useful in protecting stockholders' interests) to restrain their CEO's authority, they experienced "social distancing" by members of other boards on which they also served.[61]

Analyses consistently show that when company CEOs are relatively powerful, they can keep their jobs, scapegoat underlings, and raise their own salaries and bonuses even as their companies' performance sags.[62] For example, in 2005 the bankrupt W. R. Grace & Co. hired a new CEO who had, as part of his compensation package, a $1.75 million "Chapter 11 emergence bonus" that he was guaranteed *whether or not* the company emerged from bankruptcy.[63]

Such power might help explain why the ratio between the average wage of the rank-and-file worker in the American private sector and the average compensation of his or her chief executive officer soared from 1 to 42 to 1 to 531 over twenty years.[64] Annual CEO compensation at the top companies averages around $10 million.[65]

The Public-Sector Board. As we discussed in Chapter 1, this kind of executive power can occur in the public sector, too, and the documented dominance of school superintendents over school boards and the authority of city managers in dealing with city councils are testaments to the control that public executives can exercise over the boards to which they nominally report. But such power seems much less easily acquired in an environment in which public executives have little if any control over the selection of board members. A significant portion of public executives reports to boards of directors, such as most superintendents of education, parole officers, presidents of colleges and universities, executive directors of special districts and government corporations, the heads of almost all regulatory agencies, and (in effect) county and city managers in counties and cities with the council-manager form of government. These boards are appointed by legislatures or elected chief executives, or are elected directly by the people.

Many public-sector boards, in contrast to those in the private sector, seem to be composed disproportionately of energetic and myopic busy bodies (although, as we note in Chapter 11, the laidback boards of public authorities appear to be quite the opposite), who are far more consumed with the details of management than with the mission of their government. A five-year study of all the school boards in West Virginia, for example, found that they spent an astonishing 54 percent of their time on administration and only 3 percent on policy and oversight—which should be the sole responsibilities of boards.[66] A review of research on school boards concluded that perhaps the "greatest problem . . . is their tendency to micromanage and become bogged down in minutiae."[67]

Studies find that less than a third (the lowest response for any item tested) of both city manager and city council members give their councils a high rating for "establishing long term goals . . . and addressing real problems in the city." Council members "are ambivalent about making policy decisions . . . and instead want to expand their activity . . . in administrative matters," which, in fact, they are doing. Over time, council members are "less involved in mission . . . and more involved in administration than previously."[68]

A national survey of public-sector boards of all types concluded that nearly two-fifths of their members believed that their primary duties were either management or both management and policymaking, as opposed to just policymaking; "board governance is a prominent part of public administration in the American system of government, and it is an unusually intrusive part for public administrators who report to boards."[69]

The Independent-Sector Board. Almost all nonprofit organizations are headed by boards, and they seem to share an odd amalgam of the characteristics of corporate and public boards of directors.

As with corporate boards, independent boards tend to cede greater power to their chief executive officers than do public boards. The executive directors of nonprofit boards often serve as board members, too (emulating the corporate board but not the public one), and, when they do, their salaries are higher than when they do not serve on the board. Unsurprisingly, executive directors who serve on their boards spend much more time raising funds (perhaps to assure their higher salaries) than they do managing the programs that they were hired to manage.[70]

These kinds of arrangements can lead to precisely the same sorts of conflicts of interest that are experienced in private-sector boards. For example, many university boards have found themselves mired in questionable business deals involving their board members, such as the university foundation board that engaged in more than $30 million in deals with companies that had ties with twenty-seven of its fifty-five trustees.[71]

As with private-sector CEOs, the executive directors of nonprofit organizations sometimes receive a remarkable level of largesse from their boards, such as the New York foundation that, over just five years, tripled its president's salary to where it was nearing $1 million, or the family foundation in Chicago that, over five years, paid two family members more than $1 million, but donated only $175,000 to charities.[72] Providing executive directors and other officers with large, interest-free loans and mortgages appears to be a growing practice by nonprofit boards, and these loans total in the million of dollars.[73] As a result of incidences such as these, some prestigious independent-sector associations have called upon nonprofit organizations to follow the same strictures that Congress has imposed on corporate governance.[74]

In other ways, however, third-sector boards reflect patterns found on public boards, and these patterns may be attributable to executive directors who, by and large, are less dominant over their boards than are corporate CEOs. In a study of the boards of directors of 1,200 Canadian nonprofit organizations, it was found that, with few exceptions, the personal characteristics of board members determined who ran the organization.[75] When nonprofit boards have few women, but many older, prestigious, and well-educated men as members, the executive director or board chair calls most of the shots; high-status old men seem to associate with a lack of interest in the organization's mission, effectively ceding power to others. On the other hand, when third-sector boards have a relatively large number of women, younger members, less-educated members, and members who have high levels of commitment to the mission, the board members share power among themselves and work as an effective team.

This research on the boards of nonprofit organizations suggests that third-sector organizations can gain more dynamic board leadership for themselves if their board members are female (less than a fourth of the board members of nonprofit organizations are women[76]), young, less educated and professionally trained, and low on prestige but high on commitment.

Do Organizations Need Leaders?

Do organizations actually need these executives? Are we being conned by flashy organizational leaders whose huge and unprecedented salaries frequently go up even as the performance of the organizations that they lead goes down?

The Leadership Con? In addressing these questions, we shall focus on a specific type of leader: the "hierarchical leader." *Hierarchical leaders* are chief executive officers and persons who hold other top administrative positions in the organization's hierarchy. As our section on leadership unfolds, we shall see that not all high-level executives are leaders, and not all leaders are high-level executives. So it is important to keep in mind that, in this discussion, we are attempting to answer the question, Do organizations need *hierarchical* leaders, or leaders who are identified as leaders solely because they occupy top executive positions in the organization?

At least one writer has forcefully argued that not only do organizations not need hierarchical leaders, but also that top executives actually are counterproductive to effective organizations.[77] Executives should be exorcized from organizations altogether! Organizational leaders paramountly are committed to keeping their cushy jobs.

Their style is one of personal aloofness, an unwavering eye, a firm handshake, and a winning smile, all of which are meant to convey the message that the executive is important. They enforce excessively rigid rules that stress subservience, obedience, and loyalty (to the leaders) among members of the organization. These tactics are all designed to conceal the absence of any useful skills or knowledge on the part of the organization's executives, and to justify their existence in the organization. One is reminded, after reading these techniques of executive survival, of Mel Brooks's comment in his role as the governor in *Blazing Saddles*: "Gentlemen, we've got to protect our phony baloney jobs here!"

Leaders as Obstructionists.   If executives are such useless sycophants and con artists, then how do organizations get things done? The answer: Those who get things done in organizations are those who have specialized knowledge and skills (typically professionals) that are crucial to the achievement of organizational objectives; examples include scientists, accountants, attorneys, and professors. When it comes to getting things done, executives merely obstruct or even stymie the professionals and other specialists.

That often-heard call to corporate arms trumpeted by American business people—"Lead, follow, or get out of the way!"—is the classic dramaturgical defense by the bureaucrats of their privileged positions. But, in reality, says this critique, we do not need leaders; we do not need followers; we need only that leaders and their

followers get out of the way, so that the specialists can get on with it. In many ways, this perspective is a theoretical extension (but not one based on data) of the research reviewed earlier on cosmopolitans (who would be the equivalent of specialists) and locals (some of whom would be hierarchical leaders).

The preceding polemic frames the question. But is it possible that organizations really do not need (or would even be better off without) chief executives and top administrators?

The Limits of Leadership.   Well, yes, although the evidence indicates that organizations may not need chief executives only under highly unusual circumstances. Of greater importance, perhaps, and as we noted in the preceding chapter, "human choice" seems to be less a factor in charting the course of an organization (but especially of a public organization) than does "environmental determinism," and it is organizational leaders who make (at least in theory) the most important human choices for their organizations. The heavy impact of the task environment does, in fact, limit leadership.

There is a scholarly debate of long standing, for example, about the real power of governors to effect change in their states, with one wing contending that "there is little evidence that a governor's formal powers significantly affect policy outcomes in the fifty states. . . . [Policy] differences are attributable largely to the impact of economic development rather than to the governor's power."[78] An analysis of the budgets of big American cities over seventeen years concluded that most of the variance in urban budget allocations was attributable to characteristics in the cities themselves, rather than to the entry of new mayors.[79] Another empirical study concluded that hierarchical leadership "is not always very necessary, especially if community members do not 'need' a leader in order to be motivated to make their contribution. . . . In some situations, especially where the work or membership is intrinsically satisfying and work groups are cohesive, the presence of leader is redundant."[80]

The private sector is hardly immune in this respect, and studies of private organizations yield comparable findings. Multiyear research on large corporations found that corporate performance could be correlated far more satisfactorily with the effects of time, type of industry, and traits of specific companies than with changes in the chief executive officers of these firms.[81] A study of how baseball clubs performed over fifty-three years found that the best predictor of team performance was not a new manager, but how well the team had performed in prior years: "Although managerial succession is often precipitated by inadequate organizational performance, a change of managers typically has only a small impact on organizational performance."[82]

Leadership in Context. In a very real sense, however, these analyses obscure a fundamental point, which is that leaders can and do have an impact on their organizations, despite the intrusiveness of environmental forces. The real question is: How much impact? An expert on the American governor expresses this query within the context of state policymaking: The proponents of environmental determinism "emphasize the fact that the economic conditions in a given state at a particular time may set the parameters within which the policy process operates. However, these studies [of governors' impact on state policy] do not explain the process itself. The basic question of policy formation still remains: Who gets what, when, and where . . . ?"[83]

A thorough study of thirty-two colleges and universities and their presidents conducted over five years provides some real insight on our question. The researchers delineated four presidential "types." Presidents who initiated action and "connected" with their campuses typically were found at stable institutions, whereas presidents who reacted to events and were "distant" from their campuses were largely found at unstable institutions. These patterns accounted for twenty-seven of the thirty-two institutions and their presidents.

The remaining five presidents, however, could not be fitted into this construct, or, to quote the study,

> could not be associated with a dominant presidential type. . . . [These presidents] preside over institutions that are among the smallest in the sample. . . . [Few, if any,] current campus issues . . . emerged.

In their own interviews, these five presidents presented few or no clear commitments, and they did not describe themselves as championing specific causes or moving on any clear-cut issues. In sum, unlike the other sample presidents, it was difficult to identify what was important to these five. Moreover, their campuses were quiet and relatively uneventful, giving the impression of running "on automatic." . . . These five institutions point to a fifth presidential type, perhaps a 'non-type,' representing campuses that *do not need* their presidential leaders.[84]

So there are organizations that do not seem to "need" hierarchical leaders, or top executives. But these organizations do not strike one as particularly dynamic and appear to be few in number, uneventful, small, and smug; correspondingly, their chief executive officers seem to be unvisionary, uncommitted, bored—and quite possibly extraneous. Overwhelmingly, however, most organizational leaders do have an impact on their organization, and that impact can, depending upon the circumstances, range from the salvation of the organization to its destruction.[85]

The Evolution of Leadership Theory: Defining Leadership for the Times

Whether leaders and executives are needed or not, it is leadership that has captured the energies of researchers.

The Leadership Literature: From Trickle to Torrent

Those energies appear to be boundless, for the resultant writings are vast. One encyclopedic survey of this literature cites more than 7,800 studies on leadership.[86]

In fact, with each passing decade, the number of books and articles about leadership appears to roughly double from the preceding decade.[87] The United States is the frothing fount for most of this gusher, apparently because Americans are unusually enamored with the notion of leadership. "In America, leadership has become something of a cult concept."[88]

trust /feelings of loyalty

Not so in other countries. The French, for example, have no word that translates well as "leadership" (the French word for leader is *chef*), and are reduced, in a culture that officially fights the anglicization of its language, to referring to *le leadership* (*Zut, alors!*). Germans, Italians, Spaniards, and some Latin Americans carry some embarrassing fascist baggage in their words for leader—*führer* in German, *duce* in Italian, and *caudillo* in Spanish—which may explain their current intellectual disinclination to dwell on leadership.

The Leader as an Individual, 1910–1940

Leadership research focused in its early years on the leader as an individual.

Leadership: The Classical View.   As we noted in Chapter 3, the classical view of administrative humanity stresses the rational behavior of bureaucrats, whether this behavior is cast in economic, systemic, or physical terms. But when these same serious writers in the classical tradition cast their eye on a particular type of administrative human—the leader—their hearts beat aflutter. Rationality goes out the window and romance, drama, and mythic heroes stride in. No longer are we talking about the limitless capacities of clerks to cower and laborers to labor, but of dizzying social forces that must be brought to heel by leaders possessing transcendent qualities. "True leaders" (for the classical writers allowed for the possibility that charlatans could occupy leadership positions), in this perspective, are different; it is their destiny to command.

It was during this classical period in the evolution of leadership theory that the dominant definitions of leadership emphasized authority, control, and the centralization of power.[89] A conference on leadership held in 1927 summed up this emphasis by defining *leadership*, in notably Teutonic terminology, as "the ability to impress the will of the leader on those led and induce obedience, respect, loyalty, and cooperation."[90]

Leadership Traits.   Perhaps it was because of this kind of definition, which was popular among the early researchers on leadership, that there

emerged from the classical writings a focus on leadership "traits." The point of much of the research in this phase was to identify those unusual features of the person that were associated with leadership. Researchers would score and compare "leaders" (who often were identified by the office that they held in the organization) with "followers" on such dimensions as dominance, sensitivity, physical appearance, moodiness, masculinity, and other traits that were thought to relate to leadership.

An effort undertaken in 1948 to make some sense of these trait studies, which reviewed more than 120 of them, found that they held no particular pattern. What was needed was research that matched the personality traits of leaders with the traits of his or her followers—in other words, with the characteristics of a particular group.[91]

Leadership Behaviors.   Beginning in the 1940s, leadership theorists developed two major clusters of behaviors that they believed were useful (if for different reasons) to leaders in providing leadership, and these clusters have had a lasting impact on leadership theory.[92] One cluster was that of *consideration behaviors* that related to interpersonal warmth, concern for the feelings of subordinates, and a participative/communicative style of leadership. The second cluster of behaviors was *task behaviors.* This grouping stressed such behaviors as directness, obtaining task-related feedback, and achieving goals.

As a result of the research on leadership traits and leadership behaviors in particular, the kinds of definitions that tended to dominate leadership studies in the 1930s and 1940s emphasized both individual traits and group characteristics. Leadership was seen as a kind of social process. Eventually, this viewpoint evolved into a focus on the leader and the small group.

The Leader and the Small Group, 1940–1970

Throughout the 1940s and 1950s, the focus of leadership theory on the small group was preeminent. By the 1960s, the group-oriented approach toward leadership was dividing along two major branches. One was (and is) the "contingency" approach, and the other is the "transactional" approach. Both are highly interrelated.

Ҟ Contingency Approaches. The contingency approach to the study of organizational leadership reflects mainstream thinking in organization theory generally: managers must deal with *contingencies*—that is, unexpected or unintended events or possibilities—which can occur as a result of any number of factors, such as the organizational environment, new technologies, or different personalities. Fred Fiedler did much of the original work in contingency theory.[93]

Fiedler focused on how much a group trusted its leader. Fiedler described a *high-control* situation as one in which a leader had the trust of his or her followers, there was a clear task structure, and the leader had a high level of power to reward and punish. A situation of *moderate control* occurred when the task structure was ambivalent or the group was uncooperative. A *low-control* situation was one in which followers were not supportive of the leader, the nature of the task was unclear, and the leader's authority to dispense rewards and punishments was ambiguous.

In a high-control situation, a task-motivated leader functioned quite well. Task-motivated leaders were less effective in a moderate control situation because they frequently became anxious and moved, often inappropriately, to a quick solution; typically, they were critical and punitive toward their followers. In these moderate-control situations, a relationship-motivated leader was found to be more effective. In a low-control situation, which often amounts to a crisis situation, the task-motivated leader once again surfaces as the appropriate leader type.

Although Fiedler's contingency model has been the subject of some controversy, at least one review of empirical tests given over the years that used the contingency model found that the predictions generated by the model were largely accurate.[94]

Ҟ Transactional Approaches. A second major component of the small-group approach to leadership is transactional analysis. Unlike the contingency models, which concentrate only on the problems confronting the leader in dealing with a small group, *transactional approaches* also analyze the leader's subordinates and the problems confronting them. In other words, what kind of transactions, or exchanges, occur between and among leaders and followers that facilitate or impair both the leader's and the group's effectiveness?

Transactional approaches accept that organizational "culture affects leadership as much as leadership affects culture. . . . there is a constant interplay between culture and leadership."[95] An analysis of more than a hundred corporations found that corporate "culture matters most": Employees who worked for the same company, no matter what their jobs, were 30 percent more likely to exhibit similar leadership competencies than were employees who had the identical job, but who worked in different companies.[96]

Path-goal theory is an important feature of the transactional literature on leadership. Researchers have found that consideration behavior (the "path" in this case) by a leader is most effective (the "goal") when a follower's job is distasteful or boring, whereas, by contrast, structuring or task-oriented behavior by the leader is most effective when a subordinate's job is unstructured.[97] One study found that, when group leaders used consideration behaviors in their decision making (that is, solicited and used advice from members of the groups), the groups' "perceptions of procedural fairness" increased, and, as a result, members' "commitment to the decision, attachment to the group, and trust in its leader" also increased.[98]

Studies in the path-goal tradition also have found that subordinates who are highly dogmatic relate better to task-oriented leaders, whereas followers who are more open respond more readily to leaders who display consideration.[99] A similar investigation found that subordinates who showed a high need for personal growth in their jobs did not like a structured, task-oriented approach under any conditions, even when the task at hand was quite unstructured. By contrast, followers who showed relatively low levels of need for personal growth did not respond to consideration behaviors on the part of a leader; this seemed to be the case because these kinds of subordinates were happy in what amounted to be routine, boring work.[100]

The Leader and the Organization, 1980–Present

By the mid-1960s, there were signs that leadership researchers were moving away from the small group end and taking on what leadership meant in terms of the larger organization. Perhaps the roots of the movement can be traced to the efforts made to take Fiedler's contingency model of leadership and to expand it to the larger organizational setting.[101]

Transformation and Charisma.   Central to this expansion was James MacGregor Burns' idea of *transformational leadership*, which occurred "when one or more persons engage with others in such a way that leaders and followers raise one another to higher levels of motivation and morality."[102] The 1980s saw a movement that extended the concept of transformational leadership to, in many ways, a resurrection of Weber's notion of charisma. Max was back. *Charismatic leaders* are those "who by force of their personal abilities are capable of having a profound and extraordinary effect on followers. . . . [and charisma] is usually reserved for leaders who by their influence are able to cause followers to accomplish outstanding feats."[103]

In contrast to a non-charismatic leader, a charismatic leader is one who is opposed to the status quo, possesses an "idealized vision" of the future, incurs a great personal risk and cost, is expert in using unconventional means to transcend the existing order, is far more sensitive to the task environment, articulates goals strongly, is elitist, entrepreneurial, and can transform people in a way that they become committed to the radical changes he or she advocates.[104]

Does charisma work? The evidence is mixed.

On the one hand, a careful study of thirty-nine presidents of the United States (from George Washington through Ronald Reagan) concluded that "personality and charisma do make a difference" in presidential performance.[105] Research on thirteen, previously socialist, countries that were in the process of transforming their economies to a free-market footing concluded that those nations that were most successful had "strong leadership from executives with strong

commitment, a vision of where they would like to go, and a willingness to take risks."[106]

On the other hand, charisma can have only a negligible impact. An analysis of more than 200 middle- and upper-middle managers in the Canadian public service found that that charismatic leaders bore only a scant relationship to the motivation of followers, and was "not significantly related to unit performance."[107]

The Power Bases of Leadership.   In contrast to contingency and transactional approaches to leadership, the transformational approach (including charismatic approaches) is based on a recognition that power exists in organizations; consequently, the role of the group in legitimizing leaders may be less salient.

Researchers have identified seven bases of social power that support leaders. They are *control over information and the work environment; reward power*, or the leader's ability to positively recognize another; *coercive power*, or the opposite of reward power, which is the leader's capacity to punish; *legitimate power*, or the acceptance of the leader by others; *referent power*, or the personal attraction that a leader holds for others; *charisma*, or the personal ability and will to exert great change; and *expert power*, which refers to the perception that the leader is knowledgeable.[108]

Control over information and the work environment, and the powers of reward, coercion, and legitimacy can be seen as variations of "position power."[109] Weber's "traditional" and "legal/rational leaders," Mooney and Reiley's "titular leaders" and "true organizers," and much of the classical theory of leadership relates to a positional power base.

Referent power, charisma, and expert power can be grouped under "personal power."[110] There are some classical elements that are covered here, notably Weber's concept of charisma, but, for the most part, the small-group theories are the theories of leadership which relate to personal power bases. This is because the small-group theories almost all pertain to the leader's interactions with others.

The Power Bases of Public Leadership.   Positional power bases are less available to the leaders of public organizations than of private ones. As a consequence, charismatic leaders actually may be more common in public organizations than in private ones, simply because leaders of public organizations must rely more heavily on their own personalities to transform organizations. An intriguing analysis of ten public and thirty-five private organizations in New York found that the leaders of the public organizations had a very low level of control over some important positional power bases of leadership, notably reward power, coercive power, and legitimate power, whereas the leaders of private organizations had a very high level of control over these power bases. Public leaders, therefore, had to depend on their personal power bases to significantly change their organizations, and members of these organizations perceived their leaders to be far more inspirational and personally involved with them than did followers in private organizations.[111]

As this research implies, administrative leaders in government are more constrained than are private ones. One study of public and private leaders found that the leaders' subordinates and superiors, and the leaders themselves, believed that leaders in the public sector had considerably less discretion and authority to lead than did their private-sector counterparts.[112]

Leading the Public Organization

As one might infer from our review of the literature of organization theory in this and the preceding two chapters, leading the public agency represents a different set of challenges than does leading the private corporation. In fact, the two sectors even define successful leadership in starkly opposite terms.

Defining Successful Leadership

To appreciate effective public leadership, it is useful to first understand how the private sector defines successful leadership.

Successful Private Leadership. A good corporate leader is unlawful, unhelpful, and directive.

A careful study of the leaders of a large state government agency and a *Fortune* 10 manufacturing firm found that private-sector leaders were not seen as particularly successful by their superiors and subordinates when they monitored subordinates for legal compliance, and when they provided assistance to subordinates (indeed, even *subordinates* felt that their leaders' mentoring of them did not add to their leaders' luster). When corporate leaders emphasized directing and coordinating their company, however, their superiors and subordinates perceived them as much more effective.[113]

Successful Public Leadership. In stark contrast to the private sector, successful leadership in the public sector involves obeying the law, helping others, and letting employees do their own thing.

When government leaders stressed directing and coordinating their agency, their superiors and subordinates perceived then as much less effective. Government leaders were viewed as successful by both their superiors and their subordinates when they monitored their subordinates' work closely for compliance with laws and regulations, and when they reached out to lend a helping hand to their fellow workers to assist them in achieving their objectives.[114]

Leadership as Organizational Success. Or Not

Public executives, it appears, are seen as successful when leadership is perceived in human terms, and, unlike private executives, they are viewed as less successful when leadership is cast in organizational terms.

Research confirms this distinction, and leaders themselves in the two sectors display deep differences in how they define their own success. Leaders in the business world placed great emphasis on the achievement of organizational goals as a measure of their own effectiveness. By contrast, public leaders did not perceive that there was much of a match between their leadership abilities and actually accomplishing their agency's goals.[115]

Helping fellow employees, however, is exceptionally important to public-sector leaders. A study of 242 city managers found that an astounding 78 percent of the city managers had a "primary leadership style" (out of four possible styles) that was "high supportive and low directed behavior."[116] Public executives, it would seem, are deeply committed to mentoring coworkers and giving them the freedom to grow and mature in their jobs. Moreover, their coworkers respond very favorably to this treatment.[117]

This distinction may be ascribed to the fact that, as research consistently demonstrates, goals are considerably less focused in the public sector than in the private one,[118] and agency missions are saturated by "pervasive vagueness."[119] When organizational success itself cannot be readily understood, a condition that is common in the public sector, then leadership's success, when defined in organizational terms, is far less tenable. Hence, alternative definitions are sought and, in the public sector, the definition of effective leadership tilts toward one of effectively helping others.

Public Leadership: Vision, Communication, Work

The literature of organizational leadership can be reduced to a practical formula for the public administrator: Leadership equals vision, communication, and hard work.[120] Certainly this formula reflects the research that we have reviewed here. But how well does it work in the public sector?

Vision as Vexation.   Vision—"the presentation of an alternative future to the status quo"[121]—is not all that easily formed in the public sector, where both the status quo and the agency's future are legislated. Perhaps of greater importance, public agencies, at least at the federal level, are increasingly likely to be headed by short-term political appointees,[122] and rarely are such men and women visionaries.

Career public administrators, by contrast, often do have a vision for their agency but are frequently fated to be "number twos," not "number ones." "And 'number twos' do not have visions, or at least, do not go around shouting about them."[123]

Communication as Conundrum.   Communicating the vision can also be more difficult in the public sector than in the private one. Not only does the "number two" phenomenon impair communication, but so does much of the traditional lore of the public administrator—for instance, the need to be "neutral," to be "removed from politics" (and politics are, in essence, communication), and, to recall Louis Brownlow's famous dictum, to cultivate "a passion for anonymity."[124] These values have not enhanced the propensity of leaders of public organizations to communicate their vision of an alternative future, although many public administrators nonetheless have done so, and quite effectively.[125]

Work as Passion.   The third component of leadership is hard work, and here many public administrators excel, in part because public administration is intrinsically demanding and inspiring. Consider the example of James Forrestal, who, when secretary of defense, "worked with his staff seven days straight. When he left his office at 10:30 P.M. on Sunday, he told them to have a nice weekend."[126]

Vision, communication, work. These are the elements of leadership, irrespective of sector, public or private. Nevertheless, as with other facets of public organizations, the chore of administrative leadership in the public sector seems to be more challenging and difficult than in the corporate world.

In Part II, we reviewed the increasingly turbulent organizations that public administrators are charged with managing. In Part III, we review the methods that public administrators use to do that managing.

Notes

1. See James F. Guyot, "Government Bureaucrats *Are* Different," *Public Administration Review* 22 (December 1962), pp. 195, 202; James R. Rawls and Oscar T. Nelson, Jr., "Characteristics Associated with Preferences for Certain Managerial Positions," *Psychological Reports* 36 (June 1975), pp. 911–988; James R. Rawls, Robert A. Ulrich, and Oscar T. Nelson, "A Comparison of Managers Entering or Reentering the Profit and Nonprofit Sectors," *Academy of Management*

Journal 18 (September 1975), pp. 616–622; and Warren H. Schmidt and Barry Z. Posner, "Values and Expectations of City Managers in California," *Public Administration Review* 47 (September/October 1987), pp. 404–409; Kuo-Tsai Lion and Ronald C. Nyhan, "Dimensions of Organizational Commitment in the Public Sector: An Empirical Assessment," *Public Administration Quarterly* 18 (Spring 1994), p. 112; B. S. Young, S. Worchel, and D. J. Woehr, "Organizational Commitment Among Public Service Employees," *Public Personnel Management* 27 (Fall 1998), pp. 339–348; Hal G. Rainey, "Reward Preferences Among Public and Private Managers: In Search of the Service Ethic," *American Review of Public Administration* 16 (Winter 1982), p. 290; Dennis Wittmer, "Serving the People or Serving for Pay: Reward Preferences Among Government, Hybrid Sector, and Business Managers," *Public Productivity and Management Review* 14 (Summer 1991), pp. 369–383; J. Norman Baldwin, "Public Versus Private Employees: Debunking Stereotypes," *Review of Public Personnel Administration* 11 (Fall 1990–Spring 1991), p. 7; R. Hartman and A. Weber, *The Rewards of Public Service* (Washington, DC: Brookings Institution, 1980); Gene A. Brewer, "Work Motivation in the Senior Executive Service: Testing the High Performance Job Theory," *Journal of Public Administration Research and Theory* 10 (July 2000), pp. 531–550; Princeton Survey Research Associates and the Brookings Institution, *Health of the Public Service* (Washington, DC: Authors, 2001), http://www.brook.edu; and Leonard Bright, "Public Employees with High Levels of Public Service Motivation: Who Are They, Where Are They, and What Do They Want," *Review of Public Personnel Administration* 25 (June 2005), pp. 138–154. When one or more of these articles is particularly pertinent to making a point in the text, we shall cite it, or them, specifically.

2. Bright, "Public Employees with High Levels of Public Service Motivation," pp. 148–150.
3. Brookings Institution, *Winning the Talent War: New Brookings Survey Finds the Nonprofit Sector Has the Most Dedicated Workforce* (Washington DC: Author, 2002), p. 2. This was a survey of 1,041 nonprofit workers conducted in late 2001 and early 2002. The paper compares these finding with surveys of 1,051 federal and 1,005 private-sector employees that were conducted at approximately the same time.
4. Wittmer, "Serving the People or Serving for Pay," p. 379.
5. Princeton Survey Research Associates and the Brookings Institution, *Health of the Public Service*, Q8 and sources in note 1.
6. Bright, "Public Employees with High Levels of Public Service Motivation," pp. 138–154. This was a study of 349 responding employees in twelve major departments in a large county government in Oregon.
7. Peter D. Hart Research, *Calling Young People to Government Service: From "Ask Not . . ." to "Not Asked"* (Washington, DC: Council for Excellence in Government, 2004), p. 2. Figures are for 2004.
8. Princeton Survey Research Associates and the Brookings Institution, *Health of the Public Service*, Q8. Figures are for 2001.
9. Gene A. Brewer, "Building Social Capital: Attitudes and Behavior of Public Servants," *Journal of Public Administration Research and Theory* 13 (January 2003), pp. 5–20. The quotation is on p. 5. The data for the analysis were drawn from the 1996 American National Election Study conducted at the University of Michigan, which is "the longest-running social science survey in the world" (p. 13).
10. Paul C. Light, "The Content of Their Character: The State of the Nonprofit Workforce," *Nonprofit Quarterly* 9 (Fall 2002), p. 11. This was the same survey, cited earlier, that was conducted by the Brookings Institution, *Winning the Talent War*. Figures are for 2001–2002.
11. Brookings Institution, *Winning the Talent War*, p. 2. Figures are for 2001–2002.
12. Among the major contributors to the psychology of adult development are Carl G. Jung, *The Integration of Personality* (London: Kegan Paul, Ltd., 1940); Erik Erikson, *Childhood and Society* (New York: Norton, 1950); Daniel J. Levinson et al., *The Seasons of a Man's Life* (New York: Alfred A. Knopf, 1978); Roger Gould, *Transformations: Growth and Change in Adult Life* (New York: Simon and Schuster, 1978); and George E. Vaillant, *Adaptation to Life* (Boston: Little, Brown, 1977). For some excellent synopses of this literature from an organizational perspective, see Harry Levinson, "A Second Career: The Possible Dream," *Harvard Business Review* 61 (May/June 1983), pp. 122–129; Harold L. Hodgkinson, "Adult Development: Implications for Faculty and Administrators," *Educational Record* 55 (Fall 1974), pp. 263–274; and Richard L. Schott, "The Psychological Development of Adults: Implications for Public Administration," *Public Administration Review* 46 (November/December 1986), pp. 657–667.
13. Erikson, *Childhood and Society*, pp. 270–271.
14. Gould, *Transformations*, p. 294.
15. Vaillant, *Adaptation to Life*, p. 234.
16. Erikson, *Childhood and Society*, p. 269.
17. Manfred Kets de Vries et al., "Using the Life Cycle to Anticipate Satisfaction at Work," *Journal of Forecasting* (Spring 1984), pp. 161–172; Manfred Kets de Vries and Danny Miller, *The Neurotic Organization* (San Francisco: Jossey-Bass, 1985); and Manfred Kets de Vries, ed., *The Irrational Executive: Psychoanalytic Studies in Management* (New York: International Universities Press, 1984).
18. Nicholas Henry, "Are Internships Worthwhile?" *Public Administration Review* 39 (May/June 1979), pp. 245–257; Kenneth Oldfield, "Measuring Changes in Democratic Attitudes and Career Aspirations among Administrative Interns," *Public Productivity and Management Review* 23 (March 2000), pp. 359–370; Judith M. Labiner, *Looking for the Future Leaders of Government? Don't Count on Presidential Management Interns.* A Brookings Institution Center for Public Service Working Paper (Washington, DC: Brookings, 2003), p. 7.

19. Levinson et al., *The Seasons of a Man's Life*, p. 79.
20. Vaillant, *Adaptation of Life*.
21. Ibid., p. 228.
22. Levinson et al., *The Seasons of a Man's Life*, p. 320.
23. Manfred Kets de Vries et al., "Organizational Sleepwalkers: Emotional Distress at Mid-Life," *Human Relations* 52 (November 1999), pp. 1377–1401.
24. Michael Maccoby, *The Leader* (New York: Simon & Schuster, 1981), p. 221.
25. Kets de Vries et al., "Using the Life Cycle to Anticipate Satisfaction at Work."
26. Vaillant, *Adaptation to Life*.
27. Kets de Vries et al., "Using the Life Cycle to Anticipate Satisfaction at Work."
28. Ruth Kanfer and Phillip L. Ackerman, "Aging, Adult Development, and Work Motivation," *Academy of Management Review* 29 (July 2004), p. 450.
29. Geert Hofstede, "Motivation, Leadership, and Organization: Do American Theories Apply Abroad?" *Organizational Dynamics* 9 (Summer 1980), p. 43.
30. Nakiye Avoan Boyacigiller and Nancy J. Adler, "The Parochial Dinosaur: Organizational Science in a Global Context," *Academy of Management Review* 16 (April 1991), p. 262. See also Geert Hofstede, *Culture's Consequences: International Differences in Work-Related Values* (Beverly Hills, CA: Sage, 1980).
31. The following discussion is drawn from ibid. and Hofstede, "Cultural Constraints in Management Theories." In "Motivation, Leadership, and Organization," Hofstede observes: "The fact that data obtained within a single MNC [multinational corporation] have the power to uncover the secrets of entire national cultures can be understood when it's known that the respondents form well-matched samples from their nations: They are employed by the same firm . . . ; their jobs are similar (I consistently compared the same occupations across the different countries); and their age categories and sex composition were similar—only their nationalities differed. Therefore . . . the 'only' general factor that can account for the differences in the answers is national culture" (p. 44).
32. Hofstede, "Motivation, Leadership, and Organization," p. 54.
33. Allensbach Opinion Research Institute, National Opinion Research Center, and Pew Research Center for the People and the Press, as cited in "A Nation Apart," *The Economist* (November 6, 2003), http://www.economist.com. Data are for 2003. France, Italy, Germany, the United Kingdom, and the United States were surveyed.
34. Hofstede, "Motivation, Leadership, and Organization," p. 55.
35. Ibid. A review of international applications of (American-originated) organization development (OD) techniques—techniques that are predicated on Maslow's assumptions about human needs—certainly lends credence to this conclusion. See Alfred M. Jaeger, "Organization Development and National Culture: Where's the Fit?" *Academy of Management Review* 11 (January 1986), pp. 178–190. In fact, "cultural"

differences, in Jaeger's view, have accounted for the failure of OD applications *within* the United States! Jaeger cites studies (pp. 183–184) indicating that OD is more successful in Southern California than in New England, and that many of its operating premises are "not natural" in the U.S. State Department.
36. Hofstede, "Motivation, Leadership, and Organization," p. 58.
37. Ibid., p. 57.
38. Mark F. Peterson, Peter B. Smith et al., "Role Conflict, Ambiguity, and Overload: A 21-Nation Study," *Academy of Management Journal* 38 (April 1995), pp. 429–452.
39. Hofstede, "Motivation, Leadership, and Organization," p. 59.
40. Ibid., pp. 59–60.
41. Ibid., p. 60.
42. Alvin W. Gouldner, "Cosmopolitans and Locals: Toward an Analysis of Latent Social Roles," *Administrative Science Quarterly* 2 (December 1957 and March 1958), pp. 281–306 and 444–480, respectively.
43. See, for example, Jerald Hage and Robert Dewar, "Elite Values versus Organizational Structure in Predicting Innovation," *Administrative Science Quarterly* 18 (September 1973), pp. 279–290; Jan L. Pierce and Andre L. Delbecq, "Organization Structure, Individual Attitudes, and Innovation," *Academy of Management Review* 2 (January 1977), pp. 27–37; Everett M. Rogers, *Diffusion of Innovation*, 3rd ed. (New York: Free Press, 1983); and John R. Kimberly and Michael J. Evanisko, "Organizational Innovation: The Influence of Individual, Organizational, and Contextual Factors on Hospital Adoption of Technological and Administrative Innovations," *Academy of Management Journal* 24 (December 1981), pp. 689–712.
44. Roy L. Lewicki, "Organizational Seduction: Building Commitment to Organizations," *Organizational Dynamics* (Autumn 1981), pp. 16–19.
45. Donna M. Randall, "Commitment and the Organization: The Organization Man Revisited," *Academy of Management Review* 12 (June 1987), p. 467.
46. Thomas S. Robertson and Yoram Wind, "Organizational Cosmopolitanism and Innovativeness," *Academy of Management Journal* 26 (June 1983), p. 337.
47. Patricia A. Adler and Peter Adler, "Intense Loyalty in Organizations: A Case Study of College Athletics," *Administrative Science Quarterly* 33 (September 1988), p. 415.
48. Jean A. Wallace, "Organizational and Professional Commitment in Professional and Nonprofessional Organizations," *Administrative Science Quarterly* 40 (June 1995), p. 228.
49. Dwaine Marvick, *Career Perspectives in a Bureaucratic Setting*, University of Michigan Governmental Studies, No. 27 (Ann Arbor: University of Michigan Press, 1954). As the careful reader will observe, the publication of Marvick's research precedes Gouldner's by a good five years. Gouldner's analysis is by far the better known, so we have described it first, but one should not

infer from this ordering that we consider Marvick's analysis to be a subset of Gouldner's; far from it. Indeed, we think that Marvick's *Career Perspectives* is the more insightful work, as well as one that is more central to public administration.

50. Frank U. Sulloway, *Born to Rebel* (New York: Little, Brown, 1997).

51. Joseph C. Rost, *Leadership for the Twenty-first Century,* (New York: Praeger, 1991), p. 102.

52. John P. Kotter, "What Leaders Really Do," *Harvard Business Review* 68 (May/June 1990), p. 104. See also Kotter's, *A Force for Change: How Leadership Differs From Management* (Glencoe, IL: Free Press, 1990).

53. Kotter, "What Leaders Really Do," p. 104.

54. Rost, *Leadership for the Twenty-first Century*, p. 143.

55. William A. Brown, "Exploring the Association between Board and Organizational Performance in Nonprofit Organizations," *Nonprofit Management & Leadership* 15 (Spring 2005), pp. 379–339; and Jennifer Bright Prestonand and William A. Brown, "Commitment and Performance of Nonprofit Boards Members," *Nonprofit Management & Leadership* 15 (Winter 2004), pp. 221–228.

56. Pearl Meyer & Partners, *2004 Director Compensation* (New York: Author, 2004), p. 4. In 2004, the directors of the 200 largest U.S. corporations received an average annual compensation of $176,673, up by a fourth over five years.

57. Gary Strauss, "Do Conflicts Cloud the Objectivity of Corporate Boards," *USA Today* (March 5, 2002).

58. Jonathan D. Glater and David Leonhardt, "Bill Addressing Business Fraud Is Seen As First Step," *New York Times* (July 25, 2002).

59. See, for example, "Warren Boeker, Power and Managerial Dismissal: Scapegoating at the Top," *Administrative Science Quarterly* 37 (September 1992), pp. 410–425; M. J. Conyon and S. L. Peck, "Board Control, Remuneration Committees and Top Management Compensation," *Academy of Management Journal* 41 (April 1998), pp. 146–157; and Galal M. Elnagraset, J. Richard Harrison and Rogene A. Bucholz, "Power and Pay: The Politics of CEO Compensation," *Journal of Management and Governance* 2 (2, 1998/1999), pp. 311–334.

60. James D. Westphal and Edward J. Zajac, "Who Shall Govern? CEO/Board Power, Demographic Similarity, and New Director Selection," *Administrative Science Quarterly* 40 (March 1995), pp. 55–71.

61. James D. Westphal and Poonam Khanna, "Keeping Directors in Line: Social Distancing as a Corporate Control Mechanism in the Corporate Elite," *Administrative Science Quarterly* 48 (September 2003), pp. 361–398.

62. See, for example, Boeker, "Power and Dismissal"; Lucai Bebchuk and Jesse Fried, *Pay without Performance: The Unfulfilled Promise of Executive Compensation* (Cambridge, MA and London: Harvard University Press, 2004); and Henry L. Tosi, Wei Shen, and Richard J. Gentry, "Why Outsiders on Boards Can't Solve the Corporate Governance Problem," *Organizational Dynamics* 32 (May 2003), pp. 180–193.

63. Securities and Exchange Commission report, as cited in David S. Hilzenrath, "For Many Top Executives, It's 'Ask and You Shall Receive,'" *Washington Post* (June 27, 2005).

64. Executive Pay Watch, *Pay Watch: How Much Would You Be Making if Your Pay Had Grown as CEO Pay Has?* (Washington, DC: Author, 2001). Figures are for 1980–2000. In 1990, the ratio was 1:85.

65. Claudia H. Deutsch, "My Big Fat C. E. O. Paycheck," *New York Times* (April 3, 2005). This was a survey of 179 large representative companies. Figure (actually, an average of $9.84 million) is for 2005 and was an increase of 12 percent from the previous year.

66. Lynn Olson and Ann Bradley, "Boards of Contention," *Education Week Special Journal Report* (April 29, 1992).

67. Ellen Todras, "The Changing Role of School Boards," *ERIC Digest*, No. 84 (Eugene, OR: Eric Clearinghouse on Educational Management, May 1993), p. 1.

68. James H. Svara, "The Shifting Boundaries between Elected Officials in Large Council-Manager Cities," *Public Administration Review* 59 (January/February 1999), pp. 46, 50, 47, respectively. Data are for 1996. Svara surveyed thirty-one council-manager cities with populations greater than 200,000. The earlier survey is James H. Svara, "Dichotomy and Duality: Reconceptualizing the Relationship between Policy and Administration in Council-Manager Cities," *Public Administration Review* 45 (January/February 1985), pp. 221–232. Six large council-manager cities were surveyed.

69. Jerry Mitchell, "Representation in Government Boards and Commissions," *Public Administration Review* 57 (March/April, 1997), p. 166.

70. Edward R. Dyl, Howard L. Frant, and Craig A. Stephenson, "Governance and Funds Allocation in United States Medical Research Charities," *Financial Accountability and Management* 16 (November 2000), pp. 335–352.

71. Julianne Basinger, "Boards Crack Down on Members Inside Deals," *Chronicle of Higher Education* (February 6, 2004), pp. A1, A23–A24. The foundation was the University of Georgia's.

72. U.S. Government Accountability Office, *Tax-Exempt Sector: Governance, Transparency, and Oversight Are Critical for Maintaining Public Trust,* GAO–05–561T (Washington, DC: U.S. Government Printing Office, 2005), pp. 13–14. The GAO is citing a series of reports by the *Boston Globe* published between October and December 2003.

73. Harry Lipman and Grant Williams, "Special Report: Borrowing the Future," *Chronicle of Philanthropy* (February 6, 2004), pp. 6–14.

74. BoardSource and Independent Sector, *The Sarbanes-Oxley Act and Implications for Nonprofit Organizations* (Washington, DC: Authors, 2003).

75. Vic Murray, Pat Bradshaw, and Jacob Wolpin, "Power in and Around Nonprofit Boards: A Neglected Dimension of Governance," *Nonprofit Management and Leadership* 3 (Winter 1992), pp. 165–182.

76. Ronald G. Shaiko, "Female Participation in Association Governance and Political Representation: Women as Executive directors, Board Members, Lobbyists, and Political Action Committee Directors," *Nonprofit Management and Leadership* 8 (Winter 1997), pp. 121–138.

77. Victor A. Thompson, *Modern Organization* (New York: Knopf, 1961). See also Colin Ward, "The Organization of Anarchy," in Bernard I. Kimmerman and Lewis Perry, eds., *Patterns of Anarchy: A Collection of Writings in the Anarchist Tradition* (Garden City, NY: Anchor Books, 1966), pp. 386–296. Much of the antileadership literature is in the anarchist political tradition.

78. Thomas R. Dye, "Executive Power and Public Policy in the States," *Western Political Quarterly* 27 (December 1969), p. 938. Opposite findings exist, of course. One researcher, for example, found a quantifiable measure of the governor's clear capacity to control their agencies' legislative funding. See Ira Sharkansky, "Agency Requests, Gubernatorial Support and Budget Success in State Legislatures," *American Political Science Review* 62 (December 1968), pp. 121–226.

79. G. R. Salancik and Jeffrey Pfeffer, "Constraints on Administrative Discretion: The Limited Influence of Mayors on City Budgets," *Urban Affairs Quarterly* 12 (April 1977), pp. 475–498.

80. Eleanor Fujita, *The Evaluation of College Presidents: Dimensions Used by Campus Leaders* (College Park, MD: National Center for Postsecondary Government and Finance, 1990), p. 20. See also Steven Kerr and John M. Jermier, "Substitutes for Hierarchical Leadership: Their Meaning and Measurement," *Organizational Behaviour and Human Performance* 22 (March 1978), pp. 275–403.

81. S. Lieberson and J. F. O'Connor, "Leadership and Organizational Performance: A Study of Large Corporations," *American Sociological Review* 37 (August 1972), pp. 117–130.

82. M. P. Allen, S. K. Panian, and R. E. Lotz, "Managerial Succession and Organizational Performance: A Recalcitrant Problem Revisited," *Administrative Science Quarterly* 24 (March 1979), p. 179. On the other hand, a comparable study of basketball coaches found that new coaches who came to a team *with previous records of success* did indeed improve their teams's winning score, whereas new coaches lacking such records did not. See Jeffrey Pfeifer and A. Davis-Blake, "Administrative Succession and Organizational Performance: How Administrave Experience Mitigates the Succession Effect," *Academy of Management Journal* 29 (February 1986), pp. 72–83.

83. Coleman B. Ransone, Jr., "The Governor, the Legislature, and Public Policy," *State Government* 52 (Summer 1979), p. 119.

84. Annna Neumann and Estela M. Bensimon, *Constructing the Presidency: College Presidents' Images of Their Leadership Roles, A Comparative Study* (College Park, MD: National Center for Postsecondary Government and Finance, 1990), pp. 19–20. Emphasis added.

85. See, for example, Fujita, *The Evaluation of College Presidents*; Kerr and Jermier, "Substitutes for Hierarchical Leadership"; Alan Berkeley Thomas, "Does Leadership Make a Difference to Organizational Performance?" *Administrative Science Quarterly* 33 (September 1988), pp. 388–400; and Susan Summers Raines and Aseem Prakash, "Leadership Matters: Enterpreneurship in Corporate Environmental Policymaking," *Administration and Society* 37 (March 2005), pp. 3–22. These and other empirical analyses conclude that leadership does make a difference.

86. Bernard M. Bass, *Stodgill's Handbook of Leadership: Theory, Research, and Managerial Applications*, 3rd ed. (New York: Free Press, 1990).

87. Rost, *Leadership for the Twenty-first Century*, p. 10. There is no sign that this literary gusher is abating.

88. "American Survey: The Leadership Thing," *The Economist* (December 9, 1995), p. 31.

89. Rost, *Leadership for the Twenty-first Century*, p. 47.

90. As cited in ibid.

91. Ralph M. Stodgill, "Personal Factors Associated with Leadership: A Survey of the Literature," *Journal of Psychology* 25 (June 1948), pp. 35–71.

92. For examples of this literature, see Kurt Lewin, Ronald Lippitt, and Ralph K. White, "Patterns of Aggressive Behaviour in Experimentally Created Social Climates," *Journal of Social Psychology* 10 (March 1930), pp. 271–299; Robert L. Kahn and Daniel O. Katz, "Leadership Practices and Relation to Productivity and Morale," in Dorwin Cartwright and Alvin Zander, eds., *Group Dynamics* (New York: Harper & Row, 1953); and Robert F. Bales and Paul E. Slater, "Role Differentiation in Small Decision Making Groups," in Talcott Parsons and Robert F. Bales, eds., *Family, Localization, and Interaction Processes* (New York: Free Press, 1945).

93. Fred E. Fielder, "A Contingency Model of Leadership Effectiveness," in Leonard Berkowiz, ed., *Advances in Experimental Psychology*, Vol. 1 (New York: Academic Press, 1964); and Fred E. Fielder, *A Theory of Leadership Effectiveness* (New York: McGraw-Hill. 1967).

94. Michael J. Strube and Joseph E. Garcia, "A Meta-Analytical Investigation of Fielder's Contingency Model of Leadership Effectiveness," *Psychology Bulletins* 90 (September 1981), pp. 307–321. For a good review for this literature, we suggest J. C. Wofford and L. Z. Liska, "Path-Goal. Theories of Leadership: A Meta-Analysis," *Journal of Management* 19 (Winter 1993), pp. 857–876.

95. Bernard M. Bass and Bruce J. Avolio, "Transformational Leadership and Organizational Culture," *Public Administration Quarterly* 17 (Spring 1993), p. 113.

96. Thomas Kell and Gregory T. Carroll, "Culture Matters Most," *Harvard Business Review* 83 (May 2005) pp. 22–24.

97. Robert J. House, "A Path-Goal Theory of Leardership," *Administrative Science Quarterly* 16 (September 1971), pp. 321–338.

98. M. Audery Korsgaard, David M. Schweiger, and Harry J. Sapienza, "Building Commitment, Attachment, and Trust in Strategic Decision-Making Teams: The Role of Prodcedural Justice," *Academy of Management Journal* 38 (February 1995), p. 60.

99. Stanley E. Weed, Terance R. Mitchell, and William Moffitt, "Leadership Style, Subordinates Personality, and Task Type as Predictors of Performance and Satisfaction with Supervision," *Journal of Applied Psychology* 61 (February 1976), pp. 58–66.

100. Ricky N. Griffin, "Relationships Among Individual Task Design, and Leadership Behavior Variables," *Academy of Managment Journal* 23 (December 1980), pp. 665–683.

101. Rosemary Stewart, *Choices for the Manager* (Englewood Cliffs, NJ: Prentice-Hall, 1982). See also John R. Schemerhorn, Jr., James G. Hunt, and Richard N. Osborn, *Managing Organizational Behavior* (New York: John Wiley, 1982).

102. Burns, *Leadership*, p. 20.

103. Robert House, "A 1976 Theory of Charismatic Leadership," in James G. Hunt and Lars Larson, eds., *Leadership: The Cutting Edge* (Carbondale, IL: Southern Illinois University Press, 1977), p. 196.

104. Jay A. Conger and Rabinda N. Kanungo, "Toward a Behavioral Theory of Charismatic Leadership in Organizational Settings," *Academy of Management Review* 12 (November 1987), pp. 637–647.

105. Robert J. House, William D. Spangler, and James Woycke, "Personality and Charisma in the U.S. Presidency: A Psychological Theory of Leader Effectiveness," *Administrative Science Quarterly* 36 (September 1991), p. 364.

106. John Williamson et al., *The Political Economy of Policy Reform* (Washington, DC: Institute for International Economics, 1993).

107. Mansour Javidan and David A. Waldman, "Exploring Charismatic Leadership in the Public Sector: Measurement and Consequences," *Public Administration Review* 63 (March/April 2003), pp. 229–242. The quotation is on page 229.

108. John R. P. French, Jr. and Bertram Raven, "The Bases of Social Power," *Group Dynamics: Research and Theory*, in Dorwin Cartwright and Alvin Zander, eds. (New York: Harper & Row, 1968), pp. 238–259. French and Raven originated the five powers of reward, coercion, legitimacy, reference, and expertise. Later, Bass added charisma and Yukl added control over information and the work environment. See Bass, *Stodgill's Handbook of Leadership*, rev. ed., and Gary A. Yukl, *Leadership in Organization*, 2nd ed. (Englewood Cliffs, NJ: Prentice Hall, 1989).

109. Yukl, *Leadership in Oganizations*.

110. Bass, *Stodgill's Handbook of Leadership,* rev. ed.

111. Leanne E. Atwater and Wendy J. Wright, "Power and Transactional Leadership in Public and Private Organizations," *International Journal of Public Administration* 9 (June 1996), pp. 963–990. For some related analyses, see Patricia A. Wilson, "The Effects of Politics and Power on the Organizational Commitment of Federal Executives," *Journal of Management* 21 (Spring 1993), pp. 101–118; and Gerald T. Gabris, Keenan Grenell et al., "Management Innovation at the Local Level: Some Effects of Administrative Leadership and Governing Board Behavior," *Public*

Productivity and Management Review 23 (June 2000), pp. 486–431.

112. Robert Hooijberg and Jaepil Choi, "The Impact of Organizational Characteristics on Leadership Effectiveness Models: An Examination of Leadership in a Private and Public-Sector Organization," *Administration and Society* (September 2001), pp. 403–431.

113. Ibid.

114. Ibid.

115. Ibid.

116. George L. Hanbury II, "Leadership 'Fit' and Effectiveness: Trust and Performance," paper presented at the Annual Conference of the American Society for Public Administration, Phoenix, Arizona, March 2002, p. 27. Random surveys were sent to 600 city managers, 40 percent of whom responded to questionnaires based on the Myers-Briggs Type Indicator—Form G and *Leadership Behavior Analysis—Self*. The former is used to measure personality types, and the latter is used to measure situational leadership behavior.

117. Hoojberg and Choi, "The Impact of Organizational Characteristics on Leadership Effectiveness Models."

118. See, for example: Philip Selznick, *TVA and the Grass Roots* (Berkeley: University of California Press, 1949); Richard E. Boyatzis, *The Competent Manager* (New York: Wiley, 1982); Yuan Ting, "Analysis of Job Satisfaction of the Federal White-Collar Workforce: Findings from the Survey of Federal Employees," *American Review of Public Administration* 26 (December 1996), pp. 439–456; Yuan Ting, "Determinants of Job Satisfaction of Federal Government Employees," *Public Personnel Management* 26 (Fall 1997), pp. 313–334; and Hal G. Rainey, *Understanding and Managing Public Organizations*, 2nd ed. (San Francisco: Jossey-Bass, 1997).

119. Gerald J. Miller, "Unique Public-Sector Strategies," *Public Productivity and Management Review* 13 (Winter 1989), p. 137.

120. Unless noted otherwise, this discussion is drawn from the following sources: Mark A. Abramson, "The Leadership Factor," *Public Administration Review* 49 (November/December 1989), pp. 562–565 (our primary source); Norma M. Riccucci, "'Execucrats,' Politics, and Public Policy: What are the Ingredients for Successful Performance in the Federal Government?" *Public Administration Review* 55 (May/June 1995), pp. 219–230; Joseph N. Cayer, "Qualities of Successful Program Managers," in Robert E. Cleary and Nicholas Henry, eds., *Managing Public Programs*, (San Francisco: Jossey-Bass, 1989), pp. 121–142; James L. Perry, "The Effective Public Administrator," in James L. Perry, ed., *Handbook of Public Administration*, (San Francisco: Jossey-Bass, 1989), pp. 619–627; and Terry L. Cooper and N. Dale Wright, eds., *Exemplary Public Administrators* (San Francisco: Jossey-Bass, 1992).

121. Abramson, "The Leadership Factor," p. 563.

122. See, for example, Hugh Heclo, *A Government of Strangers: Executive Politics in Washington* (Washington, DC: Brookings, 1977); and G. Calvin MacKenzie, ed., *The In-and-Outers* (Baltimore, MD: Johns Hopkins University Press, 1987).

123. Abramson, "The Leadership Factor," p. 564.

124. Although the famous phrase is commonly attributed to Brownlow, it makes its initial appearance in a publication written by three authors. See Louis Brownlow, Charles E. Merriam, and Luther Gulick, "Report of the President's Committee on Administrative Management," *Administrative Management in the Government of the United States, January 8, 1937* (Washington, DC: U.S. Government Printing Office, 1937), pp. 1–6. Actually, the authors are referring not to career public administrators, but rather to the top White House staff; the authors write that these staffers ("probably not exceeding six in number") "should be possessed of high competence, great physical vigor, and a passion for anonymity." The quotation is on p. 5.

125. James N. Doig and Erwin C. Hargrove, eds., *Leadership and Innovation: A Biographical Perspective on Entrepreneurs in Government* (Baltimore, MD: Johns Hopkins University Press, 1987). Fourteen profiles of career public administrators who led both their organizations and the nation in their capacities as public administrators are featured in the book, and all are notable in their skill and enthusiasm in communicating their personal visions through the media.

126. Cecilia Stiles Cornell and Melvyn P. Leffler, "James Forrestal: The Tragic End of a Successful Entrepreneur," in ibid., p. 374.

Part III

Public Management

Public management is the development or application of methodical and systematic techniques, often employing comparison, quantification, and measurement, that are designed to make the operations of public organizations more efficient, effective, and increasingly, responsive. This is a considerably more crisp, concise, and narrow definition than is our definition of public administration, and its sharper focus is attributable to the larger field's encompassing of values in addition to those of efficiency, effectiveness, and responsiveness.

We begin Part III with a discussion of the pervasive phenomenon of information technology. The techniques of performance measurement, public program evaluation, and productivity improvement follow and are given a thorough review. Public finance, budgeting, and human resources management conclude our treatment of the nuts and bolts of public management.

CHAPTER **6**

Clarifying Complexity: The Public's Information Resource

Before we start managing public programs, it is prudent to clarify what problems of public management confront us. The computer has been central to this clarification.

It is often forgotten that electronic data processing originated in the public sector. A Census Bureau employee, Herman Hollerith, invented a punch card and tabulation machine for use in the 1890 census.

Today, the federal government spends about $65 billion a year on information technology.[1] Federal spending for information technology services alone nearly doubled over five years, and accounts about a third of all federal expenditures for information technology.[2] No other single organization in the United States, and likely the world, spends more money on computer technology than does the U.S. government.[3]

Computers also have made themselves felt among the grass-roots governments. All state and local governments combined spend about $50 billion per year on computers, software, and systems,[4] and it is expected that this amount will increase by more than a third every five years![5]

As the public information resource grows ever-more pervasive, a duo of devilish dilemmas has grown ever more ominous. One is the crucial need to protect the privacy of individual citizens, and the other is the equally vital need to protect the security of public data. Although both challenges overlap, they do have differences and we consider them next.

Privacy versus *Policy: The Particular Problem of the Public Computer*

In 2006, an employee of the U.S. Department of Veteran Affairs decided to do some homework and, in violation of standing but laxly-enforced regulations, took home a departmental computer. That evening, the computer was stolen, and with it, the names, Social Security numbers, and birth dates—and, for many, the telephone numbers and addresses as well—of 26.5 million military veterans. This was the largest theft of personal data from a government in history, although it did not match the forty million credit cardholders whose accounts were compromised in 2005 by hackers in a cyberattack on CardSystem Solutions.

Without doubt, databanks and information technology have assisted in making better public policy. But at what point does the collection, storage, retrieval, and sharing of social information for public purposes become an invasion of the citizen's privacy?

⚹The Meaning of Privacy *versus* Policy

There is ample reason to be alert to the presence of personal information in governments' databases, but there also is reason to be concerned when personal information is *not* present in those databases. It is in these instances that the importance of personal data in making and implementing good public policy becomes clear.

Here is an example of what we mean. The Internal Revenue Service (IRS) is the only federal agency that maintains a database of all federal taxpayers. Congress requires the IRS to keep that database confidential so that taxpayers can be protected from having their personal information disclosed to the public.

This confidentiality of taxpayer information applies to all individual and corporate taxpayers, both honest and dishonest. Unfortunately, federal agencies other than the IRS cannot know about the tax cheaters in the IRS database when they let contracts to the private sector. As a result, private contractors who *owe* substantial tax dollars to the federal government nonetheless *collect* substantial taxpayers' dollars when they are awarded federal contracts. For instance, a private health care services company received more than $300,000 in a contract from Washington, even though it owed more than $18 million in back taxes.[6]

The extent of this scam is vast. The Government Accountability Office (GAO) found that some 33,000 federal contractors owed the federal government more than $3.3 billion in back taxes. Many of these companies withheld payroll taxes from their own employees' paychecks but never sent those withholdings to the IRS. Although Washington has taken some steps to correct this situation, it still has quite a way to go.[7]

This situation also applies to the states. Another GAO study found that Washington had distributed $1.8 billion in federal contracts over the course of a single year to more than 4,600 contractors who owed the states some $17 million in unpaid taxes.[8]

This, in short, is the problem of privacy *versus* policy. On the one hand, citizens' privacy is protected. On the other hand, governments and their citizens are being exploited by tax cheats as a direct result of that protection of privacy. This example exemplifies the delicate balance between protecting the person and protecting the public. We address that central question here, focusing on the federal experience.

The End of Privacy?

Governments' use of personal information is surprisingly broad and diverse. The federal government alone collects information not only about the citizen in question, but also about his or her spouse, children, dependents, and parents. Personal identifiers recorded by federal agencies include one's legal name, maiden name, aliases, driver's license number, phone numbers, and e-mail addresses, among other identifiers. Demographic data include the date of one's marriage and divorce, educational level, occupation, height, and eye color, to list a few. Financial and legal data collected by the federal government include information on salaries, investments, net worth, credit history, child support payments, bankruptcies, litigation, and criminal and drug convictions.[9]

The GAO reports that there were 2,400 federal "systems of records" in twenty-five agencies containing personal information on an approximate median of 3,500 people per system. The GAO estimated that 70 percent of these systems contained electronic records; 12 percent were fully computerized, 58 percent combined electronic and paper records, and 31 percent were exclusively paper records.[10]

Mixing and Matching

Of even graver concern is the accelerating trend among governments to "mix and match" information on individuals, and at least fifteen major federal agencies engage in this practice.[11] *Computer matching* is the electronic comparison of two or more sets or systems of individual personal records.

Federal agencies estimate that they save "at least" $900 million each year just by sharing data with each other.[12]

Besides savings, these laws have resulted in the creation of such electronic dossiers as the IRS's Debtor Master File and the Medicaid Management Information System, among other federal systems that are extensively engaged in computer matching. The Real ID Act of 2005 creates an immense database that centralizes the information collected by the states' departments of motor vehicles, and this information may be shared not only among federal, state, and local agencies, but also with those in Canada and Mexico. The Homeland Security Act of 2002 requires the development of policies for sharing security information among agencies, and the Intelligence Reform and Terrorist Prevention Act of 2004 calls for the creation of an "Information Sharing Environment" for data on terrorism.

Twenty-seven states, 64,000 law enforcement agencies, and over a million officers participate in the Federal Bureau of Investigation's (FBI) National Crime Information Center, which stores more than 15 million individual arrest histories and the fingerprints of 41 million people.[13] It appears that the number of federal computer matches tripled in only five years, and that more than two billion separate records were exchanged during that period.[14]

A Case of Unmatched Failure

Although the practice of mixing and matching government databases is a serious issue of privacy, distressing breakdowns of public policy can be a consequence when governments fail to mix and match their data. Here is one example.

Dean Arthur Schwartzmiller may hold the world record as a serial child predator. In 2005, police discovered seven notebooks containing 36,000 separate entries by Schwartzmiller listing the names and other details of children whom, Schwartzmiller wrote, he had molested. Schwartzmiller has been arrested for child molestation in five states over the course of thirty-five years and spent twelve years in prison for his crimes. But the stunning extent of his self-described molestations had been unknown to authorities.

How did this apparent failure of public policy happen? In large part, it happened because public information was not mixed and matched.

All fifty states maintain databases that list and track sex offenders, and convicted child molesters such as Schwartzmiller are required to record in these databases where they live and work. (In 2003, the Supreme Court ruled that these registration requirements may be imposed even on offenders whose crimes took place before states had enacted such laws.) Schwartzmiller, however, simply did not register—not anywhere, not anytime. Indeed, the whereabouts of an estimated one-fourth of all convicted sex offenders are unknown because they fail to register. Because there was no national database (The U.S. Justice Department, however, initiated such a database a month after the news about Schwartzmiller broke) or any system for the states to share not only their sex offender registrations but also their arrest and conviction records for sexual crimes, Schwartzmiller, and likely other child molesters, was never tracked. This failure enabled Schwartzmiller, presumably, to continue his molestation with far greater abandon for more than three decades.

Sources: Caroline Marshall, "Child Molester Is Suspected of Hundreds of Cases," *New York Times* (June 17, 2005); Keving Johnson, "National Online Registry of Sex Offenders Launched," *USA Today* (July 20, 2005); and Donna Horowitz and Eric Malnic, "Child Advocate Calls for National Web Site for Tracking Molesters," *Los Angeles Times* (June 18, 2005).

Privacy Policies

Some 80 percent of Americans register themselves as "concerned" or "very concerned" over these trends, although Americans express considerably higher trust over the government's potential use of personal files than over how private firms may use them.[15] Increasingly, too, the courts and Congress have addressed issues of personal privacy.

The Judiciary's Zone of Privacy. In 1977, in *Whalen* v. *Roe,* the Supreme Court recognized for the first time a constitutionally protected "zone of privacy" of the individual, a concept that involved the right of people to prevent others from disclosing personal data to the public.

Over the years, the courts have developed a three-pronged test, based on the Constitution's Fourth Amendment, that should be used in balancing the rights to privacy of employees with the rights of the employer to know legitimate information about the employees. These tests are reasonableness, compelling interest, and job relatedness. Any intrusion by management into the personal lives of public employees must be *reasonable,* in that prior publication of such practices as surveillance be present, and employee consent obtained, among other factors; the employer must have a *compelling interest,* such as testing for drug use among those employees, such as air traffic controllers, who have life-and-death responsibilities; and the intrusion must be *job related* in that it cannot exceed the scope of business necessity.[16]

Congress's Privacy Legislation. Congress has recognized the value of individual privacy as well by its passage of several laws. Major ones include: the *Fair Credit Reporting Act of 1970,* which grants consumers access to their credit reports, among other measures, to ensure their accuracy; the *Privacy Act of 1974,* which grants citizens access to their federal records and prevents agencies from distributing personal information; the *Family Educational Rights and Privacy Act of 1974,* which protects the privacy of student records; the *Right to Financial Privacy Act of 1978,* which imposes certain limits on governments seeking financial information on people and limits financial institutions in how they provide such information; the *Electronic Communications Privacy Act of 1986,* which inhibits the interception and disclosure of electronic messages; the *Computer Matching and Privacy Protection Act of 1988,* which provides procedures for federal data matching; the *Financial Services Modernization Act of 1999,* which requires institutions that collect credit information to notify their customers that they are entitled to prohibit these institutions from sharing personal data with other companies; and the *Electronic Government Act of 2002,* which directs agencies to provide "privacy impact assessments" when purchasing new information technologies or initiating new collections of personal information.

In 2001, following the terrorist attacks of September 11, Congress reversed course. As one scholar phrased the new reality of security and privacy, "We must be wary of extending political authority to protect privacy without careful contemplation of the consequences."[17]

Congress responded to this wariness by passing the *USA Patriot Act of 2001,* which expands Washington's authority to monitor citizens' e-mail, Internet activities, and other electronic communications. In 2005, with the enactment of the *Real ID Act,* a national databank was created that has at least the potential for abusing citizens' privacy.

Protecting Privacy

It appears that the federal government does a reasonably good job of enforcing its privacy statutes.

An analysis by the GAO of how four representative departments handled personal information about citizens concluded that they "generally complied with key requirements and guidance pertaining to information collection, privacy, security, and records management."[18]

Another study by GAO found that compliance with the Privacy Act was "generally high" among twenty-five agencies, estimating a compliance rate of 71 percent "with the requirement that personal information should be complete, accurate, relevant, and timely before it is disclosed to a nonfederal organization." Nevertheless, compliance was "uneven," and "the government cannot adequately assure the public that all legislated individual privacy rights are being protected."[19]

Some agencies have taken it upon themselves to appoint chief privacy officers. Following the exposure of privacy abuses by IRS employees in the 1990s, the IRS appointed a "privacy advocate," and in 2001 the Postal Service, which collects a wide range of personal information, designated its first "chief privacy officer." In 2002, with the passage of the Homeland Security Act, Congress created the first statutory "privacy officer," specifically for the Department of Homeland Security, and this remains the only such position in the federal government today.

State governments are sufficiently concerned about privacy issues that they are now exploring the creation chief privacy officers, and the private sector has been appointing these officials for some time, in large part to accommodate federal privacy legislation. There is an International Association of Privacy Professionals and a Council of Chief Privacy Officers, among other groups, that bring together privacy professionals in the private sector, but no such association exists for the public sector.

The Crusade for Secure Data

In the preceding discussion, we have been describing the fears that individual citizens have concerning the misuse of computers by governments and other institutions. But the opposite pertains, too: the fears that organizations have concerning the misuse of computers by individual citizens. In a word, *hacking*, or the illegal access to computer databases by unauthorized persons.

The cost of hacking is high. Perhaps $10 billion each year is lost to corporations, nonprofit organizations, and government agencies through unauthorized intrusions into their databases.[20]

The Rise of Hacking

Hacking is burgeoning, both in public and private systems. In one major survey, 64 percent of corporate, university, and government sites reported at least one computer break-in during the preceding twelve months, and that security breaches had increased by 16 percent over the course of a single year.[21] An annual and authoritative "E-Crime Watch Survey" of security and law enforcement executives, a third of whom work in government, supports the these findings. It found that seven out of ten U.S. organizations reported at least one break-in per year, and that e-crimes had "become so commonplace" that, after fifteen years of counting them, it was discontinuing the practice.[22]

Most organizations usually do not know that their computers have been breached. One expert says that, overall, only one in 500 of these attacks is noticed,[23] although government fares slightly better in this regard. A GAO study determined that 4 percent of the successful penetrations of the Pentagon's computers were detected.[24] Still, this is not a number that conveys bragging rights.

Humiliated by Hacking

There are "at least fifty-thousand computer viruses" in the World Wide Web, and "any fool can enter, alter, and destroy even the most seemingly impregnable Web sites."[25]

No organization wants to be humiliated by "any fool" discovering its innermost secrets, and it appears that, as a result, hacking is grossly underreported. Private companies in particular underreport those break-ins of which they are aware—perhaps only 10 percent are reported—because of the adverse publicity that could result.[26] The public sector, however, is hardly immune to this syndrome. Only 27 percent of the illegal penetrations of the Pentagon's computers that were detected by the military were reported to the Defense Information Systems Agency, in accordance with procedures.[27]

It seems that the fear of embarrassing revelations over hacking is not confined to the corporate world. But failing to report hacking can only compound, and apparently is compounding, the problem.

Resistance to Hacking

There are laws designed to guard federal information, and it should not be surprising that some of those laws designed to protect privacy mentioned earlier—most notably the *Privacy Act of 1974*—also help protect security. Additional legislation that is designed to improve information security includes the *Paperwork Reduction Act of 1980*, which established the Office of Management and Budget as the agency responsible for developing information security policies and checking agency practices; the *Computer Security Act of 1987*, which broadly defines the kinds of information that are confidential, private, or secret; the *Information Technology Management Reform Act of 1996*, which reemphasizes the need to protect sensitive information; the *USA Patriot Act of 2001*, which directs the Secret Service to establish a national network of electronic crime task forces; and the *Federal Information Security Management Act of 2002* (the act is also Title III of the Electronic Government Act of that year), which requires agencies to establish comprehensive information security programs that must be evaluated annually by outside evaluators. These evaluations are done by inspectors general.

Other kinds of federal policies have been developed, too. In 1985, the Office of Management and Budget (OMB) issued *OMB Circular A-130*, "Security of Federal Automated Information Resources." Circular A-130, in conjunction with the Computer Security Act, authorizes the National Institute of Standards and Technology to certify and accredit the security of federal information systems. In 1997, the GAO listed information security as a high-risk area, and it continues to do so.

In 1998, the president issued *Presidential Decision Directives 62* and *63* in an effort to further protect federal databases. The former pertains to terrorism and is secret, but Presidential Decision Directive 63 established entities in the National Security Council, Department of Commerce, and FBI to coordinate federal security practices.

The Record of the Resistance

The success of these and other efforts has been mixed.

The Good News. There has been progress. The terrorist attacks of September 11, 2001, "changed the way federal agencies approach IT [information technology] security,"[28] and nowhere was this change more pronounced than in funding it. In the four years following 9/11, federal expenditures for computer security quadrupled,[29] and now amount to some $6 billion per year.[30]

This quadrupling in electronic security budgets has had some salutary effect. In 1998, the GAO identified "significant information security weaknesses," mostly of "poor control over access to sensitive data," in all major federal agencies.[31] By 2005, however, the OMB reported that more than three-quarters of all federal information technology systems had been "certified as secure," and this was a tripling from only three years earlier.[32]

The Bad News. All this is the good news. There is, unfortunately, some bad news. As we mentioned earlier, some two-thirds of the databanks of U.S. organizations are hacked every year,[33] and the cost and frequency of e-crimes continue to rise.[34]

At the federal level, the annual evaluations of computer security, conducted by inspectors general since 2003, give federal agencies low marks. In the first year of these evaluations, the government received an overall grade of "D," and improvement has been slow.[35]

The information security of the Department of Defense, for obvious reasons, is of considerable concern, and what we know about it is worrisome. For starters, the department's official grade for its computer security is a "D."[36] The GAO reports that there are some forty million computers around the globe that have the potential ability to break into 90 percent of the Pentagon's computer files. In a single year, as many as 250,000 attempts were made to do so, and, in the GAO's audit, the success rate was 65 percent. The GAO concluded that "the potential for catastrophic damage" resulting from these break-ins "is great."[37]

The states also have been lax, even though state governments are highly vulnerable to cyberattacks. Almost half of all state agencies have failed to adopt computer security policies that are similar to their federal counterparts, as stipulated by the Homeland Security Act of 2002.[38] Only fourteen states comply with federal mandates concerning the protection of personal data stored in information systems in the private sector, such as those in banks and insurance companies.[39]

In contrast to governments' relative success in assuring citizens' privacy in the information age, governments are still struggling to assure the security of their own data.

Knowledge Management: Managing the Public's Information Resource

As the preceding discussion posits, the public sector has problems of managing information resources that are unique to it. We call these challenges *public information resource management*, or, more simply, *knowledge management*, both of which refer to the coordination and administration of public policies and procedures for information technology, resources, personnel, and systems in the public sector.

We do not know a lot about these challenges. There is "an extremely limited body of knowledge about emerging IS [information systems] management in the public sector."[40]

We have learned, however, that the challenges of managing the public information resource differ markedly from those in the private sector. An intense comparison of over 1,000 "high-level data managers" in state governments and the private sector concluded that the public managers dealt with greater interdependence among systems, more red tape, different criteria in purchasing hardware, and more extensive "extra-organizational linkages" than did private data managers.[41]

Interviews with top information technology administrators in the public sector (again, in state governments) who had held comparable positions in the private sector found many of them to be somewhat "disheartened" over the lack of incentives available in government to produce results. Even the smallest organizational changes required far more time and effort in government than in industry. And, although they entered public service with some understanding that it would differ from the private sector, "it's been an eye-opener

for many to see just how much of their success depends on understanding the agendas of powerful interest groups and people."[42]

We also have discovered that the experiences of the national government and the subnational governments with information technology have been quite different. The federal government's record has been one of frustration, but that of state and local governments has been largely positive. We review these experiences next.

Managing the Nation's Knowledge: A Far-Flung Federal Failure?

Regrettably, the federal government's experience with computers has been as maddening as computers themselves are necessary.

By 1990, after spending more than $300 billion over the preceding two decades on its computers, it took the federal government forty-nine months, or more than four years, to buy information technology. By contrast, comparable purchases in the private sector consumed thirteen months.[43] The GAO harrumphed in 1990 that "not one major government computer system reviewed by GAO has come in under budget or on time."[44] A survey of federal senior managers confirmed, unsurprisingly, that buying information technology took so much time that they ended up "acquiring out-of-date products."[45]

An official at GAO described the feds' computer problems succinctly: "It's a loose fire hose. Money is being spewed all over the place, and it's not clear at all if things are getting better."[46]

Eventually Congress responded. In 1990, the GAO introduced its "high-risk series" listing critical areas of federal management that require concentrated attention, virtually all of which involve improvements in information resource management. In 1996, Congress passed the Information Technology Management Reform Act (also known as the Clinger-Cohen Act), which freed federal procurement officers from selecting only the lowest bid when buying computer hardware and software; streamlined purchasing of information systems; de-throned the General Services Administration as the government's czar for information systems and placed responsibility for those purchases in the agencies; and required large agencies to appoint chief information officers (CIOs) at a senior level.

Washington's Results: Mixed

Are these and other measures arresting the deterioration of knowledge management in the federal government? The evidence is mixed.

On the one hand, Washington seems to be making progress, if with glacial speed. The OMB continues to develop a government-wide strategic information resources management plan,[47] as required by the Paperwork Reduction Act of 1980. The Information Technology Management Reform Act probably has speeded, simplified, and improved the purchase of information resources, and, with little question, the act's requirement that chief information officers be appointed in the twenty-seven major federal agencies is a good and long-needed move. It is also encouraging that 70 percent of federal CIOs report directly to their agency heads.[48]

On the other hand, there remain serious challenges in designing and managing federal information systems, providing talented human resources for knowledge management, and alleviating undue burdens on the public incurred as the result of Washington's computer crisis.

Design Dilemmas, Managerial Mediocrity. The GAO found that only twenty out of ninety-six agencies had established a foundation for understanding their present and future capacities in information technology and for devising an investment plan that would transition their information systems to the future.[49] The application of strategic planning, performance measures, and prudent investment practices by agencies to their management of information technology was "uneven" and "mixed," with less than half the agencies fully using these techniques.[50] Worse, more than two-fifths of federal employees report that they do not have electronic access to information needed to do their jobs.[51]

The hands-on effects of these general problems are felt in specific and crucial areas. For one, the federal government is underfunding itself. The IRS, by its own estimate, fails to collect about 15 percent of what taxpayers owe the government,

and this failure is due to antiquated computers that are unable to adequately track tax scofflaws. Because IRS computers are incapable of recording each quarter the penalties for those uncollected taxes, Washington loses more than $800 million in interest every year.[52] In 1990, the GAO identified the collection of unpaid taxes as a "high-risk area," and in 1995 it added IRS financial management and IRS business systems modernization to its list. All are still on it.

Difficulties of design and management attenuate in matters of national security. In late 2002, the FBI signed a $170 million contract to replace with electronic records systems its paper-based systems, which were not only inefficient but likely contributed to the success of the 9/11 terrorists. Within a year, "technical and functional deficiencies"— ultimately, some 400 of them—in the contractor's first batch of software were evident. Not only did the bureau fail to notify the contractor of these problems, but it also sailed on with a $17 million testing program, even though it knew that the software would have to be scrapped. Which it was in 2005, but only after costing taxpayers $104 million in wasted expenditures. There were least four chiefs of the FBI's information technology division during this three-year period; as one member of Congress pondered, the FBI "had some real personnel problems."[53]

The Information Resource's Human Resources. So does the whole of federal information technology management.

Chief information officers are at the top of the federal knowledge-management heap but seem unhappy there and evidence a conspicuously high turnover rate. The median time in office for permanently appointed CIOs is fewer than two years.[54]

At the middle echelons of Washington's information-resource hierarchy, there is mixed evidence concerning human resources. On the one hand, an extensive study found that, over a period of twenty years, the federal civil service hired professionals and administrators with skills in information technology "at higher grade levels, promoted them faster, and paid them more" than it did other, similarly educated and experienced, employees, indicating

Washington's determination to upgrade its knowledge management. On the other hand, these same researchers found that in spite, or perhaps because, of these exceptional efforts, the feds had hired knowledge managers with less than "ideal qualitifications," who performed at the same level as did comparably educated and experienced managers and professionals in other areas and stayed in the government just as long. In short, the feds were paying more for less, or, at best, the same.[55]

The Public's Burden.   Cynical taxpayers may chalk off these federal frustrations to the usual (in their view) wasteful ways of government. Ignored in this view is that the direct cost to the public of Washington's computer crisis is real and severe.

An analysis by the GAO of the government's success in reducing its paperwork burden on the public, as mandated by the Paperwork Reduction Act, unearthed unequivocal policy failures. Congress had set a goal of reducing paperwork by 35 percent over six years, but, in fact, paperwork had increased by 17 percent, amounting to an estimated 8.2 billion "burden hours" on the public, and the burden was growing rapidly.[56]

The computer-based problems of the national bureaucracy go far beyond burdens; unless corrected they could connote bureaucratic breakdown. For example, because of "software glitches," the Social Security Administration shortchanged some 700,000 retirees by $850 million in Social Security payments, including the multiple sclerosis victim who went without payments for four years, accumulated $60,000 in medical debts, and lost her house and car. So outdated are the nation's air traffic control systems (which would cost about $7 billion to replace) that some equipment dating from the 1960s relies on vacuum tubes, and replacements must be ordered from Poland.[57]

A Sad Summation: It appears that Washington still has some way to travel if it is going to gain satisfactory productivity from its information technology. As one report put it, the federal government "has compiled a record of failure that has jeopardized the nation's welfare, eroded public safety, and squandered untold billions of dollars."[58]

Managing Knowledge at the Grass Roots

In contrast to Washington's dismal experience with its information technology, state and local governments seem to be faring rather well. Information technology professionals in the subnational governments have set some ambitious goals for themselves, with a majority stating that they have established initiatives to increase the efficiency and effectiveness of their governments; over a fifth are trying to "improve customer service;" and more than a tenth are expanding the use of information technology to "facilitate effective decision making and policy formulation."[59]

Managing Knowledge in the States.   At the state level, information resource managers have shown an understanding that organizational change often must accompany technological change. Every state has a chief information officer, twenty-seven of whom report directly to the governor.[60]

Of course, state information systems are not without issues. As we noted earlier, most states have real problems in safeguarding their data, but there are other problems, too. Forty-seven states are developing or operating child welfare information systems that are designed to detect, track, and arrest perpetrators of child abuse and neglect. Despite federal funds that have been available since 1994 for this supremely important purpose, the states report a median delay of two-and-half years in bringing their systems online, and there are also problems of data accuracy, inadequate caseworker training, and other deficiencies.[61]

Managing Knowledge in Communities.   Local government administrators feel good about computers. Ninety-two percent of municipal finance directors report that "computers have improved their government's efficiency and productivity";[62] indeed, only 5 percent of local government managers are dissatisfied with their systems.[63]

Some local governments have become the "employer of choice" for professionals in information technology, "in spite of public sector constraints."[64]

Indeed, local governments are the nation's information resource leaders, accounting for some 1,500 different applications, and the number of new digital government applications by local governments are projected to surpass by a factor of three the number of new applications introduced by the federal and state governments over the course of a decade.[65] Larger cities with higher voter registration levels are likelier to adopt new electronic services for citizens.[66]

When information systems are working effectively, the productivity of public policies can soar, and soar rapidly. The New York City Police Department saw its murder rate drop by two-thirds over just five years and ascribes this impressive occurrence to Compstat, a computer program that weekly crosscuts and analyzes performance assessments from each of its police precincts. Baltimore applied a comparable program, CitiStat, to not only law enforcement, but to other areas as well. One result is that the city was able to almost halve the blood lead levels in children in only two years. At least ten local governments across the nation have adopted their own versions of CitiStat.[67]

✳*E-Gov: Lean, Clean, and Seen Government*

The often gloomy caverns of public information resource management do have at least one bright and shining light: e-gov. *E-gov*, short for *electronic government*, is the introduction of government Web sites and portals (*portals* are integrated Web sites for targeted services) that furnish information and services, and facilitate governmental processes, for citizens, businesses, and governments themselves.

Governments are gradually realizing the vision that early dreamers once had of using computers to bring government closer to the people, and becoming more effective and efficient in the process. All federal agencies and almost all state and local agencies have Web sites, and more than half of all Americans have visited at least one.[68] Electronic government is, perhaps, a less complex managerial challenge than is the coordination of vast oceans of data that involve issues of privacy, security, and finance, but it nonetheless is an almost unconditional success in the management of the public information resource.

Federal.gov

The Government Paperwork Elimination Act of 1998 provides the basis of federal e-gov. It directs all agencies to make as much information as possible available electronically to other agencies and the public.

In 2001, the president established the President's Management Agenda, which identified the expansion of electronic government as one of six key elements in improving federal administration, and the OMB, in turn, divided this priority into ninety-one objectives expressed in twenty-five e-gov initiatives. Three years later, thirty-three of OMB's ninety-one e-government objectives had been achieved, and thirty-eight had been partially achieved.

In 2002, Congress buttressed the president's e-gov priority by passing the Electronic Government Act, which directed OMB to establish an Office of E-Government and Information Technology and required federal courts and regulatory agencies to establish more informative Web sites. The bureaucracy was responsive. The GAO concluded that, two years after the passage of the act, "In most cases . . . federal agencies have taken action to address the act's requirements within stipulated time frames."[69]

Some examples of Washington's e-government include the following. More than three-quarters of all recipients of federal benefits, such as Social Security payments, receive their benefits electronically.[70] Food stamp benefits are available through e-gov.[71] More than a fourth of federal income tax payers now file their returns online.[72] The federal government sells billions of dollars of products and property at more than 160 Web sites and is among the globe's biggest vendors on the Internet.[73]

State.gov

All the states provide forms and information electronically for purposes of professional licensing, and half permit at least partial online registration for licensing. Forty-two of the forty-three states with a personal income tax allow their citizens to perform some form of tax payment or refund online, ranging from simply downloading the tax form (all forty-two states) to online filing (twenty-three); sixteen do the same for vehicle registration.[74]

Thirty-nine states use *electronic benefits transfer*, or bankcards to deliver via automated teller machines most of the $100 billion in welfare payments that the federal and state governments distribute each year.[75] "E-procurement" is practiced in two-thirds of the states,[76] and purchasing transaction costs have been slashed by more than 90 percent as states move from paper to computers.[77] At least eighteen state arts and cultural councils have electronic grant application systems.[78]

Local.gov

Local governments have adopted e-gov with breathtaking speed.[79] Nearly all cities and counties are on the Internet, up from around half just five years earlier.[80] Over nine out ten local governments have their own Web sites.[81] The most formidable barrier to establishing local Web sites for all local governments is a lack of financial resources, but for smaller governments the primary obstacles also include a lack of technology, trained staff, and expertise;[82] it follows, perhaps, that a fourth of local governments contract out the operation and management of their Web sites to the private sector.[83]

Posting information on Web sites is the most favored form of local e-gov. At least six out of ten local Web sites or more do so.[84]

Substantive electronic transactions between citizens and their city halls or county courthouses are considerably less voluminous. Still, a surprisingly large proportion, 30 percent, of cities and counties have Web sites that let their citizens request services electronically.[85] The major obstacles to offering these more advanced personal services are laws assuring confidentially, citizen concerns over privacy, and costs.[86]

Will e-gov Reignite Government?

Polls indicate that digital government is enormously popular among Americans. Three-quarters of e-gov users believe that it has made it easier and more convenient for them to stay informed about government services; two-thirds think that it has made it easier and more convenient for them to conduct transactions with the government; and three-fifths state that the information they receive from government Web sites is reliable.[87] Even more profoundly, e-gov may be restoring Americans' faith in government. More than six out of ten of the public believe that e-gov will have positive effect on government and think that e-gov can make governments more accountable.[88] An analysis of the public's use of e-gov found that government Web site use is "positively associated with e-government satisfaction and . . . e-government satisfaction is positively associated with trust in government."[89]

Public administrators are even more delighted with e-gov than are citizens. More than eight out of ten senior employees in the federal, state, and local governments believe that digital government will have a positive impact on government, and "not a single public official" states that e-gov affects government operations negatively.[90] Almost seven out of ten local government administrators believe that e-gov has improved their governments' communication with the public, and well over half think that it has improved customer service.[91]

There is not a little irony in public administrators' comfort with The Computer, particularly in light of the fact that, "Putting services on the Web doesn't just change how governments interact with citizens. It can change how governments are run."[92] This assertion is substantiated by experience. A few city and county administrators report that e-gov already has reduced the number of staff in their governments.[93] A third of local officials state that e-government has "changed the role of staff" and more than a fourth say that it has "reengineered business processes" in their governments.[94]

✳ Best Practices for Knowledge Management

As we noted earlier, not much is known about managing information technology in the public sector, but what little there is[95] we have reduced to five guidelines that we believe have a particular salience to the management of public information resources. They are as follows:

- *Strong, skilled leadership is essential.* Clear communication of changing needs and unambiguous assignment of responsibility are critical. Public employees in particular must be pushed to "get with the program," as they tend to hunker down until this fad, too, shall pass.
- *The goals of new information systems must clearly align with legislative and agency goals and be comprehensively integrated throughout the organization.* The clearer this alignment, the likelier that legislative support will continue. A formal strategic process that uses both radical and incremental strategies and which continuously monitors progress is mandatory.
- *Organizational processes, not software or hardware, should be the focus in introducing and managing information resources.* A radical reengineering of core processes that can deliver order-of-magnitude gain is called for. It is, however, prudent to try pilot projects prior to committing the organization to wholesale change. Once the administrative processes are right, then the software can be rewritten to accommodate them. *need to achieve mission?*
- *Develop strong skills among information resource managers, strong relationships between these managers and the rest of the organization, and rigorous performance measures.* These interrelated strengths entail the establishment of clear definitions of roles and responsibilities, setting challenging goals, assuring an organization-wide perspective of information resource management projects as investments, not as overhead costs, and the inclusion of the chief information officer as a top management player—a condition not typically found in public agencies.[96]
- *Minimize risks.* Minimizing risk is especially important when an operation is critical, such as meeting payroll schedules. Politics contribute to agencies' risks, because competitive agencies or subunits will protect their traditional turfs, which new data systems can threaten; hence, wringing agreements about project specifications from department heads is both vital and tough. Unbundling projects into separate modules also reduces risk because failures are isolated, and the whole system is less likely to crash. Knowing one's capabilities is important when unbundling is undertaken, and the management of some project components are best outsourced to outside experts when one's own expertise is limited.

Clarifying Public Decisions

Public administrators interact with increasing intensity and frequency with the public information resource. Has this interaction changed the nature of their decision making?

Making Different Decisions?

Yes, probably. One study concluded that midlevel public managers actually appear to make *different kinds* of decisions depending upon whether or not they are computer literate! "When computers are involved, computer literate decision makers choose different information than computer novices and . . . the selection of computer information has an effect on the outcome of the decision."[97]

Decision makers at the top levels of organizations may be a different story, and generally, most investigators seem to agree that information technology does not affect the behavior of top-level decision makers very much one way or another. One investigator, after interviewing more than a hundred top managers and examining in detail the decision-making process in more than a dozen large companies, concluded that the computer has not had much impact on decision making at the top, although information technology has speeded the overall decision-making process in organizations by making more information more readily available to top managers.[98]

Making Better Decision?

Is information technology irrelevant to making better decisions, as some chief executive officers would have us believe? What little empirical evidence there is suggests that the use of information technology does indeed facilitate better decisions in organizations. An intensive investigation of four corporations, which assessed the effects of information technology on the strategic decision process, is particularly illuminating.

The researchers found that "the use of information technology does improve both the efficiency and, more importantly, the effectiveness of the decision-making process. . . . "Information technology resulted in higher quality . . . decisions."[99]

The utility of information systems is improving organizational performance in the public sector as well. A survey of county administrators found the adoption of information technology had "a direct effect on performance." Information technology increased the number of participants in county decision making, which improved "technical decision making" by county governments, and "as more types of technology were adopted by the organization, technical decision making improved."[100]

The Information Resource and the Future of Governance

The role of information technologies in changing how governments are run goes considerably beyond putting government services on the Web. These technologies already have transformed much of government and bode to transmute all of it.

Because of information technology, "public agencies of the welfare state appear to be quietly undergoing a fundamental change of character. . . . Window clerks are being replaced by Web sites. . . . Today, a more true-to-life vision of the term 'bureaucracy' would be a room filled with softly humming servers, dotted here and there with a system manager behind a screen."[101]

The Transmutation of Government

The public bureaucracy has been transformed by a slow but steady elimination of *street-level bureaucrats*, or those public employees who interact directly with citizens, and their replacement by a *screen-level bureaucracy*, or a routinized decision-making process in which public officials, when they are in direct contact with citizens at all, communicate with them through a computer screen.

Screen-level bureaucracies are, in turn, fading away in favor of *system-level bureaucracies*. System-level bureaucracies transfer administrative discretion (formerly a preserve of the street-level bureaucrats) to system designers and other officials who are actively engaged in data processing.

The rise of these data processors largely, perhaps entirely, terminates face-to-face interaction between citizens and administrators (with the exception of those bureaucrats, such as help-desk workers, who merely interface between citizens and system). As a result, even the possibility of public administrators exercising administrative discretion withers.[102]

The Transmutation of Governance

With the rise of system-level bureaucracies, we also are witnessing the corresponding rise of *infocracies*, or the information elites who dominate the public bureaucracy.[103] These elites derive their powers from both the bottom and the top of the bureaucratic hierarchy.

At the bottom of the hierarchy, infocrats displace street-level bureaucrats by confining the space in which they can make decisions, and their jobs thereby tend to be downgraded. At the top of the hierarchy, elected officeholders usually are "insufficiently aware of the possibilities" of the information resource, and therefore are hesitant to fully use them. "So, in the practical absence of politicians and elected officials, non-elected public officials have a free playing field," and the infocrats "know better than the people's representatives" the conditions and opinions of these representatives' own constituencies.[104]

At the level of the citizen, governance is characterized by the notorious *digital divide*, or the propensity of information technology to deepen the disadvantages of those already disadvantaged by dint of their being less able to participate in the information revolution. As street-level bureaucracies decline, the power of computer-illiterate citizens to communicate with government also diminishes. Conversely, however, as system-level bureaucracies expand, computer-savvy citizens see their relationships with government enhanced.[105]

Never before in human history has a technology so metamorphosed democracy itself. The transfiguration of democracy, however, may be the least of the computer's impact. Galileo and Copernicus showed us that human beings are not at the center of the universe; Darwin enlightened us with the knowledge that humanity is not created by God, not especially endowed with soul and reason; Freud demonstrated that the individual person is not completely rational; and the computer will yield us the insight that the human race is not uniquely capable of thinking, learning, and changing its environment.[106]

In this chapter, we have reviewed some of the ways in public administrators *clarify* some of the basic issues of public management. In the following three chapters, we address how public administrators *do* public management.

Notes

1. U.S. Government Accountability Office, *Information Security: Improving Oversight of Access to Federal Systems and Data by Contractors Can Reduce Risk*, GAO–05–362 (Washington, DC: U.S. Government Printing Office, 2005), p. 4. In 2005, the GAO stated that the U.S. government "plans to invest approximately $65 billion annually on IT."

2. U.S. General Accounting Office, *Contracting for Information Technology Services*, GAO–03–384R Contracting for IT Services (Washington, DC: U.S. Government Printing Office, 2003), p. 1. In 1997, IT services contracted out to private firms cost over $9 billion; in 2001, they cost more than $17 billion. At the time, total federal expenditures for IT were about $45 billion. See Colleen O'Hara, Diane frank, and Dan Caterinicchia. "Budget Hawks Watch IT Projects," *Federal Computer Week* (August 2001), pp. 28–30.

3. Brian Deagon, "The Government Looks at Why Huge Technology Efforts Often Fail," *Investor's Business Daily* (July 12, 1994).

4. Gary Enos, "Calling in Help," *Governing* (July 2001), pp. 55–56.

5. G2 Research, Inc., and Federal Sources, Inc., as cited in Peter Behr, "Information Technology, Please," *Washington Post* (October 9, 1995), and "The Business of Government," *Governing* (July 1994), p. 51.

6. Norm Coleman, "Tax Cheats at the Government Trough," *New York Times* (June 25, 2005). Coleman is a U.S. senator from Minnesota and chairs the Senate Permanent Subcommittee on Investigations.

7. Ibid and U.S. General Accounting Office, *Financial Management: Some DOD Contractors Abuse the Federal Tax System with Little Consequence*, GAO–04–95 (Washington, DC: U.S. Government Printing Office, 2004). In the Pentagon alone, 27,000 contractors owed more than $3 billion in unpaid taxes. It was determined that the Federal Patent Levy Program was not working, so federal agencies established the Federal Contractor Tax Compliance Task Force as a watchdog for the levy program. The situation has improved, but problems remain. Washington still fails to assure that companies' tax information is accurate; does not always aggressively prosecute tax cheaters; and does not provide an annual list of federal contractors who have been convicted of tax-related crimes or who have had tax liens placed against them.

8. U.S. Government Accountability Office, *Financial Management: State and Federal Governments Are Not Taking Action to Collect Unpaid Debt through Reciprocal Agreements*, GAO–05–697R Reciprocal Agreements for Collecting Unpaid Debt (Washington, DC: U.S. Government Printing Office, 2005), p. 2. Figures are for 2004.

9. U.S. General Accounting Office, *Information Management: Selected Agencies' Handling of Personal Information*, GAO–02–1058. (Washington, DC: U.S. Government Printing Office, 2002), p. 1.

10. U.S. General Accounting Office, *Privacy Act: OMB Leadership Needed to Improve Agency Compliance*, GAO–03–304 (Washington, DC: U.S. Government Printing Office, 2003), p. 13.

11. Anne R. Field, " 'Big Brother, Inc.' May Be Closer than You Thought," *Business Week* (February 9, 1987), p. 27, and Priscilla M. Regan, "Privacy, Government Information, and Technology," *Public Administration Review* 46 (November/December 1986), p. 631.

12. U.S. Government Accountability Office, *Taxpayer Information: Options Exist to Enable Data Sharing between IRS and USCIS but Each Presents Challenges*, GAO–06–100 (Washington, DC: U.S. Government Printing Office, 2005), Highlights page. Figure is for 2000.

13. Field, "'Big Brother, Inc.' May Be Closer than You Thought," p. 27; and Christopher Swope, "Sherlock Online," *Governing* (September 2000), pp. 80–84.

14. Field, "'Big Brother, Inc.' May Be Closer than You Thought," p. 28; and Regan, "Privacy, Government Information, and Technology," p. 631. The years were 1980–1984. New controls, however, are being introduced; from 1984 to 1989, when Congress stopped the practice, the Social Security Administration provided credit bureaus with verification of citizens' Social Security numbers.

15. Surveys by Equifax and Louis Harris and Associates, and by Yankelovich, respectively, as cited in "80% Fear Loss of Privacy to Computers," *USA Today* (September 3, 1995); and Graphic, Verification, and Usability Center, Georgia Institute of Technology, *GVU's Tenth WWW User Survey* (Atlanta: Author, 1999), which found that 80 percent of Internet users were concerned about security on the World Wide Web.

16. Don E. Cozzetto and Theodore B. Pedeliski, "Privacy and the Workplace: Future Implications for Managers," *Review of Public Personnel Administration* 16 (Spring 1996), pp. 21–31.

17. Lisa A. Nelson, "Privacy and Technology: Reconsidering a Crucial Public Policy Debate in the Post–September 11 Era," *Public Administration Review* 64 (May/June 2004), p. 259.

18. U.S. General Accounting Office, *Information Management: Selected Agencies' Handling of Personal Information*, p. 1. GAO reviewed the departments of Agriculture, Education, Labor, and State, which were selected because they were broadly representative of

how the federal government collects and processes information about individual citizens.

19. U.S. General Accounting Office, *Privacy Act: OMB Leadership Needed to Improve Agency Compliance,* Highlights page.

20. M. J. Zuckerman, "Companies Fear Losing Privacy, Customers' Trust," *U.S.A Today* (July 2, 1996).

21. Study sponsored by the FBI, as cited in U.S. General Accounting Office, *Information Security: Computer Attacks at Department of Defense Pose Increasing Risks,* GAO/AIMD–96–84 (Washington, DC: U.S. Government Printing Office, 1996), p. 3.

22. Computer Emergency Response Team, Carnegie Mellon University, *Cert/CC Statistics 1988–2005* (Philadelphia: Author, 2005), http://www.cert.org. In 1988, six instances of hacking were reported; in 2003, the final year that CERT tracked this figure, 137,529 instances were reported.

23. Zuckerman, "Companies Fear Losing Privacy, Customers' Trust."

24. U.S. General Accounting Office, *Information Security: Computer Attacks at Department of Defense Pose Increasing Risks,* p. 2.

25. Michael Specter, "The Doomsday Click," *The New Yorker* (May 28, 2001), pp. 101–102.

26. Zuckerman, "Companies Fear Losing Privacy, Customers' Trust."

27. U.S. General Accounting Office, *Information Security: Computer Attacks at Department of Defense Pose Increasing Risks,* p. 2.

28. Florence Olsen, "Input: Security Spending to Rise," *FCWCOM* (March 17, 2005), http://www.fcw.com.

29. Florence Olsen, "Input: IT Security Spending to Catch Its Breath," *FCWCOM* (July 14, 2005), http://www.fcw.com.

30. Olsen, "Input: Security Spending to Rise." In 2005, federal spending on IT security was $5.6 billion, and OMB projected that IT security spending would increase by about 4 percent per year for the next five years. See ibid. and Olsen, "Input: Security Spending to Catch Its Breath."

31. U.S. General Accounting Office, *Information Security: Serious Weaknesses Place Critical Federal Operations and Assets at Risk,* GAO–AIMD–98–92 (Washington, DC: U.S. Government Printing Office, 1996), p. 5. Two dozen major federal agencies were audited, accounting for 99 percent of federal expenditures.

32. U.S. Office of Management and Budget, "Making Government More Effective," *Budget of the United States Government, Fiscal Year 2006* (Washington, DC: U.S. Government Printing Office, 2005), p. 52. In 2005, 77 percent of federal systems were certified as secure; in 2002, 26 percent were.

33. Ibid., p. 3, and Computer Emergency Response Team, Carnegie Mellon University, *CERT/CC Statistics 1988–2005.*

34. Ibid. (both citations), and Computer Emergency Response Team, Carnegie Mellon University, *2004 E-Crime Watch Survey Shows Significant Increase in Electronic Crimes* (Philadelphia: Author, 2004), http://www.cert.org.

35. Government Reform Committee, U.S. House of Representatives, "Federal Computer Security Report Card" (Washington, DC: Author, 2005). Grade is for 2003. In 2004, the government received a "D+."

36. Ibid. Grade is for 2003 and 2004. The good news (?) is that Defense's grade for computer security tops that of the Department of Homeland Security, which has yet to exceed "F."

37. U.S. General Accounting Office, *Information Security: Computer Attacks at Department Of Defense Pose Increasing Risks,* p. 2.

38. Zeichner Risk Analytics study, as cited in Brian Krebs, "States not Ready for Cyberattacks–Report," *Washington Post* (March 21, 2003). Data are for 2003.

39. Zeichner Risk Analytics study, as cited in Jonathan Krim, "States Seen as Lax on Database Security," *Washington Post* (March 26, 2003). Data are for 2003.

40. Stephen J. Bajjaly, "Managing Emerging Information Systems in the Public Sector," *Public Productivity and Management Review* 23 (September 1999), p. 46.

41. Stuart Bretschneider, "Management Information Systems in Public and Private Organizations: An Empirical Test," *Public Administration Review* 50 (September/October 1990), pp. 536–545.

42. Thomas R. Davies, "The Inside Story," *Governing* (December 2003), p. 64. Davies interviewed top IT managers in seven states.

43. U.S. Internal Revenue Service, *Management Review of the Contracts and Acquisitions Division,* (Washington, DC.: U.S. Department of the Treasury, 1990).

44. U.S. General Accounting Office, *Facing Facts: Comptroller General's 1989 Annual Report* (Washington, D.C.: U.S. Government Printing Office, 1990), p. 27.

45. Information Technology Association of America, *Key Issues in Federal Information Technology* (Arlington, VA: Author, 1992), p. 4.

46. David McClure, quoted in Deagon, "The Government Looks at Why Huge Technology Efforts Often Fail."

47. U.S. General Accounting Office, *Paperwork Reduction Act: Record Increase in Agencies' Burden Estimates.* GAO–03–691T (Washington, DC: U.S. Government Printing Office, 2003), p. 2.

48. U.S. Government Accountability Office, Federal Chief Information Officers: Responsibilities, Reporting Relationships, Tenure, and Challenges. GAO–04–823 (Washington, DC: U.S. Government Printing Office, 2004), Highlights page.

49. U.S. General Accounting Office, *Information Technology: Leadership Remains Key to Agencies Making Progress on Enterprise Architecture Efforts,* GAO–04–40 (Washington, DC: U.S. Government Printing Office, 2003).

50. U.S. General Accounting Office, *Information Technology Management: Governmentwide Strategic Planning, Performance Measurement, and Investment Management Can Be Further Improved,* GAO–04–49 (Washington, DC: U.S. Government Printing Office, 2004), Highlights page.

51. Colleen O'Hara, "Feds Feel Job Satisfaction," *Federal Computer Week* (March 31, 2001), p. 30. Forty-one percent said this.

52. Mary Dalrymple, Associated Press, "IRS Measures $300 Billion Tax Gap, Fails to Charge Interest on Tax Penalties," *Savannah Morning News* (March 30, 2005). In 2001, according to an internal IRS analysis, the feds failed to collect from $313 billion to $353 billion (estimated), and in 2002 the IRS could have charged over $817 billion in interest if its computers had applied the penalties to cover taxpayer accounts quarterly. This situation has festered for some time. In 1996, the IRS could not collect 14 percent of the taxes owed it. See Ralph Vartabedian, "To an IRS Mired in the 60s, '90s Answers Prove Elusive," *Los Angeles Times* (December 10, 1996). See also U.S. Government Accountability Office, *Tax Gap: Multiple Strategies, Better Compliance Data, and Long-Term Goals Are Needed to Improve Taxpayer Compliance,* GAO–06–208T (Washington, DC: U.S. Government Printing Office, 2005).

53. Surveys and Investigations Staff, Appropriations Committee, U.S. House of Representatives, "confidential report" as cited in Dan Eggen, "FBI Pushed Ahead with Troubled Software," *Washington Post* (June 6, 2005). Representative Frank R. Wolf is quoted. Apparently, the FBI resisted renegotiating its contract, even after it knew that it was mired in a fiasco, because some of its officials thought that they would be able to show observers some sort of face-saving result if they hung in there. They were wrong. See also U.S. Government Accountability Office, *Information Technology: FBI is Taking Steps to Develop an Enterprise Architecture, but Much Remains to Be Accomplished,* GAO–05–363 (Washington, DC: U.S. Government Printing Office, 2005). This report concluded that the FBI relied "heavily" on contractors to develop its information technology, "but has not employed effective contract management controls in doing so" (Highlights page).

54. U.S. Government Accountability Office, *Federal Chief Information Officers,* pp. 20, 22.

55. Gregory B. Lewis and Zhenhua Hu, "Information Technology Workers in the Federal Service: More Than a Quiet Crisis?" *Review of Public Personnel Administration* 25 (September 2005), pp. 207–224. The quotations are on pp. 207 and 222. This was an examination of a 1 percent sample of federal personnel records for 1976–2003. Even though Washington was hiring IT professionals at higher than normal salaries during this period, they still lagged significantly behind the private sector, making it all the more puzzling why turnover rates are so comparable with professionals in other fields. In the mid-1990s, private industry spent 50 cents on salaries for every dollar that it expended on information systems,; the feds spent 22 cents. See Ralph Vartabedian, "U.S. Mounts High-Stakes Computer Reform Effort," *Los Angeles Times* (December 11, 1996).

56. U.S. General Accounting Office, *Paperwork Reduction Act,* pp. 4–12. Figures are for 1995–2001. Nearly half of the 17 percent increase occurred in FY 2002 alone. Almost 95 percent of these 8.2 burden hours were generated by regulatory compliance procedures.

57. Vartabedian, "Federal Computers: A System Gone Haywire?"

58. Ibid.

59. IBM/Robert H. Smith School of Business, University of Maryland study, 2002, as cited in "IT Wish List," *Governing* (September 2003), p. 54. This was a survey of the goals of government technology initiatives, based on a survey of 400 IT professionals. The precise percentages are 51, 22, and 11, respectively.

60. National Association of State-Information Resource Executives, *Issue Focus Report: The Role of the State Chief Information Officer* (Lexington, KY: Author, 2000), p. 1.

61. U.S. General Accounting Office, *Child Welfare: States Face Challenges in Developing Information Systems and Reporting Reliable Child Welfare Data,* GAO–04–267T (Washington, DC: U.S. Government Printing Office, 2003).

62. Glen Hahn Cope, "Budgeting for Performance in Local Government," *Municipal Year Book, 1995* (Washington, D.C.: International City/County Management Association, 1995), p. 51.

63. John Scoggins, Thomas H. Tidrick, and Jill Auerback, "Computer Use in Local Government," *Municipal Year Book, 1986* (Washington, D.C.: International City Management Association, 1986), p. 43.

64. G. Zhiyong Lan, Lera Riley, and N. Joseph Cayer, "How Can Local Government Become an Employer of Choice for Technical Professionals? Lessons and Experiences from the City of Phoenix," *Review of Public Personnel Administration* 25 (Fall 2005), p. 225.

65. Forester Research, Inc., as cited in "e-Gov Momentum," *Governing* (August 2001), p. 46. In 2000, local governments had roughly 1,500 e-gov applications, and the federal and state governments about 1,000 each. It was projected that, by 2006, local applications would hit 9,000, federal applications, 2,000, and state applications 3,000.

66. Christopher Weare, Juliet A. Musso, and Matthew L. Hale, "Electronic Democracy and the Diffusion of Municipal Web Pages in California," *Administration and Society* 31 (March 1999), pp. 3–27.

67. Mark A. Abramson, Jonathan D. Gould, and John M. Kamensky, *Four Trends Transforming Government* (Washington, DC: IBM Center for The Business of Government, 2003), p. 10; and Robert D. Behn, ."The Varieties of CitiStat," *Public Administration Review* 66 (May/June 2006), pp. 332–340.

68. Council for Excellence in Government, *The New E-Government Equation: Ease, Engagement, Privacy and Protection* (Washington, DC: Author, 2003), p. 1. Data are for 2003. Three-fourths of all Americans with Internet experience have visited a government web site: 59 percent of these users have visited a federal agency Web site; 54 percent have visited a state government Web site; and 43 percent have visited a local government Web site.

69. U.S. Government Accountability Office, *Electronic Government: Federal Agencies Have Made Progress Implementing the E-Government Act of 2002.* GAO–05–12 (Washington, DC: U.S. Government Printing Office, 2004), p. 2.

70. U.S. General Accounting Office, Electronic Transfers: Use by Federal Payment Recipients Has Increased but Obstacles to Greater *Participation Remain,* GAO–02–913 (Washington, DC: U.S. Government Printing Office, 2002). Figure is for 2002.

71. U. S. General Accounting Office, *Electronic Government.* GAO/T–AIMD/GGD–00–179 (Washington, DC: U. S. Government Printing Office, 2000).

72. Ibid. Figure is for 2000.

73. Graeme Browning, "Dot-gov Goes Retail," *Federal Computer Week* (May 28, 2001), pp. 21–27. This is the first survey of its kind. In 2000, Washington sold more than $3.6 billion of goods, and Amazon.com sold $2.8 billion.

74. Ellen Perlman, "The People Connection," *Governing* (September 2002), p. 32.

75. David Barstow, "A.T.M. Cards Fail to Live Up to Promises to Poor," *New York Times* (August 16, 1999). Figures are for 1999.

76. Shane Harris, "Getting Down to Business," *Governing* (September 2002), p. 42. Figure is for 2001.

77. "Slowdown Ahead for Financing E-Procurement," *Governing* (July 2001), p. 70.

78. Shavaun Rigler, "The Grantmakers: What Are They Doing? How Well Are They Doing It?" *The Grantsmanship Center Magazine* (Summer 2003), http://www.tgci.com.

79. Donald F. Norris and M. Jae Moon, "Advancing E-Government at the Grassroots: Tortoise or Hare?" *Public Administration Review* 65 (January/February 2005), pp. 64–73.

80. John O'Looney, "Use of the Internet for Citizen Participation and Service Delivery," *Municipal Year Book, 2001* (Washington, DC: International City/County Management Association, 2001), p. 28. In 2000, 96 percent of all cities and counties had Web sites.

81. David Coursey, "E-Government: Trends, Benefits, and Challenges," *Municipal Year Book, 2005* (Washington, DC: International City/County Management Association, 2005), pp. 14–21.

82. Ibid., p. 14.

83. Elvina R. Moulder, "E-Government: Trends, Opportunities, and Challenges," *Municipal Year Book, 2003* (Washington, DC: International City/County Management Association, 2003), p. 43. Figure is for 2002.

84. Coursey, "E-Government," p. 17. Figures are for 2004.

85. Ibid.. Figures are for 2004.

86. Civic Resource Group, *Cities on the Internet, 2001: E-Government Applied* (Santa Monica, CA: Author, 2001). Figures are for 2001. All 270 cities with populations of 100,000 or more were surveyed.

87. Council for Excellence in Government, *The New E-Government Equation,* pp. 2, 5. Figures are for 2003.

88. Council for Excellence in Government, *E-Government: To Connect, Protect, and Serve Us* (Washington, DC: Author, 2002), pp. 19–20. Figures are for 2001.

89. Eric C. Welch, "Linking Citizen Satisfaction with E-Government and Trust in Government," *Journal of Public Administration Research and Theory* 15 (Summer 2005), pp. 371–392. The quotation is on p. 371.

90. Council for Excellence in Government, *The New E-Government Equation,* p. 24. Figures are for 2003.

91. Coursey, "E-Government," p. 17. Figures are for 2004.

92. Ibid. In 2004, 2 percent of local officials reported this.

93. Rob Gurtwitt, "Behind the Portal," *Governing* (August 2001), p. 50.

94. Coursey, "E Government," p. 17. Figures are for 2004.

95. We have relied largely on: Bajjaly, "Managing Emerging Information Systems in the Public Sector," pp. 40–47; Bruce Rocheleau, "Prescriptions for Public-Sector Information Management: A Review, Analysis, and Critique," *American Review of Public Administration* 30 (December 2000), pp. 414–435; U.S. General Accounting Office, *Improving Mission Performance Through Strategic Information Management and Technology*; William Cats-Baril and Ronald Thompson, "Managing Information Technology Projects in the Public Sector," *Public Administration Review* 55 (November/December 1995), pp. 559–566; and National Association of State Information Resource Executives, *Best Practices in the Use of Information Technology in State Government* (Lexington, KY: Author, 2000).

96. Bretschneider, "Management Information Systems in Public and Private Organizations," p. 537.

97. Ralph F. Shangraw, Jr., "How Public Managers Use Information: An Experiment Examining Choices of Computer and Printed Information," *Public Administration Review* 46 (November 1986), p. 514.

98. Rodney H. Brady, "Computers in Top Level-Decision Making," *Harvard Business Review* 45 (July/August 1967), pp. 67–76.

99. Steve Molloy and Charles R. Schwenk, "The Effects of Information Technology on Strategic Decision-Making," *Journal of Management Studies* 32 (May 1995), pp. 288, 301.

100. Theresa Heintz and Stuart Bretschneider, "Information Technology and Restructuring in Public Organizations: Does Adoption of Information Technology Affect Organizational Structures, Communications, and Decision Making?" *Journal of Public Administration and Theory* 10 (October 2000), pp. 801–828.

101. Mark Bovens and Stavros Zouridis, "From Street-level to System-Level Bureaucracies: How Information and Communication Technology is Transforming Administrative Discretion and Control," *Public Administration Review* 62 (March/April 2002), pp. 174–175.

102. Ibid., pp. 174–184.

103. Ignace Snellen, "Electronic Governance: Implications for Citizens, Politicians and Public Servants," *International Review of Administrative Sciences* 65 (June 2002), p. 194.

104. Ibid., pp. 190–197.

105. Ibid.

106. Herbert A. Simon, *The Shape of Automation for Men and Management* (New York: Harper & Row, 1965).

CHAPTER 7

Corruption's Consequence: Public Productivity

Planted in a lush landscape of large political change and reared in reformist roots, the public productivity movement, notably the methods of performance measurement and public program evaluation, sprouted into the Saguaro cactus of public management: tall, tough, prickly, and dry.

Juicier, perhaps, are estimates of what the public may gain from improved governmental productivity. The Government Accountability Office (GAO) has stated that for every 5 percent increase in federal productivity, the federal government would save $4.5 billion, and Congress has contended that a 10 percent increase in the productivity of the federal government could reduce federal expenses by $8 billion, yet maintain present levels of service.[1]

As impressive as these numbers sound, however, governments are inherently unable to attain the same levels of productivity found in the private sector. This is because the service-intensive character of government, by its very nature, inhibits gains in public productivity.

In the private sector, notably in manufacturing and agriculture, investments can be made in technology that increase productivity by replacing labor. But government services are unable to benefit to the same degree from such investments. Most government employees, such as teachers, social workers, police, and firefighters, are direct, hands-on producers. Their services are, in effect, the final product, and the quality of that product is part and parcel of public productivity itself. Hence, it is extremely difficult to make teachers more productive by increasing their class sizes, to make social workers more productive by increasing their caseloads, or to make police and firefighters more productive by decreasing their numbers. In these instances, the quality of service inevitably suffers. "The same might be said for playing a string quartet with two instruments: More productive, perhaps, but it's not the same thing."[2]

With this caveat in mind, we enter our discussion of public productivity, focusing especially on its attendant techniques, performance measurement and public program evaluation.

Naming Things What They Are

The Chinese have a saying that, translated very roughly, means, "First, we must name things what they are." Nowhere is this sentence more salient than in the subtle and sometimes confusing world of measuring and evaluating the productivity of public management.

Government attempts to improve its own productivity can be traced back to the early nineteenth century,[3] and have focused on several broad issues, such as expenditure control, tax reduction, and accountability. At base, however, the values of efficiency and effectiveness have never been far from view and usually have been centerpieces. *Efficiency* is the accomplishment of a job using the fewest resources possible, or "the biggest bang for the buck." *Effectiveness* is the full production of the intended result.

We remind ourselves of these fundamental definitions because the terms are not as universal as one might expect. There is, for example, no word in Russian for the concept of efficiency, although there is one for effectiveness.[4] Those who ever faced the fearsome might of the Red Army can appreciate the latter point.

The basis of the public sector's effort to improve its efficiency and effectiveness is performance measurement, or what some analysts prefer to call "performance indicators," on the grounds that the term "measurement" implies an ability to precisely measure policy outcomes, even though such precision is rarely attained in the messily human arena of policy implementation.[5] *Performance measurement* is "the ongoing monitoring and reporting of program accomplishments, particularly progress towards pre-established goals."[6] Performance measurement typically must be done before a public program evaluation can be undertaken.

Public program evaluation, or *evaluation research*, is the "individual systematic studies conducted periodically or on an ad hoc basis to assess how well a program is working."[7] More amply, "program evaluation is a way of bringing to public decision makers the available knowledge about a problem, about the relative effectiveness of past strategies for addressing or reducing that problem, and about the observed effectiveness of particular programs."[8]

Program evaluation differs from performance measurement on two dimensions: focus and use. Performance measurement focuses on whether a program has achieved its measurable goals, whereas a program evaluation is broader in scope and examines a greater range of information in a larger environment. Similarly, although both are used to improve service delivery and program effectiveness, performance measurement is used mostly as an early warning system to managers should a program falter, and as a method for improving governmental accountability to the public; a program evaluation, by contrast, is a deeper inquiry into a program's performance and its context and seeks to develop a comprehensive assessment of whether the program works and how it might be improved.[9]

Productivity concludes our definitional discussion. *Productivity* is government's improvement of efficiency and effectiveness in delivering its services, or, more formally, "a ratio between inputs and outputs. Productivity is improved when increases of output are achieved per unit of input."[10] *Inputs* are the resources used by a program, such as money, people, or time. *Outputs* are the final products of a program, such as arrests made or Social Security checks sent.

Productivity is the larger environment in which the evaluations of public programs are conducted, and it is an environment that is less than tidy. One review of the literature on productivity concluded, quite accurately, that "the amazing thing about public productivity research is [that] different clusters of researchers investigate the same problems in different ways . . . the majority of researchers in one cluster are not aware, let alone familiar with, the studies of the other clusters . . . all these differences put researchers into intellectual ghettos."[11]

Despite these problems, however, public productivity constitutes an environment of optimism about the prospects of improving public management. Productivity is the *proactive* quest for better government. Although productivity includes performance measurement and program evaluation, it is more expansive in concept and its uniqueness lies in its propensity to look toward the future: What more can government do, what initiatives can it take, what innovations can it create to improve the citizens' lot by rendering government more responsive, effective, efficient, open, and honest?

Curtailing Corruption: Do Productivity Measures Help?

Productivity evolved from a simple, moral concern: to improve government by eradicating corruption. It was widely believed, and not unreasonably so, among the reformers of the nineteenth century that the elimination of political corruption was the essential first step in attaining governmental efficiency and effectiveness. But their reasoning did not end there: If governments were grossly inefficient and ineffective, the reformers held, then these governments likely were corrupt as well. This, too, was not unreasonable in the context of the times. Thus, performance and productivity measures emerged as means that demonstrated, in objective terms, whether or not governments were not only efficient and effective, but also whether or not they were corrupt. In short, performance measurement was seen as a powerful tool in eliminating corruption, and this perception still holds today.

Table 7-1 shows that performance measures and program evaluations have always been bonded, if often indirectly and unconsciously, with corruption control in the American psyche. When corruption is perceived by society as a major problem, as it was during the early twentieth century, interest in governmental productivity rises; when corruption is seen as a relatively minor annoyance, productivity efforts fade.

How do Americans perceive corruption today? And are their perceptions accurate?

Confronting Corruption

Two-thirds of American voters believe that government is corrupt,[12] and the public's perception is that corruption is growing.[13] What are the facts?

Financial fraud in the federal government appears to account for considerably less than 1 percent of the federal budget. "Nevertheless, though relatively small in terms of the percentage of the budget impacted," one analysis concluded, fraud uncovered in the federal government "has proven to be extremely costly" simply because of the immensity of the federal budget.[14]

Prosecutions launched against federal officials and others engaged in defrauding the federal government have nearly quadrupled since 1980 and now are nearing 500 indictments per year.[15] (By contrast, corruption prosecutions at the state and local levels have remained relatively flat over the same period and there are far fewer of them than

federal prosecutions.[16]) Whether these burgeoning prosecutorial levels reflect increased corruption or the increased zeal of federal prosecutors cannot be known. However, it is known that considerably fewer than half (42 percent to 46 percent) of federal employees who allegedly defrauded the government on their own were prosecuted (compared to 60 percent of those who colluded with others to defraud), a prosecutorial rate described as "low."[17]

A useful annual poll, the Corruption Perceptions Index, which is a composite survey that is based on polls of risk analysts, international businesspeople, and the general public who have dealings with public officials in 159 countries, ranks the United States seventeenth in terms of its perceived corruption.[18]

In sum, most Americans think that their governments are corrupt. The evidence supporting their perception, however, is not strong. Still, even if governmental corruption in the United States is far from systemic, there is, nonetheless, corruption.

Controlling Corruption

What can performance measures, program evaluations, and other productivity efforts do about that corruption?

Measurement and Evaluation: Revealing but Limited. Measuring and evaluating public programs do, in fact, aid public administrators in objectively determining the productivity of public programs, and if a program's productivity is abnormally low, then certain conclusions are unavoidable. Specifically, those conclusions are the program was ill conceived and is unworkable; or the program is simply not needed; or the program is poorly managed; or the program has been corrupted; or all or some of these. In other words, ascertaining the level of a program's productivity can lead, at least potentially, to the detection of corruption.

Performance measurement and program evaluation, however, are not panaceas for corruption. Nor are the many other methods of public administration that are designed to assure honesty in government, such as auditing, accounting, inspecting, and civil service reform, to list a few. Under

Table 7-1   The Evolution of Performance Measurement, Public Program Evaluation, and Productivity

Feature	Efficiency (1990–1940)	Budgeting (1940–1970)	Management (1970–1980)	Privatization (1980–1992)	New Public Management (1992–present)
Motivation	"Good government," meaning more efficient and less corrupt government	Control expenses	Efficiency and effectiveness	Reduce deficit, taxes, government expenses, and government	Reduce government expenses, increase accountability, efficiency, effectiveness, and responsiveness, empower public administrators
Dominant Level of Government	Local, federal by 1930s	Low involvement at all levels	Federal, state, and local	Federal, some local	Local, then federal
Initiators	Citizens, businesspeople, scholars, and experts, time-and-motion studies, Bureau of Municipal Research. New Deal Administration, National Committee on Municipal Standards	Budget-oriented public administrators, and operations-and-management specialists, Great Society administrators; organization development pioneers	Elected officials, followed by public administrators and academics, Urban Institute, universities	Citizens and businesspeople, universities, conservative think tanks	Public administrators, followed by elected officials, universities
Political Environment/ Working Assumptions	Politics is separate from administration; efficiency equates with better government; better government equates with the elimination of corruption	Comprehensive productivity is not explicit as a goal, and is subsumed under budgetary innovations	Public and private sectors place a high premium on productivity	Private sector can improve the public sector's productivity	Empowered public administrators can produce more accountable, effective, efficient, and responsive government
Cultural Perspectives on Corruption	Corruption is the result of misuse of government by political parties and pervades the government from top to bottom	Corruption is limited to a few dishonest individuals and groups who defraud the government when the opportunity arises	Corruption is criminal combination of waste, fraud, and abuse that actively harms taxpayers and citizens		
Methods of Corruption Control	Isolating politics from administration and making public administration increasingly professional	Applying the principles of administration in designing the organization and processes of public agencies	Law enforcement, in the form of new and more restrictive checks, procedures, and investigations of public administrators and elected officials		Empowered public administrators and new information systems can control corruption

the right conditions, corrupt public officials are quite capable of shielding themselves from investigation and maintaining their profitable positions.

How to Succeed in Corruption without Really Trying. Research conducted in four countries, including the United States, found that, unsurprisingly, public officeholders who are being investigated for corrupt practices will make a concerted effort to undermine the credibility of the process and will try to derail it. The extent to which these corrupt officials are successful depends on the degree of centralization of the political system and its openness to the media. The more centralized and "fused" that political power is in the government, and the less access that the media have to the government, the more likely that corrupt officials will survive attempts to prosecute them.[19]

Nevertheless, even in those contexts of decentralized, diffused political power and governmental openness to the media, such as those usually found in the United States, entrenched, institutionalized corruption can successfully resist efforts to eliminate it. Consider a couple of cases.

Corruption as Conquest. On occasion, an otherwise-honest public agency is effectively "captured" by a corrupt suborganization. Often this suborganization is the crucial "dominant coalition"[20] in the organization that we described in Chapter 4, and, for all intents and purposes, it is the reigning power center that really runs the larger organization. Or, at least, the corrupt subunit sufficiently intimidates the relatively uncorrupted organization that it effectively backs off.

An example is New York City's school custodians. Custodial scandals have erupted since 1924 and continue unabated. A three-year investigation of the custodians found that they were "systematically transforming their schools into enterprises for bribery, extortion, theft, and nepotism. With little accountability and broad discretion over budgets and staff, custodians gave family and lovers no-show jobs as helpers and handed them thousands of dollars in fraudulent overtime. They used school maintenance budgets to renovate

their homes. They extorted kickbacks from emergency contractors. A number did not even maintain a presence at their schools, pursuing second jobs instead."[21] With a half-billion dollar budget and 8,500 employees allegedly "working" in 1,200 schools, the custodians' corruption persists in spite of the imposition of "performance accountability," work standards, and other controls. "Most principals . . . [are] terrified of what they dubbed custodians' 'reigns of terror'."[22]

Corruption as Culture. Another context of corruption is that which defines the public culture itself, and this kind of corruption can morph into one mean monster.

Consider the case of Phenix City, in Russell County, Alabama. Over the course of a century, Phenix City and Russell County had evolved in such a way that, by the 1950s, virtually every local official had some personally rewarding connection with racketeering, primarily gambling and prostitution. Albert Patterson, a state senator, was elected Alabama's attorney general on the pledge that he would clean up corruption in the two jurisdictions, which had become embarrassments to the state.

Patterson was assassinated shortly after the election. Alabama's governor promptly asked General Walter J. Hanna to investigate, and later appointed him as the commander of a military force to take charge of the city and county. The governor declared temporary martial law in Russell County, and replaced all law-enforcement agencies and the courts with Hanna's army. One hundred fifty-two people eventually were convicted of corruption.[23]

The Corruption Cure: Political Will. Given these examples, it seems patent that the eradication of political corruption requires strategies that go far beyond the milquetoast methods of audits, investigations, performance measures, and program evaluations. But it is important to keep in mind that these and other methods cannot, in and of themselves, curtail corruption of any kind, not even ordinary, purloining-a-pen-from-the-office corruption. They were never meant to. The anticorruptive power of the standard methods of public management is limited to discouraging and detecting corruption, not in destroying it.

The actual destruction of governmental corruption requires political will by public administrators, law enforcers, lawmakers, and the people themselves. For close to a century, New York has not shown the necessary political will, and the janitors in the city's schools continue to live the good, if corrupted, life, and at the expense of students, teachers, and taxpayers. By contrast, Alabama, after a century had elapsed, did demonstrate steely political will, and corruption finally was crushed in Phenix City and Russell County.

The deeper the corruption, the more political determination will be required to eliminate it. To root out pervasive corruption entails "overhauling management, eradicating special interests, and aggressively punishing misconduct."[24] Or, as was done in Phenix City, declare martial law and send in the troops. But the uprooting of even garden-variety corruption also demands political will, if only in the form of officials and citizens reporting minor transgressions and then taking appropriate action. So our fundamental point remains: Whatever the extent of the corruption, whether it is of the garden variety or it is the garden itself, political will is the key to its curtailment.

As we have noted, a popular concern with corruption weaves its way through governmental attempts to improve public productivity. The following sections review the evolution of the productivity movement in the United States and cast that movement in terms of efficiency, budgeting, management, privatization, and, our current phase of public productivity, the new public management. We also shall address political corruption throughout this discussion, but particularly in two more guises: corruption's expanding definition in the public's mind and in the context of the new public management. Table 7-1 arrays the evolution of the productivity movement.

Efficiency for Good Government, 1900–1940

The movement to focus public resources on the attainment of higher levels of productivity in government began in the cities. At the beginning of the twentieth century, American government was concentrated at the local level; aside from the national defense budget, nearly three-fourths of all public expenditures were expended by local governments.[25] Moreover, because the functions of local governments at that time were (and still are) mostly to provide routine, physical services (such as garbage collection, fire protection, water supplies, and so forth), local governmental tasks often were receptive to improved efficiency via the techniques of scientific management (recall Chapter 3), which was a flourishing enterprise of its own during this period.

The founding in 1906 of the New York Bureau of Municipal Research (noted in Chapter 2), which conducted a variety of studies on how to make municipal government more efficient, symbolized the scientific management movement as it pertained to urban governments. The National Committee on Municipal Standards, formed in 1928, was another major contributor in the development of ways of measuring the efficiency of government services and was likely the originator of the nation's first performance measures in the public sector. Certainly, however, the publication in 1938 of the classic *Measuring Municipal Activities* by Clarence E. Ridley and Herbert A. Simon,[26] added serious impetus to the movement toward the measurement of government performance.

These early efforts at the municipal level found their way to the federal level as well. In 1912, the federal government created the Commission on Economy and Efficiency, although sustained federal interest in productivity and program evaluation began in the 1930s under the New Deal of Franklin Delano Roosevelt. The President's Committee on Administrative Management, noted in Chapter 2, which published its impressive report in 1937, is testimony to federal involvement in productivity efforts. And "efficiency" clearly was seen as the key that opened all locks to good government. As Luther Gulick noted in the report: "Efficiency is thus axiom number one in the value scale of administration. This brings administration into apparent conflict with the value scale of politics. . . ."[27]

The emphasis on efficiency during this era dovetailed neatly with a broader national concern over systematic governmental reform that

sci. mgmt
merit system
council-manager
attack corruption

focused on kicking the party hacks out of Washington, the state houses, and the county court houses, but especially out of the city halls. Public program evaluation and productivity were very much a part of the government reform movement that swept the United States during the late nineteenth and early twentieth centuries.

Office of Economic Opportunity (later retitled the Community Services Administration in 1975 and ultimately eliminated in 1981) was especially aggressive in encouraging an evaluation research component in its various projects. The Elementary and Secondary Education Act of 1965 did much to promote program evaluation in education.

Budgeting to Control Costs, 1940–1970

By 1940, the motivation to improve governmental productivity was a result less of a crusade to quash corruption and more of a concern over controlling costs. Corruption control, of course, remained a value, but it was less overt a value than it had been earlier and was subsumed into the larger effort to improve public management, with an emphasis on fiscal administration. In effect, this resulted in a view which held that organizational design could check corruption; the great public administrationist of that era, Leonard White, put it forthrightly: "Out of reform, moral in its motivation, came reorganization, technical and managerial in connotation."[28]

Corruption no longer was seen as a deep and pervasive problem in which political parties used taxpayers' monies to reward themselves via a spoils system. Instead, corruption was perceived as an occasional and sporadic phenomenon that mostly manifested itself in the form of dishonest individuals and small coteries seizing intermittent windows of opportunity for financial gain. These windows, it was felt, could be closed over time through the application of administrative principles and the installation of well-planned organizational structures and processes, and there was minimal interest in a comprehensive approach to productivity.

Nevertheless, some groundwork for later developments was being laid. The early pioneers of organization development, reviewed in Chapter 3, originated some of the basic theoretical precepts of program evaluation.[29] With the inauguration of Lyndon Baines Johnson's (LBJ's) Great Society legislation in the 1960s, social scientists rediscovered poverty, education, and similar domestic issues, and LBJ's

Managing for Efficiency and Effectiveness, 1970–1980

program eval.

By 1970, people in the public administration community were beginning to wonder what had happened to program evaluation and productivity. In 1971, a distinguished public administrationist asked, as the title of an editorial in the field's leading journal, "Why Does Public Administration Ignore Evaluation?"[30] and even four years later this author could accurately observe that "the practice of evaluation in public administration remains in its formative stages."[31]

The 1970s were an important decade for measuring, assessing, and improving public productivity. State and local governments were enthusiastic in their rediscovery and development of the methods of productivity enhancement, although Washington was almost rueful in displaying its lethargic interest in these same methods.

Federal Forward—Fitfully

A 1970 study of federal evaluation practices concluded that "the whole federal machinery for making policy and budget decisions suffers from a crucial weakness; it lacks a comprehensive system for measuring program effectiveness."[32] In that same year, a powerful senator noted to the Comptroller General of the United States (who heads the GAO) that it was "distressing that we have no real measures of the efficiency of the federal sector."[33]

Some Febrile Federal Efforts. Despite these critiques, efforts by the executive branch to improve federal productivity during the 1970s were not strong, although some innovations during this period had some surprising and satisfying long-term results.

In 1970, the Comptroller General appointed a task force that led to the creation by President Richard Nixon in the same year of the National Commission on Productivity, which eventually evolved into the National Center for Productivity and Quality of Working Life. Although the emphasis of the commission, and later the center, was on productivity in the private sector, both organizations had a public component.

The National Center for Productivity and Quality of Working Life folded in 1978, and its public-sector functions were transferred to a new group called the Center for Productive Public Management, which later became the National Center for Public Productivity. The center serves today as a national clearinghouse for public productivity studies at all levels of government.

The Inspector General. Congress's principal productivity prod during the 1970s was the establishment of inspectors general throughout the federal bureaucracy. *Inspectors general* (I.G.) are charged with exposing waste, fraud, and abuse in agencies, and to help administrators eliminate these problems.[34] I.G.s are found not only in Washington, but also in states, counties, cities, and school districts, and all governments have found them to be useful, occasionally extremely useful, in raising public productivity.

The appointment of federal I.G.s can be traced to the 1960s by a few agencies acting on their own volition, but their formal institution began with the Inspector General Act of 1978, which was broadened in 1988; currently, there are some sixty I.G. offices in as many federal agencies.[35] The I.G.s in the fourteen cabinet departments alone employ over 84,000 people.[36]

The twenty-seven inspectors general responsible for the largest federal agencies are nominated by the president and confirmed by the Senate; the remaining thirty-four I.G.s are appointed by agency heads without Senate confirmation. Uniquely, inspectors general report to both the heads of the agencies to which they are assigned *and* to Congress; moreover, they are the only presidential appointees who may communicate directly to Congress without clearance from

the Office of Management and Budget—a clear indication of their power in government.

The I.G.s have been aggressive and productive, and more than 38,000 federal employees, contractors, and others have been successfully prosecuted for corruption over a ten-year period as a consequence of investigations by inspectors general. I.G.s may recover for the federal government as much as $750 million a year in fines and penalties imposed on companies and individuals by the courts and save it $23 billion a year in retrieving questionable charges by contractors and by recommending ways to expend agency funds more astutely.[37]

In recent years, the budgets of federal inspectors general have declined, the consolidation of some I.G. offices has been proposed, and the nature of their audits has changed from traditional financial audits to performance audits. At least 60 percent of I.G. audits now are performance audits.[38] Inspectors general, according to one survey, were "very confident" about their progress, but recognize that they are at a "vulnerable junction" with regard to their resource base, independence and respect from Congress, and appreciation within the executive branch.[39]

The States Steam Forth

A survey of the states conducted in 1972 ascertained that only half of the forty-two responding state governments had a full-time program analyst in at least one agency.[40] A federal study conducted in 1978 indicated that state governments needed more evaluation research but faced significant problems in acquiring it.[41] A 1980 survey of state governments found that, while most states still did not have comprehensive, formal productivity improvement programs, there remained considerable interest in program evaluation.[42]

This interest bore results. Table 7-2 shows the significant progress that state agencies and legislatures made in conducting program analyses during the seventies. The percentage of state agencies that were conducting effectiveness evaluations nearly tripled, and those conducting productivity analyses more than doubled. By the end of the decade, over two-fifths of major state agencies were conducting such studies.

Table 7-2   Conduct of State Program Analyses, 1970, 1980, 1990, and 2000

State Agency	*Percentage of States Conducting Program Analysis*			
	1970	*1980*	*1990*	*2000*
Central budget office conducts effectiveness/productivity analyses	18/31%	53/75%	66/94%	59/59%
Most major agencies conduct effectiveness/productivity analyses	14/20%	44/41%	45/49%	50/53%
Legislature conducts effectiveness/productivity analyses	14/16%	42/39%	51/51%	53/53%
Postauditor conducts program analysis	4%	42%	38%	59%

Note: Percentages are for all fifty states and the District of Columbia.

Source: As derived from data in Robert C. Burns and Robert D. Lee, Jr., "The Ups and Downs of State Budget Process Reform: Experience of Three Decades," *Public Budgeting and Finance* 24 (Fall 2004), p. 10.

Local Leadership

As with the state governments, the base line of progress for local governments dates to the early 1970s. As Table 7-3 indicates, a national survey of local governments conducted in 1971 found that less than two-fifths of the responding governments had some form of program evaluation unit in even one agency or more. This percentage had burgeoned to nearly two-thirds, however, only five years later.

In contrast to Washington, local governments enthusiastically rediscovered program evaluation and productivity during the seventies. New York City placed a great emphasis on increasing municipal productivity, and the Urban Institute and various urban professional associations provided much of the research on new techniques of public program evaluation and productivity during this management-oriented phase.

Table 7-3   Local Governments' Use of Program Evaluation, Performance Monitoring, and Productivity Improvement Programs, 1971–2001

	1971	*1976*	*1982*	*1987*	*1993*	*2001*
	N = 354	*N = 404*	*N = 460*	*N = 451*	*N = 520*	*N = 277*
Program Evaluation	38%	64%	——	80%	75%	——
Performance Monitoring	——	28%	68%	67%	75%	88%
Productivity Improvement	——	43%	67%	54%	53%	——

Note: The 1971 survey covered cities and counties with 50,000 people or more; the 1976 through 1993 surveys covered cities with 25,000 to 1 million people; the 2001 survey covered cities and counties, but did not identify population sizes, and polled for "performance measurement," not the closely related "performance monitoring" as the earlier surveys had.

Sources: For 1971 data, Richard E. Winnie, "Local Government Budgeting, Program Planning, and Evaluation," *Urban Data Services Report* 4, No. 5 (Washington, DC: International City Management Association, May 1972); 1976 data derived from Rackham S. Fukuhara, "Productivity Improvement in Cities," *The Municipal Year Book, 1977* (Washington, DC: International City Management Association, 1977), pp. 193–200; 1982 data from Theodore H. Poister and Robert P. McGowan, "The Use of Management Tools in Municipal Government: A National Survey," *Public Administration Review* 44 (May/June 1984), p. 218; 1987 data from Theodore H. Poister and Gregory Streib, "Management Tools in Municipal Government: Trends over the Past Decade," *Public Administration Review* 49 (May/June 1989), pp. 240–248; 1993 data from Theodore H. Poister and Gregory Streib, "Municipal Management Tools from 1976 to 1993: An Overview and Update," *Public Productivity and Management Review* 18 (Winter 1994), pp. 115–125; and 2001 data from Government Accounting Standards Board, *Performance Measurement at the State and Local Levels: A Summary of Survey Results* (Washington, DC: Author, 2002), p. 5.

Privatizing for Less Government, 1981–1992

With the inauguration of Ronald Reagan as president in 1981, a new aspect was added to the ongoing development of public program evaluation and productivity. This new aspect was privatization, or the contracting out of government programs for implementation by private companies, and its impact was felt mostly, but not exclusively, at the federal level. Privatization is a large and somewhat complicated phenomenon, and we devote much of Chapter 11 to it. But its effects on public program evaluation and productivity can be reviewed here.

A Federal Fixation

The motivations underlying the privatization phase included that of improving federal productivity, but there were other, likely more central, motives, too. These included the slashing of taxes, the shrinking of government's costs, and, in its more ideological mode, reducing the size and power of the federal government itself.

Even in the face of the privatization onslaught, however, federal administrators in the 1980s nevertheless advanced the values of performance measurement, program evaluation, and productivity. In 1982, the GAO created its Division of Program Evaluation and Methodology (terminated, regrettably, in 1996), which "pioneered some of the agency's most groundbreaking studies."[43] In 1987, the GAO concluded that, despite a significant decline during the early eighties in the level of federal resources available for program evaluation research, the number of program evaluations produced by federal agencies remained about the same as in earlier years, "suggesting continued executive branch interest in obtaining evaluation information."[44] This continued federal interest of the 1980s would burst into a full-fledged federal fascination in the 1990s and beyond.

A Stabilizing Subnational Scene

Privatization also grew in state and local governments during the eighties, but the grass-roots governments never displayed the fervid fixation of the feds with privatization.

As Table 7-2 shows, the states continued their progress in adopting measures, evaluation, and productivity, although their progress had slowed and stabilized since the 1970s. By the mid-1980s, legislatures in thirty-five states had expanded existing agencies or had created new ones charged with the statewide evaluation of program effectiveness and efficiency.[45]

Local governments, long the leaders in the movement to measure performance, evaluate programs, and improve productivity, retained their position of leadership. As Table 7-3 shows, by the end of the eighties an astounding four-fifths of local governments were conducting program evaluations.

Waste, Fraud, and Abuse: The New Meaning of Corruption, 1975–Present

Since the mid-1970s, the accelerating involvement by governments in productivity efforts has been linked with an expanding view by the public of what constitutes governmental corruption. Increasingly, corruption was (and is) perceived as including not only *fraud*—that is, using dishonest means and committing illegal acts for the purpose of personal financial gain, as corruption had always been defined in the past—but "abuse" and "waste" as well.[46] The mantra of campaigning politicians—"eliminate waste, fraud, and abuse"—which is cynically touted as a painless way to both increase government services and cut taxes—emerged during the 1970s and remains with us today.[47]

Three events exploded in the 1970s and 1980s that altered, perhaps permanently, the public's perception of corruption. We consider these instances of waste, fraud, and abuse in turn.

Waste as Corruption: The Fall of New York

The first event was the unprecedented fiscal crisis in 1975 of New York City, in which the city narrowly averted default. Although some fraud was involved, the dominant dynamic in the New

York fiasco was plain waste, a condition resulting from governmental incompetence and irresponsibility, but not illegality; *waste*, to borrow one reasonable definition, is "the unnecessary costs that result from inefficient or ineffective practices, systems, or controls,"[48] and this is not a reasonable definition of corruption.

Yet, today waste is perceived as a kind of corruption. One review of the literature on government waste identified "a logical taxonomy of nine types of waste," including one category entitled "corruption, fraud, theft, and red tape."[49] Red tape equates with corruption, fraud, and theft? Similarly, the title of a mudslinging book of the 1990s put it succinctly: *Government Racket: Washington Waste From A to Z.*[50] Waste is a racket?

We should note that we are *not* dismissing government waste as a trivial matter. During the 1990s, the Government Reform and Oversight Committee of the U.S. House of Representatives issued two reports, based on research by the GAO, inspectors general, audits, and congressional testimony, which estimated that the amount of federal dollars lost to "waste, fraud, and mismanagement" per year amounted to roughly a third of the federal budget.[51] Although there were inevitable politics in these reports (both of which were issued when one party controlled Congress and the other party was in the White House), they are nonetheless sobering.

What we *are* suggesting is that waste has been added as a new dimension to the popular understanding of what constitutes corruption, and that this widened definition is not only inappropriate but has brought with it new restrictions on the discretionary judgments and administrative decisions that may be made by public administrators.

Fraud as Corruption: The Fall of Washington

During the 1980s, the public's worries over old-fashioned fraud were given renewed impetus.

Fraud of dramatic dimensions, centered in Washington's efforts to privatize the federal government by contracting out public services to private companies on an unprecedented scale, roiled through the Department of Housing and Urban Development. Unprecedented privatization was also the underlying cause of record levels of fraud in the Pentagon during this period, which has been described as "America's biggest defense scandal," resulting in the criminal convictions of nearly 100 corporate and federal executives.[52] High levels of fraud permeated Medicare, a $200 billion healthcare program for the elderly, throughout the eighties and well into the nineties. The savings and loan scandal of the 1980s—in which some $500 billion of taxpayers' dollars were used to bail out thousands of savings and loan associations that had, often fraudulently, "lost" the savings of millions of investors—was the direct result of their irresponsible deregulation by Congress. The eruption of federal fraud on a historic scale during the 1980s rendered the public much more sensitive to its presence in government, and even less tolerant of it.

Abuse as Corruption: The Fall of the White House

Between 1973 and 1975, a "third-rate burglary" (to quote President Nixon) metamorphosed into the mother of all political scandals—"Watergate." Watergate refers to Nixon's efforts to cover up his aides' burglary of the offices of the Democratic Party so that he could acquire information benefiting his reelection. The resulting scandal, besides forcing Nixon's resignation, also rendered the public extremely aware of how officeholders could abuse their authority.

Abuse of authority may be defined as the inappropriate, unethical, or illegal misuse of the power vested in one's public office. In Watergate, this abuse happened to be illegal, but the abuse of authority, while often reprehensible, is not always criminal.

Examples of inappropriate and unethical abuses are of more recent vintage. Consider the case of the special prosecutor charged (originally) in the mid-1990s with investigating some of President Bill Clinton's personal investments when he had served as governor of Arkansas, an episode known as "Whitewater." Ultimately, the special prosecutor found no provable improprieties involving Whitewater but did allege illegal acts by the president stemming from the quite unrelated matter of the president's affair with a White House intern.

The special prosecutor's zealous expansion of his initial mission was legal, but, in the view of most Americans, was an abuse of authority that was clearly inappropriate. By contrast, President Clinton's sexual exploitation of a young intern was clearly unethical (and his lying about it under oath was criminal). Both of these abuses led to the demise of the twenty-one-year-old independent prosecutor law; the impeachment, trial, and acquittal of the president by Congress; and deepened the public's perception that abuse of power, even when it is legal, nonetheless is corruption.

Waste, Fraud, and Abuse: The Blurred Lump of Corruption

In sum, "corruption" in the popular mind now is a blurred lump composed of waste, fraud, and abuse. Corruption control, in turn, no longer is seen as a matter of antipartisan political reform or clever organizational design, but rather as law enforcement. Now incompetence can equate with criminality.

The consequence of this broadened definition of corruption has been, since the 1970s, an exponential increase of standards, rules, rigidities, and investigative officers (such as inspectors general, ethics officers, auditors, attorneys, and accountants) extending well beyond the administrative controls imagined in the wildest dreams of the good-government reformers of a hundred years ago. It is precisely these new controls that have led, in part, to the fifth and current phase of performance measurement, program evaluation, and productivity: a new public management.

A New Public Management, 1992–Present

By the final two decades of the twentieth century, a number of forces—intellectual, political, and fiscal—were making themselves felt within governments. These forces included the emergence of large, high-performance corporations; innovations undertaken in other countries to reduce national deficits; initiatives begun by American cities and towns; rapid technological changes;

the end of the Cold War, with its attendant refocusing by citizens in many nations on domestic issues; a declining faith—a "trust deficit"—among Americans in their governments;[53] and last but by no means least, new restrictions on public administrators that led to their seeking new ways of managing.

Beyond Reinventing Government

These kinds of social trends resulted in an explosion of publications in the early 1990s that called for a new kind of governmental reform.[54] The most famous of these critiques was the national bestseller *Reinventing Government: How the Entrepreneurial Spirit is Transforming the Public Sector*, published in 1992, which we have chosen as the year marking the start of our current phase of the productivity movement, the new public management.

The new public management is an expanded view of "reinventing government," which began in the 1980s almost entirely at the local level.[55] These local developments led to a remarkable undertaking by President Clinton. Within three months after being sworn into office in 1993, Clinton created the National Performance Review, chaired by Vice President Al Gore. Clinton declared that "Our goal is to make the entire federal government both less expensive and more efficient, and to change the culture of our national bureaucracy away from complacency and entitlement toward initiative and empowerment."[56] In 1998, the National Performance Review was retitled the National Partnership for Reinventing Government, and in 2001 it was terminated.

Ultimately, a team of some 250 experienced federal employees from all corners of the government were assembled, the opinions of more than 30,000 citizens and hundreds of organizations from across the country were sought, and the National Performance Review released over 1,200 recommendations to the president.[57] Just how revolutionary these ideas were for reinventing the federal government is open to debate. The GAO, for example, opined that virtually all of the National Performance Review's recommendations were good—even if the GAO had itself been recommending their implementation years before the National Performance Review was even formed.[58] Still, the National Performance Review was "the longest-running reform in the history of the Federal Government."[59]

The Five Fundamentals of the New Pubic Management

At root, *the new public management* is composed of the following five ideas.[60]

- *Alertness.* Government should anticipate problems and changes before they emerge, then deal effectively with them.
- *Agility.* Government should be entrepreneurial, open, and communicative. It should empower citizens and public employees alike.
- *Adaptability.* Government should continuously improve the quality of its programs and services, and it should do so by assessing its performance with measurable results. It should alter with changing circumstances and take advantage of new opportunities.
- *Alignment.* Government should saturate itself with knowledge by effectively managing its information technology. Governments should collaborate with other governments and the nonprofit and private sectors to achieve social goals.
- *Accountability.* Government should have a clear and compelling mission that focuses on the needs of people. Government should improve its accountability to the *public interest*, which should be understood in terms of law, community, and shared values.

These ideas lead to a much greater emphasis on certain kinds of public management that have been stressed only intermittently in the past, notably performance measurement, collaboration, coalition formation, benchmarking, citizen satisfaction studies, program evaluation, strategic planning, training, team building, decentralization, downsizing, privatization, enhanced executive authority, and streamlining and innovating procurement, budgeting, and human resources. American governments have responded to these developments, and one survey of governments at all levels found that only 10 percent "had no experience" with the bundle of concepts, approaches, and techniques that we associate with the new public management.[61]

By 1996, almost two-thirds of the National Performance Review's 1,200 recommendations had been enacted (but almost none after that year), resulting in savings of more than $136 billion. By 2000, the federal government had published over 4,000 new customer service standards, scrapped some 640,000 pages of internal agency rules, and eliminated 426,200 federal jobs. Nearly 2,000 field offices and 250 programs and agencies, such as wool subsidies and the Bureau of Mines, had been shut down.[62]

A "report card" on the federal effort to introduce a new public management gave the effort a "B," noting that "no such effort has ever received such lasting high-level support."[63] A decade after the launch, more than four-fifths of senior federal administrators and three-fifths of federal managers reported that their agency's top leadership "demonstrated a strong commitment to achieving results."[64]

By the opening decade of the twenty-first century, it appeared that the federal government had made genuinely important reforms in how it purchased, procured, and acquired. Significant inroads had been made in human resources management, most notably in the decentralization of many traditional duties from the Office of the Personnel Management to the line agencies. And a basis had been established for improved financial management, results-based budgeting, performance monitoring, and strategic planning.[65]

The New State Management

The new public management also is gaining a grip in the states, but how strongly is open to debate. An analysis of the states' adoption of eleven specific reforms that express the values of the new public management (such as privatization, strategic planning, and citizen satisfaction surveys) found that, in general, from only a tenth to a fifth of the state agencies had fully implemented any of the reforms, although the extent of partial implementation was higher. "There is a clear possibility . . . that the reforms urged under the 'reinvention' banner will not be widely and quickly adopted across the states."[66]

Katrina, Crisis, and Collapse

A bit more of the New Public Management, with its emphasis on alertness, agility, and adaptability, would have been welcomed by the people of the Gulf Coast when Hurricane Katrina slammed into Alabama, Louisiana, and Mississippi on August 29, 2005, leaving more than 1,500 dead and hundreds of thousand homeless in its wake. Were governments alert, agile, and adaptable in responding to the hurricane? You decide.

Katrina, then a tropical storm, was first observed over the Central Bahamas on August 24th, five days before it struck the Gulf Coast, and a hurricane warning was issued that day.

The evacuation of people in the face of a potential natural disaster is a state and local responsibility, unless these jurisdictions are overwhelmed by events, in which case Washington may intervene. In Alabama and Mississippi, and in Louisiana outside of New Orleans, evacuations went reasonably well. In The Big Easy, however, they did not. Despite adequate warning given fifty-six hours before Katrina made landfall, the governor of Louisiana and the mayor of New Orleans, each of whom had the power to order a mandatory evacuation, delayed ordering one for New Orleans. The mayor finally ordered an evacuation just nineteen hours before the hurricane struck, and highways already were jammed with evacuees.

Orders are one thing, implementing them another. New Orleans' mayor failed to mobilize the city's busses for carrying those citizens who had no other transportation. And there were many—some 100,000 people in the city owned no car. Amtrak provided a train to evacuate New Orleanians, but, due to a lack of local coordination, it left the station almost empty. As a partial consequence of the bungled evacuation, more than 70,000 New Orleanians were trapped in floodwaters reaching twenty feet and higher, awaiting rescue. They waited many days.

Local government had collapsed. About 15 percent (figures vary, but this seems to be the approximate midpoint) of New Orleans' finest, its police officers, failed to report for duty after the hurricane made landfall. The Police Department "as an institution . . . disintegrated with the first drop of water" in dealing with its impact (Select Bipartisan Committee, p. 246).

Louisiana's governor refused to use her power to declare martial law, or even a state of emergency. She also declined the White House's proposal to place her National Guard under federal control, and requested federal aid only after the mayor had given his order to evacuate New Orleans.

The president was at his ranch in Texas when the hurricane hit, and evidently was not seriously engaged in the crisis until days after landfall. A large majority of the top officials in the Federal Emergency Management Agency (FEMA), the main federal bureau responsible for responding to disasters, held their offices more by dint of experience in party politics than in emergency management (details are in Chapter 9). Three days after Katrina struck, the director of FEMA was *still* working on an organization chart that laid out his staffing plan for the emergency.

Numerous nations offered help, ranging from rescue teams to physicians. New Mexico volunteered its National Guard. The U.S. Interior Department (which, eight months earlier, had been made a formal part FEMA's Southern Louisiana Catastrophic Hurricane Plan), offered eleven aircraft, hundreds of trucks and boats, and 4,400 law enforcement officers to FEMA. The Agency failed to respond, or ineffectually responded days or weeks later, to these and other offers of assistance.

The most critical information, that of the capacity of New Orleans' levees to hold during Katrina, was shredded. The levees were, in fact, breached on the very night that Katrina struck, but ten hours after the National Weather Service had posted a bulletin to this effect, plus reports of breaches from FEMA officials, the Army Corps of Engineers, and the Coast Guard, the Homeland Security Operations Center still was maintaining that the levees had not been breached.

Days after Katrina had made landfall, both the director of FEMA and the secretary of Homeland Security publicly contended that they were unaware that anything was seriously awry on the Gulf Coast, despite unremitting media coverage that sent a quite contrary message. The president seemed to concur with his appointees, praising his FEMA director with a phrase that may long endure in the discourse of disconnectedness: "You're doin' a heckuva job, Brownie."

Washington sent serious assistance to the region only after: nine days had elapsed *after* Katrina was spotted on August 24th; eight days *after* it glanced off Florida, causing at least two deaths; seven days *after* Hurricane Katrina had attained Category 3 dimensions, was projected to hit Gulfport and New Orleans, and Louisiana declared a state of emergency; six days *after* Mississippi and New Orleans declared states of emergency; five days *after* Katrina registered as a Category 5 hurricane, the most destructive storm possible, Alabama declared a state of emergency, and a mandatory evacuation was ordered by the mayor of New Orleans; four days *after* Katrina made landfall as a Category 3 hurricane, and New Orleans began to flood; three days *after* 80 percent of New Orleans was flooded and widespread looting had erupted; two days *after* the evacuation of 25,000 people trapped in New Orleans' Superdome began; and one day *after* some rescue efforts in New Orleans were suspended because of sniper fire. Only on the next day, September 2nd, did significant federal aid arrive, in the form of 26,000 National Guard troops.

Fraud flourished in Katrina's aftermath. The Government Accountability Office reported that, during a period of just six months after Katrina struck, "we are 95 percent confident that the range of improper and potentially fraudulent payments [by FEMA] is from $600 million to $1.4 billion," and likely was around $1 billion, a fraud rate of 16 percent of FEMA's expenditures for helping victims (GAO, Highlights page). An example: $10 million in housing assistance for displaced residents went to people who were not displaced, including 1,170 prison inmates.

People suffered, needlessly, long after the hurricane. In New Orleans alone, Katrina left an estimated 50,000 homes with "major or severe" damage, but, six months after Katrina's landfall, not one had been razed and removed. Nearly 800,000 displaced households still were living in, or moving to, rental or temporary housing at a cost of nearly $3 billion to taxpayers. "For many families," the months following Katrina were ones of "frustrations and uncertainty. . . . And the ad-hoc nature and multiple components of housing aid have only added to the confusion" (Katz, *et al.*, p. 5). One analysis found that simply using the federal government's existing Section 8 housing voucher program would have been a more cost-effective and humane approach to sheltering Katrina's homeless.

Katrina's victims focused their ire on their public administrators. One local elected official accused, "The bureaucracy has murdered people in the greater New Orleans area" (Aaron Broussard, President, Jefferson Parish, Louisiana, September 7, 2005, as quoted in Schneider, p. 515).

Sources: Select Bipartisan Committee to Investigate the Preparation for and Response to Hurricane Katrina, U.S. House of Representatives, 109th Congress, Second Session, *A Failure of Initiative: Final Report* (Washington, DC: U.S. Government Printing Office, 2006); Christopher Swope and Zach Patton, "In Disaster's Wake," *Governing* (November 2005), pp. 48–58; Brookings Institution, *Hurricane Katrina Timeline* (Washington: DC: Author, 2005). U.S. Government Accountability Office, *Hurricanes Katrina & Rita Disaster Relief: Improper and Potentially Fraudulent Individual Assistance Payments Estimated to Be between $600 Million and $1.4 Billion,* GAO-06-844T (Washington, DC: U.S. Government Printing Office, 2006). Brookings Institution, "Measuring Progress in New Orleans: A Katrina Index Update," *Update from the Brookings Metro Program* (Washington, DC: Author, 2006); Frances Fragos Townsend, Assistant to the President for Homeland Security and Counterterrorism, *The Federal Response to Hurricane Katrina: Lessons Learned* (Washington, DC: U.S. Government Printing Office, 2006), Chapter 4, http://www.whitehouse.gov/reports/katrina-lessons-learned/; Eric Lipton, "Interior Dept. Report Describes FEMA's Scant Use of Its Help," *New York Times* (January 30, 2006); Bruce Katz, Amy Liu, Matt Fellowes, and Mia Mabanta, *Housing Families Displaced by Katrina: A Review of the Federal Response to Date* (Washington, DC: Brookings, 2005); and Saundra K. Schneider, "Special Report: Administrative Breakdowns in the Governmental Response to Hurricane Katrina," *Public Administration Review* 65 (September/October 2005), pp. 515–516.

The New Local Management

The new public management in local governments, which started it all, has stabilized and now appears to be solidly entrenched.[67]

City managers are on the forefront of the new local management and support "reinvention" by better than nine to one.[68] "Nearly all" city managers "believe that taxpayers should be treated as customers, that third-party contracting and competition in service and delivery are acceptable, that government should be mission-driven and entrepreneurial, and that non-tax revenue sources should be developed."[69]

There are numerous additional indications of the local commitment to the new public management. For example, the use by local governments of collaboration and privatization is substantial, with almost half of all local services being delivered in conjunction with other organizations or via contracts with companies or nonprofit organizations,[70] and almost two-thirds of local governments engage in strategic planning.[71] Almost six out of ten cities have implemented "entrepreneurial activities," and more than seven out of ten cities have underwritten employee training programs on improving customer service and employee responses to customer complaints and have funded citizen surveys.[72]

In sum, the feds are energetically making up for lost time in adopting the new public management; the states are lagging, although there is progress; and local governments, especially cities, are still leading the movement and blazing new trails in the process.

Control or Corruption? Turbidity or Agility?

At base, the new public managers are rebelling against a core cultural current that we explored in Chapter 1: the constraint of government.

The New Public Management *versus* The Old Public Administration

As expressed in a public administrative setting, this cultural current birthed the "good government"

crusaders of the nineteenth century, who placed a high value on constraining public officials by instituting corruption controls. Beginning in the 1970s, Americans' desire to constrain government was renewed by a popular revulsion over governmental scandals and a resultant revisionist definition of corruption as waste and abuse, as well as fraud. This produced more and more layers of new and stultifying administrative restrictions, bureaucratic structures, complexities, and procedures, all designed for second-guessing line administrators. The new public managers are trumpeting: Unchain the bureaucrats from these antiquated and crushing constraints so that they may more effectively serve the public.

And there is much merit to this call. Just as, however, there also is much merit to the motivations of both the reformers of yore and corruption controllers of today. Those motivations—which can be reduced to cleaning up corrupt governments and protecting honest ones from corruption—still have real relevance, and the essence of the resistance by the old public administrators to the new public managers is the fear that a loosening of traditional administrative controls will lead to more corruption in government.

Confronting Control

Corruption in the United States is hardly on the pandemic scale that it reached in the nineteenth century—not even close. Nevertheless, are we willing to discard our need to maintain and strengthen honest government in our quest to build more responsive government?

Our answer is no. But the question itself is misleading, and our answer neither implies that the traditional, control-oriented values of public administration are working as well as their defenders contend or accepts that the adoption of the newer values underlying the new public management—alertness, agility, adaptability, alignment, and accountability—will somehow undermine honest and uncorrupted government.

It is worth noting, after all, that all of the recommendations (and then some!) of the good-government reformers of the nineteenth century had long been in place in the Pentagon even as it was being "sold" in the late twentieth century to corrupt private contractors: "Hundreds of thousands of employees had no task other than to keep scrupulously close tabs on contractors. Seventy-nine separate offices issued voluminous acquisition regulations. . . . The volume of rules equaled five times the length of Leo Tolstoy's novel *War and Peace*. The Army once promulgated fifteen pages of specifications for sugar cookies alone." It is undeniable that the traditional values and practices of public administration were firmly present—indeed, omnipresent, at least officially—in the Pentagon even as some of its officials were engaged in corruption of unprecedented proportions. "How could such dishonesty exist in a system ostensibly run according to rigid rules and absolute discipline?"[73]

Reconciling the Old and the New

One answer may be that the traditional approaches of public administration no longer provide the complete solution for controlling corruption, if they ever did. We are not suggesting that the creaky, buttoned-down values of the old public administration should be dismissively discarded, any more than we are proposing that the slick, entrepreneurial values of the new public management should be passionately embraced.

Melding Tradition with Innovation. We are suggesting, however, that introducing the values of the new public management will *not* inevitably result in less honest or less lawful government, as the critics insist, and *may* induce more alert, agile, adaptable, aligned, and accountable government, as the new public managers (perhaps rashly) promise. One close follower of developments in the new public management puts it well: "The traditional approach is not obsolete; it can never be so long as the United States is a government of laws. But it must be adapted to a new reality of shared responsibility for common purposes."[74]

In other words, both the old public administration and the new public management have their uses. Neither approach is particularly useful in exorcising corruption—that requires political will—but *both* can be very useful in spotting

the presence of corruption *and* in rendering government more agile, innovative, efficient, and effective. It is how they are used *in combination* that determines whether they succeed or fail in these missions. Consider a couple of examples of how this combination can work, or not work, in practice.

A Tacky Tangle in Texas. An analysis of the propensity of administrators in 476 Texan school districts to manipulate student scores on standardized tests[75] sheds some light on the utility of the old public administration and the new public management in confronting corruption and facilitating more supple government. The researchers found that elements of both approaches were present in the school districts: rules, red tape, and a monitoring process (or characteristics associated with the old public administration), and performance measures, results budgeting, and incentives (or features associated with the new public management). Nevertheless, "organizational cheating" among school districts was rife, and this corruption was most likely to occur when resources were scarce, demands were extreme, the daily activities of administrators were not closely monitored, and performance was linked to incentives.

Among the striking findings of this research is that the policymakers who set up the system that allowed corruption to flourish were singularly devoid of common sense. Foxes should not guard hen houses, and usually hens should not guard hen houses, either. Honor codes do not work in government. This is not rocket science.

In Texas, these commonsensical canons were violated. Fiscally strapped district administrators were responsible for increasing the budgets for their schools, which, in turn, was dependent on raising their students' test scores. Then these administrators were given sole responsibility for monitoring, administering, and reporting those scores. Is it any wonder that "organizational cheating" broke out? The hens, and only the hens, were watching there own hen house, and their scratching produced, if not educational rewards, then certainly monetary ones.

This district cheating could have been easily avoided, of course, by simply assuring that an agency that was fully independent of the school districts administered the student tests and reported the scores.

The Lone Star State Is Not Alone.   Texan school districts are by no means alone in this sorry syndrome. Variations of it are a national phenomenon.

For example, states are required by federal law to report high school graduation rates, with federal funding of state schools determined in part by how high those rates are. As in Texas, elements of both the old public administration and the new public management are present in this reporting procedure.

In another parallel with Texan school districts, the administrators who need funding are responsible for collecting and providing the data that will acquire that funding: The states calculate and report their own graduation rates. The results are predictable, with a large majority of states omitting important data, and a few not reporting any data.

Of greatest significance, however, the states are free to define "graduation rate" and to set graduation-rate goals (presumably, goals to raise those rates) in any way that they choose. This freedom has brought states to the silly season. Some states use an "irrational graduation-rate definition," such as not counting any dropouts who were not high school seniors, and set graduation-rate goals that are actually *lower* than the current graduation rates that they report to Washington.[76]

As a result, it appears that many, perhaps most, states puff their graduation rates in blowfish proportions. The manifold analyses of graduation rates essentially agree that almost a third of all high school students do not graduate on time,[77] but "in many of the state reports, these alarming numbers are nowhere to be found [and] the information they provided is of little value to school-improvement efforts."[78]

Again, as in Texas, the correction of these anomalies does not demand brightly burnished brain power. Their correction requires only that the requested data be collected in full, that an enforceable definition of *graduation rate* be provided, and that the proviso be established that goals must not be set at a level lower than present performance. These are eminently reasonable stipulations.

In sum, both the old public administration and the new public management have the potentiality

for curtailing corruption and enhancing governmental alertness, agility, adaptability, alignment, and accountability. It may be that these missions can be achieved even more fully when these two approaches are used—and used sensibly—in tandem.

As the foregoing history of the public productivity movement implies, performance measurement and public program evaluation are among its methodological foundations. We shall treat these bases in turn, starting with performance measurement.

Measuring Public Performance

The adoption and implementation of performance measures by governments are not easy chores. Research has found that state and local governments, for example, are persuaded to adopt performance measures largely by technical and rational arguments, but that actually using those performance measures in making decisions is heavily influenced by political and cultural considerations. As a consequence, although a government may have performance measures ostensibly in place, they may remain mostly unimplemented.[79] In addition, some agencies find performance measures far more useful and easier to use than others; highway safety agencies, with their straightforward, measurable mission, have found performance measures to be rewardingly productive, but child welfare programs, with a necessarily more subjective, judgmental mission, have not.[80]

The Purposes of Performance Measures

There is, in short, "no one magic performance measure," but rather different measures for different purposes, and this reality complicates further their use. One scholar has identified eight purposes of performance measures. They are

- *Evaluation*, or ascertaining the level of agency performance.
- *Control*, or assuring that subordinates are doing the right thing.

- *Budgeting*, or deciding on what programs and projects the public administrator should spend the public's money.
- *Motivation*, or inspiring all stakeholders, from staff to citizens, "to do the things necessary to improve performance."
- *Promotion*, or convincing superiors, politicians, journalists, and others that the administrator's agency is doing a good job.
- *Celebration*, or recognizing success;
- *Learning*, or determining what is working or not working and why.
- And *improvement*, or ascertaining who should do what differently to heighten performance.[81]

As this list suggests, using performance measures can be a complicated and vexing exercise in strategic thinking. Nevertheless, measuring performance has grown immeasurably as a dominating concern of the public administration community: The National Academy of Public Administration, the American Society for Public Administration, the Federal Accounting Standards Advisory Board, the Government Accounting Standards Board, and the Government Finance Officers Association have all endorsed performance measurement.[82] So have the American people. Seventy percent of the public "favor creating a system of evaluating government agencies by the [objective] results they produce rather than by the programs they initiate or the money they spend."[83]

We encapsulate next how each level of American government has responded to this professional and popular enthusiasm for the arcana of performing functions and then measuring them.

Measuring Federal Performance

If Washington was a reluctant suitor of the methods of productivity improvement in the 1970s, and an only slightly more ardent one in the 1980s, the feds bloomed into a passionate paramour of productivity in the 1990s.

Federal interest in performance measurement is clearly quickening. A 1991 survey by the GAO of 103 agencies, which accounted for three-fourths of all federal outlays, found that virtually all of them collected a large number of performance measures, but only nine agencies could be described as measuring their performance in legitimate and meaningful ways.[84] As the deputy director of management of the Office of Management and Budget phrased it, "On a scale of 10," the federal government's ability to measure performance is "about at a 2,"[85] an assessment echoed by an official of the National Academy of Public Administration, who observed, after noting that the national governments of Australia and New Zealand had been developing and using performance measures for "decades," the U.S. government "came late to this revolution."[86]

But Washington seems interested in raising this ranking. The Government Performance and Results Act of 1993 and the National Performance Review point by their titles alone to this conclusion. In 1998, Congress created the first "performance-based organization" in the federal hierarchy: the Department of Education's Office of Student Financial Assistance, followed by the Internal Revenue Service, the Federal Aviation Administration, and the Patent and Trademark Office. Performance-based organizations are managed by federal administrators who sign contracts that hold them accountable for delivering measurable results; in return for greater managerial flexibility, pay and job security are directly tied to agency performance.

In 2001, President George W. Bush launched the President's Management Agenda, which measures federal performance in six key areas.[87] By the initial years of the twenty-first century, 89 percent of federal managers reported that there were performance measures in place for their programs.[88]

Measuring State Performance

As with Washington, the state capitals made significant gains in measuring their performance during the 1990s. Essentially all state agencies, 98 percent, use at least one performance measure, and an impressive 40 percent use them in at least half of their programs.[89] All the states mandate a budget process that requests from agencies quantifiable data that provides meaningful information about program outcomes.[90] Nearly three-fourths of the states' budget agencies regularly use measures of state programs that quantify the goods or services being produced relative to their costs, and four-fifths of the states include productivity measures in their budget documents.[91]

State administrators are pleased with their states' use of performance measures. More than seven out of ten state agency administrators say that the efficiency and effectiveness of their agency have been enhanced because of performance measures.[92]

Important factors in determining a state's success in using performance measures include a clear identification of specific needs; an understanding of how the measures would be used; a desire to learn; using performance-based information in formulating budgets; legislators and governors who question agencies about their performance; providing adequate time to get performance measures in place; and strong leadership.[93] More populous states are more likely than less populous states to retain performance measures over time.[94]

Measuring Local Performance

It was in the cities where performance measurement got its start at the turn of the twentieth century, and it is in the cities where this technique is likely to be employed most thoroughly and innovatively in the twenty-first century.

Almost nine out of ten cities and counties report that they use performance measures[95] (see Table 7-3). Three-fifths of those cities that use performance measures employ them citywide, and the rest use them in selected programs.[96]

Most local administrators like performance measures. A national survey of city managers found that 61 percent of the respondents felt that, on balance, "the positive payoffs of the performance measures used in their jurisdictions were worth the cost and organizational strain of collecting these data. Less that 1 percent felt that it was not."[97] A later survey of senior local administrators determined that 95 percent rated performance measures as "very effective" (38 percent) or "somewhat effective" (57 percent).[98] In those cities that use performance measurement in all agencies, almost half, 46 percent, of urban managers attribute lower operational costs to city-wide performance measures.[99]

In more than nine out of ten cities, municipal administrators whose cities use citywide performance measures (or nearly a fourth of all cities) say that budget changes have resulted from their use, including 11 percent who said that these reallocations were substantial.[100] Twelve percent of all cities reward their departments for meeting their performance targets by granting them additional budget allocations.[101]

Linking money with measurable performance means that governments take performance seriously, and local governments may be making this linkage more strongly than any other governmental level.

Permutations of Performance Measurement

There are five generally recognized kinds of performance measures that are commonly used by governments. We describe them here, and explain the extent of their usage by the federal, state, and local governments.

Workload, or Output, Measures

Workload, or *output*, *measures*, are the most basic sort of performance measurement, and they calculate the amount of work performed or service provided. An example is tons of trash collected.

Because workload measures are relatively easy to use, governments at all levels use them the most extensively. More than half, 54 percent, of federal managers whose agencies have performance measures (or 89 percent of all federal agencies[102]) report that they use output measures to a great or very great extent.[103] Sixty-three percent of state agencies that have performance measures in at least half of their programs (or 40 percent of all state agencies) use output measures.[104] And from over half to almost four-fifths of those cities (depending on the function) that measure performance (88 percent of all cities and counties report that they use some sort of performance measure[105]) employ workload measures.[106]

Unit Cost, or Efficiency, Measures

Unit cost, or *efficiency, measures*, are more refined, and assess the monetary expense per unit of output or workload. An example is the cost of trash collected per residence.

Forty-three percent of federal administrators whose agencies use performance measures use efficiency measures extensively, and 34 percent of state agencies that use performance measures in at least half of their programs use them. Oddly, those local governments with performance measures use efficiency measures the least frequently of all types of performance measures—from over a fifth to just two-fifths, depending on the agency.

Outcome, or Effectiveness, Measures

Outcome, or *effectiveness*, *measures*, quantify the extent to which goals are attained, needs are met, and desired effects are produced. An example is counting the number of renovated homes in a neighborhood that is undergoing renewal.

Fifty-five percent of federal administrators ` report that they use effectiveness measures to a great or very great extent, and more than half, 52 percent, of state agencies say that they use them. From about a third to nearly two-thirds, depending on the function, of local governments use outcome measures.

Service Quality Measures

Service quality measures are value-based assessments of management's responsiveness to clients' needs or expectations, such as timeliness, accuracy, and courtesy. Although responsiveness sometimes can be objectively measured (for example, the time that it takes for an ambulance to arrive at an accident), determining whether or not the response is of adequate quality is often a subjective judgment. (Does an average arrival time of thirty minutes amount to adequate service quality, or should it be five minutes?)

Forty-six percent of federal administrators use service quality measures extensively. A fourth of state agencies use "quality/customer satisfaction measures." From more than a fourth to over half of local agencies, depending on the service, use service quality measures.

Citizen Satisfaction Measures

A final sort of major performance measure is the *citizen satisfaction measure*, which assesses the extent to which citizens feel that their needs have been met by a program.

Nearly half, 47 percent, of federal managers whose agencies use performance measures report that they use "customer service measures" to a great or very great degree. As noted earlier, 25 percent of state agencies that use performance measures in at least half of their programs report that they use "quality/customer satisfaction measures," although another survey found that nearly two-thirds of all state agencies had "fully or partially" initiated customer satisfaction surveys.[107] And from less than a third to more than half, depending on the function, of local government agencies that use performance measures state that they use "client or citizen satisfaction" measures.

Performance Measurement in Practice

Performance measurement is well entrenched in American governments and likely will dig deeper trenches over time. It is important, therefore, to know how to measure governmental performance. We consider next the practicalities, pitfalls, and productiveness of measuring performance

The Measurement Mire

At least eight limitations of performance measurement have been identified that public administrators should be cognizant of before they employ performance measures.[108] We briefly review them here.

Measuring the Wrong Thing. On occasion, imprecision in defining what one wants to measure results in measuring something else entirely. For instance, in determining how much government should invest in health, safety, and other public programs that deal directly with human life, it was decided that government must know how much a human life was worth. Great effort to do so has led to some remarkably inconsistent estimates, ranging from about $1 million[109] to more than $6 million,[110] depending on the federal agency making the estimate. But the real question is less the worth of a human life and more one of people's willingness to pay (through taxes) for their own health and safety. Once this distinction is understood, then we can move from a fruitless (and likely futile) attempt to estimate how much people are worth to measuring how much people are willing to pay to protect themselves, and this determination can be made through analyzing opinion polls or prices in markets where risk is a factor.[111]

Using Meaningless Measures.   Consider this: Several court house clerks, who, when asked how they collected data required for their weekly reports, replied, "We put down something that sounds reasonable."[112] Or this, written by a retired police officer: "During my more than 30 years as a cop, I produced and sometimes created crime statistics. . . . No official order was ever given to underreport or not report crimes . . . but an officer following the rulebook would soon find out from his sergeant that he had an attitude. Once sergeants decided you had a wrong attitude, it was time look for look for another job. . . . The mayor didn't like high crime stats with no arrests. Thus, the police commissioner didn't either. . . . Consequently, it was a bad idea for a rookie to report a robbery with no arrests. . . ."[113]

Both the clerks and the cops likely were doing the best they could under trying circumstances, but their approach illustrates a serious problem in the data that administrators sometimes must use in measuring performance: unreliability. The GAO determined that only five of the two dozen major federal agencies' performance reports "included assessments of the completeness and reliability of their performance data,"[114] and that twenty of these twenty-four agencies had only limited confidence in *their own* performance data; not one agency had full confidence in its own data![115] Program design issues, limited evaluation capacities, and "long-standing weaknesses in agencies' financial management" all reduced the data's credibility.[116]

Whether the motivations of public administrators to make up or distort "facts" is innocent or sinister, the result is the same: Performance measures are rendered meaningless.

Differing Interpretations of the "Same"Concept. No matter how rigidly defined, the meaning of concepts (and, hence, the measurement of them) can change according to who is using them. For example, is a "client" of a community health agency someone who occasionally phones in for advice, or is a client a regular visitor who has an ongoing file with the agency? If we interpret "client" to mean the former, then the agency's budget may fatten, but another agency using the latter interpretation may starve, even though the latter agency is likely more productive than the former.

Displacing Goals.   As we observed in Chapter 4, goal displacement occurs in all organizations, and performance measurement programs are no exception, especially when agencies want the numbers to make them look good. For example, "In Poland under communism, the performance of furniture factories was measured in the tons of furniture shipped. As a result, Poland now has the heaviest furniture on the planet."[117] Weight displaced furniture as Poland's furniture production goal because of the performance measure used. However, had the Polish communists instead stipulated free-standing items of furniture, rather than tonnage, as their measure of performance, Poland might now have the lightest—and the tiniest—furniture on the planet.

Shifting Costs Instead of Saving Costs.   Because agency programs are often measured in isolation, program managers can claim that they are saving public funds when in reality they are merely shifting costs to other programs. For example, a hospital allegedly shipped its dying patients to nursing homes shortly before they expired—a practice that not only shifted costs, but also resulted in splendidly declining mortality rates for the hospital.[118] Welfare agencies typically use "exits" as a measure of their success, but "few systemic attempts . . . are made to discover why people leave welfare, for how long, and where they go."[119]

Disguising Subgroup Differences with Aggregate Indicators. By concentrating on "the big picture," performance measures can hide critical (and perhaps, embarrassing) information. For instance, even though the U.S. Census Bureau reported an annual rise in all Americans' average income of 1.2 percent in 1996, it neglected to note that the wealthiest fifth of the population saw its income rise by 2.2 percent, but the poorest fifth witnessed its income fall by 1.8 percent. The aggregate indicator of rising average income (the good news) obscured a widening income gap between the richest and poorest Americans (the bad news).[120]

Ignoring the Limitations of Objective Measures. Even when properly done, measuring performance can take us only so far, and administrators should realize that performance measures may unfairly underrate innovative programs and overrate commonplace ones, or not account for the unintended effects of the program and its changing environment. An example of both limitations is provided by the Internal Revenue Service, which, for years, effectively had measured the performance of its agents on the basis of a single indicator: collection rates. The result was some ruthless agents, dubious practices, anguished taxpayers, and an overhauled, reorganized, and redirected Internal Revenue Service when Congress responded to rising public anger in 1998.

Failing to Address How and Why Questions. When performance measures are used in isolation, they can be useless or even counterproductive. The theory rationalizing the program could be misguided and should be replaced, important program outcomes may not be understood, poor management, under- or overfunding, and unique circumstances are all examples that would not be identified by performance measures alone.

What if, for instance, the sole employer in a town closed down? Performance measures of the town's employment agency would tell us only that the agency was failing to find jobs for unemployed townspeople. They would not tell us, however, that there were no jobs in the town.

Minimizing the Pitfalls of Performance Measurement

The potential pitfalls of performance measures are real, but at least a half-dozen precautions can be taken to minimize their peril. These include the following:[121]

- Be realistic about the political and organizational context in which the measures will be used—or not be used. As the physicians say, Do no harm.
- Assure that the measurements are at the right level and do not concentrate on outcomes over which the program has only a minimal influence.
- Always test measurements in advance.
- Review, revise, and update measures frequently.
- Actively involve stakeholders in developing and reviewing program measures.
- Use a lot of program measures, including those that measure variables other than just outcomes; organizational processes, for example, are often usefully measured.

Benchmarking Performance

Measuring performance is the foundation of benchmarking performance. *Benchmarking* may be defined as the seeking out of superior performance through systematic search for and use of best practices by using internal and external comparison assessments to stimulate higher performance.[122]

Performance measurements can, if conducted over a long enough period of time, indicate whether the productivity of a public program is going up or down, and this is important information. This simple tracking of performance is popular among governments, and it appears that about two-thirds of cities do it.[123]

Benchmarking, however, does this and more: it permits comparisons. Are we, in other words, doing this particular job *as well as* other organizations like ours which are also doing this particular job? Or are we doing it better? Or worse?

Benchmarking is making some, if slow, progress in American governments. The federal government is exploring benchmarking and has established a Federal Benchmarking Consortium, a group that includes representation from other countries engaged in benchmarking, and an Inter-Agency Benchmarking and Best Practices Council.

State governments also are increasingly aware of benchmarking. A national survey of the states found that almost three-fourths of state agencies compared their agencies' performance data with data from other government agencies, at least sometimes;[124] a half-dozen states have actually enacted legislation that specifically requires their governments to benchmark.[125]

At the local level, a national survey of cities found that a solid three-quarters of these governments are benchmarking their performance against the performance of other governments, at least occasionally,[126] and another national survey of 146 responding cities found that 70 percent used benchmarking as a common practice (19 percent) or sometimes (51 percent).[127]

An analysis of local benchmarking projects found that, although local administrators tended to have expectations of benchmarking that "soared beyond the projects' ability to deliver," they nonetheless believed that benchmarking provided some "substantial benefits," such as identifying alternative means of delivering services. Benchmarking, in and of itself, did little in the way of reducing costs or improving programs, but it did reveal where costs were possibly too high or programs might not be up to par and thereby helped local administrators in taking corrective action.[128]

Evaluating Public Programs

As we have noted, performance measurement provides the base for conducting most public program evaluations. And, as we also have observed, program evaluations run deeper—much deeper—than does performance measurement.

Public Program Evaluation, Paranoia, and Civic Virtue

Public program evaluation is more than a bureaucrat lethargically asking, "How're we doin'?" This modest question cloaks a process that can be intellectually stimulating, politically threatening, and even civically ennobling.

Because public program evaluation "is always undertaken in a context of decisions about the use of resources," it "accordingly, has implications for the acquisition, distribution, and loss of . . . power."[129] Occasionally, in fact, making better use of resources is not the real reason at all for launching a program evaluation. "Evaluation research can be invoked for a variety of purposes. . . . Sometimes evaluation is undertaken to justify or endorse an ongoing program and sometimes to investigate or audit the program in order to lay blame for failure, abolish it, change its leadership, or curtail its activities."[130]

So a program evaluation can be threatening, especially to those who are employed to manage the program being evaluated. This facet of evaluation research, however, can be overstated, and it would appear that when evaluations actually do cause programmatic changes, they rarely are draconian ones. An analysis of some 600 evaluations of municipal programs found that less than 1 percent "led to termination of the evaluated activities," but that 78 percent of these evaluations "led to adjustments of program activities."[131] Despite the aura of paranoia that sometimes seems to surround public program evaluation, evaluation research draws far short of a slash-and-burn attack on public management; it often seems to result, however, in changes designed to improve the productivity of public programs.

Evaluation research, in sum, can result in better, and even wiser, government. We review next the place of public program evaluation in each level of government.

Evaluation's Emergence

Public program evaluation has made long strides in almost all government.

Evaluating Federal Programs. With performance measurement gaining federal ground, successful program evaluation soon followed. During the 1990s, Congress enacted a series of laws designed to do just this. Together, they are of profound potential importance.

The single most significant of these laws is the Government Performance and Results Act of 1993 (less formally known as the Results Act), which moves federal administrators away from the tradition of reporting on their compliance with procedures and toward reporting on their achievement of measurable results.

But the Results Act is by no means the only legislation designed to enhance performance-based management in the federal government. In addition, Congress enacted during the final decade of the twentieth century new laws, and amended or rediscovered several older ones, to create an interlocking network of legislation designed to change in massive ways the managerial culture of the federal government. This legislation, all of which connects in some fashion with the Government Performance and Results Act, focuses on three critical areas of federal administration: information technology, fiscal controls, and financial management. The financial management legislation of the 1990s resulted in a remarkable and much needed achievement in 1998: the federal government's first-ever government-wide audited financial statements.

These laws, both old and new, are the rockbed of public program evaluation in the federal government. "Implemented together," notes the Government Accountability Office, "these laws provide a powerful framework. . . . [which] should promote a more results-oriented management and decision making process within both Congress and the executive branch."[132]

Evaluating State Programs. The clear progress that the states have made in measuring their agencies' performance seems to have been emulated in the realm of evaluating state programs. All states use some method of managing for results,[133] and as Table 7-2 indicates, the proportion of states in which most major agencies conduct effectiveness or productivity analyses more than doubled, from a fifth or fewer to half or more, over three decades. Central budget offices that conduct these analyses shot from a not even a third at best to almost three-fifths during the same period, and well over half of state legislatures now conduct them.

Evaluating Local Programs. Of all levels of government, local governments seem to have made the most significant progress in introducing public program evaluations. As Table 7-3 indicates, three-quarters of cities now report that they use program evaluations, a level which experts generally believe to be the maximum that is reasonably possible for the adoption of any innovative technique of public management. Over half of the cities now have some sort of program for improving productivity, and almost half have organized special staffs to evaluate productivity in their governments and to identify better methods to improve the delivery of services.[134]

Those local governments that are most successful in adopting productivity improvement measures are those which have a participative management style in city government, relatively high levels of privatization, an emphasis on economic development, department heads who have college educations, a comparatively low reliance on state and federal sources of revenue,[135] and extensive civil service reforms in city governments, such as the decentralization of decision-making authority concerning personnel, the creation of a senior executive service, and the elimination of veterans' preference in hiring and promoting.[136]

Public Program Evaluation in Practice

In addition to the scope and permutations of public program evaluation, there is the all-important *practice* of evaluation research. Practicing public program evaluation can be reduced to three fundamental steps: choosing the evaluators, defining the problem, and designing the evaluation.

Step 1: Selecting the Evaluators

To understand the process of public program evaluation, we must first know who the evaluators are.

Outside evaluators bring with them perspectives that differ from those of agency administrators. These differing perspectives include specificity *versus* generality (researchers are more likely to be interested in long term problem solving, while practitioners are more likely to be concerned with solving immediate problems); *status quo versus* change (practicing administrators, on the one hand, may attempt to conceal badly managed programs and to resist any change that they perceive as being potentially disruptive, while academic evaluators, on the other hand, often claim a superior knowledge of human affairs that predisposes them to dramatize the inadequacy of the administrators); and finally, academic knowledge *versus* practical experience (because the evaluator is, in fact, often an academic, the practitioner views him or her as having no "real-world" experience in or awareness of such practical problems as limited budgets and personnel resources).[137] Sometimes conflict can result from these differing perspectives.

Consequently, most experts in the field of evaluation agree that the evaluation of a program ought to be commissioned and sponsored by the highest level in an organization that has program responsibility and, on balance, evaluation that is conducted by an external agency or by a third-party consultant probably is preferable.[138] When evaluation research is commissioned by the top executives of an agency and is conducted by outside evaluators, some of the natural strains between practitioners and researchers are avoided. In addition, outside evaluators are more likely to question the basic premises of the organization; are more effective mediators because of their objectivity; and are more likely to devote their time more fully to the research problem at hand. Still, insiders have certain advantages, too, including a more detailed knowledge of the organization, and the probability that they are in a better position to be able to do continuing, long-term program evaluation.[139]

Step 2: What Is Your Problem?

To determine a decision-maker's needs, we must ask what the decision-maker's perceptions of the problem are. Is he or she dissatisfied with the effectiveness or the results of the program— or with the lack of a program—to meet a particular social mission?

Defining the Problem.   To fully understand what the goals of the program are, one should have a written statement that lists the intended benefits of the program. It should include how many of those benefits are expected to be attained and within what

time frame, identify possible recipients of adverse consequences or unintended benefits that cannot be avoided, include important qualitative features, and finally, account for multiple objectives that may conflict with each other or, conversely, be in support of one another. "The importance of taking such a comprehensive view of [program] objectives cannot be overstated. Oversimplified statements (1) will not capture all essential aspects of the effects intended, and (2) may contain implied conflicting consequences for groups other than the intended beneficiaries."[140]

Critical to defining the problem is, oddly, defining success. That is, how do we know, and when do we know, that our program is successful? Researchers have found that when program managers have clear understandings of what programmatic success means, they can upgrade their definition of success over time, and that this process enhances long-term program development and policymaking.[141]

Is Evaluating the Problem Worthwhile?   Once the agency's problem is defined, then another question arises: Is the agency's problem worth the expense and energy involved in evaluating it?

To answer this, five questions must be addressed:

- How much confidence can agency administrators have in the evaluation's findings and conclusions? That is, what is its level of *validity*?
- Will its results be useful to the agency? That, is what will be its *relevance*?
- Will the research provide the program administrators with substantially more insights than they can glean from their own observations? That is, what will be its *significance*?
- Will the value of research exceed its cost? That is, will it have *efficiency*?
- And, finally, will the study be completed in time to meet agency schedules? That is, will it be *timely*?

If the responses to these questions are affirmative, then the evaluation is worth undertaking.

Step 3: Designing the Evaluation

Once the agency's problem has been identified, then the evaluators must design their research around it.[142] This can be a very tricky business because evaluation research differs from basic research. Evaluation research is a form of applied, or "action research," because it may, wittingly or unwittingly, contribute to social action. Evaluation research, like basic research, is concerned with theory and experimental design, but its chief purpose is to evaluate comprehensively a particular activity, and to meet an agency's deadline in the process.

Because a public program evaluation is a kind of action research, certain trade-offs are inevitable. Most notably, "there is often a tradeoff between the breadth of a study and the precision of results."[143] With breadth comes fuzziness, and with clarity, narrowness.

The Study Plan. Preparing a detailed study plan is the initial step in designing an evaluation. The study plan should always include the following components:

- A clear statement of the problem
- The objectives of the research
- A careful listing of the assumptions and constraints to be used in addressing the problem
- The resources to be committed
- The methods to be employed
- Measures of the evaluation's attainment of its objectives
- Lines of communication
- Specific procedures for amending the study plan
- A schedule for completing major components of the evaluation, including a final deadline
- Specific procedures for using the results of the evaluation

The Attenuations of Action Research: Technical Challenges. Once the study plan is completed, the core design issues must be faced, and "the central scientific problems in evaluation are (a) the segregation of treatment effects per se from random variation on the one hand and from systematic biasing through uncontrolled factors that are extraneous to treatment on the other hand, and (b) the reliable measurement of these effects."[144]

Achieving control over the variables in a program for purposes of evaluating that program is unusually difficult in an action setting. When a *control group* (that is, a group of clients who are excluded from receiving the benefits of a particular experimental program designed to improve services) is set aside for purposes of comparing it with an *experimental group* (a group of clients who do receive the benefits of a particular program innovation), there is often a great deal of social and political pressure to provide the benefits of that experiment to both groups. Thus, both the program's administrators and the program's clients are reluctant to withhold services from a particular group that might benefit from those services, even though the evaluation might be ruined by doing so. Relatedly, self-selection is a problem in a program evaluation in an action setting; "it is difficult to refuse service to those who seek it and provide service to those who resist it."[145]

In short, action settings simply inhibit evaluators from using a well-controlled experimental design. In addition, hidden motives on the part of the evaluator can interfere with accurate measurement. For example, private consultants, who must make a living by securing contracts from public agencies, may dismiss technical challenges and promise too much in writing their research design. Among the more vivid examples of this is provided by a program evaluation attempted by the (now defunct) Office of Economic Opportunity in 1972, in which 120 drug treatment centers in six cities were evaluated in a study involving interviews with 9,000 present and former drug abusers. All of this was to be accomplished in thirteen months. After seven months of rather grotesque trial and error, the project was abandoned. During that time, the program evaluators (a private consulting firm) had collected data on just nine treatment centers and 1,270 clients at a cost of more than $2 million.[146]

The Attenuations of Action Research: Ethical Challenges. In designing their research, evaluators also should be cognizant of some basic ethical and moral problems associated with the conduct of program evaluation. Principal among these are problems involving privacy.

Privacy, Confidentiality, and Informed Consent. The issues of privacy and confidentiality are not unique to evaluation research, but they do assume a somewhat different tenor in this context. In program evaluation projects, *privacy* refers to the state of the individual; *confidentiality* refers to a state of information. Thus, privacy becomes a matter between the evaluator and the respondent. It hinges on the degree to which the evaluator's questions, in and of themselves, are perceived by the respondent to be prying or embarrassing. Hence, privacy is not a matter of *who* knows the answer, but of whether certain kinds of knowledge are known to *anyone* other than the respondent. The test of an invasion of privacy is to ask if the respondent will voluntarily furnish answers under conditions that appear to appropriately restrict the use of those answers.

Confidentiality refers to the question of whether an investigator's promise of confidentiality to a respondent is either sufficient or even necessary. The evaluator's promise, no matter how solemnly given, may not be sufficient because, under certain legal situations, the investigator must yield the information he or she has collected or go to jail. The legal fact of the matter is that social science research records are not protected under statutory law as a privileged communication, as are the records of lawyers and physicians.

Central to the ethical issues of privacy and confidentiality is the problem of *informed consent*, which refers to whether or not a respondent understands what he or she is agreeing to. "Lawyers have questioned the legality as well as the ethicality of experimental design and random assignment of participants to treatment for purposes of program evaluation. The grounds for such questioning include the issues of informed consent, equal protection, and the statutory (or other) authority of the agency to conduct experimental evaluations."[147]

You Got a Problem with That?   When ethical issues arise in conducting program evaluations, what do the evaluators do? More often than not, they disagree on whether or not an ethical question is even present.

When program evaluators were asked to react to a series of hypothetical ethical scenarios, disagreement ruled: "The bad news is that one voice" among evaluators "does not exist" when ethics are involved. Evaluators who are private consultants, however, "were less likely than those in other settings," such as nonprofit organizations and universities, "to believe that the scenarios portrayed unethical behavior by the evaluator."[148]

It also appears that once it is determined that ethics have been violated, researchers do, in fact, report it (at least more than nine out of ten do), but to whom they report it depends on how close they are to the research. A study of research administrators and research scientists found that the administrators were much more likely (75 percent) to report unethical practices to "externally accountable individuals," ranging from university officers to the press, whereas the scientists were much more likely (58 percent) to report such incidents to colleagues on their own research teams, and to no one else, "raising the question of whether scientists' behavior constitutes professional self-regulation or cover-up."[149]

Using Public Program Evaluations

Once a public program evaluation is completed, it is supposed to be used.

As with all things evaluative, this last and most important step is not easy. When administrators and the evaluators of those administrators' programs disagree, what should the evaluator do? Are evaluators accountable for the evaluation being used, or, once they have completed the evaluation, should they instead leave it to the tender mercies of the administrator?

Passive or Active Evaluation?

These questions lie at the heart of a consuming debate in evaluation circles. One wing argues that, because administrators are confronted by many varieties of information (social, economic, political) on which they must judge public programs (evaluation research being just one), it is appropriate for the evaluator to withdraw once the evaluation is done; the responsibility of the evaluator does not exceed that of providing adequate and accurate knowledge.[150]

The other wing of the debate contends that the evaluator has the responsibility to assume an active role in promoting the evaluation's use.[151] This wing reflects a real frustration of evaluators, that is, their perception that their evaluations are rarely used. "There is a pervasive sense that government officials do not pay much attention to the research their money is buying. The consensus seems to be that most research studies bounce off the policy process without making much of a dent in the course of events."[152]

Program evaluators, unsurprisingly, tend to place greater importance on their evaluations than do program administrators. One observer suggests that certain strategies be used by evaluators in overcoming bureaucratic resistance to their findings, and arrays these strategies along a continuum ranging from coercion and inducement, to rational persuasion, and finally to "consensual cooperation."[153]

Consensual cooperation is now the mode favored by evaluators in conducting program evaluations. The field calls this approach "collaborative modes of evaluation," by which is meant evaluators working closely with administrators in evaluating those administrators' programs. The peril, of course, in collaborative evaluations is that of "misutilization" of the evaluation by administrators, which is how evaluators describe those "serious questions about the evaluator's ability to maintain a sufficiently bias-free stance due to pressures emanating mainly from the program community"[154]—that is, from the administrators whose programs are being evaluated.

Does Public Program Evaluation Matter?

We rather favor the more passive model of how to use an evaluation. That is, less collaboration between evaluators and administrators, resulting in a greater assurance of an accurate and useful evaluation. We favor it not only because it is safer from contamination by those with interests in assuring certain findings in the evaluation, but also because the very act of program evaluation often serves a purpose that is both important and under recognized by evaluators.

Carol Weiss calls this hidden purpose "the enlightenment function," citing as evidence for its existence three major studies on the uses of evaluation research that indicate "some other process is at work."[155] This process is not the conventional wisdom of the evaluation researcher, which holds that, "to the extent that he departs from the goals and assumptions adhered to by policymakers, his research will be irrelevant to the 'real world' and will go unheeded."[156]

Weiss argues that this perception by the evaluation researcher is both cynical and naive (and likely it is overwrought, too; recall our earlier point that an analysis of hundreds of evaluations of public programs found that almost four-fifths of them resulted in programmatic changes[157]). The real utility of public program evaluation, according to Weiss, is that it is a form of social criticism and should be viewed by evaluators as such. "The enlightenment model . . . implies that research need not necessarily be geared to the operating feasibilities of today, but that research provides the intellectual background of concepts, orientations, and empirical generalizations that inform policy. As new concepts and data emerge, their gradual cumulative effect can be to change the conventions policymakers abide by and to reorder the goals and priorities of the practical policy world."[158]

The enlightenment model posited by Weiss is perhaps the most succinct and useful view of the role that public program evaluation plays in public administration. Although not rigorously scientific, it does appeal to the basic precepts of how knowledge is used. In this view, public program evaluation sensitizes policymakers. It opens new options that, over time, they are more likely to adopt because of the background data provided by an evaluation research project. Evaluation research may not be used as immediately and radically as the evaluation researcher might wish, but in the long run program evaluations are employed by policymakers, and perhaps on a broader plane than evaluation researchers realize.

In this chapter we have introduced the new public techniques and innovations for making governments more efficient, effective, accountable, and productive. Money, the public's money, is central in this effort, as we shall see in the next chapter, "The Public Trough."

Notes

1. Cited in C. Dineen, "Productivity Improvement: It's Our Turn," *The Bureaucrat* 14 (Winter 1985), pp. 10–14.

2. John E. Petersen, "Productivity Pinch," *Governing* (September 2003), p. 62. Petersen is citing the work of economist William Baumol. This is not to say that technology is incapable of producing more productivity in the public sector, as the introduction of information technology has demonstrated (see Chapters 6 and 8). But governments remain inherently less benefited than the private sector by the introduction of most new technologies.

3. U.S. Office of Personnel Management, *Investing in Federal Productivity and Quality* (Washington, DC: U.S. Government Printing Office, 1992). In 1816, the U.S. House of Representatives established a standing committee to oversee the operations of the War Department, and this may qualify as the nation's first attempt at productivity improvement in government.

4. Susan E. Knapp, "Budget Reform in Kazakstan," *IPA Report* (Summer 1998), p. 1.

5. Gerald Gaither, Brian P. Nedwek, and John E. Neal, *Measuring Up: The Promises and the Pitfalls of Performance Indicators in Higher Education* ASHE-ERIC Higher Education Report No. 5. (Washington, DC: The George Washington University, Graduate School of Education and Human Development, 1994), p. 5.

6. U.S. General Accounting Office, *Performance Measurement and Evaluation: Definitions and Relationships*, GAO/GGD–98–26 (Washington, DC: U.S. Government Printing Office, 1998), p. 3.

7. Ibid.

8. Eleanor Chelinsky, "Evaluating Public Programs," in James L. Perry, ed., *Handbook of Public Administration* (San Francisco: Jossey-Bass, 1989), p. 259.

9. U.S. General Accounting Office, *Performance Measurement and Evaluation*, p. 3.

10. Robert Birnbaum, *Leadership and Campus Productivity* (College Park, MD: National Center for Post Secondary Governance and Finance, 1990), p. 1.

11. Geert Bouckaert, "The History of the Productivity Movement," *Public Productivity and Management Review* 14 (Fall 1990), p. 83.

12. Harris Poll, "Confidence in Political Institutions, 1967–1995," *Harris Survey* (November 1995), pp. 1–4. In 1995, 66 percent of American voters thought government was corrupt. As we observed in Chapter 1, few Americans believe that public administrators are corrupt, but, obviously these views do not extend to governments as a whole.

13. The National Election Studies, "Are Government Officials Crooked, 1958–2004" (Ann Arbor: University of Michigan, 2005). In 1958, 26 percent of Americans said hardly any government officials were crooked, and 24 percent said quite a few; by 2004, these responses had altered to 10 percent and 35 percent, respectively.

14. Sandra T. Welch, Sarah A. Holmes, and Jeffrey W. Strauser, "Fraud in the Federal Government: Part I—The Perpetrators and the Victims," *Government Accountants Journal* 46 (Spring 1997), p. 24. These figures are the product of a survey of the 8,000 members of the Association of Certified Fraud Examiners; response rate was 31 percent, and 208 defalcations were reported and described in detail. Depending on the agency, losses attributable to fraud amounted from 0.03 percent to 0.40 percent of the agency's budget request. Nevertheless, these 208 defalcations added up to $157 million!

15. U.S. Bureau of the Census, *Statistical Abstract of the United States, 2006*, 125th ed. (Washington, DC: U.S. Government Printing Office, 2006), Table 327. In 1980, 123 federal officials were indicted on public corruption charges, and in 2003, 479 were.

16. Ibid. In 1980, 72 state government officials and 247 local government officials were indicted on public corruption charges. In 2003, these figures were 94 and 259, respectively.

17. Sandra T. Welch, Sarah A. Holmes, and Jeffrey W. Strauser, "Fraud in the Federal Government Part II—Characteristics of the Schemes, the Detection and Resolution of the Cases," *Government Accountants Journal* 46 (Summer 1997), p. 44.

18. Transparency International, *Corruption Perceptions Index 2005* (Berlin: Author, 2005). Figure is for 2005, when the United States was rated 7.6 on a ten-point scale. The five Scandinavian countries, New Zealand, Singapore Switzerland, Australia, Austria, Netherlands, U.K., Luxembourg, Canada, Hong Kong, and Germany, with scores ranging from 9.7 (Iceland) to 8.2 (Germany), scored better than the United States, which generally ranges from 16th to 18th in these surveys.

19. M. Maor, "Feeling the Heat? Anticorruption Mechanisms in Comparative Perspective," *Governance* 17 (January 2004), pp. 1–28. The author investigated five "anticorruption mechanisms" in the United States, Russia, Italy, and Australia.

20. James D. Thompson, *Organizations in Action: Social Science Bases of Administrative Theory* (New York: McGraw-Hill, 1967), p. 142.

21. Lydia Segal, "Roadblocks in Reforming Corrupt Agencies: The Case of the New York City School Custodians," *Public Administration Review* 62 (July/August 2002), pp. 445–446.

22. Ibid, p. 448.

23. For two good treatments of the Phenix City follies, see Alan Grady, *When Good Men Do Nothing: The Assassination of Albert Patterson* (Tuscaloosa: University of Alabama Press, 2003), and Margaret Anne Barnes, *The Tragedy and Triumph of Phenix City, Alabama* (Macon, GA: Mercer University Press, 1998).

24. Segal, "Roadblocks in Reforming Corrupt Agencies," p. 445.

25. Frederick C. Mosher and Orville F. Poland, *The Costs of American Governments: Facts, Trends, Myths* (New York: Dodd, Mead, 1964), pp. 12–15.

26. Clarence E. Ridley and Herbert A. Simon, *Measuring Municipal Activities: A Survey of Suggested Criteria and*

Reporting Forms for Appraising Administration (Chicago: International City Managers Association, 1938).

27. Luther Gulick, "Science, Values, and Public Administration," in Luther Gulick and L. Urwick, eds., *Papers on the Science of Administration* (New York: Institute of Public Administration, 1937), p. 192.

28. Leonard D. White, *The Administrative Histories: The Federalists* (New York: Macmillan, 1948), p. 16.

29. See, for example, Kurt Lewin, *Resolving Social Conflicts* (New York: Harper & Row, 1948); Ronald Lippitt, *Studies in Experimentally Created Autocratic and Democratic Groups*, University of Iowa Studies: *Studies in Children's Welfare*, Vol. 16. (No.3, 1940), pp. 45–198; and Leon Festinger and Harold Kelley, *Changing Attitudes Through Social Contact* (Ann Arbor: University of Michigan Press, 1951).

30. Orville F. Poland, "Why Does Public Administration Ignore Evaluation?" *Public Administration Review* 31 (March/April 1971), p. 201.

31. Nicholas Henry, *Public Administration and Public Affairs* (Englewood Cliffs, NJ: Prentice Hall, 1975), p. 222.

32. Joseph S. Wholey, John W. Scanlon, Hugh G. Duffy, et al., *Federal Evaluation Policy: Analyzing the Effects of Public Programs* (Washington, DC: Urban Institute, 1970), p. 23.

33. Senator William Proxmire, quoted in Thomas D. Morris, William H. Corbett, and Brian L. Usilaner, "Productivity Measures in the Federal Government," *Public Administration Review* 32 (November/December 1972), p. 754.

34. For a thorough review of the federal government's experience with inspectors general, see Paul C. Light, *Monitoring Government: Inspectors General and the Search for Accountability* (Washington, DC: Brookings, 1993).

35. Dana Priest, "Panel Inspects Inspectors General," *Washington Post* (May 27, 1992).

36. Tom Shoop, "The IG Enigma," *Government Executive* (January 1992), p. 31.

37. President's Council on Integrity and Efficiency, as cited in ibid., p. 40. Figures are for 1990.

38. Kathryn E. Newcomer, "Opportunities and Incentives for Improving Program Quality: Auditing and Evaluating," *Public Administration Review* 54 (March/April 1994), p. 150.

39. Ibid., p. 135.

40. Unpublished report conducted by the Council for State Governments and the Urban Institute, 1972, as cited in Harry P. Hatry, Richard E. Winnie, and Donald M. Fisk, *Practical Program Evaluation for State and Local Government Officials* (Washington, DC: Urban Institute, 1973), p. 17.

41. U.S. General Accounting Office, *State and Local Productivity Improvement: What Is the Federal Role?* (Washington, DC: U.S. Government Printing Office, 1978). The report said much the same for local governments, too.

42. James E. Jarrett, "Productivity," *Book of the States, 1982–83* (Lexington, KY: Council of State Governments, 1982), pp. 296–301.

43. Juliet Eilperin, "Cuts Kill GAO Evaluation Division," *Roll Call*, July 11, 1996, p. 1.

44. U.S. General Accounting Office, *Federal Evaluation: Fewer Units, Reduced Resources, Different Studies From 1980*, GAO/PEMD–87–9 (Washington, DC: U.S. Government Printing Office, 1987), p. 1.

45. Judith R. Brown, "Legislative Program Evaluation: Refining a Legislative Service and a Profession," *Public Administration Review* 44 (May/June 1984), p. 258.

46. We are indebted to two scholars for much of the original thinking in this discussion: Frank Anechiarico and James D. Jacobs, "Visions of Corruption Control and the Evolution of American Public Administration," *Public Administration Review* 54 (September/October 1994), pp. 465–473. It is worth noting that Americans' growing intolerance, and expanding definition, of corruption can be traced to the country's origins, when General George Washington's unusual expense claims to the Continental Congress raised no eyebrows. Neither did the purchase of a Pierce-Arrow, Rolls-Royce, house, and an annuity by President Woodrow Wilson's friends bother Americans in the early 1920s. Times have changed.

47. According to the Annenberg Campaign Data Base, the words "waste, fraud, or abuse" were not spoken by the presidential candidates during the 1960 campaign, but in 1980 the candidates uttered them eighty-three times, and they have shown strong appearances in presidential campaigns every since. See: Paul C. Light, *The True Size of Government* (Washington, DC Brookings, 1999), p. 88.

48. J. B. McKinney, "Concepts and Definitions," in J. B. McKinney and M. Johnstone, eds., *Fraud, Waste, and Abuse in Government: Causes, Consequences, and Cures* (Philadelphia: Institute for the Study of Human Issues, 1986), p. 5.

49. William Stanberry and Fred Thompson, "Toward a Political Economy of Government Waste: First Step, Definitions," *Public Administration Review* 55 (September/October 1995), pp. 418–427.

50. Martin L. Gross, *Government Racket: Washington Waste From A to Z* (New York: Bantam, 1992).

51. Reports by the U.S. House Government Reform and Oversight Committee issued in 1992 and 1996, as cited in: Stephen Barr, "Panel Finds Little Progress in Government Reform," *Washington Post* (October 22, 1996). The 1992 report estimated a loss of $300 billion, and the 1996 report estimated $350 billion.

52. Andy Pasztor, *When the Pentagon Was for Sale: Inside America's Biggest Defense Scandal* (New York: Scribner, 1995).

53. John M. Kamensky, "Role of the 'Reinventing Government' Movement in Federal Management Reform," *Public Administration Review* 56 (May/June 1996), pp. 248–249.

54. David Osborne and Ted Gaebler, *Reinventing Government: How the Entrepreneurial Spirit is Transforming the Public Sector* (Reading, MA: Addison-Wesley, 1992); Michael Barzelay and Basak J. Armajani, *Breaking Through Bureaucracy: A New Vision for*

Managing Government (Berkeley; University of California Press, 1992); Philip K. Howard, *The Death of Common Sense: How Law is Suffocating America* (New York: Random House, 1994); Mark Goldstein, *America's Hollow Government: How Washington Has Failed the People* (Homewood, IL: Business One/Irwin, 1992); and Larry M. Lane and James E. Wolf, *The Human Resource Crisis in the Public Sector: Rebuilding the Capacity to Govern* (New York: Quantum, 1990).

55. Paul Teske and Mark Schneider, "The Bureaucratic Entrepreneur: The Case of City Managers," *Public Administration Review* 54 (July/August 1994), pp. 336–340.

56. Cited in Al Gore, *From Red Tape to Results: Creating a Government That Works Better and Costs Less.* Report of the National Performance Review. (Washington, DC: U.S. Superintendent of Documents, 1993), p.1.

57. Al Gore, *Creating a Government That Works Better and Costs Less.* Status Report of the National Performance Review (Washington, DC: U.S. Government Printing Office, 1994).

58. U.S. General Accounting Office, *Management Reform: GAO's Comments on the National Performance Review's Recommendations*, GAO/OCG–94–1 (Washington, DC: U.S. Government Printing Office, 1994).

59. National Partnership for Reinventing Government, "Accomplishments, 1993–2000: A Summary," *History of the National Partnership for Reinventing Government* (Washington, DC: Author, 2001), p. 1.

60. The following discussion is based on Paul C. Light, *The Four Pillars of High Performance: How Robust Organizations Achieve Extraordinary Results* (Washington, DC: Brookings, 2005); U.S. Government Accountability Office, *21st Century Challenges: Transforming Government to Meet Current and Emerging Challenges*, GAO–05–830T (Washington, DC: U.S. Government Printing Office, 2005); Osborne and Gaebler, *Reinventing Government*; Barzelay and Armajani, *Breaking Through Bureaucracy*; and Robert B. Denhardt, and Janet Vinzant Denhardt, "The New Public Service: Serving Rather than Steering," *Public Administration Review* 60 (November/December 2000), pp. 549–559. The Denhardts argue that the new public management is "a cluster of ideas and practices . . . that seek, at their core, to use their private-sector and business approaches in the public sector" (p. 550), and urge that the new public management be modified into a more public-interest-intensive approach they call "the new public service," a notion that is somewhat reminiscent of "the new public administration" of the 1960s, discussed in Chapter 2. Their comparison of "the old public administration," "the new public management," and "the new public service" is valuable, and we have incorporated several of their ideas in what we still stubbornly call "the new public management."

The titles of the first four ideas that we have listed as constituting the new public management are Light's; the final title, Accountability, is ours. Light's enlightened book has contributed to our discussion in more ways than just titles, however.

For other oars churning this pond, see: Daniel W. Williams, "Reinventing the Proverbs of Government," *Public Administration Review* 60 (November/December 2000), pp. 522–534; Peri E. Arnold, "Reform's Changing Role," *Public Administration Review* 55 (September/October 1995), pp. 407–417; James D. Carroll and Dahlia Bradshaw Lynn, "The Future of Federal Reinvention: Congressional Perspectives," *Public Administration Review* 56 (May/June 1996), pp. 299–304; H. George Frederickson, "Painting Bull's Eyes Around Bullet Holes," *Governing* 6 (December 1992), pp. 60–62; Hugh T. Miller, "A Hummelian View of the Gore Report: Toward a Post-Progressive Public Administration?" *Public Productivity and Management Review* 18 (Fall 1994), pp. 59–71; and Ronald C. Moe, "The 'Reinventing Government' Exercise: Misinterpreting the Problem, Misjudging the Consequences," *Public Administration Review* 54 (March/April 1994), pp. 111–122.

61. Samantha L. Durst and Charldean Newell, "Better, Faster, Stronger: Government Reinvention in the 1990s," *American Review of Public Administration* 29 (March 1999), p. 63. Figure is for 1996; eighty governments responded to the survey.

62. National Partnership for Reinventing Government, "Accomplishments, 1993–2000," pp. 1–2. We should note that in 1996, the National Partnership claimed enactment of 380 of its 1,203 "action items," based on reports by federal agencies to the vice president. The GAO's audit revealed, however, that only 294 (or 77 percent) of these reported implementations had actually been enacted. See U.S. General Accounting Office, *Management Reform: Completion Status of Agency Actions Under the National Performance Review*, GAO/GGD–96–94 (Washington, DC: U.S. Government Printing Office, 1996). In 1998, the National Partnership discontinued tracking the accomplishment of action items because "a majority" of them had been achieved. See National Partnership for Reinventing Government, *Status of the Recommendation of NPR Recommendations* (Washington, DC: Author, 1998), p. 1. Similarly, the GAO has questioned the National Partnership's claims of savings, suggesting that not all agency savings it claims can properly be attributed to it. See: U.S. General Accounting Office, *NPR's Savings: Claimed Agency Savings Cannot All Be Attributed to NPR*, GAO/GGD–99–120 (Washington, DC: U.S. Government Printing Office, 1999).

63. Donald F. Kettl, *Reinventing Government: A Fifth Year Report Card* (Washington, DC: Brookings, 1998), p. 8.

64. U.S. Government Accountability Office, *Results-Oriented Government: GPRA Has Established a Solid Foundation for Achieving Greater Results*, GAO–04–38 (Washington, DC: U.S. Government Printing Office, 2004), p. 71. Figures are for 2003.

65. For a slightly different take on this, see the useful piece by James R. Thompson, "Reinvention as Reform: Assessing the National Performance Review," *Public Administration Review* 60 (November/December 2000), pp. 508–521.

66. Jeffrey L. Brudney, F. Ted Hebert, and Deil S. Wright, "Reinventing Government in the American States: Measuring and Explaining Administrative Reform," *Public Administration Review* 59 (January/February 1999), p. 29.

67. Richard C. Kearney, "Reinventing Government and Battling Budget Crises: Manager and Municipal Government Actions in 2003," *Municipal Year Book, 2005* (Washington, DC: International City/County Management Association, 2005), pp. 27–32. The survey found that "support for the reinventing government movement remains strong among managers and councils, although it has weakened slightly since 1997" (p. 27).

68. Barry M. Feldman, "Reinventing Local Government: Beyond Rhetoric to Action," *Municipal Year Book, 1999* (Washington, DC: International City/County Management Association, 1999), pp. 23–24. Data are for 1998, and refer to 912 council-manager cities of 10,000 people or more.

69. Richard C. Kearney, Barry M. Feldman, and Carmine P. F. Scavo, "Reinventing Government: City Manager Attitudes and Actions," *Public Administration Review* 60 (November/December 2000), p. 544. All council-manager cities with populations of 10,000 (1,484 cities) or more were surveyed in 1997.

70. Mildred Warner and Amir Hafetz, "Pragmatism over Politics: Alternative Service Delivery in Local Government, 1992–2002," *Municipal Year Book, 2004* (Washington, DC: International City/County Management Association, 2004), p. 11. Cities and counties delivered from 48 percent to 52 percent of their services using only their own employees, and they contracted out from 26 percent to 27 percent of their services to the private and nonprofit sectors in 1992, 1997, and 2002. We devote much of Chapter 11 to privatization, and some of Chapter 12 to local intergovernmental collaborative arrangements.

71. Theodore H. Poister and Gregory Streib, "Municipal Management Tools from 1976 to 1993: An Overview and Update," *Public Productivity and Management Review* 18 (Winter 1994), pp. 21–22. Figure (63 percent) is for 1993. We review governments' use of strategic planning in Chapter 10.

72. Kearney "Reinventing Government and Battling Budget Crises," p. 31. Figures are for 2003. See also Gregory Streib and Theodore H. Poister, "Performance Measurement in Municipal Governments," *Municipal Year Book, 1998* (Washington, DC: International City/County Management Association, 1998), pp. 9–15. The municipal courts' use of citizen satisfaction surveys was a unique outlier at 6 percent.

73. Pasztor, *When the Pentagon Was for Sale*, p. 10.

74. Donald M. Kettl, *Reinventing Government? Appraising the National Performance Review* (Washington, DC: Brookings, 1994), p. 54. See also: Marilyn Marks Rubin, DeWitt John, Donald F. Kettl, et al., "What Will New Governance Mean for the Federal Government?" *Public Administration Review*, 54 (March/April 1994), pp. 170–175. This is a nice synopsis of how the new public managers and the traditionalists differ in their approaches to public problems.

75. John Bohte and Kenneth J. Meier, "Goal Displacement: Assessing the Motivation for Organizational Cheating," *Public Administration Review* 60 (March/April 2000), pp. 173–182. See also Diana Jean Schemo and Ford Fessenden, "Gains in Houston Schools: How Real Are They?" *New York Times* (December 3, 2003).

76. Daria Hall, *Getting Honest about Grad Rates: How States Play the Numbers Game and Students Lose* (Washington, DC: The Education Trust, 2005), p. 6.

77. See, for example: Christopher Swanson, *Who Graduates? A Statistical Portrait of Public High School Graduation, Class of 2001* (Washington, DC: Education Policy Center, The Urban Institute, 2004); Jay Greene and Greg Foster, *Public High School Graduation and College Readiness Rates in the United States* (New York: The Manhattan Institute of Policy Research, 2005); and Paul Barton, *One-Third of a Nation: Rising Dropout Rates and Declining Opportunities* (Washington, DC: Policy Information Center, Educational Testing Service, 2005).

78. Hall, *Getting Honest about Grad Rates*, p. 1. The report is based on state figures for 2002–2003, and which were collected by the U.S. Department of Education in 2005; this was the first year that Washington received state graduation rates as required by the No Child Left Behind Act of 2001. See also U.S. Government Accountability Office, *No Child Left Behind Act: Education Could Do More to Help States Better Define Graduation Rates and Improve Knowledge about Intervention Strategies*, GAO–05–879 (Washington, DC: U.S. Government Printing Office, 2005).

79. Patricia de Lancer Julnes and Marc Holzer, "Promoting the Utilization of Performance Measures in Public Organizations: An Empirical Study of Factors Affecting Adoption and Implementation," *Public Administration Review* 61 (November/December 2001), pp. 693–705. See also Richard C. Kearney and Carmine Scavo, "Reinventing Government in Reformed Municipalities: Manager, Mayor, and Council Actions," *Urban Affairs Review* 37 (September 2001), pp. 43–66.

80. Jane Lynch, "Skewed Results," *Governing* (December 2004), pp. 42–45.

81. Robert D. Behn, "Why Measure Performance? Different Purposes Require Different Measures," *Public Administration Review* 63 (September/October 2003), pp. 586–606. The quotations are on p. 588.

82. Ronald C. Nyhan and Herbert A. Marlowe Jr., "Performance Measurement in the Public Sector: Challenges and Opportunities," *Public Productivity and Management Review* 18 (Summer 1995), p. 333, and Thomas D. Lynch and Susan E. Day, "Public Sector Performance Measurement," *Public Administration Quarterly* 19 (Winter 1996), p. 412. All these endorsements were garnered in the early 1990s.

83. A poll of 900 Americans conducted in 1994 by the Americans Talk Issues Foundation, as cited in Kevin Merida, "Americans Want a Direct Say in Decision-Making, Pollsters Find," *Washington Post* (April 17, 1994).

84. U.S. General Accounting Office, *Program Performance Measures. Federal Agency Collection and Use of*

Performance Data, GAO/GGD–92–65 (Washington, DC: U.S. Government Printing Office, 1992). See also: Amy Waldman, "You Can't Fix Anything If You Don't Look Under the Hood," *Washington Monthly* (July/August 1995), p. 35.

85. Frank Hodsoll, as quoted in Charles F. Bingham, "Installing the M-Team," *Government Executive* (January 1992), p. 25.

86. Christopher Wye, quoted in Jeff Shear, "It's Time to Win One for the GPRA," *National Journal* (October 26, 1996), p. 1042.

87. The six areas in the President's Management Agenda are human capital, competitive sourcing, financial management, electronic government, budget and performance integration, and (added in 2004) federal asset management. Quarterly scores may be accessed at www.whitehouse.gov/results/agenda/scorecard.html.

88. U.S. Government Accountability Office, *Managing for Results: Enhancing Agency Use of Performance Information for Management Decision Making*, GAO–05–927 (Washington, DC: U.S. Government Printing Office, 2005), Highlights page. Figure is for 2004.

89. Governmental Accounting Standards Board, *Performance Measurement of the State and Local Levels: A Summary of Survey Results* (Washington, DC: Author, 2002), p. 6. Figure is for 2001.

90. Julie Melkers and Katherine Willoughby, *Staying the Course: The Use of Performance Measurements in State Governments* (Washington, DC: IBM Center for the Business of Government, 2004).

91. Robert D. Lee Jr., "A Quarter Century of State Budget Practices," *Public Administration Review* 57 (March/April 1997), p. 137. Data are for 1995.

92. Governmental Accounting Standards Board, Performance Measurement at the State and Local Levels, p. 6. Figure is for 2001. See also Katherine G. Willoughby, "Performance Measurement and Budget Balancing: State Government Perspectives," *Public Budgeting and Finance* 24 (June 2004), pp. 21–39.

93. Cherlye A. Broom, "Performance-Based Government Models: Building a Track Record," *Public Budgeting and Finance* 15 (Winter 1995), pp. 3–17. The states were Florida, Minnesota, Oregon, Texas, and Virginia, and were selected from a list of eleven states that the magazine *Financial World* had ranked as the top "quality of management" states. See Katherine Barrett and Richard Greene, "The State of the States," *Financial World* (May 11, 1993), p. 10.

94. Robert D. Lee Jr., and Robert C. Burns, "Performance Measurement in State Budgeting: Advancement and Backsliding from 1990 to 1995," *Public Budgeting and Finance* 20 (Spring 2000), pp. 50–51. Population was the only independent variable of significance in this regard.

95. Governmental Accounting Standards Board, Performance Measurement at the State and Local Levels, pp. 17–18. Figure is for 2001.

96. Streib and Poister, "Performance Measurement in Municipal Governments," pp. 9–15. Figures are for 1997. All cities with populations of 25,000 or more were surveyed with a response rate of 55 percent.

97. Robert P. McGowan and Theodore H. Poister, "The Impact of Productivity Measurement Systems on Municipal Performance," paper prepared for delivery at the 1984 Annual Conference of the American Political Science Association in Washington, DC, August–September 1984, pp. 12–13.

98. Gregory Streib and Theodore H. Poister, "Performance Measurement in Municipal Governments," *Municipal Year Book 1998* (Washington, DC: International City/County Managment Association, 1998), p. 11.

99. Gregory Streib and Theodore H. Poister, "Performance Measurement in Municipal Government: Assessing the State of the Practice," *Public Administration Review* 59 (July/August 1999), pp. 331, 333. Data are for 1997.

100. Ibid., p. 333. In 1997, 23 percent of all municipalities used performance measures in all agencies, and an additional 15 percent used them in at least one major agency.

101. Julia Melkers and Katherine Willoughby, "Models of Performance-Measurements Used in Local Governments: Understanding Budgeting, Communication, and Lasting Effects," *Public Administration Review* 65 (March/April 2005), p. 184. This was a national survey of almost 300 city and county governments conducted in 2000. Four percent of county governments reward their departments in this fashion.

102. U.S. Government Accountability Office, *Managing for Results: Enhancing Agency Use of Performance Information for Management Decision Making*, Highlights page. Figure is for 2004.

103. U.S. Government Accountability Office, *Results-Oriented Government: GPRA Has Established a Solid Foundation for Achieving Greater Results*, GAO–04–38 (Washington, DC: U.S. Government Printing Office, 2004), Highlights page. The remaining references in the text concerning the use of each type of performance measurement used by federal government are from this source. All forthcoming figures are for 2003 and, as noted in the text, refer to federal administrators whose agencies have performance measures (89 percent of all federal agencies), and who use the specific measure cited to a great or very great extent.

104. Governmental Accounting Standards Board, *Performance Measurement at the State and Local Levels*, pp. 5–6. Figures are for 2001. The remaining references in the text (unless noted otherwise) concerning the use of each type of performance measurement by state agencies are from this source. All forthcoming figures are for 2001, and, as noted in the text, the percentages of state agencies that use each type of performance measure are drawn from a universe of the state agencies that use some type of performance measure in at least half of their programs (or 40 percent of all state agencies).

105. Ibid., p. 6. Figure is for 2001.

106. Poister and Streib, "Performance Measurement in Municipal Government," p. 329. Figure is for 1997. The remaining references in the text concerning the use of each type of performance measurement in local governments are drawn from this source.

All forthcoming figures are for 1997. The authors report that, in 1997, only 38 percent of the municipalities they surveyed indicated that their cities used any sort of performance measures. As we note in Table 7-3, however, 88 percent of municipalities and counties reported in 2001 that they use some sort of performance measure, and we rely on this figure in our discussion. It may be that the 1997 finding is an anomaly; as the authors themselves admit (p. 328), their 1997 figure is "a significantly lower percentage than reported by some of the earlier surveys."

107. Jeffrey L. Brudney, F. Ted Hebert, and Deil S. Wright, "Reinventing Government in the American States: Measuring and Explaining Administrative Reform," *Public Administration Review* 59 (January/February 1999), p. 23.

108. This discussion is based (with some modifications) on: Burt Perrin, "Effective Use and Misuse of Performance Measurement," *American Journal of Evaluation* 19 (Fall 1998), pp. 367–379.

109. Christopher Scanlan, "U.S. Measures Human Value, a Life-and-Death Calculation," *Philadelphia Inquirer* (September 2, 1990). Figure is for 1990 and is the product of separate calculations by OMB and the U.S. Department of Agriculture.

110. Jim Holt, "The Human Factor," *New York Times* (March 28, 2004). Figure is for 2004, and is the calculation made by the Environmental Protection Agency for the per capita cost of removing arsenic from drinking water.

111. Maureen L. Cropper and George L. VanHoutven, *When Is A Life Too Costly to Save?* (Washington, DC: Resources for the Future, 1994).

112. Perrin, "Effective Use and Misuse of Performance Evaluation," p. 374.

113. Joseph T. McNamara, "Crime Statistics—Only Game in Town," *Savannah Morning News* (February 5, 2002).

114. U.S. General Accounting Office, *Performance Reporting: Few Agencies Reported on the Completeness and Reliability of Performance Data*, GAO–02–372 (Washington, DC: U.S. Government Printing Office, 2002), p. 2. Figure is for 2000.

115. U.S. General Accounting Office, *Managing for Results: Opportunities for Continued Improvements in Agencies' Performance Plans*, GAO/GGD/AIMD–99–21 (Washington, DC: U.S. Government Printing Office, 1999).

116. U.S. General Accounting Office, *Managing for Results: Challenges in Producing Credible Performance Information*, GAO/T–GGD/RCED–00–134 (Washington, DC: U.S. Government Printing Office, 2000), p. 4.

117. "Report on Business," *Toronto Globe and Mail*, "about 1996," as quoted in Perrin, "Effective Use and Misuse of Performance Evaluation," p. 367.

118. Katherine Barrett and Richard Greene, "Poisoned Measures," *Governing* (May 1998), p. 60.

119. Perrin, "Effective Use and Misuse of Performance Measurement," p. 375.

120. Cited in ibid., p. 376.

121. The following discussion is based on ibid., pp. 367–379.

122. Christopher E. Bogan and Michael J. English, *Benchmarking for Best Practices* (New York: McGraw-Hill, 1994), p. 17.

123. Alfred Tat-Kei Ho and Anna Ya Ni, "Have Cities Shifted to Outcome-Oriented Performance Reporting?—A Content Analysis of City Budgets," *Public Budgeting and Finance* 25 (Summer 2005), p. 74. In 2002, 67 percent of twenty-one big cities tracked performance over time.

124. Governmental Accounting Standards Board, *Performance Measurement at the State and Local Levels*, p. 12. Figure is for 2001.

125. Julie Melekers and Katherine Willoughby, "The State of the States: Performance-Based Budgeting in 47 Out of 50," Public Administration Review 58 (January/February 1998), p. 69.

126. Governmental Accounting Standards Board, *Performance Measurement at the State and Local Levels*, p. 12. Figure is for 2001.

127. Streib and Poister, "Performance Measurement in Municipal Government," p. 14. Figure is for 1997.

128. David N. Ammons, Charles Coe, and Michael Lombardo, "Performance-Comparison Projects in Local Government: Participants' Perspectives," *Public Administration Review* 61 (January/February 2001), pp. 104, 106.

129. Henry W. Riecken, "Principal Components of the Evaluation Process," *Professional Psychology* 8 (November 1977), p. 405.

130. Ibid.

131. Peter Dahler-Larsen, "Surviving the Routinization of Evaluation: The Administrative Use of Evaluations in Danish Municipalities," *Administration and Society* 32 (March 2000), p. 70.

132. U.S. General Accounting Office, *Managing for Results: The Statutory Framework of Performance Management and Accountability*, GAO/GGD/ AIMD–98–52 (Washington, DC: U.S. Government Printing Office, 1998), p. 1.

133. Moynihan and Ingraham, "Look for the Silver Lining," p. 469.

134. Poister and Streib, "Municipal Management Tools from 1976 to 1993," pp. 115–125.

135. David H. Foly and William Lyons, "The Measurement of Municipal Service Quality and Productivity," *Public Productivity Review* 10 (Winter 1986), pp. 21–33.

136. Jonathan P. West, "City Government Productivity and Civil Service Reforms," *Public Productivity Review* 10 (Fall 1986), pp. 45–59.

137. Caro, "Evaluation Research," pp. 13–15.

138. Riecken, "Principal Components of the Evaluation Process," p. 405.

139. Caro, "Evaluation Research," p. 17.

140. U.S. General Accounting Office, *Evaluation and Analysis to Support Decision-Making*, p. 14.

141. Mary E. Poulin, Phillip R. Harris, and Peter R. Jones, "The Significance of Definitions of Success in Program Evaluation," *Evaluation Review* 24 (October 2000), pp. 516–536.

142. Much of this discussion on evaluation design is drawn from, U.S. General Accounting Office, *Evaluation and Analysis to Support Decision-Making*, especially pp. 11–41; Caro, "Evaluation Research," especially pp. 23–27; and U.S. General Accounting Office,

Designing Evaluations, GAO/PEMD-10.1.4 (Washington, DC: U.S. Government Printing Office, 1991).

143. U.S. General Accounting Office, *Evaluation and Analysis to Support Decision-Making*, p. 13.

144. Riecken, "Principal Components of the Evaluation Process," p. 398.

145. Caro, "Evaluation Research," p. 24.

146. H. Donald Messer, "Drug Abuse Treatment: An Evaluation That Wasn't," in *Program Evaluation at HEW: Research Versus Reality*, Part 1: *Health*, James G. Abert, ed. (New York: Marcel Dekker, 1979), pp. 113–168.

147. Riecken, "Principal Components of the Evaluation Process,"p. 408.

148. Michael Morris and Lynette R. Jacobs, "You Got a Problem with That? Exploring Evaluators' Disagreements about Ethics," *Evaluation Review* 24 (August 2000), pp. 384–406. The quotations are on pp. 384 and 403. Questionnaires were returned by 397 members of the American Evaluation Society; 40 percent worked in universities, 19 percent in business or consulting, and 15 percent in nonprofit organizations.

149. Neil S. Wenger, Stanley G. Kornman, Richard Berk, and Honghu Liu, "Reporting Unethical Research Behavior," *Evaluation Review* 23 (October 1999), p. 553. A survey was conducted of 924 scientists and 140 research administrators working under federal grants. The 58 percent figure includes the 6 percent of scientists who would not report the violation at all; only 1 percent of administrators would not report it.

150. See, for example, Carol H. Weiss, "Evaluation for Decisions: Is Anybody There? Does Anybody Care?" *Evaluation Practice* 9 (Spring 1988), pp. 5–19.

151. See, for example: M. O. Patton, "The Evaluator's Responsibility for Utilization," *Evaluation Research* 9 (Summer 1988), pp. 5–24.

152. Carol H. Weiss, "Research for Policy's Sake: The Enlightenment Function of Social Research," *Policy Analysis* 3 (Fall 1977), p. 532.

153. Thomas V. Bonoma, "Overcoming Resistance to Change Recommended for Operating Programs," *Professional Psychology* 8 (November 1977), pp. 451–463.

154. Lynn M. Shulha and J. Bradley Cousins, "Evaluation Use: Theory, Research, and Practice Since 1986," *Evaluation Practice* 18 (Fall 1997), p. 200.

155. Weiss, "Research for Policy's Sake," p. 535.

156. Ibid., p. 544.

157. Dahler-Larsen, "Surviving the Routinization of Evaluation," p. 70. To be fair, we should note that the 600 evaluations were conducted in Danish cities, not American ones.

158. Weiss, "Research for Policy's Sake," p. 544.

CHAPTER **8**

The Public Trough: Financing and Budgeting Governments

In government, money is blood. Currency courses through the body politic, carrying with it civic health or public pestilence, depending upon how governments derive and disburse their dollars.

In this chapter, we attempt to convey an understanding of both finance and budgeting in the public sector. We begin with the price that Americans are willing to pay for their governments and then move to an explanation of public finance, problems of tax systems, the role that the federal government plays in the national economy, the meaning of deficits and debt, congressional budget making, agency strategies for acquiring budgets, and the evolution of budgetary theory.

How Much Should Governments Cost?

Government has a self-regulating price in the marketplace. Liberals may froth that government should have more money, and conservatives may fume that government should have less, but in fact there are limits on the price that Americans are willing to pay for their governments. Americans do not mindlessly demand lower taxes and less government; in reality, they insist that government deliver more, and at a relatively fixed price.

Increasingly, governments must compete with other economic forces that are taking greater shares of Americans' incomes. Since 1972, the portion of personal income allocated by families to basic needs, notably food, clothing, transportation, and savings, has fallen to accommodate the rising costs of two other necessities. Those necessities are: health care, the cost of which doubled over thirty years, and other services, particularly financial services, that increased by some 50 percent over the same time frame.[1]

These trends in home economics have had an impact on just how much Americans are willing to pay for their governments, and the grass-roots tax revolt launched against governments' growing cost, beginning in the 1970s, has yielded policymakers some notion of a realistic price of government. Since 1972, the price that Americans pay for government has remained fairly constant. Over the course of thirty years, Americans have paid from 35 percent to 37 percent of their personal incomes for all governments at all levels. The federal government displays the greatest variation during this time period, ranging from 20 percent to 22 percent in its share of personal income, although since 2001, the federal share of personal income has fallen below 20 percent as a result of unprecedented federal tax cuts initiated by President George W. Bush. State governments accounted for 7.3 percent to 8.3 percent of personal income, and local governments took from 6 percent to 6.6 percent of personal income over thirty years.[2]

Within these ranges of Americans' willingness to pay for government, governments use a variety of means to fund the execution of public policy. We consider these means next.

Public Finance: Paying for Public Policy

First, some basics: *Public finance* is the raising by governments of revenues that are then expended to fund public policies. *Revenue* is the money that government collects to expend in support of public policies. *Expenditures*, or *outlays*, are the money that governments spend to fund public policies.

All governments use two categories of revenue and expenditure in financing their activities: a general fund and special funds. Together, the general fund and the special funds comprise a government's total revenues and its total expenditures.

The General Fund

The *general fund* is comprised of those revenues that may be expended for any purposes that the government chooses. The general fund receives what often is called *general-purpose revenue*, or *general revenue*, and the money spent from it usually is dubbed *general fund expenditures*, or *discretionary spending*. When budget battles erupt in Congress and in state and local legislatures, it is the general fund that typically is at stake.

Taxes are the principal source of revenue for the general fund in all governments, and those taxes that contribute to the general fund are called a *general tax*. The type of general tax that each level of government primarily relies upon for its general revenue differs markedly, however, and over the years each governmental level has established "ownership" of a particular tax. That is, the federal government effectively "owns" the income tax, state governments dominate the sales tax, and local governments traditionally have relied on the property tax as their main source of general revenue. We explain in greater detail these and other taxes in the ensuing discussion.

Special Funds

Special funds are comprised of those revenues that may be expended only for specific, preestablished purposes. The principal justification for this arrangement is that some special funds underwrite public policies that are so vital that they must be protected by law from the political tides and their accompanying opportunists, who might divert the funds needed for these policies to other, lesser but popular, purposes. An example of this sort of special fund is Social Security, a federal program that taxes workers and their employers for the sole purpose of providing retirees with a monthly stipend; those tax revenues cannot be used for any other purpose.

Another rationale for special funds is that some special funds are self-funding; that is, they pay not only for policies that benefit the public, but they pay for themselves, too. Typically, these special funds rely on *user fees*, which are charges to citizens who use specific governmental services, such as colleges, bridges, and government-owned enterprises.

Washington's Special Funds. More than half of all federal dollars are found in special funds.[3] In large part, this condition is the result of congressional decisions to allocate increasingly expansive portions of federal revenues by formula.

Some of these formulas are tied to the growth or shrinkage of a particular type of population, and government payments to citizens in these populations grow or shrink automatically as the number of eligible recipients increases or decreases; an example is federal unemployment insurance. Other formulas are based on the economy and are indexed for inflation and deflation; an example is Social Security.

Irrespective of the formula used, these programs are called *entitlements* on the logic that a person meeting the qualifications of an entitlement program is entitled to his or her payments by right. Most of these programs are linked to economic fluctuations. Of the federal government's sixteen major entitlement programs, eight are tied to the consumer price index and another three are partially indexed. Together, entitlements add up to massive transfers of federal revenues. Almost a third of Americans receive some kind of cash benefit from the federal general government, and over a fifth of all U.S. households receive from Washington a benefit other than cash.[4]

The entitlement programs constitute a class of federal expenditures that federal policymakers call *relatively uncontrollable outlays* that are spent for *mandatory and related programs.* These are mostly entitlement programs (such as Social Security and Medicare) that must be funded, and interest on the national debt, which must be paid.

This uncontrolled spending by Washington is rising steadily and inexorably. In 1962, mandatory and related programs accounted for less than a third of federal spending: Twenty-six percent of federal spending funded mandatory programs, and 6 percent went to pay interest on the debt, leaving a relatively comfortable 68 percent of federal revenues in its general fund and available for discretionary programs. By 2005, the portion of federal revenue that had to be spent on mandatory and related programs had nearly doubled to a disquieting 61 percent: Fifty-four percent of federal spending was drawn for mandatory programs, and 7 percent went to paying interest on the debt. The proportion of federal expenditures that was being spent from the general fund at the discretion of Congress had been reduced by more than two-fifths from forty-three years earlier to a mere 39 percent.[5]

State and Local Special Funds. The special funds of state and local governments do not consume the share of revenue and expenditure that they consume in the federal government, but they nonetheless account for a significant portion of state and local finance.

Trusts, Charges, and Enterprises. State and local special funds pertain to three categories of revenue and expenditure. They are insurance trusts, current charges for services, and government-owned utilities and liquor stores. Together, these three types of special funds generate what are known in state and local governments as *other than general revenue*, or income that may be spent only by or for insurance trusts, specific services, utilities, or liquor stores. Over a tenth of all state dollars, and more than a fifth of all local revenue, are other than general revenue that resides in these special funds.[6]

Insurance trusts are comprised of revenue generated by and expended for unemployment insurance, workers' compensation, and retirement funds for public employees. Insurance trusts are the most important special fund in state governments, where they account for about three-quarters of all other-than-general-revenue dollars.[7]

Charges are fees for specific services. Charges include a welter of diverse payments, such as college tuition; school lunch sales; hospital charges to patients; rents for public housing; bridge and highway tolls; and payments paid to governments by people who use their parks, airports, seaports, sewerage, recreation, trash collection, and other specialized services. Charges are the most significant special fund in local governments, where they constitute more than half of all other than general revenue.[8]

Finally, customer payments that are collected and spent by certain government-owned enterprises comprise our third category of special fund. Specifically, these enterprises include *utilities* (that is, electric and gas power plants, waterworks, and public transit) and *liquor stores.*

Most user charges, utility payments, and liquor store sales are administered by public authorities or special districts that are financed not only by the charges and payments that these entities collect, but also by legislative appropriations, municipal bonds, and borrowing. We explain this facet of public finance in Chapter 11.

Some Unofficial Forms of Special Funds. Insurance trusts, charges, and utilities and liquor stores constitute the totality of state and local special funds that are officially recognized by the public finance community, and we provide more details about them later in our discussion. One could credibly argue, however, that there are other sorts of fiscal categories that, while not technically designated as special funds, nonetheless function as special funds.

For example, the grants-in-aid that state and local governments receive from other governments bear a distinct resemblance to special funds. Although these grants are considered to be general revenue and discretionary expenditures, they almost always come with stringent conditions attached about how the grants must be spent and on what, thus rendering them analogous to special funds.

Another sort of unofficial special fund is the designation of general revenue for special purposes. California is a conspicuous example. Californians have used the initiative to not only slash property taxes, but also to then limit how general tax revenues can be spent.

California's budgetary limits are both burgeoning and draconian. The number of initiatives on the California ballot rocketed from nine in the 1960s to sixty-one in the 1990s. Most of these initiatives mandated new programs that taxpayers had to fund, or specified the percentage of general revenue that must be dedicated to the funding of new programs—and to some old programs as well.

As a consequence, the vast bulk of the Golden State's general revenue is earmarked for specific programs, ranging from a guaranteed minimum spending on schools to funding California's "three strikes" life-sentencing of criminals. The governor and the legislature may exercise discretionary spending over a passing thin slice of the state budget—estimates are from only 15 percent to perhaps 20 percent.[9]

In short, although special funds in state and local governments are relegated technically to trusts, charges, and government-owned enterprises, their characteristics are prominent in other areas of state and local finance as well.

With these two broad categories of public money—general funds and special funds—in mind, we consider next, by each level of government: the sources from which governments garner the revenues they need to pay for public policies; the principal taxes that American governments levy; and what the federal, state, and local governments spend their money on.

Financing the Federal Government

During the course of most of the past century and all of this one, the federal government, unlike state and local governments, has had a consistent revenue flow in the form of taxes.

Federal Revenue

The primary source of federal revenue is the *personal*, or *individual*, *income tax*, which is a general tax on the annual income of each person. The personal income tax accounts for almost 44 percent of all federal revenue.[10]

Social insurance and retirement receipts account for nearly 38 percent of all federal revenue. This category includes old-age and survivors insurance (or Social Security); disability insurance (nine separate major programs, targeted, for the most part, at people aged fifty to sixty-four); hospital insurance (or Medicare); unemployment insurance; and relatively small sums paid toward the retirement funds of federal and railroad employees. Social Security and Medicare, which are retirement and health insurance programs for people aged sixty-five and older, are the heavy hitters here, and account for more than four-fifths of all social insurance and retirement receipts.[11]

The *corporation*, or *corporate*, *income tax* is a general tax on the annual profits of businesses. It accounts for 11 percent of all federal revenue.[12]

The *excise tax* is a general tax on specific items that usually is paid by the manufacturer. The main federal excise taxes are placed on companies that make gasoline, alcoholic beverages, telephone systems, and tobacco products, and all excise taxes account for less than 4 percent of all federal revenues.[13] The revenue generated by excise taxes has fallen precipitously; in 1950, excise taxes accounted for more than a fifth of total federal revenue.[14]

The Income Tax

Together, personal and corporate income taxes account for more than six out of every ten tax dollars collected by *all* governments, including those governments that do not impose income taxes.[15]

No other tax comes close to equaling the revenue productivity of the income tax, particularly the individual income tax.

Income taxes may be progressive, proportional, or regressive. A *progressive income tax* taxes higher incomes at a higher rate than it taxes lower incomes. A *proportional income tax* taxes all incomes, high and low alike, at the same rate, which is why a proportional income tax also is called a *flat tax*. A *regressive income tax* taxes higher incomes at a lower rate than it taxes lower incomes. The federal government and all other governments in the United States that levy income taxes try, at least nominally, to apply a moderately progressive tax rate.

Washington's Income Taxes.   Between them, Washington's taxes on personal and corporate incomes amount to more than half, 55 percent, of all federal revenues.[16] Although the personal income tax has remained quite steady as a proportion of all federal revenue over the past half-century, the corporate income tax has declined significantly, falling from 29 percent of total federal revenue in 1950 to 11 percent today.[17]

For the nation's first 125 years following the ratification of the Constitution, the federal government was prohibited from taxing the income of citizens directly. Taxing companies, however, was another matter, and the first federal corporate income tax was enacted in 1909.

The rise of the income tax as an unparalleled revenue harvester, however, began with the ratification, in 1913, of the Sixteenth Amendment to the Constitution. The Sixteenth Amendment permitted the federal government to tax all incomes, and the feds quickly rose to the occasion. Today, Washington rakes in almost four-fifths of all income-tax dollars collected by all governments.[18]

State and Local Income Taxes.   Besides the federal government, forty-three states and a few local governments also levy the personal income tax, and forty-five states and a few local governments use the corporate income tax. Wisconsin was the first state to impose an income tax (both personal and corporate) in 1911.[19]

Although the state individual income tax has been steadily rising as a revenue source, from not much more than a fourth of all state tax revenue in 1980 to nearly one-third today, the corporate income tax has been plummeting precipitously, from almost a tenth of all state tax revenue in 1980 to half that today.[20] The slippage of the state corporate income tax has been attributed to changing economies in the states and, perhaps of even greater importance, to shrewd tax planning by corporations[21] that occurs in tandem with a cutthroat competition among state governments that are lowering their corporate income taxes to lure companies to relocate to their states.[22]

Fourteen states permit at least some types of their local governments to tax personal income. Philadelphia was the first local government to levy an individual income tax in 1938.

Paying for Social Security and Medicare: Washington Thanks You for Your Contributions

We noted earlier that, after the personal income tax, the principal source of federal revenue is social insurance and retirement receipts, and this category is dominated by Social Security and Medicare. These two massive programs are funded by what is called, with unfortunate coyness, "insurance contributions." *Insurance contributions* are actually a compulsory payroll tax, and they derive their name from the Federal Insurance Contributions Act (FICA) of 1935, which underwrites Social Security and Medicare exclusively. The payroll taxes collected through FICA account for more than a third, 34 percent, of total federal revenue—quite a jump from 1950, when these taxes amounted to less than 8 percent of all federal revenue.[23]

Both employers and employees pay this tax in equal shares, and their combined tax rate has quintupled from about 3 percent of payrolls in 1950 to over 15 percent today.[24] The payroll tax rate is not adjusted for the size of one's paycheck and, with one regressive exception, it is a proportional, or flat, tax that taxes all those who pay it at the same tax rate.

The exception is the Social Security portion of FICA, which comprises more than four-fifths of the payroll tax. The Social Security component stops after an employee has been paid a set amount (currently $90,000) for the year, and then restarts at the beginning of the next calendar year. (For example, if an employee were paid $180,000 for the year, then FICA would disappear from his or her paycheck after June, and reappear in January of the following year.) If an employee's annual pay does not exceed the preestablished payroll limit, then the tax never stops.

Unlike the Social Security tax, the Medicare component of FICA has no payroll cap and is a true flat tax. Medicare contributions continue forever, regardless of how much one is paid.

Federal Expenditures

The federal government spends three-fifths, of its money on what are known as *payments for individuals*, which are federal grants for individual persons. About four-fifths of these payments for individuals are in the form of direct payments to them (examples include Social Security and Medicare, among others), and the remainder is delivered in the form of federal grants to state and local governments that are passed on to individual citizens (examples include welfare payments, such as Temporary Assistance for Needy Families, among others). Almost 18 percent of federal dollars is allocated to national defense; less than 8 percent pays the interest on the national debt; and 6 percent funds other grants.[25]

Taxing Times: Rethinking Federal Taxes

The criteria for a good tax system are equity, economic efficiency, simplicity, transparency, and administerability.[26] These qualities co-exist in a zero-sum environment; that is, no one value can be expanded or contracted without affecting the others, so adjusting tax policies will always be a delicate and difficult exercise.

The federal tax structure has come under increasingly withering criticism for allegedly violating each of these five standards.

Equity

A particular criticism of the federal tax structure concerns equity, specifically the existence of a large number (about 150) of *preferential provisions*, or exemptions, from taxes. The largest of these exemptions include: the exclusion of employer contributions to medical insurance premiums and medical care; the deductibility of mortgage interest on owner-occupied homes; and the net exclusion of pension contributions and earnings. Since 1974, the number of these exemptions more than doubled, the tax revenue lost to the federal government because of them tripled, and all exemptions are estimated to amount to 7.5 percent of the gross domestic product (GDP).[27]

Efficiency

Economists are in general agreement that the federal tax structure imposes significant efficiency costs, although exactly how much those costs are is difficult to measure due to the enormous complexity of the American economy. Still, partial estimates "suggest that the overall efficiency costs imposed by the tax system are large–on the order of several percentage points of GDP."[28]

Simplicity

A major component of economic efficiency is the tax structure's *simplicity*–that is, what it costs taxpayers to comply with tax policy. As with overall efficiency costs, we do not know the precise price of complying with federal tax policies, but the more comprehensive studies suggest a magnitude of 2 percent to 5 percent of GDP.[29]

Transparency

A *transparent tax structure* is one that taxpayers are able to understand, and the indications are that the federal tax system is becoming less transparent over time. According to the Government Accounting Office (GAO), "Numerous tax provisions have made it more difficult for taxpayers to understand how their tax liabilities are calculated, the logic behind the tax laws, and what other taxpayers are required to pay."[30]

Administerability

Finally, *adminsterability* is a quality found in tax systems that allows the government to collect taxes easily and cost-effectively. Adminsterability is not merely the responsibility of the Internal Revenue Service (IRS), which consumes a budget of more than $10 billion to process over 130 million individual income tax returns annually. Administering the tax code is also done by taxpayers, employers, banks, tax professionals, and others. The administrative costs to these other parties are more difficult to determine, but estimates range from $100 billion to $200 billion per year.[31]

Despite these impressively large expenditures, however, about 15 percent of federal taxes owed go uncollected each year, mostly due to "persistent levels of noncompliance"[32] by taxpayers and, as we described in Chapter 6, a persistent level of administrative incapacity in the IRS to enforce taxpayer compliance. If Washington were able to collect these taxes, Congress could eliminate almost all the annual federal deficits. So administerability is a tax-system component that is as important as the word itself is awful.

Financing State Governments

When we leave the world of Washington and consider the financing of states and their local governments, new categories of revenue emerge. One is *intergovernmental revenue*, which is money that governments receive from other governments. Governments usually acquire intergovernmental revenue by requesting grants-in-aid offered by other governments, and we explore "fiscal federalism," as it is often called, in Chapter 12.

The other revenue category is *own source revenue*, which is money that governments generate from their own sources. Most own source revenue is the product of state or local taxes.

State Intergovernmental Revenue

Almost three out of ten dollars, 28 percent, of all state revenue comes from other governments. Almost all of this state intergovernmental revenue is in the form of grants from the federal government (accounting for 26 percent of state revenue), although local governments also contribute a small amount (amounting to 2 percent of state revenue).[33] Over the years, intergovernmental revenue provided by Washington has remained fairly stable as a proportion of all state revenue.[34]

State Own Source Revenue

The remaining three-fourths of state revenue derives from the states' own sources. More than two-fifths, 42 percent, of all state revenue (and some three-quarters of all own source revenue) is generated by state taxes. About 13 percent of all state revenue derives from insurance trusts, the next highest revenue source. Charges for specialized services, such as hospitals and housing, constitute 8 percent of total state revenue. The clear leader in this category is charges for higher education (that is, mostly tuition), which account for almost 5 percent of total state revenue.[35]

State Taxes

The most important tax for the states is the *sales tax*, which is a general tax on the sale price of goods and services that usually is paid at the point-of-sale, such as a retail store. The sales tax accounts for more than a fifth of total state revenue and half of all state tax revenues. It is followed by the individual income tax, which amounts to about 14 percent of total state revenue and a third of state tax revenue. Taxes on the income of corporations account for 2 percent of total state revenue and 5 percent of tax revenue.[36]

The Sales Tax

Forty-five states use the sales tax, and it has long held the title as the states' primary tax. Prior to Mississippi's invention of the sales tax in 1930, states relied heavily on the property tax.

A Regressive Tax. The sales tax is inherently regressive because it is, at root, a tax on consumption. Although the sales tax taxes all consumers at the same rate, its burden inevitably falls on those consumers who are poor. Because the poor must spend a greater proportion of their money on essentials, such as medicine and food, than the rich, the poor effectively are taxed at a higher rate than are the wealthy.

States have attempted to alleviate the more regressive elements of the sales tax by exempting basic necessities. For example, forty-three of the forty-five states with the sales tax exempt prescription drugs; thirty exempt residential consumers of electricity and gas; and twenty-five exempt groceries.[37] Nevertheless, although the regressivity of the sales tax may be moderated by these and similar exemptions, its structurally regressive nature cannot be eliminated.

Issues of Inequity, Intricacy, and Obscurantism. In addition, the sales tax seems to be uncommonly buffeted by the political winds of the day, and it has been criticized for its lack of equity, simplicity, and transparency.[38] Powerful (or at least stealthy) legislators have been known to exempt favored constituents from the sales tax with no apparent economic or philosophic rationale for doing so.

The Florida legislature, for example, has exempted some 440 transactions from its sales tax, thereby exempting more than two-fifths of all purchases and slashing sales tax revenue by more than three out of every ten sales tax dollars.[39] Charges for charter fishing trips in Florida's waters are exempt, but not charges for fishing rods; charges for lap dancing in the state's "gentlemen's clubs" are exempt, but not charges for movie tickets; food for ostriches and racehorses is exempt, but not food for cats and dogs; lawn mowing services are exempt, but not lawn mowers; pool services for Florida's swimming pools are exempt, but not the chemicals needed to clean those pools; tattooing, body piercing, tanning services, satellites, space vehicles, adult escort services, haircuts, and a lot of products (notably seed, feed, and fertilizer) purchased by farmers, who are a potent lobby in any state, are all exempted from Florida's sales tax.[40] One state senator confessed that he had voted unwittingly for many of these exemptions because they had been "sneaked through."[41]

Florida is by no means the exception, and many other states have exempted from their sales tax businesses that seem of questionable merit.

Thirty state legislatures have exempted the sale of custom computer programs; thirteen states exempt repairers; eight exempt hotel rooms; seven exempt telecommunications services; and three states exempt contractors.[42] The logic justifying these and other exemptions is not obvious.

The Decline of the State Sales Tax. In part because of its regressive nature and clouded transparency, the long reign of the state sales tax is being challenged by the rise of the state personal income tax. During the 1950s, the sales tax generated three times the revenue of personal and corporate income taxes, accounting for almost three-fifths of all state tax revenues, compared to the income tax's less than one-fifth.[43] Today, the sales tax generates only a fourth more revenue than does the income tax and accounts for half of all state tax revenue; the individual and corporation income taxes are catching up rapidly and now contribute close to two-fifths of state tax revenue.[44]

The Rise of the Local Sales Tax. In contrast to the decline of the sales tax in the states, it is flourishing among local governments. The number of states that permit at least some of their local governments to levy sales taxes has leaped from one in 1950[45] to thirty-four today.[46] As a consequence of these state policies, local governments in more than half the states impose the sales tax.[47]

State Expenditures

The states' largest single expenditure is for public welfare, at almost a fifth of all state outlays. Public welfare is followed by expenditures for education, at 13 percent, more than four-fifths of which is for higher education. Insurance trust expenditures account for 12 percent, most of which is for employee retirement pensions, and highways amount to 5 percent, of all state outlays.[48]

Financing Local Governments

Of all levels of government, local governments (that is, counties, municipalities, townships, school districts, and special districts) have experienced the greatest fiscal turmoil. As we explain in greater detail in Chapter 12, local governments, once the reigning fiscal actor in the federal structure, have slipped in their financial stature and now collect and spend less money than do either the federal government or the fifty state governments.

Local Intergovernmental Revenue

More than any other level of government, local governments depend on other governments to keep them going. Intergovernmental revenue is the largest single source of revenue for local governments and constitutes an impressive 37 percent of all local revenue.[49]

Almost nine out of ten dollars in local intergovernmental revenue are provided by the state governments, and the remainder is transferred directly by the federal government to local governments.[50] However, approximately one-third of the intergovernmental revenue that localities receive from their states has actually been contributed by the federal government in the form of pass-through grants.[51] *Pass-through grants* are funds granted by the federal government to the states with the stipulation that the funds be passed on by the states to their local governments for use in specific programs. If we count these pass-through grants as intergovernmental revenue that localities receive from Washington, rather than from the states, then the proportion of intergovernmental revenue that local governments receive from the feds (in both pass-through grants and direct federal aid) quadruples from about a tenth of all local intergovernmental revenue to some two-fifths of their intergovernmental revenue and expands from 11 percent of total local revenue to an estimated 15 percent.[52]

In sum, although the states have always sent the most substantial subsidies to their local governments, Washington also is a large, and largely hidden, source of local revenue.

Local Own Source Revenue

The remaining three-fifths of local revenues come from local sources. Local taxes are the largest single source here, accounting for over a third of total local revenue (and more than three-fifths of all

local own source revenue). Charges for particular services contribute almost 14 percent to all local revenue; the largest of these sources is hospital charges to patients, at 4 percent of total local revenue. Utility revenue accounts for 8 percent, and revenue from interest earnings amounts to less than 3 percent, of all local revenue.[53]

Local Taxes

The *property tax*, an ancient form of taxation, is a general tax on personal wealth. With the sole exception of special districts, which rely primarily on user fees for their revenue, the property tax is the leading source of own source revenue for all local governments. This mainstay tax accounts for a fourth of their total revenue, and more than seven out of every ten tax dollars received by local governments. The sales tax comes in at 4 percent of total local revenue, and 16 percent of all local tax dollars. Individual income taxes account for less than 2 percent of total revenue and 4 percent of local tax dollars.[54]

The Property Tax

Local governments levy property taxes on the basis of how much a property is worth. To determine a property's value, governments (counties usually are responsible for the administration of the property tax) hire and train professional assessors, who may choose from the following assessment methods: base the property's value on how much the property last sold for (a method sometimes dubbed, with heavy irony, "welcome stranger"); estimate the price that it currently would fetch in the open market; estimate how much it would cost to replace it; or estimate how much sustainable net income it will produce. Once the assessment is made, the property tax is levied on a predetermined fraction (say, 30 percent) of the property's assessed value.

Another Regressive Tax.   As with the sales tax, the property tax has some regressive elements. Although a taxpayer first must have wealth (in the form of property) to pay the property tax, and this precondition can render the property tax potentially progressive, the property tax nonetheless has a disproportionately heavy impact on people with mid-to-low incomes.

As a practical matter, the property tax concentrates on people's homes as its major source of revenue. Middle-class homeowners have a relatively large portion of their wealth tied up in their residences. By contrast, the wealthy often salt away their wealth in other ways, such as in stocks and bonds that are not subject to the property tax, and have proportionately less of their wealth parked in their homes. Hence, the property tax collects a greater proportion of the middle class's wealth than it collects from the wealthy.

Poor people, who usually do not own their own homes but instead rent their residences, pay property taxes, too, if indirectly. The owners of these rental properties simply pass on the cost of their property taxes to their renters. As with the middle class, then, there also is a regressive element in the property tax as it affects low-income households.

Relieving Regressivity. State governments have attempted to ameliorate the regressivity of the local property tax through two main mechanisms: circuit breakers and differential treatment of residential and commercial properties.

A *circuit breaker* is a device that prevents electrical circuits from overloading, and it has lent its name to a policy that automatically "trips" when the property tax reaches a certain percentage of a taxpayer's income. The property taxpayer is relieved, usually through rebates or income-tax credits, from paying property taxes that exceed this percentage. Thirty-five states have circuit-breaker programs, and two-thirds of these states offer circuit breakers to renters as well as to homeowners. One state, Oregon, offers a circuit-breaker program to renters only.[55] Because circuit breakers often are poorly publicized and application procedures can be onerous, however, it appears that perhaps less than half of eligible property owners take advantage of circuit breakers.[56]

The second major way that states have tried to introduce some progressivity into the local property tax is by assessing or taxing residential property less than commercial property. This practice shifts some of the tax burden from home renters and owners to those property owners who use their property to turn a profit.

Four-fifths of the states protect homeowners through *homestead exemptions*, which exempt, or at least shield, from property taxes some portion of the value of everyone's home; homestead exemptions, of course, do not apply to commercial properties.[57] Half the states either assess residential property at lower levels (eighteen) or tax residential property at lower rates (seven) than commercial property.[58]

While admirable, and to some degree effective, these attempts to transform the local property tax into a progressive tax ultimately fail because the property tax, as with the sales tax, is structurally regressive, and thus is not subject to significantly progressive change.

Unpopular and Unpredictable. Public opinion polls consistently indicate that the local property tax is the most disliked tax among Americans,[59] and their disdain may reflect its unpredictability. For example, those homeowners with fixed incomes who are faced with rapidly rising property values and costs of living can face real hardships as a result of the property tax, which rises with the rising value of the property, and possibly lose their homes.

The unpredictability of the property tax is structural. The property tax is difficult to administer equitably, depending, as it does, on the competence and consistency of government assessors who assess the value of individual properties as the basis for determining how much money in property taxes property owners must pay. More often than not, unfortunately, consistency in assessing properties is erratic, and "this lack of uniformity is the greatest problem for operation of the property tax."[60]

Chip Chipping Away. Although the property tax remains the paramount tax for local governments, state governments are chipping away at its local prominence. Forty-two states have imposed some form of restriction on the levying of local property taxes, including limitations on the tax's rate, the amount of revenue it may generate, or the assessed value of property.[61]

The growing propensity of state legislatures to permit their local governments to introduce new kinds of taxes also has cut into the property tax's share of local revenue. As late as the 1960s, the local sales tax accounted for less than 7 percent, and the local income tax for about 3 percent, of all local tax dollars. Since then, the sales tax has doubled its share, and the income tax has more than tripled its portion, of local tax revenues. The property tax, which accounted for almost nine out of every ten local tax dollars in the 1960s, has slipped by nearly a fourth.[62]

In part because local legislators know how deeply the property tax is disliked by their constituents, they try hard to avoid raising it, even though the property tax is their wellspring of own source revenue. This legislative reluctance to hike property taxes has, of course, diminished the revenue clout of the property tax, too. Typically, local governments search out other producers of own source revenue rather than raise the property tax.[63]

Parting with the Property Tax. The most consistent replacement for withering revenue from the property tax is increasing local user fees. A quarter century after California voters in 1978 enacted Proposition 13, which slashed local property taxes in the state, California's municipal governments had grown much more reliant on charges and fees and had not increased their reliance on the sales tax as much as expected.[64]

Another analysis of 162 large cities across the country over twenty-four years came up with quite comparable findings. In these cities, the property tax shrank as a revenue source and was replaced by growth in the local income and sales taxes in those cities that had these taxes. As in California, however, user fees were the replacement mainstay for the property tax and experienced the most dramatic growth. User fees more than doubled in dollars collected per capita over the two dozen years, and leaped from 11 percent of these cities' revenue to 18 percent. The growth in user fees alone more than compensated for the decline in the property tax.[65]

In short, local governments will almost always turn to the user fee, whether it is in the form of customer payments to government-owned enterprises or charges for public services, to compensate for declining revenue from the property tax. The user fee also is the favored alternative to avoid raising the property tax—and not just the property tax, but any local tax. Nearly nine out of ten cities and towns use funds derived from local enterprises, and nearly seven out of ten increase service charges, rather than raise taxes; both of these approaches are growing over time.[66]

Local Expenditures: A Money Menagerie

Although local governments display a modicum of consistency in how they collect revenues (that is, most local governments rely heavily on intergovernmental revenue and the property tax), no consistencies are apparent in how local governments spend those revenues. The nation's 87,849 local governments are a diverse lot, with manifold missions; meaningful averages concerning expenditures, as a consequence, are not possible. For example, counties spend a far greater share of their money on welfare than does any other type of local government; a plurality of special districts, by contrast, spend all of their revenues solely on natural resources. We explain these and other fiscal variations among local governments in the box in Chapter 12.

Taxing Times: The Fiscal Future of States and Communities

The U.S. economy is in the throes of thrashing change. We review some of these economic trends, and examine their implications for the tax bases of state and local governments.

The Information Revolution and the Tax Base

Contrary to conventional wisdom, the shift from manufacturing to a service economy seems not to have eroded the revenue provided by state and local taxes. Of infinitely greater significance is the rise of the information economy. The sales and property tax systems are not designed to—and, in fact, cannot—track fiscal flows generated by such intangible assets as databases, software, formulas, copyrights, and trademarks, and it is these new forms of property that are growing dramatically as a share of GDP.[67]

Similarly, the rise of electronic commerce, such as that conducted on eBay, represents a rising type of economic transaction that is virtually exempt from not only the sales tax, but from the corporate income tax as well.[68] For the moment, e-commerce does not represent a particularly significant share (about 2 percent) of total retail sales, but it is growing extremely rapidly at more than one-fourth per year.[69] Over time, states and localities are losing tax revenue to these new kinds of property and commerce.

In an initial effort to counter this growing tax drain, eighteen states meticulously designed a simplified and harmonized sales tax collection system for online retailers that was activated in 2005. The system is strictly voluntary for retailers, although a tax amnesty component encourages their joining. If successful, it could lead to a mandatory tax collection system for online retailers, but only if Congress and the president concurred; any interstate tax must be enacted by federal law.[70]

Competing for Companies

Add to these trends the increasingly cutthroat competition among state and local governments to induce service and manufacturing firms, and the jobs they bring, to relocate to their jurisdictions. One poll found that, over two decades, all fifty states had increased the level and variety of financial and tax incentives for luring new businesses to their states, and thirty-eight states had increased their use of these incentives during the previous five years.[71]

As at least a partial consequence of these policies, the burden of state and local *personal* taxes and fees on individual taxpayers burgeoned by more than a fourth over the course of just thirteen years, but the burden of state and local *corporate* income taxes on businesses was almost halved.[72] Increasingly, citizens are bearing the tax costs of government's competition for more companies.

What's a Government to Do?

The traditional taxes on sales, property, and corporations are facing possible obsolescence in an information age. State and local governments appear to be their own worst enemies in their manic competition for companies, and the jobs and revenue that accompany them. What are governments to do?

No one seems to know. "No solution presents state and local policymakers with a clear win-win situation, in which they could halt or reverse the decline in the revenue productivity of their taxes without sacrificing autonomy, competitiveness, neutrality, or administrative simplicity."[73] But the taxing portents of these accelerating economic developments are nonetheless worrisome and serious for state and local governments.

The Federal Government and the National Economy

As the preceding discussion implies, public finance ebbs and flows in a far vaster ocean: the national economy. Although the economy channels those ebbs and flows, government also affects the economy's currents, so it is important that public administrators have some understanding of these interrelationships.

In reviewing government's economic role, it is worth recalling that the U.S. economy is not a command economy, but a capitalist one. Hence, federal economic policies have only a relatively marginal effect on the economy. Other, stronger forces have a greater impact. For example, the astonishing surge forward that the economy took in the mid- to late-1990s was largely a result of revolutionary developments in information technology that contributed to a booming stock market, and to a slowdown in health spending due to managed care. Enlightened federal policy was a positive factor in this surge, but a comparatively small factor.[74]

The topic of government and the economy is largely the preserve of economists, who practice a profession not known for agreement. As a distinguished economist once remarked,

"Ask five economists and you'll get five different answers—six if one went to Harvard."[75] With this caveat very much in mind, we enter our discussion.

The Money Supply and the Federal Spigot

A healthy economy—by which is meant full employment, stable prices, and sustained economic growth—depends upon how much money is circulating in it. The amount of capital circulating in the economy is called the *money supply*. If there is too little money in the economy, recession, even depression and deflation, can result because people do not have enough money to buy goods and services. If there is too much money, inflation, even hyperinflation, can result because people must pay too high a price for goods and services.

The effects of recession and inflation are the same: an ailing economy. People are spending too little, either because they have not enough money in first place, or they have money, but prices are too high. In both cases, the determining factor of economic health is the supply of money.

Government plays an important role in determining how much money is circulating in the economy, but of all levels of government, the national government is by far the most potent. Federal expenditures account for roughly a fifth of the gross domestic product (GDP). By contrast, all state and local outlays combined, as a percentage of GDP, amount to about half of the federal figure.[76] It follows that the "federal spigot"—that is, how much money the federal government spends, taxes, and borrows—plays a highly significant role in determining the amount of money circulating in the economy. Shut off the fiscal flow from the federal spigot and the economy may be parched; open wide the flow from that spigot and the economy may be flooded.

The Heart of the Matter: Government Spending

Depending on one's point of view, federal taxes or federal deficits are the governmental causes of Americans' economic woes. Both views are wrong. The potential threat that the federal government poses for the economy is neither a confiscatory tax rate nor an irresponsible level of borrowing. Or, to put it more precisely, taxing and borrowing are not the *underlying* threats to the economy. Government spending is the heart of the matter.

Government spending affects how much money is circulating in the economy. If government spends too little when the economy is in recession, its stingy spending shrinks even further the already low supply of money needed to invest in enterprises that would have helped the economy grow. This low level of federal spending effectively encourages the recession to deepen and spread.

If government spends too much when the economy is healthy, its reckless spending "crowds out" once available money that could have been invested in enterprises that would have helped the economy grow. This high level of federal spending can undermine a healthy economy in any number of ways—recession, inflation, or stagflation (a grim combination of a stagnant economy and inflationary prices) are all possible.

Government spending, in short, is the engine of government's impact, for good or ill, on the economy.

Taxing and Borrowing.   Federal spending may be financed in only two ways: by taxing or by borrowing.

Taxation is the more familiar of the two. If government's tax revenues match government's spending, then government spending is covered and the federal budget is balanced. This is all well and good—provided, however, that the government is not spending so much that the correspondingly high tax rates do not withdraw too much money from the economy. To do so would induce an economic slowdown.

The second way that government spending is financed is by borrowing money. Borrowing must be undertaken when government's revenue falls short of government's spending. When annual government spending exceeds its annual income, the resulting difference is called a *deficit*. When government borrows too much money (that is, government's deficit spending is too high a percentage of GDP), the government is withdrawing too much money from the economy and thereby undermining the economy's vitality.

Whether the government is taxing too much or borrowing too much, both the cause and the effect are the same. The cause in both cases is too much government spending. The effect in both cases is an unhealthy economy.

An Aside on Supply-Side Economics. There is a school of economic thought that holds that too much emphasis is placed on the deleterious economic impact of borrowing and deficit spending, and not enough credit is given to the stimulative effects of low rates of taxation. This school, which gained particular currency during the 1980s, is called supply-side economics.

Supply-side economics contends that, if taxes were slashed dramatically, those lower tax rates would hugely increase the supply of money in the economy. This increased money supply, in turn, would generate significantly more revenue for government—so much more revenue, in fact, that government no longer would need to borrow to finance its programs. Even though the tax rate would be lower, government revenue would be higher because of the increased productivity that the lower tax rate induced. It would be the best of all possible economic worlds: low taxes and low-to-nonexistent deficits—even, perhaps, government surpluses that would facilitate even deeper tax cuts.

Sadly, the evidence supporting supply-side economics is, at best, mixed. Supply-side economics assumes that if taxes were lower, citizens would save more, and those savings could be invested in businesses, thereby spurring the economy to new heights. But the record indicates that lower taxes have little if any impact on Americans' saving rates, which, at *minus* 1 percent to 2 percent of disposable personal income, already are below bottom-scrapingly low and getting lower.[77] Moreover, the negative national savings rate "is not only low by historical standards but has been well below that of other major industrial countries over the past few decades."[78] Europeans joke that if an American is given a dollar, he or she will spend $1.25.

In fact, in the United States, lower taxes seem to roughly correlate with *lower*, not higher, savings.[79] This perverse pattern occurs (at least since 1980) because, when the federal government cuts taxes, it rarely cuts spending and therefore must borrow to cover expenses. Increased borrowing, of course, means more spending in deficit, and deficit spend-

ing withdraws money from the economy that people and businesses might otherwise save and invest.

Facts are stubborn things. The mulish fact that cannot be circumvented is that government spending is the culprit. Whether government finances its spending through taxing or borrowing is almost immaterial.

Forms of Federal Economic Policy

Federal economic policy is based on the Keynesian idea that economic health can be improved through governmental action. If government wants to heat up a cooling and depressed economy, then it should borrow more, spend in deficit, and lower taxes and interest rates. These adjustments add to the money supply. If, on the other hand, government wants to cool down an overheated and inflationary economy, then it should borrow less or not at all, generate surpluses, and raise taxes and interest rates. These alterations withdraw money circulating in the economy.

To make these adjustments, the federal government relies on two forms of economic policy: fiscal policy and monetary policy. We consider these in turn.

Fiscal Policy. *Fiscal policy* is the federal government's effort to assure a healthy economy through its spending, taxing, and borrowing decisions. Fiscal policymaking is centered in Congress and the White House, and fiscal policy usually is expressed in the form of the federal budget. The size of that budget, the amount of revenue coming in to support it, tax rates, the price of public policies enacted by Congress, and the level of federal borrowing and deficit spending, number among the factors that constitute fiscal policy.

Monetary Policy. *Monetary policy* is the federal government's effort to assure a healthy economy by adjusting the money supply to control economic fluctuations. Monetary policymaking is centered in the Federal Reserve Board (known colloquially as "the Fed") and its twelve member Federal Reserve banks. The Federal Reserve Board and its banks are independent from Congress and the president because the policymakers who set up the Fed in 1913 believed that it should be isolated from those who might want to manipulate the money supply for political advantage.

The Federal Reserve Board uses three main monetary tools in influencing the economy. They are open-market operations, the discount rate and the federal funds rate, and the reserve requirement. We consider these in turn.

Open-Market Operations. *Open-market operations* are the Fed's most commonly used tool and refer to the Federal Reserve Board buying or selling bonds issued by the federal government. If the Federal Reserve wishes to cool down the economy, then it sells these securities in the open market. The effect of selling them is to exchange the bonds for money that was circulating in the economy, thereby reducing the money supply. If the Fed wishes to stimulate the economy, then it buys federal bonds. The effect of purchasing these securities is to trade money for bonds, thereby increasing the money supply.

The Discount and Federal Funds Rates. The *discount rate* and the *federal funds rate* are the rates of interest at which member banks can borrow money from the Federal Reserve or from each other. Adjusting these rates exerts a more powerful effect on the economy than does open-market operations, since these rates of interest directly impact interest rates throughout the economy. If the Fed hikes its interest rates for borrowing money from the Federal Reserve, then all interest rates rise, and economic activity is slowed, thereby reducing inflationary pressures. If the Fed lowers its interest rates, then all interest rates decline, and economic activity is accelerated.

The Reserve Requirement. Finally, the Federal Reserve Board can adjust the *reserve requirement*, which is the money that the Fed's member banks are mandated to keep in reserve to cover their outstanding loans. These reserves are a percentage of the total amount that the banks have in outstanding loans (usually about 10 percent of their loans' value), and member banks must keep these reserves on deposit. If the Federal Reserve raises the reserve requirement, then the banks have less money to loan, and they may even have to call in some loans to build up their reserves.

The effect, of course, is to reduce the money circulating in the economy and to decelerate economic activity. If the Fed lowers the reserve requirement, then the banks have more money to loan, more money is thereby injected into the economy, and the economy is stimulated.

Understanding Deficits and Debt

Few federal phenomena cause more consternation, but are as little comprehended, than deficits and debt. One poll found that "a sweeping majority," 70 percent, of Americans worried about the size of the federal deficit "some" or "a lot," but not much more than a third, 35 percent, were willing to cut government spending (and services) to balance the budget, and even fewer, 18 percent, were inclined to raise taxes to do so. What is perhaps the most effective strategy for controlling deficits, that of cutting spending *and* raising taxes, was favored by just 1 percent.[80]

Understanding Deficits. From 1950 through 2004, the American population grew by 91 percent;[81] the number of people holding jobs in the civilian labor force more than doubled, burgeoning by 145 percent;[82] and the gross domestic product exploded by more than forty-one times.[83] Over the course of those fifty-four years, the federal budget balanced in four of them.[84] During the remaining half century the federal government spent in deficit.

We bring up these figures because they illustrate that federal borrowing and its resultant deficits do not necessarily weaken the economy. Many economists think that a low level of deficit spending, one that does not exceed around 2 percent of the gross domestic product, does little if any harm (other than adding to the debt),[85] and under certain circumstances, such as a recession or depression, deficit spending can actually help restore the economy's health.

Nevertheless, spending in deficit can be a risky business. When deficits attain high levels, and these high levels are sustained over time, many economists worry that too much money is being drawn from the economy.[86] Economists seem to agree that "over the long-term, the costs of federal borrowing will be borne by tomorrow's workers and taxpayers. . . . [and will] inevitably result in declining GDP and future living standards."[87] Conversely, lowering deficit spending can result in substantial benefits. The GAO has projected that a permanent deficit reduction of only 1 percent as a share of GDP would, after fifty years, amount to nearly $2,000 in real higher income for every man, woman, and child in the United States.[88]

Understanding Debt. Big deficits bring big debt. The last year that the nation had no debt was 1835 and, from the nation's first fiscal year of 1797, the federal debt as a percentage of the gross domestic product "rose substantially *only* as the result of wars and recessions."[89]

After 1980, however, this pattern changed radically. In just twenty-seven years, the national debt increased by more than ten times.

Of greater concern, even though the times were mostly peaceful and prosperous, the gross federal debt as a percentage of GDP more than doubled from a third of GDP in 1980 to over two-thirds today. The federal debt weighs in at a hefty $9 trillion plus change.[90]

Reducing the national debt is beneficial because, as with reduced deficits, lower debt frees more private capital for investment, and thereby promotes economic growth. In addition, lower debt frees existing public funds that are used to pay down the debt so that they may be used for future public benefits or emergencies. In short, large debt can bring with it an unhealthy economy and inflexible public policies. Balancing the federal budget would, over time, reduce, or even eliminate, the national debt, an improbable development that nonetheless would improve people's lives.

A Founder on Debt

Most informed observers agree that, when national deficits and debt burgeon, they do so less as a result of economics, and more as a consequence of inadequate political will. The nation's first Secretary of the Treasury, Alexander Hamilton, made this very point more than two centuries ago, noting that, when the burdens of public debt grow too heavy on the citizenry, "convulsions & revolutions . . . are a Natural offspring."

To extinguish a Debt which exists and to avoid contracting more ideas are almost always favored by a public feeling and opinion; but to pay Taxes for one of the other purpose, which are the only means of avoiding the evil, is always more or less unpopular. These contradictions are in human nature. And the lot of a Country would be enviable indeed, in which there were not always men ready to turn them to the account of their own popularity or to make other sinister account. . . .

The consequence is, that the Public Debt swells, 'till its magnitude becomes enormous, and the Burthens of the people gradually increase 'till their weight becomes intolerable. Of such a state of things great disorders in the whole political economy, convulsions & revolutions of Government are a Natural offspring.

[My previous report] suggests the idea of *"incorporating as a fundamental maxim* in the SYSTEM of PUBLIC CREDIT of the United States, *that the creation of Debt should always be accompanied with the means of extinguishment*—that this is the true secret for rendering public credit immortal, and that it is difficult to conceive a situation in which there may not be an adherence to the Maxim" and it expresses an unfeigned solicitude that this may be attempted by the United States.

Alexander Hamilton
Secretary of the Treasury
"Report on a Plan for the Further
Support of Public Credit"
January 16, 1795

Congress's Quixotic Quest: Decreasing Deficits

Nineteen-eighty was a fiscal benchmark. The year marked the beginning of serious federal deficits that had little if any relation to economic downturns or girding for war. In just three years, federal deficits doubled as a percentage of the GDP, rising from 3 percent of GDP in 1980 to an astonishing 6 percent in 1983. Within the brief span of a dozen years, federal deficits quintupled; from 1980 through 1992, federal deficit spending soared from less than $74 billion to more than $290 billion (or nearly 5 percent of GDP).

Observers attribute this quintupling to the Omnibus Budget Reconciliation Act of 1981, which cut taxes substantially (it reduced individual income taxes by about a fourth) but not spending. The act has been described as a "watershed" that "resulted in a legacy of large deficits."[91] Before 1980, conservatives had routinely accused Washington of "tax-and-spend" profligacy; after 1980, this profligacy was better described as "borrow and spend"—or, as some wags would have it, "spend and spend."

Federal policymakers grew concerned that the deepening deficits of the 1980s and early 1990s threatened the nation's economic structure, and Congress launched a long, and quixotic, quest to lower deficit spending.

Failure: The Balanced Budget and Emergency Deficit Control Acts of 1985 and 1987

Initially, Congress enacted two laws designed to bring the deficit under control: the Balanced Budget and Emergency Deficit Control Acts of 1985 and 1987, known as "Gramm-Rudman-Hollings I and II" after their legislative sponsors. The 1985 act was designed to achieve a balanced budget by 1990, which the 1987 act extended to 1993, through "sequestration." *Sequestration* referred to a series of automatic spending cuts that would come into play if the federal budget did not fall within $10 billion of targeted deficit reductions.

The president would cut all agencies' budgets proportionately (that is, he would sequester their funds), although the two biggest spenders of deficit dollars, interest payments and most entitlement programs, were exempt.

Congress avoided the unpleasantness of sequestration by adopting overly optimistic economic forecasts in its budget making, and Gramm-Rudman-Hollings never lived up to expectations. But the historic and unprecedented point was made (perhaps unintentionally) that the budget process was no longer policy neutral, that it now should be used to reduce the deficit by reducing spending—and not, with equal logic, reduce the deficit by raising taxes, which was not an option under the acts.

Success: The Budget Enforcement Act of 1990

When it became clear that the Balanced Budget and Emergency Deficit Control Acts had failed in lowering deficit spending, Congress got relatively tough and passed the Budget Enforcement Act of 1990. This act also was designed to reduce the deficit via spending cuts, but it did so by requiring that budget increases in one program must be fully off set with reductions in another. Caps were set on discretionary spending for each fiscal year that prohibited spending to grow as rapidly as inflation. The anagram used to describe what had become a zero-sum budget-making game in Congress was PAYGO, for "pay-as-you-go." These spending caps, and with them, PAYGO, were set in the legislation to expire automatically in 2002, which they did.

Sense and Sensibility: The Omnibus Budget Reconciliation Act of 1993

Three years following the passage of the Budget Enforcement Act (which proved useful in reducing the deficit), Congress enacted a budget that likely was critical in righting deficit spending. The Omnibus Budget Reconciliation Act of 1993 was starkly different from its predecessor of 1981, which had accelerated deficit spending. Rather than cutting taxes, as the 1981 act had done, the 1993 act raised taxes by some $250 billion and cut programs by a similar amount over five years. Commonsensical though it may appear, this combination of higher taxes and lower spending could have resulted in an economic recession (which is one reason that the Senate passed it by only one vote), but it seemed to help reduce deficit spending: beginning in 1993, federal deficits steadily declined.

Irrelevancy: The Balanced Budget Act of 1997

Between 1995 and 1997, Congress and the White House engaged in unusually bitter wrangling over the deficit, even though deficit spending had been declining steadily since 1992. In 1997, a complicated compromise was achieved in the form of the Balanced Budget Act, which sailed through both chambers by large margins, and was signed by the president.

The Balanced Budget Act of 1997 promised to eliminate federal deficit spending by 2002. (In this it failed.) It was to delete deficits by reducing federal spending (other than for entitlement programs and interest on the debt) by 12 percent through the use of stringent spending caps. It also cut federal taxes by $152 billion.[92]

Nirvana Attained? The Budget Surpluses

In 1999 (Fiscal Year 1998), the federal government not only had no deficit but showed its first surplus—an impressive $70 billion—in twenty-nine years. In 2000, the surplus hit $127 billion, and in 2001, $236 billion. No longer were budget makers bemoaning bodacious "deficits as far as the eye can see."[93] Instead, they were touting stupendous surpluses—at one point, the Congressional Budget Office (CBO) was projecting a stunning $5.6 trillion in surpluses over a decade[94]—for as far as the equally visionary could envision.

Though welcome, the three budgetary surpluses of 1999–2001 were not wholly deserving of full-throated cheering. Federal surpluses include revenue generated by Social Security taxes and, to a much lesser degree, revenue from the U.S. Postal Service (which accounts for less than 3 percent of the revenue from the two sources). Revenues from Social Security and the Postal Service are officially classified as *off-budget* revenues (that is, they do not appear in the federal budget) and generate in the neighborhood of $200 billion per year.[95] If these off-budget revenues were *not* counted against the budget deficits, then they would have more than wiped out each of the budget surpluses in 1999 and 2000 (thereby converting these surpluses into deficits) and would have eradicated most of the largest surplus of $236 billion in 2001.

It is important to note this off-budget component because, although the Social Security tax is, at present, a rich source of revenue, unless changes are made it could become a dark hole of debt. By 2017, the cost of paying Social Security benefits is projected to exceed its income from the payroll tax. The Social Security Trust Fund still will be able to pay full benefits, thanks to interest income, but, beginning in 2027, the Trust Fund's balances will begin to dry up. The Trust Fund will be exhausted by 2041, when Social Security will be able to pay less than three-fourths of its promised benefits.[96] "Absent reform, the nation will ultimately have to choose between persistent, escalating federal deficits, significant tax increases, and/or dramatic budget cuts of unprecedented magnitude."[97] So understanding the crucial and perilous place of Social Security revenue in calculating federal surpluses (and, for that matter, in calculating the totality of federal finance) is worthwhile.

Back to the Future?

As the United States entered the second millennium, Washington's interest in diminishing its deficits dimmed.

Congress and Spending. Congress increasingly disregarded its own budget process, and from 1999 onward, revenue-and-expenditure targets either were surpassed by wide and unprecedented margins, or concurrent budget resolutions simply were not passed.[98] From 2000 through 2002, Congress violated with a vengeance the pay-as-you-go fiscal policies that it had established in the Budget Enforcement Act of 1990 and indulged in "a spending frenzy that vitiated discretionary spending caps."[99] In 2000, Congress exceeded its own caps on discretionary spending by 9 percent above the legal limit; in 2001 by 15 percent; and in 2002 by 24 percent.[100] The act's spending caps expired in late 2002 and were not renewed.

Congress showed some real creativity in violating the Budget Enforcement Act. Among other innovations, Congress declared over $30 billion in each of the three years to be "emergency spending," a category that was exempted from the act's spending caps. (Between 1991 and 1998, emergency spending averaged about $7 billion annually.) "Emergencies" funded by Congress included the decennial census, an item that had appeared in the Constitution for the preceding 210 years, so it was not as if Congress had not been alerted of its imminence.[101]

These congressional accounting tricks soon added up and were compounded by President George W. Bush's refusal to veto any spending bill that Congress sent him. Federal spending as a percentage of GDP had been declining steadily since 1992. Beginning in 2001, however, federal spending as a percentage of GDP actually grew.[102]

The President, Congress, and Revenue Reduction. Expanding federal spending was accompanied by dramatically shrinking federal revenue. In 2001, at President Bush's urging, Congress passed the Economic Growth and Tax Relief Reconciliation Act, which slashed federal taxes by a record $1.6 trillion over ten years. Within only two years, federal revenue as a percentage of the economy spiraled to levels so low that they had not been witnessed since 1959.[103]

In each of the years following 2001, the president and Congress enacted legislation that expanded, extended, accelerated, or deepened federal tax cuts.[104] The projected revenue lost to the federal government as a consequence of these cuts amounts to more than $3.3 trillion, or close to 2 percent of the gross domestic product, over thirteen years.[105]

They're Back: The Return of the Deficits. Between Congress's predisposition to trash its own fiscal policies, and the president's and Congress's determination to simultaneously increase spending and radically reduce revenue, deficits, unsurprisingly, returned. In 2002, the deficit logged in at a substantial $159 billion. In 2003, the deficit hit an all-time dollar record of $375 billion, only to be surpassed in 2004 when the deficit attained $413 billion; each of these deficits amounted to approximately 3.6 percent of the GDP.

In 2005, thanks to a 15 percent surge in federal revenue after years of decline, the deficit slipped to $319 billion. Even though the deficit in 2005 was the third largest ever, it amounted to a not-too-worrisome 2.6 percent of GDP.

A Dismal Science: Deficits, Debt, and Democracy

Congress and the White House have yet to address the fundamental fiscal doubt held by economists about democracy. That doubt is as follows: Democracies are unable to avoid burying future generations in debt due to the need of elected policymakers to be elected and reelected. Elected officeholders assure their reelection by giving voters more and more benefits, lower and lower taxes with which to pay for them, and larger and larger deficits. Eventually, these accrued deficits create a public debt so humongous that it crushes some future generation to the point that it overthrows democracy as its form of government. The nation's first secretary of the treasury understood this doubt well, as the box in this chapter indicates.

Washington's continued resistance to fiscal responsibility could have grave consequences. The real issue nationally is less one of a balanced budget and more one of the creation of a national fiscal policy. A distinguished economic historian phrases this overriding crisis well: "It is not that the size of the debt itself is the problem . . . Instead, it is the recent trend that is ominous. For that trend results not from a deliberate political decision to spend in deficit [a decision often made, for example, when a nation goes to war], but rather from nothing more than the sum of myriad decisions regarding taxing and spending that, collectively, now substitutes for fiscal policy. In a very real sense, the federal government *has* no fiscal policy, for the tail of political expediency has long wagged the dog of prudent policy in Washington."[106]

Public Budgeting: Spending for Public Policy

Over the years, government agencies have developed number of strategies and tactics that facilitate their defending and acquiring their budgets.

A number of scholars have addressed what it means for an agency head to be a politician in securing an agency's funding, and a review of some of their thinking on the topic is worthwhile.[107] Although they broach the federal budgetary process almost exclusively, the same basic rules apply to state and local governments as well. Politics requires the use of strategies and tactics, and the politics of the budgetary process is no exception. As Aaron Wildavsky observed in his classic essay on the topic: "What really counts in helping an agency get the appropriations it desires? As several informants put it in almost identical words, 'It's not what's in your estimates but how good a politician you are that matters.' "[108]

To be a good budgetary politician requires the use of what Wildavsky labeled "ubiquitous" and "contingent strategies."[109] We prefer the more easily understood terms, *standing strategies* and *opportunistic tactics*, and consider them in turn.

Standing Strategies for Securing Budgets

Standing strategies (or what Wildavsky called *ubiquitous strategies*) are pervasive and used on a continuing basis by an agency; their purpose is to build confidence in the agency in the agency's budget source and the public, and to add to its clientele. There are at least three types of standing strategies.

Find, Serve, and Use a Clientele for the Services You Perform. The thought here is that an agency, when threatened, mobilizes its clientele. A case in point is the former Office of Economic Opportunity (OEO). When the OEO was budgetarily emasculated under the Nixon administration, various organizations representing the poor rose to its defense, fighting a remarkable rearguard action in the courts in an effort to preserve OEO. Although OEO can be faulted on other strategy counts (eventually it was dismantled), the OEO unquestionably had found and used a clientele. A number of observers felt that OEO had politicized and organized "the forgotten fifth" in the United States to a point at which the poor were better equipped to fend for themselves when it came to passing and implementing federal legislation, with or without OEO.

Establish Confidence in the Mind of the Reviewer That You Can Carry Out the Complicated Program (Which He or She Seldom Understands) Efficiently and Effectively. Here, the key notion is that if legislators believe in your abilities, you can get just about anything you want. Exemplary in this regard is the National Science Foundation (NSF), founded in 1950. An early fear held by a number of citizens was that NSF would become an all-powerful "science czar" of the United States. Through the strategic use of a low administrative profile, academic trappings, and capitalizing on a popular romanticism concerning science, the foundation not only eliminated this worry but eventually was operating in a budgetary environment that permitted an awesome degree of latitude: science could (and should) be funded solely for the sake of science, and fellow scientists were deciding who among them should be awarded NSF grants. The foundation's premise—that science should be funded according to what happened to interest scientists rather than for the achievement of larger social goals—ultimately came under some hard questioning in

Congress. But for many years NSF enjoyed an impressive degree of budgetary success despite a virtual absence of accountability in terms of what it did with the money.

Capitalize on the Fragmentary Budgetary Review Process. A notable example of this strategy is provided by the Air Force. Throughout most of the 1950s, the Air Force practiced "phased buying." This meant that the Air Force bought parts for a larger number of weapons than its appropriations request indicated it intended to purchase. As a result, Congress and the president were left with little choice but to authorize the purchase of the remaining parts if any of the weapons were to be useful. For many years, this questionable use of the fragmentary review process worked handsomely, but in 1957, after a public furor arose, Secretary of Defense Charles Wilson ended the practice. In effect, however, "phased buying" continues under a new guise, which is the research and development contract. The Defense Department argues (with some reason) that productive research cannot be scheduled rigidly by the calendar, so R&D projects are extended (often reluctantly) year after year by Congress, on the logic that there is little choice if the research is to pay off.

Opportunistic Tactics for Securing Budgets

Opportunistic tactics (or what Wildavsky called *contingent strategies*) are designed to capitalize on unusual opportunities perceived by the agency that might defend or expand its base. As with standing strategies, there are three types.

Guard Against Cuts in Old Programs. There are a number of ways for an agency to defend its programs. A favorite tactic is to cut the most popular program that the agency has, on the logic that citizen complaints will get back to legislators more speedily. When the National Institutes of Health (NIH) decided to start a dental research program, it was concerned that Congress would insist that it fund it by transferring existing funds from other programs. To preempt this, the NIH proposed that it fund dental research by cutting its

most popular programs—heart, cancer, and mental health research. Because of constituent pressure, Congress restored these funds and approved the whole package.

Inch Ahead with Old Programs. It is always easier to get new appropriations if they are made to look like old programs. A favored device for accomplishing this is the numbers game. The National Institutes of Health, for example, long have engaged in this tactic by reducing the number of its research grants ("Look! We're economizing!"), but increasing the dollars in them (thus inching ahead).

Add New Programs. The final tactic used by agencies is the incremental addition of new programs. Because the new and novel often are distrusted by those empowered to distribute money, efforts are made by the agency to make its new program look as old and as dull as possible. Variations of this approach include the contention that the new program is only temporary, that it is exceedingly small and thus hardly worth examination, that it is merely a logical continuation of an old program, that it is an attempt to reduce some sort of backlog in the agency, and that it will save money.[110]

Occasionally, agencies' efforts to add new programs deteriorate into what has been described as "the sort of haggling more likely to be found at a car dealership than a Senate conference room." Consider an example of this haggling in action: "Air Force officials assured cost-conscious lawmakers that they had swung a deal to get . . . Raptor fighter jets for the bargain-basement price of $110 million each. Of course, if they wanted a few extras that could lump another $40 million to $60 million onto the sticker price. Only when pressed did they acknowledge that one of the extras happens to be the engine." As one representative noted ruefully, "I've learned that you've got to ask exactly the right question at exactly the right time."[111]

If the foregoing review of budget-acquiring strategies and tactics sounds cynical, it is. To be cynical, however, is not necessarily to be scrofulous. Bureaucrats-as-politicians are capable of using cynical means for the sake of noble ends, and this phenomenon is well exemplified by the budgetary process.

Public budgeting, in brief, is draped with the trappings of professionalism, technology, and expertise, but it is also a system of values, biases, and politics.

The Evolution of Public Budgeting: Variations, Viewpoints, and Values

The centrality of the budget to governance is why it is important to understand the evolution of budgetary thinking by public officials.[112] The development of the budget can be categorized into seven periods: traditional, or Line-Item Budgeting, with its control orientation; Program/Performance Budgeting, with its management emphasis; Planning-Programming-Budgeting, with its economic planning focus; Budgeting-by-Objectives, with its emphasis on budgetary decentralization; Zero Base Budgeting, with its stress on ranking program priorities; Target Base Budgeting, with its centralizing overtones; and Budgeting for Results, which incorporates the values of the new public management into the budgetary process. As with our other reviews of how various concepts evolve in public administration, the time periods associated with each of these phases is not as neat as we indicate; some levels of government, for example, continue to develop one concept of budgeting while other levels move onto new concepts—or regress to old ones.

There is a method to this madness. The evolution of new budgeting formats is driven by evolving public opinion about the proper role of government. In its early stages, when governments had to prove to their taxpayers that they could be trusted with their money, the budget emphasized controlling costs, accounting for finances, and improving efficiency. Later, particularly during the Depression, when Americans wanted government to proactively solve problems for which the private sector was largely blamed, the effectiveness of public programs came into greater budgetary focus.[113] In recent years, both of these missions have been reflected in the public budget.

In each of our seven budgeting thrusts, the idea of what a budget is, could be, or should be, has assumed a different cast. (Table 8-1 summarizes these casts, and you may wish to refer to it throughout the chapter.) Nevertheless, the essential meaning of the word "budget" has remained unaltered. To borrow a classic definition, a *budget* is "a series of goals with price tags attached."[114] There are, of course, other and lengthier definitions of budget, but this pithy one-liner has the blessed advantage of being unmysterious, accurate, and short, so we shall rely on it.

Line-Item Budgeting, 1921–1939

All governments have always had some form of budget. From the days of the ancient courts of Egypt, Babylon, and China, something was needed to keep track of expenses, and this very basic document was the earliest form of the budget as we know it. But in American public administration, the refinement of the budget document was a product of reformist pressures of the early twentieth century.

The Line-Item Budget and Administrative Reform

These pressures took at least three forms, all associated with the Progressive Movement, that had lasting consequences.

A Push for Progressive Reform.   One such pressure was the drive to establish a *consolidated executive budget*, or a comprehensive budget formulated in the executive branch by the elected chief executive, subject to approval by the legislature. The value behind this drive was one of ousting financial corruption in government, and the way to accomplish this goal was to consolidate public financial management bureaus under the chief executive.

This thrust related to a second pressure, which was the *administrative integration movement.* The proponents of administrative integration advocated the functional consolidation of agencies, the abandonment of various independent

Table 8-1   Some Differences Among Budgetary Concepts

Feature	Line-Item (1921–39)	Program/ Performance (1940–65)	Planning- Programming- Budgeting (1965–72)	Budgeting- by-Objectives (1972–77)	Zero-Base- Budgeting (1977–80)	Target- Base-Budgeting (1980–92)	Budgeting for Results (1993–Present)
Basic orientation	Control	Management	Planning	Management	Decision making	Control and attainment of a single, system-wide mission	Management
Scope	Inputs	Inputs and outputs	Inputs, outputs, effects, and alternatives	Inputs, outputs, and effects	Alternatives	Mission-specific inputs and mission-specific effects	Inputs and outputs; alternatives as they relate to optional delivery methods
Personnel skills	Accounting	Management	Economics and planning	Managerial "common sense"	Management and planning	Political, coordinative, and knowledge relevant to system-wide mission	Management, planning, and communications
Critical information	Objects of expenditures	Activities of agency	Purposes of agency	Program effectiveness	Purpose of program or agency	Does program or agency further the system-wide mission?	Activities of agency
Policymaking style	Incremental	Incremental	Systemic	Decentralized	Incremental and participatory	Systemic and aggressive	Incremental, participatory, and decentralized
Planning responsibility	Largely absent	Dispersed	Centralized	Comprehensive, but allocated	Decentralized	Centralized	Joint with central budget agency
Role of the budget agency	Fiscal propriety	Efficiency	Policy	Program effectiveness and efficiency	Policy prioritization	Attainment of a system-wide mission	Assure accountability

boards, and the enhancement of the chief executive's appointive and removal powers, among similar reforms designed to assure efficiency and coordination in government.

The third pressure was the desire of political reformers to build in administrative honesty by *restricting the discretionary powers held by public administrators.* Thus, innovations such as centralized purchasing, standardized accounting procedures, and expenditure audits emerged. All related directly to the notion that the budget was a useful device for controlling public administrators (if in a purely negative way) and ensuring honesty in government.

The Budget and Accounting Act of 1921.   Among other results of these forces, the Budget and Accounting Act of 1921 was enacted. This centralized federal budget formation in the newly created Bureau of the Budget (retitled in 1970 to the Office of Management and Budget, or OMB), which then reported to the treasury secretary but now to the president, and established the General Accounting Office (retitled in 2004 to the Government Accountability Office), which reports to Congress, as the congressional check on federal expenditures. The Budget and Accounting Act was historic legislation that gave the federal government, for the first time, an executive budget process and also influenced the budgeting process in some state governments.[115]

What Is Line-Item Budgeting?

Most people know what a budget looks like. Each line on a sheet of paper has an item (for example, pencils, 112) on the left side followed by a cost ($5.00) on the right side; hence, the traditional budget acquired its descriptive title of "line-item," or "objects-of-expenditure." A *Line-Item, or Objects-of-Expenditure, Budget* is simply the allocation of resources according to the cost of each item, from paperclips to personnel, used by a government agency.

Honesty, Efficiency, and Inflexibility.   The Line-Item Budget rapidly became associated with governmental honesty, efficiency, and less propitiously, inflexibility. In 1923 Charles G.

Dawes, as first director of the Bureau of the Budget, wrote: "The Bureau of the Budget is concerned only with the humbler and routine business of government. . . . it is concerned with no question of policy, save that of economy and efficiency."[116] As a result of these very limited objectives, the Line-Item Budget emphasized such factors as skilled accountancy, the employees and equipment needed to run an office or program and their costs, incremental policymaking throughout government, dispersed responsibility for management and planning, and a fiduciary role for the budget agency. Technical definitions of items were stressed (for example, pencils, 112, with 1/2-inch erasers, wood, No. 2 grade lead, 6" × 1/4"), and the use of such phrases as "watchdog of the treasury" were common, indicating the mentality of this control-oriented stage of budgetary thought.

Inputs and the Budgetary Treatment of Paperclips and Parks.   The Line-Item Budget covers *inputs* only, meaning that it deals only with what it takes to make a project continue—discs, desks, and secretaries. Consider two examples, paperclips and parks. Under a Line-Item Budget, the only policy-related questions that a public administrator would be channeled into asking are: How many paperclips do we need and what will they cost? Or how many parks do we need and what will it cost to build and maintain them?

We shall refer again to paperclips and parks as examples of how each successive concept of the budget changed the policy-related questions that pertained to them. The point is that the budget represents a way of thinking about, measuring, and evaluating public policy.

The Governmental Utility of Line-Item Budgeting

The Line-Item Budget fulfills a vital financial function: It shows public administrators what they are spending their money on in detail. Occasionally, however, it is used for missions for which it is not designed. As we shall see, the absence of abstraction inherent in, and the simplicity of, the Line-Item Budget do not render it suitable for larger purposes, and it is best used at the lower levels of the organization. Occasionally, this is not fully appreciated by executives, and when it is not, use of the Line-Item Budget can result "in micro-management at the macro level."[117]

Program/Performance Budgeting, 1940–1964

Although lone voices were heard throughout the 1920s and 1930s advocating a budget attuned to identifying broader programs and government performance, as well as objects of expenditure, the meaningful shift to this kind of thinking came with President Franklin D. Roosevelt's New Deal.

The New Deal and the Need for a New Budget

A number of historical factors influenced this movement. One was the firm establishment of the control techniques advocated by the line-item budgeteers. With the setting up of accurate accounting, purchasing, and personnel practices, budgeting as a concept was released from many of its traditional watchdog duties. Second, the government was expanding enormously, and there emerged a corresponding need to centralize and coordinate managerial activities more effectively. The budget provided the obvious salient tool for systematically coordinating government management. Third, government was increasingly perceived as an institution that delivered benefits, and the budget in turn was seen as a means by which the appropriate managerial delivery systems could be measured. With the New Deal, these factors congealed. Between 1932 and 1940 federal spending more than doubled. The President's Committee on Administrative Management recommended (in the form of Luther Gulick's and Lyndall Urwick's oft-mentioned report of 1937) that the Bureau of the Budget shed its control orientation in favor of a managerial emphasis, and that the bureau be used to coordinate federal administration under presidential leadership. In 1939, the Bureau of the Budget was transferred from the Treasury Department to the newly founded Executive Office of the President. The bureau's staff was increased by a factor of ten, it developed new methods of statistical coordination and budgetary apportionment, and it increasingly drew its personnel from the ranks of public administration rather than from accounting. Executive Order 8248 officially expressed the new managerial role of the Bureau of the Budget: "to keep the President informed of the progress of activities by agencies of the Government with respect to work proposed, work actually initiated, and work completed, together with the relative timing of work between the several agencies of the Government; all to the end . . . to prevent overlapping and duplication of effort."[118]

Clarifying Programs and Performance

The strengthening bond between budgets and management that began during the New Deal illustrated with increasing clarity two growing problems of federal management, but which expressed themselves in the form of the budget.

The Programs Problem.   One problem was the rapidly deteriorating coherence of the budget document itself, and this incoherence made management more difficult. The Line-Item Budget had no capacity to show policymakers what public money was being spent for, other than to list objects of expenditure, such as paperclips, pencils, and pens. The Line-Item Budget is unable to address policy and was never meant to.

This blindness to public policies and programs that is inherent in the Line-Item Budget was growing increasingly problematic. The first Hoover Commission observed that the federal budget of 1949 was 1,625 pages long with approximately one-and-a-half million words, and questioned its utility as a document that facilitated more coordinated and effective public management. The Hoover Commission advocated organizing the budget by "programs."[119]

The Performance Problem.   The second problem involved the gnawing question of whether the money being budgeted for public programs was actually doing any good. Under the guidance of its director, Harold D. Smith (1939–1946), the

Bureau of the Budget became preoccupied with originating measures of work performance and performance standards and linking these new measurements and standards to an agency's budget in an effort to determine that agency's efficiency, effectiveness, and overall level of performance. These efforts commonly were called "functional budgeting" or "activity budgeting." In 1949, the first Hoover Commission gave this budgetary innovation one of the names by which we know it: "Performance Budgeting."

The Emergence of Program/Performance Budgeting. The Hoover Commission's report brought swift results. In 1949, Congress passed amendments to the National Security Act of 1947, which established Program/Performance Budgeting in the Defense Department, and in 1950, Congress enacted the Budgeting and Accounting Procedures Act, which emplaced the Program/Performance Budgeting in the remaining federal agencies. A new budgetary age was at hand.

What Is Program/Performance Budgeting?

We call it *Program/Performance Budgeting*, but this kind of budget is known either as a *Program Budget*, emphasizing its budgeting of public programs, or a *Performance Budget*, stressing its focus on agency performance and its measurement. In reality, when it was introduced to the nation in the mid-twentieth century, it did both, so we call it *Program/Performance Budgeting*, and define it as a system of resource allocation that organizes the budget document by operations and programs, and "links performance levels" of those operations and programs "with specific budget amounts."[120]

Inputs and Outputs. Program/Performance Budgeting covers more administrative activities than had the traditional Line-Item Budget. Now *outputs* as well as *inputs* were considered. Budget officers saw their mission not only as one of precise and controlled accounting, but also the development of program classifications, the description of an agency's program and its performance, and the exploration of various kinds of

work/cost measurements. Managerial, as opposed to accounting, skills were stressed; activities of the agency were given precedence over the purchase of items required to run the office; management responsibility became newly centralized, although planning responsibility remained dispersed; policymaking remained incremental; and the role of the budget agency evolved from a fiduciary to an efficiency function.

Of Paperclips and Parks. What did this new role of the budget signify for our original examples of paperclips and parks? Under a Line-Item Budget, an administrator asked only input-related questions: How much will it cost next year to assure an adequate supply of paperclips for the office? How much will it cost next year to assume adequate maintenance of the parks for the public?

Under a Program/Performance Budget, an administrator was pushed into asking not only *input*-related questions, but *output*-related questions as well. In terms of programs, the Program/Performance Budget asks: To what programs do paperclips and parks pertain? Do we have a paperclips program? Do we have a parks program?

In terms of performance, the Program/Performance Budget asks: How many papers will be clipped? How many people will be served by the parks? We might anticipate administrative studies to be generated that would survey the average number of papers clipped per paperclip, or the average number of persons visiting each park. In short, how did paperclips and parks *perform*?

The Governmental Utility of Program/Performance Budgeting

Among the more lasting impacts of the Program/Performance Budgeting phase on American governments was its displacement (but not the exclusion) of budgeting by objects of expenditure (e.g., "pencils, 112") with budgeting by programs (e.g., "accounting program"). The Program/Performance Budget allowed public administrators to haul themselves out of the micromire of the Line-Item Budget and view a much bigger picture of the programmatic purposes of the public budget.

The other pillar of Program/Performance Budgeting—that is, its focus on measuring results and linking those results with agency budgets—was less successful. Nevertheless, the very fact that governments had tried hard to match budget dollars with agency performance represented a new, and notably persistent, notion about the role of the governmental budget: Budgets no longer were merely a means of controlling expenditures; they also were a way to fulfill public purposes.

Planning-Programming-Budgeting, 1965–1971

Program/Performance Budgeting swept through governments and its two defining elements quickly became commonplace. But another result was that its limitations became increasingly aggravating.

An Emerging New Standard for Budgetary Theory

What really was happening was that public administrators and policy makers wanted the budget to inform them more about public policies than the Program/Performance Budget was able to do.

The Policy Problem. While Program/Performance Budgeting represented a step forward in budgetary theory, it did not delve into the deeper levels of government. Unquestionably, Program/Performance Budgeting made a significant contribution in attempting to devise measurements of a program's effectiveness, and this was to the public's good. But, as one New York state legislator exclaimed after looking over his state's Program/Performance Budget, "Who the hell cares how much a pound of laundry costs?"[121]

Such data represent needed knowledge, to be sure, but ultimately the more important issue is a policy issue: Which programs are the most important? (In the case of the New York legislator, he would want to know why the state is washing laundry in the first place.) After this policy issue

is resolved, then we can begin evaluations of a program's performance.

The Performance Problem (Again). There was another problem with Program/Performance Budgeting: Despite high initial expectations, half of it, the performance half, was not working well. As the second Hoover Commission's report circumspectly noted with exquisite tact in 1955, "the installation of performance budgeting . . . has met with varying degrees of success."[122] This was a polite way of saying that Washington's Program/Performance Budget had largely failed in linking federal programs with their real costs and performance.

The Emergence of Planning-Programming-Budgeting. These concerns eventually led to the displacement of Program/Performance Budgeting in government by Planning-Programming-Budgeting (PPB). PPB-related notions had their origins in industry. As early as 1924, General Motors Corporation was using variants of PPB, and during World War II the Controlled Materials Plan of the War Production Board relied on PPB concepts.

In 1961, Robert McNamara, the chief executive officer of Ford Motor Company, became secretary of defense. The Defense establishment that he entered was beset by almost cutthroat competition among the services, each of which was vying for control of as many new weapons systems as it could acquire, and it was a competition that McNamara was convinced was undermining the nation's defense. McNamara and his "whiz kids" (a not entirely affectionate appellation given the McNamara team by the military) shook up the services by reestablishing central control of the military services through the imposition of Planning-Programming-Budgeting. McNamara began phasing in PPB in 1961, and, over a decade, PPB became the Pentagon's budgeting system, which it remains to this day.

President Lyndon B. Johnson was sufficiently impressed that in 1965 he ordered PPB to be applied throughout the federal government. By 1967 the Bureau of the Budget had instructed the use of PPB in twenty-one agencies, with a final goal of thirty-six agencies.

What Is PPB?

PPB, also known as *Planning-Programming-Budgeting System*, or *PPBS*, is a system of resource allocation designed to improve government efficiency and effectiveness by establishing long-range planning goals, analyzing the costs and benefits of alternative programs that would meet these goals, and articulating programs as budgetary and legislative proposals and long-term projections.[123]

Inputs, Outputs, Effects, and Alternatives. PPB is concerned not only with *inputs* and *outputs*, but also with *effects* and *alternatives*. Hence, PPB is associated with budget officers who have skills in economic analysis, as well as in accountancy and administration. The purposes of various programs become the chief concern, as opposed to their objects of expenditure or activities. Decision making becomes less incremental and more systemic throughout the bureaucracy. Finally, the budgetary agency is seen more than ever before as a policy-making body—a far cry from Dawes's statement in 1923 about budgeting being concerned with the "humbler and routine business of government."

Of Paperclips and Parks. How does this broadened scope of the budget affect the questions that we have been asking about our examples of paperclips and parks? With inputs, you recall, we ask only: How much will a year's supply of paperclips or a year's program of park maintenance cost? With outputs, we must ask: How many papers will our paperclips clip, or how many people will visit the parks?

With the additions of effects and alternatives our budget-related questions become considerably more sophisticated and penetrating. For example, in order to determine the effects of our paperclips, we must ask: What effect do the clipped papers have on the agency and its mission? Does paper clipping them facilitate the achievement of agency goals? Does the process expedite anything, or should paperclips be abandoned as an item on the budget? How do we measure the effects of the paperclips program on agency goals? After determining paperclips' effect on the accomplishment of the agency's

mission, we then must ask about alternatives. Should we use staples instead? Is there an optimal paperclip/staple mix? Do other alternatives exist?

Parks present a similar dilemma. When we ask about the effects of parks, we also must ask: What are parks really meant to do? The answer, of course, is that the purpose of parks is to provide recreation to the public—to allow citizens to "re-create." Yet, we soon discover that recreation is not much of an answer, particularly when we try to measure the effects of the park program. It is no longer enough to count visitors per day to each park—that is, to measure the park's performance, or output. Now we must ascertain whether or not each visitor is "re-creating" in the park—whether he or she is having fun. That chore is not only difficult, but it also may be impossible. For instance, we may discover that after midnight the park is visited entirely by muggers, rapists, and victims—not an entirely unwarranted assumption, given urban crime patterns.

This kind of thinking, which is enabled by PPB, also forces us to consider more systemic questions about parks. We may find out that the recreation function of a city affects other urban functions, such as crime control. If it is discovered that parks correlate positively with crime, we may wish to reconsider the utility of parks in light of the total urban system. At the very least, the role that parks play in the larger urban system will be clarified by asking questions about the effects of parks, and planning for public policy presumably will be made more precise, responsive, and rigorous.

Finally, we can consider alternatives to parks. Would public libraries provide more opportunities for recreating among the citizenry, and should monies allocated for parks be used instead for libraries? Might not many neighborhood miniparks provide more effective recreation than a few superparks? These and other alternatives would come up for evaluation under a PPB budget.

The Governmental Utility of Programming-Planning-Budgeting

PPB is, perhaps, the single most comprehensively "rational" budgeting system ever perpetrated in the United States. Has PPB's rationalism brought benefits, or do its rigid convolutions amount to not much more than a wearisome headache for public administrators?

An analysis of budgeting in the states found that rigorously rational budgeting does bring some positive results. Most notably, rational budgeting that incorporates a systemwide approach, two features that virtually define PPB, "reduces expenditures in aggregate."[124] In other words, rational and systematic budgetary practices bring about cost savings and more effectively expended dollars by governments. This is, of course, precisely what public budgeting is meant to do.

Budgeting-by-Objectives, 1972–1977

With the abandonment of PPB by the federal government (with the notable exception of the Defense Department) in the late 1960s, budgeteers turned to a new concept of budgeting (or, more precisely, to a variant of project management): Management-by-Objectives (MBO). MBO got its start in the private sector, and in 1954, Peter Drucker wrote a book entitled *The Practice of Management*, which generally is thought to be the first major expression of the MBO concept.[125]

What Is Budgeting-by-Objectives?

MBO may be defined as "a process whereby organizational goals and objectives are set through the participation of organizational members in terms of results expected."[126] When used as a budget system, MBO morphs into *Budgeting-by-Objectives (BBO)*, which may be defined as a process whereby resources are set through the participation of organizational members in terms of results expected, *and resources are allocated according to the degree to which organizational goals and objectives are met.*

Inputs, Outputs, and Effects. We have seen how PPB was concerned with inputs, outputs, effects, and alternatives as a budgetary posture. By contrast, BBO is in many ways a return to the world of Program/Performance Budgeting, especially in the sense that it emphasizes that persistent and pesky *bete noir* of budgeting, the assessing and funding of agency performance.

BBO is concerned with *inputs, outputs,* and *effects,* but not necessarily with alternatives. It deals primarily with agency performance and the effectiveness of governmental programs, but when it comes to pushing policymakers to ask what else—or what "other"—might government do to accomplish a particular social mission, BBO appears to be at somewhat of a loss. BBO has a managerial orientation that stresses, in terms of personnel skills, something called "common sense." It is concerned paramountly with program effectiveness, and its policymaking style is decentralized. In terms of planning—and very much *un*like PPB—BBO is comprehensive in one sense (i.e., it sets operational goals centrally), but it allocates the implementation of that comprehensive planning responsibility to on-line managers. Thus, the budgetary agency becomes concerned chiefly with program effectiveness and efficiency, much in the style of Program Performance Budgeting of the 1950s.

Of Paperclips and Parks. In relating BBO to our ongoing examples of paperclips and parks, we do not ask what the alternatives to paperclips and parks might be available in accomplishing the mission of the agency. Instead, we merely ask: How much does it cost to keep us in paperclips and parks? What do paperclips and parks actually do for us? How effective are paperclips in achieving the agency's mission? How effective are parks in achieving society's objectives? We do not ask, however, what alternatives there are to paperclips or to parks.

The Governmental Utility of Budgeting and Managing by Objectives

In concluding our discussion of BBO, we should note the some general findings about its foundation, MBO.

There is a significant body of empirical research on the results of applying MBO in the public sector that, when casually perused, is inconclusive in drawing conclusions about

MBO's usefulness. This is the case mainly because the researchers themselves often reject each others' methodologies on the basis of their own unfounded assumptions. As two researchers put it, "MBO has been a fundamental part of the movement to strengthen management capacity in the public sector. Yet, it often seems to be undervalued by the public administration professional and academic communities."[127]

In an unusually thorough and important analysis of thirty major investigations of governments' experience with MBO, which focused on their methodological approaches, it was found that, in every one of the thirty studies, productivity and performance gains resulted from MBO and were accurately and legitimately reported. When top management was strongly committed to MBO, "MBO programs result in large productivity gain."[128] Large indeed—an average of 58 percent gains in productivity in those studies where percentage gains were estimated.

Local governments in particular have found MBO to be useful. In these governments, MBO has proven itself to be quite "versatile, with objectives targeted on quality enhancement, cost control, productivity improvement, and special problem solving. . . . Thus, we would expect to see more complete application of MBO in cities in the future. . . ."[129]

Budgeting and managing by objectives remains a useful budgetary/management/productivity tool.

Zero Base Budgeting, 1977–1980

Although President Gerald Ford had continued BBO, a new face in the White House brought with it a new budgeting concept. The new face was Jimmy Carter, a nonestablishmentarian fresh from Georgia who had had a good experience with a concept called Zero Base Budgeting (ZBB) when he was governor. Indeed, Carter was the first elected executive to introduce ZBB to the public sector,[130] although the U.S. Department of Agriculture can be properly credited with its original development in the 1960s.[131]

What Is Zero Base Budgeting?

ZBB is the allocation of resources to agencies on the basis of those agencies periodically reevaluating the need for all of the programs for which the agency is responsible and justifying the continuance or termination of each program in the agency budget proposal. In other words, an agency reassesses what it is doing from top to bottom from a hypothetical "zero base."

Alternatives. The odd aspect about ZBB is that it really does not pay much attention to inputs, outputs, and effects. Rather, it fixates on *alternatives.* What are our options? Although ZBB does ask some vague questions about the outputs and effects of existing policies, its core query is: What should we do instead?

In practice, ZBB employs two steps. The first step is the development of "decision packages" for each agency with each package containing a summary analysis of each program within the agency. These packages are ranked by the agency head in accordance with his or her perception of overall agency priorities.

The second step requires that each decision package be evaluated by top management to determine whether it is justified for further funding. Programs that are considered ineffective or to have outgrown their usefulness are discarded, modified, or combined with other programs. In short, ZBB asks, what would we do with this agency's funds if they were not already committed? To determine such options, practitioners of ZBB identify each decision unit, analyze each decision unit within a decision package, evaluate and rank all decision packages to develop the appropriations request, and finally prepare a detailed operating budget that reflects those decision packages approved in the budget appropriations.

Of Paperclips and Parks. So what impact would ZBB have on an agency's use of paperclips or a city's parks program? For one, a great many more public managers would be talking about both topics as the decision-making process progressed. ZBB pushes participation at all levels, and this is likely to the good. But the inputs, outputs, and effects of paperclips and parks would be incidental considerations; decision makers would be concentrating on alternatives.

At the agency level, for example, the head of the Office of Paper Fastening Technologies would be deciding between purchasing more paperclips, staples, tape, or glue, but at the top level, the city manager might be choosing between purchasing more paperclips or closing more parks. These decisions would be formulated as decision packages and cast in terms of the agency's or government's broadly-defined program or purpose. Ultimately, paperclips and parks would be rank-ordered in terms of their relative usefulness to the government's overall mission.

The Governmental of Utility of Zero Base Budgeting

Does ZBB work? One review of empirical research on the experiences of federal, state, and local governments with ZBB concluded that it works within narrow limits and certain circumstances.[132] Specifically;

- ZBB is by no means as radical as its name implies; programs virtually never are cut to zero. Typically, government agencies submit their "cut back" decision packages at levels ranging from 75 to 90 percent of last year's budgets.
- ZBB is useful for comparing programs and assisting decision makers in deciding which ones they want to spend more on and which ones they want to spend less on. ZBB cannot (as was often touted in the 1970s) identify issues, set objectives, or determine alternative ways of conducting programs.
- ZBB can coexist on reasonably friendly terms with other budgetary concepts and processes. It adapts easily. In this sense, ZBB is a marginal and incremental budgetary tool, one not central to budgeting and management in the way that PPB is.
- Program managers clearly feel that they participate more in the budgetary process, and communication among all levels of the government bureaucracy is enhanced when ZBB is introduced. These are perhaps the most conclusive findings of the research.
- However, unless ZBB is introduced carefully, program managers can become parochial in their use of it and fail to see larger issues.

- Paperwork increases with ZBB, but its expansion appears to be controllable. Not all observers agree with this conclusion, however, and one authority contends that, at the federal level, ZBB "became mired in mammoth amounts of paperwork, probably even more so" than PPB.[133] Another study concluded that federal paperwork exploded by an average of 229 percent during ZBB's first year of implementation![134]
- ZBB does not seem to reduce government spending by the federal and state governments, where expenditures are largely obligated by formula-based public programs, but most local administrators believe ZBB to be quite useful in holding down costs.

Target Base Budgeting, 1980–1992

Prior to 1980, the introduction of a new budgeting system was high theatre. The Line-Item Budget was established by historic legislation. The unveiling of the Program/Performance Budget followed the publication of the prestigious report by the first Hoover Commission, urging its adoption. PPB amounted to a wrenching revolution from the top orchestrated by President Johnson. BBO was introduced and used in part by President Nixon as a tactic to enhance the power the White House at the expense of the Budget Bureau. ZBB, mandated with flourishes and fanfare by President Carter, suffused every aspect of his presidency.

After 1980, the tradition of dramatically trumpeting a new budgeting system withered. As one observer put it, "There has not been a major drive to install a new [budget] system since President Carter promulgated the Zero Base Budgeting system." Nevertheless, although budgeting systems "no longer get much attention, each system has had a lasting effect. Their legacies continue to influence budget practices."[135]

Target Base Budgeting (TBB) was the first budgeting system to reflect these new realities. It was introduced quietly, even stealthily; it and its successor, Results Budgeting, include many features found in earlier budget systems; and it transformed the budget process, and even the process of government, in fundamental ways.

What Is Target Base Budgeting?

TBB, also known as *Target Budgeting, Fixed-Ceiling Budgeting*, and *Top-Down Budgeting*, is a method of allocating resources to agencies in which agency spending limits (and, often, agency goals, too), or "targets," are set by the elected chief executive of the government.

Agency heads are permitted to attain their goals in the manner that they deem to be most effective within these centrally set spending limits, and are expected to demonstrate progress in the achievement of agency goals in next year's budget request. Increasingly, agencies are provided with budgetary incentives by chief executive officers to attain their goals. Often, a second part of the budget request is also present, which is those agency fund requests that are not part of the target, but which the agency still wants, and these are ranked by priority.

TBB is driven by revenues, and in this respect TBB is an unusually realistic budget system. Whether the revenue base is determined by economic conditions beyond the control of policymakers, or by conscious political choices, such as tax caps, is irrelevant: Budgeting targets will have a much better likelihood of reflecting available revenues because the chief executive is setting the targets.

TBB Plays Well with Others. There are a number of elements of ZBB present in TBB, and most of them work to the advantage of TBB as an easily implemented budget system. These elements include a premium on prioritization; agency budget requests based on service levels, whether current or desired; or a requirement by the chief executive that the agency propose a budget that is supportive of new government policies. "Target base budgeting is a version of zero-base budgeting without a lot of the extra work. Instead of examining all programs or providing alternative scenarios with multiple budgets, target budgeting is based on one figure. . . ."[136] Because it gives greater reign to agency heads in attaining goals, TBB also relates well with BBO, and, because it also centralizes goal setting, TBB also relates well to the new governmental emphases on performance measures and strategic planning.

The Burial of Bottom-Up Budgeting. Despite its emphasis on decentralizing the management of funds to agency heads, TBB clearly empowers the central administration to set expenditure and programmatic goals; therefore, TBB (or Top-Down Budgeting) is a complete reversal of the traditional budgetary process in government, which is "bottom-up."

In other words, in a traditional budget-making process, agencies send their spending requests upward toward the budget director and the elected chief executive. These requests are filtered through a series of discussions and hearings, and planning ceilings for each agency are established under the general guidance of the director of the budget. Ultimately the chief executive approves or disapproves of the director's recommendations, and agency heads may appeal the recommendations of the director. While this system is still more or less in place, it is largely *pro forma*. The real system of budgeting now is from the top downward.

Inputs and Effects. Because TBB is so mission specific that outputs and alternatives are not major factors. Outputs are viewed merely as a means to an end—the attainment of the government's highly focused mission. Alternatives are irrelevant, since the government already knows precisely what it wants.

Thus, *inputs* and *effects* are the salient variables, and these are expressed in highly mission-specific terms. How much money can we accrue (by raising taxes, cutting other programs, spending in deficit—whatever) to achieve our mission? Will we obtain the effects of that mission that we desire?

One fact emerges very clearly in TBB: Budgeteers and elected executives know their mission and budget exclusively for that mission. The policymakers of a government can deal with the budget as a whole and use it to advance whatever mission they are pursuing. The skills needed to implement TBB are political and coordinative, plus a knowledge of the system, especially knowledge about what is needed from the system to advance the mission. Government's policy-making style is aggressive, centralized, and highly focused.

Of Paperclips and Parks.   In terms of how TBB would deal with paperclips and parks, it might push us into choosing either paperclips or parks to the exclusion of all other public programs. Let us say that we, as the government's top policymaker, chose paperclips. Parks would wither, as would all other public programs, to the extent that we could politically defend and advance our mission, that is, paperclips. The paperclip mission would flourish, by contrast, because every penny that we could prise from parks—and every other public program—would be directed to paperclips.

The Governmental Utility of Target Base Budgeting

Even though TBB has been introduced discreetly and quietly into all levels of American governments, its impact has been substantial, and perhaps revolutionary. Paradoxically, TBB has both given new freedoms to line managers and new powers to central ones.

Of perhaps greater significance, TBB has reversed the very flow of the budget-making process itself. Under TBB, public executives inform agencies what budget levels they may request. No longer do public executives scurry to merely meet agencies' budgetary demands.

Cutback Management: Responding to the Reality of Red Ink

TBB was one response that the grass-roots governments accorded their reduced financial circumstances that had appeared in the 1980s; the other was a pastiche of methods used to reduce government spending. Unlike the federal government, which can and often has engaged in deficit spending, almost all state and local governments must, by law, balance the books. The late 1970s through the early 1990s were an era of reduced revenues— a "decade of red ink,"[137] to borrow one description—for the public sector, and state, but particularly local, governments developed systematic ways of responding to these new realities. These methods are called "cutback management,"

and they are very much a part of the package of Top-Down Budgeting.

Cutback management is the collection of techniques that have been developed by practicing public administrators to reduce costs or eliminate public programs when confronted by fiscal constraints.[138] These techniques of cutback management include short-term and long-term approaches.

Cutting Back for the Short Term

Short-term cutback management includes techniques that do little more than buy time. We consider some of them here.

Hiring Freezes.   A *hiring freeze* simply means that no one new is hired and relies on a process of natural attrition (i.e., employees retiring or leaving the agency voluntarily for other jobs) to effect cost savings. Hiring freezes can disadvantage some units of government more than others if, for whatever reason, some agencies lose more employees to attrition than do other agencies, and yet, like those other units, still are not allowed to hire replacements. One remedy to these problems is to permit the hiring of one person for every three lost by attrition until an established level is reached.

Undifferentiated Budget Cuts.   "Across-theboard" budget cuts constitute another short-term method of cutback management, and this approach has the advantage of relieving the senior public administrator of considerable stress, since it is, essentially, mindless: A 10 percent cut in the budgets of all units may be an easy decision for the chief executive to make, but it is insensitive to the varying needs and services of those units. Typically, unilateral budget cuts harm those agencies that have a high proportion of skilled workers providing sophisticated services, such as a science laboratory, while they do not have a major impact on agencies which deliver a routine service, such as mowing highway medians, that simply can be slowed down to accommodate a budget cut.

Other Short-Term Tactics.   Reducing temporary employees, deferring maintenance, and postponing equipment purchases also are relatively stressless decisions for the senior public administrator to make when implementing cutbacks, and, also like hiring freezes and unilateral budget cuts, have the advantage of buying time for the longer haul. Ultimately, these techniques are short-term approaches and often harbor hidden long-term costs. To actually reduce expenditures permanently requires more thought.

Cutting Back for the Long Term

Reducing expenditures permanently requires longer term approaches to cutback management. Some of these approaches are quite direct, and others less so.

Reorganizing Government.   Streamlining government agencies and their programs through reorganization is often touted as a way of achieving direct cost savings, and we include it in our list precisely because it is cited so frequently. Regrettably, however, governmental restructuring is almost impossible to accomplish in any meaningful way, and in those few instances when government is reorganized, the reorganization rarely, if ever, saves money.

As we explained at length in Part II, particularly in Chapter 4, public organizations are far more vulnerable to external pressures than are private ones. Restructuring governments and agencies is thus more challenging because outside powers, in the form of the iron triangle of agency, legislature, and special interest, resist it, and almost always successfully. When a rare reorganization of government does take place, the notion of enhanced efficiency is, almost always, simply not present. As the National Commission on the Public Service concluded, reorganizations of the federal government "virtually never" realize greater cost savings,[139] and analyses of restructuring in state governments arrive at comparable conclusions.[140]

New Technologies.   Although, as we noted in Chapter 7, service-intensive governments cannot derive savings from technological innovations to the same extent as product-intensive corporations,[141] new technologies nonetheless can

achieve some degree of direct cost savings in the public sector. Perhaps the most significant technology that has saved governments money is information technology, which we discussed in Chapter 6.

An indirect example of how information technology saves public funds is provided by the shrinkage of the federal workforce as Washington expands its information technology. In 1989, clerical workers accounted for nearly one in seven federal employees; today, they account for about one in thirteen. As one former federal secretary observed, "The stuff I did 15 or 16 years ago is no longer necessary. Now we all need some level of computer literacy."[142]

Productivity Improvement.   Another method of saving money directly is to improve productivity. As we detailed in Chapter 7, all levels of government are deeply engaged in improving productivity in the form of performance measures, benchmarking, program evaluation, and other methods.

Using Alternative Delivery Systems.   At root, *alternative methods of service delivery* rely on governments using people, who are not full-time employees of the government sponsoring the program, to deliver their programs. Often, these methods are less costly than is the traditional approach of providing services with full-time government workers, and they include contracting out services to companies and nonprofit organizations and using lower cost personnel, such as part-timers and volunteers, among other approaches. We consider these methods in detail in Chapter 11.

Rearranging Intergovernmental Relations. Another way to cut costs is to rearrange the relationships among governments. Those rearrangements that have a particular pertinence to achieving direct cost savings include various kinds of intergovernmental service agreements; annexation of adjacent territory by municipalities; consolidation, or the merging of two or more local governments; and regional approaches to governing. These methods often facilitate the attainment of simpler and more effective governmental processes and enhance economies of scale in service delivery, thereby reducing costs. We consider them more fully in Chapter 12.

Prioritizing Programs. Our final long-term approach to cutback management is prioritizing programs, and then cutting the lowest ranked programs.

Prioritizing programs, somewhat surprisingly, is still relatively new in governmental budget making, but it is at least making rapid headway. In 1975, fewer than three out of ten state budgets ranked priorities among programs, but today more than eight out of ten do so.[143]

How program priorities, low and otherwise, are determined by agency administrators can be a painful process that requires sophistication and sensitivity to reduce the conflict that is inherent in making such choices. Practicing public administrators seem to agree that the following steps should be taken in determining program priorities when faced with cutbacks.[144]

- Be sure that all interested parties are informed of the need for cutbacks, and solicit their views on those cutbacks.
- Determine the criteria for how priorities should be set. While these criteria should be determined by the chief executive, the views of other employees in the agency should be carefully considered, and if possible, implemented.
- Establish a preliminary and tentative priority list based on the explicit criteria that have been developed for priority setting.
- Attempt to build some public consensus through various meetings and hearings to develop a final priority list.
- Insure that various elected officials and other pertinent decision makers approve of the priority list.
- Understand that there will never be complete agreement in the priority-setting process but keep trying to explain why the priorities have been set in the manner that they have to the public at large and to agency employees.
- Public executives faced with cutting public programs should remain calm, professional, honest, open, and unflappable in the process of setting priorities. Cutback management is, above all, a process of conflict reduction.

Budgeting for Results, 1993–Present

A new budgeting phase is emerging, and it re-invokes, for at least the third time in the evolution of the budget, the vexing problem of paying for measurable performance, rather than shelling out public money to government agencies simply because the agencies are there. This phase is usually called Budgeting for Results, and its debut can be traced to 1993, when the federal Government Performance and Results Act (also known as the Results Act) was enacted and the National Performance Review released its recommendations for budgetary reform.

What Is Budgeting for Results?

Budgeting for Results, or *Results Budgeting*, also known as *Mission Budgeting*, *Entrepreneurial Budgeting*, *Performance Budgeting*, and *Performance-Based Budgeting*,[145] is a system of resource allocation that links the disbursement of funds to performance measures. Results Budgeting is, most definitely, a return to the traditions of Program/Performance Budgeting of the 1950s.

Results Budgeting and Program/Performance Budgeting. As with Program/Performance Budgeting, Budgeting for Results has, as its basic orientation, a heavy emphasis on management. Also like Program/Performance Budgeting, its policymaking style is incremental. Unlike Program/Performance Budgeting, however, Budgeting for Results uses a policymaking style that is participatory and decentralized, as well as incremental.

The kinds of public administrators needed to budget for results must be, as they were in the case of Program/Performance Budgeting, solid managers. But they also must be excellent planners and communicators. The critical information that must be communicated under Budgeting for Results is, as in Program/Performance Budgeting, information about the activities of each agency, with a focus on efficiency, effectiveness, and accountability. Planning is a joint affair between the agency and a central office, usually the budget office (under classic Program/Performance Budgeting, planning is dispersed and does not receive much attention). The role of the budget office is to assure, above all else, accountability. This is yet another difference that Budgeting for Results has with Program/ Performance Budgeting, which makes efficiency the budget agency's chief concern.

Inputs and Outputs.   Again like Program/ Performance Budgeting, Budgeting for Results has a scope that is essentially limited to *inputs* and *outputs*, although there is a notable concern with the "quality" of those outputs that may not be as noticeable in Program/Performance Budgeting. One could argue that the scope of Budgeting for Results also includes the development of alternatives. It does, kind of, but essentially only as such alternatives might apply to delivery mechanisms, such as contracting out *versus* direct servicing, for existing policy, and not to the introduction of new, alternative policies.

Of Paperclips and Parks.   So, in terms of how Budgeting for Results would deal with paperclips and parks, it would ask essentially the same questions that Program/Performance Budgeting would ask: How many papers are being clipped? How many people are being served by the parks? But Budgeting for Results also is likelier to ask about alternatives for delivery. Could we clip papers and serve park visitors more efficiently, effectively, and responsively by privatizing our management of paperclips and parks? Or engaging in intergovernmental agreements? Or by using vouchers or volunteers? Or other options?

The Governmental Utility of Budgeting for Results

With some exceptions, Results Budgeting is a return to the performance component of Program/Performance Budgeting. If—and it is a big if—governments can accurately determine excellent agency performance and reward them with larger budgets, and sanction poor agency performance with lesser budgets, then governments that are more efficient, effective, and valued by the citizenry should emerge.

Governments have tried this before (in fact, they have never completely stopped trying since budgeting for performance first surfaced in the mid-twentieth century), often with disappointing consequences. But the clear determination of governments in the twenty-first century to methodically and meticulously marry money with measurable results may be unprecedented. If Budgeting for Results fulfills the investment being placed in it, it will have a rare governmental utility indeed.

In this chapter, we have reviewed how governments tax, spend, and budget. How governments undertake these financial responsibilities is a product of values, politics, and choices. In the next chapter, we review values, politics, and choices in a more human context: public human resource management.

Notes

1. David Osborne and Peter Hutchinson, *The Price of Government: Getting the Results We Need in an Age of Permanent Fiscal Crisis* (New York: Basic Books, 2004) p. 45. Figures are for 1972–2002.

2. Ibid., pp. 44–47. Figures are for 1972–2002.

3. U.S. Government Accountability Office, *Comptroller General's Forum: The Long-Term Fiscal Challenge*, GAO–05–282SP (Washington, DC: U.S. Government Printing Office, 2005), p. 47. There are twenty-six major mandatory programs. The largest ones, in order of the most dollars expended, are: Social Security, Medicare, Medicaid, federal employee retirement, unemployment compensation, food and nutritional assistance (largely food stamps and school lunches), the earned income tax credit, Supplemental Security Income, and veterans' benefits. For the full list, see U.S. Office of Management and Budget, "Historical Tables," *Budget of the United States Government, Fiscal Year 2007* (Washington, DC: U.S. Government Printing Office, 2006), Table 8.5.

4. As derived from data in U.S. Bureau of the Census, *Statistical Abstract of the United States, 2006*, 125th ed. (Washington, DC: U.S. Government Printing Office, 2006), Tables 530, 531. In 2003, over 32 percent of persons with income who were fifteen or older received one or more benefits in the forms of Social Security, railroad retirement, Supplemental Security income, public assistance, veterans' payments, unemployment compensation, workers' compensation, military retirement, federal employee pensions, and Pell grants. In 2002, 20 percent of U.S. households received at least one federal means-tested noncash benefit, notably food stamps, school lunches, public housing, and Medicaid.

5. U.S. Government Accountability Office, *Comptroller General's Forum: The Long-Term Fiscal Challenge*, p. 47. Discretionary spending declined by 37 percent, 1964–2004. Even by 1984, 55 percent of federal expenditures went to mandatory and related programs: Forty-two percent was spent from special funds, and 13 percent to pay interest on the debt; 45 percent was spent on discretionary programs.

6. As derived from data in U.S. Bureau of the Census, *Statistical Abstract of the United States, 2006*, Table 427. Figures include current charges and expenditures, utility and liquor store revenues and expenditures, and insurance trust revenue and expenditures in 2002. In 2002, over 12 percent of state revenue and more than 22 percent of local revenue were in these funds.

7. As derived from data in ibid. Figure is for 2000.

8. As derived from data in ibid. Figure is for 2000.

9. John E. Petersen, "Going for Broke," *Governing* (November 2003), p. 70. After almost a half-century of these micromanaging initiatives, it is hardly surprising that the finances of the Golden State and its local governments are bleak. The municipal bond ratings of the state government and California's local governments have slipped from a consistent AAA by all three major credit rating agencies in the 1980s to the lowest rated state in the country, and deficit spending is the rule, not the exception. California's abysmal bond rating is attributable not only to the hamstringing of its finances by populist initiatives, but also to other factors. The legislature's requirement that there must be a two-thirds majority vote to adopt a budget has led to a dysfunctional tyranny of the minority, and legislative term limits have ensured that California's legislators will always remain dilettantes.

  In 2005, Californians overwhelmingly defeated Proposition 76, an initiative sponsored by the governor that would have slowed spending and loosened the grip of special interests on the state's general fund.

10. As derived from data in U.S. Bureau of the Census, *Statistical Abstract of the United States, 2006*, Table 464. Figure is for 2005.

11. As derived from data in ibid. Figure is for 2005. Social Security was enacted in 1935, its coverage was extended to survivors and dependents in 1939, and disability Insurance was added in 1956; these are all Social Security programs, and are called, officially, Old-Age, Survivors, and Disability Insurance, or OASDI. Hospital insurance was added in 1965, and refers to Part A of Medicare.

12. As derived from data in ibid. Figure is for 2005.

13. As derived from data in ibid. Figure is for 2005.

14. U.S. Bureau of the Census, *Statistical Abstract of the United States, 1951*, 72nd ed. (Washington, DC: U.S. Government Printing Office, 1951), Table 354. In 1950, the excise tax accounted for 21 percent of all federal revenues.

15. As derived from data in U.S. Bureau of the Census, *Statistical Abstract the United States, 2006*, Table 418. Figure is for 2004 and pertains to all "current tax receipts," but does not include "contributions for government social insurance," for example, Social Security and Medicare. When these contributions are included, the income tax accounted for 43 percent of governments tax receipts in 2004.

16. As derived from data in ibid. Figure is for 2005.

17. U.S. Bureau of the Census, *Statistical Abstract of the United States, 1951*, Table 354. Figures are from 1950 through 2003. In 1950 the personal income tax accounted for 49 percent of federal revenue, and in 1980 it accounted for 47 percent. As late as 1980, the corporate income tax accounted for 13 percent of all federal revenue.

18. As derived from data in U.S. Bureau of the Census, *Statistical Abstract of the United States, 2006*, Tables 418, 464. Figure is for 2004.

19. Actually, Hawaii was the first state to enact personal and corporate income taxes in 1901; it was not a state, however, when it did so, but a territory.

20. As derived from data in U.S. Advisory Commission on Intergovernmental Relations, *Significant Features of Fiscal Federalism, 1980–81*, M–132 (Washington, DC: U.S. Government Printing Office, 1981), pp. 41, 44; and U.S. Bureau of the Census, "Table 1. Summary of State and Local Government Finances by Level of Government: 2002–03," *Census of Governments, 2002*. http://www.census.gov/ovs/estimate/03s100us.html. In 1980, the state individual income tax accounted for 27 percent of all state tax revenue, and in 2003 it accounted for 32 percent. The state corporate income tax accounted for almost 10 percent of total state tax revenue in 1980, but only 5 percent in 2003.

21. Gary Cornia, Kelly D. Edmiston, David L. Sjoquist, et al., "The Disappearing State Corporate Income Tax," *National Tax Journal* 58 (March 2005), pp. 115–139.

22. Robert Tannenwald, *Are State and Local Revenue Systems Obsolete?* (Washington, DC: National League of Cities, 2004).

23. As derived from data in U.S. Bureau of the Census, *Statistical Abstract of United States, 2006*, Table 481, and *1951*, Table 354. Current figure is for 2003. In 1950, federal revenues totaled slightly more than $37 billion, and what were then known as "employment taxes" (that is, Social Security revenue) amounted to almost $2.9 billion. We should note that self-employed workers "contribute" to Social Security and Medicare through the Self-Employment Contributions Act at the same rate as that of FICA.

24. C. Eugene Steuerle, *Contemporary US Tax Policy* (Washington, DC: Urban Institute, 2004), p. 38. FICA currently levies on both employers and employees a combined 12.4 percent payroll tax to fund Social Security and a 2.9 percent tax to fund Medicare.

25. U.S. Bureau Census, *Statistical Abstract United States, 2006*, Table 461. Figures are for 2005.

26. U.S. Government Accountability Office, *Understanding the Tax Reform Debate: Background, Criteria, and Questions*, GAO–05–1009SP (Washington, DC: U.S. Government Printing Office, 2005). Much of the following discussion is from this source.

27. U.S. Government Accountability Office, *Government Performance and Accountability: Tax Expenditures*

Represent a Substantial Federal Commitment and Need to Be Reexamined, GAO–05–690 (U.S. Government Printing Office, 2005). Figures are for 2004. In 2004, there were 146 exemptions, or what are technically called *tax expenditures*.

28. U.S. Government Accountability Office, *Understanding the Tax Reform Debate*, p. 40.

29. U.S. Government Accountability Office, *Tax Policy: Summary of Estimates of the Cost of the Federal Tax System*, GAO–05–878 (Washington, DC: U.S. Government Printing Office, 2005).

30. U.S. Government Accountability Office, *Understanding the Tax Reform Debate*, p. 49.

31. Ibid., p. 51.

32. U.S. Government Accountability Office, *Tax Gap: Multiple Strategies, Better Compliance Data, and Long-term Goals Are Needed to Improve Taxpayer Compliance*, GAO–06–208T (Washington, DC: U.S. Government Printing Office, 2005). Highlights page. The good news is that the tax gap is closing over time, if glacially. Each 10 percent reduction in the tax gap would translate into $25 billion more in additional annual revenue.

33. As derived from data in U.S. Bureau of the Census, "Table 1." Figures are for 2002–2003.

34. As derived from data in American Council on Intergovernmental Relations, *Significant Features of Fiscal Federalism, 1995*, Vol. 2 (Washington, DC: Author, 1998), p. 52. In 1980, the federal contribution to state revenues was 22 percent.

35. As derived from data in U.S. Bureau of the Census, "Table 1." Figures are for 2002–2003.

36. As derived from data in ibid. Figures are for 2002–2003.

37. U.S. Advisory Commission on Intergovernmental Relations, *Significant Features of Fiscal Federalism, 1995*, Vol. 1, M–197 (Washington, DC: U.S. Government Printing Office, 1995), pp. 89–90. Figures are for 1994.

38. One thorough review puts the matter succinctly: "As state sales taxes operate in practice, they flagrantly violate all the primary criteria [for a fair and effective tax:] . . . economic neutrality, equity, simplicity, and transparency." See Charles E. McClure, Jr., "Rethinking State and Local Reliance on the Retail Sales Tax: Should We Fix the Sales Tax or Discard It?" *Brigham Young University Law Review* 2000 (1, 2000), pp. 77–130. The quotation is on p. 85.

39. George F. Will, "A Taxing Challenge," *Washington Post* (February 6, 2005).

40. Ibid. and Michael Sandler, "State Sales Tax 'Not in Synch'," *St. Petersburg Times* (August 7, 2003).

41. Quoted in Sandler, "State Sales Tax 'Not in Synch.'"

42. U.S. Advisory Commission on Intergovernmental Relations, *Significant Features of Fiscal Federalism, 1995*, Vol. 1, pp. 89–90. Figures are for 1994.

43. As derived from data in U.S. Advisory Commission on Intergovernmental Relations, *Significant Features of Fiscal Federalism, 1980–81*, p. 44.

44. As derived from data in U.S. Bureau of the Census, "Table 1." Figures are for 2002–2003.

45. Scott Mackey, *Critical Issues in State-Local Fiscal Policy*, Part 2, *A Guide to Local Option Taxes* (Denver, CO: National Conference of State Legislatures, 1997).

46. National Conference of State Legislatures, "Local Option Sales Taxes," *Legisbrief* 6 (August/September 1998), p. 1. This figure was attained in 1998, and was still valid in 2006. Twenty-six states allow counties, municipalities, townships, and special districts to levy sales taxes; six permit only counties to do so; and two authorize only municipalities.

47. John R. Bartle, "Trends in Local Government Taxation in the 21st Century," *Spectrum: The Journal of State Government* 76 (Winter 2003), pp. 26–29.

48. As derived from data in U.S. Bureau of the Census, "Table 1." Figures are for 2002–2003.

49. As derived from data in ibid. Figure is for 2002–2003.

50. As derived from data in ibid. Figures are for 2002–2003, when states provided 89 percent of local intergovernmental revenue, and Washington provided 11 percent in direct grants to localities.

51. David B. Walker, *The Rebirth of Federalism: Slouching toward Washington*, 2nd ed. (New York: Chatham House, 2000), p. 227. Figure is the average for seven selected years from 1957 through 1990.

52. As derived from figures in U.S. Bureau of the Census, "Table 1." Figures are for 2002–2003. We have assumed that one-third of federal aid to the states continues to be pass-through grants to local governments.

53. As derived from data in ibid. Figures are for 2002–2003.

54. As derived from data in ibid. Figures are for 2002–2003.

55. David, Baer, *State Programs and Practices for Reducing Residential Property Taxes* (Washington, DC: AARP Public Policy Institute, American Association of Retired Persons, 2003), p. ii. Figures are for 2003.

56. Andrew Reschovsky, *The State Role in Providing Property Tax Relief* (Madison, WI: Department of Political Science, University of Wisconsin, no date). http://www.leg.state.nv.us.

57. Baer, *State Programs and Practices for Reducing Residential Property Taxes*, p. ii. Figure is for 2003.

58. Ibid., p. iii. Figures are for 2000.

59. U.S. Advisory Commission on Intergovernmental Relations, *Changing Public Attitudes on Governments and Taxes*. Reports S–1 through S–23 (Washington, DC: U.S. Government Printing Office, 1972–1994); John Kincaid and Richard L. Cole, "Public Opinion on Issues of U.S. Federalism in 2005: End of the Post-2001 Pro-Federal Surge?" *Publius* 35 (Winter 2005), p. 175; and Richard L. Cole, John Kincaid, and Alejandro Rodriguez, "Public Opinion on Federalism and Federal Political Culture in Canada, Mexico, and the United States, 2004," *Publius* 34 (Summer 2004), p. 206.

60. John L. Mikesell, *Fiscal Administration: Analysis and Applications for the Public Sector* (Homewood, IL: Dorsey, 1982), p. 230.

61. Baer, *State Programs and Practices for Reducing Residential Property Taxes*, p. ii. Figure is for 2003.

62. As derived from data in: U.S. Advisory Commission on Intergovernmental Relations, *Significant Features of Fiscal Federalism, 1980–81*, p. 44; and U.S. Bureau of the Census, "Table 1." Current figures are for 2002–2003.

63. Richard C. Kearney, "Reinventing Government and Battling Budget Crises: Manager and Municipal Government Actions in 2003," *Municipal Year Book, 2005* (Washington, DC: International City/County Management Association, 2005), p. 31.

64. Christopher Hoene, "Fiscal Structure and the Post-Proposition 13 Fiscal Regime in California's Cities," *Public Budgeting and Finance* 24 (December 2004), pp. 51–72.

65. Bruce A. Wallin, *Budgeting for Basics: The Changing Landscape of City Finances* (Washington, DC: Brookings, 2005), p. 6. Figures are for 1977–2000 and are based on 162 cities that had populations of at least 100,000 in 1977. The property tax's contribution to general revenue in these cities declined by almost 6 percent, while the user fees' contribution increased by nearly 7 percent.

66. Kearney, "Reinventing Government and Battling Budget Crises," p. 31. Figures are for 2003.

67. Tannenwald, *Are State and Local Revenue Systems Becoming Obsolete?* pp. 7–26.

68. Ibid.

69. U.S. Bureau of the Census, *E-Stats* (Washington, DC: U.S. Government Printing Office, 2005), http://www.census.gov/mrts/data. In the third quarter of 2005, 2.4 percent of total resale sales were conducted electronically, and represented an increase of 27 percent from the third quarter of 2004. For a review of the Internet taxation issue, see Amy F. Haas, "Internet Taxation: The Battle Begins!" *Journal of State Taxation* 23 (Summer 2004), pp. 43–50.

70. Christopher Swope, "Internet Sales Taxes Are a Giant Step Closer," *Governing* (August 2005), p. 56.

71. Keon Chi and Drew Leatherby, *The States and Business Incentives: An Inventory of Tax and Financial Incentives Programs* (Lexington, KY: Council of State Governments, 1997).

72. As derived from data in Tannenwald, *Are State and Local Revenue Systems Becoming Obsolete?* p. 29. Figures are for 1986–1999.

73. Ibid., p. iv.

74. Douglas Holtz-Eakin, director, Congressional Budget Office, as cited in: David E. Rosenbaum, "The Deficit Disappeared, but That Was Then," *New York Times* (September 21, 2003).

75. Edgar R. Fiedler, as quoted in http://view.atdmt.com.

76. As derived from data in U.S. Office of Management and Budget, *Historical Tables, Budget of the United States Government, Fiscal Year 2007*, Table 15.3. Figures are for 2005. Outlays by state and local governments refer to expenditures from their own sources of revenue and do not include federal and state grants.

77. U.S. Department of Commerce, Bureau of Economic Analysis, "Personal Saving Rate," http://www.bea.gov/briefrm.saving.htm. In the first quarter of 2005, the personal saving rate dipped below 1 percent, a low that had not been seen since 1933, at the height of the Great Depression, and in the second quarter it neared minus 2 percent. In 1980, personal saving as a percentage of disposable personal income was about 11 percent.

See U.S. Government Accountability Office, *Social Security Reform: Answers to Key Questions*, GAO–05–193SP (Washington, DC: U.S. Government Printing Office, 2005), p. 31.

78. U.S. Government Accountability Office, *Federal Debt: Answers to Frequently Asked Questions, An Update*, GAO–04–485SP Federal Debt (Washington, DC: U.S. Government Printing Office, 2004), p. 44. Between 1984 and 2002, the United States ranked sixth out of seven industrialized countries in its average gross national saving rate.

79. Research and Policy Committee, Committee for Economic Development, *Exploding Deficits, Declining Growth: The Federal Budget and the Aging of America* (Washington, DC: Author, 2003), p. 8.

80. Associated Press/Ipsos survey of 1,000 adults taken in 2005, as cited in Robert Tanner, Associated Press, "Headed for a Crash?" *Savannah Morning News* (September 4, 2005).

81. U.S. Bureau of the Census, *Statistical Abstract of the United States, 1951*, Table 4; and U.S. Bureau of the Census, *Statistical Abstract of the United States, 2006*, Table 2. In 1950, the U.S. population was slightly less than 154 million, and in 2004 it was slightly less than 294 million.

82. Ibid. (*1951*), Table 204; and ibid. (*2003*), Table 576. In 1950, nearly 60 million people were employed in the U.S. civilian labor force, and in 2004 more than 147 million people were working in it.

83. Ibid. (*1951*), Table 303; and ibid. (*2006*), Table 650. In 1950, the gross national product amounted to almost $279 billion in current dollars; in 2001, the GDP toted up to more than $11 trillion, $735 billion in current dollars. Another way of expressing this growth is that the economy grew by over 4,100 percent.

84. The years in which the federal budget balanced (actually, there were surpluses) during this period were 1970, 1999, 2000, and 2001 (or Fiscal Years 1969, 1998, 1999, and 2000).

85. See, for example, Louis Uchitelle, "Politicians May Be Up in Arms about Government Deficits, but Economists Aren't," *New York Times* (November 8, 1996); John Cassidy, "Ace in the Hole," *The New Yorker* (June 10, 1996), pp. 36–43; John M. Berry, "The Deficit Is (a) Still Really Big, or (b) No Big Deal," *Washington Post* (March 24, 1994); and Louis Uchitelle, "The Pitfalls of a Balanced Budget," *New York Times* (February 21, 1995). According to these reports, the economists interviewed agreed that federal deficit spending that did not exceed 2 percent of the GDP was manageable; however, when deficits neared 5 percent of the GDP, they became worried.

86. The National Association of Business Economists describes the federal deficit as the single most significant problem facing the U.S. economy. See: "America's Deficits: A Flood of Red Ink," *The Economist* (November 6, 2003), http://www.economist.com. A bipartisan coalition of three economic think tanks charges that "Allowing a fiscal imbalance [as a result of deficit spending] of this magnitude to continue will do significant harm to the budget and the economy...." See Committee for

Economic Development, Concorde Coalition, and Center on Budget and Policy Priorities, *Mid-Term and Long-Term Deficit Projections* (Washington, DC: Authors, 2003), p. 19. The former chair of the Federal Reserve Board agrees, warning that deficits pose "a significant obstacle to long-term stability." See Alan Greenspan, as quoted in Robert B. Reich, "The Mixed-Up Politics of the Deficit," *New York Times* (May 11, 2004).

87. U.S. Government Accountability Office, *Federal Debt*, pp. 39, 41. The GAO notes (p. 39) that "The fiscal policies in place today—absent substantive entitlement reform and dramatic changes in tax and spending policies—will result in large, escalating, and persistent deficits that are economically unsustainable over the long term. In other words, today's policies cannot continue forever."

88. Ibid., pp. 41–42. The figure is in constant dollars, and the years covered are 2003–2054.

89. Ibid., p. 17. Emphasis added.

90. U.S. Office of Management and Budget, *Historical Tables, Budget of the United States Government, Fiscal Year 2007*, Table 7.1. Figures are estimated for 2007. In 1980, the gross federal debt was less than $910 billion and amounted to less than 33 percent of the GDP; in 2007, at an estimated $9.3 trillion, it accounted for almost 68 percent.

91. Philip G. Joyce, "Congressional Budget Reform: The Unanticipated Implications of Federal Policymaking," *Public Administration Review* 56 (July/August 1996), p. 317.

92. Robert Greenstein, *Looking at the Details of the New Budget Legislation: Social Program Initiatives Decline Over Time While Upper-Income Tax Cuts Grow* (Washington, DC: Center on Budget and Policy Priorities, August 12, 1997), p. 11.

93. The phrase was probably first enunciated in 1983 by OMB Director David Stockman, who was predicting annual deficits of at least $200 billion. See "A Plea from David Stockman," *Washington Post* (April 20, 1983).

94. U.S. Congressional Budget Office, *Budget Options, Part I*, Table I. The years covered are 2002–2011. CBO has since adjusted its February 2001, projection, based on "current policies and assumptions."

95. U.S. Office of Management and Budget, *Budget of the United States Government, Fiscal Year 2007*, Table 1.1. These funds would be included in the budget according to generally accepted accounting practices, but Congress excludes them by law.

96. U.S. Government Accountability Office, *Social Security Reform: Answers to Key Questions*, p. 22.

97. U.S. General Accounting Office, *Social Security Reform: Analysis of a Trust Fund Exhaustion Scenario Illustrates the Difficult Choices and the Need for Early Action*, GAO–03–1038T (Washington, DC: U.S. Government Printing Office, 2003), p. 1.

98. Research and Policy Committee, Committee for Economic Development, *Exploding Deficits, Declining Growth*, pp. 11–12. We are referring to the process established by the Congressional Budget and Impoundment Control Act of 1974, explained later in the chapter.

99. Alan Schick, "The Deficit That Didn't Just Happen: A Sober Perspective on the Budget," *Brookings Review* 20 (Spring 2002), p. 46.

100. As derived from data presented in Figure 2-1 in: Research and Policy Committee, Committee for Economic Development, *Exploding Deficits, Declining Growth*, p. 11.

101. Philip G. Joyce and Roy T. Meyers, "Budgeting During the Clinton Presidency," *Public Budgeting and Finance Review* 21 (Spring 2001), p. 8.

102. Robert Kogan, *Swelling Deficits: Increased Spending Is Not the Principal Culprit* (Washington: DC: Center on Budget and Policy Priorities, 2003), p. 1. Growth in federal spending is for 2001–2003.

103. Isaac Shapiro, *Federal Income Taxes, As a Share of GDP, Dropped to Lowest Level since 1942, According to Final Budget Data* (Washington, DC: Center on Budget and Policy Priorities, 2003), p. 1. In 2003, total federal revenue as a share of GDP dropped to 16.6 percent. Federal income taxes dropped to 8.6 percent of GDP, the lowest level since 1942. Inadequate information technology in the IRS, and Congress's budgetary stinginess, also have cut federal revenue. Antiquated computers reduce federal revenue by 15 percent, and the number of IRS auditors shrank by 28 percent, 1995–2002. See Mary Dalrymple, Associated Press, "IRS Measures $300 Billion Tax Gap, Fails to Charge Interest on Tax Penalties," *Savannah Morning News* (March 30, 2005) and Paul Krugman, "Business as Usual," *New York Times* (October 22, 2002.) In 2005, federal fortunes reversed, and there was 15 percent surge in revenue. Federal spending in that year grew by 8 percent.

104. Period covered is 2001–2005.

105. William G. Gale and Peter Orszag, *Bush Administration Tax Policy: Revenue and Budget Effects* (Washington, DC: Tax Policy Center, 2004), p. 1. Period covered is 2001–2014. The tax cuts enacted in 2001 are set to expire in 2014 if Congress fails to make them permanent.

106. John Steele Gordon, *Hamilton's Blessing: The Extraordinary Life and Times of our National Debt* (New York: Walker, 1997), p. 5. Emphasis is original.

107. Aaron Wildavsky, *The Politics of the Budgetary Process*, 2nd ed. (Boston: Little, Brown, 1974); Richard A. Fenno, Jr., *The Power of the Purse: Appropriation Politics in Congress* (Boston: Little, Brown, 1966); and Jesse Burkhead, *Government Budgeting* (New York: John Wiley, 1956).

108. Wildavsky, *The Politics of the Budgetary Process*, p. 64.

109. The following discussion of budgetary strategy is drawn from ibid., pp. 63–127.

110. Quoted in ibid., p. 120.

111. Jeffrey McMurray, Associated Press, "Tight Budgets Heighten Scrutiny of F/A-22 Raptor," *Savannah Morning News* (April 4, 2004). The representative quoted is John Murtha of Pennsylvania.

112. Much of the following discussion, at least as it pertains through the 1960s, is based on: Bertram M. Gross, "The New Systems Budgeting," *Public Administration Review* 29 (March/April 1969), pp. 113–137; and Allen

Schick, "The Road to PPB: The Stages of Budget Reform," *Public Administration Review* 26 (December 1966), pp. 243–258.

113. Janet M. Kelly, "A Century of Public Budgeting Reform: The 'Key' Question," *Administration and Society* (March 2005), pp. 89–109.

114. Wildavsky, *The Politics of the Budgetary Process*, p. 4.

115. Irene S. Rubin, "Early Budget Reformers: Democracy, Efficiency, and Budget Reforms," *American Review of Public Administration* 24 (September 1994) pp. 229–252.

116. Charles G. Dawes, *The First Year of the Budget of the United States* (Washington, DC: U.S. Government Printing Office, 1923), p. ii.

117. Verne B. Lewis, "Reflections on Budget Systems," *Public Budgeting and Finance* 8 (Spring 1988), p. 7.

118. Executive Order 8248, as quoted in Schick, "The Road to PPB," p. 250.

119. Commission on Organization of the Executive Branch of Government, *Budgeting and Accounting* (Washington, DC: U.S. Government Printing Office, 1949), p. 8.

120. U.S. General Accounting Office, *Performance Budgeting: State Experiences and Implications for the Federal Government*, GAO/AFMD–93–41 (Washington, DC: U.S. Government Printing Office, 1993), p. 1.

121. Quoted in Allen Schick, *Budget Innovation in the States* (Washington, DC: Brookings, 1971), p. 127.

122. Quoted in U.S. General Accounting Office, *Performance Budgeting: Past Initiatives Offer Insights for GPRA Implementation*, GAO/AIMD–97–46 (Washington, DC: U.S. Government Printing Office, 1997), p. 34.

123. This definition is based on one contained in ibid., p. 35.

124. Christopher G. Reddick, "Testing Rival Theories of Budgetary Decision-Making in the US States," *Financial Accountability and Management* 19 (Winter 2004), pp. 315–335. The author examined state budgeting practices as conducted from 1960 to 1996. The quotation is on p. 315.

125. Peter Drucker, *The Practice of Management* (New York: Harper & Row, 1954).

126. Jong S. Jun, "Management by Objectives and the Public Sector, Introduction," *Public Administration Review* 26 (January/February 1976), p. 3.

127. Theodore H. Poister and Gregory Streib, "MBO in Municipal Government: Variations on the Traditional Management Tool," *Public Administration Review* 55 (January/February 1995), p. 54.

128. Robert Rodgers and John E. Hunter, "A Foundation of Good Management Practice in Government: Management by Objectives," *Public Administration Review* 52 (January/February 1992), p. 34.

129. Poister and Streib, "MBO in Municipal Government," p. 55.

130. See Peter A. Phyrr, "The Zero Base Approach to Government Budgeting," *Public Administration Review* 37 (January/February 1977), p. 7; and Thomas P. Lauth, "Zero-Base Budgeting in Georgia State Government: Myth and Reality," *Public Administration Review* 38 (September/October 1978), pp. 420–430.

131. Aaron Wildavsky and Arthur Hammond, "Comprehensive Versus Incremental Budgeting in the Department of Agriculture," *Administrative Science Quarterly* 10 (December 1965), pp. 321–346.

132. Frank D. Draper and Bernard T. Pitsvada, "ZBB—Looking Back After Ten Years," *Public Administration Review* 41 (January/February 1981), pp. 76–83. The principal studies of ZBB's use in the public sector are: Allen Schick, *Zero-Base 80: The Status of Zero-Base Budgeting in the States* (Washington, DC: National Association of State Budget Officers and The Urban Institute, 1979); Perry Moore, "Zero-Base Budgeting in American Cities," *Public Administration Review* 40 (May/June 1980), pp. 253–258; and, for the federal experience, Frank D. Draper and Bernard T. Pitsvada, *A First Year's Assessment of ZBB in the Federal Government—Another View* (Arlington, VA: Association of Government Accountants, 1978); Frank D. Draper and Barnard T. Pitsvada, "Congress and Executive Branch Budget Reform: The House Appropriation Committee and Zero-Base Budgeting," *International Journal of Public Administration* 2 (3, 1980), pp. 331–374; Comptroller General of the United States, *Streamlining Zero-Base Budgeting Will Benefit Decision-Making*, PAD–79–74 (Washington, DC: U.S. General Accounting Office, 1979); and Comptroller General of the United States, *Budget Formulation: Many Approaches but Some Improvements Are Needed*. Report to the House Committee on Government Operations, PAD–80–31 (Washington, DC: U.S. General Accounting Office, 1980). See also Thomas H. Hammond and Jack H. Knott, *A Zero-Based Look at Zero-Base Budgeting* (New Brunswick, NJ: Transaction, 1980), for a more general treatment.

133. Harry P. Hatry, "The Alphabet Soup Approach: You'll Love It!" *Public Manager* 21 (Winter 1992–1993), p. 9.

134. Cited in U.S. General Accounting Office, *Performance Budgeting: Past Initiatives Offer Insights for GPRA Implementation*, p. 49.

135. Lewis, "Reflections on Budget Systems," p. 4.

136. Irene S. Rubin, "Budgeting for Our Times: Target Base Budgeting," *Public Budgeting and Finance* 11 (Fall 1991), p. 6.

137. Penelope Lemov, "The Decade of Red Ink," *Governing* (August 1992), pp. 22–26.

138. Much of the following discussion is based on the chapter by Frank Sackton, "Financing Public Programs Under Fiscal Constraints," in Robert E. Cleary and Nicholas Henry, eds., *Managing Public Programs: Balancing Politics, Administration, and Public Needs* (San Francisco: Jossey-Bass, 1989), pp. 147–166. Among the better examples of the cutback management literature are: Charles H. Levine and Irene Rubin, eds., *Fiscal Stress and Public Policy* (Beverly Hills, CA: Sage, 1980); E. K. Keller, ed., *Managing With Less* (Washington, DC: International City Management Association, 1979); G. W. Wynn, ed., *Learning from Abroad—Cutback Management: A Trinational Perspective*

(New Brunswick, NJ: Transaction Books, 1983); and Charles Levine, Irene S. Rubin, and G. Wolohojian, *The Politics of Retrenchment: How Local Governments Manage Fiscal Stress* (Beverly Hills, CA: Sage, 1981).

139. National Commission on the Public Service, *Urgent Business for America: Revitalizing the Federal Government for the 21st Century*, Report of the National Commission on the Public Service (Washington, DC: U.S. Government Printing Office, 2003), p. 36.

140. Richard C. Elling, *Public Management in the States: A Comparative Study of Administrative Performance and Politics* (Westport, CT: Praeger, 1992).

141. John E. Petersen, "Productivity Pinch," *Governing* (September 2003), p. 62.

142. Michael A. Fletcher, "A Sea Change in the Secretarial Pool," *Washington Post* (May 11, 2000). Susie M. Grant is quoted.

143. Robert C. Burns and Robert D. Lee, Jr., "The Ups and Downs of State Budget Process Reform: Experience of Three Decades," *Public Budgeting and Finance* 24 (Fall 2004), p. 4. In 1975, 28 percent of state budgets ranked priorities, and in 2000, 81 percent did. These polls include the District of Columbia,

144. Sackton, "Financing Public Programs Under Fiscal Constraints," pp. 147–166.

145. Dan A. Cochran, "Entrepreneurial Budgeting: An Emerging Reform?" *Public Administration Review* 53 (September/October 1993), pp. 445–454.

CHAPTER 9

Managing Human Resources in the Public Sector

Two-thirds of Americans have jobs, and 16 percent of this labor force, or more than twenty-one million workers, are employed by governments.[1] Managing them is a challenge of no modest dimensions.

The traditional field of personnel administration has expanded its intellectual boundaries and now is called "human resource management." *Public human resource management* is the administration of and policymaking for people and positions in the public sector.

Who Wants to Work for Government?

A basic human resource challenge for governments is that of finding people of talent, commitment, and energy who want to work in them. In other words, recruiting applicants of high quality. Quality, however, must be understood in relative terms, and what might have been perceived as a superior applicant a decade ago may not be so regarded today.

A Rising Bar

This shifting standard is the result of both private and public employers' rising expectations of their employees. For example, a survey of twenty-one large corporations in a representative array of industries found that close to three-fourths of the firms reported that they had raised the levels of numeracy, literacy, and cognition needed by employees over the last five years, and 71 percent, as a consequence, perceived an "overall reduction in candidates with necessary skills."[2] A similar phenomenon is happening in the public sector. Nearly three-fourths of thirty-three federal agencies surveyed foresaw higher skill and educational levels being needed for their own workforces.[3]

A Shrinking Pool?

About one American prefers working in government for almost every three Americans who would rather work in business. "Governments face an enormous challenge in attracting the best and brightest of the younger generation into public service. . . . and the pool seems to be shrinking," according to a major study of American attitudes toward government employment. The survey found that the proportion of respondents who preferred government employment dropped by one-third, from 28 percent to 19 percent, over a ten-year period. By significant margins, people of color, veterans, Democrats, and older citizens preferred government jobs more than white people, those who have not served in the military, Republicans, and younger Americans.[4] Nearly one-third of Americans born before 1940 prefer public-sector jobs, but less than one-fifth of those born since 1960 prefer them, and "the desire to work for government is likely to continue declining."[5] Only a third of young adults say that the idea of government service appeals to them, and this represents a decline from two-fifths only two years earlier.[6] No doubt, their parents, teachers, and other older people have had a hand in this decline. Only 11 percent of parents, and 24 percent of high school teachers, rank government as the most desirable career choice,[7] and more than half, 54 percent, of adults would not recommend to young people that they "start their careers in politcs/government."[8]

These views seem to be having an impact on more highly educated young people. Just 26 percent of recent college graduates say that they are "very interested" in working for government, compared to nearly three times that proportion, 73 percent, who say that they are "just somewhat" or "not at all interested" in working for government.[9]

Governments, in short, may not be able to attract the talent needed to run them well. To stave off this looming "crisis in public service," the federal government has attempted to assure its bureaucrats the "freedom to manage," and to make federal jobs "more challenging, more satisfying, and more fulfilling."[10] A nonprofit Partnership for Public Service was founded in 2001 designed to attract more talent to the federal government.

A Less Talented Pool?

A shrinking pool of prospective public administrators could imply a less talented pool, and there is some concern about the prospects of recruiting able people to the public service. Most federal supervisors, for example, think that the quality of their applicant pools has declined—less than a third, in fact, perceive the quality of applicants for entry-level professional and administrative jobs to have improved.[11] At the state level, analysts who developed a statistical model of hiring professionals concluded that "the size of the applicant pool for career professional positions is not likely to be large [and] the quality of the applicant pool is not likely to be very strong."[12]

And they may be right. Although almost half of the entering employees of the federal government have college diplomas in specifically useful fields, less than 3 percent have any training in political science or public affairs, and are "largely untutored in the most basic structural, procedural, and institutional knowledge of government."[13] Surveys have found that not only do most college students fail to regard the government as their first choice as an employer,[14] but also that the better students are much less likely to consider public service as their top employment preference; just 5 percent of college students admitted to honor societies rank the government as their "most preferred employer," compared to 34 percent who prefer large corporations.[15]

So, who wants to work for the government? Fewer people than a few decades ago, and possibly fewer people of talent.

Who Works for Government?

In light of these realities, how successful have governments been in their recruiting? Have they hired people of competency and commitment? In general, despite the possible decline in the quality of the potential labor pool, the answer is that they have.

The Public Workforce

Objective evidence suggests that the federal workforce remains one of high quality. A comparison of applicants who declined or accepted offers of federal employment found "little difference in the education levels and grade point averages" between the two groups,[16] although a later analysis determined that, over a four-year period, educational levels had declined slightly among new federal hires.[17] An extensive study concluded that a rise in the quality of federal workers was the major reason accounting for the proportional increase over sixteen years of employees who occupied higher positions in the federal hierarchy.[18]

As we detail later, state and local governments also employ workers of high quality, and that quality is rising over time; this acceleration has been particularly rapid in state governments. Measures of education and professionalism for state and local employees have been steadily rising for decades and long have matched or surpassed comparable measures for federal employees.[19]

Keeping Public Talent

Have governments been able to retain their employees, or are the more able ones departing for other sectors? The patterns are mixed.

At the federal level, surveys indicate that, although 37 percent of federal employees claim that they plan to look for another job in the coming year, more than half of these same respondents state that they would actually accept another job only if it were still in government, and less than a tenth would take another job only if it were outside government.[20] However, few federal employees actually leave, and those who do depart may not be the best. At least one analysis, based on a massive data set, found that there was "no evidence to support the conclusion that the federal government is losing its most capable employees," a finding "consistent with previous research on the exit quality of federal employees."[21]

Regrettably, the same cannot be said for state and local governments, where there is a brain drain. States are losing high-quality male employees and managers, and local governments are losing high-quality minority and female employees and clerical workers.[22]

Some good news: Not all government workers who leave their governments are heading for the greener pastures of corporate America. Almost a fourth, 23 percent, of those federal, state, and local employees who leave their governments acquire jobs in other governments.[23]

Every public employee works in at least one of four "systems" of human resource management, each one of which represents differing values and philosophies. One is the Civil Service System. The remaining three—the Collective, Political Executive, and Professional Public Administration systems—have evolved, at least

to some degree, as reactions to the Civil Service System.

The Civil Service System: The Meaning of Merit

The civil service has been the historic heart of public administration. The general *Civil Service System*, or *merit system*,[24] is career personnel who have tenure and who are administered according to "traditional merit practices."[25]

The Meaning of Merit

What are these practices? The central traditional merit practices are position, tests, and civil-service sovereignty.

The Position. Most centrally, the overriding practice of the merit system is the emphasis that is placed on the *position*: defining its duties, responsibilities, requirements, and qualifications. The Civil Service System assumes: that government positions can be scientifically, objectively, and correctly classified; that the best person can be scientifically, objectively, and correctly placed in each position; and that pay, based on the principle of equal pay for equal work, can be scientifically, objectively, and correctly determined for each position.

Hiring by Score. Traditional merit practices also focus on how public administrators are hired. Entry into the civil service is determined by the "merit" of applicants, and merit, traditionally, is determined by the score one earns on competitive entrance examinations. Gender, race, religion, family, politics, connections, and other nonmeritorious factors are irrelevant. Egalitarianism and political neutrality reign supreme.

A Sovereign Civil Service. Finally, the "merit principle," as it often is called, also demands that human resource management be sovereign and separate from the rest of government, and that the hiring and staffing decisions made by personnel administrators must be unilateral and final. To do otherwise ultimately would undermine the objectivity and neutrality of the merit principle itself, which would, in turn, lead to less efficient, more partisan, and more corrupt government.

Sounds good, but there were problems. Most notably, a sovereign civil service led to a highly regulated civil service. "The merit system, as the civil service personnel system came to be called, created passive roles for both managers and personnel specialists in a system of centralized regulation and compliance," and this emphasis on "compliance with regulations became the central focus of the personnel system."[26]

The Murkiness of Merit.   These essentially ethical and faith-based (faith, that is, in science, not religion) values underlie the Civil Service System. As we shall see throughout our discussion of public human resource management systems, however, "Developments since World War II have

---

The First Reform

Although the civil service of the United States got off to a good start at the nation's founding (it would have been hard to get off to a bad start with Washington, Adams, Jefferson, Madison, and Monroe as its first presidents), problems of patronage and politics surfaced, beginning in the 1840s. The following passage describes these issues, and what was done about them.

When independence was declared in 1779, over four-fifths of the states required that, to vote, male citizens must own land or have paid taxes (often the two were one and the same), but by 1830, only half of the states retained such stipulations. When this dramatic expansion of the suffrage was combined with a populist candidate—in the form of Andrew Jackson (1829–37) in the election of 1828—voting participation more than tripled from only four years earlier and surpassed half of the eligible voters for the first time in American history.

Contrary to conventional wisdom, Jackson's pattern of top appointments actually was quite similar to those of his establishmentarian predecessors, and, although Jackson seems to have tried to reach out to lower rungs of American society in making his major appointments, these exceptions were not appreciable in number. John Tyler (1841–45) was the first president who implemented a comprehensive spoils system, a practice that reached its apex with the presidency of Abraham Lincoln (1861–65), whose "sweep of people from office was the most extensive in United States history" (Cayer, p. 22).

It is difficult for those of us reared in an environment of largely honest government to appreciate the extent—and the brazenness—of the spoils system in the 1800s. After an election, newspaper advertising typically swelled with such announcements as, "WANTED—A GOVERNMENT CLERKSHIP at a salary of not less that $1000 per annum. Will give $100 to anyone securing me such a position." Following the election of 1880, newly elected President James A. Garfield, according to a government archive, found "hungry office-seekers lying in wait for him like vultures for a wounded bison."

The corrupt excesses of the spoils system eventually resulted in a reform movement determined to rid government of those bureaucrats who owed their office to no more than party hackwork. The assassination of President Garfield by a deranged office-seeker in 1881 (who helpfully shouted his support for the spoils system immediately after shooting the president) effectively assured national legislation of civil service reform.

befogged the meaning of merit principles and confused the content of merit systems."[27]

The Scope of Merit

Merit systems made steady progress in all American governments over the course of the twentieth century. In the twenty-first century, however, there is clear and growing evidence of shrinkage.

The Faltering Federal Merit System. At the federal level, the progress made by merit systems began in 1884, following the passage of the Civil Service Act, which in that year covered not much more than one out of every ten federal civilian employees. Its coverage steadily expanded and, a century after the act's enactment, well over nine out of ten federal civil servants were managed under its auspices.[28]

Since then, the coverage of Washington's Civil Service System has declined precipitously. We

---

After just two years following Garfield's assassination, Congress passed the Civil Service Act (the Pendleton Act) of 1883. The act created a bipartisan Civil Service Commission (which was succeeded in 1978 by the Office of Personnel Management) responsible to the president and charged with the duty of filling government positions by a process of open, competitive examinations. Civil service reform spread almost instantly. New York enacted its own civil service act in the same year that Congress passed the federal version; Massachusetts did so the following year; and eight more states had passed civil service acts by 1920.

There were at least two enduring and interrelated effects of the Civil Service Act, one moral and the other political—or, more precisely, apolitical.

The reformers associated the reformed civil service "with morality, with a connotation of 'goodness' vs. 'badness,' quite apart from the purposes for which people were employed." This connotation resulted in "government by the good," or government by ethical public administrators in contrast to corrupt political machines, at least in eyes of the intellectuals (Mosher, pp. 68, 66).

A related effect of the Civil Service Act was the firm establishment of the idea that the government bureaucracy was politically and administratively neutral. In 1907, President Theodore Roosevelt (1901–09) mandated Civil Service Rule I, which prohibited almost seven out of ten federal workers from participating in political campaigns and barred the solicitation of political contributions from federal employees. These reforms were strengthened and broadened by the Political Activities Act (the Hatch Act) of 1939. Although in 1993 Congress allowed federal employees to participate in political campaigns, they still may not be candidates in partisan elections or engage in political activity while on duty.

Over time, the civil service commissions at the federal, state, and local levels, and the personnel departments that they spawned, evolved into buffers against political pressure brought on by elected officials. In this development, public personnel administration as a field gradually was disassociated from the substantive and managerial functions of government. To put it far too crassly but clearly: The bureaucrats responsible for getting a job done and the bureaucrats responsible for keeping government neutral and apolitical (and, hence, moral) became increasingly distinct entities.

Sources: Erik W. Austin, *Political Facts of the United States Since 1789* (New York: Oxford University Press, 1989); N. Joseph Cayer, *Public Personnel Administration in the United States*, 2nd ed. (New York: St. Martin's, 1986); Ann Gerhart, "A New Deal," *Washington Post* (March 28, 2005); Frederick C. Mosher, *Democracy and the Public Service*, 2nd ed. (New York: Oxford University Press, 1982); and O. Glenn Stahl, *Public Personnel Administration*, 8th ed. (New York: Harper & Row, 1983).

can trace this decline, at least in part, by following how many civilian employees are covered by the General Schedule, which is the federal government's main position classification and pay system for the general civil service.

By the early 2000s, the General Schedule's coverage had fallen from more than nine out of ten career employees two decades earlier to fewer than eight out of ten.[29] About half of all civilian workers were exempt from at least some of the traditional regulations associated with the civil service.[30]

During the mid-2000s, Congress enacted legislation that, in essence, removed an additional two-fifths of federal civilian employees from the merit system.[31] So, in very rough terms, the traditional Civil Service System covers only, at best, four out of ten of all federal civilian employees; the rest are in other human resource systems or in agencies that have radically weakened traditional civil service policies. The General Schedule "is broken. It cannot repaired. . . . At this stage it has no defenders."[32]

This evisceration of the federal Civil Service System has been so sudden, so swift, and so severe that the Government Accountability Office (GAO), which has itself been freed from the General Schedule, warns that "the federal government is quickly approaching the point where 'standard governmentwide' human capital policies and processes are neither standard nor governmentwide," and urges that steps be taken "to avoid further fragmentation within the civil service."[33] Failure to take these steps will assure greater inconsistencies that will result in increasingly unfair practices within the federal workforce.

State and Local Merit Systems. Congress encouraged state and local governments to adopt merit systems with the 1939 amendments to the Social Security Act, which mandated merit systems in states receiving federal assistance. These amendments, of course, produced merit systems in all states that did not already have them.

By the 1970s, every state had at least a major portion of its employees working under the merit system.[34] Since then, there has been some significant deterioration of the merit principle in the states, and we review this deterioration later in the chapter.

Merit systems are prevalent in American local governments. Excluding education, civil service protection covers an estimated 95 percent of municipal employees,[35] and two dozen states require their cities to adopt merit systems.[36] The merit principle is used less extensively in counties, although nineteen states require its use in their counties, at least to some degree.[37]

The Profession of Public Human Resource Management

Nearly 620,000 people are employed as professional human resource managers and professionals in the United States, and over 13 percent, or more than 80,000 of these managers and professionals, work in the public sector.[38] Over two-fifths of public human resource managers are women, more than nine out of ten are college graduates, and they have long career histories in their field and in government.[39] Public personnel administrators appear to have a high job satisfaction, and most perceive their jobs as being a long-term professional career.[40]

What do public human resource managers do? In essence, they are charged with refining and enforcing the merit system. Their major duties, listed in the approximate order of the most time that they devote to them, are recruiting and hiring; benefits administration; pay administration; developing human resources policy, such as retirement plans or the constraints on political involvement by public employees; position classification; training and development; processing grievances; performance appraisals; performance measurement; brokering conflict; managing diversity; and collective bargaining, among other activities.[41]

Hiring Bureaucrats

Hiring new employees of high quality is an important task in all governments. A study of white-collar jobs in the federal government found that, when robust selection procedures were used, a 17 percent increase in productivity accompanied their use.[42]

Unfortunately, the evidence indicates that governments are not particularly adept at hiring. Almost three-fourths of Americans report that no one (including, presumably, government human resource agencies) has *ever* asked them if they would consider working in government and the small percentage who have been asked is declining significantly over time.[43]

We consider here how the processes of hiring employees take place in the national, state, and local governments.

A Federal Sojourn.   Between 1955 and 1974, the federal government gained most of its new recruits to the civil service through the Federal Service Entrance Examination, its first "universal" instrument for selecting college graduates for entry into management positions, and which tested general verbal and quantitative skills. In 1974, it was replaced with the Professional and Administrative Career Examination, which tested not only general competencies but also attempted to gauge the professional training of applicants. Blacks failed this examination in substantially greater numbers than did whites, and in 1981 the Office of Personnel Management signed a consent decree in which it agreed to eliminate its use.

Between 1981 and 1990, the finding of an entry-level administrative position in the federal government was, as the director of the Office of Personnel Management phrased it, "intellectually confusing, procedurally nightmarish, inaccessible to students and very difficult to explain,"[44] and it was unclear at best that a more representative or talented federal service was being hired.[45]

The courts demanded that the federal government develop a replacement examination, and in 1990, the Office of Personnel Management introduced a new "universal" test for selecting applicants for entry-level management positions in the federal government, called Administrative Careers With America. Administrative Careers With America proved disappointing. Few agencies used it to hire people,[46] so, four years after its introduction, the Office of Personnel Management essentially abandoned the test, although it is still used, if rarely.

A Federal Frustration.   The recruiting and hiring of new federal employees is no longer a major activity; with federal downsizing, a relatively small number, around 80,000, new hires are made per year, of whom about a tenth are for entry-level professional and administrative positions.[47] One observer has noted that "since it appears that so little recruiting is being done at the national level, describing the problem [of attracting talent] as a 'recruitment' problem may be a misnomer."[48]

Even in the face of low levels of hiring, however, federal recruitment remains beset with problems. As many as a third of all federal job openings are never publicly announced,[49] which may account for the fact that more than seven out of ten "new" federal hires are federal employees drawn from their own agency (46 percent) or other federal agencies (25 percent), and only 29 percent are truly "new hires" brought in from outside the federal bureaucracy.[50] Filling competitive service positions consumes more than three months, on average.[51]

One survey found that, relative to workers in the nonprofit and private sectors, federal workers were more likely to describe the hiring process that they had experienced as confusing and slow by margins better than two-to-one. Only three-quarters of federal workers said that their hiring process had been fair, compared to nine out of ten workers in the nonprofit and private sectors.[52]

Of graver importance, Washington may not be hiring the right applicants for its jobs. Almost two-fifths of federal employees think that their agencies are failing to hire people with the right skills.[53] If true, the reason is apparent: The main assessment methods that the federal government uses to select applicants for hire—assigning points based on applicants' self-reported training and experience—"is the least effective available predictor of job performance."[54]

The Federal Future.   Beginning in the 1990s, Washington began to rethink its recruitment and hiring processes. In 1994, the federal government moved to the World Wide Web and voice mail as its main means of recruiting and hiring. Called USA Jobs, citizens may use the Internet or call a toll-free number to learn of federal job openings by category and location. (See Appendix E for details.)

Also in that year, the Office of Personnel Management abandoned its infamous "Standard Form 171: Application for Federal Employment," a monstrous, multipaged affair that had been the cornerstone of federal hiring practices since 1938, and replaced it with some 650 "delegated examining units," which are agency-based offices that are authorized "to examine applicants for virtually every position in the competitive civil service."[55]

In an effort to further speed and simplify the federal hiring process, President Bill Clinton in 2000 issued Executive Order 13162, which created the Federal Career Intern Program as an alternative to competitive examinations, which traditionally has been the feds' primary hiring method. Of all the means that the federal government uses for hiring, the Federal Career Intern Program is the only one that has increased the number of new, outside hires in recent years, and now more new federal hires are executed through its auspices than through any other hiring method.[56]

Hiring in State Governments.   At the state level, it appears that hiring problems may reflect those of the federal government. One survey found that nearly six out of ten state agency heads thought that the most serious impediment to recruitment was low salaries; almost four out of ten cited the complexity of personnel procedures for recruiting; and nearly three out of ten faulted these procedures for hiring.[57] Researchers have concluded that "the hiring process will move very slowly" in the states for the foreseeable future.[58]

Hiring in Local Governments.   Locally, hiring continues to expand, and local governments rely on reasonably straightforward methods to recruit. The most popular recruitment tool is to simply announce available jobs. Six out of ten cities and counties post job vacancies on their Web sites, and almost six out of ten of those local governments that do not yet do this plan to do so.[59]

This practice this followed by the more proactive approach of soliciting recommendations from minority and women's organizations, state and private employment agencies, unions, and professional organizations. Cities and counties

also use internships as a recruiting tool.[60] Local governments rely heavily on written tests to hire—95 percent of large cities use them, at least sometimes, for entering into certain positions and the practice is growing.[61]

Classifying Bureaucrats

Once hired, bureaucrats are classified. The position classification system is a core tenet of the civil service, irrespective of governmental level.

Washington's General Schedule.   In 1923, as a result of increasingly vocal dissatisfaction over the lack of rigor in federal pay policies (federal supervisors had unlimited autonomy to determine the pay of workers), and an ongoing commitment to establishing equal work for equal pay, Congress passed the Classification Act. The act established what is now the Classification Programs Division of the Office of Personnel Management to group public positions into rational classes on the bases of comparable duties, responsibilities, and skills.

A new and more comprehensive Classification Act was enacted in 1949. This act established the dominant classification and pay system for the federal government, the General Schedule. The General Schedule is comprised of fifteen grades for white-collar workers, and within these grades there are more than 450 job categories called "series." At the very top are the 8,000 members of the Senior Executive Service, which in 1978 replaced what were widely but informally known as the "supergrades," or Grades 16 through 18, as the grades for these executives.

At the dawn of the twenty-first century, some three-quarters of federal civilian employees were clearly covered by the General Schedule. Today, the extent of the General Schedule's coverage is considerably less clear due to recent regulations and legislation, noted earlier.

Classifying at the Grass Roots.   Almost all state governments, and virtually all local governments, now have position classification systems. A dozen states require their cities to adopt classification plans.[62] Most cities and counties use a single classification system for all employees, although many (as with the federal government) use different classification plans for different kinds of employees, such as clerks, trades people, professionals, and executives. The smaller the jurisdiction, the more likely there will be multiple classification systems.[63]

Within this context, however, there is a turning away by state and local governments from classification systems that replicates what is happening at the federal level. "The position classification technology that has prevailed" in governments since the early years of the twentieth century "is under full retreat in large numbers of subnational jurisdictions."[64]

Broadbanding.   Some observers believe that position classification systems have grown overly complicated and calcified. The average number of job classifications in a state government, for instance, is around 2,000.[65] As a consequence, various groups associated with reforming government have recommended *broadbanding, paybanding,* or *salary banding,*[66] all of which refer to the reduction of job classifications into broad bands of job "families." Broadbanding job classifications is generally thought to facilitate more effective recruiting and to be a necessary first step before more flexible and agile managerial reforms can be successfully installed.

Washington is moving with increasing speed toward paybanding.[67] The National Commission on the Public Service has recommended that the fifteen pay grades in the General Schedule be roughly halved in number.[68]

The grass-roots governments also are turning to salary banding. Thirty states reduced their job classifications during the 1990s (although fifteen added more),[69] and one survey found that 56 percent of cities had consolidated some position classifications.[70]

Paying Bureaucrats

The position classification of bureaucrats is the foundation for determining their pay.

Public and Private Pay.   Overall, public employees do well compared to private workers.

But the compensatory perks of public employment pool in blue-collar ponds. In general, blue-collar and lower-level white-collar government workers are paid as much or more, and usually have better benefits, than their counterparts in the private sector.[71]

As one ascends the organizational ladder, however, these comparative advantages diminish and eventually disappear. When one reaches the topmost rungs, the pay and benefits of government executives do not remotely approach the stratospheric levels of their corporate counterparts, who often enjoy multimillion-dollar compensation packages, yet manage funds of comparable or lesser size.[72]

In part, this condition persists because Americans do not like paying their top public servants well. One survey found that only 13 percent of the citizenry thought that the salaries of public administrators should be raised "to encourage the best people to go into government,"[73] so keeping public-sector salaries competitive with private-sector salaries is a delicate business.

Nowhere is this delicacy more in evidence than in the federal civil service.

Raising and Reforming Federal Salaries. There are four pay systems for federal civilian employees: the General Schedule; the Federal Pay Wage System, which covers some 300,000 blue-collar workers; the Postal Field Service System, and various remaining pay systems that are of limited scope, such as that of the Foreign Service.

In part because of presidential recalcitrance, the salary situation for federal administrators was, by the early 1990s, reaching critical conditions.[74] Frustrations over compensation and advancement were the major reasons given by more than seven out ten federal employees who left the civil service for the private sector—where they earned, on the average, a fourth higher salaries![75]

In 1990, Congress took a significant step toward rectifying the problem of federal pay by enacting the Federal Employees Pay Comparability Act. The act represented a new federal pay system and implemented large pay hikes for top federal administrators.

The Federal Employees Pay Comparability Act sets federal pay by a position's comparability with the private sector and by locality (73 percent of federal employees work in places other than the District of Columbia[76]). The act proved to be breakthrough legislation that speedily reinvigorated the federal service. The proportion of top federal administrators who were satisfied with their salaries burgeoned by nearly eightfold following its passage,[77] and the percentage of all federal workers who were satisfied with their salaries almost doubled.[78]

Doing Good and Doing Well at the Grass Roots. In general terms, public workers at the grass roots are paid well—arguably, quite well.

The total compensation costs (that is, employee pay plus benefits) of all state and local government employers are nearly $35 per hour worked. The total compensation costs for private-sector employers are less than $24 per hour worked. So the compensation costs of state and local employers are over two-thirds more than those of private employers. For many years, the compensation costs of both sets of these employers have each been consistently increasing at exactly the same rate—slightly more than 3 percent annually—so it is likely that these disparities will continue well into the future.[79]

Of course, the compensatory advantage of state and local employees relative to those in the private sector concentrates at the lower end of the pay scale, just as it does for all public workers, and pertains much less, if at all, to grass-roots executives. Still, if top state and local administrators earn less than the chief executive officers of large companies, they appear to earn more than their federal counterparts.

Even after the passage of the Federal Employees Pay Comparability Act, the compensation of federal executives is not "on a par . . . with counterpart positions in state or local government."[80] As a respected British publication put it, "The secretaries of state and defense . . . are paid less than the city manager of Phoenix, Arizona, and the director of higher education in Georgia."[81]

Appendix E has more detailed information on government salaries at all levels.

Training Bureaucrats

Public administrators usually may avail themselves of ongoing training programs designed to hone their skills. Training is beneficial for numerous reasons, not the least of which is public employee happiness; 60 percent of local government employees who receive training benefits report that they "like their jobs very much," compared to only 48 percent who do not receive such benefits.[82]

The principal purpose of training is to enhance employee productivity, and it generally appears to be successful in doing so. The Australian government—often cited as a model of efficient and effective public administration—spends an impressive 5 percent of its budget on employee training, and Australians cite upgraded training programs as being the "most useful" of their government's innovations.[83] Similarly, "the most effective private firms" spend from 3 percent to 5 percent on training.[84]

Regrettably, many American governments fall somewhat short of these standards.

Training Feds. Most in-service training in the federal government emerged when the Government Employees Training Act was enacted in 1958. As a further stimulus President Lyndon B. Johnson issued Executive Order 11348 in 1967, which resulted in the founding of what is now the Office of Training and Development and Regional Training Centers around the country. A year later, Johnson followed this up with the inauguration of the Federal Executive Institute.

Although some 200,000 federal employees participate in training programs each year, it appears that in the past Washington has undervalued the role of training. The federal government spends not much more than 1 percent of its budget on training,[85] and, worse, federal administrators are prone to focus on agency training programs when they need to cut budgets, and to cut them back more than other programs.[86]

There are indications that these traditional attitudes are changing for the better. Federal managers report a steady rise over a half-dozen years in their training for seven tasks that pertain to results-oriented government, such as developing performance measures. From a third to a half of federal agencies, depending on the activity, now provide, arrange, or pay for such training.[87]

There is still some way to go. Although more than half of all federal employees think that they receive adequate training to do their jobs, over a fourth do not and feel "unprepared to perform the basic tasks of their jobs"; these figures are fairly stable over time. The number of federal workers who say that they need more training to do their jobs effectively, however, has risen from less than a third to almost half over eight years.[88]

Training at the Grass Roots. The states evidence a considerable interest in improving their training for their employees, and training is a growing area. But at least one survey of state training practices has concluded that there are some serious deficiencies, including a lack of follow-up analyses on whether training had the desired impact, and the need to improve ways in which training needs are assessed.[89]

Forty-six states impose training requirements on municipal employees, although most do so only for police and firefighters (only seven states impose training requirements for "other" city employees); forty-five states do so for county employees, including thirteen for employees "other" than police officers.[90]

Some training programs for state and local administrators are conducted in-house or by professional societies, such as state municipal leagues, but many (likely most) are done by universities.[91] One survey found that about four-fifths of state and local officials report that they have used university-based institutes for a variety of services and rank them as comparable to services furnished by the private sector; state and local administrators give their highest marks to university-based training programs of all types of services offered.[92]

Rating Bureaucrats' Performance

The great majority of public administrators are formally graded, or rated, on how well they perform their duties. This practice is known as *performance rating, performance assessment,* or *performance appraisal,* all of which refer to the

evaluation of an employee's actual achievements and productivity in his or her job.[93]

The merit principle, at least in its original manifestation, never really addressed the idea that bureaucrats should produce results. True, the merit principle pushed, and pushed hard, for governmental efficiency, but, during the time that governments were adopting the merit principle, efficient government meant merely honest government. If a government was not corrupt, then it was, by definition, efficient; it is, after all, challenging for a government to be efficient when its officials are regularly plundering the public till.

Hence, for many decades, an efficient, effective, and productive public administrator was, as a practical matter, defined as one who simply did not break laws and commit criminal acts. "Performance" was assessed in terms of how closely a bureaucrat adhered to regulations. Not a particularly high standard, perhaps, but one that was needed, certainly, in the second half of the nineteenth century and well into the twentieth.

This perspective began to alter in the 1940s. In 1949, the first Hoover Commission first proposed the use of performance ratings in government,[94] and the federal government, forty-nine states (Rhode Island is the exception),[95] and over four-fifths of cities and counties[96] now use performance assessments.

The Pit of Performance Assessment. In general, performance rating is one of the public sector's most complicated and vexing administrative activities.[97] Public administrators are much more critical of performance assessment than are their counterparts in business.[98] Only a fifth of federal employees report that their performance appraisal system motivates them to do a better job, or even improve job-related communications between them and their supervisors![99] A survey of human resource managers found that nearly a third were "unsatisfied" or "very unsatisfied" with their organizations' performance assessment systems.[100] The problem, regrettably, is that the system of performance appraisal "stinks," and "employee reviews have devolved into an odious ritual that employees and managers alike would just as soon avoid."[101]

Rater bias, fuzzy performance standards, inadequate documentation and communication, process errors, and little or no training in the area are a few of the factors that reduce both the reliability and the reputation of public-sector performance rating.[102] Moreover, some public officials are far less susceptible to performance assessments than are others. Service to clients, for instance, can be measured by how many calls an administrator answers per hour, and how often his or her answers satisfy callers. But how does one quantify the performance of the international staff of the U.S. Treasury, which is supposed to monitor developments in the international economy, coordinate with other governments, and push for certain policies?[103]

One of the few clear benefits of performance appraisals, as they are currently administered, is a mostly negative one. Performance assessments document the performance of employees, or at least supervisors' opinions of that performance, and this documentation provides a vital paper trail that can justify negative actions, such as demotions and terminations, should these be deemed necessary.

The Prospects for Performance Assessment.
There is a flickering glimmer of hope on this human resource horizon, however. Increasingly, governments are realizing that if they are to improve their administration, they must create appraisal systems that are valid, positive, and respected. Research and the experience of other nations with performance appraisal[104] indicate that to successfully assess individual performance requires both personal and systemic approaches.

Assessor-to-Assessed. At the one-on-one, supervisor-to-subordinate level, it is increasingly appreciated that those administrators doing the assessing must be adequately trained in leading, managing, and communicating, including, certainly, setting clearly expressed performance measures that communicate precisely what is expected.[105] To mitigate against personal favoritism in the rating process, "independent reasonableness reviews" by outside agencies, such as human resource offices, and the emplacement of transparency and accountability mechanisms, such as publishing the overall results of performance appraisals, are necessary accoutrements.[106] Governments also are moving toward performance assessments that emphasize individual and flexible goal setting and casting performance appraisers as coaches rather than judges.[107]

System-to-Assessed. At the systemic level, governments should work hard at building meaningful consensus throughout their agencies for performance assessment systems, including developing a set of values and objectives to guide performance assessment.[108] Performance ratings work best when individual and organizational goals are closely aligned; individual competencies, as well as individual performance, are assessed; pay is linked not only to individual performance, but to overall organizational performance as well; and there is an agency-wide commitment to results-oriented performance management.[109]

Successful Performance Assessment Is Possible.
In essence, the research on performance appraisal seems to be in agreement on a single central point. That point is that performance assessment can work effectively only when it is embedded in the context of larger, integrated management systems that focus coherently on improving performance across the board—culturally, organizationally, and personally.[110]

When governments incorporate these values into their performance appraisal systems, the results can be dramatic. Washington State did so in 1998, replacing a traditional system that had registered a disapproval rate of 93 percent among the state's employees with a new performance assessment system that emphasized communication and collaboration and eliminated rating scales. Today, surveys of Washington's employees register a satisfaction level of 97 percent, "a staggering figure, considering the typical employee attitude toward performance appraisal."[111]

Rating Bureaucrats' Nonperformance

The dark side of performance appraisal is that it sometimes fails to identify "poor performers," or "nonperformers," as incompetent government employees are officially described.

Federal Incompetence. Precisely how many poor performers work for the federal government resides to some degree in the eye of the beholder, and the GAO admits that "the exact number of poor performers in the federal government is unknown."[112] Whatever the number, though, research suggests that even a few poor performers can have a negative impact on the productivity of the entire public workplace.[113]

Federal employees themselves report that up to a fourth of their coworkers "are not up to par," a figure that is essentially the same as estimates made by employees in the private sector about their coworkers.[114]

Deeper investigation finds both better and worse news. The better news is that there may be fewer poor performers than federal workers think; the worse new is that they are well-ensconced poor performers.

In unique and intensive interviews of 200 federal supervisors, it was determined that less than 4 percent of federal workers and supervisors could be classified as poor performers. Less than 4 percent of the federal workforce may not appear to be a major problem, until one calculates the numbers—about 54,000 permanent federal employees are viewed as poor performers. These poorly performing federal employees are deeply entrenched in their jobs, and average an astonishing fourteen years in the federal employ![115]

In light of such a depressing datum, it is little wonder that the public seems to regard government jobs as sinecure for life, and there are egregious examples in the federal workforce to feed the public's perception. Consider these examples: the part-timer who broke a Labor Department secretary's jaw when she complained about filing delays; the part-timer received a transfer, a permanent job, and a nearly $4,000 raise. Or the federal biologist who was let go because it took him four months to do what his supervisors could do in two days; he was reinstated because no one had explained what "too slow" meant. Or the letter carrier who was reinstated after pleading guilty to statutory rape on the logic that the victim was not on his route. Or the secretary fired for incompetence who was reinstated and transferred because coping with poor bosses had "induced a mental handicap that had to be tolerated."[116]

Fewer than 11,500 federal employees, or a fraction of 1 percent of the federal civilian workforce, are fired outright or leave voluntarily for reasons of poor performance (roughly a third), misconduct, or "other conduct-related deficiencies" each year, and another 1,400 or so are demoted or denied automatic salary increases because of poor performance.[117] These are not insignificant numbers, but, as the U.S. Merit Systems Protection Board itself notes, "removing or demoting inadequate performers still remains relatively rare in the civil service."[118]

Dealing with Federal Incompetents. Washington has not been effective in dealing with incompetents.

Sincere Supervisors. Federal supervisors are conscientious in trying to deal positively with poor performers. Well over half have supervised employees who had problems of performance (30 percent of supervisors), or conduct (7 percent), or both (22 percent), over the preceding two years; nearly nine out of ten supervisors who had to deal with these issues counseled the employee (and spent a remarkable five hours a week, on average, doing so[119]); fewer than one-in-ten took no action.[120] Nevertheless, the allocation of poor-performance assessments is negligible, and less than one-third of 1 percent of federal employees receive an "unacceptable" performance rating.[121]

Most federal managers seem to be at least trying to do their jobs in dealing with poor performers and miscreants. Are they doing their jobs effectively? To some degree, yes, they are. Nearly half of supervisors report that counseling improved employee performance, and over a third stated that taking formal action did so.[122]

Supine Systems. The federal system of dealing with incompetents, however, seems to be another matter. "Federal employee surveys and other indicators over at least the last 18 years suggest that most employees, including supervisors themselves, judge the response to poor performance to be inadequate."[123]

Fully two-thirds of federal employees believe that their organizations do not do a good job of disciplining poorly performing employees, compared to less than half in the private sector.[124]

Another survey found that not even a third of federal employees felt that their government did very or somewhat well in disciplining poor performers, compared to more than half of workers in the nonprofit and private sectors.[125]

The apparent inability of the feds to deal with their own incompetents waxes even more perplexing when we realize that federal employees have essentially no greater legal protections than do workers in any other sector. As one federal report observed, "legal protections for employees in the non-Federal sector are similar . . . to those in the Federal sector. This is true in both public [i.e., state and local] and private employment."[126]

At least part of the problem of dealing with federal incompetents is a tangled appeals process involving no fewer than five federal agencies, each of which varies in their authority, and each with its own procedures and body of case law. Any given case may be brought before one *or more* of these agencies, which, of course, further extends and confuses the appellate process.[127]

In sum, the problem of dealing with poor performers may be the single most serious human resource management problem in the federal government.

State Incompetents.   State governments also must deal with incompetent, but well-protected employees. A third of state agency heads think that personnel rules and procedures make it difficult to discipline or discharge poorly performing state employees.[128]

Nevertheless, states seem to be slowly limiting the rights of appeal that their employees long have had.[129] As a result, perhaps, the rate at which state employees are dismissed appears to at least marginally surpass that of the federal government.[130]

Local Incompetents.   It appears that local managers have taken greater care than have their counterparts in Washington and the states to assure themselves of some authority when dealing with nonperforming employees. A national survey of American cities found that 91 percent of those municipalities that have collective bargaining agreements with public employee unions (and more than nine out of ten cities do have such agreements) insert a management rights clause in at least one of their contracts.[131]

In addition, employee appeals of disciplinary action seem to be handled with much more dispatch in municipal governments than in the federal one, where federal employee complaints to the Equal Employment Opportunity Commission are backlogged for more than nine months.[132] The average length of time that it takes to resolve grievances in over nine out of ten cities, by contrast, is fewer than three months.[133]

Securing Bureaucrats' Jobs

The popular image of the Civil Service System is one of a job for life. But is it accurate? Do, in fact, government employees actually have more secure jobs than private-sector employees?

You bet they do.

If we use stability as an indirect measure of job security (and it is an unusually informative measure), we find that the median job tenure over two decades for all government workers is 80 percent longer than it is for employees in private companies. Private-sector workers have a median tenure of 3.6 years, a median that has held flat for twenty-one years. Public-sector employees, by contrast, not only have a much longer tenure, but their tenure has also lengthened over time, from a median tenure of six years to seven years over the same period.[134]

These astonishing statistics are reinforced by additional data. An analysis of the "quit rates" in the federal civil service over a twelve-year period concluded that "quit rates in federal white-collar employment have been remarkably stable . . . and remain the same as, or lower than, those in most private firms."[135]

In sum, the popular perception of remarkably secure government jobs is borne out by the evidence.

The Morphed Meaning of Merit

The Civil Service System is predicated on the merit principle, and the long-standing definition of *merit system* is "a personnel system in which comparative merit or achievement governs each individual's selection and progress in the service and in which the conditions and rewards of performance contribute to the competency and continuity of the service."[136]

As our review of the Civil Service System implies, this standard definition of merit has been seriously weakened in practice. Although there is some merit-based selection of applicants for government jobs, achievement, other than simply time in grade, is hardly a factor when pay and promotions are distributed in merit systems. In the federal General Schedule, and in many other public pay systems, employees who perform acceptably progress only after waiting periods that are stipulated by law have elapsed. In addition, rewarding government employees for performance is, as a practical matter, rarely, if ever, done in merit systems. Conversely, few public employees are disciplined, demoted, or dismissed for nonperformance in these systems. The entrenched job security of government employees in merit systems, a security that is far firmer than in the private sector, is a reflection of these realities.

Without putting too fine a point on it, the practice of merit in the Civil Service System no longer reflects its commonly accepted meaning. One is reminded of "newspeak," the sinister and perverted language demanded of the populace by the thought police in George Orwell's *1984*: War is peace; freedom is slavery; ignorance is strength.[137] To which we might add, merit is sinecure.

The Collective System: Blue-Collar Bureaucrats

Our second public personnel system is the *collective system*, and it refers primarily to blue-collar workers whose jobs are administered via agreements between management and organized workers. The core value of the collective system is worker solidarity; in a word, *unions*.

Unions *versus* Merit: The Basic Differences

At root, there are two philosophic differences between the Collective System and the Civil Service System. One difference concerns the notion of *sovereignty*. The Civil Service System holds that a public position is a privilege, not a right, and that each public servant is obliged to uphold the public trust accorded to him or her by a paternalistic government. Conversely, the Collective System holds that employees are on an equal footing with employers, and that they have a right to use their collective powers as a means of improving their conditions of employment. The Civil Service System sees this contention as a threat to the sovereignty of the state, whereas the collective system views the traditions of the civil service as redolent of worker exploitation.

The second difference concerns the concept of *individualism*. The Civil Service System long has valued the ideal that the individual worker be judged for a position on the basis of his or her unique merits for performing the duties of a particular job; the Collective System argues that the identity of the individual should be absorbed in a collective effort to better the conditions of all workers. Hence, the relations of the individual with his or her government employer are replaced by a new set of relations that exists between the government employer and a collective "class" of employees.

Among the conflicts that result from these fundamental differences between the two systems of sovereignty and individualism are: disputes over employee participation and rights (equal treatment *versus* union shop); recruitment (competitive tests *versus* union membership); promotion (performance *versus* seniority); position classification and pay (objective analysis *versus* negotiation); working conditions (determination by legislatures and management *versus* settlement by negotiations); and grievances (determination by civil service commissioners *versus* union representation to third party arbitrators).

These are very basic differences with the concept of merit.

The Scope of Organized Labor

At its apex, in 1953, organized labor included almost a third of all nonagricultural employees in the nation. Nearly 36 percent of private-sector employees were in unions, and less than 12 percent of public-sector workers were organized.[138]

Since then, overall union membership has spun down a steep spiral, and the relative sizes of private and public union membership have more than reversed. Less than 13 percent of all workers in the United States are members of labor unions. Not even 8 percent of American workers in the private sector are in unions.[139] Union membership in the private sector has regressed to levels last seen during the Great Depression,[140] when the hope of millions of jobless Americans was to just find work, not to find justice at work.

In contrast to the private sector, unionization in the public sector tripled over the past half-century. Almost 37 percent of all government employees, or more than 7.4 million public-sector workers, belong to unions. Government workers now form the backbone of organized labor. Although public employees comprise far fewer than two out of ten workers in the national labor force, they number almost five out of ten workers who are members of unions.[141]

The Federal Collective System.   Nearly one out of three, 28 percent,[142] of all federal civilian employees belong to about 125 unions or similar organizations in roughly 2,200 bargaining units, figures that have remained fairly constant over the years.[143] Three unions are dominant, representing some three quarters of organized labor's members who are employed by the federal government. They are the American Federation of Government Employees, the National Federation of Federal Employees, and the National Treasury Employees Union. In addition, most of the 786,000 employees of the U.S. Postal Service, a government corporation, are represented by the Postal Workers Union and the National Association of Letter Carriers.

The Grass-Roots Collective System.   Almost 31 percent of state employees and over 41 percent of local employees are members of unions.[144] Firefighters have long led the list as the most heavily organized of public employees, followed by teachers and police. These and other occupational groups are represented by nearly 34,000 bargaining units.[145] The most significant unions at the state and local levels are the National Education Association, the American Federation of State, County, and Municipal Employees, the American Federation of Teachers, the Fraternal Order of Police, and the International Association of Fire Fighters.

Representation* versus *Membership.   All public unions represent slightly more workers than those who actually pay dues to them. Unions represent almost 41 percent of all public employees— 33 percent of federal workers. 35 percent of state employees, and nearly 46 percent of local workers.[146] Employees who are represented by unions, but who do not belong to them, are nonetheless included in any benefits that the unions may have negotiated with management.

The Right to Organize, the Right to Bargain

State and local policies on government negotiations with organized employees are of two types. The *collective bargaining* approach permits decisions on salaries, hours, and working conditions to be made jointly between employee and employer representatives. The *meet-and-confer* tack says only that both sides must meet and confer over these issues, but that management has the final decision.

Although federal employees had secured the right to organize in 1912 with the passage of the Lloyd-La Follette Act, the right to negotiate collectively was resisted until the 1960s, and the initial indications that attitudes were shifting on these issues came not from Washington but from state and local governments. In 1959, Wisconsin passed the first law allowing its local governments to bargain collectively, and today thirty-five states authorize their cities to engage in collective bargaining with at least some of their employees,[147] and twenty-eight states authorize their counties to do so.[148]

Judging by their written policies, the great majority of states and localities prefer the collective bargaining approach. Forty-two states have a labor-relations policy,[149] and public employees in thirty states possess collective bargaining rights;[150] only three states have specified the use of meet-and-confer bargaining.[151] Ninety-four percent of all cities engage in collective bargaining with their employees.[152]

Bargaining With and Striking Against the Public Employer

Overall, the collective-bargaining relationships between public administrators and public unions are not good. A large-scale analysis of two national surveys of public-sector negotiators concluded that, "We should be very concerned when only a minority of union and management negotiators indicate their relationships are improving (as opposed to staying the same or getting worse) and when less than 10% of negotiators indicate their relationships are both cooperative and improving."[153]

The federal government and the state and local governments have gained experience in dealing with organized labor over the years, but their experiences are quite different.

The Feds and Unions. Federal activity in the field of collective bargaining is marked by President John F. Kennedy's Executive Order 10988 of 1962. The order stated that certain conditions of employment could be bargained for collectively between agency management and employees; wages, hours, and fringe benefits, however, were excluded.

The first major strike by federal employees occurred in March 1970, when about 200,000 postal workers staged an unprecedented walkout. For the first time, federal representatives bargained on salaries (subsequently ratified by Congress), and later Congress legislated the right of postal employees to bargain collectively for wages.

Although the federal government has made some progressive moves in recognizing organized labor, it also has shown itself to be increasingly tough in dealing with unions. In 1978, President

Jimmy Carter signed Public Law 95-610, which prohibits union organization of the armed forces and punishes any member of the armed forces who might join a military labor organization. Unions that try to enlist soldiers and sailors for the purpose of organizing them into a collective bargaining unit also are subject to stiff penalties.

Also in that year, Congress passed the Civil Service Reform Act. Under the act, federal employees have the right to join unions, but strikes and slowdowns are prohibited.

In 1981, Washington showed that it meant business when it was dealing with organized federal workers when it decertified—that is, no longer recognized a union as the official representative of its members—the Professional Association of Air Traffic Controllers. In effect, this act eliminated the union and deprived virtually all of its members of their jobs. Decertifying the union was an unprecedented and historic action that dismissed some 11,000 air traffic controllers (President Ronald Reagan famously said, "They weren't fired. They quit."), and likely strengthened the hand of public administrators in all governments when dealing with unions.

In 1993, President Bill Clinton issued Executive Order 12871, in which he required, for the first time, agencies to negotiate, presumably downward, with unions "the numbers, types, and grades of employees assigned to any organizational subdivision," and to bargain on issues dealing with equipment, technology, assignments, and other topics. This was a significant expansion of the scope of federal bargaining, and it was an expansion that unions wanted much more than did federal managers.[154]

In 2001, President George W. Bush issued Executive Order 13203, allowing agencies discretion to adopt a labor-relations strategy best suited to their own needs.

Bargaining at the Grass Roots. The history of collective bargaining at the state and local levels is more contentious than at the federal one, and there is a number of ways that have been designed over the years to reach agreements between labor and management when they bargain collectively.

State and local governments are becoming increasingly innovative in bargaining with their employees, and there is a growing use of *goldfish-bowl bargaining*, or *sunshine bargaining*, in which the public is made aware of negotiations as they are happening. Traditionally, particularly in the private sector, negotiations are done behind closed doors. About a dozen states have enacted sunshine bargaining statutes,[155] and nearly 14 percent of cities have opened their negotiations with employees to the public.[156]

Money and Unions. Unions of public employees have been a factor in raising salaries, benefits, and pensions of government workers, and these costs to public budgets are relatively apparent. A study of employee compensation in the state governments found that "state employee union density" was "the most consistent and important determinant of compensation."[157]

It also seems that these costs are not especially onerous. One analysis found that state employees who worked in unionized state governments had about 7 percent higher wages than did their counterparts who worked in nonunionized governments.[158] Related research indicates that the wage increases negotiated by public-sector unions generally have less of a financial impact on their governments than the wage increases negotiated by private-sector unions have on their companies.[159]

An intriguing analysis of the finances of 162 large cities also lends indirect credence to the idea that unions do not have a particularly profound impact on local budgets. The study found that, out of eleven designated "spending areas," that of salaries and wages had withered over twenty-four years, from an average of 50 percent of the cities' general expenditures to less than 43 percent. Spending on salaries and wages tied with libraries for the lowest rate of growth, too. The cities' spending per capita on salaries and wages increased by only a fifth during the two dozen years, whereas average spending for all eleven areas grew by almost twice that rate.[160]

Mediating with Unions. Should labor and management reach an impasse, *mediation*, or the voluntary use of an impartial third party to resolve

differences and suggest compromises, can be introduced. *Conciliation* is an option, too, and it differs from mediation in that the third party may not suggest solutions to problems. State governments and the federal government, usually in the form of its Federal Mediation and Conciliation Service, provide mediators and conciliators in disputes between labor and management.

When mediation or conciliation fail, as they occasionally do, arbitration may be brought in, especially if some essential public service is involved. *Arbitration* is a formal process of hearings and fact finding, and it may be *voluntary,* in which both sides agree beforehand to accept the arbitrator's decision, or *compulsory* (also known as *binding*), in which both sides must, under law, accept as final the arbitrator's decision. In 2001, the U.S. Supreme Court ruled that employers may compel their workers to take job-related disputes to arbitration.[161]

Arbitration, both voluntary and compulsory, seems to be a favored recourse among public employees, and one analysis found that 23 percent of the grievances filed in the public sector resulted in a demand for an arbitration hearing![162] Termination cases are by far the most frequently filed grievances in which arbitration is demanded by public employees, and this pattern holds for private-sector employees, too.[163]

Public labor does well in arbitration. Most analyses are quite consistent in concluding that public unions win more arbitrations than do private unions.[164] Organized labor likes arbitration as a means of settling disputes with government employers, and with some reason.

Still, arbitration has proven to be a useful tool in minimizing the disruptions of public services when dealing with organized labor. An analysis of strikes by teachers during the 1970s, when public employee strikes were at their all-time high and teachers were leading most of them, found that state binding arbitration laws were "the policy choice most likely . . . to minimize the level of teacher strike activity. . . . while the impact of strike prohibitions and penalties is less clear."[165]

Slow Downs and Strikes at the Grass Roots. Only thirteen states directly protect their public employees' right to strike, although each of these states places clear restrictions on that right,[166] and four states permit certain categories of local employees to strike.[167] Nevertheless, when state and local workers grow sufficiently dissatisfied with their conditions and feel that they have the clout to change them, they go on strike—or at least engage in work slowdowns. "Blue flu" (meaning a police slowdown), "red rash" (firefighters), and "Human Error Day" (when municipal workers in San Diego misplaced everything from files to phone calls) are variants of these slowdowns.

Strikes and work stoppages by state and local employees peaked in 1979 at 536, and both the number of strikes and stoppages and the length of their duration have been in remission since. The number of strikes and work stoppages by state and local employees has been fewer than thirty a year since 1986.[168]

The dramatic downturn in strikes and stoppages among public workers is attributable both to tougher governments and to a public disaffection with public unions. Some of this disaffection has been brought on by the unions themselves, and some observers point to 1979, the peak year for strikes by public employees, as the year when the citizenry turned on unions of government workers; it was in 1979 that New Orleans police struck just prior to Mardi Gras, effectively canceling the holiday and costing the business community millions. These kinds of stunning gaffes in public relations—like strikes themselves—rarely happen anymore.

How Powerful Are Public Unions?

As the benighted episode of 1979 in New Orleans implies, public unions, during the 1970s in particular, flexed large muscles. They began employing full-time staffs whose sole responsibility was to analyze state and local budgets (as they do to this day) for the sole purpose of winkling out public funds that could be redirected to their members.[169] The attitude of public unions toward their public employers was expressed succinctly during this period by the pension specialist of the American Federation of State, County, and Municipal Employees who, when asked where the money for higher pensions for his members would be coming from, replied, "That's the government's problem. Just because there is a pinch for money, it's no excuse to make the employees do without."[170]

Organized labor has made progress in governments, and the public sector remains the lifeblood of the union movement. The glory days have been waning since the early eighties, however, and, beginning in the mid-1990s, it was apparent that "public sector unionism . . . has topped out, both in membership and market share," with declines evident in both.[171]

So, how powerful are public unions today? More powerful when they work with public employers than when they work against them.

The Political Executive System: Politics in Administration

At quite the opposite end of the scale, or that end where the blue-collar bureaucrats assemble to form the Collective System, are the political executives. *Political executives* are those public officials appointed to an office without tenure, who have significant policymaking powers, and who are outside the civil service system. They have been called "the true nexus between politics and administration."[172]

The paramount values of the Political Executive System are those of developing and implementing a policy agenda for the elected chief executive. In contrast to the Civil Service System's emphasis on the position, and the Collective System's focus on unions, the Political Executive System fixates on *policy*.

Political Executives in Washington

Some 3,500, less than 3 percent of the 126,000 federal employees who occupy the top three rungs of the federal career ladder, are political executives who are nominated or appointed directly by the president.[173] Contrast this number to the roughly 100 political appointees available to each of the prime ministers of Britain, France, and Germany.[174]

The number of political executives in the federal government "is not fixed and varies depending on who does the counting and how positions are defined. . . . What is important is the trend toward more political appointees for each presidential administration. The direction of this trend is not in dispute."[175] That direction is: up.

An Increase in Intellect. As a group of men and women in the public employ, political executives exhibit certain systemic tendencies. Most notably, perhaps, is the emphasis on intellect. Over half of the politically appointed executives hold advanced degrees,[176] and their level of education places them, on average, on a somewhat higher educational plane than their careerist counterparts.[177]

A Decrease in Partisanship. For at least most of the second half of twentieth century, there has been a declining emphasis on partisanship in the political executive personnel system. An intensive study of assistant secretaries found that a mere 10 percent were appointed primarily by dint of "service to party."[178] Another analysis found that the proportion of top-level presidential appointees who were affiliated with the president's party never exceeded 70 percent and dipped as low as 56 percent.[179] Contrast this percentage with the 90 percent of the government's top echelon appointees who were Democrats or closely affiliated with the president's party in Franklin Roosevelt's administration.[180]

Although partisanship is in historic decline, it is by no means absent from the presidential appointment process. In the box in Chapter 7, we noted that when Hurricane Katrina struck the Gulf Coast in 2005, the initial federal response to this Category 3 storm was late, weak, and bumfuzzled. This response may have been caused, in part, by a decline in professional talent in the Federal Emergency Management Agency (FEMA), the feds' central organization for dealing with such crises. When Katrina made landfall, five of the eight highest executives in FEMA, including its director, and his immediate predecessor, had come "to their posts with virtually no experience in handling disasters" but did have significant partisan backgrounds. Three of the agency's five chiefs for natural disasters and nine of its ten regional directors were in acting positions because many of

FEMA's seasoned professionals had quit over a deepening disgust with falling funding and promotion through patronage.[181]

Sometimes the traditional merit principle looks pretty good.

The Rise of the White House Loyalty Test. One should not infer that the diminishing role of partisan fealty in the selection of federal political executives means that there is a lessened demand for personal loyalty. Indeed, loyalty to the occupant of the White House (including, it appears, loyalty to the president's ideology) appears to be a qualification of rising importance.

No one can dispute the desirability of a democratically elected chief executive establishing his or her control over the policymaking and policy-executing apparatus of the executive branch, and appointing loyalists in key positions is an important means of establishing this control. But there are problems. For one, establishing pervasive, centralized control over the political appointee system is simply very difficult to achieve. One former presidential personnel assistant, who was notorious for his belief in the necessity of the president controlling the appointment process, later admitted, "It's an awfully difficult job just to handle the *presidential* appointees. . . . if you try to do too much, you may be diluted to the point where you're not as effective."[182]

Perhaps more fundamentally, it is unclear that White House dominance over the political executive system is needed to achieve competent bureaucratic responsiveness to presidential policy. Surveys of all presidential appointees who served over a period of more than forty years found that from nearly eight in ten to over nine in ten (depending on the administration) thought that career executives were competent and responsive.[183]

Ironically, it appears that those presidential appointees who are the most effective in advancing the president's agenda are effective *not* because of loyalty to their president or his ideology, but instead are effective because of the opportunities for change available in the agency that the appointee heads, and the appointee's own managerial abilities, personality, and plan for attaining his or her goals.[184]

A Question of Quality: Assessing Federal Political Executives

In short, competence counts. Do federal political executives have it?

Most career administrators doubt it. A survey of members of the Senior Executive Service found that the high esteem in which career executives are held by political executives is far from reciprocal. A mere 18 percent of the service's career members believed that political appointees have "good leadership qualities," and only 15 percent thought that these appointees have "good management skills."[185]

Baroquely Burdensome: The Appointment Process. It is possible that presidents no longer are able to attract the kind of top talent to work for them that they once were. Certainly the increasingly lengthy and baroque political appointment process stands as an impediment to appointing top executives to federal offices, regardless of their talent. In the early 1960s, the average time that it took to nominate and confirm a presidential appointee was less than two and a half months; by the early 1990s, the process consumed, on average, over eight months, and this remains the average confirmation time in the 2000s.[186]

In addition, Congress's concerns with conflicts of interest have required sacrifices that not all highly qualified prospects for administrative positions may be willing to make. An astonishing 250,000 federal employees must report each year the full details of their personal finances, and almost 25,000 of these administrators must disclose these details to the public.[187] To comply with federal regulations, 41 percent of presidential appointees resigned posts (often board memberships) in corporations or other organizations, 32 percent sold stock or other assets, and 14 percent created blind or diversified trusts that placed control (and knowledge) of their personal assets in the hands of others.[188] Demanding that political executives not only undergo an exhausting confirmation process, but sacrifice financially as

well, could result (and perhaps has resulted) in well-qualified prospects being unwilling to serve in Washington.

An Avaricious Elite? On the other hand, there is some evidence to suggest that the political executives who do run the appointments gauntlet (almost a fourth of the presidential appointees who served in the 1980s and 1990s describe the appointments process as "embarrassing," and a fifth found it "confusing"[189]), and ultimately are appointed, may be in it mostly for the money.

Between 1964 and 1984, 39 percent of presidential appointees said that "accomplishing important public objectives" was the "most satisfying part of the job," and only 2 percent said "enhancing your long-term career opportunities" brought the greatest satisfaction. Between 1984 and 1999, however, only 15 percent of presidential appointees derived their greatest satisfaction from achieving public goals, and 10 percent stated that enhancing their career opportunities brought them the most satisfaction. Fully 30 percent said that, once appointed, they earned "a lot more" money, and only 6 percent earned "a lot less."[190]

Are these the kinds of top federal executives that the nation needs? Money-grubbing political hacks who are unfazed by an often mortifying appointments process, who are uninterested in serving the public interest, and who see their chance to make their "big money" in the federal service?

The Experience Quotient: Our New Understanding of Executive Quality

One of the most distinctive characteristics of federal political executives is their relative inexperience in public administration.

"A Government of Strangers"? Research (aptly entitled *A Government of Strangers*) found that the average tenure of an undersecretary or assistant secretary was fewer than twenty-two months.[191] It appears that even these brief tenures of political appointees are getting briefer over time,[192] and that the higher political executives rise, the likelier they are to leave quickly. One analysis found that the average tenure of the political appointees in the Senior Executive Service was about eighteen months in one position, and even briefer in the higher positions.[193]

By contrast, career bureau chiefs in the federal government average about twice the time in their positions—more than three years—than do political executives.[194]

These figures are somewhat misleading, in that they deal only with how long federal executives have held a single position. In fact, presidentially appointed executives, on average, have more than nine years of experience in a variety of governmental positions.[195] Still, nine years are not a lot when compared to an average of nearly twenty-six years of governmental experience that reside under the belts of senior executives who have made the federal service a career.[196]

The Importance of Experience. The federal government offers a unique insight into an age-old argument about who makes the best public executives: career bureaucrats or political appointees. There are two reasons for this uniqueness. First, only the federal government can provide a significant population of political appointees who are "in-and-outers," or those political executives who have more experience in sectors other than in the public one. State and local governments have political executives, too, but they are fewer in number, and often have spent most, if not all, of their careers in their governments.

Second, only the federal government (and this is a recent development) has a single system in which each of its agencies is graded for its comparative performance against all other agencies.[197] Once such a system is in place, then we can gain a reasonably accurate idea about the administrative quality of the heads of those agencies. Moreover, we can compare those agency heads on all kinds of dimensions, including their professional experience and the graded performance of their agencies under their leadership of them.

When we make these comparisons, it turns out that experience matters. In fact, experience matters

more than we ever knew, and it has a direct bearing on our understanding of the roles that political executives and career executives play in the performance of their agencies.

A seminal analysis of 242 federal bureau chiefs found that politically appointed bureau chiefs got "systematically lower management grades than bureau chiefs drawn from the civil service." Why? The career civil servants had twice as much governmental experience: "Career managers have more direct bureau experience and longer tenures and these characteristics are significantly related to management performance."[198] Long governmental experience of agency heads, in brief, strongly correlates with superior agency performance.

After reviewing these data, the question becomes obvious: How can a government of strangers—or, more to the point, ignoramuses in the ways of federal management, who do not serve long enough to learn about their jobs or each other—intelligently administer the national government of the world's largest and most complex democracy? That early advocate of competent government, Alexander Hamilton, were he alive, would have been appalled. If high-level public administrators were to stay only briefly in office, Hamilton wrote, it would "occasion a disgraceful and ruinous mutability in the administration of government."[199] Words that are worth remembering in our present day.

Political Executives at the Grass Roots

In contrast to developments over the past four decades at the federal level, the Political Executive System of public personnel administration at the state and local levels is tilting more in favor of career administrators. Political patronage is down, and public professionalism is up.

The Departure of Patronage. The Supreme Court has been involving itself in the area of patronage-based political appointments since 1976, and the clear drift of its decisions (and those of lower courts as well) has been one of reducing the power of patronage in state and local governments.[200]

The Passing of State Patronage.   Perhaps the most important antipatronage case is that of *Rutan* v. *Illinois Republican Party.* In 1990, the Supreme Court ruled, in a five-to-four decision, that party affiliation could not play a part in the hiring, promoting, or transferring of most of Illinois's 60,000 gubernatorial appointees. The governor of Illinois was shocked, saying the decision "turns politics on its head."[201]

Other states that traditionally have had large numbers of political appointees—Indiana, Massachusetts, New York, North Carolina, Pennsylvania, and West Virginia—have taken steps to reduce the power of partisan politics in their personnel systems as a direct consequence of *Rutan.* As one observer notes, "Nobody wants to be sued. They tend to pay attention to a major decision like this."[202]

The Passing of Local Patronage.   What is true for the states is even more in evidence among local governments, where reformist pressures have their roots. Today, four-fifths of all American cities have nonpartisan professional chief administrative officers,[203] most of whom have powers that any political appointee would envy. In more than half, 57 percent, of all cities (including those cities that do not have city managers), city managers have the sole authority to develop the municipal budget,[204] and in almost two-fifths, 39 percent, they have the exclusive power to appoint department heads.[205]

The Entry of Professionalism.   As patronage passes from the grass-roots governments, professionalism enters. Educational attainments of top state and local administrators are now comparable to their federal counterparts, which was not the case, especially among state administrators, some forty years ago. Perhaps more significantly, and very much *un*like federal political executives (who are "outta here"—"here" being Washington, D.C.—after only two years), state and local political executives are careerists, with long histories as public administrators.

Professional State Executives.   In the states, interest in developing a cadre of educated and experienced public executives bloomed in the 1960s as part of administratively inspired reorganizations that swept most state governments for three decades.[206] These state executive systems typically cover less than 1 percent of a state's employees.[207]

Analyses consistently show that the quality and professionalism of top state administrators are steadily rising.[208] A careful study of state agency heads that has been conducted periodically since 1964 is one of them,[209] and it traces the dramatic increase in the educational levels of state agency heads over four decades. In 1964, more than a third of state agency heads (who are gubernatorial appointees) did not have a bachelor's degree. (By contrast, only a tenth of their federal counterparts had not completed college.[210]) Forty percent held a graduate degree. By 1994, however, only 6 percent had not completed college, and 60 percent had earned their graduate degree, mostly in management and public administration.[211] These numbers raised state executives to an educational par with their federal counterparts.[212]

A second indication of a deepening professionalism is that more state agency heads have chosen state public administration as a career. Seventy percent of state agency heads came to their positions from other positions in government (whether federal, state, or local), and almost nine out of every ten state administrators in this 70 percent came from other positions in state government. On average, state agency heads have fifteen years of working in state government under their belts.[213] These are the statistics of committed professionalism.

Professional Local Executives.   Local governments evidence a pattern that parallels that of the states. Local interest in developing a deep pool of executive talent associates with the dramatically accelerating adoption, beginning immediately after World War II, by local jurisdictions of the council-manager and similarly professional forms of government.[214]

As with state and federal executives, top local administrators are well educated, with only 10 percent lacking a bachelor's degree, and 63 percent holding a graduate degree, most of which are master's degrees in public administration. In another match with state agency heads, city managers are committed to their professions, and they have spent an average of more than seventeen years as a local government administrator.[215]

This long experience of local executives contributes to more effective local government, much in the manner that it contributes to superior federal performance, described earlier. An analysis of municipal budget officers found that the longer the tenure of these local financial leaders, the more smoothly, efficiently, and effectively they managed local funds.[216]

The Professional Public Administration System: Embracing the Professions of Politics and Management

The two overriding values of public human resource management for the future will be those of "professionalism" and "management."[217] The Professional Public Administration System acknowledges these realities, and embraces as the essence of its profession both "politics" (as in *public*) and "management" (as in *administration*). This is new.

The central value of the Professional Public Administration System is not position, union, or policy. Its overriding value is *public administration.*

The Professional Public Administration System is the result of a triad of developments that either altered the realities of public administration and public human resource management, or changed popular perceptions about both enterprises. These three boulders on which the Professional Public Administration System rests are the National Civil Service League's Model Public Personnel Administration Law of 1970; the national reaction to the Watergate scandal of 1973–1975; and the Civil Service Reform Act of 1978. We consider them in turn.

The Model Public Personnel Administration Law of 1970

The formulation of the sixth Model Public Personnel Administration Law of 1970 by the now-defunct National Civil Service League is important for two reasons. First, the league,

founded in 1881 as the Civil Service Reform League and presided over in its early years by Woodrow Wilson, wielded immense prestige and power in the personnelist (as it is called) community of practitioners and scholars. Second, the league's model law represented the consensus of opinion in that critical community. This consensus reflected "a sea change in the views of the cognoscenti about what the public service should be and how it should be governed."[218]

The Model Public Personnel Administration Law of 1970 replaced the league's previous model law of 1953, and it was a radically different document from all of its five predecessors. Rather than emphasizing the protection of the civil service against partisan patronage and similar transgressions, the 1970 model law incorporated management as its overriding value. "Personnel administration must be regarded as a part of management, not a protector against it."[219] Five years following the model law's release, over half of all subnational governments had made their personnel systems more responsive to executive leadership.[220]

Watergate and the Muffled Mouthpiece for "Merit"

But if the public personnel administration community was for the first time passionately embracing the importance of public management, the public was beginning to have quite a different reaction to the behavior of public managers. In a word, Watergate, a crucible that seared the nation from 1973 through 1975, was the direct product of a president's criminality and that of his public administrators.

Even though the line civil service was essentially uninvolved in Watergate, the public bureaucracy did not fare well in the public mind. "However justified or unjustified they may have been, the effects of Watergate unquestionably were to tarnish the reputation of the public service in general. . . . And the U.S. Civil Service Commission, which had been set up in part as a watchdog of the integrity of the civil service system, did not attack, or growl, or even bark until the affair had ridden most of its course. . . .

Watergate generated doubts in the nation as a whole . . . about the public service as a whole, both career and noncareer."[221]

Perhaps, many citizens thought, the old public personnel merit system was not all that meritorious and was in need of replacement.

The Civil Service Reform Act of 1978

If public human resource managers were notably weak-kneed when it came to protecting the merit principle from dilution by the White House, they seemed positively ferocious in using it to harass federal managers who were trying to administer their public programs. Surveys revealed high levels of frustration among federal executives and managers over inadequate authority to hire and promote their own employees, and they appeared to attribute at least some of the reasons for their lack of managerial authority to the heavy hands of the personnel administrators.[222]

Because the Civil Service Commission seemed not to be doing its job when it should have been, and doing it all too avidly when it should not have been, pressures were generated for far-reaching changes in the personnel practices of the federal government. In his 1978 State of the Union address, President Jimmy Carter said that reform of the civil service was "absolutely vital,"[223] and the director of the U.S. Civil Service Commission backed him up with report after consternating report about the lack of control and authority held by federal administrators.[224]

As a consequence of these initiatives, there ensued a hugely ambitious and deep-reaching study of public personnel administration involving more than 1,500 practitioners, scholars, organizations, and other sundry experts. Ultimately the Civil Service Reform Act of 1978 was enacted, thus replacing the Pendleton Act, which, for ninety-five years, had been the civil service policy of the United States.

The Civil Service Reform Act enacted into law three new offices for human resource management. One of these is the Office of Personnel Management, which replaced the Civil Service Commission. The Office of Personnel Management advises the president on personnel matters and coordinates the government's personnel programs.

The Act also established a bipartisan, three-member Merit Systems Protection Board, which adjudicates employee appeals and conducts investigations of allegations that federal personnel laws have been violated. It has the power to order agency compliance with its rulings.

Finally, the act legislated the Federal Labor Relations Authority, which is charged with conducting investigations and developing and enforcing federal policy for labor relations. It was the Federal Labor Relations Authority that in 1981 decertified the nation's air traffic controllers, noted earlier.

Perhaps of greatest significance, the act created the Senior Executive Service, which we have mentioned throughout this chapter. The Senior Executive Service amounts to a professional administrative class in the European tradition. Senior executives may be assigned, reassigned, or removed on the basis of their ability or performance. Political executives may constitute no more than 10 percent of the service's some 8,000 positions, and 45 percent of its positions must be reserved for career federal administrators. The Senior Executive Service is managed by the Office of Personnel Management.

"The main thrust of the Carter reforms, repeated in virtually all the speeches and arguments of their supporters, was management."[225]

A Pair of Professional Profundities: Performance and Pay

The Professional Public Administration System has given rise to an overriding dynamic that is profoundly expressive of its values. It is the idea that public employees should be paid for their professionalism and performance.

A Question of Compensation: Does Merit Mean Meretricious?

We noted earlier that governments' use of the term, *merit,* comes heaped with baggage, and so it is with governments' use of the phrase, *merit pay.* Since the mid-twentieth century, the term, merit pay, is rarely uttered in governments and, although still popular in the private sector, where "pay for performance is a virtually universal policy for white-collar workers. . . . the phrase is no longer used widely in the public sector."[226]

The implications of this linguistic lapse are worrisome and hint that the merit principle itself has morphed into a culture of entitlement that saturates the public bureaucracy.

In addition to the possibility that American governments may be staffed by some leechlike employees as a result of financial disincentives that are structured into the merit system, public pay is beset with a passel of other problems. The federal government provides a rich reservoir of examples. Although half of federal employees report that they are satisfied with their pay,[227] they nonetheless give their pay plans low marks for fairness. Over a fourth of federal employees say that ensuring that employees received equal pay for equal work is a major problem—a perception shared at "every level of the pay scale."[228] As an official in the Office of Personnel Management put it, the current "system allows the manager to be precisely wrong. What the manager needs is the opportunity to be roughly right."[229]

As a consequence of these conditions, governments, starting in the late 1970s, began to rethink how they paid their bureaucrats and turned to the idea of paying them for their performance. *Pay for performance*, also known as *pay for contribution*, or *pay for competence*, links pay, in whole or in part, to individual, group, and/or organizational performance.[230]

The foundation of performance pay is the rating of individual workers' performance, reviewed earlier. Without a credible system of performance appraisal in place—a challenge of no mean dimensions—paying for performance is a non-starter.

We consider next governments' use of performance pay.

The Federal Experience with Performance Assessment and Performance Pay

Washington's history of performance pay has been one of lethargy, indecision, and, finally, the prospect of implementation.

Assessing Federal Administrators.   In part, this historical hesitancy has been a function of the enormously difficult problem of assessing the performance of federal administrators, a problem that has its own history.

In 1984, Congress amended the Civil Service Reform Act of 1978, setting up the Performance Management and Recognition System as the means of rating the performance of federal employees. By virtually every account, this legislation was a bad joke. One observer encapsulated the situation neatly: "The current personnel system was last overhauled in 1978, based on ideas from the 1950s that were built on research conducted in the 1930s, using data collected in the 1920s by scholars trained in the 1910s."[231]

But there were weaknesses in the new system that went far beyond that of outdated scholarship. The Performance Management and Recognition System established five ratings that were soon rendered virtually meaningless by organized labor and members of Congress representing districts close to Washington, where large numbers of federal employees voted. These interests derailed plans to limit the proportions of employees being appraised who could be included in each of the five categories (thereby forcing a wide distribution of ratings), resulting in more than 99 percent of federal employees being rated every year as "Outstanding," "Exceeds Fully Successful," or "Fully Successful."[232] (Research suggests that, in the typical workgroup, from only 15 percent to 20 percent of workers are considered to be extraordinarily productive by their coworkers.)[233] In addition, studies indicated that the ratings were unevenly distributed by just about any category one chose—grade, gender, geography, and ethnicity—so the federal employee evaluation system was "widely perceived as a failure by workers, members of Congress, and university researchers."[234]

As a consequence, Congress in 1993 allowed the sun to set on the Performance Management and Recognition System, and in 1996, the Office of Personnel Management decentralized its personnel evaluation to the agencies, which could adopt pass/fail criteria, develop their own ratings, and rate teams of employees as well as individuals, among other innovations. It appears that many federal agencies, perhaps most, opted for the simplest and least informative assessment, that of pass/fail.[235]

Paying Federal Performers. Washington cloned its early experience with performance assessment in its early grappling with performance pay. Although the Civil Service Reform Act of 1978 requires merit pay increases for midlevel supervisors and managers (grades 13–15), it does not specify how these increases should be implemented. For the ensuing thirty years or so following its passage, Congress failed to establish a well-planned, adequately funded system, and instead undertook a series of spasmodic efforts to link pay with performance.

Stymied Progress. These attempts were sporadic and, unsurprisingly, progress remained elusive. Analyses conducted during this period suggested that performance pay did not deliver as hoped—in other words, it seemed not to heighten worker productivity in governments.[236] Federal agencies appeared to be increasingly disillusioned with performance pay, and during the last half of the 1990s, all major federal offices were cutting back on their use of monetary performance incentives.[237] Surveys of federal employees show that, agency by agency and year after year, these workers consistently rate "performance-based rewards and advancement practices" lower than any other personnel practice.[238]

After almost three decades of federal floundering with performance pay, fewer than 40,000 federal employees were covered by pay-for-performance systems,[239] including the top 8,000 federal executives, seven out of every ten of whom were earning precisely identical salaries![240]

Renewed Efforts. With the inauguration of President George W. Bush in 2001, performance pay was reenergized. In that year, "strategic human capital management," focusing especially on the need for performance pay, was included in Bush's new President's Management Agenda and was added to the GAO's "high-risk series" as a concern that warranted constant attention and improvement. Also in 2001, the president authorized the restructuring of the Senior Executive Service's pay system in a way that clearly emphasized rewarding the performance of top federal executives.

In 2002, Congress passed the Homeland Security Act, which included a requirement that a performance-based personnel management system be implemented in the Department of Homeland Security. The National Defense Authorization Act of 2004 created the National Security Personnel System, which greatly facilitates the implementation of performance pay in the Pentagon. The practical result of these two laws has been to introduce performance pay systems and related reforms that cover nearly 750,000 federal employees, or some two-fifths of all federal civilian workers.

In 2003, Congress authorized up to $500 million to be appropriated to a new Human Capital Performance Fund to be used by the Office of Personnel Management for special increases for high performers. The fund will limit these awards to 15 percent of federal civilian employees, a proportion that reflects research concerning the actual percentage of high performers found in a typical workforce.[241] Whether Congress will actually allocate adequate monies to the Fund, and not cave again to special interests as it did in the 1980s, are open questions.

Although Washington seems committed to reaching a point where it can pay all its employees for their performance, and not pay them for their nonperformance, "the shift to pay for performance," to quote one understated assessment, "is going to be difficult."[242] Nevertheless, most knowledgeable observers think that paying for performance "would be a huge improvement over the current system, which fails at virtually every task it undertakes."[243]

Paying Performers at the Grass Roots

The grass-roots governments also are entering the complex world of performance pay. Among state and local governments, "compensation systems are being gradually disconnected from job classes, thereby giving supervisors greater discretion on the assignment of salaries based on . . . performance."[244]

Thirty states use pay-for-performance in at least one agency, and this number is growing.[245] Almost six out ten states use individual performance bonuses, and over a third use group performance bonuses, in frequencies ranging from "rarely" to "often" (14 percent use individual bonuses, and 2 percent use group bonuses, often).[246]

Over a third of local governments,[247] and perhaps twice that number (depending on how researchers define pay-for-performance),[248] use pay-for-performance plans. Close to half of the largest counties pay for performance "very often" (36 percent) or "often" (11 percent); only a fourth never use performance pay.[249] More than two-thirds of local personnel directors give pay-for-performance plans a "very useful" rating, with the remainder saying they are "somewhat useful."[250]

Does Human Resource Management Impair Public Administration?

The irony of today's phase of public human resource management is that policymakers increasingly believe public personnel administration can best improve the management of government by getting out of the way—or even by getting out of government altogether.

Equity or Effectiveness?

Increasingly, policymakers are of the opinion that the traditional functions of human resource management in the public sector are obsolete. Job classification and analysis—a basic tenet of public personnel administration—is an example. Agency administrators typically must bargain with human resources managers about how high or low a position should be ranked in the agency hierarchy, and what kinds of qualifications prospective applicants should have. Often agency heads, who are interested in strategic and effective management, and personnel administrators, who want uniformity and fairness in the classification system, find themselves at odds.

An extensive national survey supports this view. It found that public human resource administrators consistently placed values associated with the equity of all employees at the top of their value structure, followed by values that are more associated with line managers—notably, efficiency, professionalism, and implementing the chief executive's agenda, in that order.[251]

In the opinion of most public human resource managers, employee equity trumps agency effectiveness. This is an ongoing and fundamental tension in public administration.

Ignorance or Irrelevance?

In addition to holding different organizational values, human resource managers may not comprehend the wide-ranging professional and administrative needs of the more general public administrator.

Line administrators harbor few qualms about expressing their frustration over what they deem to be administrative obtuseness of human resource managers. At the federal level, one out of three administrators complain that the chief human resources bureau of the federal government, the Office of Personnel Management, accords them little or no help in recruiting, developing, or utilizing employees, and this was the highest negative response in the survey.[252] A national study of state governments found that "The general picture that emerges . . . is one of administrators trapped by rigid, slow, and cumbersome systems that are incapable of meeting government's human resources needs."[253]

More to the point, perhaps, research indicates that better human resource management processes seem not to be terribly important in recruiting and retaining organizational talent. In other words, the connection between a strong human resource management office and able general administrators is, at best, obscure.[254]

After reviewing this research, Catbert comes to mind. Catbert is one of the more memorable characters in the popular comic strip *Dilbert*, and he invariably is identified as the perennially "evil director of human resources." In the opinion of many public administrators, it seems, Catbert rules.

Are Governments Dismantling Human Resource Management?

As a consequence of these entrenched and tightening tensions between agency administrators and personnel managers in government, we are witnessing a decentralizing and diminishing of public human resource agencies. Consider some facts.

Federal Developments. At the federal level, Washington, beginning in the 1960s and perhaps earlier, has effectively exempted specialized professionals from its official civil-service regulations, apparently in response to the resistance displayed by these professionals to traditional civil-service rigidities.[255] As we have mentioned, the General Schedule's coverage of employees is shrinking, and a majority of all federal civilian workers have been exempted from at least some policies in the traditional civil service,[256] or are in different personnel systems altogether.[257]

The decline of the Civil Service System has had some predictably deleterious effects on the federal government's chief bureau for human resource management. Between 1993 and 1998, the Office of Personnel Management eliminated nearly half of its employees, "a far greater reduction than that of any other Federal agency."[258] Today, a much reduced Office of Personnel Management directly administers not much more than the federal retirement system.

Grass-Roots Reform. An extensive and ongoing study of human resource management in state and local governments provides some enlightening findings about how these governments are reforming how they manage their human resources. Approximately 200 innovations in state and local human resource management have been unearthed by this analysis, a finding that leads to at least two conclusions. One is that 200 innovations in any field is a startlingly large number, and the other is that subnational jurisdictions are deeply committed to rethinking and reforming how they treat their people.[259]

State Developments. Perhaps the most revolutionary developments in the reform of public human resource management are occurring in the states.

States' Decentralization of Civil Service. As in Washington, states also are decentralizing their personnel functions. Sixteen states have contracted out at least some of their personnel programs and services to the private sector.[260] Forty-six states have decentralized a core function of all human resource bureaus—that of hiring employees—to the line agencies, and the remainder are mixed systems; only nine states retain the recruitment of new employees in a central personnel office.[261] "That a number of states have achieved high levels of personnel deregulation suggests it is more than just another administrative reform fad."[262]

States most likely to decentralize their human resource management share certain characteristics. They tend to have relatively weak public unions; Republican-controlled governments; high administrative professionalism;[263] high legislative professionalism; low levels of state unemployment; and plentiful state resources.[264]

States' Elimination of Civil Service. Three states—Florida,[265] Georgia,[266] and Texas—have, for all intents and purposes, eliminated their civil services. Among other reforms, these states moved in the direction of what is known as *at will employment*—that is, employees serve at the sufferance of their supervisors and are not protected by the merit system. They may be hired, promoted, reorganized, transferred, demoted, and fired immediately at the will of their supervisor.

Public administrators in all three states believe that civil service reform (or, perhaps more accurately stated, civil service evisceration) has served them well. Hiring, promoting, reassigning, and firing have been eased, accelerated, and streamlined; "patronage hiring appears to proceed along typical levels," with no unusual spike in political hiring or firing; the prospects of the early retirement of high-salaried employees are enhanced; and the line agencies' responsibilities for human resource management increase. These reforms seem to be most successful when they are accompanied by some sort of centralized quality-control that yields coherence to state personnel practices, and weds those practices to statewide strategic human resource planning.[267]

Local Developments. It appears that human resource management is a bit of a sore spot among local governments, and apparently provides the greatest impetus for local governments to undertake reform measures across the board. An analysis of counties that had implemented significant governmental reforms found that 70 percent of their reforms related to human resource management policies.[268]

Among these reforms is privatization, and local governments are privatizing the management of their human resources at an accelerating pace. This outsourcing has significant implications because all governments long have treated personnel administration as a core, inherently governmental, function that properly should remain in-house; contracting it out implies its diminishing worth in the eyes of policymakers.

Over the course of a decade, the proportion of cities and counties that privatized personnel services more than doubled, from less than 4 percent to almost 9 percent, far outpacing the average growth in privatization of all local services, which grew by less than a tenth over the same period. Nearly 11 percent of local governments deliver their human resource services via public-private partnerships, a practice that also is expanding over time.[269] These are not large numbers, but their growth, and the implications of that growth, is notable for the traditional civil service.

A Modest Proposal

The structure and functions of human resource agencies are changing. Perhaps such traditional activities of public personnel administration as job classification and analysis, human resources planning, performance appraisal, selection, discipline, and dismissal should be turned over to agency administrators, or even outsourced to other sectors.

It is still desirable, however, that other traditional activities of public personnel administration be retained in one or more separate staff units, such as departments of human resources, on the grounds that they are less directly critical to the management function or can be handled more effectively by a central agency. These activities include training, employee development, labor relations, research, and the administration of wages, salaries, benefits, and services. Of particular importance is employee development and training, activities that government personnel departments have not emphasized in the past.

Human resource management in the public sector does have a future. Nevertheless, it is a future that will require some adaptation.

Race, Sex, and Jobs: The Challenge of Affirmative Action

Perhaps nowhere has that adaptation been more challenging than in the national effort to give all people a more equal chance to get ahead.

Although it is in decline, prejudice is still present in American society, and it is working against women, people of color, the disabled, and older citizens.[270] In the context of employment, we find such phenomena as "sticky floors" (or jobs with limited potential for promotion), "glass ceilings" (organization-wide limitations on advancement for certain groups), and "glass walls" (fields that employ few minorities or women).[271]

To counter such prejudices and phenomena, American governments have originated the policy of "affirmative action." *Affirmative action* is a policy that argues for the hiring and promoting of members of disadvantaged groups on the grounds that jobs should be open to as many people as possible.

The Federal Impact: A Tortuous Evolution

The legal history of affirmative action (a term that, technically, applies only to executive orders issued by the president, but which commonly includes agency directives, laws, and court decisions as well) is a clouded and confused one. What has been "conspicuously evident" about the evolution of affirmative action "is that these various laws and rules grew without a strong governmental or legal theory binding them coherently together . . . and thus weakening their effectiveness and giving the courts unclear directions in interpreting them."[272]

Roots. The roots of this difficult legal history can be traced to 1941, when President Franklin D. Roosevelt issued Executive Order 8802, which barred discrimination by race, religion, or national origin in industries with federal contracts. After a hiatus of two decades, President John F. Kennedy followed with his Executive Order 10925 of 1961, which encouraged the employment of minorities but had no enforcement procedures attached to it.

LBJ: The Archangel of Affirmative Action. The archangel of affirmative action, however, was President Lyndon Baines Johnson (LBJ). It was Johnson who, largely by sheer force of personality, pushed through the Civil Rights Act of 1964, Titles VI and VII of which prohibit all forms of discrimination in public- and private-sector hiring. The act included, for the first time, women, Hispanic Americans, Native Americans, and Asian Americans, as well as African Americans, as groups whose rights are protected by federal law.

Johnson followed this historic legislation with Executive Order 11246 of 1965, which directed all companies and organizations that were working under contracts with the federal government to take "affirmative action" (marking the debut of this phrase) to provide equality of opportunity, irrespective of race, religion, or national origin. No longer were minorities' rights merely protected, as the Civil Rights Act had stipulated; now minorities were to be hired and promoted aggressively. This was new. It is not surprising that Executive Order 11246 has been described as "the most important affirmative action document in the government."[273]

In 1967, Johnson issued Executive Order 11375, which added women, for the first time, to the ranks of those who are specifically protected by affirmative action.

Age Discrimination. Following Johnson's administration, Congress largely took the lead in protecting the rights of additional groups, and congressional attention initially focused on the elderly. In 1967, Congress passed the Age Discrimination in Employment Act, which prohibited discrimination in employment because of age. The act was amended in 1974 and 1981 and now prohibits compulsory retirement in most jobs for reasons of age and protects all workers from age discrimination who are forty years old or older. The act covers some seventy-five million Americans, or about half of the nation's labor pool.

Setting Aside for Minorities and Women. In the late 1970s, Congress began what are known as *set-aside programs*, or federal policies that require federal, state, and local governments to reserve (or "set aside") a percentage of their contracts for businesses that are owned by minorities or women. Federal minority set-aside programs are conducted principally under the aegis of Small Business Administration's "8 (a) program," which certifies firms seeking to qualify as Disadvantaged Business Enterprises, and the Pentagon's "1207 Program." Companies owned by minorities and women receive over 8 percent of federal contract dollars, and uncounted proportions of state and local contract budgets.[274]

The first set-aside program appeared in the Public Works Employment Act of 1977. It was challenged in the courts by white contractors, who argued that it violated both equal protection under the Constitution and due process of law, and was upheld by the Supreme Court in 1980 in the case *Fullilove* v. *Klutznick.*

Limiting Set-Asides at the Grass Roots. Within a decade, however, the Court began to backtrack. In 1989, in *City of Richmond* v. *Croson,* the Court held that Richmond could not set aside 30 percent of its contracting dollars for minority business enterprises, as it had done, unless there was a compelling government interest to sponsor the program, and the remedy was "narrowly tailored" to alleviate the problem. Richmond's set-aside program met neither test, and thus was unconstitutional. This was new.

The lasting result of *Croson* was that it forced state and local governments to launch *disparity studies*, or analyses designed to show that race-conscious, set-aside programs were needed—or not. An examination of these studies concluded that, "In nearly all of the disparity studies in our sample, there was little serious evaluation of race-neutral activities."[275] This conclusion seems to indicate that state and local governments are prepared to "talk the talk" of the Supreme Court by churning out disparity studies, but "walk the walk" by continuing their proactive affirmative action traditions.

Limiting Set-Asides in Washington. In 1996, the Supreme Court extended to the federal government the standards for state and local governments that it had set sixteen years earlier in *Croson.*

The Court decided five-to-four in *Adarand Constructors, Inc.* v. *Peña* that federal contracts awarded on the basis of race were subject to "strict scrutiny."

In response to *Adarand*, the White House instructed agencies not to use racial, ethnic, or gender-based affirmative action classifications in their human resource management programs without explicit approval from the Justice Department. *Adarand* forced the federal government to suspend (but not necessarily cancel) set-aside programs that designated specific, numerical goals for awarding contracts to businesses owned by minorities and women, affecting at least $1 billion in minority set-aside contracts.[276]

How much these actions actually affected businesses owned by minorities and women, however, is debatable. One analysis of the impact of *Adarand* concluded that "constitutional flexibility to establish racial, ethnic, and gender goals and timetables to promote federal workforce diversity simply may not make much difference, except possibly for the smallest minority groups."[277]

Disabled Americans. In 1990, Congress enacted the Americans with Disabilities Act, which defined the disabled as a group entitled to basic civil rights and prohibited discrimination against the disabled in employment and accommodations. The act essentially eclipsed earlier legislation, notably the Architectural Barriers Act of 1968 and the Rehabilitation Act of 1973.

The Americans with Disabilities Act defines *disability* as a "physical or mental impairment that substantially limits one or more of the major life activities" of a person. This wording is unusually inclusive and applies to some forty-five million Americans, or about 15 percent of the population. Scholars have called the Americans with Disabilities Act "one of the most sweeping nondiscrimination pieces of legislation since the Civil Rights Act of 1964."[278] The courts, however, have been busy with their dustpans, and employers have won more than nine out of ten of the suits brought under the Act's auspices.[279]

Sexual Orientation. In 1998, President Bill Clinton issued Executive Order 13087, which, for the first time, stated that it was federal policy that a person's sexual orientation should not be a basis for the denial of a job or promotion in the federal civilian workforce. Twenty-six states and the District of Columbia have prohibited discrimination in employment on the basis of sexual orientation. More than 200 local governments have enacted comparable policies.[280]

Oddly, it appears that gay men may the victims of *negative* discrimination relative to heterosexual men in the workplace, but that lesbian women may be the beneficiaries of *positive* discrimination relative to heterosexual women. A large-scale analysis of this issue found that homosexual men earned from 14 percent to 16 percent less than heterosexual men, but that homosexual women earned from 20 percent to 34 percent more than did heterosexual women.[281] In any event, "relatively few" formal allegations of discrimination on the basis of sexual orientation, according to the GAO, have followed the enactment of these laws.[282]

A Summing Up. In sum, the federal government forbids discrimination by any employer on the basis of race, religion, sex, national origin, age, and disability. The federal employer, the nation's capital, and some states and localities also prohibit discrimination on the basis of sexual orientation. Together, these *protected classes*, as they are called, constitute an impressively large chunk of the American population, and about nine out of ten American adults are protected by federal affirmative action policies.

Federal Enforcement of Affirmative Action

All three branches of the federal government have taken an affirmative enforcement stand on affirmative action.

Congressional Enforcement. The critical law in the enforcement of affirmative action is the Equal Employment Opportunity Act of 1972. The act established the Equal Employment Opportunity Commission, which investigates charges of employment discrimination from around the nation, and may fine employers in all sectors if it finds discrimination.

Judicial Enforcement. Perhaps the judiciary's most notable innovation in enforcement is that of "disparate impact." *Disparate impact*, or *adverse impact*, holds that employees who allege discrimination in the workplace do not have to prove that their employer deliberately tried to discriminate against them, but only that they have been disproportionately harmed by workplace policies. Hence, employers can be fined and required to change workplace policies, even though they have not intentionally discriminated.

Over the years, the Supreme Court, citing Title VII of the Civil Rights Act of 1964, has applied the doctrine of disparate impact in cases involving discrimination on the basis of sex, religion, and race. In 2005, the Court, citing the Age Discrimination in Employment Act, extended disparate impact to age discrimination.[283]

Executive Enforcement. LBJ's Executive Orders 11246 and 11375 cover some 200,000 government contractors and subcontractors, employing nearly a fourth of the nation's labor pool. They are enforced by the Department of Labor's Order Number 4 of 1971, which charges the Department's Office of Federal Contract Compliance Program to implement it. In 1978, the Labor Department issued Revised Order Number 4, which set specific goals and timetables for organizations and companies with federal contracts to establish effective plans for affirmative action. It was this order that was largely responsible for the expansion of affirmative action offices in universities, organizations, agencies, and corporations, because most employers were now required to develop, update, and implement specific affirmative action goals. In addition, the Federal Communications Commission (FCC), also beginning in the 1970s, enforces affirmative action among the nation's 5,000 radio stations and 1,500 television stations, which typically do not hold federal contracts. In 1990, the Supreme Court upheld that the FCC may take race into account in distributing broadcast licenses.[284] A variety of federal agencies, such as the Federal Reserve Board, the Comptroller of the Currency, and the Department of Housing and Urban Development, among others, enforce affirmative action among the nation's banks, mortgage companies, and insurance companies.

Affirmative Action and the Grass-Roots Governments

Among the first institutions to feel the impact of these federal forays were state and local governments, where the bulk of public positions—some nineteen million jobs—are found. When Washington introduced affirmative action programs to the nation in the 1960s, the indications are that subnational governments initially resisted implementing these programs' goals.[285] But, over time, this changed, and local public administrators in particular led this change. A national survey of cities conducted in the early 1970s found that city managers were *"far and away* the principal initiators of affirmative action in their governments."[286]

Today, over two-thirds of cities and counties have government-wide affirmative action policies, up from about half fifteen years earlier. Over 95 percent of these local policies cover minorities, nine out of ten include women, and well over three quarters address the disabled.[287]

These numbers imply real public progress, and, as noted, this progress seems to be attributable to the public bureaucrats.

"Reverse Discrimination" and the Quota Question

How is success measured in affirmative action? Can an employer succeed by merely promising (earnestly, of course) to review the job applications of a few more people in the "protected classes"? Or does success require the dismissal of all mentally and physically fit white men under forty years of age, and their replacement by people from those same classes?

These are queries that bring us quickly to the question of quotas. *Quotas* in public personnel administration refer to the argument that the traditional entry and promotion qualifications of the civil service, such as high test scores, should be reduced or waived for the disadvantaged until the number of women, minority group members, and disabled and older Americans working in government at all ranks at least equals their proportion of the population at large. If 10 percent of a city's population, for instance, were African American, it would then follow that blacks should be allocated 10 percent of the jobs available in city hall.[288]

The rub, of course, is that some well-qualified mentally and physically fit white men under forty could be not be hired, trained, or promoted in a system of quotas that must be filled by disabled Americans, minorities, women, or anyone over forty. When this happens, the charge of "reverse discrimination" is occasionally leveled.

The "Quota Bill" of 1991.   In 1991, Congress took a forthright stand on this issue by passing the Civil Rights Act of that year, which made it much more difficult—and costly—for employers to fire workers in the protected classes. Opponents, in fact, derided the Civil Rights Act of 1991 as a "quota bill."

Unexpectedly, the legislation seems to have backfired. One analysis found that, because the act made it much easier for protected workers who had been fired to prove discrimination and increased by significant margins the damages that a successful plaintiff could collect for discrimination, employers tried to find new ways to cut their losses.

This they did. Only about a fifth of all workers who are let go are actually fired for cause, so it is not a major problem for management to mix in those protected workers whom it actually wants to dismiss with a larger group that includes white men; it is just a matter of waiting for a downturn to trigger layoffs. But this practice makes discrimination much more difficult to prove.

As a consequence, the overall rate at which protected workers are terminated has remained the same as it was before the 1991 law came into effect. African American men are now fired for cause much less frequently, but this reduction has been canceled out by much more frequent layoffs of black men. For white men, the ratio of firings to layoffs has stayed the same.[289]

In brief, the Civil Rights Act of 1991 was a factor in ending "a decades-long trend of greater labor-market integration," and the gains that minorities and women had made in "historically unwelcoming sectors." Employers were taking "fewer chances" on hiring "untested protected workers."[290]

Congress, in sum, has shown itself to be less than adroit in addressing the quota question. The judiciary, however, has made its own attempts to do so for decades, and, as a result, has found itself deeply immersed in the effort to make fairer the working lives of all Americans.

Two Defining Decisions.   The most famous reverse discrimination case is *Regents of the University of California* v. *Bakke*, in which Allan Bakke, a white male, was denied admission to the University of California's medical school because that institution had set aside a portion of each entering class for "approved minorities." In 1978 the Supreme Court, in a five-to-four decision, ruled against the university, holding that Bakke should have been admitted to the medical school on the basis of the Civil Rights Act of 1964. Of greater significance, all nine justices agreed that affirmative action programs *per se* were neither unconstitutional nor illegal, and that being from a minority group could, in the justices' view, "be deemed a 'plus' in a particular applicant's file."

A year following the *Bakke* ruling, the Supreme Court heard a second case that came to be known as the "blue-collar *Bakke*" decision. In *Weber* v. *Kaiser Aluminum and Steel Corporation and United Steel Workers Union*, Brian Weber, a white lab technician, charged discrimination against whites in a training program that mandated that half of its available positions be filled by whites and the other half be filled by blacks. The Court held that employers could consider race as one of many factors not only in training policies, but in hiring and promotion policies as well.

In effect, both decisions outlawed the use of quotas but left some leeway for colleges and employers to improve the odds for minority applicants and employees.

Two Definitive Decisions. For the next quarter-century, the judiciary churned out a series of largely ambivalent rulings about the legitimacy of affirmative action and quotas. For the most part, these decisions wobbled either for or against diversity; forthrightly rejected quotas in words, but often permitted them in practice; and micromanaged the administration of affirmative action policies. As a result of this judicial hemming and hawing, there was a growing national uncertainty about the future of affirmative action.

Finally, in 2003, the Supreme Court decided a pair of cases that, relatively definitively and forcefully, addressed whether racial preference programs unconstitutionally discriminated against whites.

Both cases were brought by the University of Michigan. In the first case, *Gratz* v. *Bollinger*, decided in a six-to-three ruling, the Court stated that the university's undergraduate admissions policy, which amounted to a point system designed in part to increase diversity, was ill-conceived as a means achieving that diversity and was ruled unconstitutional.

In the second case, *Grutter* v. *Bollinger*, decided five-to-four, the Court held that the university's law school used a less structured admissions policy than it used for undergraduate admissions. The law school's policy took race into account, although less so than did the university's

undergraduate admissions policy. The Court ruled that the university's admissions policy for its law school was constitutional.

Of greatest importance, however, both decisions acknowledged that the University of Michigan had a compelling interest in increasing campus diversity, and that this goal was constitutional. By implication, the encouragement of diversity throughout society was also constitutional.

Tests: The Validation Vexation

A dimension of affirmative action that is closely related to reverse discrimination is that of testing applicants for jobs or promotions. This brings us to the problem of *test validity*, or the level of confidence that employers can reasonably have in the power of examination scores to predict how well or how badly an applicant will fare in a particular job. As we shall see, minorities and, to a lesser degree, women score lower, on average, than do whites and men on employment and promotion tests, so test validity has real relevance in assuring that governments are not practicing policies that have a disparate impact

To mitigate against this problem of adverse impact, Congress and the courts have focused especially on two kinds of test validity. The first is whether the test actually examines for qualifications that are really needed to do the job in question; these qualifications can include special skills, particular levels of general cognitive ability, and minimum education requirements, among others. The second sort of test validity is whether the test is fair to minority and women applicants. We consider these types in turn.

Qualification Validity. In 1971, the Supreme Court rendered its decision in the landmark case, *Griggs* v. *Duke Power Company*. The Court ruled that the Civil Rights Act of 1964 prohibited discriminatory employment practices against blacks in a private company, thereby barring those employment practices that operate to exclude members of disadvantaged groups when those practices cannot be shown to relate to job performance.

Testing for Cognitive Ability. In its *Griggs* decision, the Court effectively banned general cognitive ability tests (that is, "intelligence" tests) and minimum education requirements, unless the scores on those tests and the education requirements could be shown to relate to job performance. This caused problems. The "dilemma in deciding whether to use cognitive ability tests for selection boils down to a choice between using what is likely the single best predictor of job performance and incurring adverse impact or utilizing other, less effective predictors and potentially increasing minority representation in the workforce."[291]

The Courts and Cognition. Governments are understandably frustrated by what they take to be the courts' apparent position that entry and promotion examinations that test for general cognitive ability are illegal. Yet, a closer examination reveals that, over the years, the judiciary has been reasonably consistent on this issue and has not excluded the use of intelligence tests that are well conceived and administered.

A study of twenty-two lawsuits that challenged cognitive-based testing over a period of twelve years, found that most of these lawsuits were race-based claims and pertained to civil service jobs.

A clear pattern emerged in how the courts decided these cases. If the agency or company had used a professionally developed test that had been validated, preferably by using test-validation experts who relied on professional standards, and if the results from those tests were used properly when setting cutoff scores, then the courts generally supported the organization that relied on such tests to determine who should be hired and promoted.[292]

Cultural Validity. Writing a test so that it yields some predictive power in terms of an applicant's prospective performance in a specific job is one sort of test validity. Another is writing a test so that it does not disqualify wholly qualified applicants, and this possibility is called "culturally biased" testing.

Cultural bias refers to the tendency of those highly educated people who write examinations to unwittingly slant the phrasing and nuances of their test questions in ways that reflect their own culture. Thus, people taking an examination who are not members of the dominant culture are unfairly handicapped in their chances to score as well as those examinees who have been reared in the prevailing culture.

Local government managers consistently identify "test results" as the single greatest disqualifier of minorities seeking employment, followed by minimum education requirements.[293] Typically, African Americans score lower than whites on cognitive ability tests, as do Hispanic Americans, although their scores are slightly closer to whites than are those of African Americans.[294] Women score lower than men on these exams, but gender gaps are narrower than are racial gaps among these scores.[295]

Two important cases, *Albemarle Paper Company* v. *Moody,* decided in 1975, and *State of Connecticut* et al. v. *Adele* (1982), firmly established the principle that cultural bias in testing is against the law. In *Albemarle*, the Court ruled that culturally biased tests were illegal, even though the employer was not discriminating intentionally, and in *Connecticut* the justices held that, even though the state had promoted more blacks than whites, using a test that nevertheless was culturally biased still was illegal.

In short, the judiciary is not against testing. But it is against tests that are invalid.

Governments' Response. The courts' decisions on test validity challenged a fundamental foundation of the merit system: the use of tests to determine applicants' entry into government, and the subsequent careers of public administrators and other government workers. The ways in which governments have responded to this challenge vary.

As we noted earlier, the federal government was barred by the courts for a decade from using a common written test for entry into the federal service because of problems of cultural bias, and in essence the federal government as a whole has abandoned "universal" application tests. Competitive entry examinations are still used extensively by Washington, mostly at the agency level, but their use is in precipitous decline, and only about a fourth of new federal administrators and professionals are hired through tests.[296]

By contrast, as we also observed earlier, the grass-roots governments continue to use written tests extensively, and their use, in contrast to federal trends, seems to be rising.[297] Of greater importance, however, state and local governments have taken the problem of test validity fairly seriously. A survey of every major state and local public personnel system (outside of education) in 1970 indicated that only 54 percent of them validated any tests in any way regardless of type—written, oral, or whatever.[298] But a second survey taken five years later found that 87 percent had initiated test validation procedures.[299]

All in all, Congress, the courts, and the bureaucracies of federal, state, and local governments have moved in a constructive way to match talent with fairness in employment.

Women's Work?

At least two issues are present in governments' attempts to end discrimination in employment that are of special relevance to women, although none of them is necessarily the sole preserve of women. They are comparable worth and sexual harassment. We review these issues here.

The Curious Question of Comparable Worth. "Comparable worth" is a newer wrinkle in the fabric of affirmative action.

Comparing the Value of Work.   *Comparable worth* means that employees should be paid the same rate of pay for performing tasks that involve roughly the same levels of importance, knowledge, stress, skills, and responsibilities, even though the tasks themselves may be quite different. The unit of analysis used in comparable worth is not individual positions, such as a secretary, but whole position classifications, such as all secretaries. When one job classification is judged to be of comparable worth to another job classification (for example, if what secretaries do is deemed to be comparable to what highway repair workers do), then employees in both classifications must be paid at a comparable rate. As a practical matter, comparable worth works to raise the salaries of employees in position classifications dominated by women.

Comparable worth relies on the idea that the social value of occupations can be compared, and this can be a tricky business. For example, are the musicians in a city's symphony orchestra worth "more" to society than the workers in the municipal waterworks? The contributions of the musicians may elevate and inspire our souls, but we need potable water. Because the theory of comparable worth leads to these kinds of questions, the chair of the U.S. Commission on Civil Rights (a man) called the concept "the looniest idea since Looney Tunes came on the screen,"[300] and the director of the U.S. Office of Personnel Management (a woman), in testifying against comparable worth in Congress, stated that pressures for its adoption were "perplexing at best."[301] Women's rights groups immediately took sharp issue with both officials.

Implementing Comparable Worth.   Much of the interest in comparable worth associates with the case of *American Federation of State, County, and Municipal Employees (AFSCME)* v. *State of Washington*, in which the Ninth Circuit Court of Appeals overruled the lower court and held in 1985 that Washington State was not required to award back pay to 15,500 state employees in position classifications dominated by women. The Civil Rights Act did not obligate Washington, in the court's ruling, "to eliminate an economic inequality which it did not create." Ultimately, the case was settled out of court, and Washington State agreed to set new pay levels for some 60,000 state employees, at a cost of $571 million, in an effort to bring women's salaries in line with those of men.

Despite the judiciary's ambivalent-to-negative views on comparable worth, states and communities have been notably progressive in confronting the issue of their women employees being paid less than men in jobs that are equally demanding. Only five states have not undertaken some sort of activity in the area of comparable worth, and twenty states have raised pay for women as a result of such activity. Eight states have enacted laws establishing the principle of comparable worth for all state employees.[302] Almost 10 percent of cities and nearly 12 percent of counties have enacted comparable worth policies.[303]

Implementing comparable worth policies is, paradoxically, both economical and difficult. In the eight states that have enacted comparable worth laws, aggregate pay gaps between female and male employees ranged from 14 percent to 31 percent, although closing these gaps required a relatively modest expenditure that ranged from 1 percent to 4 percent of the total state payroll. Even so, introducing comparable worth has resulted in such anomalies as intensified pay compression between lower and higher ranks, including some workers being paid more than their own supervisors; major slippages in the pay of state employees relative to their counterparts in the private sector; and men leaving state employment in greater numbers after comparable worth had been introduced.[304]

Whether comparable worth is "looney," progressive, or merely "perplexing," it will be an issue for some time to come, in part because the people seem to be for it, perhaps by as much as three to one.[305]

The New Meaning of Sex at Work. Clearly not looney but perhaps as perplexing is another personnel policy that has a particular (but not exclusive) applicability to women: sexual harassment. *Sexual harassment* is a comment or act made or permitted by a coworker in the workplace, including a workplace environment, which is interpreted by another coworker to have sexual overtones, and causes discomfort in, or is offensive to, the worker. Sexual harassment can range from the contemptible (such as a superior demanding sexual favors from a subordinate as the price of continued employment) to the boorish (for example, a pattern of vulgar jokes by a peer).

Most private firms, the federal government, at least two-thirds of the states (only eight states clearly fail to address this issue),[306] and almost 90 percent of local governments[307] have policies prohibiting sexual harassment. Despite these prohibitions, the number of sexual harassment charges being filed by employees around the country with the Equal Employment Opportunity Commission is growing at a rate five times faster than all other types of discrimination charges

combined, and now number almost 16,000 a year, or approximately a fifth of all charges received by the commission.[308]

Who Harasses and Where? The federal government has been surveying its employees about incidents of "unwanted sexual attention" since 1980 and has found that more than two-fifths of women and nearly a fifth of men report such incidents occurring over the preceding two years.[309]

Almost four-fifths of unwanted sexual attention reported by federal workers comes not from workers' supervisors but from coworkers or other employees. Because supervisors are not involved, it is unlikely that the courts would consider this kind of attention to be sexual harassment. Twenty-eight percent of female and 14 percent of male federal workers report that an immediate or higher level supervisor was responsible, and this sort of attention could qualify as sexual harassment. If so, the costs are high: The federal government estimates that sexual harassment costs it over $160 million per year.[310]

Perspective, of course, is pertinent, and it appears that sexual harassment in the public sector does not attain its levels in the private sector. Twenty-two percent of those federal workers who have worked outside the government believe that there is more sexual harassment in these nonfederal workplaces, compared to 7 percent who think there is less.[311] One survey of more than 400 women executives in private industry found that nearly two-thirds reported that they had been sexually harassed—a significantly higher proportion than in government.[312] Another survey of workers in the private sector found that over two-fifths of the official complaints made about sexual harassment allege that direct or other supervisors were the ones doing the harassing—again, a significantly higher proportion than in government.[313]

The Court Weighs In. In 1986, the Supreme Court heard its first sexual harassment case in *Meritor Savings Bank* v. *Vinson.* The Court stated that Title VII of the Civil Rights Act of 1964 covered sexual harassment, in effect declaring sexual harassment to be a form of discrimination.

In 1992, the Court really got tough in the case of *Franklin* v. *Gwinnett County Public Schools,* in which the Supreme Court reversed the ruling of two lower courts and ruled that students (and, by inference, employees) who have been victims of sexual harassment could sue their schools (or employers) for damages.

In 1998, the Court decided three important cases that did much to clarify the legalities of sexual harassment. The first was *Oncale* v. *Sundowner Offshore Services,* in which the justices unanimously overturned a lower court's ruling and found that harassment could occur in same-sex situations. In other words, sexual harassment is not sex, but conduct.

The other two cases, *Fanagher* v. *City of Boca Raton* and *Burlington Industries, Inc.,* v. *Ellerth,* were decided *au pair* in seven-to-two decisions. The Court held that employers are always legally liable for their supervisors' harassment of employees which results in tangible adverse actions (such as demotion or firing) taken against those employees, whether or not the employers knew about the harassment. But the Court also afforded employers some protection if the employer could show that there were antiharassment policies and complaint procedures in place which displayed "reasonable care" by the employer in preventing and correcting harassment. If harassed employees chose to ignore these policies and procedures, then they could expect little if any protection from the judiciary. It is likely that the courts now will be building case law over what "reasonable care" means in practice.

The judicial history of sexual harassment could be having an impact not only on managers, who now can be sued over their failure to deal with it, but on workers, too, especially government workers. In 1980, only 65 percent of male federal employees stated that pressuring an employee for sexual favors constituted harassment; fourteen years later, 93 percent said so.[314]

The Effects of the Efforts

When it comes to affirmative action, everyone has pitched in: governments, businesses, nonprofit organizations, and the people themselves. Has this effort been successful?

The Federal Record. Over time, the federal government has increased the representation of minorities and women in its workforce.

Minority Federal Workers and Executives. People of color comprise nearly 31 percent of the American population, almost 29 percent of the private sector's labor force, and more than 31 percent of federal employees. Almost 18 percent of federal civilian workers are African American (whose proportion of the total American resident population is 13 percent, and over 10 percent of the private sector's workforce); 7 percent are Hispanic Americans (who number 13 percent of the total population; and over 13 percent of the private sector's labor force); and over 7 percent are other minorities (who account for 5 percent of the population and over 5 percent of the workforce).[315]

These are encouraging figures. Moreover, the proportion of minorities working in the federal government's lower grade levels in going down, and the percentage of those working in its upper grades is going up. Fourteen percent of the top federal executives are African American, Hispanic American, or are from other minority groups.[316]

Table 9-1 provides details, and it indicates that, over twenty-four years, minority progress in the federal government has been steady and, in several instances, dramatic.[317]

Women Federal Workers and Executives. A similar configuration is evident for women in the federal employ. Women comprise 51 percent of the American population, almost 47 percent of the private sector's labor force, and nearly 45 percent of the full-time civilian employees who work in the federal government.[318] As Table 9-1 shows, women have made substantial progress, with over a fourth of top posts occupied by women—almost a seven-fold expansion over two-dozen years.

The State and Local Record. As Table 9-2 shows, similar patterns can be found at the state and local levels.

Minority Grass-Roots Workers and Executives. Thirty-one percent of all full-time state and local employees (excluding educators) are African

Table 9-1 **Percentages of Federal Full-Time Civilian Black, Hispanic, and Women Employees, by General Schedule and Related Grades, 1980 and 2003**

Grade Range	1980			2003		
	Black	Hispanic	Women	Black	Hispanic	Women
Total Executive/Senior Pay Levels ($$$$$)	5%	Fewer than 50	4%	7%	3%	26%
Grades 13–15 ($$$$)	5	2%	8	11	4	33
Grades 9–12 ($$$)	9	3	19	15	8	47
Grades 5–8 ($$)	20	4	46	24	9	65
Grades 1–4 ($)	24	5	74	24	9	64
Totals, All Employees	15	4	45	17	7	45

Notes: Percentages have been rounded and are expressed as a percentage of all federal employees in each grade range. Covers executive branch, General Schedule, and related employees only. Excludes employees in the Postal Service, Wage Pay System, and other pay systems. Some grade ranges for women varied slightly in 1980 from those in 2003. For women only, Grades 9–12 in the table were actually Grades 11–12 for women in 1980; Grades 5–8 were Grades 7–10 in 1980; and Grades 1–4 were Grades 1–6 in 1980. Grades 13–15 were the same for women in 1980 and 2003. The grade range, "Total Executive/Senior Pay Levels," is identical in 1983 and 2003, but for women it covers only the Senior Executive Service in both years.

Sources: As derived from data in U.S. Office of Personnel Management, *The Fact Book, 2004* (Washington, DC: U.S. Government Printing Office, 2005), pp. 10, 11, 28, 52, 74; U.S. Bureau of the Census, *Statistical Abstract of the United States, 2006,* 125th ed. (Washington, DC: U.S. Government Printing Office, 2006), Table 485; and U.S. Bureau of Census, *Statistical Abstract of the United States, 1982–1983,* 103rd ed. (Washington, DC: U.S. Government Printing Office, 1982), Tables 460 and 457.

Americans, Hispanic Americans, or are from other minority groups, but, as with the federal government, disproportionately large numbers of minorities are found at or near the bottom rungs of the state and local employment ladders.

Nevertheless, African Americans have made steady progress in all occupational categories over twenty-four years, and Hispanic Americans have at least doubled their representation in every category.

Table 9-2 **Percentages of Full-Time Black, Hispanic, and Women Employees in State and Local Governments (Excluding Education), by Occupation, 1980 and 2003**

Occupational Category	1980			2003		
	Blacks	Hispanic	Women	Black	Hispanic	Women
Officials/Administrators ($$$$)	6%	2%	23%	11%	5%	37%
Professionals ($$$)	9	3	44	15	7	37
Technicians ($$)	12	4	39	16	8	43
Blue Collar/Clerical ($)	19	5	40	22	10	42
Totals, All Employees	16	4	41	19	9	45

Notes: Percentages have been rounded and are expressed as a percentage of all state and local employees in each occupational category. The occupational category, "Blue Collar/Clerical," includes Protective Services, Paraprofessionals, Administrative Support, Skilled Craft, and Service Maintenance.

Sources: As derived from data in U.S. Bureau of the Census, *Statistical Abstract of the United Sates, 2006,* 125th ed. (Washington, DC: U.S. Government Printing Office, 2006), Table 454, and U.S. Bureau of the Census, *Statistical Abstract of the United States, 1982–1983,* 103rd. ed. (Washington, DC: U.S. Government Printing Office, 1982), Table 504.

Top spots, however, still need work. Few minorities head state agencies. Less than 11 percent of all state agencies are headed by minority executives. Less than 7 percent are African American, and less than 3 percent are Hispanic. However, these numbers are rising over time.[319]

At the local level, there is less progress. Only 5 percent of the highest appointed local executives, city and county managers, are minorities, but, as with state executives, these figures are going up.[320]

Women Grass-Roots Workers and Executives. Forty-five percent of all full-time state and local employees (again excluding educators) are women. As Table 9-2 indicates, relatively large numbers of women are found in the upper rungs of the grass-roots occupational ladders.

In the states, more than 29 percent of gubernatorially appointed department heads are women, a proportion that is rising, if unsteadily.[321]

At the local level, 12 percent of the top appointed executives in municipalities and counties are women, and this proportion is rising.[322] A fourth of the executive directors of public authorities, most of which are recognized by the U.S. Census Bureau as stand-alone local governments, are women.[323] "Of the three levels of government, the local level has apparently had the greatest progress toward gender equity."[324]

The Third Sector Record. Sixteen percent of nonprofit employees are people of color; 7 percent are African American and 4 percent are Hispanic. From two-thirds to three-fourths of employees in the independent sector are women.[325]

Almost 15 percent of the executive directors of nonprofit associations, and over 17 percent of the presidents and board chairs, are women. Although these numbers do not qualify as embarrassingly low, given the large volume of women working in the independent sector, it is perhaps perplexing that more do not have the top jobs. Women are more likely to occupy these positions when the association has a smaller budget, is relatively new, is in some city other than Washington, DC, and has a relatively large percentage of women serving on its board.[326]

A Palpably Progressive Public Sector

Many of the public- and nonprofit-sector numbers that we have just reviewed can and should be larger. But context, as we often have pointed out, is worth comprehending, and assessing the nation's progress toward more diverse workplaces is no exception.

A More Welcoming Workplace. Without question, minorities and women have fared far better in the public sector than they have in the private one.

At the national level, analyses indicate that "federal agencies are on a par, or even ahead, of their corporate counterparts in the initiation of new recruitment, training, and development" of members of disadvantaged groups.[327]

State and local agencies seem even further ahead, and there are proportionately more women and African Americans (but not Hispanic Americans) working in technical, professional, and managerial positions in these governments than in the private sector. Moreover, they (including Hispanics) are paid more than are their counterparts in commerce. "In the aggregate, state and local governments are doing considerably better than the private sector in living up the challenge of attaining sexual and racial-ethnic employment equity," establishing a record that is "quite impressive."[328]

A More Promoting Workplace. The public sector's achievements extend to the very top strata. As we have noted, from 5 percent to 14 percent of the nation's top public executives, depending on the level of government, are minorities. Compare these figures to the private sector, where the chief executive officers of the *Fortune* 500 companies who are minorities ranges, in any given year, from nil to an infinitesimal fraction of 1 percent.[329]

Similarly, as we also observed earlier, from 12 percent to 29 percent of the country's top public administrators at all governmental levels are women. By contrast, a very small fraction of 1 percent of the chief executive officers of the *Fortune* 500 companies are women, although this tiny proportion is rising, glacially, over time.[330]

These statistics imply that women have a tougher time getting ahead in the private sector than they do in the public one, and research indicates that this is the case. Studies of two large firms, for example, concluded that there was statistically significant evidence that women managers "are viewed with suspicion and that their commitment and competence are overtested" when decisions on advancements are being made.[331] Another study of the private sector found that, even though female managers were more aggressive in pursuing promotions and had higher performance scores than did males, men nevertheless were offered more promotions per years of service than were women.[332]

Compared to the private sector, then, minorities and women in the public sector, and, to a somewhat lesser degree, in the nonprofit sector, are both doing well and doing good.

A Demographic Solution?

In light of the enormous effort that has been expended by governments and nonprofit organizations to provide more opportunities for minorities, women, and other protected classes, it is ironic that any prospects for a fairer future for these populations may have little to do with that effort. After almost a half century of implementation, "only a small fraction of the public"—a modest 16 percent—"reports having been directly affected by affirmative action programs," whether for good or ill.[333]

Demographics may "implement" more diversity in the workplaces of all three sectors than affirmative action policies have yet done.

The Endangered White Male.   Here is why. The percentage of white males in the total U.S. civilian labor force (that is, workers in all sectors) has been in steady decline since 1940, when they constituted 69 percent of the civilian labor force.[334] Today, this proportion has slipped by almost a third to less than 45 percent, and the Bureau of Labor Statistics projects that this proportion will slide further, to less than 43 percent, by 2012.[335]

This loss of white males in the workforce is due to the fact that the country's supply of young white men is shrinking, although less so in recent years.[336] White males still will comprise the largest single category of workers, but, increasingly, minorities and women will take and are taking their place.

The Rise of Minorities and Women.   Between 1980 and 2004, the proportion of minority workers in the total U.S. civilian labor force expanded by 70 percent, from 17 percent to almost 29 percent. It is projected that minority workers will constitute nearly a third of all workers in the civilian labor force by 2012.[337] The largest increases likely will be among Asians and Hispanics.[338]

Women are expected to continue to enter the work force at a faster rate than men.[339] Today, women comprise 46 percent of the civilian labor force, and their share is projected to stabilize over the next decade while men's share will continue its gradual decline.[340]

When we add these demographic changes to what appears to be a propensity among both women and minorities to enter the public sector at a more rapid rate than the private sector, then it is possible that we may look forward to governments staffed far more by women and people of color than they are now, and that there will continue to be more women and minorities working in government relative to corporate America in the future as well.[341]

Notes

1. U.S. Bureau of the Census, *Statistical Abstract of the United States, 2006,* 125th ed. (Washington, DC: U.S. Government Printing Office, 2006), Tables 451, 452. Figures are for 2003.
2. Gary W. Loveman and John J. Gabarro, "The Managerial Implications of Changing Work Force Demographics: A Scoping Survey," *Human Resource Management* 30 (Spring 1991), p. 15. See also American Management Association, as cited in "A Crash Course in the Three Rs?" *Business Week* (May 20, 1996), p. 31. In 1990, 26 percent of job applicants lacked basic reading and math skills; in 1995, 33 percent.
3. U.S. Merit Systems Protection Board, *Evolving Workforce Demographics: Federal Agency Action and Reaction* (Washington, DC: U.S. Government Printing Office, 1993), p. 29. Twenty-four agencies held this view. Figure is for 1992.
4. Gregory B. Lewis and Sue A. Frank, "Who Wants to Work for the Government?" *Public Administration*

Review 62 (July/August 2002), pp. 395–344. In 1998, 62 percent of 2,609 respondents stated that they preferred a job in private business, 24 percent preferred working for the government, and 14 percent could not choose between them. This article focuses on that 24 percent. The quotation is on p. 401. The years covered are 1989–1998. The data source is the General Social Survey conducted by the National Opinion Research Center at the University of Chicago.

5. Ibid., p. 401.

6. Peter D. Hart Research, *Calling Young People to Government Service: From "Ask Not" . . . to "Not Asked"* (Washington, DC: Council for Excellence in Government, 2004), p. 3. Figure is for 2004.

7. Harris Poll, as cited in Paul C. Light, "To Restore and Renew: Now Is the Time to Rebuild the Federal Government Public Service," *Government Executive* (November 2001), http://www.brook.edu, p. 7. Figures are for 2000.

8. Pew Research Center, as cited in Partnership for Public Service, *Public Opinion on Public Service*, Poll Watch, PPS–05–3 (Washington, DC: Author, 2005), p.4. Figure is for 1998.

9. Panetta Institute, as cited in ibid., p. 2. Figures are for 2001.

10. President George W. Bush, quoted in David S. Broder, "A Crisis in Public Service," *Washington Post* (October 21, 2001).

11. U.S. Merit Systems Protection Board, *The Changing Federal Workplace*: *Employee Perspectives* (Washington, DC: U.S. Government Printing Office, 1998), p. 25. Figure is for 1996.

12. James B. Conant and Dennis L. Dresang, "Retaining and Recruiting Career Professionals," in Frank D. Thompson, ed., *Revitalizing State and Local Public Service: Performance, Accountability, and Citizen Confidence* (San Francisco: Jossey-Bass, 1993), p. 127.

13. Larry M. Lane and James E. Wolf, *The Human Resource Crisis in the Public Sector: Rebuilding the Capacity to Govern* (New York: Quorum Books, 1990), p. 77.

14. U.S. Merit Systems Protection Board, *Attracting Quality Graduates to the Federal Government: A View of College Recruiting* (Washington, DC: U.S. Government Printing Office, 1988).

15. National Commission on the Public Service, *Leadership for America: Rebuilding the Public Service* (Washington, DC: Author, 1989).

16. U.S. General Accounting Office, *Federal Recruiting: Comparison of Applicants Who Accepted or Declined Federal Job Offers*, GAO/GGD–92–61BR (Washington, DC: U.S. Government Printing Office, 1993), p. 3.

17. U.S. Merit Systems Protection Board, *Competing for Federal Jobs: Job Search Experiences of New Hires* (Washington, DC: Author, 2000), pp. 4–5. In 1994, 50 percent of new federal hires had four-year college degrees, compared to 40 percent in 1998.

18. Gregory B. Lewis, "Grade Creep in the Federal Service?" *American Review of Public Administration* 27 (March 1997), pp. 4–21. We are referring to higher grades in the General Schedule. The years covered were 1977 through 1993.

19. See, for example, Julia E. Robinson, "The Role of the Independent Political Executive in State Governments: Stability in the Face of Change," *Public Administration Review* 58 (March/April 1998), pp. 119–128, and Tari Renner, "The Local Government Management Profession at Century's End," *Municipal Year Book, 2001* (Washington, DC: International City/County Management Association, 2001), pp. 38–39.

20. U.S. Merit Systems Protection Board, *The Federal Workforce for the 21st Century: Results of the Merit Principles Survey 2000* (Washington, DC: U.S. Government Printing Office, 2003), p. 15. Figures are for 2000.

21. Phillip C. Crewson, "Are the Best and the Brightest Fleeing Public Sector Employment? Evidence from the National Longitudinal Study of Youth," *Public Productivity and Management Review* 20 (June 1997), p. 368.

22. Ibid.

23. Ibid.

24. Stahl is precisely correct when he writes the that the civil service is different from the merit system. The civil service refers to the corpus of government civilian employees, who may, in theory, be managed by political patronage as well as by a merit system. A merit system, by contrast, is a personnel management system. We have chosen to use as one the terms *civil service system* and *merit system* on the logic that almost all governments in the United States purport, at least ostensibly, to manage their civil services with a merit system. See O. Glenn Stahl, *Public Personnel Administration*, 8th ed. (New York: Harper & Row, 1983), p. 35.

25. Frederick C. Mosher, *Democracy and the Public Service*, 2nd ed. (New York: Oxford University Press, 1982), p. 145.

26. Collleen A. Woodard, "Merit by Any Other Name— Reframing the Civil Service First Principle," *Public Administration Review* 65 (January/February 2005), p. 110.

27. Mosher, *Democracy and the Public Service*, pp. 217–218. The foregoing discussion is based loosely on pp. 217–221.

28. Stahl, *Public Personnel Administration*, p. 42. In 1980, the federal merit system officially covered 94 percent of federal civilian employees.

29. National Commission on the Public Service, *Urgent Business for America: Revitalizing the Federal Government for the 21st Century* (Washington, DC: U.S. Government Printing Office, 2003), p. 27. Figure is for 2002.

30. U.S. General Accounting Office, *Human Capital: OPM Can Better Assist Agencies in Using Personnel Flexibilities*, GAO–03–428 (Washington, DC: U.S. Government Printing Office, 2003), p. 7. Figure is for 2003. These employees were exempted, at least partially, from what are known as "Title 5 laws" (for Title 5 of the *United States Code*), which deal in part with classification, appointment, pay and benefits, and adverse action.

31. The legislation is the National Defense Authorization Act of 2004 and the Homeland Security Act of 2002. We detail these laws later in the chapter.

32. Howard Risher, "How Much Should Federal Employees Be Paid? The Problems with Using a Market Philosophy in a Broadband System," *Public Personnel Management* 34 (Summer 2005), p. 121.

33. U.S. Government Accountability Office, *Human Capital: Selected Agencies' Statutory Authorities Could Offer Options in Developing a Framework for Governmentwide Reform*, GAO–05–398R Human Capital Authorities (Washington, DC: U.S. Government Printing Office, 2005), p. 1.

34. Stahl, *Public Personnel Administration*, pp. 38, 41.

35. Andrew W. Boessel, "Local Personnel Management," *Municipal Year Book, 1974* (Washington, DC: International City Management Association, 1974), pp. 92–93. Gear is for 1974.

36. U.S. Advisory Commission on Intergovernmental Relations, *State Laws Governing Local Government and Administration*, M-186 (Washington, DC: U.S. Government Printing Office, 1993), p. 49. Figures are for 1990.

37. Ibid. Figure is for 1990.

38. As compiled from data in Bureau of Labor Statistics, U.S. Department of Labor, *Occupational Employment Statistics, 2004* (Washington, DC: Author, 2004), http://stats.bls.gov/oes/current/oes. In November 2004, there were in the United States 58,610 human resources managers (10,050 of whom worked in government); 32,610 training and development managers (2,100 were in government); and 53,320 compensation and benefits managers (3,280 in government). There were 173,160 employment, recruitment, and placement specialists (20,670 of whom worked in government); 95,800 compensation, benefits, and job analysis specialists (14,490 were in government); 206,140 training and development specialists (30,900 in government); and 168,580 human resources, training, and labor relations specialists (13,330 in government).

39. Steven W. Hays and Richard C. Kearney, "Anticipated Changes in Human Resource Management: Views from the Field," *Public Administration Review* 61 (September/October 2001), pp. 585–597. Data are for 1998. This was a national survey of 984 public personnelists at all levels of government and includes some consultants and professors of human resource management. The response rate was 33 percent.

40. Myron D. Fottler and Norman A. Townsend, "Characteristics of Public and Private Personnel Directors," *Public Personnel Management* 6 (July 1977) p. 252. and American Society of Personnel Administrators, *The Personnel Executive's Job* (Englewood Cliffs, NJ: Prentice Hall, 1977).

41. Hays and Kearney, "Anticipated Changes in Human Resource Management," p. 593. Data are for 1998.

42. A. L. Schmidt, et al., "The Economic Impact of Job Selection Methods on Size, Productivity and Payroll Costs of the Federal Work Force: An Empirically Based Demonstration," *Personnel Psychology* 39 (Spring 1986), pp. 1–30.

43. Peter D. Hart Research, *Calling Young People to Government Service*, p. 7. In 2004, 73 percent of young American adults said that no one had ever asked them about working in government. In 2002, 62 percent said this.

44. Constance Horner, as quoted in Judith Havemann, "New Federal Job Exams Set for June," *Washington Post* (April 22, 1990).

45. Carolyn Ban and Patricia W. Ingraham, "Retaining Quality Federal Employees: Life After PACE," *Public Administration Review* 48 (May/June 1988), pp. 708–725.

46. U.S. Merit Systems Protection Board, *Entering Professional Practices in the Federal Government* (Washington, DC: U.S. Government Printing Office, 1994). The study covered 1984 through 1994. Only 19 percent of applicants who entered federal service did so by taking any kind of competitive examination. Nearly a third were hired directly by the agency, and almost a fourth were promoted from within.

47. U.S. Merit Systems Protection Board, "Are New College Grads Landing Government Jobs?" *Issues of Merit* (September 2002), p. 6. In 2001, a total of 81,391 appointments into full-time nonseasonal federal positions were made. Of these, 47,053 were "career-conditional appointments" (the typical mode of entry for new permanent employees who have no previous civilian government service). Only 8,325 of the 47,053 career-conditional appointees were hired into entry-level professional and administrative positions, and only 3,149 of these were in the 21- to 25-year-old age group, or the group most likely to make federal administration a lifelong career.

48. Conant and Dresang, "Retaining and Recruiting Career Professionals," p. 127.

49. U.S. Office of Personnel Management, as cited in Light, "To Restore and Renew." Figure is for 1999.

50. U.S. Merit Systems Protection Board, "Who Gets Selected for Federal Jobs?" *Issues of Merit* (August 2001), pp. 1–3. Figures are for 2001, and are drawn from a survey of federal supervisors. See also U.S. Merit Systems Protection Board, *Help Wanted: A Review of Federal Vacancy Announcements* (Washington, DC: U.S. Government Printing Office, 2003).

51. U.S. General Accounting Office, *Human Capital: Opportunities to Improve Executive Agencies Hiring Processes*, GAO-03–450 (Washington, DC: U.S. Government Printing Office, 2003), p. 3.

52. Paul C. Light, "The Content of Their Character: The State of the Nonprofit Workforce," *Nonprofit Quarterly* 9 (Fall 2002), p. 11. In 2000 and 2001, 37 percent of 1,051 federal workers said that their hiring process had been simple, 18 percent said that it had been fast, and 75 percent said that it had been fair. The corresponding figures for 1,140 nonprofit employees were 72 percent, 44 percent, and 90 percent, respectively. For 1,005 private-sector workers, the numbers were 75 percent, 53 percent, and 90 percent, respectively.

53. U.S. Office of Personnel Management, *Human Capital Survey, 2002: What Do Federal Employees Say?* (Washington, DC: U.S. Government Printing Office, 2003), p. 22. Federal respondents are evenly divided on this. In 2002, 38 percent of federal employees said their work unit was hiring people with the wrong skills, and 39 percent said it was hiring people with the right skills.

54. Partnership for The Public Service, *Asking the Wrong Questions: A Look at How the Federal Government Assesses and Selects Its Workforce* (Washington, DC: Author, 2004), p. 1.

55. U.S. Merit Systems Protection Board, *The Role of the Delegated Examining Units: Hiring New Employees in a Decentralized Civil Service* (Washington, DC: U.S. Government Printing Office, 1999), p. vi.

56. U.S. Merit Systems Protection Board, *Building a High Quality Workforce: The Federal Career Intern Program* (Washington, DC: U.S. Government Printing Office, 2005). From 2000 through 2004, the total number of hires under the FCIP increased 28 percent. Hiring through competitive examinations decreased from 48 percent in 2000 to 26 percent to 2004.

57. Richard C. Elling, Lyke Thompson, and Valerie Monet, "The Problematic World of State Management: The More Things Change the More They Remain the Same," paper Presented at the Annual Meeting of the Midwest Political Science Association, Chicago, 2003. Figures are for 2000–2001.

58. Conant and Dresang, "Retaining and Recruiting Career Professionals," p. 127.

59. David Coursey, "E-Government: Trends, Benefits, and Challenges," *Municipal Year Book, 2005* (Washington, DC: International City/County Management Association, 2005), p. 17. Figures are for 2004.

60. Siegrun Fox Freyss, "Continuity and Change in Local Personnel Policies and Practices," *Municipal Year Book, 1996* (Washington, DC: International City/County Management Association, 1996), pp. 11–17.

61. Lana Stein, "Merit Systems and Political Influence: The Case of Local Government," *Public Administration Review* 47 (May/June 1987), p. 267. Lana Public safety positions are the highest scorer in this regard, with 97 percent of large cities reporting that they use written tests for determining hires in the police field, followed by positions in fire departments and clerical jobs; the lowest use of written examinations (15 percent) is for positions as sanitation workers. About 45 percent of cities use written tests for entry level professional positions. Stein sent questionnaires to personnel departments in 172 cities with 100,000 people or more, and obtained a response rate of 86 percent. Data are for 1986.

62. U.S. Advisory Commission on Intergovernmental Relations, *State Laws Governing Local Government Structure and Administration*, p. 49. Figure is for 1990.

63. N. Joseph Cayer, "Local Government Personnel Structure and Policies," *Municipal Year Book, 1991* (Washington, DC: International City/County Management Association, 1991), p. 9.

64. Steven W. Hays, "Trends and Best Practices in State and Local Human Resource Management," *Review of Public Personnel Administration* 24 (October 2004), pp. 265–266.

65. Jonathan Walters, "Untangling Albany," *Governing* (December 1998), p. 20.

66. National Commission on the State and Local Public Service, *Hard Truths/Tough Choices: An Agenda for State and Local Reform.* First Report. (Albany: State University of New York, 1993), p. 27; National Academy of Public Administration, *Modernizing Federal Classification: An Opportunity for Excellence* (Washington, DC: National Academy of Public Administration, 1991); and Al Gore, *From Red Tape to Results: Creating a Government that Works Better and Costs Less. Reinventing Human Resource Management: Report of the National Performance Review* (Washington, DC: U.S. Government Printing Office, 1993).

67. National Commission on the Public Service, *Urgent Business for America*, pp. 41–42. In 2002, five agencies had broadbanding: Office of Personnel Management, National Institute of Standards and Technology, Internal Revenue Service, Federal Aviation Administration, and Government Accountability Office. The Departments of Homeland Security and Defense are implementing broadbanding.

68. Ibid, p. 27. The Commission recommended that the fifteen grades be consolidated into six to eight broadbands.

69. Sally Coleman Selden, Patricia Wallace Ingraham, and Will Jacobson, "Human Resource Practices in State Government: Findings from a National Survey," *Public Administration Review* 61 (September/October 2001), p. 604. Data are for 1991–1998. Forty-nine states responded to the national survey.

70. J. West, "City Personnel Management: Issues and Reforms," *Public Personnel Management* 13 (Fall 1984), pp. 317–334.

71. Steven Gold and Sarah Ritchie, "Compensation of State and Local Employees: Sorting out the Issues," in Frank Thompson, ed., *Revitalizing State or Local Public Service*, (San Francisco: Jossey-Bass), pp.163–196; and M. L. Miller, "The Public/Private Pay Debate: What Do the Data Show?" *Monthly Labor Review* (May 1996), pp. 18–29.

72. Ibid., both citations.

73. Kevin Merida, "Americans Want a Direct Say in Political Decision-Making, Pollsters Find," *Washington Post* (April 17, 1994). The 1994 survey of 900 citizens was conducted by the Americans Talk Issues Foundation.

74. Commission on Executive, Legislative, and Judicial Salaries, *High Quality Leadership: Our Government's Most Precious Asset* (Washington DC: U.S. Government Printing Office, 1987), and Task Force on the Senior Executive Service, Twentieth Century Fund, *The Government's Managers* (New York: Priority Press Publications, 1987). See also Task Force on Pay and Compensation, *Report of the Task Force on Pay and Compensation to the National Commission on the Public Service* (Washington, DC: National Commission on the

Public Service, 1989). Between 1970 and 1987, the purchasing power of federal administrators fell by as much as two-fifths, while the purchasing power of corporate executives rose by more than two-thirds.

75. U.S. Merit Systems Protection Board, *Why Are Employees Leaving the Federal Government? Results of an Exit Survey* (Washington, DC: U.S. Government Printing Office, 1990). The reasons cited most frequently for resigning after pay and advancement were organizational management concerns, with 17 percent—a distant second.

76. U.S. Office of Personnel Management, *The Fact Book: Federal Civilian Workforce Statistics, 2004* (Washington, DC: U.S. Government Printing Office, 2005), p. 74. Figure is for 2004.

77. U.S. Merit Systems Protection Board, *Working for America: A Federal Employment Survey* (Washington, DC: U.S. Government Printing Office, 1990), and U.S. General Accounting Office, *Senior Executive Service: Opinions about the Federal Work Environment.* GAO/GGO–92–63 (Washington, DC: U.S. Government Printing Office, 1992). In 1989, 11 percent of SES executives were satisfied with their salaries; in 1991, 78 percent were.

78. U.S. Merit Systems Protection Board, *The Changing Federal Workplace: Employee Perspectives* (Washington, DC: U.S. Government Printing Office, 1998), p. 28. In 1989, 28 percent of all federal workers were satisfied with their salaries; in 1992, 42 percent; and in 1996, 50 percent.

79. Ken McDonnell, "Facts from EBRI: Compensation Costs in the Private and State/Local Public Sectors," *EBRI Notes* 26 (March 2005), pp. 10–15. In 2004, private-sector employer compensation costs were $23.76 per hour worked, up from $13.42 in 1987. Compensation costs for state and local governments were $34.72 per hour worked, up from $22.31 in 1991. Compensation costs for both sectors had risen at an annual rate of 3.3 percent. Benefits as a percentage of total compensation costs were over 30 percent for all workers (the private and public sectors were not separated), and over 36 percent for "public administration." The analysis was conducted by the Employee Benefit Research Institute and was based on data from the Bureau of Labor Statistics.

80. National Commission on the Public Service, *Urgent Business for America*, pp. 23–24. Between 2000 and 2001, the salaries of Cabinet officers lost more than half of their value with respect to median family income.

81. "Federal Pay: Better at the Top," *The Economist* (January 10, 1987), p. 35.

82. Victor S. De Santis and Samantha L. Durst, "Job Satisfaction Among Local Government Employees," *Municipal Year Book, 1997* (Washington, DC: International City/County Management Association, 1997), p. 10.

83. Donald F. Kettl, *Reinventing Government? Appraising the National Performance Review* (Washington, DC: Brookings, 1994), p. 20.

84. National Commission on the Public Service, *Leadership for America: Rebuilding the Public Service*, p. 43.

85. Kettl, *Reinventing Government?* p. 20. In 1993, Washington spent 1.3 percent of its budget on training.

86. U.S. General Accounting Office, *Training Budgets: Agency Budget Reductions in Response to the Balanced Budget Act*, GAO–GGD–86–98BR (Washington, DC: U.S. Government Printing Office, 1986), p. 2. The GAO's analysis of fifty-six federal agencies in 1986 found that forty-two of them cut training budgets in an effort to comply with the Deficit Control Act (i.e., the Gramm-Rudman-Hollings balanced budget act), and that thirty of the agencies cut their training budgets by 10 percent or more, even though the Act required a reduction of only 4.3 percent.

87. U.S. General Accounting Office, *Results-Oriented Government: GPRA Has Established a Solid Foundation for Achieving Greater Results*, GAO–04–38 (Washington, DC: U.S. Government Printing Office, 2004), p. 84. Figures are for 1997–2003.

88. U.S. Merit Systems Protection Board, *The Federal Workforce for the 21st Century*, p. 7. Figures are for 1992–2000.

89. George R. Gray, et al., "Training Practices in State Government Agencies," *Public Personnel Management* 26 (Summer 1997), pp. 187–202. The authors surveyed 323 state agencies in thirty states; response rate was 43 percent.

90. U.S. Advisory Commission on Intergovernmental Relations, *State Laws Governing Local Government Structure and Administration*, p. 49. Figures are for 1990.

91. Charles J. Spindler, "University-Based Public Sector Management Development and Training," *Public Productivity and Management Review* 15 (Summer 1992), p. 447.

92. Joseph W. Whorton Jr., Frank K. Gibson, and Delmer D. Dunn, "The Culture of University Public Service: A National Survey of the Perspectives of Users and Providers," *Public Administration Review* 46 (January/February 1986), pp. 39–40. Seventy-nine percent of local administrators and 80 percent of state administrators reported using universities for training, research, technical assistance, or education at least once over the last three years. See also James D. Slack, "Information, Training, and Assistance Needs of Municipal Governments," *Public Administration Review* 50 (July/August 1990), p. 453. Forty-nine percent of mayors and city managers said they had been contacted by universities regarding training services.

93. We have selected this definition of performance rating because results-based appraisal systems are what governments are moving toward. There are, however, other types, such as trait-based and behavior-based appraisal systems that have little, if anything, to do with productivity. For an explanation of these systems, see Everett M. Berman, James S. Bowman, Jonathan P. West, and Montgomery Van Wart, *Human Resource*

Management in Public Service: Paradoxes, Processes, and Problems (Thousand Oaks, CA: Sage, 2001), pp. 259–286.

94. Commission on Organization of the Executive Branch of the Government, *Personnel Management A Report to the Congress* (Washington, DC: U.S. Government Printing Office, 1949).

95. Selden, Ingraham, and Jacobson, "Human Resource Practices in State Government," p. 605.

96. Freyss, "Continuity and Change in Local Personnel Policies and Practices," p. 15. The precise figure is 81 percent.

97. Gary E. Roberts, "Perspectives on Enduring and Emerging Issues in Performance Appraisal," *Public Personnel Management* 27 (Fall 1998), pp. 301–320.

98. Hal G. Rainey, Carol Traut, and Barry Blunt, "Reward Expectancies and Other Work-Related Attitudes in Public and Private Organizations: A Review and Extension," *Review of Public Personnel Administration* 5 (Summer 1986), pp. 50–72.

99. U.S. Merit Systems Protection Board, *The Federal Workforce for the 21st Century*, p. 26. Figure is for 2000. This was also true in 1996. See U.S. Merit Systems Protection Board, "Director's Perspective: Performance Appraisals Are Not Performance Management," *Issues of Merit* (August 2001), pp. 1–3.

100. A "recent survey" conducted by the Society for Human Resource Management and Personnel Decisions International, as cited in Dayton Fandray, "The New Thinking in Performance Appraisals," *Workforce* 80 (May 2001), pp. 36–40. The figure was 32 percent.

101. Jonathan Walters, "I Have to Talk to You About Your Job . . ." *Governing* (March 2001), pp. 44–45.

102. Dennis M. Daley, *Performance Appraisal in the Public Sector* (Westport, CN: Quorum, 1992).

103. "Reforming Government Pay," *Washington Post* (July 28, 2005).

104. U.S. General Accounting Office, *Results-Oriented Cultures: Insights for US Agencies from Other Countries' Performance Management Initiatives*, GAO–02–862 (Washington, DC: U.S. Government Printing Office, 2002). The countries surveyed were Australia, Canada, New Zealand, and the United Kingdom.

105. U.S. Government Accountability Office, *Human Capital: Symposium on Designing and Managing Market-Based and More Performance-Oriented Pay Systems,* GAO–05–832SP (Washington, DC: U.S. Government Printing Office, 2005).

106. U.S. General Accounting Office, *Posthearing Questions Related to Pay for Performance,* GAO–03–793R Pay for Performance (Washington, DC: Author, 2003), pp. 1–2.

107. Tom Coens and Mary Jenkins, *Abolishing Performance Appraisals: Why They Backfire and What to Do Instead* (San Francisco: Berrett-Koehler, 2000).

108. U.S. Government Accountability Office, *Human Capital: Symposium on Designing and Managing Market-Based and More Performance-Oriented Pay Systems,* Highlights page.

109. U.S. General Accounting Office, *Results-Oriented Cultures,* Highlights page.

110. See, for example, Howard Risher, *Pay for Performance A Guide for Federal Managers,* Human Capital Management Series (Washington, DC: IBM Center for the Business of Government, 2004), p. 5; George T. Mikovich and Alexandra Widgor, *Pay-for-Performance: Evaluating Performance Appraisal and Merit Pay* (Washington, DC: National Academy of Sciences Press, 1991); U.S. General Accounting Office, *Results-Oriented Cultures: Creating a Clear Linkage between Individual Performance and Organizational Success,* GAO–03–488 (Washington, DC: U.S. Government Printing Office, 2003); and U.S. General Accounting Office, *Major Management Challenges and Program Risks: Office of Personnel Management,* GAO–03–115 (Washington, DC: U.S. Government Printing Office, 2003).

111. Hays, "Trends and Best Practices in State and Local Human Resource Management," p. 267.

112. U.S. Government Accountability Office, *Issues Related to Poor Performers in the Federal Workplace,* GAO–05–812R Poor Performers in the Federal Workplace (Washington, DC: U.S. Government Printing Office, 2005), p. 2.

113. U.S. Merit Systems Protection Board, *The Federal Workforce for the 21st Century*, p. 24.

114. Light, "To Restore and Renew," p. 13. Figures are for 2001. Federal workers said that almost 24 percent of their coworkers were less than able, compared to 26 percent of private-sector employees, in the opinions of their coworkers. The higher one ascends the federal hierarchy, the less incompetence is perceived. Another survey found that 14 percent of federal employees felt that their coworkers were performing below reasonably expected levels. See U.S. Merit Systems Protection Board, *The Federal Workforce for the 21st-Century,* p. 23. Figure is for 2000.

115. U.S. Office Personnel Management, *Poor Performers in Government: A Quest for the True Story* (Washington, DC: U.S. Government Printing Office, 1999). 3.7 percent were viewed as poor performers. The average tenure of fourteen years refers to "rehabilitated poor performers"; no tenures were given for unrehabilitated poor performers.

116. James B. King, then-director of the Office of Personnel Management, as cited in Frank Greve, "Civil Service Can Be a Job for Life," *Baltimore Sun* (November 29, 1993).

117. U.S. Merit Systems Protection Board, *Federal Supervisors and Poor Performers* (Washington, DC: U.S. Government Printing Office, 1999), pp. 15–16. In 1997, over 3,550 federal employees "were separated from their jobs" for unacceptable performance, "either directly through removal or indirectly through their own voluntary actions in lieu of management action." Another 7,900 "separations" related to conduct. One

hundred employees were demoted for poor performance, and another 1,275 were denied pay raises. This report is a useful summary of the three large "MSPB Merit Principles Surveys" conducted in 1989, 1992, and 1996, and other sources.

118. Ibid., p. 8.
119. U.S. General Accounting Office, *Performance Management: How Well is the Government Dealing with Poor Performers?* GAO/GGD–91–7 (Washington, DC: U.S. Government Printing Office, 1990), pp. 32–33.
120. U.S. Merit Systems Protection Board, *Federal Supervisors and Poor Performers*, pp. 13, 17. In 1996, 88 percent of supervisors counseled re poor performance and 87 percent for both poor performance and misconduct; 17 percent took formal action against poor performers and 26 percent did so against both poor performance and misconduct; 33 percent gave less-than-satisfactory performance ratings for poor performance, and 334 percent for both poor performance and misconduct; and 8 percent took no action in both categories.
121. U.S. Government Accountability Office, *Issues Related to Poor Performers in the Federal Workplace*, p. 11. Figure is for 2003.
122. U.S. Merit Systems Protection Board, *Federal Supervisors and Poor Performers*, p. 19. In 1996, 48 percent of supervisors said counseling "made things better," and 37 percent said formal action did so.
123. Ibid., p. 8.
124. "Federal vs. Private: Whose Workforce Is Better?" *Government Executive* (November 2001). http://www. brook.edu. In 2001, 67 percent of federal employees and 47 percent of private employees said this.
125. Light, "The Content of Their Character," p. 15. In 2001–2002, 30 percent of federal employees, and 52 percent each of nonprofit- and private-sector employees said this.
126. U.S. Office of Personnel Management, *Poor Performers in Government*, p. 33.
127. National Commission on the Public Service, *Urgent Business for America*, pp. 40–41. The five federal appellate bodies are the Merit Systems Protection Board, the Office of Special Counsel, the Federal Labor Relations Authority, the Office of Personnel Management, and the Equal Employment Opportunity Commission. These agencies are free to review each other's decisions, and often do, further confusing the process.
128. Elling, Thompson, and Monet, "The Problematic World of State Management."
129. See Jerrell D. Coggburn, "Personnel Deregulation: Exploring Differences in the American States," *Journal of Public Administration Research and Theory* 11 (April 2001), pp. 223–244; and Jonathan Walters, *Life after Civil Service Reform: The Texas, Georgia, and Florida Experiences*. Human Capital Series (Washington, DC: IBM Endowment for the Business of Government, 2002).
130. Richard C. Elling, "Dissin' the Deadwood? Patterns in the Dismissal of Civil Servants in American State

Bureaucracies," paper Presented at the Annual Meeting of the Southwestern Political Science Association, San Antonio, Texas, 1999. Elling found that the average annual dismissal rates for 1993 through 1995 in eighteen states average about 1 percent, which is higher than the federal dismissal rate of a fraction of 1 percent.
131. Unless noted otherwise, this paragraph is drawn from, Robert Hebdon "Labor-Management Relations in the United States, 1999," *Municipal Year Book, 2000* (Washington, DC: International City/County Management Association, 2000), pp. 22–27.
132. U.S. Equal Employment Opportunity Commission, *Annual Report on the Federal Workforce for Fiscal Year 2004* (Washington, DC: U.S. Government Printing Office, 2005). In 2004, agencies took 280 days, on average, to investigate a complaint. This is an improvement over a few years earlier. In 1998, "the average age of cases in agencies' inventories" was 446 days. See U.S. General Accounting Office, *Equal Employment Opportunity: Complaint Caseloads Rising, With Effects of New Regulations on Future Trends Unclear*, GAO/GGD–99–128 (Washington, DC: U.S. Government Printing Office, 1999), p. 1.
133. Hebdon, "Labor-Management Relations in the United States, 1999," p. 23.
134. Craig Copeland, "Employee Tenure: Stable Overall, but Male and Female Trends Differ," *EBRI Notes* 26 (March 2005), pp. 2–10. Figures are for 1983–2004. This was an analysis by the Employee Benefits Research Institute based on 2004 data from the U.S. Census Bureau's Current Population Survey. Public employee tenure actually peaked in 1998 at 7.5 years.
135. Gregory B. Lewis, "Turnover and the Quiet Crisis in the Federal Service," *Public Administration Review* 51 (March/April 1991), p. 154. The years analyzed were 1976 through 1988.
136. Stahl, *Public Personnel Administration*, p. 35.
137. George Orwell, *1984* (New York: Harcourt Brace Jovanovich, 1949).
138. Seymour, Martin Lipset, and Ivan Katchanovski, "The Future of Public Sector Unions in the U.S.," *Journal of Labor Research* 23 (Spring 2001), p. 230.
139. U.S. Bureau of Labor Statistics, *Union Members in 2005* (Washington, DC: Author, 2006), Table 3. http://www.bls.gov.news.release/union2.nr0.htm. Figures are for 2005.
140. Joel Cutcher-Gershenfeld and Thomas Kochan, "Taking Stock: Collective Bargaining at the Turn of the Century," *Industrial and Labor Relations Review* 58 (October 2004), p. 3.
141. As derived from data in U.S. Bureau of Labor Statistics, *Union Membership in 2005*, Table 3. Figures are for 2005, when over 16 percent of U.S. labor worked for government, and 47 percent of all union members worked for government. In that year, there were more than 7.4 million government workers who belonged to unions, and another 832,000 who were represented by unions.
142. Ibid. Figure is for 2005.

143. U.S. Office of Personnel Management, *Union Recognition and Agreements in the Federal Government* (Washington, DC: U.S. Government Printing Office, 1991), pp. 6–7.

144. U.S. Bureau of Labor Statistics, *Union Members in 2005*, Table 3. Figures are for 2005.

145. U.S. Bureau of the Census, *Statistical Abstract of the United States, 1986*, 106th ed. (Washington, DC: U.S. Government Printing Office, 1986), Table 714. Figure is for 1982.

146. U.S. Bureau of Labor Statistics, *Union Membership in 2005*, Table 3. Figures are for 2005.

147. Hebdon, "Labor-Management Relations in the United States, 1999," p. 22. Figure applies to police and firefighters.

148. U.S. Advisory Commission on Intergovernmental Relations, *State Laws Governing Local Government and Administration*, p. 49. Figure is for 1990.

149. John Thomas Delaney and Raymond D. Horton, "Managing Relations with Organized Employees," in James L. Perry, ed., *Handbook of Public Administration*, (San Francisco: Jossey-Bass, 1989), p. 439.

150. Richard C. Elling, "Administering State Programs: Performance and Politics," in Virginia Gray and Russell L. Hansen, eds. *Politics in the American States: A Comparative Analysis*, 8th ed., (Washington, DC: CQ Press, 2004), p. 278. Figure is for 2001.

151. David A. Dilts, William J. Walsh, and Constanza Hagmann, "State Labor-Management Relations Legislation: Adaptive Modeling," *Journal of Collective Negotiations in the Public Sector* 22 (1, 1993), p. 80.

152. Hebdon, "Labor-Management Relations in the United States, 1999," p. 23.

153. Cutcher-Gershenfeld and Kochan, "Taking Stock," p. 15.

154. Not much more than half of agency officials wanted to expand the scope of bargaining, but all union officials did. Four-fifths of "neutral experts," however, favored an expansion, indicating that it likely is a good idea. See Gore, *From Red Tape to Results*, p. 81.

155. Marvin J. Levine, "The Status of State 'Sunshine Bargaining' Laws," *Labor Law Journal* 30 (November 1980), p. 713.

156. Chambers, "Labor Management Relations in Local Government," p. 92. Figure is for 1988.

157. Richard C. Kearney, "The Determinants of State Employee Compensation," *Review of Public Personnel Administration* 23 (Winter 2003), p. 305.

158. Dale Belman, John Heywood, and John Lund, "Public Sector Earnings and the Extent of Unionization," *Industrial and Labor Relations Review* 50 (April 1997) pp. 610–628.

159. Richard T. Kearney, with David G. Carnevale, *Labor Relations in the Public Sector*, 3rd ed. (New York: Marcel Dekker, 2001).

160. Bruce A. Wallin, *Budgeting for Basics: The Changing Landscape of City Finances* (Washington, DC: Brookings, 2005), pp. 8–9. Figures are for 1977–2000. Cities with populations of at least 100,000 in 1977 were studied. Per capita library spending grew by 19.9 percent and spending for salaries/wages by 20.1 percent.

161. The case was *Circuit City Stores, Inc. v. Adams.*

162. G. W. Bohlander, "Public Sector Grievance Arbitration: Structure and Administration," *Journal of Collective Negotiations in the Public Sector* 21 (2, 1992), pp. 271–286.

163. Debra J. Mesch and Olga Shamayera, "Arbitration in Practice: A Profile of Public Sector Arbitration Cases," *Public Personnel Management* 25 (Spring 1996), p. 123.

164. For research showing that management wins more frequently than labor in private-sector arbitrations, see ibid., p. 125; P. A. Zirkel, "A Profile of Grievance Arbitration Cases," *Arbitration Journal* (Spring 1983), pp. 35–38, and Debra J. Mesch and D. R. Dalton, "Arbitration in Practice: Win, Lose, or Draw?" *Human Resource Professional* 44 (December 1992), pp. 27–41, 45. Zirkel found that management won 54 percent of the cases and labor 25 percent. Mesch and Dalton found 48 percent for management, and less than 38 percent for labor.

For research showing that labor wins more frequently than management in public-sector arbitrations, see, for example, D. A. Dilts and E. C. Leonard, Jr., "Win-Loss Rates in Public Sector Grievance Arbitration Cases: Implications for the Selection of Arbitrators," *Journal of Collective Negotiations in the Public Sector* 18 (3, 1989), pp. 337–334, and M. Rahnama-Moghadan, D. A. Dilts, and A. Karim, "The Arbitration of Disciplinary Matters in the Public Sector: Does Objective Evidence Make a Difference?" *Journal of Collective Negotiations in the Public Sector* 21 (1, 1992), pp. 151–157.

165. Dane M. Partridge, "Teacher Strikes and Public Policy: Does the Law Matter?" *Journal of Collective Negotiations in the Public Sector* 25 (1, 1996), p. 3.

166. Carolyn Ban and Norma Ricci, "Personnel Systems and Labor Relations: Steps Toward a Quiet Revitalization," in Thompson, ed., *Revitalizing State and Local Public Service*, p. 79. Figure is for 1990.

167. U.S. Advisory Commission on Intergovernmental Relations, *State Laws Governing Local Government Structure and Administration*, p. 49.

168. Walters, "The Chastening of the Public Employees," p. 29.

169. Llewellyn M. Toulmin, "The Treasure Hunt: Budget Search Behavior by Public Employee Unions," *Public Administration Review* 48 (March/April 1988), pp. 620–630.

170. Quoted in Sterling Spero and John M. Capozzola, *The Urban Community and Its Unionized Bureaucracy* (New York: Dunellen, 1973), p. 218.

171. Leo Troy, "Has Public Sector Unionism Topped Out?" *Government Union Review* 17 (Spring 1996), p. 1. Between 1994 and 1995, public union membership slipped by more than 2 percent, and market share by nearly 1 percent. More recent data confirm this decline. See U.S. Bureau of Labor Statistics, *Union Membership in 2005*, Table 3.

172. Frederick C. Mosher, *Democracy and the Public Service* (New York: Oxford University Press, 1968), p. 166.

173. Joseph A. Ferrara and Lynn C. Ross, *Getting to Know You: Rules of Engagement for Political Appointees and Career Executives*, 2004 Presidential Transition Series (Arlington, VA: IBM Center for the Business of Government, 2005), p. 8. Figures are for 2003, and include grades GS 14–15 (the two top grades in the General Schedule) and the approximately 8,000 members of the Senior Executive Service.

174. Pfiffner, "Political Appointees and Career Executives," p. 57.

175. Ibid., p. 58.

176. Ferrara and Ross, *Getting to Know You,* p. 9. Figure is for 1992, but the authors provide some evidence that it is still roughly correct.

177. David E. Lewis, *Political Appointments, Bureau Chiefs, and Federal Management Performance* (Princeton, NJ: Princeton University, Woodrow Wilson School of Public and International Affairs, 2005), p. 35. Data are for 2004. This was a seminal comparison of 242 federal bureau chiefs. Three-fourths of this group were political appointees, and a quarter were career executives in the Senior Executive Service.

178. Dean E. Mann and Jameson W. Doig, *The Assistant Secretaries: Problems and Processes of Appointment* (Washington, DC: Brookings, 1965), p. 120.

179. Roger G. Brown, "Party and Bureaucracy: The Presidents Since JFK," paper prepared for the 1981 Annual Meeting of the American Political Science Association, New York: September 3–6, 1981. Tables 1–10. This analysis included all cabinet, subcabinet, policymaking officials, judges, and ambassadors, from 1960 through 1978. The percentage of appointees who were members of the president's party that were appointed by Kennedy was 70 percent, Johnson 56 percent, Nixon 70 percent, Ford 61 percent, and Carter 61 percent. The Carter appointees cover only 1977 and 1978. After 1978 information on partisan affiliation became unavailable on a systemic basis.

180. David T. Stanley, Dean E. Mann, and Jameson W. Doig, *Men Who Govern* (Washington, DC: Brookings, 1967), p. 24.

181. Spencer S. Hsu, "Leaders Lacking Disaster Experience: 'Brain Drain' at Agency Cited," *Washington Post* (September 9, 2005).

182. Fred Malek, presidential personnel assistant in the Nixon Administration, as quoted in Pfiffner, "Political Appointees and Career Executives," pp. 63–64. Emphasis is original.

183. National Academy of Public Administration, *Leadership in Jeopardy: The Fraying of the Presidential Appointments System* (Washington, DC: Author, 1985), p. 67, and Paul C. Light and Virginia L. Thomas, *The Merit and Reputation of an Administration: Presidential Appointments on the Appointments Process* (Washington, DC: Brookings, 2000), pp. 9, 31, 32.

184. A 1985 survey of five agencies during the Reagan administration by Laurence Lynn, as cited by George C. Edwards III, "Why Not the Best? The Loyalty-Competence Trade-Off in Presidential Appointments," *Brookings Review* 19 (Spring 2001), pp. 12–16.

185. U.S. Merit Systems Protection Board, *The Senior Executive Service: Views of Former Federal Executives* (Washington, DC: U.S. Government Printing Office, 1989), p. 20. Both political appointees and fellow career executives rank career executives considerably higher on these and every other dimension surveyed. A GAO study brought comparable results. See U.S. General Accounting Office, *Senior Executive Service: Opinions About the Federal Work Environment,* GAO/GGD–92–63 (Washington, DC: U.S. General Accounting Office, 1992).

186. National Commission on the Public Service, *Urgent Business for America,* p. 19. See also Task Force on the Presidential Appointment Process, *Obstacle Course* (New York: Twentieth Century Fund, 1996); and Light and Thomas, *The Merit and Reputation of an Administration.*

187. National Commission on the Public Service, *Urgent Business for America,* p. 21. Figures are for 2001.

188. National Academy of Public Administration, *Appointee Survey Data Base.* (Washington, DC: Author, 1985). The report covered 1979 through 1984.

189. Light and Thomas, *The Merit and Reputation of an Administration,* p. 10.

190. Ibid., pp. 4–6.

191. Hugo Heclo, *A Government of Strangers: Executive Politics in Washington* (Washington, DC: Brookings, 1977).

192. C. Brauer, "Tenure, Turnover, and Postgovernment Employment Trends of Presidential Appointees," in G. Calvin MacKenzie, ed., *The In-and-Outers* (Baltimore, MD: Johns Hopkins University Press, 1987), pp. 1–29.

193. Ingraham, "Building Bridges or Burning Them?" p. 429.

194. Lewis, *Political Appointments, Bureau Chiefs, and Federal Management Performance,* p. 35. Figure is for 2004. It was found that career bureau chiefs served more than thirty-eight months in a position, compared to sixteen to twenty months for political appointees.

195. Ferrara and Ross, *Getting to Know You,* p. 9. Figure is for 1992. The authors provide some evidence that it has not changed much since then.

196. Ibid. Figure is for 2003, and refers to about 122,500 career senior executives.

197. This federal grading system is called the PART program, introduced in 2004. Its scoring is not perfect, but "the scores almost certainly capture some of the variance in true management quality among federal programs. . . ." See Lewis, *Political Appointments, Bureau Chiefs, and Federal Management Performance,* p. 8.

198. Ibid., pp. 4, 2.

199. Alexander Hamilton, "No. 72," in Clinton Rossiter, ed. *The Federalist Papers* (New York: New American Library, 1961), p. 436.

200. David K. Hamilton, "The Continuing Judicial Assault on Patronage," *Public Administration Review* 59 (January/February 1999), pp. 54–62.

201. James R. Thompson, as quoted in Jeffrey L. Katz, "The Slow Death of Political Patronage," *Governing* (April 1991), p. 58.

202. Stephen Allred, as quoted in ibid., p. 62.

203. Susan A. MacManus and Charles S. Bullock III, "The Form, Structure, and Composition of America's Municipalities in the New Millennium," *Municipal Year Book, 2003* (Washington, DC: International City/County Management Association, 2003), p. 12. Figure is for 2001.

204. Ibid, p. 11. Figure is for 2001.

205. Tari Renner and Victor S. DeSantis, "Municipal Form of Government: Issues and Trends," *Municipal Year Book, 1998* (Washington, DC: International City/County Management Association, 1998), p. 34. Figure is for 1996.

206. James Conant, "Management Consequences of the 1960–1990 'Modernization' of State Government," in John J. Gargan, ed., *Handbook of State Government Administration* (New York: Marcel Dekker, 2000). Twenty-six states reorganized their governments, 1965–1990.

207. Frank P. Sherwood and Lee J. Breyer, "Executive Personnel Systems in the States," *Public Administration Review* 47 (September/October 1987), p. 411.

208. See, for example, Deborah D. Roberts, "A New Breed of Public Executive: Top Level Exempt Managers in State Government," *Review of Public Personnel Administration* 8 (Spring 1988), pp. 20–36; and Robinson, "The Role of the Independent Political Executive in State Governance," pp. 119–128.

209. Cynthia J. Bowling and Deil S. Wright, "Change and Continuity in State Administration: Administrative Leadership across Four Decades," *Public Administration Review* 58 (September/October 1998), pp. 429–442.

210. Mann and Doig, *The Assistant Secretaries*, p. 120. In 1964, 90 percent of the assistant secretaries and deputy agency administrators were college graduates.

211. Bowling and Wright, "Change and Continuity in State Administration."

212. Ferrara and Ross, *Getting to Know You*, p. 9.

213. Bowling and Wright, "Change and Continuity in State Administration."

214. In 1945, there were 622 municipalities that had a council manager plan; by 2004, 3,475 had it. Between 1945 and 1969, the number of municipalities that had the plan had burgeoned by almost three-fourths. See "Inside the *Year Book*," *Municipal Year Book, 2005* (Washington, DC: International City/County Management Association, 2005), p. x.

215. Renner, "The Local Government Management Profession at Century's End," pp. 38–39. Figures are for 2000. In 1994, nearly half, 45 percent, of city managers and chief administrative officers had M.P.A. degrees. See Victor S. DeSantis and Charldean Newell, "Local Government Managers' Career Paths," *Municipal Year Book, 1996* (Washington, DC: International City/County Management Association, 1996), p. 4. Another survey found that 79 percent had a graduate degree, and that 62 percent of these city managers held M.P.A.s. See Craig M. Wheeland, "Council Evaluation of the City Manager's Performance," *Municipal Year Book, 1995* (Washington, DC: International City/County Management Association, 1995), p. 14.

216. Carolyn Cain, Enamul Choudhury, and James C. Clingermayer, "Turnover, Trust, and Transfers: An Examination of Local Government Budget Execution," *International Journal of Public Administration* 27 (August/September 2004), pp. 557–576. This was a study of municipal budget leaders in metropolitan Cincinnati.

217. Mosher, *Democracy and the Public Service*, pp. 109, 238–239.

218. Ibid., p. 103.

219. Ibid.

220. Couturier, "The Quiet Revolution in Public Personnel Laws," pp. 150–159. Three hundred thirty-eight public personnel systems responded to the survey. Sixty-three percent were influenced by the law, and 55 percent had acted on it.

221. Mosher, *Democracy and the Public Service*, pp. 104–105.

222. U.S. Office of Personnel Management, *Federal Employee Attitudes, Phase I: Base Line Survey, 1979, Government-Wide Report* (Washington, DC: U.S. Government Printing Office, 1979), p. 25.

223. Jimmy Carter, *State of the Union Message*, January 19, 1978.

224. A good example is Allan K. Campbell, "Civil Service Reform: A New Commitment," *Public Administration Review* 38 (March/April 1978), especially pp. 101–102.

225. Mosher, *Democracy and the Public Service,* p. 107.

226. Risher, *Pay for Performance*, pp. 4, 7, citing the glossary on the Web site of WorldatWork, formerly the American Compensation Association.

227. U.S. Merit Systems Protection Board, *The Federal Workforce for the 21st Century,* p. 11. In 1996, 50 percent of federal workers said that they were satisfied with their pay, and in 2000, 49 percent.

228. U.S. Office of Personnel Management, *Adherence to the Merit Principles in the Workplace: Federal Employees' Views* (Washington, DC: U.S. Government Printing Office, 1997), p. 3.

229. James E. Clovard, deputy director, OPM, as quoted in National Academy of Public Administration, *Modernizing Federal Classification: Operational Broad Banding Systems Alternatives* (Washington, DC: Author, 1995), back cover.

230. Ibid., p. 7.

231. Light, "To Restore and Renew," p. 15. See also Larry M. Lane, "Public Sector Performance Management," *Review of Public Personnel Administration* 14 (Summer 1994), p. 27.

232. U.S. Office of Personnel Management, *The Fact Book, 1999: Federal Civilian Workforce Statistics* (Washington, DC: U.S. Government Printing Office, 1999), p. 71. Figures are for 1991–1996. After 1999,

OPM ceased collecting these statistics "ostensibly because it could not figure out how to present data from the increasing number of pass/fail systems in its appraisal statistics." See Light, "To Restore and Renew," p. 12.

233. Risher, *Pay for Performance*, p. 41.
234. Stephen Barr, "OPM Shucks 'One-Size-Fits-All' Annual Employee Reviews for Designer Versions," *Washington Post* (August 23, 1995).
235. U.S. General Accounting Office, *Posthearing Questions Related to Pay for Performance*, GAO-03–793R Pay for Performance (Washington, DC: Author, 2003), p. 2.
236. See J. Edward Kellough and Haoran Lu, "The Paradox of Merit Pay in the Public Sector," *Review of Public Personnel Administration* 13 (Spring 1993), pp. 45–46. Jone L. Pearce and James Perry, "Federal Merit Pay: A Longitudinal Analysis," *Public Administration Review* 43 (July/August 1983), pp. 315–325; Mikovich and Widgor, *Pay-for-Performance*; and Joan E. Pynes, *Human Resource Management for Public and Nonprofit Organizations* (San Francisco: Jossey-Bass, 1997).
237. U.S. Government Accounting Office, *Human Capital: Using Incentives to Motivate and Reward High Performance*, GAO/T–GGD–00–118 (Washington, DC: Author, 2000). Between 1995 and 1999, the use by twenty-four agencies of performance incentives declined in terms of both dollars awarded and employees who received them. On the other hand, this analysis also found that other sorts of monetary awards are increasing. The *Washington Post* reported that in 2002 some two-thirds of all federal civilian employees receive some form of cash award or paid time off, and the typical award was less than 2 percent of salary. Some critics allege that, in some agencies, awards "are spread like peanut butter," with everyone getting something. This information is provided in Risher, *Pay for Performance*, p. 17.
238. Risher, *Pay-for-Performance*, p. 4. The author is citing the average responses found in the four Federal Human Capital Surveys, conducted by the Office of Personnel Management, 1989–2000.
239. Ibid., p. 7. Figure is for 2004.
240. National Commission on the Public Service, *Urgent Business for America*, p. 31. Figure is for 2001. This condition was largely due to pay compression of the six pay levels in the Senior Executive Service.
241. Risher, *Pay for Performance*, p. 41.
242. Ibid., p. 10.
243. Paul C. Light "The End of the Civil Service?" *Washington Post* (May 9, 2003). In 2003, the National Commission on the Public Service called for the abolishment of the General Schedule, and the Council for Excellence in Government also has supported the idea of far-reaching change in federal human resources management. See Gerhart, "A New Deal." In 1991, the National Academy of Sciences also added its support to pay for performance. See Mikovich and Wigdor, *Pay-for-Performance*.

244. Hays, "Trends and Best Practices in State and Local Human Resource Management," p. 266.
245. J. Edward Kellough and Sandy Coleman Selden, "Pay-for-Performance in State Government," *Review of Public Personnel Administration* 17 (Winter 1997), pp. 5–21. Figure is for 1994.
246. Selden, Ingraham, and Jacobson, "Human Resource Practices in State Government," p. 605. Figures are for 1998.
247. Gregory Streib and Lloyd Nigro, "Pay-for-Performance in Local Governments: The Views of Personnel Directors," *International Journal of Public Administration* 18 (12, 1995), pp. 1775–1794.) Figure (36 percent) is for 1992.
248. Freyss, "Continuity and Change in Local Personnel Policies and Practices," p. 15. Figure (70 percent) is for 1995. See also Richard C. Kearney, Barry M. Feldman, and Carmine P. F. Scavo, "Reinventing Government: City Manager Attitudes and Actions," *Public Administration Review* 60 (November/December 2000), pp. 535–548. This national survey found that 47 percent of city managers had "recommended setting aside funds for employee incentives" in 1997.
249. Sally Coleman Selden, "Human Resource Management in American Counties, 2002," *Public Personnel Management* 34 (Spring 2005), p. 81. Figures are for 2002. Thirty-six out of forty counties responded to the survey.
250. Streib and Nigro, "Pay-for-Performance in Local Governments," p. 1781. Figure (67 percent) is for 1992.
251. Hays and Kearney, "Anticipated Changes in Human Resource Management," p. 592. Ironically, the protection of public employees from political influences—the central value underlying to the passage of the Civil Service Act of 1883 that created the modern civil service—was ranked dead last out of eight possible values by public H. R. managers.
252. U.S. Merit Systems Protection Board, *Civil Service Evaluation: The Evolving Role of the US Office of Personnel Management* (Washington, DC: U.S. Government Printing Office, 1999), p. 24. Twenty-three major departments were surveyed. Figure is for 1997.
253. Coggburn, "Personnel Deregulation," p. 227.
254. Perhaps the most famous of these analyses is Ed Michaels, Helen Hatfield-Jones, Beth Axelrod, *The War for Talent* (Cambridge, MA: Harvard Business School Press, 2001). See also Baruch Lev, *Intangibles: Management, Measurement, and Reporting* (Washington, DC: Brookings, 2001).
255. Mosher, *Democracy and the Public Service*, pp. 140–141. Mosher first reported this development in the original edition of his book (p. 131), which was published in 1968.
256. U.S. General Accounting Office, *Human Capital: OPM Can Better Assist Agencies in Using Personnel Flexibilities*, p. 7. Figure is for 2003.
257. Not only have the departments of Homeland Security and Defense been effectively removed from the General Schedule, but Washington is also outsourcing its human

resource management. An analysis of eight selected agencies found that all of them were using alternative means of service delivery, primarily privatization, "for the full range of their human capital efforts." See U.S. General Accounting Office, *Human Capital: Selected Agencies' Use of Alternative Service Delivery Options for Human Capital Activities*, GAO–04–679 (Washington, DC: U.S. Government Printing Office, 2004), p. 3. Data are for 2004.

258. U.S. Office of Personnel Management, *Federal Human Resources Management for the 21st Century* (Washington, DC: U.S. Government Printing Office, 1997), p. 8. Figures are for 1998. OPM was reduced from approximately 6,200 employees to 3,250.

259. Hays, "Trends and Best Practices in State and Local Human Resource Management," pp. 256–275. The study referred to is conducted by the Annie E. Casey Foundation and was launched in 1999. It focuses on state and local human service providers. The article is based on this research.

260. As derived from data in Keon S. Chi, Kelley A. Arnold, and Heather M. Perkins, "Privatization in Government: Trends and Issues," *Spectrum: The Journal of State Government* 76 (Fall 2003), p. 16. Figure is for 2002.

261. Selden, Ingraham, and Jacobson, "Human Resource Practices in State Government," p. 600.

262. Coggburn, "Personnel Deregulation," pp. 233–244. The quotation is on p. 241.

263. Ibid.

264. J. Edward Kellough and Sally Coleman Selden, "The Reinvention of Public Personnel Administration: An Analysis of the Diffusion of Personnel Management Reforms in the States," *Public Administration Review* 63 (March/April 2003), pp. 165–176.

265. For a good report on Florida's civil service reform, see James S. Bowman, Mark G. Gertz, Sally C. Gertz, and Russell L. Williams, "Civil Service Reform in Florida State Government: Employee Attitudes One Year Later," *Review of Public Personnel Administration* 23 (Winter 2003), pp. 286–301.

266. For a thorough and excellent explanation of Georgia's innovation, see Charles W. Gossett, "Civil Service Reform: The Case of Georgia," *Review of Public Personnel Administration* 22 (March 2002), pp. 94–113.

267. Walters, *Life after Civil Service Reform*, pp. 5, 12.

268. Selden, "Human Resource Management in American Counties, 2002," p. 61. Figure is for 2002.

269. Mildred Warner and Amir Hefetz, "Pragmatism over Politics: Alternative Service Delivery in Local Government, 1992–2002," *Municipal Year Book, 2004* (Washington, DC: International City/County Management Association, 2004), pp. 10–11. Data are for 1992–2002. In 1992, 8 percent of personnel services were delivered through public-private partnerships.

270. For a couple of good analyses of long-term trends of racial and gender inequalities in the United States, see: Reynolds Farley, "Racial Trends and Differences in the United States 30 Years After the Civil Rights Decade," *Social Science Research* 26 (September 1997), pp. 235–262; and M. Therese Seibert, Mark A. Fossett,

and Dawn M. Baunach, "Trends in Male-Female Status Inequality, 1940–1990," *Social Science Research* 26 (March 1997), pp. 1–24. The former article finds that as racial diversity increases, inequities are reducing (especially for blacks), although some severe problems remain; the latter article concludes that gender inequities "declined sharply" during the 1980s but still remain.

271. We are grateful to Elling, "Administering State Programs," p. 276, for the provision of these terms.

272. Reginald Wilson, *Affirmative Action: Yesterday, Today, and Beyond* (Washington, DC: American Council on Education, 1995), p. 6.

273. Bob Zelnick, *Backfire: A Reporter's Look at Affirmative Action* (Washington, DC: Regnery, 1996), p. 29.

274. Mitchell F. Rice and Maurice Mongkuo, "Did *Adarand* Kill Minority Set-Asides?" *Public Administration Review* 58 (January/February 1998), p. 82. Figures are for 1994.

275. George R. La Noue and John C. Sullivan, "Race Neutral Programs in Public Contracting," *Public Administration Review* 55 (July/August 1995), p. 354.

276. Rice and Mongkuo, "Did *Adarand* Kill Minority Set-Asides?" p. 85, and *Federal Register*, cited in Ann Devroy, "Affirmative Action Rules are Revised," *Washington Post* (May 23, 1996).

277. Lorenda A. Naylor and David H. Rosenbloom, "*Adarand*, Grutter and Gratz: Does Affirmative Action in Federal Employment Matter?" *Review of Public Personnel Administration* 24 (June 2004), p. 150.

278. Pan S Kim, "Disability Policy: An Analysis of the Employment of People with Disabilities in the American Federal Government," *Public Personnel Management* 25 (Spring 1996), p. 73. In 1999, the Supreme Court ruled in three cases that the ADA did not apply to people whose condition could be corrected.

279. American Bar Association, as cited in Laurie Asseo, "High Court Limits Disabilities Law," *Washington Post* (June 22, 1999). 700 cases from 1992 through 1997 were analyzed.

280. Charles W. Gosset, "Lesbians and Gay Men in the Public-Sector Workforce" in Norma M. Riccucci, ed., *Public Personnel Management: Current Concerns, Future Challenges*, 4th ed. (New York: Longman, 2006), pp. 76–77. Figures are for 2005.

281. Dan A. Black, Hoda R. Makar, Seth G. Sanders, and Lowell J. Taylor, "The Earnings Effects of Sexual Orientation," *Industrial and Labor Relations Review* 56 (April 2003), pp. 449–470. This investigation was based on the General Social Survey data from 1989–1996.

282. U.S. General Accounting Office, *Sexual Orientation-Based Employment Discrimination*: States' Experience with Statutory Provisions, GAO–02–878R (Washington DC: US Government Printing Office, 2002).

283. The case was *Smith* v. *City of Jackson*.

284. The case was *Metro Broadcasting* v. *Federal Communications commission*.

285. See Thompson, *Personnel Policy in the City*, pp. 112–130.

286. Robert J. Huntley and Robert J. McDonald, "Urban Managers: Organizational Preferences, Managerial Styles, and Social Policy Roles," *Municipal Year Book, 1975* (Washington, DC: International City Management Association, 1975), p. 157. Emphasis has been added.

287. Moulder, "Affirmative Action in Local Government," pp. 47–52. Data are for 1989. In 1974, 46 percent of cities had affirmative action plans for women and 55 percent for minorities. See: Huntley and McDonald, "Urban Managers," p. 157.

288. This is not as clear-cut as it may appear. The Supreme Court ruled unanimously in 1987, in *St. Francis College v. Al-Khazraji*, that Arabs and other ethnic groups no longer could be counted as whites in discrimination suits but must be treated, to quote the Court, as "identifiable classes of persons" who may have been victims of discrimination "solely because of their ancestry or ethnic characteristics."

289. Paul Oyer and Scott Schaefer, "Sorting, Quotas, and the Civil Rights Act of 1991: Who Hires When It's Hard to Fire?" *Journal of Law and Economics* 45 (April 2002), pp. 41–68.

290. Paul Oyer and Scott Shaefer, "The Bias Backfire," *Harvard Business Review* 82 (November 2004), p. 26.

291. Elizabeth L. Schoenfelt and Leslie C. Pedigo, "A Review of Court Decisions on Cognitive Ability Testing, 1992–2004," *Review of Public Personnel Administration* 25 (September 2005), p. 272.

292. Ibid., pp. 271–287.

293. Moulder, "Affirmative Action in Local Government," p. 51; and Eveline R. Moulder, "Affirmative Action: The Role Local Governments are Playing," *Municipal Year Book 1986* (Washington, DC: International City Management Association, 1986), p. 26.

294. See, for example, James L. Outtz, "The Role of Cognitive Ability Tests in Employment Selection," *Human Performance* 15 (Spring 2002), pp. 161–171, and Kevin R. Murphy, "Can Conflicting Perspectives on the Role of g in Personnel Selection Be Resolved?" pp. 173–186, in the same issue. African Americans typically score one standard deviation lower than whites on cognitive ability tests.

295. Earl Hunt, "When Should We Shoot the Messenger? Issues Involving Cognitive Testing, Public Policy, and the Law," *Psychology, Public Policy, and Law* 2 (September/December 1996), pp. 486–505.

296. U.S. Merit System Protection Board, *Building a High-Quality Workforce*, p. 24. In 2001, 48 percent of "total accessions" in professional and administrative positions (GS grades 5, 7, and 9) were admitted to the federal employ through competitive examinations, specifically the Office of Personnel Management's Certificates of Eligibles (in which OPM ranks applicants' education, veterans' status, and other variables that often include a written examination and then submits its top three recommendations to the agency for selection); agencies' delegated examining units; and the Administrative Careers with America written test. By 2004, only 26 percent of all accessions were made through these test-based means. By contrast, employees hired through the Federal Career Intern Program had increased from 1 percent in 2001 to 28 percent in 2004.

297. Stein, "Merit Systems and Political Influence," p. 267.

298. Jean Couturier, "Court Attacks on Testing: Death Knell or Salvation for the Civil Service System," *Good Government* 88 (Winter 1971), p. 12.

299. Couturier, "The Quiet Revolution in Public Personnel Laws."

300. Clarence M. Pendleton, Jr., quoted in Associated Press, "Rights Panel Chief Scoffs at Idea of Comparable Pay for Women," *New York Times* (November 17, 1984).

301. Constance Horner, quoted in Mike Causey, "Comparable Worth Plans," *Washington Post* (April 22, 1987).

302. Susan E. Gardner and Christopher Daniel, "Implementing Comparable Worth/Pay Equity: Experiences of Cutting-Edge States," *Public Personnel Management* 27 (Winter 1998), pp. 475–489.

303. Cayer, "Local Government Personnel Structure and Policies," p. 9.

304. Gardner and Daniel, "Implementing Comparable Worth/Pay Equity," and U.S. General Accounting Office, *Pay Equity: Washington State's Efforts to Address Comparable Worth*, GAO/GGO–92–87BR (Washington, DC: U.S. General Accounting Office, 1992).

305. James E. Campbell and Gregory B. Lewis, "Public Support for Comparable Worth in Georgia," *Public Administration Review* 46 (September/October 1986), pp. 432–437; and Mark A. Emmert, "Public Opinion of Comparable Worth: Some Preliminary Findings," *Review of Public Personnel Administration* 6 (Fall 1985), pp. 69–75.

306. Cynthia S. Ross and Robert E. England, "State Governments' Sexual Harassment Policy Initiatives," *Public Administration Review* 47 (May/June 1987), p. 261. Data are for 1985.

307. Cayer, "Local Government Personnel Structure and Policies," p. 12. Over 87 percent of cities and over 88 percent of counties have policies forbidding sexual harassment.

308. As derived from data in U.S. Equal Employment Opportunity Commission, "Charge Statistics," and "Sexual Harassment Charges," http://www.eeoc.gov/ staff. Between 1992 and 2000, sexual harassment charges filed with the EEOC grew by over 50 percent; the remaining types of charges (i.e., discrimination based on race, sex, disability, age, religion, and national origin) grew by less than 11 percent. In 1980, 3,661 sexual harassment charges were filed with the EEOC; in 1991, 6,883; in 2000, 15,836. Sexual harassment charges have exceeded 15,000 every year since 1995.

309. U.S. Merit Systems Protection Board, *Sexual Harassment in the Federal Workplace* (Washington, DC: U.S. Government Printing Office, 1995). Figures for both sexes (44 percent for women, 19 percent for men) are for 1994, but the numbers are fairly stable over time. The 94 percent of the employees who did not

intend to file charges said, in about even numbers, that they were not going to do so because either the "attention" was not serious or that they did not trust the government to be responsive. The 1994 survey was sent to 13,200 federal workers with a response rate of 61 percent.

310. Ibid., p. 19. Figures are for 1994.

311. Ibid.

312. 1993 survey by the UCLA Graduate School of Management and Korn Ferry International, as cited in ibid., p. 20.

313. American Management Association survey of large U.S. corporations, as cited in Kirsten Downey Grimsley, "Co-Workers Cited in Most Sexual Harassment Cases," *Washington Post* (June 19, 1996). Not quite 50 percent of private-sector workers who lodged sexual harassment complaints did so against peers, over 26 percent against their direct supervisors, over 17 percent against "other supervisors," and nearly 7 percent against customers or vendors.

314. U.S. Merit Systems Protection Board, *Sexual Harassment in the Federal Workplace*, p. 7.

315. U.S. Office of Personnel Management, *The Fact Book, 2004*, p. 48, for federal and private-sector workforce employment percentages, and as derived from data in U.S. Bureau of the Census, *Statistical Abstract of the United States, 2006*, Table 13, for population percentages. All data are for 2003.

316. U.S. Bureau of the Census, *Statistical Abstract of the United States, 2006*, Table 485. Figure is for 2003.

317. For additional analyses, see U.S. General Accounting Office, *The Public Service: Issues Confronting the Federal Civilian Workforce*, GGD-94-157 (Washington, DC: U.S. Government Printing Office, 1994), and Salomon A. Guarjardo, "Minority Employment in U.S. Federal Agencies: Continuity and Change," *Public Personnel Management* 25 (Summer 1996), pp. 199–208.

318. U.S. Office of Personnel Management, *The Fact Book, 2004*, p. 48. Data are for 2003.

319. Center for Women in Government and Civil Society, State University of New York at Albany, *Appointed Policy Makers in State Government: Five-Year Trend Analysis: Gender, Race, and Ethnicity* (Albany, NY: Author, 2004), p. 2. Figure is for 2003.

320. Renner, "The Local Government Management Profession at Century's End," p. 37. Figure is for 2000.

321. Center for Women in Government and Civil Society," *Appointed Policy Makers in State Government*, p. 4. Figure is for 2003.

322. Renner, "The Local Government Manager at Century's End," p. 37. Figure is for 2000. Prospects seem good for enlarging this proportion. In 1991, 34 percent of assistant city managers were women. See Joy Pierson Cunningham, "Fostering Advancement for Women and Minorities," *Public Management* 14 (June 1992), p. 23.

323. Jerry Mitchell, "Education and Skills for Public Authority Management," *Public Administration Review* 51 (September/October 1991), pp. 429–437.

324. Gayle A. Lawn-Day and Steven Ballard, "Speaking Out: Perceptions of Women Managers in the Public Service," *Review of Public Personnel Administration* 16 (Winter 1996), p. 42.

325. Light, "The Content of Their Character," p. 8.

326. Ronald G. Shaiko, "Female Participation in Association Governance and Political Representation: Women as Executive Directors, Board Members, Lobbyists, and Political Action Committee Directors," *Nonprofit Management and Leadership* 8 (Winter 1997), pp. 121–139.

327. Eleanor V. Laudicina, "Managing Workforce Diversity in Government: An Initial Assessment," *Public Administration Quarterly* 19 (Summer 1995), p. 170.

328. Nelson Dometrius and Lee Sigelman, "Assessing Progress Toward Affirmative Action Goals in State and Local Governments: A New Benchmark," *Public Administration Review* 44 (May/June 1984), pp. 244–245. Data are for 1980. See also Gregory B. Lewis and David Nice, "Race, Sex, and Occupational Segregation in State and Local Governments," *American Review of Public Administration* 24 (December 1994), pp. 393–410.

329. Lisa Genasli, "Women, Minority Executives Remain Few," *Philadelphia Inquirer* (September 27, 1994). In 1994, two *Fortune* 500 CEOs were minorities.

330. "The 2005 Fortune 500: Women CEOs," *Fortune*. http://www.fortune.com/fortune/fortune500/articles/. In 2005, nine *Fortune* 500 CEOs were women.

331. Alison M. Konrad and Kathy Cummings, "The Effects of Gender-Role Congruence and Statistical Discrimination on Managerial Advancement," *Human Relations* 50 (October 1997), pp. 1305–1328.

332. Kathleen Cannings and Claude Montmarquette, "Managerial Momentum: A Simultaneous Model of the Career Progression of Male and Female Managers," *Industrial and Labor Relations Review* 44 (January 1991), pp. 212–228.

333. Pew Research Center for the People and the Press, *Conflicted Views of Affirmative Action*, (Washington, DC: Author, 2007), p. 3. Figure is for 2003,

334. Judith J. Friedman and Nancy Di Tomaso, "Myths about Diversity: What Managers Need to Know About Changes in the U.S. Labor Force," *California Management Review* 38 (Summer 1996), pp. 54–77.

335. As derived from data in U.S. Bureau of the Census, *Statistical Abstract of the United States, 2006*, Table 577. Current figure is for 2004.

336. Friedman and Di Tomaso," Myths about Diversity," p. 58.

337. As derived from data in U.S. Bureau of the Census, *Statistical Abstract of the United States, 2006*, Table 577. Current figure is for 2004. There are some anomalies in theses figures, as, beginning in 2003, the Current Population Survey allows respondents to choose more than one race, if they wish. The figures cited in the text represent people who selected that particular racial group only, and exclude people who reported that they belonged to more than one race. Prior to 2003, the Current Population Survey allowed respondents to report only one racial group.

338. U.S. General Accounting Office, *The Changing Workforce: Demographic Issues Facing Employers*, GAO/T–GGD-92–61 (Washington, DC: U.S. Government Printing Office, 1992), pp. 1–7.

339. Friedman and Di Tomaso, "Myths about Diversity," p. 58.

340. As derived from data in U.S. Bureau of the Census, *Statistical Abstract of the United States, 2006*, Table 577. Current figure is for 2004.

341. Friedman and Di Tomaso, "Myths about Diversity." But see also Audrey J. Cohen, "Predictors of Public and Private Employment for Business College Graduates," *Public Personnel Management* 22 (Spring 1992), p. 167. This and other research suggests that minority college graduates are considerably more favorably disposed toward working in the public sector than are white college graduates.

Part **IV**

Implementing Public Policy

In the fourth and final part of *Public Administration and Public Affairs*, we explain how to get things done. Although we touched upon certain aspects of getting things done in Chapter 4, notably in our discussion of administration in organizations, in Part IV we take a broader view.

Implementation is the execution and delivery of public policies by organizations or arrangements among organizations. It is perhaps the most "hands-on" facet of public administration, but the subject of implementation is, surprisingly and justifiably, theoretical and often abstract. This is both an irony and a paradox in the study of the implementation of public policy.

We approach the complex arena of public policy execution in slices of narrowing breadth. That is, we treat first the making of public policy itself; then the implementation of public policy by the three sectors; then by only the public sector; and finally by individual public administrators.

Hence, in the introductory chapter to Part IV, we explain what is being implemented—that is, public policy, or, more specifically, the various models of how public policy is made, delivered, and adjusted.

The following two chapters focus on the institutions that governments use to implement public policy, such as companies, public authorities, nonprofit organizations, government-sponsored enterprises, and other governments. These and other devices have extended the reach of government far beyond its nominal station. One researcher calculates that the federal government spends only 7 percent of its budget on the civilian programs that federal administrators directly implement,[1] and another analyst concludes that the number of federal civilian employees is not fewer than 1.9 million, as Washington contends, but in reality is more than 14.4 million![2]

The disparity is attributable to the number of employees working, ostensibly, for businesses, nonprofit organizations, and state and local governments, but whom Washington either funds through contracts and grants, or simply mandates subnational governments to hire. When we define the federal workforce to include these "indirect" employees, then about two out of every five American households has someone in them who is working for the federal government.[3]

In similar fashion, state and local governments extend their influence by using the same institutions and methods. Some have called these arrangements "government by proxy,"[4] which has resulted in a "shadow workforce" that toils in "the shadow of government."[5]

Finally, and perhaps of greatest importance, we focus on the specific area of ethical decision-making by individual public administrators in the formulation and implementation of public policies, and close our book with some thoughts on the passion of public administration.

Notes

1. Donald F. Kettl, *Government by Proxy* (Washington, DC: Congressional Quarterly Press), 1988.
2. Paul C. Light, *Fact Sheet on the New True Size of Government* (Washington, DC: Center for Public Service, Brookings Institution, 2003), p. 4. In 2002, the federal government had almost 1.76 million civilian workers on its payroll, contracted out nearly 5.17 million jobs to private employers, effectively ordered state and local governments to hire an estimated 4.65 million employees through mandates (estimate is for 1996), and paid state and local governments to employ 2.86 million workers through federal grants-in-aid. These figures do not include almost 1.46 million military personnel and 875,000 Postal Service workers. If these two groups were included, the total would be almost 16.77 million federal workers in 2002.
3. Ibid., p. 3.
4. Kettl, *Government by Proxy.*
5. Paul C. Light, *The True Size of Government* (Washington, DC: Brookings, 1999).

CHAPTER 10

Understanding and Improving Public Policy

Public policy is what public administrators implement, so it is sensible to begin our section on implementation with a discussion of how public policy is perceived, analyzed, and understood.

Public policy is a course of action adopted and pursued by government. *Public policy analysis* is the study of how government policies are made and implemented and the application of available knowledge to those policies for the purpose of improving their formulation and implementation.[1]

"Policy analyst" is an official job description in the federal civil service, most state capitols, and many large local governments, and "policy analysis is one of the established knowledge industries" in the United States.[2] In Washington, the enactment of the Government Performance and Results Act of 1993 and the Office of Management and Budget's far-reaching decision in 1994 to staff its critical resource management offices with policy analysts, secured the place of policy analysis in the federal structure. Moreover, policy analysis has an impact on actual policy. A study of the influence on legislators of nonpartisan policy research organizations in nineteen states found that these organizations "—even those in highly politicized environments—have a significant impact on policymaking, mainly by providing information and analysis decision-makers but also in influencing public policy outcomes."[3]

Political Science, Public Administration, and Policy Analysis

One way of understanding the subfield of public policy is to bisect it into broad branches. One branch is substantive, processual, descriptive, and objective. That is, it is concerned with the substance of some issue (such as the environment, crime, or whatever) and produces books and articles that often are entitled "The Politics of . . ." some substantive area. This branch focuses on the process of a public policy—that is, how the policy process works in a specific field—and attempts to describe that process objectively.

This is the branch dominated by political scientists, and we call it the *incrementalist paradigm* of public policymaking and implementation. It relates to the first part of our definition of public policy analysis: "the study of how government policies are made and implemented."

The second branch is theoretical, effectual, prescriptive, and normative. That is, it is concerned with the development of theories of public policymaking, and the outputs and effects of those theories in practice. It focuses on prescribing better ways of making and implementing better policies, regardless of the substantive issues and areas that the particular public policy may address.

283

This is the branch dominated by public administrationists, and we call it the *rationalist paradigm* of public policymaking and implementation. It relates to the second part of our definition of public policy analysis, "the application of available knowledge to [government] policies for the purpose of improving their formulation and implementation." Both paradigms offer several models of policy making, which we review in this chapter.

More recently, strategic planning has surfaced as a relatively practical paradigm of public policymaking which, in many ways, reconciles the differing perspectives of the incrementalist and rationalist paradigms. We conclude the chapter with a discussion of strategic planning and its application in the public and nonprofit sectors.

The Incrementalist Paradigm of Public Policymaking and Implementation

In some ways, we have already considered, at least obliquely, the incrementalist paradigm of public policy in Part II on Public Organizations. "Satisficing," organizational "drift," "bounded rationality," and "limited cognition," among other terms found in organization theory, reflect the basic idea of the incrementalist paradigm.

The various writings of Charles E. Lindblom are associated most closely with incrementalism and, in fact, it was he who is as responsible as anyone for the notion's name, *disjointed incrementalism*, as a description of the policymaking process.[4] *Disjointed*, in this context, means that the analysis and evaluation of conditions and alternative responses to perceived conditions are uncoordinated and occur throughout society; *incrementalism* means that only a limited selection of policy alternatives are provided to policymakers, and that each one of these alternatives represents only an infinitesimal change in the status quo.

Before Lindblom made the incrementalist idea more academically legitimate (and pompous) by dubbing it "disjointed incrementalism," he called the concept "muddling through."[5] Muddling through, as a term, not only is a more colorful description of the policymaking process, but is also clearer and self-explanatory.

Basically, the incrementalist paradigm posits a conservative tendency in public policymaking; new public policies are seen as being variations on the past. The public policymaker is perceived as a person who does not have the brains, time, and money to fashion truly different policies; he or she accepts the policies of the past as satisficing and legitimate. There are also certain "sunk costs" in existing policies that probably would be impossible to retrieve if a radically new course were taken, and this discourages innovative action. Incrementalist policies are nearly always more politically expedient than are policies that necessitate basic redistributions of social values. As one scholar of political feasibility put it, "what is most feasible is incremental."[6] An illustration of the incrementalist paradigm is shown in Figure 10-1.

Attempts to understand the incrementalist paradigm of public policymaking and implementation can be categorized along six emphases: elitism, groups, systems, institutionalist, neo-institutionalist, and organized anarchy. We consider each in turn.

Figure 10-1   The Incrementalist Paradigm of Public Policymaking and Implementation

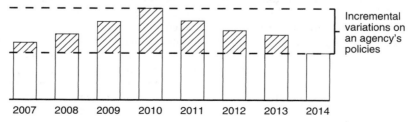

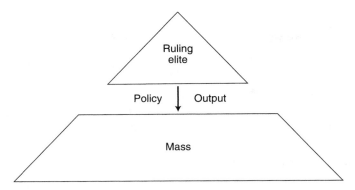

Figure 10-2   The Elite/Mass Model of Public Policymaking and Implementation

The Elite/Mass Model

In cursory form, the elite/mass model contends that a policymaking/policy-executing elite is able to act in an environment characterized by apathy and information distortion and thereby govern a largely passive mass. Policy flows downward from the elite to the mass. Society is divided according to those who have power and those who do not. Elites share common values that differentiate them from the mass, and prevailing public policies reflect elite values, which may be summed up as preserve the status quo. Finally, elites have more money, more education, and more status than the mass. Perhaps the classic expression of elite theory can be found in C. Wright Mills's *The Power Elite*.[7] A diagrammatic version of elite theory that relates it to public administration is found in Figure 10-2.

The Group Model

A second model of incrementalist public policy is the group model. In these days of questionable campaign contributions and powerful vested interests, the notion of pressure groups and lobbies also has relevance. Another way of describing the group model is the "hydraulic thesis," in which the polity is conceived of as being a system of forces and pressures acting and reacting to one another in the formulation of public policy. An exemplary work that represents

the group model is Arthur F. Bentley's *The Process of Government.*[8]

Normally, the group model is associated with the legislature rather than the bureaucracy, but it also has long been recognized by scholars that the "neutral" executive branch of government is buffeted by pressure groups, too. The numerous studies by political scientists on federal regulatory agencies, for example, all point to the same conclusion: The agency ultimately is "captured" by the group that it is meant to regulate, and its administrators grow increasingly unable to distinguish between policies that are beneficial to the interests of the public and policies that are beneficial to the interests of the groups being regulated. What is good for the group is good for the nation, in the eyes of the regulators.[9] Figure 10-3 illustrates the group model.

The Systems Model

A third emphasis in the incrementalist public-policy literature is the systems model. The systems model relies on concepts of information theory (especially, feedback, input, and output) and conceives of the process as being essentially cyclical. Policy is originated, implemented, adjusted, re-implemented, re-adjusted, *ad infinitum.*

The systems model is concerned with such questions as, what are the significant variables and patterns in the public policymaking system? What constitutes the "black box" of the actual

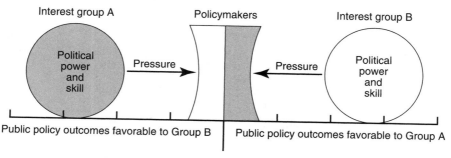

Figure 10-3   The Group Model of Public Policymaking and Implementation

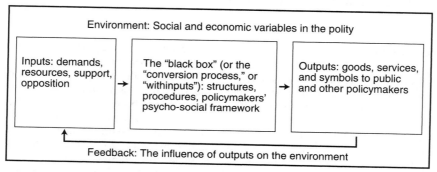

Figure 10-4   The Systems Model of Public Policymaking and Implementation

policymaking process? What are the inputs, "withinputs," outputs, and feedback of the process? A representative author of this literary stream is David Easton, particularly his *The Political System*.[10] The emphasis is diagrammed in Figure 10-4.

The Institutionalist Model

We include in the incrementalist literature the traditional institutionalist model. The institutionalist model focuses on the organization chart of government; it describes the arrangements and official duties of bureaus and departments, but customarily it has ignored the living linkages between them. Constitutional provisions, administrative and common law, and similar legalities are the objects of greatest interest; the behavioral connections between a department

and the public policy emanating from it are of scant concern. Carl J. Friedrich's *Constitutional Government and Democracy* is a representative work.[11]

With the onrush of the behavioral revolution in political science, institutional studies of the policy process were swept aside in favor of studies that relied more heavily on the group, systems, and elite/mass models, in about that order of emphasis. Illustratively, an institutionalist model would look like the diagram in Figure 10-5.

The Neo-institutionalist Model

The institutionalist model has experienced a resurrection, of a sort, that might best be described as neo-institutionalism, and it rests on a considerably more sophisticated analytical plane. There are a number of contributors to this stream,[12]

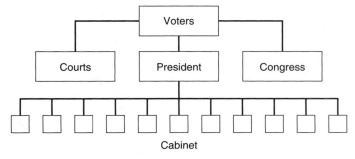

Figure 10-5   The Institutionalist Model of Public Policymaking and Implementation

although Theodore J. Lowi has done much of its groundbreaking thinking. Neo-institutionalism is an attempt to categorize public policies according to policymaking subsystems. For example, Lowi classifies policies by four "arenas of power":

redistributive, distributive, constituent, and regulative. These are shown in Table 10-1.

Arenas of Power. In a *redistributive* arena of power, for instance, power is "redistributed"

Table 10-1   The Neo-institutionalist Model of Public Policymaking and Implementation

	Target of Government Coercion	
Probability of Government Coercion	*Conduct of Individual*	*Conduct of System*
Remote	*Distributive* policy arena, for example, agricultural subsidies	*Constituent* policy arena, for example, reapportionment of legislature
	Political behaviors and characteristics	*Political behaviors and characteristics*
	Decentralized	Centralized
	Disaggregated	Systemic
	Local	National
	Partisan/electoral	Ideological
	Logrolling	Partisan/electoral
	Legislatively centered	Logrolling
		Legislatively centered
Immediate	*Regulative* policy arena, for example, elimination of fraudulent advertising	*Redistributive* policy arena, for example, progressive income tax
	Political behaviors and characteristics	*Political behaviors and characteristics*
	Decentralized	Centralized
	Disaggregated	Systemic
	Local	National
	Special interests	Ideological
	Bargaining among groups	Special interests
	Bureaucratically centered	Bargaining among groups
		Bureaucratically centered

throughout the polity on a fundamental scale. Redistributive policies tend to be highly ideological and emotionally charged for particular groups, involving a fight between the "haves" and "have-nots," but having low partisan visibility. Usually these battles are centered in the bureaucracy. Lowi, in fact, considers redistributive policies to be concerned with "not use of property but property itself, not equal treatment but equal possession, not behavior but being," and believes, because of the secrecy enshrouding the redistributive policy process, that the policy process which takes place primarily in the government bureaucracy has received the least study by social scientists.[13]

Lowi's remaining policymaking subsystems are less far-reaching in scope.

Coercion: Probability and Targets.   As Table 10-1 indicates, the neo-institutionalist approach is predicated on two dimensions: the probability of coercion and the target of coercion. The *probability of coercion* may be *remote* or *immediate*. In the regulative policy arena, for example, the possibility of coercion is quite immediate because violators of federal regulations may be punished. Moreover, violators of federal regulations may be punished as individuals; a company violating the Sherman Antitrust Act, for example, will be punished as an individual company.

Thus, we come to the *target of coercion*, which may be *individual* or *systemic*. In constituent and redistributive policy arenas, the government attempts to manipulate the conduct of the system itself through, for example, changes in the federal reserve discount rate, which can have a huge impact on the level of investments in the national economy. Yet these kinds of policies do not single out individuals as targets for coercion.

Lowi argues that from these policy arenas, which are determined by the target and probability of government coercion, emerge certain identifiable types of political behavior.[14]

The Organized Anarchy Model

A final major model of the incrementalist paradigm is the organized anarchy model of public

policymaking, and it is illustrated in Figure 10-6. John W. Kingdon's classic, *Agendas, Alternatives, and Public Policies*, is an exemplary empirical representative of this literature.[15]

Streams of Problems, Politics, and Policies.   Basic to the model is the presence of three "streams" that flow largely independently of one another and which constitute the policymaking process.

The Problems Stream.   The first of these is the *problems stream*, which involves focusing the public's and policymakers' attention on a particular social problem, defining the problem, and either applying a new public policy to the resolution of the problem or letting the problem fade from sight. Problems typically are defined in terms of *values*, such as conservative or liberal orientations; *comparisons*, such as the United States versus Iran; or *categories*—for example, is public transit for the disabled a "transportation" problem or a "civil rights" problem? Categorizing the problem becomes quite significant in how the problem is resolved.

The Political Stream.   The second stream is the *political stream.* It is in the political stream that the *governmental agenda*—in other words, the list of issues or problems to be resolved—is formed. The primary participants in the formulation of the governmental agenda comprise the *visible cluster* of policy actors, or those participants who are most readily seen on the public stage. They include high-level political appointees and the president's staff; members of Congress; the media; and interest groups. A consensus is achieved by bargaining among these participants, and at some point a "bandwagon" or "tilt" effect occurs that is a consequence of an intensifying desire by the participants to be "dealt in" on the policy resolution and not to be excluded.

The Policy Stream.   The third stream is the *policy stream.* It is in the policy stream that the *decision agenda*, or "alternative specification," is formulated. The decision agenda is the list of alternatives from which a public policy may be selected by policymakers to resolve a problem. Here the major forces are not political, but intellectual and

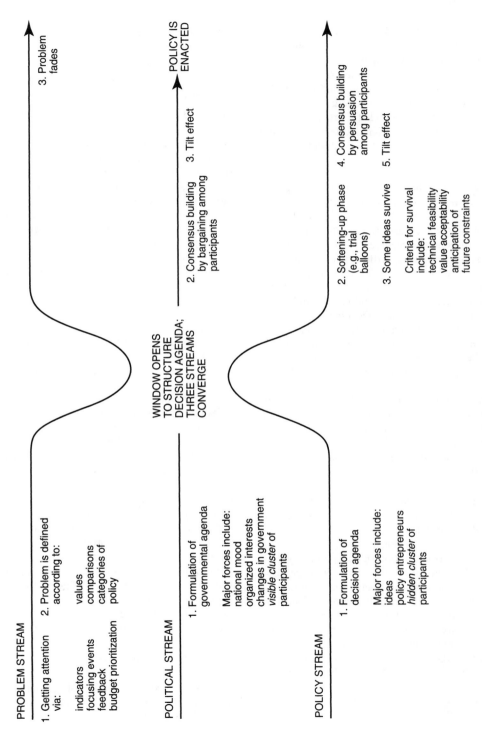

Figure 10-6 The Organized Anarchy Model of Public Policymaking and Implementation

PROBLEM STREAM

1. Getting attention
via:

indicators
focusing events
feedback
budget prioritization

2. Problem is defined
according to:

values
comparisons
categories of
policy

3. Problem
fades

POLITICAL STREAM

WINDOW OPENS
TO STRUCTURE
DECISION AGENDA;
THREE STREAMS
CONVERGE

1. Formulation of
governmental agenda

Major forces include:
national mood
organized interests
changes in government
visible cluster of
participants

2. Consensus building
by bargaining among
participants

3. Tilt effect

POLICY IS
ENACTED

POLICY STREAM

1. Formulation of
decision agenda

Major forces include:
ideas
policy entrepreneurs
hidden cluster of
participants

2. Softening-up phase
(e.g., trial
balloons)

3. Some ideas survive

Criteria for survival
include:
technical feasibility
value acceptability
anticipation of
future constraints

4. Consensus building
by persuasion
among participants

5. Tilt effect

personal. Ideas and the role of the *policy entrepreneur*, or the person who holds a deep and long abiding commitment to a particular policy change, are paramount. The major participants in the formulation of the decision agenda are called the *hidden cluster* of policy actors. These include career public administrators; congressional staffers; and interest groups (interest groups, in Kingdon's analysis, are significant actors in both the visible and hidden clusters).

Phases.   The policy stream moves from the formulation of a decision agenda to a "softening-up phase" in which "trial balloons" are released and a variety of suggestions are made both publicly and privately about how to resolve a particular problem. These ideas survive according to the criteria of whether they are technically feasible; whether they are acceptable to broad social values; and what future constraints—such as budgetary limitations and the prospects of political acceptance and public acquiescence—are anticipated by the actors in the policy stream. Unlike the political stream, consensus (or the "short list" of policy alternatives) is developed not by a bargaining process, but by the use of persuasion and rational argumentation among the participants in the policy stream. As in the political stream, however, a "bandwagon" or "tilt" effect occurs, and this happens when problems can be connected with alternative solutions and the solutions themselves are not perceived as being "too new" or radical.

Windows and Agendas.   When these three streams—problem, politics and policy—meet, a public policy can result. Kingdon calls these convergences *windows*. Windows open when there is a shift in the national mood (usually indicated by transformative elections) or new popular perceptions. When the window opens and results in a restructuring of the *governmental agenda*, it could be solely the result of occurrences in either the problem stream or the political stream. But for a window to open that results in a restructuring of the *decision agenda* requires the joining of all three streams. In this latter case, the role of the policy entrepreneur is critical.

In many ways, the organized anarchy model is a very satisfying explanation of how public policy is made. It teases out the process's messiness, disjointedness, humanity, and luck.

The Rationalist Paradigm of Public Policymaking and Implementation

Rationalism attempts to be the opposite of incrementalism. As an intellectual endeavor, rationalism tries to learn all the value preferences extant in a society, assign each value a relative weight, discover all the policy alternatives available, know all the consequences of each alternative, calculate how the selection of any one policy will affect the remaining alternatives in terms of opportunity costs, and ultimately select that policy alternative which is the most efficient in terms of the costs and benefits of social values.

Much of the rationalist paradigm deals with the construction of public policies that assure better public policies. Yehezkel Dror (as good a representative as any of the rationalists) calls this concern *metapolicy*, or policy for policymaking procedures.[16]

The rationalist approach offers a variety of intellectual directions. Most notably, it is concerned with the nature of public goods and services,[17] the relationships between formal decision-making structures and human propensities for individual action[18] and for collective action,[19] the requisites of constitutional government and corresponding patterns of collective action,[20] the interstices between producers, performance, consumer interests, and the provision of public goods and service,[21] and the broad implications of technological innovation.[22]

Diagramed, the rationalist paradigm renders public policy formation into a linear flow chart, as Figure 10-7 demonstrates. There are, of course, subsets, and these include the rational choice model, and the exclusion/consumption model.

The Rational Choice Model

In 1963, a modest collection of scholars met to discuss, in their words, "developments in the 'no-name' field of public administration."[23] Since

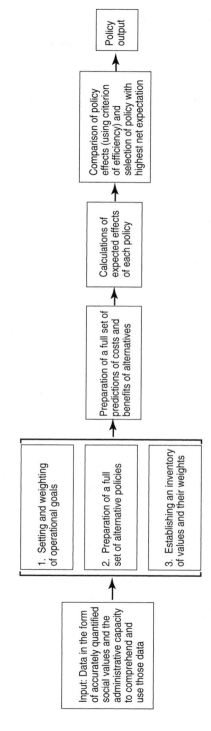

Figure 10-7 The Rationalist Paradigm of Public Policymaking and Implementation

then, names have been acquired, and they include "rational choice," "public choice," and "political economy."[24] In its more applied mode (reviewed in Chapter 12), this literature is often called "metropolitan organization" or "local public economies."

Using the concepts of rational choice, we can assess public policy in new ways. Consider, for example, the problems of air pollution, energy conservation, and the role of the automobile, which accounts for most of the air pollutants and fuel consumption in the United States. Rather than passing a flatly stated law that says little more than "Thou shalt not pollute nor use too much gas," a political economist would likely turn instead to the tax structure. He or she would reason that if a particular citizen chose to buy a Ferrari rather than a Prius, the general citizenry should not have to bear the common costs of that citizen's choice (that is, the extra pollutants emitted and fuel consumed by the Ferrari), but neither should all the other citizens be denied the Ferraris if they really want them. Thus, a special tax should be established that taxes cars according to the pollutants they emit and the energy resources they consume; the more pollutants and gas, the higher the tax. In this method, the individual citizen still can buy a Ferrari, but the costs of the purchase to the general citizenry will be offset by the special tax that the owner is forced to pay by using that tax for pollution abatement and energy research programs. Such is the nature of assessment in the public choice literature.

Optimality. On a more sophisticated plane, rational choice is concerned with "Pareto optimality," a concept originally developed by the economist Vilfredo Pareto. Or, more exactly (and because optimality is supremely difficult to achieve in any context), rational choice concerns "Pareto improvements," and the notions of trade-offs and externalities. A *Pareto improvement* is "a change in economic organization that makes everyone better off—or, more precisely, that makes one or more members of society better off without making anyone worse off."[25]

Pareto optimality may be illustrated with reference to public choice in graphic form. Figure 10-8 posits a hypothetical social value ("*X*") relative to

the accomplishment of all other social values. The *indifference curve* refers to the combination of values about which society is indifferent (at least up to a point); the *value achievement curve* indicates the optimal combination of values that it is possible for government to encourage given limited resources. The point of optimal achievement of Value *X* and the optimal achievement of all other social values constitutes the point of *Pareto optimality.* The closer that society gets to the point of Pareto optimality is considered a Pareto improvement.

Tradeoffs. Figure 10-8 also illustrates what the rational choice writers mean by "trade-offs." A *trade-off* refers to what value is being exchanged (and the social costs and benefits incurred in such an exchange) for what other value. In other words, every time Value *X* is achieved more fully, all other values are correspondingly reduced in achievement; the benefits gained by increasing resource input into Value *X* must decrease resource input into all other values.

Externalities. Executing public policies is a process that is far from tidy, and policies meant to solve problems in one social arena can cause problems in others. When a public policy in one sphere of social action affects other spheres of social action, the manner in which the other spheres is affected is called an *externality*, or *spillover effect*; that is, the effects of a public policy in one sphere "spill over" into other spheres. Externalities may be positive or negative, intended or unintended. For example, a *positive, intended* spillover effect of reducing corporate taxes might be to raise employment levels. A *negative, unintended* externality of the same public policy might be to reduce the financial resources available to the government for welfare programs.

The Exclusion/Consumption Model

A variation[26] of the rationalist paradigm deals with what kinds of goods and services should be delivered by government, and what kinds should be delivered by other sectors. Table 10-2 diagrams the following discussion, and the reader may wish to refer to it.

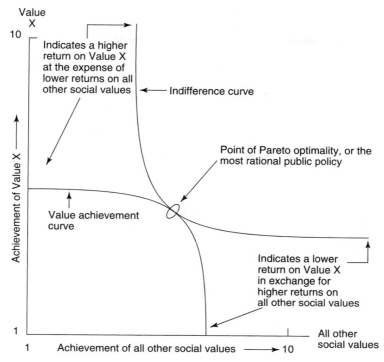

Figure 10-8   Pareto Optimality

Table 10-2   Goods and Services According to the Criteria, of Exclusion and Consumption

	Consumption/Use	
Exclusion	*Individual Use*	*Joint Use*
Feasible	Private goods and services (a bag of groceries, a haircut, a meal in a restaurant)	Toll goods and services (cable television, telephone service, theaters, libraries, electric power)
Unfeasible	Common-pool goods and services (water in a public well, fish in the ocean, air to breathe)	Collective, or public, goods and services (peace and security, public safety, pollution control, weather forecasts, public television, radio)

Excluding and Consuming.   To determine what policies government should be responsible for, two concepts are used: exclusion and consumption. *Exclusion* refers to the degree of control that both the buyer and seller have over a particular commodity; in other words, how easy is it to exclude users or owners from using or owning a particular good or service? Most goods are like a bag of groceries; for a buyer to walk out of a supermarket with a bag of groceries requires that both the buyer and seller agree to a price. In this case (which is the most common one in the real world), the seller exercises a high level of exclusionary control.

But other goods and services are not so easily controlled. For example, a lighthouse has a very low level of exclusivity. All ships within sight of the lighthouse can benefit from its service. Exclusion, in short, is a matter of economics rather than choice. Some goods and services can be excluded from the marketplace more readily than others.

The second major point used by public choice theorists in this stream of literature is that of *consumption*, or *use*. Some goods and services may be consumed, or used, *jointly* (that is, simultaneously) by many consumers without being diminished in either quality or quantity, while other goods and services are available only for *individual* rather than joint consumption. An example of joint consumption would be a television broadcast. All viewers may "consume" a television program "jointly" without the program being diminished in either quality or quantity. A fish and a haircut provide examples of individual consumption of a good and a service. Once they are consumed by an individual, no one else has access to them.

Goods and Services. Using the notions of exclusion and consumption, we can begin to classify goods and services according to four kinds of "pure forms": private, toll, common-pool, and collective goods and services.[27]

Private Goods and Services. *Private goods and services* are pure, individually consumed goods and services for which exclusion is completely feasible. There is no problem of supply. The marketplace provides private goods readily, and this supply is based on consumer demand. Government's role in the supply of private goods and services is largely limited to assuring their safety (such as in building inspections), honest representation (such as weights and measures), and so forth.

Toll Goods and Services. *Toll goods and services* are pure, jointly consumed goods and services for which exclusion is completely feasible. As with private goods, toll goods can be supplied easily by the marketplace, and excluding consumers

from using them is entirely practicable. But unlike private goods, consumption of toll goods is joint rather than individual. This is because many toll goods are natural monopolies, which means that as the number of users increases, the cost per user decreases. Examples include cable television, electric power, and water supplies. In the case of toll goods, government action may be required to assure that monopolies are created and granted in the first place and then regulated so that proprietors do not exploit their monopolistic privileges unfairly.

Common-Pool Goods and Services. *Common-pool goods and services* are pure, individually consumed goods and services for which exclusion is not feasible. The sky and air are common-pool goods. In the case of common-pool goods we do have supply problems, and this differentiates common-pool goods from both private goods and toll goods. There is neither a requirement to pay for common-pool goods nor any means to prevent their consumption; they are, in the short term, "free."

Common-pool goods bring us to the problem of what Garrett Hardin called the "tragedy of the commons"[28]—that which belongs to everyone belongs to no one, and the problem of common-pool goods is that they can be easily squandered to the point of exhaustion. An example would be the clean air supply. Until government imposed regulations on the emission of air pollutants, the air was a "free good," at least from the perspective of the industrialist who could use it as a vast dumping bin for pollutants. The air was, in this sense, a "commons." Government has a much larger role in the administration of common-pool goods than it does in private and toll goods because it makes sense for government to regulate common-pool goods so that they are not destroyed by over-consumption.

Public Goods and Services. Finally, there are *collective*, or *public*, *goods and services*, which are pure, jointly consumed goods and services for which exclusion is not feasible. The marketplace cannot supply these goods because they are used simultaneously by many people, and no one can be excluded from consuming them. Individuals have an economic incentive to exploit collective goods without paying for them, and to thus become what public choice theorists call *free riders*, or people who benefit from goods and services but do not pay for them. National defense, broadcast television, and police protection provide examples of collective goods.

Collective goods differ from common-pool goods on the basis of consumption. Common-pool goods are individually consumed (and, because of this, may be completely consumed), while collective goods are jointly consumed without diminishing the quality or quantity of the goods and services themselves.

It is in the area of collective goods that government has the greatest responsibility for management and regulation. When we realize that such basic services as police protection is considered a collective good in this construct, the importance of government intervention in the marketplace seems obvious.

The Problems of the Paradigms

The incrementalist and rationalist paradigms of public policy diverge forcefully from each other. The incrementalists want to *understand* public policy and how it is made, whereas the rationalists want to *improve* public policy and how it is made. Because of these divergent perspectives, in part, the incrementalists and rationalists have lodged some arch accusations at each other, and these criticisms have some merit.

Criticisms of the Incrementalist Paradigm

The rationalists have criticized incrementalism on several grounds, and "muddling through" has been derided as "a form of tiptoeing naked and buttocks-first into history."[29] Examples of such mindless incrementalism include the American experience in Vietnam, which was entered into by increments.

Negotiating for Nothing? A major criticism of the incrementalist paradigm is that it is based on a negotiating concept. Unfortunately, bargaining tends to be far more successful in making policy when resources are relatively unlimited and there

is something extra to divide up among the participants. In times of scarcity, however, other methods (usually rational methods) must be found to make hard choices.

The Beagle Fallacy. A related criticism is "the beagle fallacy," or the fact that beagles have a superb sense of smell but very limited eyesight and often will miss a rabbit that is directly in front of them but downwind.[30] Incrementalists, in other words, ignore the obvious. Because incrementalism is a bargaining concept, the real objectives of participants often are deliberately hidden by the participants themselves. In this criticism, incrementalists are viewed as skilled players in a poker game, but none of them admits that the objective of the other players is to win money.

The Vision Thing. A third criticism of incrementalism is that the incrementalists are singularly deficient in imagination. They have no vision. Only what is, is real to the incrementalists. As one critic has put it, "Like beautifully muscled illiterates, incrementalists . . . have overdeveloped powers of political calculation and underdeveloped powers of social imagination."[31] Related to this charge is the concern that incrementalists are so wrapped up in political gamesmanship, they actually become anti-intellectual in their approach to the solution of social problems.

Curmudgeonly Conservatism. Finally, incrementalism is an inherently conservative approach. Drastic and far-reaching transformations are eschewed in favor of tinkering. As change becomes more rapid and more endemic in America's technobureaucracy, the innate conservatism of incrementalism becomes less responsive and more counterproductive.

Criticisms of the Rationalist Paradigm

These are not untoward criticisms of the incrementalist approach. Nevertheless, the rationalists also have their critics.

Does Anyone Read Plans? For example, incrementalists are quick to point to the fact that there is often a wide gap between planning (an activity held particularly dear by the rationalists) and the actual implementation of the resultant plan. It is, regrettably, undeniable that many plans have been written only to collect dust on many shelves, even though these plans had cost considerable sums of time and money to develop.[32]

People Are Not Powerless. Another problem is that rationalists often ignore the role of the individual policy actor in making policy. To be implemented and to work, a plan must be more than computer runs and printouts; a plan requires people and leadership to make ideas happen. The "policy entrepreneur" is critical in both developing and implementing public policies in government.[33]

Policymaking Is Not Linear. A third criticism is that the rationalists are far too mechanical in their approach to what is, in reality, a complex form of life—the policy process. As one critic has noted, "we can no longer profitably discuss our world and its future in simple linear terms . . . for the evidence all around us is of multi-dimensional, complex actions."[34]

They Are Just Wrong. A fourth criticism of the rationalists' approach is that the predictions it makes often are wrong, or it fails to make predictions when there appears to be ample evidence warranting certain predictions. The rationalists have a less than terrific record as forecasters of future events.[35]

Rationalism Costs. Finally, it has been alleged that the effort to "gin up" large-scale, comprehensive planning programs ends up spending more than the plans ultimately save their investors or the taxpayers. "In most states, it is very probable that the new costs of data manipulation have been met largely by reducing the support of the activities which are measured."[36] Planning in the comprehensive, rationalist mode, in short, costs more than it saves. (Or so say its critics; practicing public administrators, as we see later in this chapter, would appear to disagree with this criticism.)

These are the main criticisms that the incrementalists and rationalists allege about each other. But criticisms, no matter how accurate, are not always constructive. "What is needed . . . is a strategy that is less exacting than the rationalistic one, but not as constricting in its perspective as the incrementalist approach."[37]

The Strategic Planning Paradigm of Public Policymaking and Implementation

This "third approach" has since acquired the title of "strategic planning," or, less frequently, "strategic decision making" or "strategic management," and it is an eminently useful concept in that it attempts to combine the strongest features of incrementalism and rationalism, yet avoid their pitfalls.

Strategic planning as we know it emerged in the world of business, Alfred Chandler Jr., first called attention to the practical emergence of strategic planning in major American corporations in 1962,[38] and strategic planning appears to have made corporations more productive organizations. One review using "meta-analytic data drawn from twenty-six previously published studies" concluded that "strategic planning positively influences firm performance. . . ."[39]

Strategic planning is neither the personal vision of the chief executive officer nor a collection of unrelated plans drawn up by department heads. Strategic planning is done by the top line officers of the organization, from the chief executive officer through the upper levels of middle management. It is not done by planners. As one planning official wrote, "First we ask: who is leading the planning? If it is a planner . . . we are in trouble."[40]

The strategic plan does not substitute numbers for important intangibles, such as human emotions, but it does use computers and quantification to illuminate choices. What a strategic plan does is place line decision makers in an active rather than in a passive position about the future of their organization. "The aim of strategic planning is to place the unit in a distinctive position relative to its environment."[41] To do this requires that strategic planning be highly participatory and tolerant of controversy.

In these ways, strategic planning is an attempt to reconcile the incrementalist and rationalist approaches to the problem of public policy formulation.

Strategic Planning: The Public and Nonprofit Experiences

Strategic planning has been adopted extensively by governments at all levels, and by the third sector, too. *Public strategic planning* may be defined as the development, articulation, prioritization, and communication of significant policy goals by public and nonprofit organizations, and the integration of those goals into the management, budgeting, and performance measurement systems of these organizations. Figure 10-9 synthesizes the main features of public strategic planning.

A variation of public strategic planning, and one that is increasingly popular, is called *scenario planning*, which involves the creation of alternative narratives about the future based on different decisions, made by many players, as each narrative progresses. Scenario planning augments the strategic plan.

Strategic planning in the public sector differs from its form in the private one. An analysis of strategic planning in local governments concluded that, "governmental strategic planning probably should be judged by different standards than private-sector, corporate strategic planning"; none of the governments and agencies "was able

to follow the linear, sequential planning models of the business policy textbooks, and none was able to prepare a public-sector equivalent of the slick corporate strategic plan."[42] The International City/County Management Association reflects this thinking in its recommendation that "a well-crafted" public strategic plan will amount, on average, to a modest five to seven pages.[43]

The Scope of Public Strategic Planning

Public strategic planning has had an undeniable impact on all three levels of government, and on the nonprofit sector as well.

Federal Strategic Planning. At the national level, the Government Performance and Results Act of 1993 requires, for the first time in federal history, that agencies submit multiyear strategic plans to Congress and the Office of Management and Budget. The first-ever government-wide strategic plans appeared in 1998, which, in the words of the act, provides "a single cohesive picture of the annual performance goals for the fiscal year."

State Strategic Planning. The states seem enamored with strategic planning. All the states require, either legislatively or by administrative

Figure 10-9   The Strategic Planning Paradigm of Public Policymaking and Implementation

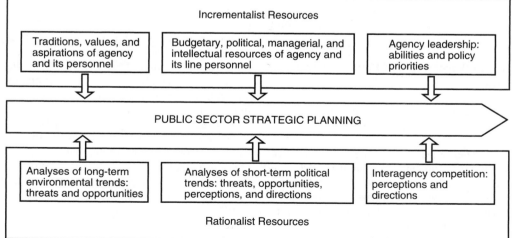

Incrementalist Resources

| Traditions, values, and aspirations of agency and its personnel | Budgetary, political, managerial, and intellectual resources of agency and its line personnel | Agency leadership: abilities and policy priorities |

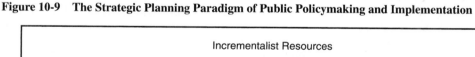

PUBLIC SECTOR STRATEGIC PLANNING

| Analyses of long-term environmental trends: threats and opportunities | Analyses of short-term political trends: threats, opportunities, perceptions, and directions | Interagency competition: perceptions and directions |

Rationalist Resources

means, strategic planning regarding their agencies' missions, goals, and objectives.[44] The percentage of governors who provide written "overall policy guidance" to their agencies (clearly strategic planning) in preparing agency budget requests has increased steadily from a third in 1970 to almost four-fifths today, and over half of the governors furnish this policy guidance "by other means."[45] Nearly two-fifths of state agencies have fully implemented strategic plans, and almost four-fifths have "partially or fully" implemented strategic plans; strategic planning, in fact, has the highest rate of implementation of any of eleven managerial innovations surveyed in the states.[46]

Local Strategic Planning.   Nearly half, 45 percent, of cities use strategic planning citywide, and this figure has grown, if marginally, over the years. The larger the city, the more likely that it will have a comprehensive, citywide plan in place. More than a third, 34 percent, of cities have completed a full cycle of at least one strategic plan over the last five years.[47]

Nonprofit Strategic Planning.   The nonprofit sector also plans strategically, although "many nonprofit organizations do not use strategic planning."[48] Third-sector organizations that are more likely to employ strategic planning are larger, have boards that focus on policy issues rather than on administration, more sophisticated managers, and which (and this seems to be especially important) are being prodded by outside funding sources to plan.[49]

The Implementation of Public Strategic Planning

Developing and implementing a strategic plan in the public sector is far from easy.

Federal Implementation.   The federal government's first government-wide plan has much work that remains to be done in two "critical areas": strengthening weak agency plans aimed at improving performance, and the attainment of "an integrated, governmentwide perspective throughout the plan."[50] These are daunting challenges, but progress, though slow, seems at least to be present. Seven out of ten federal managers report that they consider "strategic goals to a great or very great extent in allocating resources," and this proportion is steadily rising.[51]

State Implementation.   The adoption by state agencies of strategic planning is closely related to a new governor assuming office, when the state's fiscal health is sound, when the agency has a history of dealing with the private sector, and when similar agencies in neighboring states have adopted it.[52] Strategic planning in state agencies seems to undergo an evolution in which it ultimately becomes part of a broader quality management program.

Local Implementation.   At the local level, some research indicates that local managers must overcome some significant technical and political obstacles in implementing strategic planning. It is possible that technical difficulties in local strategic planning are of greater significance than are political obstacles. An analysis of local public authorities in Britain found that "the problems of rational planning are largely technical," such as shortages of resources or expertise, "rather than political."[53]

An analysis of local governments in Minnesota found that a government or public agency is the most likely to succeed in initiating and completing a strategic plan if it has several characteristics in place. They include the presence of a "powerful process sponsor" (that is, one or [typically] more major figures who endorse the idea of strategic planning, even if tepidly); a strong "process champion" (a skilled administrator who knows what he or she is doing and believes in strategic planning); an agency-wide expectation of disruptions and delays; and a willingness to be flexible about what, precisely, a strategic plan really is.[54]

A survey of all cities and towns with populations of 25,000 or more found that municipalities are putting their money where their plan is. More than four-fifths of these local governments link the budget to their strategic plan. Almost two-thirds of these jurisdictions base the salary increases of their managers on accomplishing the objectives stipulated in their strategic plans.[55]

These techniques of implementation have brought results. Local officials in those municipalities that have completed one strategic plan estimate that two-fifths, on average, of the plan's goals were accomplished, and in those communities where multiple rounds of planning have been completed, the average estimate rises to three-fifths of goals achieved.[56]

Nonprofit Implementation. Perhaps the most significant internal variable for a nonprofit organization to begin strategic planning is that its stakeholders agree on organizational goals, an agreement that may be more difficult to achieve than in the private or even public sectors. "The most critical external factor [is] a funding source requirement to submit a plan of action, leading several authors to conclude that nonprofits plan when they have to plan." This is "one of the strongest research findings" in the field.[57] In other words, if a third-sector organization is to plan and then implement its plan, it must have, first, members who agree on what they want their organization to do, and, second, have major donors who insist that the organization plan strategically. This appears to be an uncommon combination.

The Limitations of Public Strategic Planning

Beginning a strategic plan requires considerable effort in any sector, but especially so in the public one. Although strategic planning has been described as a "hearty, public-sector perennial,"[58] it is clear that it is a perennial whose heartiness is the product of growing in thinner soil: The intrusiveness of the public sector's working environment makes strategic planning a tougher (and likely less satisfactory) job than it is in the private sector.

The Impact of the Environment. For example, a thorough comparison of four federal agencies and twelve *Fortune* 500 companies concluded that, because the companies had clearer goals, clearer measures of performance, and were less influenced by outside forces than were the agencies, strategic planning was used much more extensively by the companies than the agencies, simply because it was easier for the companies to do.[59]

More broadly, the public organization's political environment reaches into the organization's inner workings that severely curtail corporate-style strategic planning. The "pervasive vagueness" of agency missions; environmental constraints in the form of interest groups, media, and other forces that render "bold moves" by public sector executives "almost completely impossible"; the uniquely omnipresent need to be sensitive to how a policy will be perceived, not just what it will do; arbitrary time constraints, such as budget and election cycles, that can rush or delay strategic decisions in ways that they no longer are strategic; and coalitions which are usually prone to disintegrate prior to the complete implementation of a strategic plan—all these and more limit the use of strategic planning in the public sector.[60] One study of city managers and mayors in council-manager cities concluded that the single greatest obstacle to successful strategic planning in these municipalities was the "need to gain greater control over the external political environment."[61]

The Larger, but Perilous, Purpose of Public Strategic Planning. At root, strategic planning is a "disciplined effort to produce fundamental decisions and actions that define what an organization . . . is, what it does, and why it does it."[62] And it is in implementing this larger purpose that public strategic planning seems to have a special relevance.

This focus on the larger picture, however, does have its perils. By openly identifying and emphasizing big, inspiring organizational goals, morale can suffer if the public organization fails to attain those goals—typically because of budget reductions over which the public agency has no control. In the context of the public sector, strategic planning tends to over promise (or, at least, to raise expectations), and if promises are unkept, disappointment and malaise can seep through the organization.

The Symbolic Uses of Nonprofit Planning? Success in strategic planning also seems limited in the nonprofit sector, it for quite different reasons. In the third sector, strategic failure may be less a function of dashed hopes, as it is in government, and more a consequence of organizational cynicism.

Because "coercive pressure" that is brought to bear by external funding sources seems to be the primary reason why independent organizations work up strategic plans at all, it is less likely that their plans will actually be strategic. Instead, the plan "may be largely symbolic . . . and the planning process may be decoupled from other strategic activities," such as improving performance.[63] The nonprofit strategic plan, in other words, may not be a shaper of organizational dynamism (as it is meant to be), but rather a sitter on dusty office shelves (as it too often is, in all sectors).

The Benefits of Public Strategic Planning

While potentially perilous, public strategic planning is not necessarily ineffective. If a public or nonprofit organization can complete a strategic plan, then it has been able to identify issues, prioritize them, and formulate ways of—for example, strategies for—dealing with them. But just how effective public strategic plans are—that is, do they measurably facilitate public and third-sector administrators in achieving their goals and resolving issues?—is not clear; one review of the literature concluded that "no careful study of the effectiveness of governmental strategic planning has been done," although it is known that those public administrators who develop and complete strategic plans believe that their efforts are worthwhile.[64]

Public Strategic Benefits. In a survey of state administrators' use of strategic planning, it was found that the ability of strategic planning to articulate and prioritize goals was its single most valued feature, with 90 percent rating its utility in "clarifying agency priorities" and "management directions" as its most important contribution to their agencies.[65]

Local administrators, too, give high marks to strategic planning. Among those municipalities that have completed at least one strategic plan, more than four-fifths are very satisfied (33 percent) or satisfied (52 percent) with its implementation and goal achievement. A remarkable 93 percent of administrators in these cities state that strategic planning is worth the time and expense that it entails (only 2 percent say that it is not). Almost nine out of ten local administrators say that

completing the strategic plan was beneficial or very beneficial in terms of focusing the city council's agenda on important issues, and providing their communities with "a genuine sense of mission."[66]

Nonprofit Strategic Benefits. Using strategic planning in the independent sector seems to reap more measurable rewards than in the governmental sector. Strategic planning associates with nonprofit organizational growth, both in funding and membership; higher performance; greater effectiveness in attaining the nonprofits' social and organizational mission; and improved effectiveness by their boards of directors.[67]

By and large, the research on strategic planning in the public and nonprofit sectors suggests that public strategic planning is worth the considerable effort it requires.

Strategic planning is a means of implementing public policy, and, as such, is one of the approaches to public policy and its implementation that we have reviewed in this chapter. Aside from the techniques of public management themselves, which we explained in Part III, public policies are implemented through a rich variety of forms of intersectoral and intergovernmental arrangements. We consider these methods in the next two chapters.

Notes

1. This definition is based loosely on Harold D. Lasswell, *A Pre-view of Policy Sciences* (New York: American Elsevier, 1971), pp. 1–2.
2. William N, Dunn, *Public Policy Analysis: An Introduction,* 2nd ed. (Englewood Cliffs, NJ: Prentice Hall, 1994), p. 50.
3. John A Hird, "Policy Analysis for What? The Effectiveness of Nonpartisan Policy Research Organizations," *Policy Studies Journal* 33 (Spring 2005), pp. 83–105. The quotation is on p. 83.
4. Charles E. Lindblom, *The Policy Making Process* (Englewood Cliffs, NJ: Prentice Hall, 1968).
5. Charles E. Lindblom, "The Science of Muddling Through," *Public Administration Review* 19 (Spring 1959), pp. 79–88.
6. Ralph K. Huitt, "Political Feasibility," in Austin Ranney, ed., *Political Science and Public Policy* (Chicago: Markham, 1968), p. 274. We should note, however, that, although we agree largely with Huitt's assessment, far-reaching policy change can be both fast and rational—that is, not incremental. Nonincremental

policymaking has occurred, for example, in Medicaid policy in Arizona, Michigan, and Tennessee. See Carol S. Weissert and Malcolm L. Goggin, "Nonincremental Policy Change: Lessons from Michigan's Medicaid Managed Care Initiative," *Public Administration Review* 62 (March/April 2002), pp. 206–216.

7. C. Wright Mills, *The Power Elite* (New York: Oxford University Press, 1956).

8. Arthur F. Bentley, *The Process of Government* (Bloomington, IN: Principia Press, 1949). First published in 1908.

9. For a good review of how this works, see Louis M. Kohlmeier, *The Regulators: Watchdog Agencies and the Public Interest* (New York: Harper & Row, 1969). For an explanation of why it works this way, see Murray Edelman, *The Symbolic Uses of Politics* (Urbana, IL: University of Illinois Press, 1964).

10. David Easton, *The Political System* (New York: Knopf, 1953).

11. Carl J. Friedrich, *Constitutional Government and Democracy* (Boston: Little, Brown, 1941).

12. See, for example, Theodore J. Lowi, "Decision-Making versus Policy-Making: Towards an Anecdote for Technocracy," *Public Administration Review* 30 (May/June 1970), pp. 134–139; Theodore J. Lowi, "Four Systems of Politics, Policy and Choice," *Public Administration Review* 32 (July/August 1972), pp. 298–310; Randall B. Ripley, "Introduction: The Politics of Public Policy," *Public Policies and Their Politics: An Introduction to the Techniques of Government Control*, Randall B. Ripley, ed. (New York: Norton, 1966), pp. i–xv.

13. Theodore J. Lowi, "American Business, Public Policy, Case Studies, and Political Theory," *World Politics* 16 (July 1964), p. 691. But see also Theodore J. Lowi, "Population Policies and the American Political System," *Political Science and Population Studies*, Richard L. Clinton, William S. Flash, and R. Kenneth Godwin, eds. (Lexington, MA: D. C. Heath, 1972), pp. 25–53. For an attempt at integrating some of the contributors to this literature, see Leonard Champney, "Public Goods and Policy Types," *Public Administration Review* 48 (November/December 1988), pp. 988–994.

14. Lowi, "Population Policies and the American Political System," pp. 29–33.

15. John W. Kingdon, *Agendas, Alternatives, and Public Policies*, 2nd ed. (New York: Harper Collins, 1995). Kingdon addressed federal policymaking. For a similarly structured analysis of state policymaking, see Virginia Gray and David Lowery, "Where Do Policy Ideas Come From? A Study of Minnesota Legislators and Staffers," *Journal of Public Administration Research and Theory* 10 (July 2000), pp. 573–597.

16. Yehezkel Dror, *Public Policy Making Reexamined* (San Francisco: Chandler, 1968), p. 8.

17. See Otto Eckstein, *Public Finance,* 2nd ed. (Englewood Cliffs, NJ: Prentice Hall, 1967); Robert L. Bish, *The Public Economy of Metropolitan Areas* (Chicago: Markham, 1971); and L. L. Wade and R. L. Curry Jr.,

A Logic of Public Policy: Aspects of Political Economy (Belmont, CA: Wadsworth, 1970).

18. Gordon Tullock, *The Politics of Bureaucracy* (Washington, DC: Public Affairs Press, 1965); and Anthony Downs, *An Economic Theory of Democracy* (New York: Harper & Row, 1957).

19. Mancur Olson, *The Logic of Collective Action* (Cambridge, MA: Harvard University Press, 1965).

20. James M. Buchanan and Gordon Tullock, *The Calculus of Consent: Logical Foundations of Constitutional Democracy* (Ann Arbor: University of Michigan Press, 1962).

21. Garrett Hardin, "The Tragedy of the Commons," *Science* 162 (December 13, 1968), pp. 1243–1248; and Joseph J. Seneca, "The Welfare Effects of Zero Pricing of Public Goods," *Public Choice* 7 (Spring 1970), pp. 101–110.

22. Early examples include Lynton Keith Caldwell, *Environment: A Challenge to Modern Society* (Garden City, NY: Natural History Press, 1970), and Nicholas Henry, "Copyright, Public Policy, and Information Technology," *Science* 182 (February 1, 1974), pp. 384–391.

23. Vincent Ostrom and Elinor Ostrom, "Public Choice: A Different Approach to the Study of Public Administration," *Public Administration Review* 31 (March/April 1971), p. 203.

24. For two good, if wildly different, discussions of the huge impact that the "rational choice" school has had on public administration and political science (but especially the latter), see William C. Mitchell, "Political Science and Public Choice: 1950–70," *Public Choice* 98 (March 1999), pp. 237–249; and Jonathan Cohn, "Revenge of the Nerds: Irrational Exuberance," *The New Republic* 221 (October 25, 1999), pp. 25–31.

25. E. J. Mishan, *Economics for Social Decisions: Elements of Cost-Benefit Analysis* (New York: Praeger, 1972), p. 14.

26. Vincent Ostrom and Elinor Ostrom, "Public Goods and Public Choices," in *Alternatives for Delivering Public Services*, E. S. Savas, ed. (Boulder, CO: Westview Press, 1977), pp. 7–14; and E. S. Savas, *Privatizing the Public Sector: How to Shrink Government* (Chatham, NJ: Chatham House Publishers, 1982). See also, Hardin, "The Tragedy of the Commons," and Seneca, "The Welfare Effects of Zero Pricing of Public Goods."

27. Savas, *Privatizing the Public Sector*, p. 33. Much of the following discussion is drawn from Savas, pp. 29–52.

28. Hardin, "The Tragedy of the Commons."

29. George Keller, *Academic Strategy: The Management Revolution in Higher Education* (Baltimore, MD: The Johns Hopkins University Press, 1983), p. 111.

30. Harold Enarson, "The Art of Planning," *Educational Record* 56 (Summer 1975), p. 173.

31. Keller, *Academic Strategy*, p. 113.

32. See, for example, David Clark, "In Consideration of Goal-Free Planning: The Failure of Traditional Planning Systems in Education," *Educational Administration Quarterly* 17 (Summer 1981), pp. 42–60.

33. Kingdon, *Agendas, Politics, and Public Policies*. But see also Joseph Schumpeter, "The Creative Response in Economic History," *Journal of Economic History* 7 (November 1947), pp. 149–159.

34. Derek Viray, *Planning and Education* (London: Routledge and Kegan Paul, 1972), p. 4.

35. For examples of critiques of the forecasting weaknesses of the rationalists models, see Paul Ward and Benjamin Ward, *What's Wrong with Economics?* (Basic Books, 1972); Seymour Martin Lipset, "The Limits to Futurology in Social Science Analysis," in Seymour Martin Lipset, ed., *The Third Century: America as a Post Industrial Society* (Cooper Institution Press, 1979), pp. 3–18; and William Ascher, "Forecasting Potential of Complex Models," *Policy Sciences* 13 (May 1981), pp. 247–267.

36. Emerson Schuck, "The New Planning and the Old Fragmentism," *Journal of Higher Education* 48 (September/October 1977), pp. 494–602.

37. Amitai Etzioni, *The Active Society* (New York: Free Press, 1968), p. 283. See also Amitai Etzioni, "Mixed Scanning: A Third Approach to Decision Making," *Public Administration Review* 27 (December 1967), pp. 385–392.

38. Alfred Chandler Jr., *Strategy and Structure: Chapters in the History of the Industrial Enterprise* (Cambridge, MA: Massachusetts Institute of Technology Press, 1962).

39. C. Chet Miller and Laura B. Cardinal, "Strategic Planning and Firm Performance: A Synthesis of More than Two Decades of Research," *Academy of Management Journal* 37 (December 1994), p. 1649.

40. Michael Aiken and Jerald Hage, "The Organic Organization and Innovation," *Sociology* 5 (January 1971), p. 80.

41. Richard Cyert, as quoted in Keller, *Academic Strategy,* p. 147.

42. John M. Bryson and Wiliam D. Roering, "The Initiation of Strategic Planning by Governments," *Public Administration Review* 48 (November/December 1988), pp. 995–1004.

43. International City/County Management Association, "Strategic Planning: A Guide for Public Managers," *IQ Report* 34 (August 2002), p. 9.

44. Julia Melkers and Katherine Willoughby, *Staying the Course: The Use of Performance Measurements in State Governments* (Washington, DC: IBM Center for the Business of Government, 2004).

45. Robert C. Burns and Robert D. Lee, Jr., "The Ups and Downs of State Budget Process Reform: Experience of Three Decades," *Public Budgeting and Finance* 24 (Fall 2004), p. 5. In 2000, 77 percent of governors provided their agencies with overall policy guidance in writing, and 53 percent did so by other means.

46. Jeffrey L. Brudney, F. Ted Hebert, and Deil S. Wright, "Reinventing Government in the American States: Explaining Administrative Reform," *Public Administration Review* 59 (January/February 1999), p. 23.

47. Gregory Streib and Theodore H. Poister, "The Use of Strategic Planning in Municipal Governments," *Municipal Year Book, 2002* (Washington, DC: International City/County Management Association, 2002), pp. 18–25. Data are for 2001.

48. Melissa M. Stone, Barbara Bigelow, and William Crittenden, "Research on Strategic Management in Nonprofit Organizations: Synthesis, Analysis, and Future Directions," *Administration and Society* 31 (July 1999), p. 383. Much of our discussion of nonprofit strategic planning is drawn from this excellent review of sixty-five empirically based journal articles published from 1977 through 1998.

49. Ibid., pp. 378–423.

50. U.S. General Accounting Office, *The Results Act: Assessment of the Governmentwide Performance Plan for Fiscal Year 1999,* GAO/AIMD/GGD-98-159 (Washington, DC: U.S. Government Printing Office, 1998), p. 2.

51. U.S. General Accounting Office, *Results-Oriented Government: GPRA Has Established a Solid Foundation for Achieving Greater Results,* GAO-04-38 (Washington, DC: U.S. Government Printing Office, 2004), p. 43. Figure is for 2003. In 1997, 64 percent of federal managers so reported.

52. Frances Stokes Berry, "Innovation in Public Management: The Adoption of Strategic Planning," *Public Administration Review* 54 (July/August 1994), pp. 322–329. Figures are for 1992.

53. George A. Boyne, Julian S. Gould-Williams, Jennifer Law, et al., "Problems of Rational Planning in Public Organizations: An Empirical Assessment of the Conventional Wisdom," *Administration and Society* 36 (July 2004), p. 328.

54. Bryson and Roering, "Initiation of Strategic Planning by Governments."

55. Theodore H. Poister and Gregory Streib, "Elements of Strategic Planning and Management in Municipal Government: Status after Two Decades," *Public Administration Review* 65 (January/February 2005), pp. 49–50. Figures are for 2001.

56. Ibid., p. 51. Figures are for 2001.

57. Stone, Bigelow, and Crittenden, "Research on Strategic Management in Nonprofit Organizations," pp. 391, 408.

58. Gerald J. Miller, "Unique Public-Sector Strategies," *Public Productivity and Management Review* 13 (Winter 1989), p. 133.

59. Richard E. Boyatzis, *The Competent Manager* (New York: Wiley, 1982).

60. Miller, "Unique Public-Sector Strategies," pp. 137–138.

61. Gregory Streib, "Strategic Capacity in Council-Manager Municipalities: Exploring Limits and Horizons," *International Journal of Public Administration* 15 (9, 1992), p. 1737.

62. Bryson and Roering, "Initiation of Strategic Planning by Governments," p. 995.

63. Stone, Bigelow, and Crittenden, "Research on Strategic Management in Nonprofit Organizations," p. 409.

64. Bryson and Roering, "Initiation of Strategic Planning by Governments," p. 1003.

65. Frances Stokes Berry and Barton Weschler, "State Agencies' Experience with Strategic Planning: Findings from a National Survey," *Public Administration Review* 55 (March/April 1995), p. 165.

66. Streib and Poister, "The Use of Strategic Planning in Municipal Governments," pp. 23–24. Data are for 2001.

67. Stone, Bigelow, and Crittenden, "Research on Strategic Management in Nonprofit Organizations," p. 391.

CHAPTER **11**

Intersectoral Administration

In Chapter 2, we observed that government is giving ground to governance; that is, the public, private, and independent sectors increasingly are administering public programs, delivering public services, and implementing public policies through contractual or collaborative arrangements. We call the implementation of these arrangements *intersectoral administration*, or the management and coordination of the relationships among governments and organizations in the private and nonprofit sectors for the purpose of achieving specific policy goals.

Figure 11-1 illustrates the major characteristics of the three sectors and arrays them on a public–private continuum.

In its more applied and narrower mode, as practiced by public administrators, intersectoral administration often is called (without much ado over being precise) "privatization," "contracting out," "procurement," "acquisitions management," or "outsourcing." *Outsourcing* is more commonly associated with the private sector and refers to American corporations shipping jobs long held by American workers to cheaper workers in other countries. But outsourcing applies to the public sector as well. Government jobs are not necessarily outsourced to other nations (although this can, apparently, happen[1]), but they

can be and are outsourced to other sectors and other governments.

Increasingly, "sourcing" has become the verb of choice, although it has a broader meaning than outsourcing. *Sourcing* is the process of choosing the appropriate method and entity for delivering or implementing a particular public program. The definitional and practical distinction between sourcing and outsourcing is that sourcing allows the public sector, as well as the private and nonprofit sectors, to be considered in the determination of how a public policy should be delivered and implemented.

The methods of policy delivery and implementation are many. Public administrators making sourcing decisions may choose not only the traditional method of using their own government's employees to implement their government's policies, but instead might also elect to use private companies, nonprofit organizations, government corporations, other governments, subsidies, joint ventures, franchises, free-market mechanisms, volunteers, or vouchers, to name a few.

In sum, public administrators are growing increasingly aggressive in discovering and using innovative means of implementing public policy. We review the more important of these innovations in this and the following chapter.

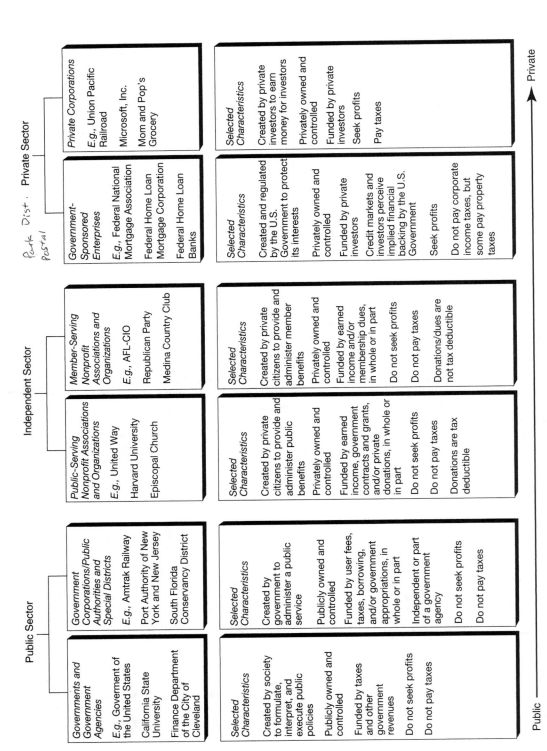

Figure 11-1 Organizations and Characteristics of the Public, Independent, and Private Sectors

304

Why Collaborate?

Governments' decision, whether by design, default, or defeat, to collaborate with businesses and nonprofit organizations in implementing public policies, actually stems from several positive impulses (and a few negative ones).[2] They include the following:

- *Savings.* Savings often can be realized. For example, civil service rules on pay scales and benefits may be skirted by using private contractors who pay only minimum wages and offer few benefits to their employees, or by using volunteers. As we discuss later, the prospect of savings is a major motivator for public administrators to collaborate.
- *Fiscal easements.* Collaboration with nongovernmental organizations can bypass cumbersome fiscal procedures and raise revenues in ways that more constitutional approaches inhibit.
- *Personnel easements.* Collaboration with private or third-sector organizations permits the government to hire specialists and people of unusual talent, without paying as much attention to the usual and sometimes inconvenient personnel policies enacted by governments.
- *Experimentation.* Collaboration with outside organizations permits the government to experiment with new policies and new delivery systems. Using other sectors, rather than their own agencies, to experiment with new policies and procedures appears to be highly valued among public administrators, or at least among the more talented public administrators. One survey of cities that privatized, or were seriously considering privatizing, found that these cities did so, in part, because they had "innovative managerial and institutional strengths."[3]
- *Lowered political risk.* Often, fewer political risks are borne by government when collaboration is used. The government becomes a less visible, less direct actor when public policies are implemented by organizations other than governments. The government can always terminate a relationship if the experiment fails, with relatively muted objection by an affected public. Empirical studies indicate that risk avoidance, particularly the avoidance of political risks, is a major motivation in exercising the outsourcing option among public officials.[4] One such analysis found, for example, that "elected officials are using private contractors to delegate responsibility for a controversial service."[5]
- *Image enhancement.* There is not a little boost in image for governments that collaborate. The personnel working for government can be expanded through agreements with private and nonprofit organizations, even though the official size of the civil service remains the same or is actually reduced. When government partners with businesses, in particular, an aura of businesslike efficiency extends to government, and, at last, the venerable *cri de guerre* that "government should be run like a business" appears to have been answered. Collaboration, in brief, can enhance the image of lean but effective government.
- *Greater leverage.* Collaboration leverages public programs. It permits government agencies to benefit from, and have their services enhanced by, the existence of private- and independent-sector organizations that already may be doing what the government wishes to do.
- *Economic development.* Collaboration can assist the economic development of a jurisdiction, especially local jurisdictions, by channeling public funds to companies and nonprofit organizations in the jurisdiction through contracts, grants, and subsidies. Then these organizations can put more people on their payrolls.
- *Emergency management.* Occasionally, government must collaborate with other sectors when emergencies or near-emergencies occur. For example, volunteers and nonprofit organizations are used extensively by governments during natural disasters.
- *Cost clarification.* A particular (and important) form of collaboration, contracting out the delivery of government services to the private and nonprofit sectors, clarifies the true costs of public programs by placing those programs in the competitive marketplace. Governments' costs to deliver services can be accurately compared with the costs incurred by companies or independent organizations to provide the same services.

These motivations of governments to collaborate with the private and nonprofit sectors in the implementation of public policies have spawned a dizzying array of arrangements. We consider these institutional arrangements under the broad rubrics of privatization, public enterprises and public authorities, and the independent sector.

An American Orthoxy

Other than governments themselves, businesses are the primary providers of public goods and the dominant deliverers of public services. It is this relationship between governments and profit-seeking companies that constitutes the basis of privatization.

Privatization occurs when government contracts to sell its assets to, or buy goods or services from, a privately owned, profit-seeking company for the purpose of implementing specific policy goals. This is not a particularly sophisticated definition, but it is clear, cogent, and concrete.

It appears that American governments may engage in the privatization of service delivery more deeply and widely than do governments in any other nation,[6] but they also sell their public assets to the private sector. Both types of privatization are covered in our definition.

The heavy use by American governments of the private sector to execute public policies relates to some deep, underlying belief sets that may be unique to the American political culture. In the United States, there exists a pervasive faith that "business is better"—that private enterprise is more efficient and effective in getting the job done than is "the incredible bulk" of government. It is a notion that can be traced to the earliest American thinking about public administration as a profession: from Woodrow Wilson's characterization of it as "a field of business" in his founding essay of 1887 (recall Chapter 2), to the municipal research bureaus of the early twentieth century (mentioned in preceding chapters), which "were not supported by the broad public . . . [but] by a small number of wealthy business people. . . . It is not surprising in this context that the staff of research bureaus gave deference in their publications to the wonders of business efficiency, regardless of the accuracy of the claim."[7]

These orthodoxies have had a profound effect at all levels of government. They have worked to encourage policymakers to abjure public administrators in favor of using nongovernmental administrators to implement public programs.[8]

We review next the selling of public assets, the purchase of private goods, and the privatization of public services by each level of government, beginning with the national government.

The Privatization of the People's Property: A Forthcoming Federal Fire Sale?

The federal government is profoundly into the business of selling its assets. The only survey of how many of its goods that Washington purveyed to purchasers over the World Wide Web found that the federal government had sold off more than $3.6 billion of its property—goods ranging from helicopters to horses—in just one year. By contrast, Amazon.com, the nation's largest private marketplace on the Internet, sold about a third less. The federal government may be the single largest Internet vendor in the world.[9]

Increasingly, Washington is interested in ridding itself of real estate, and federal real property adds up to real money. Washington's real property assets are worth more than $335 billion. Of the three billion, three hundred forty-seven million square feet that are owned or leased by the federal government worldwide, 90 percent is owned.[10]

Federal real estate is controlled by more than thirty federal agencies. Two-thirds of this owned space is the property of the Pentagon. Yet, the Pentagon's force structure has been reduced by 36 percent since the fall of the Berlin Wall in 1989, and, despite five rounds of base closures since then, the department states that it still has considerably more property than it needs.[11]

Maintaining excess property is costly. The Pentagon estimates that it is spending from $3 billion to $4 billion per year to maintain unneeded facilities, the Department of Energy puts the tab at $70 million, and Veterans Affairs pegs it at $35 million annually.[12]

The GAO has stated that, even though the federal government has reduced its workforce by several hundred thousand people; a number of agency missions have been changed; and technological innovations have altered workplace needs, many buildings have not been reconfigured to accommodate those needs; "the federal portfolio of real property assets in many ways still largely reflects the business model and technological environment of the 1950s."[13]

Washington may be on the verge of igniting the fire sale of the century.

The Privatization of Federal Policy: Public Programs and Private Profit Seekers

Over time, federal administrators have gravitated toward the use of contracting with private companies for goods and services as their primary means of implementing domestic, and some foreign, public policies.

By 1961 federal contracting with corporations was so pervasive that President Dwight D. Eisenhower, former Supreme Commander of Allied Forces in World War II and a pro-industry Republican, coined the term, "military-industrial complex," warned Americans of its "grave implications," and stated that its "total influence—economic, political, even spiritual—is felt in every city, every State house, every office of the Federal government."[14] By any standard, Ike's statement was stunning in its implications for democratic government, and he thought it of sufficient importance that it constituted his Farewell Address to the nation.

Big Bucks: The Scope of Federal Contracting

The federal government spends at least $305 billion in the form of close to twelve million "contract actions" each year,[15] amounting to about one-fourth of all federal discretionary spending.[16] It is anticipated that contract spending will continue to grow.[17]

The Department of Defense long has reigned as the most formidable federal purchaser, but, with the end of the Cold War, its share of acquisitions has slipped from more than four-fifths of all federal contract dollars in 1985[18] to less than two-thirds today.[19] About three-quarters of all remaining contract dollars are spent by just a half-dozen civilian agencies.[20] Listing largest expenditures first, federal contracts are let for: services, supplies and equipment, research and development, and construction.[21]

To place Washington's contracting with corporate America in perspective: Federal contract costs have long surpassed by large margins, by more than half, the costs of the federal civilian payroll.[22] The number of employees who work indirectly for Washington under federal contracts with private businesses—nearly 5.17 million workers—is almost three times the number of federal civilian employees and represents a growth of nearly 14 percent over a dozen years.[23] These ratios are remarkable testaments to the clout of commerce.

Federal Privatization: Policies and Procedures

As Washington's commitment to privatization grows, privatization's complexities grow, too.

Baseline Legislation. Congress took an interest in privatization more than a half-century ago and enacted legislation that set some broad rules of the game. These legal foundations of privatization include the *Armed Services Procurement Act of 1949* which, mandates advertised bidding for Defense and other agency contracts; the *Truth-in-Negotiations Act of 1962*, which requires contractors to support their bids with data; the *Competition in Contracting Act of 1984*, which established a bidding and appeals system that later was significantly simplified, but still stands in principle; and the *Procurement Integrity Act of 1988*, which prohibits contract officers from discussing employment prospects with, and slipping inside information to, contractors with whom they are negotiating.

Office of Management and Budget Circular A-76. While important, these and other statutes are not the essence—or, more precisely, the philosophy—of federal privatization policy, which is expressed primarily in administrative regulations. The first of these appeared in 1955, when the Bureau of the Budget (now the Office of Management and Budget or OMB) issued Bureau of the Budget Bulletin Number 55-4, which stated straightforwardly that government would rely on the private sector for commercial goods and services so that it would not be competing with business.

In 1967, the bureau altered this philosophy with what is now OMB Circular A-76, "Performance of Commercial Activities." OMB Circular A-76 states that it remains the government's policy "to rely on competitive private enterprise to supply the commercial and industrial products and services it needs," although, as the directive reluctantly notes (and this is the shift from the 1955 policy), the government should itself perform those functions that "are inherently governmental in nature, being . . . so intimately related to the public interest as to mandate administration by government employees."

OMB Circular A-76 appears to allow all functions that are not governmental in natural to be contracted out.[24] Within this broad parameter, individual federal managers may decide on their own to contract out; Title VII of the Civil Service Reform Act of 1978 authorizes federal administrators to "make determinations with respect to contracting out."

The Federal Activities Inventory Act of 1998. In 1998 Congress passed, and the president signed, the blandly entitled Federal Activities Inventory Act. This legislation, in conjunction with OMB Circular A-76, has waxed into a foundation of federal sourcing policy.

The act agencies to annually classify all their civilian positions in terms of "competable commercial," "noncompetable commercial," and "inherently government." Each year, approximately one-fourth of all federal civilian positions are consistently categorized as *competable commercial positions*, which means that they are subject to "public–private competitions" that assess their suitability for privatization.[25] The philosophy underlying the Federal Activities Inventory Act (the acronym of which is FAIR) is that government should not be engaged in the business of business—that is, competing unfairly with the private sector in commercial activities.

Reams of Red Tape: Privatization Procedures. The federal contracting system that these laws and circulars have established is one of inordinate complexity. The Office of Federal Procurement Policy, established in 1984 by Congress in the OMB, is responsible for developing procurement systems for the federal government. This is done through the Federal Acquisition Regulation, a document in excess of 1,600 pages, plus agency

supplements amounting to another 2,900 pages. By contrast, the Australian government's procurement regulations total ninety-three pages.[26]

Washington's core acquisition workforce exceeds 58,000 almost half of whom are contracting officers who occupy middle-management grades and are responsible for the business aspects of federal contracting. Contracting officers can make or break federal contracts.

Understanding "Inherently Governmental"

We have noted that a central value of Washington's privatization philosophy is one of government retaining those functions that are intimately related to the public interest. Precisely what these inherently governmental functions are can be a bit elusive, but some seem clear.

One is war. Presumably, the constitutional power to make war should not be contracted out.

Yet, at least to some degree, war has been privatized. Washington has hired more than 25,000 private contractors to assist with its military operations in Iraq, or about one contracted worker for every ten soldiers there. The Pentagon is quick to state that, "We have issued no contract for any contractor to engage in combat," and technically this is true.[27]

Contractors themselves, however, think otherwise. With Iraq's frustratingly floating fronts, the Defense Department's contractors are ghosting into shadow soldiers. Civilian contractors have been killed in action, and at least one contractor who lost his life in Iraq was awarded posthumously the military's Purple Heart and Bronze Star.[28] "'We're really in an unprecedented situation here. . . . Civilian contractors are working in and amongst the most hostile parts of a conflict. . . . [and contractors have] engaged every combatant with precise fire.' . . . 'The line is getting blurred . . . and it is likely to get more blurred,' with private security companies lobbying for permission to carry heavier weapons."[29]

Blurred, indeed. A private consultant, under contract with the Pentagon, even wrote the Defense Department's policies for civilian contractors on the battlefield![30]

So, even though some federal functions, such as engaging in combat, may be inherently governmental in any normal sense of the phrase,

Washington nonetheless has shown that it is capable of privatizing even some of these core public programs, too.

The Process of Federal Privatization

The privatization process has been described as an "integration-operation-separation model."[31]

Integration: Public Agency Meets Private Profit-Seeker

The integration phase is "politically overloaded . . . the primary task of the contracting officer is to balance political demands and supports with budgetary restrictions and governmental needs."[32]

Contracts and Circumvention. Accordingly, firms are integrated into the federal fold in two principal ways: by soliciting bids for federal business through advertising, or by quiet invitation and negotiation. In the latter case, a company may be awarded a *negotiated competitive contract*, which involves bargaining with a small number of preselected firms, with one or more being selected, or a *sole source contract*, in which a federal contracting officer unilaterally selects the corporation that seems most qualified.

Sole source contracts are by far the most favored by federal administrators, and even though federal law requires competitive bidding for almost all federal contracts, its use is rare. The federal government itself officially admits that close to two-fifths of its procurement contracts are not "awarded competitively,"[33] but by "the calculations of most authors and government reports, approximately 85 percent of contract expenditures" are never let for bid.[34]

How do federal agencies circumvent the bid procedure? Much of this circumvention is legal, if still questionable. Contracting officers have the power to waive bidding requirements, and they often waive with gusto. A review by the GAO of federal investigations on this topic found that from over three to nearly nine out of ten federal contracts had their competition requirements waived, with most

reporting that roughly four-fifths of all contracts had these regulations waived. Typically, these waivers were improper, unfair, or unjustified.[35]

In addition, federal agencies are not above using guile. All federal contracts are supposed to be listed in the official government Web site, FedBizOpps. Although fully two-thirds of these contracts already have been awarded (or virtually so) without competitive bidding, much of the remaining third appears to have been quietly let by federal officials under the table to favored contractors, and advertising them in FedBizOpps is strictly *pro forma*. The site's Webmaster has noted several "scams" that agencies use to avoid competitive bidding, such as miscoding a contract in the advertisement so that potential bidders can never find it ("That happens pretty often"); mentioning a particular firm in the ad itself ("That's a pretty clear tipoff that there's not going to be any competition"); and mandating absurdly brief deadlines for bids. In addition, billions of dollars worth of federal contracts are never advertised at all in FedBizOpps. As one federal contractor put it, "Anybody who believes you read [FedBizOpps] and get your contracts is out of it. You'd starve."[36]

Low-Balling and Lying. Private companies tend to understate their cost estimates to secure the contract. But it is a practice in which agencies are complicit: "One of the things that we have got to stop doing in our contracting is playing games—the government and contractor. . . . We know that if we tell the [Pentagon] . . . how much something is really going to cost, they may scrub it. And they know that if they tell the Congress how much it's really going to cost, Congress may scrub it. So you start in with both sides knowing that it is going to cost more."[37]

Low-balling the projected cost of the project, of course, is hardly the exclusive preserve of the Defense Department and its contractors; indeed, it appears to be universal. A study of 258 transportation infrastructure projects (that is, railways, roads, bridges, and tunnels) built between 1910 and 1998 in twenty countries (including the United States) on five continents found that the contractors' *estimated* cost of the project fell, on average, by a substantial 28 percent short of their *actual* cost! These differences remained remarkably consistent over time. The researchers stated that the "overwhelming statistical significance" of their analysis forced them to conclude that "the cost estimates used to decide whether such projects should be built are highly and systematically misleading . . . and [are] best explained by strategic misrepresentation, that is, lying."[38]

Operation: Agencies, Companies, and Intimacies

The operations phase of federal privatization is redolent of private contractors and public officials harboring personal, implicit goals; huge sums of money; conflicts of interest; and the heavy hand of lobbyists representing special interests in shaping public policy.

Lobbyland.   The lay of the lobbying landscape is lush and loaded with lagniappe.It is not surprising, therefore, that the employment opportunities for lobbyists are proliferating. Between the early 1970s and the mid-1980s, the number of American trade associations, which typically function as lobbyists, doubled.[39] In the 1970s, few Washington law firms engaged in lobbying, generally contending that such legislative and regulative grubbing was beneath them. Today, "virtually all of them have bustling lobbying practices,"[40] and there are least 800 political action committees registered in the nation's capital.[41]

There are some 33,000 Washington lobbyists who are officially registered with Congress, as required by law, and this number grows, on average, by more than 9 percent per year.[42] Some political scientists believe that the real number of lobbyists is much higher than those registered, and is closer to 90,000.[43]

These Washington lobbyists (the 33,000 registered ones, that is) spend more than $2 billion per annum in a relentless effort to tilt federal legislation and regulations their way. The money that lobbyists spend in Washington to influence public policy has burgeoned by almost half over just five years.[44]

In 1995, Congress passed the Lobbying Disclosure Act, under which Lobbyists must register with Congress, disclose the identity of their clients, the issues being lobbied, and how much is being paid to lobby. A year after the act's passage, the number of officially registered lobbyists more than tripled.[45]

But knowing who lobbyists are still is a far cry from blunting their more pernicious influence on federal policymakers. The Lobbying Disclosure Act, for all its strengths, nevertheless fails to illuminate a number of relevant facts that might do so, such as requiring that lobbyists disclose precisely whom in the government they lobbied and when.

Loopholes also aerate other lobbying laws. Although the Ethics Reform Act of 1989 prohibits former federal executives from lobbying not only their own former agencies, but also in their area of expertise, for a year following their departure from government, its efficacy seems doubtful. And in 2000, in his last full month in office, President Bill Clinton revoked a long-standing ban on former federal employees lobbying federal agencies for five years after they left the federal employ and also terminated a lifetime ban on former employees lobbying for foreign interests.[46]

In sum, "many rules governing [the conduct of lobbyists] remain deliberately vague, and the House Ethics Committee [which, ostensibly, controls lobbying in Congress] has been paralyzed because of dysfunction and partisan disputes." As one representative put it, "the scandal here is not that the rules were broken; the scandal is the rules themselves."[47]

Revolving Doors.   A singular manifestation of the lobbying syndrome is the "revolving door." The *revolving door* refers to government officials who retire or resign, especially from jobs that involved agency contracts with the private sector, and all-too-often end up as highly salaried executives in the company with which they dealt as a legislator, staffer, or administrator.

Just as opportunities to lobby expand, the whirl of the revolving door accelerates. In the 1970s, only 3 percent of retiring members of Congress became Washington lobbyists; in the 1990s, 23 percent did. Similar patterns appear for congressional staffers, and, over a nine-year period, the average tenure for top aides in the House declined by 27 percent, with most citing a desire for more money as their primary reason for leaving; the same trend is evident for top Senate aides.[48] Since 1998, more than 2,200 former federal employees have registered as federal lobbyists, plus some 225 former White House aides and about 250 former members of Congress.[49]

"There's a Lot of Money Involved." We have implied that lobbyists are highly paid. They are. To place the matter in perspective, consider the case of the forty-six-year-old congressional staffer who moved from his $132,000 job with the Joint Committee on Taxation to a $1 million-a-year job with the accounting firm, PriceWaterhouseCoopers.[50]

The salaries of White House officials and cabinet secretaries who left the Clinton administration increased by four-to-five times.[51]

In an attempt to explain why so many of her congressional colleagues resist reforming the phenomenon of the revolving door, a member of Congress observed that, "It's because there's a lot of money involved."[52] One is reminded by her observation of a phrase used by American youth: "Duh."

Separation: The Unfulfilled Act

The final phase in the contracting cycle is that of separation, or how the government terminates contractors and resolves disputes.

Neither termination nor dispute resolution are simple acts since agencies typically accept goods and services from contractors over a prolonged period of time. Thus, "government contractual relationships may be more like treaties than contracts in that often no real separation occurs."[53]

Federal Contracting: A Critique

It is tempting to engage in cheap shots about the condition of federal privatization, in part because some examples of federal contracting incompetence are so, frankly, shocking.

Cases in Contracting Incompetence

We succumb to temptation. Consider a couple of recent cases.

In 2004, the Department of Defense awarded a $293 million contract to a British firm to coordinate more than fifty private security companies in Iraq and to provide its own force as well. The firm had been in existence for not much more than a year, had virtually no experience in security coordination, and had never had a major contract in Iraq (it did not even appear on the State Department's list of recommended security companies for Iraq). Its chief officer had founded a company that had violated the United Nations's arms embargo in Sierra Leone and had been a key figure in an army mutiny in New Guinea. The contract was awarded by the Army transportation command in Fort Eustis, Virginia, a command that had no obvious experience in dealing with the private security industry, and the deal was described as "possessing a logic that would do only Kafka proud."[54]

At least a third of the American interrogators who were implicated in the severe mistreatment of prisoners in Iraq's infamous Abu Ghraib prison were not U.S. soldiers, but private business people hired by the federal government. They were hired not by the Pentagon (as one might reasonably assume), however, but through a computer services contract overseen by a Department of the Interior office in Arizona. In apparent violation of federal acquisition regulations, the contract was written by an employee of the firm that won the contract, and the contract was never opened for bid. The contracting process was so convoluted that the Army could not determine who wanted to hire private interrogators in the first place.[55]

Contracting Incompetence: The Systemic Problem

By the 1990s it was clear as crystal that federal contracting verged on chaos. There was and is an absence of any kind of central record keeping by governments concerning their contractors; no kind of central control over service quality, prices charged to clients, and cost overruns.[56]

Slowly, a more complete portrait of federal contracting practices is emerging, and the picture is not pretty. In the early 1990s, federal purchases of less than $100,000 took an average of three months to complete, compared to one to four weeks in the private sector.[57] Time is money. An independently conducted analysis concluded that federal procurement laws added cost, but no value.[58]

What is the price of these procurement policies and procedures? Careful analyses indicate that federally imposed requirements add up to 12 percent or more in additional contract costs, and each 1 percent saved per year in total federal purchases of equipment and supplies amounts to $700 million.[59]

The Beltway Bandits: Service Contracting and the Curious Question of Consultants

Thus far, we have been focusing mostly on Washington's use of *procurement contracts*, or legal agreements to purchase goods. But service contracts warrant our attention, too, if for no other reason than federal contracts for services account for more than 60 percent of Washington's contracting dollars, and service contracts are expanding.[60]

The rise of service contracting is new. In 1985, service contracts amounted to only 23 percent of all contracting dollars.[61] As an indication of the growing importance of service contracting, Congress in 2003 passed the Services Acquisition Reform Act, which enhances recruitment and training for service contracting, appoints Chief Acquisition Officers in civilian agencies, and creates incentives for performance-based service contracts.

Consultants and Chaos

A *federal service contract* is a legal agreement for the provision of training, leasing, technical, professional, logistical, social, or managerial support.[62] As a practical matter, this often means that federal administrators hire outside consultants to advise them on a host of issues. The OMB states that over 52,000 private companies furnish the federal government with the expertise and advice of their employees.[63]

Private consultants to federal agencies operate in a netherworld of dank and bureaucratic murk. The GAO has stated that it is unable to ascertain precisely how much Washington spends on consultants.[64]

An analysis by the GAO of the Departments of Energy's and Defense's use of consultants found that, after assessing cost, quality, and service delivery, using government employees instead of consultants would have saved significant amounts of money—from over a fourth to more than half.[65]

More anecdotal, but revealing, evidence on the utility of the "Beltway bandits" abounds. (The derogatory designation derives from the Beltway encircling Washington.) Consider some statements by federal contract officers:[66]

> "The bottom line on contracts—pure paper studies. . . . The public gets . . . maybe 10 percent of their money's worth."
>
> Of one $250,000 study, described as "an unintelligible pile of papers," a federal administrator said, "Nothing was received and we paid thousands for it. It really is a lot of gobbledygook. . . . As a taxpayer, I'm sick."
>
> "We're so busy trying to shovel money out the door, we don't have time to see what happens to it after it leaves. All the money could be stolen and I wouldn't know it. . . . The place is a madhouse."

The waste, and the opportunities, are also recognized by the more enlightened contractors. A board member of the Institute of Management Consultants observes: "It's a game. . . . Government comes to us and wants help in identifying their problems, but they don't seem to be able to use the material. They could spend much less and get more for it."[67]

"It looks like a conspiracy, but really it's chaos."[68] So stated one of the nation's leading experts on governing-by-contracting, and likely he is accurate.

The Shadow Government

Chaotic incompetence is one thing. Policy manipulation, however, is another.

A serious problem emerges when "advice" from private consultants waxes into policy executed by public administrators. The GAO has called Congress's attention to this fundamental dilemma in formal reports dating from 1961. As one of them put it, "Federal agencies have used contractors . . . to perform work that should be done by Federal employees because it involves basic management decisions . . . it is sometimes difficult to tell where 'advice' stops and 'performance' begins."[69] Or, as a top official of GAO put it more pithily, "We've seen situations where an agency contracts out so much of its data gathering and policy analysis that it thinks it has control, but the consultant is, in effect, making the decision."[70]

In 1980, Washington addressed this concern by releasing OMB Circular A-120, "Use of Advisory and Assistance Services." The circular prohibits the use of consultants in "performing work of a policy, decision making, or managerial nature, which is the direct responsibility of agency officials." Regrettably, the effectiveness of the circular over the years seems negligible.

In short, private interests may be guiding and forming public policies and engaging in government activities in ways that are inappropriate and which run counter to the general welfare. A review by the GAO of contracts for consultants' services in four major federal agencies found that over a fifth of the contracts appeared to involve "inherently governmental functions."[71] These are fundamental concerns. They deal with who makes, and implements, public policy in an advanced democracy—representatives of the public interest or of private interests.

Contracting in Corruption: A Capital Case

All too frequently, basic honesty can be as difficult to identify as simple efficiency in the federal contracting culture. The Department of Defense, as Washington's Croesus of contracting (the Pentagon is the world's largest, richest bureaucracy, with a budget that exceeds the economies of all but a dozen nations), provides an enlightening example.

Buying Bullets *versus* Hitting Bullets

On the one hand, the Pentagon seems able to purchase many goods both efficiently and honestly. A comparison of the department's and companies' costs in buying over 676,000 identical electronic and engine parts, amounting to more than \$60 million, found that Defense paid much less (over 14 percent less for electronics, and nearly 32 percent less for engine parts) than did the business sector. These savings were credited to the fact that Defense "was already using commercial practices commonly followed by large firms," including tough bargaining.[72]

On the other hand, these felicitous findings must be placed in context. By and large, they deal with simple transactions, such as buying bullets, and not complex systems, such as researching, developing, and building a missile defense shield, which has been described as "bullets hitting bullets." When the Pentagon acquires sophisticated products, efficiency often is the loser, and, to some degree, this is understandable: It is, after all, easier to buy bullets than it is to underwrite the R&D needed for a weapons system that redefines technological capacity—and whose capacity, if any, is unknown when contracts are being let. It is this situation, regrettably, that can facilitate malfeasance on a very large scale.

Over just seven years, twenty-five of the 100 largest contractors for the Pentagon were found guilty of procurement fraud, some of them more than once.[73] "Operation Illwind," begun covertly in the mid-1980s by the U.S. Justice Department, recovered over \$24 million in fines and forfeitures and ultimately resulted in over 100 convictions for corruption.[74] Between the mid-eighties and mid-nineties, the Pentagon's purchases of new weapons fell by about 70 percent, but the fines and civil recoveries collected ballooned by a factor of eleven, and the number of contractors under investigation for fraud grew from a fourth of the 100 largest defense contractors to over two-thirds.[75]

Why Fraud?

Why does fraud continue unabated?

The Structure of Fraud. In part, it is because the structure and practice of privatization itself are unusually corruptible. Of the twenty-five "high-risk" federal operations identified by the GAO as unduly vulnerable to "fraud, waste, abuse, and mismanagement,"[76] more than a third involve "large procurement operations or programs delivered mainly by third parties."[77]

There is, however, another, more ominous reason: With few exceptions, the federal government keeps coming back for more. Even though the Federal Acquisition Regulation requires officials to let contracts only to "responsible sources" that have a "satisfactory record of integrity and business ethics," not one of the twenty-five major corporations convicted of defrauding the federal government in the 1980s and 1990s was barred from further contract work with the federal government.[78] The number of suspensions and debarments issued by all federal agencies to contractors averages about 5,700 annually[79]—hardly a large proportion (indeed, infinitesimal) of the close to twelve million contracts that Washington lets each year.[80]

Of greater importance, however, the big enchiladas of federal contracting, those that reap the biggest bucks, are almost never suspended or debarred, despite long records of serious, including some criminal, violations. (It is speculated, and not unreasonably, that there are few, if any, other contractors that could take over the big, complex projects that these big, complex companies manage, so suspension or debarment are not realistic federal options.[81]) Over a period of fourteen years, the top ten federal contractors shelled out almost $3 billion in fines and penalties for 280 instances of proven or alleged misconduct, but not one of them was suspended or debarred.[82] "The government system for debarring and/or suspending contractors is broken."[83]

The Culture of Fraud. The reason why the federal government keeps contracting with proven felons relates, in part, to technical glitches that may hide from agencies an astonishing 99 percent of the suspensions and debarments that other agencies have levied on their prospective contractors for past violations.[84] However, in the view of some, the larger problem is a contracting culture in the federal bureaucracy, particularly in the Pentagon, that places scant value on acquiring one's money's worth. As a former procurement officer for the Air Force put it, "It doesn't matter if you screw everything up, as long as you keep the dollars flowing."[85]

When this entrenched bureaucratic culture (which places a premium on hiding the bad news, whether it is corruption or cost overruns, for the sake of assuring an unimpeded flow of funding from Congress) is combined with the daunting political difficulties of separating, even in the face of criminal convictions, contractor from agency (which, as we discussed earlier, are conjoined more by "treaty" than by contract), then the vast dimensions of the problem become clearer. Corruption in contracting will never be controlled as long as careers depend more on maintaining that flow of federal dollars than on managing it.

Ethical Fogs

There are also a couple of situations that, while less directly corrupt, exist in an ethical twilight zone.

Stiffing the Law. One is that federal contractors may violate federal laws that are unrelated to their contractual performance, but still be awarded new federal contracts. For example, over a tenth of federal contract dollars, according to one study, have gone to companies convicted of labor law violations.[86] Nearly a fifth of federal contract dollars, according to another analysis, flow to corporations that have been convicted of seriously violating federal health and safety regulations, including violations that resulted in the deaths of thirty-five workers in some of those companies over the course of a single year.[87]

On the day before he left office in 2002, President Clinton banned federal contracts being let to bidders who had a history of breaking environmental, health, safety, and other laws, a regulation that was promptly terminated by his successor, President George W. Bush.[88] So this particular moral quandary remains entrenched in the federal contracting culture.

Stiffing the Taxpayer. A second quandary is one that we explained in Chapter 6, but it warrants a brief reprise here. It concerns those companies that are awarded federal contracts but pay no taxes because they are headquartered in tax haven countries. During the course of a single year, these offshore companies received close to $1 billion in federal contracts, yet cost the U.S. treasury an estimated $4 billion in lost tax revenue.[89] The GAO adds that, in its analysis, "large tax haven contractors . . . were more likely to have a tax cost advantage [in competing for federal contracts] than large domestic contractors."[90]

In short, taxpayers are stiffed twice—first by the contractors who pay no taxes, and then by the government that pays these contractors with taxpayers' money. And, to add insult to injury, federal contractors who pay taxes are at a competitive disadvantage with those contractors who do not.

Reforming Federal Privatization

Slowly, Washington began to act on its dawning recognition that federal privatization was flirting with fiasco.

In 1990, Congress enacted the Defense Acquisition Workforce Improvement Act, which ordered the Defense Department to establish a separate career path for its acquisitions specialists. In the following year, the Defense Acquisition University was founded as an equivalent to the prestigious National Defense University. In 1996, Congress extended this thinking to the other agencies and created, as part of OMB's Office of Federal Procurement Policy, the Federal Acquisition Institute, designed to improve the training and capability of the civilian procurement workforce.

Four Fundamental Reforms

But the most potentially far-reaching reforms occurred in the form of four new laws and a singular revision of the government's core procurement policy.

The first of these policies is the Government Performance and Results Act of 1993, which requires agencies to measure performance—including the performance of contractors. Regrettably, Washington still has some way to travel on this road, and it appears that less than 15 percent of contracts meet performance-based criteria.[91]

The remaining three laws focus more directly on contracting. One is the Federal Acquisition Streamlining Act of 1994, which dramatically simplifies the buying of smaller items, those amounting to less than $100,000. The Information Technology Management Reform Act of 1996 empowers federal procurement officers to shorten the time that it takes to buy information technology. Also, in 1996, Congress enacted the Federal Acquisition Reform Act, and in many ways this is the most important of the three laws. It tossed out a wide range of federal regulations, which, for the most part, had been designed to assure fairness to bidders and low prices, but not top value for the dollar.

A Radically Revised Sourcing Policy

These four laws are extraordinarily significant reforms of federal privatization policy, and it appears that they have had a salutary effect on federal contracting. Still, none of them affected the fundamental federal philosophy of privatization, OMB Circular A-76, and Washington ultimately included that policy in its thinking.

In 2003 the OMB comprehensively rewrote OMB Circular A-76. The revised circular identifies ten "guiding principles for sourcing policy," including: the establishment of a sourcing process that "would permit public and private sources to participate in competition for work currently performed in-house . . . work currently contracted with the private sector, and new work."[92]

The GAO summarized these reforms well: "The federal government is dramatically changing the way it purchases goods and services by relying more on judgment and initiative versus rigid rules for making purchasing decisions."[93]

Privatizing in the States

Although Washington's privatization is substantial, it is, in many ways, dwarfed by the privatization that occurs among the grass-roots governments. The estimated dollars spent through contracts by state governments and their local governments are about a fourth more than the dollars that the federal government spends on privatization.[94]

At least some agencies in every state, privatize in some fashion.[95] The states spend about a fifth of their operating budgets on contracts, a proportion that is higher when state-delivered Medicaid benefits are included.[96]

No Sale: The Husbanding of State Assets

Until the 1990s, Washington actively discouraged states and their local governments from selling their assets by requiring that those subnational governments that sold, or even leased, infrastructure projects that had been built with some federal funding had to repay all previous federal grants invested in those projects. In 1992, President George Bush issued Executive Order 12803, which not only terminated this policy, but also directed all grant-making federal agencies to cooperate with state and local governments that wished to privatize such assets. In 1996, Congress legislated that the Federal Aviation Administration encourage the privatization of state and local airports.

These federal initiatives appear to have had little effect on state governments. Although 14 percent of state officials report that "asset sales . . . are used" in their states (hardly a large number in itself),[97] only a fraction of 1 percent of state agencies had actually *sold* state assets over the preceding five years.[98]

This reluctance by the states to sell their assets is not a product of the states possessing few assets to sell. Not only do state governments own land and buildings, but public enterprises, too. One analysis concluded that the states and their local governments could gain hundreds of billions of dollars if they simply sold off their government enterprises, such as roads, airports, waterworks, and utilities, that are (in the opinion of the analysts) more appropriately owned and managed by the private sector.[99]

Privatizing State Services

States much prefer privatizing by contracting out services to the private sector, and more than seven out of ten state agencies do so.[100] Almost nine-tenths of state officials report that, of the ten types of privatization listed in a national survey, contracting out services is one of the "methods of privatization used" in their states. The runner-up type of state privatization, that of public–private partnerships, is tightly tied to contracting out, and close to half of state administrators report that it is used in their states.[101]

Three-fifths of all state agencies contract with for-profit companies to deliver one or more of their services, and states contract more frequently with corporations than they contract with independent organizations and other public agencies to deliver services.[102] Education and transportation agencies contract with corporations the most.[103]

Why States Privatize. Saving money is a primary reason that state administrators privatize their programs. More than two-thirds of state directors of budget and legislative service agencies, and almost two-fifths of the heads of departments in the executive branch, report that "cost savings" were the primary reason that they had privatized some services.[104]

A lack of specialized personnel or expertise is another important motivator, with more than half of these same officials citing it as their primary reason to privatize. Greater managerial flexibility, speedier program implementation, and higher quality service also rank as top reasons for state privatization.[105] State employee associations and elected officials are the most commonly cited obstacles to state privatization efforts.[106]

Costs and Quality. Half of state agency heads and almost a third of state directors of budget and legislative service agencies report that the savings obtained from privatization are quite small, and do not exceed 5 percent. On the other hand, almost three out of ten agency heads (but only a pittance, 4 percent, of the directors of state budget and legislative service agencies) say that privatization has saved them more than 15 percent of their budgets.[107] Overall, barely a third of state officials report lowered costs when they privatize services.[108]

State administrators seem largely pleased with the quality of privatized services. One survey found that almost half, 49 percent, of state agency heads thought that quality improved when they contracted out services, 35 percent reported that there was no effect on quality, and only 9 percent felt that quality decreased.[109]

The States Resistant

States simply privatize less than the federal government, and even local governments. As noted, despite federal encouragement, states sell essentially none of their assets. And, although most state agencies have privatized at least one program, a modest 5 percent of state agency heads report that they have fully implemented the privatization of any major programs, and less than a fourth report even "full or partial" implementation.[110] Almost three out of ten of state agencies contract with no one to deliver any of their services—not corporations, not nonprofit organizations, not other government agencies.[111]

By contrast, the federal government sells a third more goods on the Internet than does the planet's biggest Internet vendor,[112] spends about a fourth of its discretionary funds on contracts,[113] and hires at least three times as many civilian employees through contracts with companies than it has on its own payroll.[114] Similarly, nearly a quarter of cities and counties sell some of their assets every five years,[115] and these governments deliver over two-fifths of all their services through partnerships with the private sector and contracts with for-profit companies.[116]

Although there are signs of change,[117] of all levels of government, the states traditionally have been the most resistant to privatization.

Privatizing by Local Governments

Almost four-fifths of local administrators believe that "privatization will represent a primary tool to provide local government services and facilities."[118] Privatization by local governments takes two main forms: selling assets, and contracting with companies to deliver local services.

Selling Local Assets

Although local governments, as with the federal and state governments, own public enterprises, such as waterworks and airports that they could sell to the private sector, they rarely do so. Instead, the assets that local governments sell are almost entirely land and unneeded buildings, and even here local governments display a less-than-enthusiastic interest in selling. One survey found that only 24 percent of cities and counties had sold assets over a five-year period, and only 21 percent planned to sell them over the next two years. Among those local governments that sell assets, almost 70 percent sell vacant land and about 36 percent sell buildings.[119]

Privatizing Local Services

The far more common form of privatization at the local level is contracting with companies and organizations to deliver public services. Virtually all cities and counties contract out some of their services[120] and, at one time or another, "contracts have been used for every service local governments provide."[121]

Cities and counties deliver about half of all their services by using only their own employees, and this proportion has been stable over twenty years.[122] Local governments concentrate their use of their own employees on support services, with more than four-fifths of personnel, payroll, secretarial, and public relations services being delivered by their own employees.[123]

Another 23 percent of local services, on average, are delivered in part by governments' own employees and in part by employees in the private sector—about the same percentage as two decades prior. The leaders here are street repair, tree trimming, and operating cultural and arts programs.[124]

Local service contracting with for-profit firms accounts for 18 percent of all local services,[125] up modestly from over 15 percent twenty years earlier.[126] This slow increase may be partly attributable to newer local governments enthusiastically buying in to the business-is-better ideology. When Sandy Springs (population 90,000), Georgia, and Centennial (population 104,000), Colorado, incorporated in the early 2000s, they eschewed the very concept of public employees. Sandy Springs placed only its public safety personnel on the public payroll, and Centennial hired only thirty municipal workers; everything else was, and remains, privatized.[127]

Local governments contract with for-profit companies most frequently in the areas of vehicle towing (by far the most common), followed by legal services, and solid waste collection and disposal.[128]

To Privatize or Not to Privatize? Local Pressures and Public Programs

The decision to privatize a local service can be difficult and often controversial.

Why Local Governments Contract

Local governments contract out their services for a variety of reasons. Some of these reasons are conscious and rational, but others are less so.

Rational Reasons to Contract. By far the most common incentive for cities and counties to privatize services is an internal attempt to cut costs. Eighty-eight percent of local officials cite cost-cutting as their main reason to privatize, followed by external fiscal pressures (half of all officials).[129]

That almost nine out of ten local administrators believe that privatization could save their governments money marks a major change in their perception. In the early 1980s, not much more than two-fifths of local managers thought that privatization saved money.[130]

Less Rational Reasons to Contract. Saving money is an eminently rational reason to privatize services. But there are other, murkier motivations for local governments to contract, too.

Contracting among Friends. Friends, or at least familiarity, matter. An analysis of major national surveys on local contracting found that there were indications that "elected officials are using private contractors to . . . reward electoral constituencies,"[131] and there are reports that the relationships between local politicos and private firms that have contracts with their governments are growing increasingly cozy, with the predictable result of financial scandals erupting in local governments.[132] In fact, when there is high turnover among local officials, contracting out

services goes into a steep decline, implying that there must be an existing foundation of familiarity between local officials and contractors before contracts are let.[133]

A study of local government partnering with nonprofit associations found that "social factors" count for a lot. Such social factors as employees in the agency and the association who had "genuine affection for each other" are more important in both sectors than any economic benefits that might result from the collaborative arrangement.[134]

A Symbiotic Relationship? Bureaucracy matters. An analysis of more than 1,000 Texan school districts found that the more bureaucrats in a local government, the more those bureaucrats will contract with other sectors to do their jobs for them. This relationship holds true even though local contracting is not positively associated with district performance." For each 1 percent increase in central office administrators as a percentage of total employment, there was a 0.32 percentage point increase in contracting by the government. "Contracting, thus, is associated with more top-heavy district organizations. . . . The long-term result is a process that feeds on itself."[135]

Good Times. Finally, money matters. Analyses of local governments have found that, even though cost savings leads the list of rational reasons to contract out services, governments contract more frequently when they have more money, not less, in their coffers.[136] Although cities that are controlled by the Republican Party tend to contract more with the private sector than cities in which the Democrats are in power,[137] it appears that good economic times may trump partisan ideology in the decision to privatize.[138]

Why Local Governments Do Not Contract

Local reluctance to contract out services is not only low, but is also diminishing over time. Almost six out of ten of all cities and counties report that they encounter *no* obstacles to privatizing, and this figure rises with every survey.[139] Nevertheless, there are some local disincentives to privatization.

Employee Opposition. Fifty-six percent of the two-fifths of cities and counties that have encountered impediments to privatization report that opposition from their own employees is the single greatest obstacle, and this is the highest percentage (no other comes even close to half) out of a dozen possible responses.[140] Moreover, employee resistance is growing.[141]

Opposition by local public employees to privatization is a serious barrier to privatization because, in part, local government workers are unusually active in local politics. Some estimates have it that local employees out-vote other local voters in local elections by ratios ranging from two-to-one to six-to-one.[142]

Organized labor likely plays a large hand in the opposition of local employees to privatization. Nearly a third of those municipal and county officials who encounter impediments to outsourcing cite restrictive labor contracts as an obstacle, and these restrictions rank as the third most frequently cited impediment.[143]

It appears, however, that the role of unions in local privatization is more complex than one might think. It may be that when unions are successful and win large salaries and benefits for their members, more contracting out of local services results because governments want to reduce these increasingly onerous labor costs. An analysis of national polls on this topic revealed that, "Contrary to our hypothesis, public unionization increased the likelihood of private for-profit delivery. . . . Unionization may not be the barrier to privatization it was once thought to be."[144]

Pouting Politicos. Forty-four percent of local administrators who encountered obstacles to privatization cite opposition from elected officials as the second most significant impediment, a proportion that is growing over time.[145]

The reluctance among local politicians to outsource government jobs likely stems, at least in part, from their concerns about the enthusiasm, noted earlier, of local employees to turn out in large numbers to vote in local elections; but they also may reflect the views of a cautious electorate, who seem largely leery about turning over the delivery of public services to private corporations. Thirty

percent of local administrators who must deal with barriers to outsourcing report that opposition from citizens is a factor and, as with resistance by employees and politicians, local administrators state that citizen opposition also is growing.[146]

Cautious Citizens. American attitudes about privatization have bobbled over the years, but, in general, most Americans express doubts about the private sector's ability to deliver public services.[147]

The most recent national polls, conducted in the late 1990s and early 2000s, found that less than a sixth of Americans reported that they had "the most confidence" in the private sector to deliver public services. The remainder said that they had the most confidence in the public or nonprofit sectors to deliver these services.[148]

The point stands that, in one of the globe's major bastions of capitalism, government generally is more trusted than corporations to deliver public programs efficiently.

Riffed: What Happens to Public Employees When Local Governments Privatize?

Perhaps the most salient fear, or at least concern, underlying the resistance to privatization by public workers, politicians, public administrators, and the public is the fate of those who lose their government jobs as a consequence of contracting them out.

This is an important worry. Here is what we know.

• *A relatively small number of public workers lose their jobs to privatization.* Estimates range from 5 percent to 7 percent of the local workforce.[149]

• *Those local workers who lose their jobs receive little public assistance.* Only three out of ten receive any benefits.[150] Only 9 percent of local governments develop programs to minimize the adverse effects of privatization on their displaced employees.[151]

• *Privatization creates jobs as well as eliminates them.* Because jobs are shifted from government to the private sector, the jobs lost and gained are essentially a wash; "in most cases, the job loss in the private sector is offset by at least an equal amount in private industry."[152]

• *Pay by local governments and pay by local government contractors is about the same, but the fringe*

benefits offered by contractors are less generous.
Half of the contractors offer fewer benefits, and only
16 percent offer more.[153]

• *Local employees of color appear to lose their jobs
to privatization at a faster rate than white employees.*
This seems to be especially the case in cities with populations of 100,000 to 500,000 and may be a consequence of
a propensity by local governments to outsource services,
such as sanitation, that are disproportionately peopled
by minorities.[154]

In sum, local governments face some serious
obstacles to privatizing services. It appears, however, that they could ameliorate some of the resistance to privatization by being more sensitive to
those employees whose jobs are in jeopardy.

Local Contracting: Management and Cost

Does privatization help? Do companies manage
local services better and more cost-effectively
than local governments?

The Management of Competition, Companies, and Quality

Local governments appear to have a relatively
firm, if occasionally tenuous, grip on their management of private contractors. Thirty-nine states
set purchasing standards for their local governments, and a dozen require their local governments
to centralize their purchasing function in a single
office, although centralized purchasing is the norm
for almost all local governments anyway.[155]

Competing for Local Contracts.   In addition,
competitive bidding, while not as common a
practice as it perhaps should be, seems to be used
frequently by subnational governments. Thirty-
seven states require their local governments to
competitively bid all purchases exceeding a specified amount (thirty-two), or of a designated type
(five).[156] Only 18 percent of local governments
select any contractors on a sole-source basis,[157]
in contrast to the estimated 85 percent of all contracts that are negotiated with a single company
by federal agencies.[158]

Local Government Oversight.   Oversight of a
company's performance by local officials, while
less than systematic, at least seems to be a matter
of concern. Not quite half, 47 percent, of all cities
and counties evaluate private service delivery.[159]
Cost and compliance with service standards are
the top items assessed by those local governments
that evaluate privatized service delivery, and
monitoring citizen complaints and analyzing data
are the chief means that they use to conduct their
evaluations.[160]

An analysis of national studies found that,
when local governments take back a service that
they had contracted out for delivery, the reason is
"primarily associated with problems of monitoring . . . [and] many governments do not monitor
but instead bring work back in house when they
are dissatisfied with contractor performance."[161]
Local governments' propensity for changing service delivery arrangements is particularly pronounced among smaller, poorer governments.[162]

Larger, richer local governments, by contrast,
not only change service providers less frequently
than do smaller, poorer governments, but they also
create monitoring mechanisms for private contractors far more frequently. A poll of the sixty-six
biggest cities in the United States revealed that
92 percent formally monitored their privatized
services for quality and effectiveness,[163] or almost
twice the national average.[164]

The Quality of Privatized Local Services.
Finally, local administrators express themselves as
satisfied with the quality of privatized services.
No respondents in a survey of large American
cities pronounced themselves as being "dissatisfied" with privatization;[165] nearly three-fourths,
72 percent, of local administrators in another poll
rated the quality of their services delivered by private contractors as "very favorable";[166] and a third
of these managers in yet two more surveys believe
that privatization improves service quality.[167]

Still, the actual behavior of local administrators
suggests that they harbor at least some reservations about the quality of privatized services.
More than a fifth, 22 percent, of cities and counties that privatized one or more services over
the last five years brought those services back
in-house. The great majority, 73 percent, of these

governments did so at least in part because they were not satisfied with the quality of service delivered by private companies.[168]

Independent researchers who conduct empirical analyses are less than effusive about the quality of privatized services. One unusually solid review of these analyses concluded that "there is no discernible relationship one way or the other. In other words, as best we know at present, contracting does not reduce or increase quality, as a general rule."[169]

In sum, in comparison with the federal and state governments, local governments are doing an unusually good job of managing privatization.

The Cost Question

Both the reports of local administrators and analyses conducted by independent researchers generally find that privatization normally saves local governments money. These savings usually fall short of the claims made by privatization zealots, with some claiming savings of 50 percent;[170] typically, these savings in reality do not exceed 30 percent, and then only rarely.[171] Of course, savings, if any, depend on the specific service and where it is located, and sometimes privatizing a service can cost local governments considerably more than if they delivered it themselves.[172] Privatization by no means guarantees savings.

Local Administrators' Assessments. Local managers' estimates of these savings vary, with one national survey of cities and counties revealing that 41 percent of them reported savings of 20 percent or more in services that were privatized, another 39 percent reported savings of 10 percent to 19 percent, and 18 percent reported savings of only 9 percent or less.[173] These savings perceived by local managers are substantial, but less than whopping.

And a significant minority of local managers are not only dissatisfied with the cost of privatized services but also act on their dissatisfaction. Of the more than one-fifth of cities and counties that withdraw a service from privatization and bring it back in-house, over half do so because the cost savings of the privatized service are insufficient,

and more than a third do so because their local government's efficiency has improved to the point that government can provide the service more cost-effectively than the private sector.[174]

Independent Researchers' Assessments. Independently conducted empirical research yields an additional perspective to the cost question and, as with local administrators' reports, suggests that the privatization of local services does result in overall savings. There is a large number of quantitative studies on the cost-effectiveness of outsourcing (perhaps the most thorough compilation unearthed 129 of them conducted over nineteen years[175]), but we are only recently gaining a sense of what they, on the whole, say.

This research finds that, on average, governments save 6 percent to 12 percent when they contract out services to the private sector. The largest privatization savings are in cleaning, maintenance, and refuse collection (19 percent to 30 percent). Other privatized services not only save less but also are more difficult to pin down in terms of how much they save, and savings seem to depend on local circumstances.[176]

In summary, the most consistent report from local administrators about privatization, and the most consistent finding from independent researchers, is that contracting with the private sector usually, but not always, correlates positively with lower costs in delivering a service.

But correlation is not causation.

Is Business Better? The Case for Competition

In 1986, the Michigan town of Ecorse (population 12,000) was in such dire financial straits that it became the first government in the history of the United States to be placed in receivership.[177] By 1990, the court-appointed receiver reported a budgetary surplus, and Ecorse's fiscal health was restored.

How did this happy turnabout happen? Ecorse contracted out almost every municipal service it had to the private sector, and the resultant "urban legend" holds that the "Ecorse experiment shows that . . . privatized services have the power to weed out incompetence and inefficiency, and the private sector can respond to changing conditions much more quickly than can bureaucracies."[178]

Oh? Is business really better? Is the orthodoxy actually true? Do, in fact, private companies deliver public services less expensively and more satisfactorily than governments, or is something else at work?

It has been observed that competition, not companies, is the real factor in lowering the price of service delivery: "*Public versus private* matters, but *competitive versus noncompetitive* usually matters more."[179] We consider next the evidence for this assertion.

Kinds of Competition

Competition can occur in two ways: bidding and sourcing.

⌐*Competitive Bidding.* The fact that over four-fifths of local governments rely almost exclusively on competitive bidding in letting contracts[180] is a major confirmation that local governments, at least (less enthusiasm can be generated for the federal government on this score), have integrated competition with service delivery.

It seems self-evident that transparent, competitive bidding lowers prices. But if evidence is needed, consider the federal experience. When two or more private-sector bidders are competing for the same federal contract, some $100,000 *more* in bids per full-time equivalent position is generated than when there is just one bidder.[181]

Or, conversely, reflect on the views of those who bid. A unique survey of almost 3,300 companies that had contracts with county governments found that a leading concern of these contractors was that "competition from other firms" pushed "prices too low for the firm to compete." Almost three out of ten of these business executives objected to local governments pushing for rock-bottom prices.[182]

And for some final evidence, note Nigeria. When Nigeria transitioned in 1999 from a corrupt military dictatorship to a reasonably lawful democracy, a new, reformist government required competitive bidding for government contracts to build public works and then, prudently,

checked those bids against bids for comparable projects listed on the Internet. The average costs of public works projects in Nigeria were slashed by 40 percent.[183]

⌐*Competitive Sourcing.* The second way that competition is assured is when governments themselves compete with the private, independent, and public sectors in providing services. This arrangement is known as *competitive sourcing* (in the federal government) or *managed competition* (the term favored by state and local governments) and is the process in which public-sector organizations compete with organizations in the private and nonprofit sectors, and with other public-sector organizations, to provide a public service.

The potential advantages of competitive sourcing are significant. Not only does managed competition broaden and maximize the competitive field, but also when an agency is underbid by a business, nonprofit organization, or other public agency, its energies can turn to an examination of why it lost the bid, thus promoting more efficient agency operations in the future.

The emergence of competitive sourcing, or managed competition, in governments is dramatic evidence that public administrators believe that competition, not privatization, is the key to better government. We review this emergence next.

Competitive Sourcing: The Federal Experience

Even though privatization is burdened with bounteous ideological baggage, a condition that sometimes discourages empirical investigation, Washington nonetheless displayed an early interest in trying to ascertain the actual economies of public *versus* private delivery of governmental services.

During the 1970s, federal efforts to better comprehend privatization evolved into what became known as the "A-76 process," so called because the process is an attempt to implement the policies expressed in OMB Circular A-76. At base, the *A-76 process* is an extended exercise in competitive sourcing, and this exercise includes

→vouchers–competition to improve school

analyzing individual positions for their appropriateness in the federal government.

The federal government seems convinced that its A-76 process has brought significant savings. During the first two decades of the Pentagon's A-76 competitions, average savings were 31 percent, and since then these savings have increased to an average of 42 percent.[184] Moreover, savings from these competitions were sustained over time, and performance remained the same or improved after the competitions—provided that new A-76 competitions remained a possibility.[185]

The OMB calculates that the A-76 process currently saves the federal government, including the Pentagon as well as civilian agencies, considerably more than a half-billion dollars each year. Net savings per federal position amount to 27 percent per year, a proportion that is rising rapidly, with the greatest savings per position in information technology, maintenance, and property management. And these efforts are cost-effective. For every one dollar that Washington spends to conduct A-76 competitions, it saves twenty dollars.[186]

In the early years of these A-76 cost comparisons, private contractors won over half of federal public–private competitions, giving understandable pause to federal workers.[187] Today, however, about nine out of ten competitions are won by in-house federal agencies.[188]

More to the point, competitive sourcing does not necessarily lead to large layoffs of federal employees, Studies indicate that from about 3 percent to 8 percent of federal employees are involuntarily separated as a result of the commercial sector being chosen to perform a particular governmental activity,[189] a proportion that is comparable to, if not less than, that of local governments.[190]

Managed Competition: The Grass-Roots Experience

Local governments also are adopting competitive sourcing at a rapid rate, and, in fact, it was these governments that invented it.

Managed competition originated in Phoenix in the 1970s, and the local version often involves dividing a city into competitive service districts. Although it seems to work best in large cities, over a third, 35 percent, of all municipalities engage in managed competition by allowing their departments to compete for service delivery contracts, and this represents a tripling in local managed competition in less than a decade.[191]

There is a spate of research suggesting that competition, whether it is in the form of competitive bidding or managed competition, not contracting with businesses, is the central variable in lowering the cost of delivering services by American local governments.[192]

What the Studies Say: Competition is the Key

In fact, research is surprisingly consistent in concluding that competition, not the private sector as such, greatly enhances the likelihood of more efficient government, whether that government is at the national, state, or local level. At the national level, the GAO reports that, "Agencies' experience with the Circular A-76 process suggests that competition is a key to realized savings, regardless of whether functions are eventually performed by private sector sources or retained in-house."[193]

The great majority of all studies conducted worldwide support the GAO's important assessment. A comprehensive, global review of essentially all independent analyses of privatization at all governmental levels, but mostly American and local, summarized them succinctly: "Cost reductions are attained whether public or private sector organizations win contracts. This finding, that there was no general tendency for private provision to be any more cost-effective than public provision of services under contract, is a significant one."[194]

It sure is. The conclusion of this thorough review (probably the most thorough review to date) of the empirical research on privatization is that no single sector is innately superior as a deliverer of public services. This finding flies in the face of those ideologues who insist that the private sector invariably delivers public services more cost-effectively than governments. Business is not better. In practice, any sector—public, non-profit, or private—can deliver public services and implement public programs at a comparable level of quality and at a lower cost, but only if they are competing among themselves to do so.

Herbert Simon, Nobel laureate and a godfather of both public administration and business administration, put it well when he referred to "the falsity of an equally common claim: public and nonprofit organizations cannot, and on average do not, operate as efficiently as private businesses."[195]

They can and do. Competition is the key.

Practical Privatization: Lessons Learned

When all is said and done, what do we know about the practice of privatization? What should public administrators keep in mind when contracting with private companies? Here are seven major lessons learned.[196]

- *Strong public support and a political champion probably are prerequisites for privatization.*
- *Select potential candidates for privatization carefully.* Public programs that have a distinctive business profile (such as state lotteries, trash collection, airports, utilities, and college dormitories) are the easiest to contract out successfully.
- *Privatize gradually.* Wholesale, rapid privatization often reduces political support.
- *Develop an accurate costing system before contracts are solicited.* Define outputs, set benchmarks, and use *activity-based costing,* an accounting technique that covers all the expenses of providing a service.[197]
- *Inject the maximum amount of competition possible.* Certainly this includes competitive sourcing, as well as competitive bidding.
- *Use well-defined contracts that set performance measures and incorporate evaluation procedures.*
- *Mitigate the impact of privatization on displaced public employees.* Advise them of benefits and help them find jobs. This not only reduces employee resistance to privatization but also is the ethical thing to do.
- *Recognize that the weakest links in the contracting process for all three levels of government are*

those of managing the contract and achieving accountability. It is these two areas that require the greatest attention from public administrators when privatizing services.[198]

The Public's Enterprises: Vast and Varied

We have been describing how governments contract with businesses to implement public policies. But governments also *create* businesses to implement their policies, and these creations are called public enterprises.

A *public enterprise* is a market-oriented service provided by government to the people. An example is a state-supported telephone company.

Considered from one perspective, the United States has few public enterprises. Many governments in Africa, Asia, Europe, and Latin America own and operate far more public enterprises than do governments in the United States. State-owned businesses in Western Europe, for example, account for 9 percent, on average, of their countries' gross domestic products (GDPs), excluding government services, and in Central Europe, before the collapse of communism, state-owned enterprises accounted for an astonishing 85 percent of national GDPs. By contrast, state-owned enterprises in the United States account for 1 percent of the nation's economy.[199]

This is not to say that American public enterprises are trivial. Although a definitive census of public enterprises is nonexistent,[200] they nonetheless are a major means by which American governments and their surrogates implement public policies. Many public enterprises are far-reaching in scope, and they are found at every level of government.

Although there are few federal enterprises, at least when compared to the thousands of state and local ones, some are immense undertakings. Examples include the provision of electricity and other benefits to nearly nine million people in the Tennessee Valley, a contiguous territory that meanders through seven states; transporting all of the nation's twenty-five million railroad travelers; and the daily delivery of mail to more than two hundred eighty-one million people. Some federally-sponsored enterprises are even larger, such as those multi-trillion dollar federal entities that Americans rely on to help them purchase homes and to loan farmers money at low interest rates.

Portentous public enterprises also flourish at the grass roots, and their scope is surprisingly broad. State or local governments own and operate water purification plants, housing, sewerage, swimming pools, cemeteries, parks, highways, health programs, recreational facilities, hospitals, airports, transportation systems, seaports, bridges, environmental protection and economic development projects, parking lots, electrical power plants, and gas works, to list a few.[201]

Local governments own and operate essentially all of the nation's commercial airports, 85 percent of the country's municipal water supplies and wastewater plants, four-fifths of all local public transportation systems, a fourth of the nation's electrical plants (more than 2,000 electric utilities serving over 16 million customers), and 800 municipal natural gas utilities that are bankrolled by 3.6 million customer accounts.[202]

The public enterprises of the grass-roots governments are powerful players in the country's commerce.

Managing the Public's Enterprises: The Public Authority and Other Quasi Governments

The vast majority of public enterprises are owned and operated by public authorities. Despite their power and importance, however, public authorities remain mysterious, veiled, and enigmatic entities that function on the fringes of the public domain.

A *public authority*, also known as a *government corporation, special authority*, or *public-benefit corporation*, among other monikers, is a legislatively created organization that performs a market-oriented service. The federal government uses the term *corporation*, and state and local governments generally prefer the terms *authority* or *district*.

The scholarly community generally accepts President Harry S. Truman's criteria to be used when deciding when a "corporate form of organization" is appropriate to conduct public programs. They are when the program is predominantly of a business nature; is revenue producing and potentially self-sustaining; involves a large number of business-type transactions with the public; and requires a greater flexibility than the customary type of appropriations budget ordinarily permits.[203] Figure 11-1 lists some of the characteristics of public authorities.

The Inchoate Administration of Federal Enterprises

Most of Washington's public enterprises are conducted by convoluted "hybrid organizations" that have been described as "the emerging federal quasi government."[204]

Washington's Government Corporations. Many of these federal hybrid organizations fall loosely under the category of government corporation, but so little is known about them that we do not even know how many there are. Estimates of the number of federal corporations range from a low of eighteen to a high of fifty-eight,[205] and the GAO reports that "no comprehensive descriptive definition" of federal corporations exists.[206]

Federal corporations may be wholly owned by the government, or ownership may be shared with the private sector. Most are wholly owned.[207]

Many of these public authorities have a large fiscal impact. An analysis by the GAO of twenty-two "self-reported," mostly small, federal corporations found that they had annual gross outlays that exceeded the combined gross outlays of the Departments of Commerce, Education, and Energy.[208]

Washington's Government-Sponsored Enterprises. The hybrid organizations that conduct the most vital and enormous federal enterprises are called government-sponsored enterprises. *Government-sponsored enterprises* are "financial intermediaries" created by the U.S. government that direct "capital to particular sectors of the economy,"[209] notably to housing and agriculture. To do this, they borrow money from banks and then loan it to eligible recipients at low interest rates.

Power and Privacy. The first government-sponsored enterprise was created by Congress in 1916. Their number has not grown much since then, and today there is a grand total of just five government-sponsored enterprises.[210] Despite their modest number, however, these unique federal entities possess immense and expanding economic power, with almost $7 trillion in financial obligations.[211]

The federal government classifies its government-sponsored enterprises as private-sector corporations, and with some reason. Perhaps the most telling reason is that three, including the biggest ones, of the five sell their stock on the New York Stock Exchange,[212] and at least one, Freddie Mac, is among the nation's heaviest corporate contributors to political parties.[213] In 2006, the Federal Election Commission levied against Freddie the largest fine $3.8 billion for violating election laws in U.S. history.

Nevertheless, government-sponsored enterprises exhibit many of the same features of government corporations: They appear to fulfill all the Truman criteria; they were created by Congress; they are supervised by federal agencies; they are exempt from federal, state, and local corporate income taxes; and they have the implicit backing of the federal treasury should any of the recipients of their loans default (hence, the low interest rates). So, like ducks, government-sponsored enterprises look, walk, and quack a lot like public authorities. Figure 11-1 sketches their basic features.

Fannie, Freddie, and Financial Fears. Two government-sponsored enterprises are the gorillas in the room. The Federal National Home Mortgage Association, known as Fannie Mae or simply Fannie, and the Federal Home Loan Corporation, known as Freddie Mac or Freddie, own more than four-fifths of all the assets owned by all government-sponsored enterprises.[214] Fannie Mae usually ranks as the largest, or as one of the three largest, corporations in America, and Freddie Mac normally ranks around the sixth largest.[215]

Fannie and Freddie were chartered by Congress in 1938 and 1970, respectively, to assure a stable market for mortgages and are the nation's biggest source of housing finance. Together, they hold or guarantee almost half of all home mortgages in the United States.[216] This formidable financial power is regulated by the Office of Federal Housing Enterprise Oversight, a little-known bureau created in 1992 that is tucked away in the Department of Housing and Urban Development.

How effective federal oversight of these two enormous government-sponsored enterprises has been is debatable. In 2003, the chief executive officer and other top executives at Freddie Mac were fired, and in 2004 their counterparts at Fannie Mae also were ousted, for the improper accounting of billions of dollars that was designed to burnish their stocks' images on Wall Street. The dishonesty of these two financial giants paralleled the accounting scandals and corporate corruption that had erupted in 2002, causing the bankruptcies of such major firms as Arthur Andersen, Enron, and WorldCom, among others.

The prospect of Fannie or Freddie also going under chills federal policymakers, and understandably so. The financial obligations of these government-sponsored enterprises are so gigantic that their default would place the entire economy in crisis. Congress very likely would bail them out, at enormous cost, just as it bailed out in 1987 another government-sponsored enterprise, the Farm Credit System, when it ran into financial difficulties.

Whether they are run by federal corporations, government-sponsored enterprises, or some other sort of hybrid organization, federal enterprises play for big stakes. They are not large in number, but they are colossal in their economic impact.

State and Local Public Authorities. Or Are They Special Districts?

In contrast to the federal experience in managing public enterprises, which is characterized by a multiplicity of diverse and complicated legal and organizational arrangements, state and local governments rely on a more straightforward approach. In general, public enterprises at the grass roots either function as subordinate agencies of state or local governments, or are operated by public authorities that are headed by boards of directors that have considerable autonomy. It is on these independent public authorities that we shall concentrate.

What Do State and Local Public Authorities Do? State and local public authorities are involved in a variety of businesses. What is perhaps the single most thorough national survey of these authorities found that the leaders were public housing (45 percent of all state and local authorities); environmental protection, principally sewerage, solid waste disposal, and pollution control (18 percent); economic development (14 percent); public-use facilities, such as parking lots, parks, pools, garages, gardens, galleries, golf courses, tennis courts, convention centers, beaches, stadiums, museums, and zoos (7 percent); transportation, including not only bridges and roads, but also mass transit (4 percent); health care facilities, such as hospitals and nursing homes (3 percent); ports (2 percent); utilities, including waterworks and gas and electricity plants, and education, primarily student loans and campus construction (1 percent each); and a variety of other programs. Five percent of public authorities operate more than one enterprise.[217]

Counting Corporations. As with federal corporations, just how many state and local authorities there are is unknown, although "many scholars have suggested that there are between 10,000 to 12,000," the bulk of which were founded after 1950.[218] But no one really knows, and the estimates range, somewhat astonishingly, from 5,000 to 18,000.[219]

The number of state and local public authorities, however, likely is much more. We say this because many grass-roots public authorities seem to be indistinguishable from special districts. And there are 35,356 special districts that are chartered by state or local governments and recognized as governments by the U.S. Census Bureau.

Public Authorities or Special Districts? The similarities between independent public authorities and special districts are plentiful and profound. In essence, both are special-purpose governments. (Details about special districts can be found in the box in Chapter 12.)

There are, of course, some differences between these two types of special-purpose jurisdictions, but not many. The clearest and most consistent difference is that public authorities, by definition, are created by legislatures, whereas the creation of special districts usually requires the approval of the jurisdiction's voters. Even here, however, foggy practice obscures clear definition, and some special districts have been chartered solely by legislatures.[220]

It is also posited that the allegedly more managerial, technical, and commercial public authorities are run by appointed boards and are funded by user fees. By contrast, the more political, communal, and governmental special districts are run by popularly elected boards and are funded through their power to tax.[221] The evidence supporting these contentions, however, is not present. In reality, public authorities and special districts display an utter mishmash of governance and finance that effectively renders them indistinguishable from one another.[222]

Public authorities and special districts are blithely unbothered by these definitional debates and, as a practical matter, define themselves in terms of whatever works. As one scholar of the genre observes, "while it might not seem right to equate government corporations with special districts, there is also nothing exactly wrong with this equation."[223]

The Evolution of the Public Authority

All levels of government—federal, state, and local—have created public authorities to manage their public enterprises. But the experiences of each level of government in creating government corporations, and how their public authorities have evolved over time, vary widely.

The Federal Experience

The first federal corporation (or, at least, a clear precursor thereof) is generally thought to be the First Bank of the United States, chartered in 1792. The purchase by the federal government of the Panama Railroad Company in 1903, however, marks Washington's involvement with government corporations as we presently (more or less) define them.

With the onslaught of the Great Depression, Washington took a renewed interest in the government corporation. By 1953, Washington was "the largest electric power producer in the country, the largest insurer, the largest lender and the largest borrower, the largest landlord and the largest tenant, the largest holder of grazing land and timberland, the largest owner of grain, the largest warehouse operator, the largest ship owner, and the largest truck fleet operator."[224]

Such public enterprise did not rest easily with corporate America. The U.S. Chamber of Commerce, investor-owned utilities, and the National Association of Manufacturers, among other special interests, launched a concerted lobbying drive to induce the feds to evict themselves out of "competition" with the private sector. During the 1950s, through a series of executive orders, most of the federal government's corporations were reorganized or dismantled. Ironically, they were replaced over time with the federal contracting culture that Eisenhower so eloquently decried in his Farewell Address of 1961.

The Grass-Roots Experience

During the eighteenth century, various kinds of cooperative associations arose in states and communities that could reasonably be identified as primitive (in some cases, sophisticated) public authorities. They dealt with civic, educational, and even ecclesiastical affairs.

In the early 1800s, state governments dramatically accelerated their use of public authorities and chartered such "bodies corporate" as banks and builders—notably builders of bridges, turnpikes, and canals, including New York's massive Erie Canal system. The states, in fact, chartered all bodies corporate during the nineteenth century, whether public corporations or private ones, and the demarcation between the two was dim. Not infrequently, a relationship would develop between individual legislators and corporate interests to expedite the applications of business charters. Over time, these relationships reached

such an intimacy that major scandals erupted in many states, and both states and municipalities often would default on their debts because their governments had invested in questionable business projects that had gone under. These defaults occurred well into the 1920s.

A Progressive Push. As a consequence of these statewide and local defaults on debt, and also as a result of the Progressive Movement that was sweeping the nation around the turn of the twentieth century, virtually all state constitutions contain prohibitions not only on debt, but against lending or granting state or local money or credit to individuals or firms as well. These archaic constitutional clauses render it difficult for a state or local government to finance a variety of capital projects, such as roads and other improvements, which sometimes are truly needed.

But if the Progressives were largely responsible for making it more difficult for subnational governments to finance projects, they were at least equally responsible for making it easier to establish government corporations that could finance those same projects. Progressives were instrumental in drafting and lobbying for the first state incorporation laws, which delineated the differences between a public and a private corporation, thus establishing a system for elected officials to enact statutes for the creation of public authorities. One of the nation's largest government corporations, what is now the Port Authority of New York and New Jersey with over 9,000 employees, was chartered during this period (in 1921), and at least one scholar has contended that "the history of the modern-day government corporation truly began" with its founding.[225]

The Federal Factor. Even though the progressive movement was a momentous motivator, the federal government is the single entity most responsible for the proliferation of subnational special authorities. Most notably, interest on almost all the bonds they issue is exempt from the federal income tax,[226] although there is no constitutional reason why this interest should be exempted.

It was Franklin Roosevelt, however, who saw in the subnational public authority a new means of battling the Depression and brought federal involvement in state and local corporations to an unprecedented intimacy. FDR did this in two, highly interrelated ways: first, by encouraging state and local governments to enact new legislation that would ease the creation of government corporations and, second, by promoting the issuance of revenue bonds by those corporations.

First, Roosevelt drafted "model legislation" for state and local governments to follow in creating government corporations. These and other initiatives brought quick results. By 1948, forty-one of the forty-eight states had adopted variants of FDR's model legislation, and twenty-five states had authorized their local governments to set up public authorities entirely by local initiative.

Government corporations finance their projects by issuing revenue bonds. A *revenue bond* is a type of municipal bond that pays back its buyers, plus interest, with the revenues generated by the project that the revenue bond funds. And it was the revenue bond that furnished FDR his second avenue for jump-starting the economy.

Roosevelt made state and local public authorities an offer they could not refuse. He, in effect, said that Washington would buy all the revenue bonds that they could issue, Between 1931 and 1936, the number of states permitting their sale rose from thirty-one to forty. Today, all states allow their use.

Mysteries, Money, and Might: The Unexplored Economy of the Grass-Roots Authority

The economic power of state and local government corporations is both impressive and often overlooked. Public authorities employ 3 percent of the national labor force and account for 15 percent of the nation's fixed investment.[227] State and local public authorities invest more dollars in new capital facilities than all state and municipal governments combined.[228]

Borrowing and Bonding

Public authorities support themselves by borrowing money in the nation's money markets, by grants from their sponsoring governments, and by charging user fees to customers who use the facilities they build. Most of their budgets, however, are borrowed, Public authorities, in fact, are the largest single category of borrower in the municipal bond market and borrow more money than all state and local governments combined.[229] Public authorities borrow their money by issuing municipal bonds.[230]

Municipal bonds are popular among bond buyers because the interest income that they generate is exempt not only from federal taxes, as we have noted, but also typically is exempt from state and local taxes, too, including income taxes.[231] This tax-exempt status is unique and renders municipal bonds uniquely marketable,

There are two major kinds of municipal bonds: general obligation bonds and revenue bonds.

General Obligation Bonds. General obligation bonds traditionally are the safest from the standpoint of the buyer because they ostensibly have the full faith and backing of the government issuing them; these governments commit themselves to raising taxes, if need be, to cover the obligations incurred by these bonds. Because of their presumed security, they typically pay relatively low (but tax free) interest to their buyers. State, county, municipal, and township governments, as well as school districts, issue general obligation bonds.

Revenue Bonds. Revenue bonds are the other major type of municipal bond, and the bond market generally considers revenue bonds to be riskier for investors than are general obligation bonds. Revenue bonds are bought on the assumption that the project that they fund (such as toll roads, parking garages, or college dormitories) will generate enough revenue to pay back their buyers and then some. As with general obligation bonds, income derived from revenue bonds also is exempt from taxes. Public authorities and special districts issue revenue bonds.

Revenue bonds have become the bond of choice over the past thirty years. In 1970, revenue bonds accounted for slightly more than a third of all bonds issued by state and local governments, including public authorities.[232] Today, they account for two-thirds, although this proportion is in decline from their high point of the mid-1980s, when four-fifths of all municipal bond sales were revenue bonds.[233]

Public Debt: The Primacy of the Public Authority

Big borrowing, of course, brings big debt. In 1970, less than a third of all state and local long-term debts (long-term debts comprise almost all state and local debt) were being incurred by public authorities and special districts.[234] Three decades later, this proportion had more than doubled, and public authorities and special districts now account for more than two-thirds of all state and local long-term debt.[235] This debt "exerts a massive influence on the patterns of development in the nation, an influence that is largely insulated from public debate."[236]

It's Good Being King: Public Authorities and Their Surfeit of Freedom

These fiscal realities have contributed to an independence of economic and political action that any company executive or elected politician would envy. Public authorities, though chartered by governments, are rarely controlled by them.

The Federal Corporation: Faltering Controls

By most accounts, federal corporations were reasonably well controlled until the 1970s. The Truman criteria concerning their appropriate establishment and the Government Corporation Control Act of 1945, which is the basic policy governing federal authorities, were followed conscientiously. Beginning in the late 1970s, however, federal control eroded, largely because of pressures brought by special interests and oozing oversight.

An analysis by the GAO found that few federal corporations (in fact, none) complied with all of fifteen major federal statutes that pertained to

ethical, honest, open, and well-managed government, including the Government Corporation Control Act![237] "Legislation has been enacted and executive action has been taken which ignore the [Truman] criteria and conflict with both the letter and the spirit" of the Government Corporation Control Act.[238]

There are a number of examples of these faltering controls:[239]

- Federal corporations have been established, such as the Legal Services Corporation, which produce no revenues, thus violating Truman's principal criterion for their creation.
- Some federal corporations, such as the Corporation for Public Broadcasting, are exempt from the Government Corporation Control Act.
- Other corporations, such as the Federal Deposit Insurance Corporation, have been improperly classified as to the extent of their federal ownership, thus freeing them from federal budget reviews.
- Government-sponsored enterprises, such as Fannie Mae, are not subject to the Government Corporation Control Act.

There are additional examples of failing federal control over federal corporations, and given the significance of their economic impact (not to mention that of government-sponsored enterprises), the deterioration of government control is of genuine and legitimate concern.

The Grass-Roots Authority: Large, Lax, and Liberated

At the subnational levels, the situation is even looser, a condition that is ascribable in part to the disinterest of municipal bondholders in scrutinizing the operations of public authorities as long as their tax-free interest flows unimpeded.

Initiating and Ignoring Public Authorities. New York and Pennsylvania developed the two basic models for creating government corporations. In New York, public authorities are individually chartered by the state legislature. In Pennsylvania, however, local governments can create government corporations through a number of different devices, and with little or no interference from the state. Most states, more than two-thirds, use the Pennsylvanian approach; in fact, only New York and Maine require that the state legislature enact specific legislation to establish each government corporation.[240]

In most state governments, no single department even maintains an accurate listing of active public corporations.[241] Nor do these authorities even report their finances to the Securities and Exchange Commission—which all private businesses must do. In fact, the municipal bond market, which has as its foundation the government corporation, is the only major securities market that remains virtually free from oversight by the Securities and Exchange Commission.[242] Yet, the municipal bond market, is the second largest securities market in the nation.[243]

Governing Government Corporations. State and local public authorities are headed by boards of directors, typically of three members or more who usually serve without compensation. Board directors tend to have business or professional backgrounds, and the disinterest of many of them in the affairs of the authorities that they head has been amply documented, with a significant number of board members appointing surrogates to attend board meetings, but who, in fact, rarely attend. Vacancies on these boards are frequent.[244]

It is not precisely known, but likely about half of these board members are elected by the public, and half are appointed by elected officials.[245] The practical difference between being elected or appointed to the board, however, is trivial. Candidates for election to the governing boards tend to run without opposition.[246] Passing few voters turn out in these elections, and a turnout of 2 percent to 5 percent is considered to be "unusually high."[247]

It is perhaps not surprising that at least one researcher has found elected boards to be no more responsive to popular opinion than appointed boards.[248] However, another analyst found that elected boards relied the less on the property tax as a source of revenue than did appointed boards, implying that property owners who voted in board elections might have some impact on board policies.[249]

The boards of government corporations work in an unusually unconstrained environment. Board members serve staggered, fixed terms, and almost never may be fired by the officials who appointed them, or by anyone else, except for cause (that is, by breaking the law). Public oversight of these boards is minimal. An examination of public authorities in Georgia found that, despite a stern open-meetings law, many authority board meetings were not advertised; about six citizens, on average, attended these meetings; and the press did not regularly attend nearly two-thirds of board meetings (for over a third of the authorities, in fact, the media never attended board meetings).[250]

—Administering Authorities. An important duty common to most public authority boards is the appointment of an executive director. In over four-fifths of government corporations, executive directors are appointed by their boards, and the remainder are appointed by the chief elected executive officer or legislature of the government that chartered the corporation.[251]

Independently conducted surveys, all taken at roughly the same time, confirm that, in comparison to city managers (who are their closest counterparts), the executive directors of public authorities have much more secure jobs,[252] are considerably less educated,[253] and are significantly less experienced in their professions.[254] "In a fundamental difference . . . authority executives deal with fewer competing demands and expectations" than do city managers.[255] Another survey supports this finding and found that majorities of both authority executives (63 percent) and city and county managers (58 percent) agreed (unusually so, for they agreed on nothing else) that authority executives were far freer of political pressures than were city and county managers.[256]

This freedom from demands, expectations, and pressures enjoyed by authority executives appears to have economic consequences. A thorough analysis of special-purpose governments found that the costs of their services were higher per capita than were the same services provided by general-purpose governments, such as counties and cities.[257]

The Power of the Public Authority.   We do not mean to imply that authority executives lack power, because they clearly have it, as studies consistently confirm.[258] Some, indeed, have exercised enormous power, as the career of New York's Robert Moses personifies.[259] (We relate Moses's remarkable career in Chapter 13.)

"The successes of public authorities have, in fact, motivated much of the criticism of them. Critics on the left seek a more purposeful, dynamic, and democratically controlled public sector. Those on the right seek to reduce the scope of government enterprise, or at least check its growth, and to limit its activities to those that aid private endeavors, . . . public authorities have withstood such assaults practically unscathed and continue to claim rights of independent management."[260]

Libertine Liberties?

How well have public authorities used their rights of independent management? The answer is decidedly mixed, and there is a plentitude of examples of poorly managed special authorities at all levels of government.[261]

At the federal level, it is clear that some major government corporations have failed to meet their missions of becoming financially self-sustaining. Amtrak, the nation's passenger railroad, has systematically reduced service and collected growing federal subsidies that have averaged close to a billion dollars per year since its founding in 1971. Similarly, the Tennessee Valley Authority skims about $100 million in subsidies from Washington every year.

In the states and communities, examples of incompetence by public authorities abound. Consider the following.

• The Port Authority of New York and New Jersey built in 1992 a $21 million luggage tunnel at a major airport without first checking if the airlines wanted it. They did not. The tunnel remains unused and boarded up.

• The Port Authority was being true to its own traditions. In the 1980s, it built a $25 million fish market, which, by all accounts, is a "dismal failure" because fishing boats rarely use it.

• New York's Dormitory Authority in the 1990s awarded millions of dollars in construction contracts to firms banned by other public agencies because of the firms' ties to organized crime and their long records of violations.

• The Louisiana Public Facilities Authority in 1984 sold $41 million in bonds to build housing, contracted with developers to do so, retired the bonds in 1987, and never built the housing.

• In fact, public housing, which engages the energies of close to half of all government corporations, is a particular administrative sore point. In the early 1990s, Washington unilaterally took over the nation's worst public housing, expelling in the process the local housing authorities which had managed them with an awesome ineptness. Examples include the chair of the New York City authority who redecorated her office in pink at a cost of $350,000, and the one-fourth of public housing units in New Orleans that were vacant because they were unfit for human habitation (and this was *before* Hurricame Katrina struck).[262]

Corruption is present as well, and numerous instances of fraud, kickbacks, extortion, embezzlement, and other crimes have been documented that involved millions of dollars and which had been committed by board members, executive directors, or employees of public authorities at all levels of government.[263]

Has there been a misuse of managerial freedom by government corporations? Yes; the examples are too legion to conclude otherwise. Is this misuse endemic? We do not know.

The Independent Sector: Experiences in Interdependence

Perhaps no sector in the maze of intersectoral administration has become more prominent more quickly than has the independent sector. Also known as the *nonprofit, third,* or *emerging sector,* the *independent sector* is those organizations, associations, and institutions that do not seek profits, are not created by governments, and are privately owned. Figure 11-1 provides details.

The Scope of the Independent Sector

Nine out of ten American adults belong to at least one of America's 1.6 million nonprofit associations.[264] There are two types of independent-sector organizations. *Public serving organizations*, or *public-benefit organizations*, include universities, foundations, and churches, among others, and they exist to provide benefits to the public. There are about 1.2 million of them. *Member-serving organizations* include labor unions, political parties, and private clubs, among others, and they exist to provide benefits to their members. There are about 400,000 of them.[265]

Both public-serving and member-serving organizations are exempt from federal taxes, and most are exempt from state and local taxes, too. Public-serving organizations are exempt from federal taxes under Section 501(c) (3) of the Internal Revenue Code; hence, one of their monikers is "501(c) (3) organizations." Unlike virtually any other type of tax-exempt entity, however, taxpayers may deduct from their taxable income the value of donations to 501(c) (3) organizations.[266]

The tax-exempt sector employs 9 percent of the American workforce, a labor pool that is the equivalent to that of the Food and Lodging economic sector,[267] and employment growth in the nonprofit sector significantly outpaces those in the private and public sectors.[268] Nine out of ten of all nonprofit employees are employed by public-serving nonprofit organizations, and when we add about 6.3 million volunteers who devote their energies to the third sector, nonprofit organizations account for 11 percent of all paid and voluntary employment in the United States.[269]

The spending of all tax-exempt entities account for 11 percent to 12 percent of the U.S. GDP,[270] an amount exceeding the GPD of Canada. The revenues of public-serving nonprofit organizations account for about two-thirds of all nonprofit revenue,[271] and their primary revenue sources are fees and charges (such as the tuition paid by students at independent colleges), at a steady 51 percent; government grants and contracts, at 37 percent and rising; and private giving, at a modest 12 percent and falling.[272]

In sum, public-benefit organizations, with two-thirds of the emerging sector's organizations and revenues and nine-tenths of its employees, dominate the third sector. We provide next an example of how these organization work with governments in implementing public policy.

A Case of Governance: The Emerging Sector of Human Services

Human services are a classification of government policy that encompasses health services and hospitals, cultural and recreational services, higher and vocational education, and social services. *Social services* refer to job training; residential and child day care; and individual and family services, notably welfare, food stamps, and public housing.[273] Though reasonable, these listings are neither hard and fast nor even complete, and the literature occasionally uses the terms, "human services" and "social services," interchangeably.

The United States is unique in the degree to which it relies on nonprofit organizations to deliver these kinds of benefits. Alexis de Tocqueville, in touring America in 1831 and 1832, observed how different Americans were from Europeans in their enthusiasm for banding together in support of a good cause, and we see the results of this cultural characteristic today: "The United States went a different route from Europe in creating the American welfare state. American policymakers used the tax system and direct subsidy as a way of delivering services. . . . The United States has created a welfare state through nonprofit organizations, the vast majority created since 1950."[274]

An Intersectoral Governance. As we have noted, nonprofit public-service organizations acquire, on average, close to two-fifths of their budgets from governments. These orgaizations deal mostly with human services, and government's contributions to their budgets range from a tenth for cultural programs to more than half of all revenue collected by social services.[275]

One study found that 42 percent of *all* government spending for delivering health care (excluding hospitals), housing and community development, employment and training, arts and culture, and other social services went to nonprofit organizations, and another 19 percent went to for-profit companies. In other words, more than six out of ten of the public sector's dollars expended on these vital programs are contracted out![276]

These substantial sums slide through many circuitous loops in the governmental hierarchy before they reach the citizens for whom they are intended.

The Federal Loop. "Unfortunately, no comprehensive statistical data sources track the flow of federal support to nonprofits."[277] Researchers think, however, that over half of all federal grant dollars dedicated to social services either are passed through state and local governments to nonprofit organizations, or are sent directly to nonprofit organizations, compared to virtually zero in 1960.[278]

The State Loop. Slightly more than half of all state agencies contract with nonprofit organizations to deliver services.[279] Although we do not know the precise extent to which state governments rely on the independent sector to deliver human services in particular, we do know that, when a state agency uses a subsidy to deliver a public service, it is highly likely that it is subsidizing a nonprofit organization to deliver that service. We also know that, on average, 8 percent of all state services are delivered through subsidies. This proportion, however, is considerably higher in state human service agencies; almost 25 percent of state health agencies, 16 percent of state social service bureaus, and 9 percent of state mental health offices use subsidies to deliver their services, and these are the leading state agencies in the use of subsidies.[280] It appears from this pattern of indirect evidence that state governments work closely with nonprofit organizations in the delivery of human services.

The states also administer the largest federal welfare program—the $16.5 billion block grant called Temporary Assistance to Needy Families, created by Congress in 1996—and they rely to a significant degree on the independent sector to help them do so. Forty-nine states contract out 13 percent of these federal welfare funds (or more than $1.5 billion) in the form of some 5,400 contracts per year, and almost nine out of ten, 88 percent, of these contracted dollars are funneled by the states to nonprofit organizations.[281]

The Local Loop. Over 8 percent of all local services, on average, are funneled to not-for-profit organizations for delivery,[282] the same percentage

that it was twenty years earlier.[283] The leading local services contracted out to the independent sector are all human services.

Operating shelters for the homeless is handily the most common program, with more than six out of ten homeless shelters managed by nonprofit organizations that are funded by local governments. The operation of close to half of all local drug and alcohol treatment programs and cultural and arts programs are contracted by local governments to third-sector organizations. More than three out of ten mental health facilities and programs, museums, and day care centers, and over a fourth of programs for the elderly and child welfare, are contracted out by local governments to nonprofit groups.[284]

An Intimate Governance. Although the field of human services is managerially messy and difficult to sort out, it nonetheless is the "government-nonprofit partnership that forms the core of human service delivery systems in the United States."[285] It is a core comprised of strong and intimate bonds; as another analysis concluded, "Public sector agencies and nonprofit sector agencies reported virtually identical resource dependence on each other."[286]

This interdependence likely will intensify. President George W. Bush's "faith-based initiative," launched in 2001, is exploring new ways of working with the third sector to deliver and enrich federally funded human services.

An Accountable Governance? In part because human and social services are conducted through an intensely intimate, extraordinarily complex, and deeply intersectoral administration, questions of accountability invariably arise. A thorough review of this research uncovered a copious and consistent compendium of crippled accountability, including low administrative capacity on the part of both public and nonprofit entities; "goal divergence" between public and private policies and procedures; an overreliance on public funds by nonprofit agencies; sinister "equity implications for clients"; ill-conceived performance measures; a lack of competition; diminished service quality; mission drift; "deprofessionalization"; and "poorly defined and inadequately enforced accountability mechanisms."[287] Other than that, Mrs. Lincoln, how was the play?

There are some pinpoints of light on this dreary horizon. For example, the faith-based segment of the nonprofit sector appears to be performing quite credibly in helping governments with their human services. A survey of 587 faith-based nonprofit organizations and congregations that were administering $124 million in government contracts to provide social services in fifteen states, found that 87 percent of these faith-based contractors believed that these public funds had enabled them to serve more clients. These contractors take the constitutional separation of church and state seriously, and 70 percent segregated their government funding from their private funds.[288]

Additional research suggests that human services contracting conducted in a less sectarian context also can achieve acceptable levels of accountability. An analysis based on five case studies of publicly-let contracts for human services in Kansas concluded that "the state has achieved moderate to high levels of accountability."[289]

The Third Sector and the Other Two: Questions of Performance and Impact

Although human services is an important and revealing examples of governance by the third sector, there is some systematic empirical research (not a lot) that yields insight on the interrelationships of the three sectors in terms of performance and public impact. We close our discussion of the emerging sector with a brief review of some of these findings.

• *Nonprofit organizations and for-profit companies seem to perform at comparable levels of quality and service in delivering public services.* An analysis of job-training centers found that nonprofit centers were *not* more likely (as one might reasonably assume) than for-profit centers to serve more disadvantaged clients; neither type of center was consistently more effective in increasing their clients' earning and employment rates; and both types performed better when monetary incentives were included in their government contracts.[290] "What is clear is that nonprofits are competing increasingly with for-profit firms, and in an amazing variety of forms."[291]

• *Government funding has a significant, and positive, relationship with third-sector organizations.* The larger the percentage of public revenues relative to charitable donations in an nonprofit organization's budget, the more likely that the organization will be larger in membership yet smaller in both its board size and its administrative staff (and most clearly so in the cases of those nonprofits that are no longer new); more racially diverse in its board, staffers, and volunteers; and use fewer volunteers and be less dependent on its own earned income.[292] Government, it appears, tends to fund winners in the third sector; companies, citizens, foundations, and charities tend to fund losers.

• *Citizens' confidence in the third sector's ability to deliver public policies seems to be high and increasing over time.* When asked in whom they had "the most confidence to deliver services on the public's behalf," 42 percent of the general public said government, 29 percent cited nonprofits, and a modest 17 percent said "private contractors."[293] Five years later, when college seniors were asked this same question, a screechingly bottom-scraping 6 percent said government was the institution in which they had the most confidence to deliver services, a stunning 44 percent cited nonprofits, and about the same proportion, 16 percent, as five years earlier, said "businesses that serve the government."[294]

• *Both government and business elites evidence considerable faith in the capacity of nonprofit organizations to deliver public services and manage programs effectively and efficiently.* Federal and business managers were asked to identify which institution—the federal government, state and local governments, businesses, or nonprofit organizations—would they have "the most confidence in" to implement four public-relevant functions. Nonprofit organizations essentially swept the field, with federal and business managers usually giving higher ratings to the independent sector than they gave to their own institutions.[295] Americans believe in their independent sector—often, even more than they believe in the sector in which they themselves work!

The three sectors' use of each other is a major means of implementation. In the next chapter, we consider another means: governments' use of each other.

Notes

1. It appears that some public jobs, mostly in information technology and services, may have been outsourced, at least indirectly through public contracts with American

companies, to other nations, for essentially the same reasons that private companies outsource jobs: Money is saved. In the public sector, however, offshoring jobs is even more controversial than it is the private sector, for obvious reasons. See Alan Greenblatt, "Offshoring Hits Home," *Governing* (May 2004), p. 54.

2. Unless noted otherwise, the following discussion is drawn largely from Ira Sharkansky, "Government Contracting," *State Government* 53 (Winter 1980), pp. 23–24; Donna Wilson Kirchheimer, "Entrepreneurial Implementation in the US Welfare State," paper presented the 1986 Annual Meeting of the American Political Science Association, Washington, DC, August 20 8–31, 1986; and Jeffrey D. Greene, *Cities and Privatization: Prospects for the New Century* (Upper Saddle River, NJ: Prentice Hall, 2002), p. 8; and some of the author's own thoughts.

3. Gerald W. Johnson and John G. Heilman, "Metapolicy Transition and Policy Implementation: New Federalism and Privatization," *Public Administration Review* 47 (November/December 1987), p. 468.

4. Ibid.

5. James C. Clingermayer, Richard C. Feiock, and Christopher Stream, "Governmental Uncertainty and Leadership Turnover: Influences on Contracting and Sector Choice for Local Services," *State and Local Government Review* 35 (Fall 2003), p. 150.

6. Graeme D. Hodge, *Privatization: An International Review of Performance* (Boulder, CO: Westview, 2000). Hodge's thorough analysis of quantitative studies of privatization found that only 4 percent of 164 empirical analyses that dealt with the sale of public enterprises to the private sector were done in the United States, whereas 66 percent of 129 comparable studies that dealt with contracting out services were conducted in the United States.

7. Irene S. Rubin, "Who Invented Budgeting in the United States?" *Public Administration Review* 53 (September/October 1993), p. 443.

8. Annmarie Hauk Walsh, *The Public's Business: The Politics and Practices of Government Corporations* (Cambridge, MA: MIT Press, 1978), p. 40. For an interesting extension of this critique, see Julia Beckett, "The 'Government Should Be Run Like a Business' Mantra," *American Review of Public Administration* 30 (June 2000), pp. 185–200.

9. Graeme Browning, "Dot.gov goes Retail," *Federal Computer Week* (May 28, 2001), pp. 21–27. Figures are for 2001. Amazon.com sold $2.8 billion worth of products in 2001.

10. U.S. General Accounting Office, *Federal Real Property: Executive and Legislative Actions Needed to Address Long-Standing and Complex Problems*, GAO–03–839T. Testimony before the Committee on Government Reform, House of Representatives, June 5, 2003. Statement of Bernard L. Ungar (Washington, DC: U.S. Government Printing Office, 2003), p. 2.

11. U.S. General Accounting Office, *High-Risk Series: Federal Real Property*, GAO–03–122 (Washington, DC: U.S. Government Printing Office, 2003), pp. 5, 9.

12. Ibid., p. 11.

13. Ibid., p. 8.

14. Dwight D. Eisenhower, *Farewell Address to the Nation* (January 17, 1961), p. 2.

15. Federal Procurement Data System, *Federal Procurement Report* (Washington, DC: Author, 2004), p. 2. Figures are for 2003. The FPDS is the single best source for federal acquisition data, but it does not report a lot of federal or federally related contract actions, such as all contracts totaling less than $25,000 and contracts let by some agencies, such as the U.S. Postal Service (the largest), which spent $9.1 billion on goods, services and construction in 1999. Hence, the figures in the text are very conservative. See U.S. General Accounting Office, *Federal Acquisition: Trends, Reforms, and Challenges*, GAO/T–OCG–00–7 (Washington, DC: U.S. Government Printing Office, 2000), pp. 4–6.

16. U.S. General Accounting Office, *Federal Procurement: Spending and Workforce Trends*, GAO–03–443 (Washington, DC: U.S. Government Printing Office, 2003), p. 8. Figure, 24 percent, is for 2001.

17. Ibid., pp. 9–10.

18. As derived from data in U.S. General Accounting Office, *Federal Acquisition: Trends, Reforms, and Challenges*, p. 2. In 1985, DOD accounted for 82 percent of contract dollars.

19. As derived from data in Federal Procurement Data System, *Federal Procurement Report*, p. 5. In 2003, DOD accounted for 64 percent of contract dollars.

20. U.S. General Accounting Office, *Acquisition Workforce: Status of Agency Efforts to Address Future Needs*, GAO–03–55 (Washington, DC: U.S. Government Printing Office, 2002), p. 1. The agencies are General Services Administration, National Aeronautics and Space Administration, and the Departments of Energy, Veterans Affairs, Treasury, and Health and Human Services.

21. Federal Procurement Data System, *Federal Procurement Report*, pp. 7–8. Data are for 2003. The Federal Procurement Data System does not separate service contracts in its analyses. In the FPDS classification, "Other Services and Construction" (in which construction typically amounts to less than a fifth of the category) accounts for 49 percent of federal contract dollars, supplies and equipment amounts to 34 percent, and R&D for 12 percent.

22. Ibid., p. 2, and U.S. Bureau of the Census, *Statistical Abstract of the United States, 2006*, 125th ed. (Washington, DC: U.S. Government Printing Office, 2006), Table 482. In 2003, federal payrolls surpassed $143 billion, which amounted to 47 percent of the $305 billion that Washington spent on contracts in the same year.

23. Paul C. Light, *Fact Sheet on the New True Size of Government* (Washington, DC: Center for Public Service, 2003), p. 5. Figure is for 2002. "Contractor jobs" grew by 560,000, 1990–2002.

24. U.S. General Accounting Office, *Government Contractors: Are Service Contractors Performing Inherently Governmental Functions?* GAO/GGD–92–11 (Washington, DC: U.S. Government Printing Office, 1991), p. 19.

25. U.S. General Accounting Office, *Competitive Sourcing: Greater Emphasis Needed on Increasing Efficiency and Improving Performance*, GAO–04–367 (Washington, DC: U.S. Government Printing Office, 2004), p. 6. Approximately half of all federal civilian positions are classified as competable commercial and non-competable commercial. Noncompetable commercial positions are exempt from competition because of legislative prohibitions or other reasons.

26. Al Gore, *From Red Tape to Results: Creating a Government That Works Better and Costs Less. Reinventing Federal Procurement. Accompanying Report of the National Performance Review* (Washington, DC: U.S. Government Printing Office, 1993), p. 3.

27. David Barstow, "Security Companies: Shadow Soldiers in Iraq," *New York Times* (April 19, 2004). Barstow is quoting the Pentagon's Mark J. Lumer.

28. Ariana Eunjung Cha and Renae Merle, "Line Increasingly Blurred between Soldiers and Civilian Contractors," *Washington Post* (May 13, 2004).

29. Barstow, "Security Companies." Barstow is quoting, respectively, Michael Battles, co-founder of Custer Battles; and Patrick Toohey, vice president of Blackwater. Both are security companies with employees in Iraq.

30. Jonathan Werve, *Contractors Write the Rules* (Washington, DC: The Center for Public Integrity, 2004). The company, Military Professionals Resources, Inc., wrote Field Manual 100–21, also known as *Contractors on the Battlefield*. A principal author of the manual told an interviewer that, although he was provided with "some basic guidelines" from the Army, "for the most part, however, this was a clean slate."

31. Phillip J. Cooper, "Government Contracts in Public Administration: The Role and Environment of the Contracting Officer," *Public Administration Review* 40 (September/October 1980), p. 461.

32. Ibid., p. 462.

33. Federal Procurement Data Center, *Federal Procurement Reports, FY 97* (Washington, DC: Author, 1997), p. 12.

34. Cooper, "Government Contracts in Public Administration," p. 463.

35. As derived from data in U.S. General Accounting Office, *Contract Management: Civilian Agency Compliance with Revised Task and Delivery Order Regulations*, GAO–03–983 (Washington, DC: U.S. Government Printing Office, 2003), pp. 22–24. This was a review of eleven investigations by GAO, inspectors general, and others from 1998 to 2002, which found that from 45 percent to 88 percent of contracts had competition requirements excepted. This source also contains a separate investigation, which found that 31 percent of twenty-six contracts "were issued using exceptions to the fair opportunity process" (Highlights page). See also U.S. Government Accountability Office, *Contract Management: Guidance Needed to Promote Competition for Defense Task Orders*, GAO–04–874 Washington, DC: U.S. Government Printing Office, 2004), p. 3. In 2004, thirty-four out of seventy-four multiple-award contracts and federal supply schedule orders (46 percent) had their competition requirements waived.

36. John O'Mally, editor of *Commerce Business Daily*, and Vince Villa, Washington consultant, as quoted in "Most Ads for Contractors Meaningless," *Washington Post* (June 25, 1980). The references in this article were to *Commerce Business Daily*, a five-day-a-week publication that was discontinued and replaced in 2002 by FedBizOpps. Although the title and format of federal bidding opportunities were changed, we assume that the basic facts recounted in the text remain unaltered.

37. Gordon Rule, quoted in William Proxmire, *Report from the Wasteland: America's Military Industrial Complex* (New York: Praeger, 1970), p. 83. Rule was a civilian cost containment expert for the Navy.

38. Bent Flyvberg, Mette Skamris Holm, and Soren Buhl, "Underestimating Costs in Public Works Projects: Error or Lie?" *Journal of the American Planning Association* 68 (Summer 2002), pp. 279–295. The quotation is on p. 279.

39. *The Washington Monthly*, as cited in Todd S. Purdum, "Go Ahead, Try to Stop K Street" *New York Times* (September 9, 2006).

40. Jill Abramson, "The Business of Persuasion Thrives in Nation's Capitol," *New York Times* (September 29, 1998).

41. Lobbyists.info, Home page, https://www.lobbyists.info. This is the Web site for *Washington Representatives*. Figures are for 2005.

42. PoliticalMoneyLine and Rogan Karsh, Syracuse University, as cited in Purdum, "Go Ahead, Try to Stop K Street." In 2005, there were 32,890 registered lobbyists in the District of Columbia. In 1999, there were 14,690.

43. Morris P. Fiorina and Paul E. Peterson, *The New American Democracy* (Needham Heights, MA: Allyn and Bacon, 1998), p. 213.

44. PoliticalMoneyLine and Rogan Karsh, as cited in Purdum, "Go Ahead, Try to Stop K Street." In 2004, registered Washington lobbyists spent over $2.1 billion, an increase of 46 percent from 1999, when they spent less than $1.5 billion.

45. U. S. General Accounting Office, as cited in Juliet Ellperin, "From Obscurity at GAO, Terry Deaver wrote the Report that Made Lobbying Disclosure Reform a Political Reality, *"Roll Call* (January 22, 1996).

46. Associated Press, "Former Defense Secretary Sets Up Consulting Firm," *Savannah Morning News* (January 24, 2001).

47. Purdum, "Go Ahead, Try to Stop K Street." Representative Martin T. Meehan is quoted.

48. Abramson, "The Business of Persuasion Thrives in Nation's Capitol." In 1987, the average tenure for "most administrative assistants" in the House was 5.5 years; in 1996, it was four years.

49. Center for Public Integrity, as cited in Purdum, "Go Ahead, Try to Stop K Street," Figures are for 1998–2003.

50. Abramson, "The Business of Persuasion Thrives in Nation's Capitol."

51. Susan Baer, "'Revolving Door' Spins Fast as Ever for Ex-Clintonites," *Baltimore Sun* (December 1, 1996).

52. Representative Marcy Kaptur, as quoted in Gary Lee, "Trade, National Security, and the Revolving Door," *Washington Post* (April 13, 1992).

53. Cooper, "Government Contracts in Public Administration," pp. 462–463.

54. P. W. Singer, "Nation Builders and Low Bidders in Iraq," *New York Times* (June 15, 2004).

55. Ibid., and P. W. Singer, "A Contract the U.S. Military Needs to Break," Washington Post (September 12, 2004).

56. Sharkansky, "Government Contracting," pp. 23–24.

57. Gore, *From Red Tape to Results*, p. 28.

58. Center for Strategic and International Studies, *Integrating Civilian and Military Technologies: An Industry Survey* (Washington, DC: Author, 1993).

59. Information Technology Association of America, *Key Issues in Federal Information Technology* (Arlington, VA: Author, 1992), p. 4.

60. U.S. General Accounting Office, *Contract Management: Comments on Proposed Services Acquisition Reform Act*, GAO–03–716T (Washington, DC: U.S. Government Printing Office, 2003), p. 1. Figure is for 2001.

61. U.S. General Accounting Office, *Federal Acquisition: Trends, Reforms, and Challenges*, p. 6.

62. Federal Procurement Data System, *Federal Procurement Report*. Our definition of *federal service contract* is derived from information in this source.

63. U.S. Office of Management and Budget, as cited in Frank Greve, "Hired Guns Running the U.S.," *Philadelphia Inquirer* (May 19, 1992). Figure is for 1992.

64. U.S. General Accounting Office, as cited in Stuart Auerbach, "Disclosure Rules on Consultants Held Insufficient," *Washington Post* (November 2, 1990).

65. "Draft analysis" by the General Accounting Office, as cited in Stephen Barr, "Federal Workers Cost Government Less Than Consultants, GAO Says," *Washington Post* (March 3, 1994).

66. The federal contract administrators, in order of quotation, are Roy Higdon, Environmental Protection Agency; David Webb, Health, Education and Welfare; and William Stevenson, Department of Energy. All are cited in Jonathan Neumann and Ted Gup, "An Epidemic of Waste in U.S. Consulting, Research" *Washington Post* (July 22,1980).

67. William Farris, cited in ibid.

68. Daniel Guttman, appearing on the program *60 Minutes*, CBS Television Network (November 30, 1982).

69. U.S. General Accounting Office, *Civil Servants and Contract Employees*, p. 6.

70. Al Stapleton, as quoted in "Consultants: New Target for Budget Trimmers," *U.S. News and World Report* (December 1, 1981), p. 40.

71. U.S. General Accounting Office, *Government Contractors: Are Service Contractors Performing Inherently Governmental Functions?* p. 5. GAO reviewed 108 consulting contracts let by the Departments of Transportation, Energy, and Defense, and the Environmental Protection Agency and found twenty-eight that may have involved "inherently governmental functions."

72. Joseph Besselman, Ashish Arora, and Patrick Larkey, "Buying in a Businesslike Fashion—And Paying More," *Public Administration Review* 60 (September/October 2000), p. 421.

73. Richard W. Stevenson, "Many Caught but Few Are Hurt for Arms Contract Fraud in U.S.," *Washington Post* (November 12, 1990). Period was 1983–1990.

74. Ronald J. Ostrow and John M. Broder, "New Indictments a Possibility in Pentagon Probe," *Philadelphia Inquirer* (November 26, 1990).

75. Derek Vander Schaaf, deputy inspector general of the Pentagon, as cited in Ralph Vartabedian, "Defense Fraud Cases Boom Amid Cutbacks," *Los Angeles Times* (March 26, 1995). Between 1986 and 1995, defense spending on weaponry declined by about 70 percent, but fraud-related collections increased elevenfold, attaining $1.2 billion in 1995. In 1985, twenty-five of the Pentagon's top 100 contractors were being investigated for fraud; in 1995, sixty-eight were.

76. U.S. Government Accountability Office, *GAO's 2005 High-Risk Update*, GAO–05–350T (Washington, DC: U.S. Government Printing Office, 2005), pp. 2, 3. Four areas dealt specifically with contract management in Defense, Energy, NASA, and "interagency contracting." The GAO's high-risk areas typically fluctuate from twenty-five to thirty, depending on the year.

77. Steven Goldsmith and William D. Eggers, "Government for Hire," *New York Times* (February 21, 2005).

78. Stevenson, "Many Caught but Few Are Hurt For Arms Contract Fraud in U.S."

79. U.S. Government Accountability Office, *Federal Procurement: Additional Data Reporting Could Improve the Suspension and Debarment Process*, GAO–05–479 (Washington, DC: U.S. Government Printing Office, 2005), p. 5. Figure is for 1995–2004. A *suspension* is a temporary exclusion of a contractor pending the completion of investigation or legal proceedings. A contractor can be suspended if he or she has been indicted, other federal agencies are conducting an investigation, or a serious accusation has been made. A *debarment* is a fixed-term exclusion, usually not exceeding three years. A contractor can be debarred if he or she has been convicted of fraud, other crimes, or a "willful failure to perform." It appears that most, perhaps two-thirds, of "excluded" (a term encompassing both suspension and debarment) contractors are debarred.

80. Federal Procurement Data System, *Federal Procurement Report*, p. 2. Figure is for 2003.

81. Anne Marie Squeo, "Are Firms Too Big to Debar?" *Wall Street Journal* (June 10, 2003).

82. Scott Amey, "Suspension and Disbarment: The Record Shows That the System is Broken," *Federal Times* (March 21, 2005), http://www@federaltimes.com. Figures are for 1990–2003. By contrast, in 2003 and 2004, 43,000 firms, all of them small, had been banned from further federal contracts.

83. Danielle Brian, *Contract Debarment and Suspension: A Broken System* (Washington, DC: Project on Government Oversight, 2003), p. 1.

84. U.S. Government Accountability Office, *Federal Procurement: Additional Data Reporting Could Improve the Suspension and Debarment Process*, pp. 2–3. Figure is for 2003.

85. Quoted in Russell Mitchell, "It Was Mr. Fixit Vs. The Pentagon—and the Pentagon Won," *Business Week* (December 24, 1990), p. 52.

86. U.S. General Accounting Office study, as cited in John M. Biers, "Billions in U.S. Contracts Go to Labor Law Violators," *Baltimore Sun* (February 15, 1995). In 1993, $23 billion in federal contracts was awarded to eighty companies that had violated federal labor laws.

87. U.S. General Accounting Office study, as cited in *Chicago Tribune*, "Federal Dollars for Safety Violators," *Washington Post* (September 3, 1996). In 1994, $38 billion in federal contracts were awarded to 261 companies that had seriously violated federal health and safety laws.

88. Ellen Nakashama, "Clinton Contractor Rule Is Suspended," *Washington Post* (March 31, 2001), and David S. Broder, "Bush's Stealthy Pursuit of a Partisan Agenda," *Washington Post* (January 2, 2002). Clinton's ban became effective on January 19, 2001, was suspended by Bush on March 30, 2001, and officially killed on December 27, 2001. Industry had lobbied intensely against the ban, since it was first floated in 1997 as a pledge by Vice President Al Gore to labor leaders. There are, however, thirteen *statutory disbarments* (as of 2005), which are exclusions based on laws, executive orders, or regulatory authority other than the Federal Acquisition Regulation. For details, see U.S. Government Accountability Office, *Federal Procurement: Additional Data Reporting Could Improve the Suspension and Disbarment Process*, pp. 23–24.

89. U.S. House Ways and Means Committee's Democratic staff, as cited in Jonathan D. Salant, Associated Press, "Companies Relocate to Escape Taxes," *Savannah Morning News* (May 27, 2003). In 2001, these tax haven companies were awarded $846 million in federal contracts.

90. U.S. General Accounting Office, *International Taxation: Tax Haven Companies Were More Likely to Have a Tax Cost Advantage in Federal Contracting*, GAO–04–856 (Washington, DC: U.S. Government Printing Office, 2004), Highlights page. There are not many of these large tax haven contractors; in 2001 GAO analyzed only 50 out of 3,524 large contractors.

91. As derived from data in U.S. General Accounting Office, *Contract Management: Civilian Agency Compliance with the Revised Task and Delivery Order Regulations*, Highlights page and p. 22. See also U.S. General Accounting Office, *Contract Management: Guidance Needed for Using Performance-Based Service Contracting*, GAO–02–1049 (Washington, DC: U.S. Government Printing Office, 2002), p. 3. In 2001, 11 percent of some 360,000 service contracts were performance-based.

92. U.S. General Accounting Office, *Competitive Sourcing: Implementation Will Be Key to Success of New Circular A-76*, GAO–03–943T (Washington, DC: U.S. Government Printing Office, 2003), Highlights page.

93. U.S. General Accounting Office, *Acquisition Management: Agencies Can Improve Training on New Initiatives*, GAO–03–281 (Washington, DC: U.S. Government Printing Office, 2003), Highlights page.

94. In 2003, state governments and their local governments spent an estimated $400 billion through contracts, and in 2003 Washington spent at least $305 billion on contracts. See, respectively, Jonathan Walters, "Going Outside," *Governing* (May 2004), p. 26, and Federal Procurement Data System, *Federal Procurement Report*, p. 2.

95. Keon S. Chi, Kelley A. Arnold, and Heather M. Perkins, "Privatization in State Government: Trends and Issues," *Spectrum: The Journal of State Government* 76 (Fall 2003), pp. 12–21. In 2002, 450 state budget and legislative service agency directors and the heads of those executive agencies dealing with personnel, education, health and human services, corrections, and transportation were polled. The response rate was 77 percent. The survey is a follow-up, with some variations, to one conducted in 1997: Keon S. Chi and Cindy Jasper, *Private Practices: A Review of Privatization in State Government* (Lexington, KY: Council of State Governments, 1998). A somewhat more limited but comparable survey was conducted in 1992; see Keon S. Chi, "Privatization in State Government: Options for the Future," *State Trends and Forecasts* 2 (2, 1993), pp. 2–33.

There is not much in the way of national surveys of state privatization practices. As one of the few of these notes (p. 436), the states "have received remarkably little attention in the privatization literature." See Deborah A. Auger, "Privatization, Contracting, and the States: Lessons from State Government," *Public Productivity and Management Review* 22 (June 1999), pp. 435–454. The article is based on a national survey of state privatization practices conducted from 1995 through 1997. See also National Governors Association, *An Action Agenda to Redesign State Governments: Reports of the State Management Task Force Strategy Groups* (Washington, DC: Author, 1994).

96. John R. Bartle and Ronnie LaCourse Korosec, *Procurement and Contracting in State Government, 2000* (Syracuse, NY: Syracuse University Government Performance Project, 2001), p. iv. Figure is for 2000.

97. Chi, Arnold, and Perkins, "Privatization in State Government," p. 15. Figure is for 2002.

98. Chi and Jasper, *Private Practices*, p. 14. Figure is for 1997.

99. Robert W. Poole Jr., David Haarmeyer, and Lynn Scarlett, *Mining the Government Balance Sheet: What Cities and States Have To Sell*. Policy Study No. 139 (Washington, DC: Reason Public Policy Institute, 1992), p. 2. The "preliminary estimate" was $227 billion in 1992.

100. Jeffrey L. Brudney, Sergio Fernández, Jay Eungha Ryu, and Deil S. Wright, "Exploring and Explaining Contracting Out: Patterns among the American States," *Journal of Public Administration Research and Theory* 15 (July 2005), p. 393. Figure is for 1998.

101. Chi, Arnold, and Perkins, "Privatization in State Government," p. 15. In 2002, 87 percent of about 450 state administrators reported that their states contracted out services, 45 percent used public–private partnerships, and 32 percent used grants and subsidies. These were handily the three leading types of state privatization.

102. As derived from data in Yoo-Sung Choi, Chung-Lae Cho, Deil S. Wright, and Jeffrey L. Brudney, "Dimensions of Contracting for Service Delivery by American State Administrative Agencies: Exploring Linkages between and Intergovernmental Relations and Intersectoral Administration," *Public Performance and Management Review* 29 (September 2005), p. 50. Figure is for 1998. Fifty-one percent of state agencies contract with nonprofit organizations to deliver services, and 44 percent do so with other agencies.

103. Chi and Jasper, *Private Practices*, p. 14. Data are for 1997.

104. Chi, Arnold, and Perkins, "Privatization in State Government," p. 14. Figures are for 2002.

105. Ibid. Figure is for 2002.

106. Chi and Jasper, *Private Practices*, p. 8. Data are for 1997. See also U.S. General Accounting Office, *Privatization: Lessons Learned by State and Local Governments*, GAO/GGD–97–48 (Washington, DC: U.S. Government Printing Office, 1997). This was an analysis of five states, Georgia, Massachusetts, Michigan, New York, and Virginia, and a city, Indianapolis.

107. Chi, Arnold, and Perkins, "Privatization in State Government," p. 15. Figures are for 2002.

108. Brudney, Fernandez, Ryu, and Wright, "Exploring and Explaining Contracting Out," pp. 393–420. Figures are for 1998.

109. Choi, Cho, Wright, and Brudney, "Dimensions of Contracting for Service Delivery by American State Administrative Agencies," p. 50. Figures are for 1998 and refer to state contracting with nonprofit organizations and other government agencies, as well as with private corporations.

110. Jeffrey L. Brudney, F. Ted Hebert, and Deil S. Wright, "Reinventing Government in the American States: Measuring and Explaining Administrative Reform," *Public Administration Review* 59 (January/February 1999), p. 23. Data are for 1995. Chi and Jasper, *Private Practices*, found comparable levels of privatization: Forty-three percent of agency heads had privatized *less* than 5 percent of their services. Of the managerial innovations available to state administrators, privatization appears to rank among the least attractive to them.

111. Choi, Cho, Wright, and Brudney, "Dimensions of Contracting for Service Delivery by American State Administrative Agencies," p. 50. Figure is for 1998.

112. Browning, "Dot.gov Goes Retail."

113. U.S. General Accounting Office, *Federal Procurement: Spending and Workforce Trends*, p. 8.

114. Light, *The True Size of Government*, p. 22.

115. Irwin T. David, "Privatization in America," *Municipal Year Book, 1988* (Washington, DC: International City Management Association, 1988), p. 52.

116. Mildred Warner and Amir Hefetz, "Pragmatism over Politics: Alternative Service Delivery in Local Government, 1992–2002," *Municipal Year Book, 2004* (Washington, DC: International City/County Management Association, 2004), p. 11. Figure is for 2002.

117. For a good review of this change, see Walters, "Going Outside," pp. 22–29.

118. David, "Privatization in America," p. 41.

119. Ibid., p. 52. The period covered for these figures is 1982–1987.

120. Ibid., p. 44. To be precise, 99 percent of local governments.

121. Rowan Miranda and Karlyn Andersen, "Alternative Service Delivery in Local Government, 1982–1992" *Municipal Year Book, 1994* (Washington, DC: International City/County Management Association, 1994), p. 28.

122. Warner and Hefetz, "Pragmatism over Politics," p. 10, and Elaine Morley, "Patterns in the Use of Alternative Service Delivery Approaches," *Municipal Year Book, 1989* (Washington, DC: International City Management Association, 1989), p. 36. Current figure is for 2002.

123. Warner and Hefetz, "Pragmatism over Politics," p. 10. The first ICMA survey on this topic was conducted in 1982. See Harry P. Hatry and Carl F. Valente, "Alternative Service Delivery Approaches Involving Increased Use of the Private Sector," *Municipal Year Book, 1983* (Washington, DC: International City Management Association, 1983), pp. 199–217. "All local services" refers to sixty services surveyed in 1982 and sixty-seven services in 2002. The 1982 survey covered 3,130 cities, with 46 percent responding ($N = 1,433$), and 1,570 counties, with 24 percent responding ($N = 347$). The 2002 survey covered 3,689 cities, with 27 percent responding ($N = 985$), and 1,681 counties, with 18 percent responding ($N = 298$). In 1982, 51 percent all local services were delivered by local governments' own employees. Specific services listed are for 2002.

124. Ibid (both citations). Specific services listed are for 2002. In 1982, 22 percent of all local services were delivered by mixes of governments' own employees and private employees. In 1992, the percentage of services delivered by mixes of public and private employees slipped to less than 17 percent, but climbed steadily upwards since then. Warner and Hefetz, "Pragmatism over Politics," p. 11.

125. Warner and Hefetz, "Pragmatism over Politics," p. 11. Data are for 2002.

126. As derived from data in Hatry and Valente, "Alternative Service Delivery Approaches Involving Increased Use of the Private Sector," pp. 216–217. Figure is for 1982.

127. Alan Greenblatt, "Observer," *Governing* (February 2006), pp. 17, 18.

128. Warner and Hefetz, "Pragmatism over Politics," P.13. Data are for 2002.

129. Ibid. Figures are for 2002.

130. Patricia M. Florestano and Stephen B. Gordon, "A Survey of City and County Use of Private Contracting," *The Urban Interest* 3 (Spring 1981), p. 25.

131. James C. Clingermayer, Richard C. Feiock, and Christopher Stream "Governmental Uncertainty and Leadership Turnover: Influences on Contracting and Sector Choice for Local Services," *State and Local Government Review* 35 (Fall 2003), p. 157. The ICMA surveys of 1988 and 1992 on alternative delivery methods, as well as other national sources, were used in this study. Services examined were confined to elderly and mental health programs.

132. Alan Greenblatt, "Sweetheart Deals," *Governing* (December 2004), http://governing.com.

133. Clingermayer, Feiock, and Stream, "Governmental Uncertainty and Leadership Turnover," p. 156. When there was high turnover among local elected and appointed officials, local contracting with all sectors— not just the private one, but the public and nonprofit sectors, too—fell precipitously.

134. Mary M. Shaw, "Successful Collaboration between the Nonprofit and Public Sectors," *Nonprofit Management and Leadership* 14 (Fall 2003), pp. 107–120. The quotation is on p. 107. Another study, this of a state transportation department, found comparable correlations. "Positive contractor relationships" between public administrators and contractors, "and years of working with contractors outside the agency are associated with more favorable perceptions of privatization's personal impacts [on public administrators. . . . and its] impacts on the agency." See Leisha DeHart-Davis and Gordon Kingsley, "Managerial Perceptions of Privatization: Evidence from a State Department of Transportation," *State and Local Government Review* 37 (3, 2005), pp. 228–241. Quotation is on p. 236.

135. Laurence J. O'Toole Jr. and Kenneth J. Meier "Parkinson's Law and the New Public Management? Contracting Determinants and Service-Quality Consequences in Public Education," *Public Administration Review* 64 (May/June 2004), pp. 342–352. The quotations are on pp. 342, 348–349, respectively. Data were collected from 1997–1999.

136. Pascale Joassart-Marcelli and Juliet Musso, "Municipal Service Provision Choices within a Metropolitan Area," *Urban Affairs Review* 40 (March 2005), pp. 492–519; Thomas Pallesen, "A Political Perspective on Contracting Out: The Politics of Good Times, Experiences of Danish Local Governments," *Governance* 17 (October 2004), pp. 573–587; and Jeffrey D. Greene, "Cities and Privatization: Examining the Effect of Fiscal Stress, Location, and Wealth in Medium Sized Cities," *Policy Studies Journal* 24 (Spring1996), pp. 135–144.

137. Clingermayer, Feiock, and Stream, "Governmental Uncertainty and Leadership Turnover," p. 158.

138. Pallesen, "A Political Perspective on Contracting Out."

139. Warner and Hefetz, " Pragmatism over Politics," p. 14. Figure is for 2002. In 1992, less than 48 percent of local governments reported that they had encountered no obstacles in implement a private service delivery.

140. Ibid. Figures are for 2002 .

141. As derived from data in David, "Privatization in America," pp. 43–47. No apparent savings was cited

by 59 percent of cities and counties, and a loss of program control by 51 percent. Figures are for 1988. In 1992, opposition from local government employees accounted for 54 percent, and in 1997 for 60 percent (an anomaly), of the obstacles to privatization. See Warner and Hefetz, "Pragmatism over Politics," p. 14.

142. Unidentified studies cited by Paul E. Peterson, "The New Politics of Federalism," *Spectrum: The Journal of State Government* 78 (Spring 2005), p. 7.

143. Warner and Hefetz, "Pragmatism over Politics," p. 14. Figure is for 2002.

144. Clingermayer, Feiock, and Stream, "Governmental Uncertainty and Leadership Turnover," p. 156. See also Mildred Warner and Robert Hebdon, "Local Government Restructuring: Privatization and Its Alternatives," *Journal of Policy Analysis and Management* 20 (Spring 2001), pp. 315–336.

145. Warner and Hefetz, "Pragmatism over Politics," p. 14. Figure is for 2002. In 1997, opposition from elected officials accounted for 42 percent of the impediments to privatization, and in 1992, 39 percent. In 1988, "political impediments" were cited by 42 percent of local jurisdictions and "public opinion" by 24 percent. See David, "Privatization in America," pp. 43–47.

146. Ibid. Figure is for 2002 and has ranged from 31 percent to 30 percent since 1992. In 1988, 24 percent of local officials cited "public opinion" as an impediment to privatization. See David, "Privatization in America," p. 43.

147. U.S. Advisory Commission on Intergovernmental Relations, *Changing Public Attitudes on Government and Taxes, 1985* (Washington, DC: U.S. Government Printing Office, 1985), pp. 25–29, and Hart-Teeter Poll, *Findings from a Research Project about Attitudes Toward Government* (Washington, DC: Council for Excellence in Government, 1997), p. 11.

148. Brookings Institution, as cited in Partnership for Public Service, *Public Opinion on Public Service* (Washington, DC: Author, 2005), p. 6. In 1998, 17 percent of the general public expressed the most confidence in private contractors to deliver services, and in 2002, 16 percent of college seniors said this.

149. James D. Ward, "Exploring Unintended Consequences of Privatization, 1979 to 1999," paper presented at the National Conference of the American Society of Public Administration, San Diego, 2000, p. 3. This is a useful review of the research.

150. Stephen Moore, "How Contracting Out City Services Impacts Public Employees," in Paul Seidenstat, ed., *Contracting Out Government Services* (Westport, CT: Praeger, 1999), pp. 211–218. This chapter is based on one of the most comprehensive surveys on the topic: National Center for Employment Policy, US. Department of Labor, *The Long-Term Employment Implications of Privatization* (Washington, DC: U.S. Government Printing Office, 1989).

151. As derived from data in Warner and Hefetz, "Pragmatism over Politics," pp. 10, 14.

152. Moore, "How Contracting out City Services Impacts Public Employees," p. 214.

153. Ibid. See also Christi Clark, Robin A. Johnson, and James L. Mercer, "Impact of Privatization and Managed Competition on Public Employees," in Robin A. Johnson and Norman Walzer, eds, *Local Government Innovation: Issues and Trends in Privatization and Managed Competition* (Westport, CT: Quorum Books, 2000), pp. 191–210, especially pp. 194–195.

154. Ward, "Exploring Unintended Consequences of Privatization," p. 6.

155. U.S. Advisory Commission on Intergovernmental Relations, *State Laws Governing Local Government Structure and Administration,* M–186 (Washington, DC: U.S. Government Printing Office, 1993), p. 43. Figures are for 1990.

156. Ibid. Figures are for 1990.

157. Sergio Fernandez and Hal G. Rainey, "Local Government Contract Management and Performance Survey: A Report," *Municipal Year Book, 2005* (Washington, DC: International City/County Management Association, 2005), pp. 3–4. Figure is for 2003–2004. The proportion of local contracts that are let competitively is remarkably stable over time, but slowly growing. Twenty-two percent of cities and counties used sole-source bids in 1988. See David, "Privatization in America," p. 51. An earlier survey found that more than 97 percent of American cities required sealed bids on purchasing contracts in 1979. On the other hand, nearly 87 percent of these same cities permitted bidding to be waived under certain circumstances. See Dan H. Davidson and Solon G. Bennett, "Municipal Purchasing Practices," *Municipal Year Book, 1980* (Washington, DC: International City Management Association, 1980), pp. 236–237.

158. Cooper, "Government Contracts in Public Administration," p. 463.

159. Warner and Hefetz, "Pragmatism over Politics," p. 15. Data are for 2002.

160. Elaine Morley, "Patterns of Use of Alternative Service Delivery Approaches," *Municipal Year Book,* 1989 (Washington, DC: International City Management Association, 1989). p. 40-42.

161. Mildred Warner, with Michael Ballard and Amir Hefetz, "Contracting Back In: When Privatization Fails," *Municipal Year Book, 2003* (Washington, DC: International City/County Management Association, 2003), p. 36.

162. Joassart-Marcelli and Musso, "Municipal Service Provision Choices within a Metropolitan Area," p. 515.

163. Robert J. Dilger, Randolioh R. Moffett, and Linda Struyk, "Privatization of Municipal Services in America's Largest Cities," *Public Administration Review* 57 (January/February 1997), p. 24. Figure is for 1995.

164. Warner and Hefetz, "Pragmatism over Politics," p. 15. In 2002, 47 percent of all cities and counties monitored private contractors.

165. Dilger, Moffet, and Struyk, "Privatization of Municipal Services in America's Largest Cities," p. 23.

166. David Osborne and Ted Gaebler, *Reinventing Government: How the Entrepreneurial Spirit Is Transforming the Public Sector* (Reading, MA: Addison-Wesley, 1992), p. 89.

167. Florestano and Gordon, "A Survey of City and County Private Contracting," found that 32 percent of local officials thought that privatization resulted in better quality services in 1981; and David, "Privatization in America," found that 33 percent thought so in 1988.

168. Warner and Hefetz, "Pragmatism over Politics," p. 15. Figures are for 2002.

169. Hodge, *Privatization,* p. 156.

170. William D. Eggers, *Rightsizing the Government: Lessons from America's Public Sector Innovators* (Los Angeles: Reason Foundation, 1993).

171. Hodge, *Privatization,* p. 155.

172. When Phoenix, Arizona, switched from entertaining bids from private refuse collectors to collecting refuse itself, costs fell by over two-thirds. See R. Johnson, "Privatization Issues: Experience in Phoenix, Arizona." 46th Conference of Local Government Engineering, Melbourne, Australia, February 19–20, 1990.

173. David, "Privatization in America," p. 39. Any savings accrued likely came from salaries and benefits. See, for example: Rowan Miranda, "Privatization and the Budget-Maximizing Bureaucrat," *Public Productivity and Management Review* 17 (Summer 1994), pp. 355–369; John D. Donohue, *The Privatization Decision: Public Ends, Private Means* (New York: Basic Books, 1989), p. 131; and John Rehfuss, *Contracting Out in Government: A Guide to Working with Outside Contractors to Supply Public Services* (San Francisco: Jossey-Bass, 1989), p. 201.

174. Warner and Hefetz, "Pragmatism over Politics," p. 15. In 2002, 51 percent of local administrators who had brought privatized services back in-house thought their cost savings were insufficient, and 36 percent believed that local government efficiency had improved.

175. Hodge, *Privatization,* p. 78. Much of our discussion of savings derives from this impressive source, which is among the most comprehensive of the literature. Hodge unearthed 299 studies worldwide published between 1971 and 1995 that dealt with service contracting. One hundred twenty-nine of these proved suitable for analysis (that is, they presented empirical findings, published between 1976 and 1995). Sixty-six percent of these 129 analyses dealt with the United States, followed by Britain (16 percent), Australia (11 percent), and Canada (3 percent); 58 percent analyzed local governments, 18 percent studied state governments, and 7 percent addressed federal governments.

Other reviews of empirical research focus exclusively on American local governments, and their basic findings do not deviate from Hodge's. See, for example, George A. Boyne, "Bureaucratic Theory Meets Reality: Public Choice and Service Contracting in U.S. Local Government," *Public Administration Review* 58 (November/December 1998), pp. 474–484, and E. S. Savas, "Policy Analysis for Local Government:

Public vs. Private Refuse Collection," *Policy Analysis* 3 (Winter 1977), pp. 49–74.

176. Hodge, *Privatization,* p. 155. These percentages are "mostly from local government, mostly U.S. in origin."

177. Ecorse is, in fact, the only government to be placed into receivership by court order. Washington, DC, however, shares Ecorse's distinction of having effectively been placed into receivership, but not by order of the court. In 1995, Congress passed Public Law 104–8, which established the District of Columbia Financial Responsibility and Management Assistance Authority (known as the D.C. Control Board), which oversaw the District, emasculated the Home Rule Act of 1974, and transferred almost all fiscal authority from the mayor and council to the authority, its chief financial officer, and its inspector general. In 2001, as stipulated in the 1995 legislation, the board self-terminated because the District had shown a balanced budget over the preceding five years.

178. Robert T. Kleiman and Anandi P. Sahu, "Privatization as a Viable Alternative for Local Governments: The Case of a Failed Michigan Town," in *Contracting Out Government Services*, p. 163.

179. Donohue, *The Privatization Decision*, p. 131. Emphasis is original.

180. Fernandez and Rainey, "Local Government Contract Management and Performance Survey," pp. 3–4. Figure is for 2003–2004.

181. Office of Management and Budget study, as cited in David Perera, "OMB: Competitive Sourcing Spends $1 to Save $20," *Federal Computer Week* (September 27, 2005), http://www.fcw.com.

182. Susan A. MacManus, "Why Businesses are Reluctant to Sell to Governments," *Public Administration Review* 51 (July/August 1991), p. 334. Other negative views of business people about doing business with county governments included slow payment of bills (the top ranked), communication difficulties, bid specifications, and excessive paperwork.

183. Sebastian Mallaby, "The Democracy Trap," *Washington Post* (April 25, 2005).

184. Jacques Gansler, *Moving Toward Market-Based Government: The Changing Role of Government as the Provider*, 2nd ed. Series in Market-Based Government (Washington, DC: IBM Center for the Business of Government, 2004). Figures are for 1975–1993 and 1994–2001. See also Christopher M. Snyder, Robert P. Trost, and R. Derek Trunkey, "Bidding Behavior in the Department of Defense's Commercial Activities Competitions," *Journal of Policy Analysis and Management* 20 (Winter 2001), p. 37.

185. Gansler, *Moving Toward Market-Based Government*.

186. Executive Office of the President, Office of Management and Budget, *Competitive Sourcing: Report on Competitive Sourcing Results, Fiscal Year 2003 and 2004* (Washington, DC: U.S. Government Printing Office, 2004), pp. 10, 11, 15. In 2003 and 2004, annualized gross savings averaged $522 million. It was only in FY 2004 that Congress first required all agencies to report annually on their competitive sourcing efforts.

Section 647 (b) of the Transportation, Treasury, and Independent Agencies Appropriations Act of 2004 enacted this government-wide policy, known as the "Section 647 reporting requirement." Agencies must report the number of competitions, the number of federal employees studied under the competitions, incremental costs, and savings, among other items.

187. In 1981–1987, contractors won 55 percent of the competitions in civilian agencies. See U.S. Office of Management and Budget, *Budget of the United States Government, Fiscal Year 1990* (Washington, DC: U.S. Government Printing Office, 1989), pp. 3-118–3-119. The Pentagon displayed quite comparable rates. See Gansler and Lucysanhyn, *Competitive Sourcing*, p.6.

188. Executive of the President, Office of Management and Budget, *Competitive Sourcing: Report on Competitive Sourcing Results, Fiscal Year 2003 and 2004*, p. 8. In 2004, it was determined that in-house organizations would provide the service in 91 percent of the competitions, which is "about the same" as that reported in 2003.

189. Federal studies as cited in Executive Office of the President, Office of Management and Budget, *Competitive Sourcing: Conducting Public–Private Competition in a Reasoned and Responsible Manner* (Washington, DC: U.S. Government Printing Office, July 2003), p. 2, and Gansler and Lucyshyn, *Competitive Sourcing*, p. 6.

190. Ward, "Exploring Unintended Consequences of Privatization, 1979 to 1999," p. 3. An estimated 5 to 7 percent of local government jobs are lost to privatization.

191. Robin A. Johnson and Norman Walzer, "Privatization and Managed Competition: Managed Fad or Long-Term Systematic Change for Cities?" in *Local Government Innovation*, p. 182. Figure is for 1997.

192. See, for example, Walter J. Primeaux, "An Assessment of Efficiency Gained through Competition," *Review of Economics and Statistics* 59 (February 1977), pp. 105–113; Dilger, Moffitt, and Struyk, "Privatization of Municipal Services in America's Largest Cities," p. 24; Jim Flanagan and Susan Perkins, "Public/Private Competition in the City of Phoenix, Arizona," *Government to Finance Review* 11 (June 1995), pp. 7–12; and Rowan Miranda and Allan Lerner, "Bureaucracy, Organizational Redundancy, and the Privatization of Public Services," *Public Administration Review* 55 (March/April 1995), pp. 193–200.

193. U.S. General Accounting Office, *Competitive Contracting: The Understandability of FAIR Act Inventories Was Limited*, GAO/GGD–00–68 (Washington, DC: U.S. Government Printing Office, 2000), p. 5.

194. Hodges, *Privatization*, p. 119. As noted earlier, this is an analysis of global studies of privatization, but two-thirds are U.S. studies and over half are of local governments.

195. Herbert A. Simon, "Why Public Administration?" *Journal of Public Administration Research & Theory* 8 (Winter 1998), p. 11.

196. Unless noted otherwise, this discussion is based on Seidenstat, "Theory and Practice of Contracting Out in the United States," pp. 18–20.

197. For a couple of clear, brief explanations of activity-based costing, see L. Martin, "How to Compare Costs between In-House and Contracted Services," in Colorado Municipal League, *Public Private Cooperation* (Denver, CO: Author, 1994), pp. 24–37, and "Introduction to Activity-Based Costing," *IQ Service Report* 30 (February 1998). For a more thorough explanation, see Gary Cokins, *Activity-Based Cost Management in Government* (Vienna, VA: Management Concepts, 2002).

198. Jocelyn M. Johnson, Barbara S. Romzek, and Curtis H. Wood, "The Challenges of Contracting and Accountability across the Federal System: From Ambulances to Space Shuttles," *Publius* 34 (Summer 2004), pp. 155–175. This was a study of six contracting cases, two each for the federal, state, and local governments. These issues are not confined to the United States but are international in scope. Interviews and surveys of 1,164 "front-line officials" in Australia, the Netherlands, New Zealand, and the United Kingdom uncovered similar problems of contract management and accountability. See Mark Considine, "The End of the Line? Accountable Governance in the Age of Networks, Partnerships, and Joined-Up Services," *Governance* 15 (January 2002), pp. 21–41.

199. E. S. Savas, *Privatization and Public–Private Partnerships* (New York: Chatham House, 2000), p. 11, and Branko Milanovic, *Liberalization and Entrepreneurship: Dynamics of Reform in Socialism and Capitalism* (Armonk, NY: M. E. Sharpe, 1989), pp. 15, 20. These researchers are not including Washington's government-sponsored enterprises in their tally of state-owned businesses in the United States. As we explain in the text, these enterprises technically and officially are classified as private-sector corporations. However, they do share many characteristics of government corporations.

200. Mitchell, *The American Experiment with Government Corporations* (Armonk, NY: M.E. Sharpe, 1998), p. 19.

201. This list is drawn from the following sources: Jerry Mitchell, "The Policy Activities of Public Authorities," *Policy Studies Journal* 18 (Summer 1990), pp. 928–942, and U.S. Bureau of the Census, *Census of Governments, 2002*, Vol. 1, No. 1 (Washington, DC: U.S. Government Printing Office, 2002).

202. Robert W. Poole Jr., *Revitalizing State and Local Infrastructure: Empowering Cities and States to Tap Private Capital and Rebuild America*. Policy Study No. 190 (Washington, DC: Reason Public Policy Institute, 1995), pp. 3–4, and Mitchell Denning and David J. Olson, "Public Enterprise and the Emerging Character of State Service Provisions," paper presented at the Annual Meeting of the American Political Science Association, New York, September 3–5, 1981, pp. 6, 9.

203. Harry S. Truman, *Budget Message*. House Document No. 19, 80th Congress, 1st Session (Washington, DC: U.S. Government Printing Office, 1948), pp. M57–M61.

204. Ronald C. Moe, "The Emerging Federal Quasi Government: Issues of Management and Accountability," *Public Administration Review* 61 (May/June 2001), pp. 290–312. Although most of the federal corporations that were perceived as competing with business were dismantled during the 1950s, Washington has since created a number of less commercially threatening (and smaller) public authorities and "hybrid organizations" that are not quite public authorities. Among the better known of these obscure organizations are the thirty-nine federally funded research and development centers. These are agency-created and owned nonprofit organizations that conduct research for the feds. Other agency-related nonprofit corporations are under the direct control of the agency, such as the Department of Agriculture's National Pork Board. Others voluntarily affiliate with agencies as "adjunct organizations" and are recognized as such by federal statute, such as the Interior Department's National Park Foundation. Venture capital funds constitute one of the newer forms. These are private, nonprofit corporations created by Congress and funded by federal appropriations; most of them are authorized by the Support for Eastern European Democracy Act of 1999. There are others, and they are multiplying. Although the Government Corporation Control Act of 1945 prohibits agencies from creating government corporations without explicit Congressional authorization, agencies are doing so. An example is the Federal Asset Disposition Association, created in 1995 by the Federal Savings and Loan Insurance Corporation.

205. Harold Siedman, *Politics, Position, and Power: The Dynamics of Federal Organization*, 3rd ed. (New York: Oxford University Press, 1980), p. 238; Walsh, *The Public's Business*; U.S. General Accounting Office, *Congress Should Consider Revising Basic Corporate Control Laws*, GAO/PAD–83–3 (Washington, DC: U.S. Government Printing Office, 1983); National Academy of Public Administration, *Report on Government Corporations* (Washington, DC: Author, 1981); Congressional Research Service, *Administering Public Functions at the Margin of Government: The Case of Federal Corporations*, CSR Report 83–236 (Washington, DC: Author, 1993); and Denning and Olson, "Public Enterprise and the Emerging Character of State Service Provisions." Siedman's count of eighteen federal corporations is the lowest, but none are high. Walsh lists nineteen federal corporations; the Congressional Research Service located thirty-one; the National Academy of Public Administration found thirty-five; the GAO concluded that there are forty-seven; and Denning and Olson unearthed fifty-eight.

206. U.S. General Accounting Office, *Government Corporations: Profiles of Existing Government Corporations*, GAO/GGD–96–14 (Washington, DC: U.S. Government Printing Office, 1995), p. 2.

207. Ibid., and National Academy of Public Administration, *Report on Government Corporations*.

208. U.S. General Accounting Office, *Government Corporations: Profiles of Existing Government Corporations*, p. 6.

209. U.S. Office of Management and Budget, *Special Analyses: Budget of the United States Government, Fiscal Year 1990* (Washington, DC: U.S. Government Printing Office, 1989), p. F-21.

210. U.S. Office of Management and Budget, "Government-Sponsored Enterprises," *Budget of United States, Fiscal Year 2007* (Washington DC: U.S. Government Printing Office, 2006), pp. 1229–1234. Figure is for 2006. The five government-sponsored enterprises, in order of their congressional chartering, are as follows.

The institutions of the Farm Credit System (FCS) was founded in 1916. Its mission is to provide privately financed credit to rural areas. The institutions comprising the FCS are the Agricultural Credit Bank, the Farm Credit Banks, and direct lender associations. They are regulated by the Farm Credit Administration (FCA), an independent federal agency.

The Federal Home Loan Bank System, comprised of twelve Federal Loan Banks known as FHLBanks, was chartered in 1932. FHLBanks facilitate the extension of credit to more than 8,000 member banks and other financial institutions. It is regulated by the Federal Housing Finance Board.

The Federal National Mortgage Association (Fannie Mae, 1938), and the Federal Home Loan Mortgage Corporation (Freddie Mac, 1970); details on both are provided in the text.

The Federal Agricultural Mortgage Corporation (Farmer Mac), founded in 1988, facilitates mortgages for farms and rural homes. It is supervised by the FCA.

Until 2006, the Student Loan Marketing Association (Sallie Mae, chartered in 1972) was a publicly traded GSE that facilitated loans to students. In that year, it was loosed from federal strings and now functions as as more fully privatized entity.

211. U.S. General Accounting Office, *Government-Sponsored Enterprises: A Framework for Strengthening GSE Governance and Oversight*, GAO–04–269T (Washington, DC: U.S. Government Printing Office, 2004), p. 1. GSEs had more than $6.8 trillion in obligation in 2004.

212. Ibid, p. 4, and Daniel Gross "Sallie Mae Sallies Forth," *Slate* (August 27, 2002). Fannie Mae, Freddie Mac, and Farmer Mac are publicly traded. The remaining GSEs are member-owned cooperatives.

213. Data gathered by PoliticalMoneyLine, as cited in Charles R. Babcock, "Mortgage Giants Stir Congress," *Washington Post* (July 11, 2003). In 2001–2002, Freddie Mac, at more than $4 milllion, was the largest corporate contributor of unlimited "soft-money" donations to the political parties.

214. As derived from data in U.S. General Accounting Office, *Government-Sponsored Enterprises: A Framework for Strengthening GSE Governance and Oversight*, p. 4, and U.S. Bureau of the Census, *Statistical Abstract of the United States, 1995*, 115th ed. (Washington, DC: U.S. Government Printing Office, 1995), Table 529. In 2003, they accounted for 81 percent of all GSE financial obligations, and in 1991 they accounted for 83 percent all GSE securities and guarantees outstanding.

215. Jonathan G. S. Koppell, "Hybrid Organizations and the Alignment of Interests: The Case of Fannie Mae and Freddie Mac," *Pubic Administration Review* 61 (July/August 2001), p. 469.

216. "How Fannie and Freddie Make Their Money," *Wall Street Journal* (May 3, 2004). In 2003, the two GSEs held or guaranteed over 47 percent of all residential mortgages in the U.S.

217. Mitchell, "The Policy Activities of Public Authorities," pp. 928–942. Figures are for 1989. Mitchell examined government reports, mailing lists from public agencies and professional associations, identified organizations that issue revenue bonds, and obtained the reports of more than 300 "likely public authorities." He uncovered 6,352 state and local public authorities (and forty-five federal ones) in the United States.

218. Jerry Mitchell, "Education and Skills for Public Authority Management," *Public Administration Review* 51 (September/October 1991), p. 436.

219. Annmarie Hauk Walsh concludes that there are from 5,000 to 7,000 public authorities, a number which excludes authorities that are not organizationally independent of government agencies. Donald Axelrod, using, more or less, Walsh's criteria, pegs the number at around 6,000, as does Jerry Mitchell, who, with impressive precision, states that there are 6,352. Later Walsh, with David Mammen, says that there are about 10,000 public authorities. But Charles E. Lindblom contends that if those public corporations are counted which are authorized to issue general obligation bonds, the number jumps to around 18,000. See: Walsh, *The Public's Business*, p. 5; Mitchell, "Education and Skills for Public Authority Management," p. 436; Charles E. Lindblom, *Politics and Markets: The World's Political Economic Systems* (New York: Basic Books, 1977), p. 114; Annmarie Hauk Walsh and David Mammen, *State Public Corporations: A Guide for Decision Making* (New York: Institute for Public Administration, 1983); and Donald Axelrod, *A Budget Quartet: Critical Policy and Management Issues* (New York: St. Martin's Press, 1989), p. 28.

220. For example, many seaport authorities, which the Census Bureau classifies as special districts, were created by legislatures rather than by voters. See Mitchell, *The American Experiment with Government Corporations*, p. 29.

221. James Leigland, "The Census Bureau's Role in Research on Special Districts: A Critique," *Western Political Quarterly* 43 (June 1990), pp. 362–380.

222. In terms of governing, in almost half of special districts, the board members are not elected, but appointed, and this proportion is growing over time. *Sources:* As derived from data in U.S. Bureau of the Census, *Census of Governments, 1992*, Vol. 1, No. 2, *Popularly Elected Officials* (Washington, DC: U.S. Government Printing Office, 1995), p. 19, and U.S. Bureau of the Census, *Census of Governments, 1977*, Vol. 1, No. 2, *Popularly Elected Officials* (Washington DC: U.S. Government Printing Office, 1978), p. 10.

In terms of financing, less than half of special districts are even permitted to levy taxes, and their main source of revenue, by far, is not taxes, but user fees. User fees, such as charges for water, recreation, or public housing, account for nearly two-fifths of special districts' income; for every one dollar that special districts collect in taxes, they haul in almost four dollars in user fees. *Source:* As derived from data in U.S. Bureau of the Census, *Census of Governments, 2002*, Vol. 4, No. 2, *Finances of Special Districts* (Washington, DC: U.S. Government Printing Office, 2004), Table 2.

Compounding this confusion is that many public authorities and special districts mix these criteria, having appointed boards and taxpayer funding, or elected boards and are self-financing.

223. Mitchell, *The American Experiment with Government Corporations*, p. 14.

224. Walsh, *The Public's Business*, p. 290. Unless noted otherwise, the following discussion is drawn from this source.

225. Mitchell, *The American Experiment with Government Corporations*, p. 27.

226. It is not widely known, but Congress does not exempt certain kinds of municipal bond issues from federal taxes on the grounds that the activities they fund do not provide a significant benefit to the public. For example, bond issues for investor-led housing, local sports facilities, refunding a refunded issue, and funding a local government's underfunded pension plan are not exempt from federal taxation.

227. Denning and Olson, "Public Enterprise and the Emerging Character of State Service Provisions," pp. 6, 9.

228. Walsh, *The Public's Business*, p. 6.

229. As derived from data in U.S. Bureau of the Census, *Statistical Abstract of the United States, 2006*, Table 434. Datum is for 2002 and refers to issues of long-term state and local government securities issued by districts, local authorities, and state authorities.

230. Sometimes it is good to define basics, and, although we assume that most readers know what a *bond* is, here is its definition: a certificate of ownership of a specified portion of a debt due to be paid by a government or corporation to an individual holder and usually bearing a fixed rate of interest.

231. Some states exempt from taxation only those municipal bonds issued by them or their local governments, but not the bonds issued in other states.

232. As derived from data in U.S. Bureau of the Census, *Statistical Abstract of the United States, 1992*, 112th ed. (Washington, DC: U.S. Government Printing Office, 1992), Table 458. In 1970, revenue bonds accounted for 34 percent of bond sales.

233. As derived from data in U.S. Bureau of the Census, *Statistical Abstract of the United States, 2006*, Table 434. In 2002, revenue bonds accounted for 65 percent of all municipal bond sales, and in 1985 for 80 percent.

234. As derived from data in U.S. Bureau of the Census, *Statistical Abstract of the United States, 1992*, Table 458. Refers to issues of long-term state and local government securities issued by special districts and statutory authorities. In 1970, 31 percent of long-term state and local debt was attributable to these entities. Fifteen years earlier, the figure was much the same—28 percent in 1955—indicating the stability of the public authority's role until 1970.

235. As derived from data in U.S. Bureau of the Census, *Statistical Abstract of the United States, 2006*, Table 434. Refers to issues of long-term state and local government securities issued by districts, local authorities, and state authorities. In 2002, over 67 percent of long-term state and local debt was attributable to these entities.

236. Walsh, *The Public's Business*, p. 289.

237. U.S. General Accounting Office, *Government Corporations: Profiles of Existing Government Corporations*, pp. 2–3.

238. Harold Siedman, "United States Experience: The Need to Reassert the Government Corporation Control Act of 1945," *Public Administration and Development* 18 (August 1998), p. 297.

239. The following discussion is drawn from ibid., pp. 295–299.

240. Walsh, *The Public's Business*, p. 6.

241. Ibid.

242. George L. Shepard, "Let There Be Light: The SEC's New Regulations for the Municipal Securities Market," *Public Budgeting and Finance* 16 (Summer 1996), pp. 133–141. The author notes that monies have been "regulated less strictly than other security markets" (p. 133). There are some limited signs that the federal government is tightening up on its lax regulation of the muni market. See ibid; and "Focus on Municipal Bonds: The Audit Age," *Governing* (May 1998), pp. 57–58, for details.

243. Diane Kittorwer, "A Mini Market Slowdown," *Governing* (November 2000), p. 86.

244. John Carver, *Boards That Make a Difference* (San Francisco: Jossey-Bass, 1990); Joel Sokloff, *Handbook for Commissioners* (Washington, DC: National Association of Housing and Redevelopment Officials, 1980); and Mitchell, *The American Experiment with Government Corporations*, p. 95.

245. The Census Bureau reports that special districts, many of which, as we have explained, are likely public authorities, have a board membership averaging five members, 52 percent of whom are elected and the remainder are appointed. But the percentage of appointed board members is rising over time at the expense of elected board members. See U.S. Bureau of the Census, *Census of Governments, 1992*, p. 19.

246. Nancy Burns, *The Formation of American Local Governments: Private Values in Public Institutions* (New York: Oxford University Press, 1994), pp. 12–13.

247. Ibid, p. 12. Burns is referring to special districts, but it is highly unlikely that they differ much in this regard with public authorities.

248. Michael A. Molloy, "Local Special Districts and Public Accountability," paper presented at the Annual Meeting of the Midwest Political Science Association, Chicago, 2000.

249. Nicholas Bauroth, "The Influence of Elections on Special District Revenue Policies: Special Democracies or Automatons of the State?" *State and Local Government Review* 37 (3, 2005), pp.193–205.

250. Donald T. Wells and Richard Scheff, "Performance Issues for Public Authorities in Georgia," in *Public Authorities and Public Policy: The Business of Government*, Jerry Mitchell, ed. (New York: Praeger, 1992), p. 172. Ninety-five public authorities in Georgia were examined.

251. Mitchell, "Education and Skills for Public Authority Management," pp. 429–437. Mitchell surveyed 6,352 public authorities in 1990 and obtained a response rate of 60 percent.

252. Ibid. and Tari Renner, "Appointed Local Government Managers: Stability and Change," *Municipal Year Book, 1990* (Washington, DC: International City Management Association, 1990), pp. 30–35. The Renner survey was conducted in 1989. Authority executives had tenures of nearly eight years, compared to over five for city managers.

253. Mitchell, "Education and Skills for Public Authority Management," and Victor S. De Santis and Charldean Newell, "Local Government Managers' Career Paths," *Municipal Year Book, 1996* (Washington, DC: International City Management Association, 1996), p. 5. The De Santis and Newell survey was conducted in 1994. Eighteen percent of authority executives had not completed college, compared to 4 percent of local government managers.

254. Ibid. (both citations). Only 38 percent of authority executives had been previously employed by an authority compared to 100 percent of city managers who had worked for a city.

255. Mitchell, "Education and Skills for Public Authority Management," pp. 434–435.

256. Wells and Scheff, "Performance Issues for Public Authorities in Georgia," pp. 174–175. Of the questionnaire's ten items comparing public authorities to general-purpose governments, this was the only area of agreement between the two sets of administrators, although they came close to agreeing that public authorities could hire specialized personnel more easily. Authority executives and city and county managers disagreed, often strongly, on everything else, such as which type of government cost less and performed better, with pluralities or majorities in each group responding that its type of government was superior to the other. Forty-two authority directors and city and county managers responded to this portion of the survey.

257. Kathryn A. Foster, *The Political Economy of Special-Purpose Governments* (Washington, DC: Georgetown University Press, 1997).

258. James Leighland and Robert Lamb, *WPPSS: Who Is to Blame for the WPPSS Disaster* (Boston: Ballinger, 1986); Burns, *The Formation of American Local Governments*; and Walsh, *The Public's Business*.

259. Robert A. Caro, *The Power Broker: Robert Moses and the Fall of New York* (New York: Knopf, 1974). We detail some of Moses's power at the conclusion of this book.

260. Walsh, *The Public's Business*, p. 4.

261. The following examples are drawn from Mitchell, *The American Experiment with Government Corporations*, pp. 96, 107, 116, and 117, respectively. Mitchell presents a plethora from which to draw, and these are but a small sampling.

262. Ibid., p. 108. The U.S. Department of Housing and Urban Development began taking over public housing from local public authorities and began managing them directly in the 1990s, focusing on housing projects in Chicago (all of them), San Francisco (all of them), Washington, Baltimore, Newark, Louisville, and other cities. By any standard, these government corporations managed public housing with astounding incompetence, as the U.S. Secretary of Housing and Urban Development learned when, while touring public housing in San Francisco, he happened upon a drug deal! For additional examples, see Carey Goldberg, "San Francisco Housing Authority Serves as Model of Decay," *New York Times* (May 24, 1996); Katherine Boo, "Misery's New Landlord," *Washington Post* (October 18, 1996); and Sharon Cohen, "Unlivable Public Housing Being Razed to Make Way for New Homes, Hopes," *Chicago Tribune* (April 12, 1996).

263. Mitchell, *The American Experiment with Government Corporations*, pp. 112–127; Donald Axelrod, *Shadow Government: The Hidden World of Public Authorities—and How They Control Over $1 Trillion of Your Money* (New York: Wiley, 1992); and Diana Henriques, *The Machinery of Greed: Public Authority Abuse and What to Do About It* (Lexington, MA: Lexington Books, 1986).

264. American Association of Retired Persons survey, as cited in American Society of Association Executives, *Why Are Associations So Important?* http://www.asaenet.org, and Lester K. Salamon, *America's Nonprofit Sector: A Primer*, 2nd ed. (New York: The Foundation Center, 1999), p. 22.

265. Salamon, *America's Nonprofit Sector*, p. 22. Figures are for 1996. The GAO states that there were "over 1.5 million tax-exempt entities" in 2003, two-thirds (over 960,000) of which were "charities." See U.S. Government Accountability Office, *Tax-Exempt Sector: Governance, Transparency, and Oversight Are Critical for Maintaining Public Trust*, GAO–05–561T (Washington, DC: U.S. Government Printing Office, 2005), p. 5.

266. U.S. Government Accountability Office, *Tax-Exempt Sector*, Section 503 (c) of the Internal Revenue Code specifies twenty-eight types of entities that are eligible for tax exempt status; over 1.5 million were exempt in 2003.

267. Ibid, p. 10. Figure is for 2002. Salamon, in *America's Nonprofit Sector*, p. 22, using a slightly narrower definition of the nonprofit sector that excludes such entities as armed forces insurance organizations established before 1880, states that the nonprofit sector accounted for 7 percent of total paid employment in 1995.

268. Independent Sector, *Employment in the Nonprofit Sector* (Washington, DC: Author, 2004). Between 1997 and 2001, nonprofit employment grew at an annual rate of 2.5 percent, the private sector grew by 1.8 percent annually, and the public sector grew by 1.6 percent.

269. Salamon, *America's Nonprofit Sector*, p. 22. Figures are for 1995–1996.
270. U.S. General Accountability Office, *Tax-Exempt Sector,* p. 9. Figures are for 1998–2002. Other analysts, using a somewhat narrower scope of the tax-exempt sector that excludes such entities as black-lung benefit trusts and cemetery companies, place the nonprofit sector's share of the economy at less than 9 percent in 1996. See Salamon, *America's Nonprofit Sector*, p. 22.
271. Salamon, *America's Nonprofit Sector*, p. 36.
272. Lester M. Salamon, *The Resilient Sector: The State of Nonprofit America* (Washington, DC: Brookings, 2003), p. 52.
273. Salamon, *America's Nonprofit Sector*, p. 55.
274. Peter Dobkin Hall, as quoted in Stanley Meisler, "Thinking Locally Spreads Globally," *Los Angeles Times* (June 13, 1995). Hall is an expert on nonprofit organizations.
275. Salamon, *The Resilient Sector*, p. 54. Figures are for 1997.
276. Lester M. Salamon, "Government and the Voluntary Sector in an Era of Retrenchment: The American Experience," *Journal of Public Policy 6 (January–March 1986)*, p. 7. Figures are for 1982.
277. Alan J. Abramson, Lester J. Salamon, and C. Eugene Steuerle, "The Nonprofit Sector and the Federal Budget: Recent History and Future Directors," in *Nonprofit and Government: Collaboration and Conflict*, Elizabeth T. Boris and C. Eugene's Steuerle, eds (Washington, DC: Urban Institute Press, 1999), p. 100.
278. Michael Lipsey and Steven Rathgeb Smith, "Nonprofit Organizations, Government, and the Welfare State," *Political Science Quarterly* 104 (Spring 1990), pp. 625–648. See also Lester M. Salamon, "Partners in Public Service: The Scope and Theory of Government-Nonprofit Relations," in Walter W. Powell, ed., *The Nonprofit Sector: A Research Handbook* (New Haven, CT: Yale, 1987), pp. 293–321. In 1980, Washington channeled 52 percent of its social services dollars, and 32 percent of its training and employment expenditures, to nonprofits.
279. As derived from data in Choi, Cho, Wright, and Brudney, "Dimensions of Contracting for Service Delivery by American State Administrative Agencies," p. 50. Figure, 51 percent, is for 1998.
280. Chi and Jasper, *Private Practices*, p. 14. Figure is for 1997.
281. U.S. General Accounting Office, *Welfare Reform: Interim Report on Potential Ways to Strengthen Federal Oversight of State and Local Contracting*, GAO–02–245 (Washington, DC: U.S. Government Printing Office, 2002). Figure is for 2001. The remaining 12 percent goes to for-profit corporations. Only South Dakota did not contract these services.
282. Warner and Hefetz, "Pragmatism over Politics," p. 11.

283. As derived from data in Hatry and Valente, "Alternative Service Delivery Approaches Involving Increased Use of the Private Sector," pp. 216–217.
284. Warner and Hefetz, "Pragmatism over Politics," p. 11. Specific services listed are for 2002.
285. Salamon, "Government and the Voluntary Sector in an Era of Retrenchment," p. 7.
286. Judith R. Saidel, "Resource Interdependence: The Relationship Between State Agencies and Nonprofit Organizations," *Public Administration Review* 51 (November/December 1991), p. 546.
287. David M. Van Syke, "The Mythology of Privatization in Contracting for Social Services," *Public Administration Review* 63 (May/June 2003), pp. 296–315. The quotations are on p. 298. The author conducted his own research as part of this article, and found that social services contracting among public and nonprofit managers in New York state was characterized by an absence of competition and low public-management capacity.
288. John C. Green and Amy L. Sherman, *Fruitful Collaborations: A Survey of Government-Funded Faith-Based Programs in 15 States* (Akron, OH: Bliss Institute, University of Akron; and Indianapolis, IN: Hudson Institute, 2002). Data are for 2002.
289. Barbara S. Romzek and Jocelyn M. Johnston, "State Social Services Contracting: Exploring the Determinants of Effective Contract Accountability," *Public Administration Review* 65 (July/August 2005), pp. 436–449. The quotation is on p. 436.
290. Carolyn J. Heinrich, "Organizational Form and Performance: An Empirical Investigation of Nonprofit and For-Profit Job-Training Service Providers," *Journal of Policy Analysis and Management* 19 (Spring 2000), pp. 233–261. See also Kristen Gronsberg, "Poverty and Nonprofit Organization Behavior," *Social Science Review* 64 (June 1990), pp. 208–241.
291. Burton D. Weisbrod, "The Future of the Nonprofit Sector: Its Entwining with Private Enterprise and Government," *Journal of Policy Analysis and Management* 16 (Summer 1997), p. 543.
292. Melissa Middleton Stone, Mark A. Hager, and Jennifer J. Griffin, "Organizational Characteristics and Funding Environments: A Study of a Population of United Way-Affiliated Nonprofits," *Public Administration Review* 61 (May/June 2001), pp. 276–289.
293. Brookings Institution, as cited in Partnership for Public Service, *Public Opinion and Public Service*, p. 6. Figures are for 1998.
294. Brookings Institution as cited in ibid. Figures are for 2002.
295. Princeton Survey Research Associates and the Brookings Institution, *Health of the Public Service* (Washington, DC: Authors, 2001). Figures are for 2001.

CHAPTER **12**

Intergovernmental Administration

Domestic public policy is implemented not merely by government, but by governments. The administration of a "single" public policy often involves a pastiche of funding sources and public administrators interacting through all levels of government, and the field of public administration calls this pastiche *intergovernmental relations*, or the series of financial, legal, political, and administrative relationships established among all units of government that possess varying degrees of authority and jurisdictional autonomy. These relationships are called *federalism* when applied more narrowly to the federal government's relations with state governments, and the states' relationships with each other, although, in this book, we usually use these terms interchangeably. *Intergovernmental administration*, sometimes called *intergovernmental management*, is the management and coordination of the relationships among governments for the purpose of achieving specific policy goals.[1]

Thousands and Thousands of Governments

Relations among American governments are extraordinarily complex—hardly surprising when we consider the enormous number of governments

thriving in the United States. Table 12-1 identifies the 87,507 governments in the United States by type and indicates their fluctuations in twenty-year increments since 1942, when the first census of governments was taken.

Most of the proliferation of municipalities occurred in the years following World War II, particularly around the fringes of big cities, and was largely due to unplanned metropolitan growth. For instance, a village near Minneapolis was incorporated for the single purpose of issuing a liquor license. Bryan City, California, was created so that a circus owner could zone for animal populations as he saw fit. The town of New Squier, New York, was established so that a kosher slaughterhouse could be operated. Gardena, California, was founded so that its residents might play poker legally.[2]

Other types of local governments are changing, too. Educators, convinced that they could save money by implementing economies of scale, began consolidating school districts in the 1930s, reducing their proportion of all types of local governments from the greatest number of local governments to the second smallest over fifty-five years. (The 3,034 counties have always occupied the slot reserved for the lowest number of local governments.) This reduction was offset by the growth of special districts, which rose from the second smallest proportion of all governmental types to the largest over the same period.

Table 12-1   Number of Governmental Units, by Type: 1942, 1962, 1982, and 2002

Type of Government	1942	1962	1982	2002
Total	155,116	91,237	81,831	87,900
U.S. government	1	1	1	1
State governments	48	50	50	50
Local governments	155,067	91,186	81,780	87,849
Counties	3,050	3,043	3,041	3,034
Municipalities	16,220	18,000	19,076	19,431
Townships	18,919	17,142	16,734	16,506
School districts	108,579	34,678	14,851	13,522
Special districts	8,299	18,323	28,078	35,356

Source: U.S. Bureau of the Census, *Statistical Abstract of the United States, 2006,* 125th ed. (Washington, DC: U.S. Government Printing Office, 2006), Table 415.

The Constitution and the Courts: Setting the Rules

How these thousands of American governments act and react to each other is based on broad rules of the game set by the Constitution and court decisions.[3]

Distinct National and State Responsibilities

Section 8 of Article I of the Constitution is instrumental in making distinctions between national and state responsibilities. It delegates seventeen specific powers to the national government, including defense, general welfare, and commerce, and leaves the remaining powers to the states. These remaining powers are now known as "reserved powers," a phrase taken from the Tenth Amendment, which was added rather hastily by the Founders in response to such populist rabble-rousers as Patrick Henry. The Tenth Amendment was designed to grant the states a more visible and defined territory for exercising their powers. Section 9 of Article I also dealt with state and federal responsibilities by preventing the national government from doing certain things, such as suspending the writ of *habeas corpus*, and also forbidding the states from doing certain things, such as entering into treaties with foreign nations and coining money.

Separate National and State Identities

The second area of constitutional federalism deals with establishing and maintaining the separate identities between the nation and the states. For the nation, perhaps the most significant statement is in Article VI: "This Constitution and the Laws of the United States . . . shall be the Supreme Law of the Land." The most important clause for the states is Section 2, Article IV, which stipulates that "no new States shall be Formed or Erected within the jurisdiction of any other State; nor any State be formed by the junction of two or more States, or Parts of States, without the Consent of the Legislature of the States concerned."

Integrating Nation and States

Finally, the Constitution deals with the integration of the national and state governments, primarily by providing for cooperation among them in the performance of certain functions. For example, the states and the nation cooperate in amending the Constitution and electing a president. Congress, in effect, is an assembly of national officials who have vital linkages with the states, and this, too, is politically integrating. This arrangement, of course, was designed by the founders, who were leery of according too much power to the new national government. As James Madison noted in *The Federalist*, "a local spirit will infallibly prevail much more in the members of Congress than a national spirit will prevail in the Legislatures of the particular states."[4]

Necessary and Proper Implied Powers

These three major features of the relations between the state governments and the national government—distinct responsibilities, separate identities, and national and state integration—were refined by the courts over time. Without question, the most influential single case in this process of refinement was *McCulloch* v. *Maryland*, which was settled by the Supreme Court under Chief Justice John Marshall in 1819.

Marshall and his colleagues supported the expansion of national powers under the commerce clause of the Constitution (that is, the final sentence of Section 8, Article I), which gave the national government a powerful ability to interpret what was "necessary and proper" in the way of making policy under the Constitution.

The case involved the state of Maryland's attempt to tax the second United States Bank, which was located in Maryland, but soon waxed into an argument over whether the United States could even form a bank. Alexander Hamilton, as secretary of the treasury, had proposed a national bank and argued that it could be established under a strong national government, which could and should adopt such measures because they were "implied powers" under the Constitution, even though the Constitution did not specifically authorize such policies as the establishment of the bank. The Marshall Court agreed with Hamilton. Hence, Congress had the ability to adopt appropriate measures for the realization of the powers granted to it by the Constitution to do whatever is "necessary and proper to implement its specified functions."

This notion of implied powers is with us today, and, with the exception of the Civil War, remains the single strongest statement of national power as opposed to state power. Table 12-2 lists the principal powers of the federal government and the implied powers of the states.

Table 12-2   The Constitution's Federal Divisions of Powers

Major Powers of the Federal Government

Tax for federal purposes

Borrow on the nation's credit

Regulate foreign and interstate commerce

Provide currency and coinage

Conduct foreign relations and make treaties

Provide an army and navy

Establish and maintain a postal service

Protect patents and copyrights

Regulate weights and measures

Admit new states

"Make all laws which shall be necessary and proper" for the execution of all powers vested in the U.S. government

Major Implied Powers of the States

Tax for local purposes

Borrow on the state's credit

Regulate trade within the state

Make and enforce civil and criminal law

Maintain a police force

Furnish public education

Control local government

Regulate charities

Establish voting and election laws

"Powers not delegated to the United States by the Constitution, nor prohibited by it to the states are reserved to the states respectively, or to the people."

The Evolution of Intergovernmental Administration

Operating within the formal rules of the game established by the Constitution and by subsequent judicial interpretation, localities, states, and the nation have gone through a number of phases in their administrative relationships. We can discern at least four such phases, often overlapping in time, but each possessing its own set of unique characteristics.[5]

The Layer Cake: Dual Federalism, 1789–1930

The Constitution recognizes only two levels of government: national and state. Hence, the terms "dual federalism" and "layer cake federalism," indicating that during the nation's first 140 years, the federal and state governments stuck to their very separate knitting in their very separate spheres of constitutional authority. For example, when Congress in 1854 did try (unusually) to transfer funds to the states to help them treat their indigent insane, the president vetoed the bill on the logic that to encourage the states to "become humble suppliants for the bounty of the Federal Government [would reverse] their true relation to this Union."[6]

With the outbreak of the Civil War in 1861, however, there were some changes in federalist thinking and the nation entered a period of dented dual federalism. From 1865 to 1869, the country (at least the victorious northern half of it) enacted the Thirteenth, Fourteenth, and Fifteenth Amendments to the Constitution. These new civil rights policies legitimized federal involvement in heretofore sacrosanct state affairs, and, at least for a while, Reconstruction implemented this involvement.

The federal judiciary also began to penetrate state sovereignty. Between 1794 and 1860, the Supreme Court voided sixty state laws, or about one per year, on average. Between 1860 and 1937, however, the Court overruled 525 state laws, or nearly seven per year.[7] Dual federalism, if dinged and dented, still survived, but "the pitiful position in 1860 of the national government was ended."[8]

The Marble Cake: Cooperative Federalism, 1930–1960

With the election of Franklin Delano Roosevelt as president in 1932, the layer cake of federalism sagged and whorled into "marble cake federalism." By 1937, the Supreme Court had become enthusiastic over FDR's battle against the economic Depression, and, in its enthusiasm, "the post-1937 Court sanctioned a permanent enlargement in the scope of Federal power."[9] Nation,

states, and localities faced up to the challenges of not only the Depression, but also later those of World War II and the Cold War, as an intergovernmental team.

The Pound Cake: Co-optive Federalism, 1960–1980

In our third phase of federalism, the layer cake briefly reemerged, but the top layer promptly crushed the bottom layers. The federal government grew heavier, more dominant, and more demanding in the intergovernmental construct. Perhaps "pound cake" could serve as our on-going pastry metaphor of federalism during its co-optive phase, because state and local governments were being pounded by Washington.

With the election of John F. Kennedy as president in 1960, federalism was dominated by Washington pragmatists. Problems—many of which festered not in Washington but in subnational jurisdictions—had to be solved, and the federal government was the government to solve them. It did this by hurling money, mandates, and regulations at state capitals and town halls in the form of hundreds of highly discrete and specialized grants programs.

Subnational governments were being bribed, in effect, to implement national goals, as defined by Washington. And, especially, in the 1970s, states and communities were more than willing to pay the regulatory price of federal largesse. As one acerbic observer noted during this period, "if Washington offered grants for cancer implants, cities would line up to apply."[10] By the end of the decade, federal co-optation had replaced intergovernmental cooperation, and state and local governments verged on truly becoming "humble suppliants" of a federal satrap.

The Crumble Cake: Competitive Federalism, 1980–Present

Around 1980, there were signs that the intergovernmental cake was beginning to loosen, and deteriorate, into a "crumble cake." "Competitive Federalism," or "Fend-for-Yourself Federalism," emerged.[11]

Falling Federal Funding. The federal government's fiscal preeminence in the intergovernmental system began to dissipate after 1978, when the federal government's contribution to the finances of state and local governments peaked as a share of their budgets, although Washington continues to regulate subnational governments with enthusiasm.

The feds' withdrawal of their fiscal support of subnational governments has resulted in a situation in which all governments have had to become more innovative and more competitive to deliver services. But "competition" no longer refers to state and local governments competing among themselves for federal grants, as it did during the phase of co-optive federalism. Today, competition means that all governments are competing with each other for revenues, regardless of the source. "The essence of Competitive Federalism is that now Washington policymakers as well as state and local officials must go back, hat-in-hand, to a common source—the nation's taxpayers. . . . Washington does not have the inside track in the emerging intergovernmental race for taxpayer support."[12]

Falling Faith in the Feds. Indeed not. Public opinion polls taken since 1972 show that the federal government steadily slipped (aside from a two-year upsurge following the terrorist attacks of 2001[13]) in the public's perception as the most efficient and effective level of government, relative to state and local governments, from nearly four in ten Americans to fewer than three in ten.[14] With the exception of 2002–2004, following 9/11,[15] state governments, long the butt of American political humor, have commanded more respect from Americans than has the federal government for several years[16] (more than half of the public, in fact, believes that public programs "would get better" if they were shifted from Washington to the state capitals, compared to less than a tenth who think that they would get worse[17]), whereas local governments first surpassed the federal government in Americans' esteem in 1979[18] and have been the level of government in which citizens express the greatest confidence ever since.[19]

More than six out of ten Americans believe that the federal government "has too much power."[20] Two-thirds of Americans feel that devoluting federal programs to state and local governments is "a promising direction for making government work better," and this proportion is growing.[21] As a consequence, federal administrators must compete with state and local administrators as never before to earn the respect and trust of their taxpayers if they are to increase their government's revenues. Fend for yourself.

The States Renascent? Or Ambiguous Federalism?

The long-term, growing respect among Americans for their state governments likely reflects substantive reality, as a variety of studies show that states have made impressive improvements politically and administratively.

The Capable States. The number and variety of tasks that the states do—that is, their policy scope—have expanded enormously over the past half-century. One study found that "state governments were a key force in the growth of the national and local governments" during the final half of the twentieth century,[22] and the number of state agencies, each with a unique policy mission, has doubled since the 1940s.[23]

As we observed in Chapter 9, the quality of public administrators in the states has improved as their responsibilities have expanded. Consequently, state governments are measurably more responsive and capable than they were in the early 1980s;[24] a periodic "report card" on state management accords the states a "B-minus,"[25] a grade that puts state governments on a par with the nation's thirty-five largest and wealthiest cities.[26]

In sum, state governments are doing more things and doing them more ably than ever before.

Congressional Appreciation of State Governments. During the 1990s and early 2000s, these pleasant developments began having an impact not only on the public's perception of the states, but also on the views of the federal policymakers, too.

In 1996, Congress enacted, and the president signed, the Personal Responsibility and Work Opportunity Reconciliation Act, which reversed some sixty years of federal policy by terminating most of the federal government's welfare programs, including its central one, and turned welfare over to the states in the form of a $16.5 billion block grant. The act has been described as "the biggest shift in social policy since the Depression."[27]

Also significant is the fact that Congress, beginning in the 1980s, began reinstating the states as recipients of federal assistance, rather than bypassing the states in favor of giving federal aid directly to local governments. In 1978, only 71 percent of all federal aid went to the states,[28] but today, almost nine out of ten grant dollars flow directly to the states, a proportion that has not been seen since the 1950s, when Cooperative Federalism was in flower.[29]

Judicial Appreciation of State Governments. The most significant change in federal perceptions of state competence, however, was occurring in the judicial branch. In 1995, the Supreme Court, in *United States* v. *Lopez*, reversed nearly six decades of its own constitutional interpretations and held that the Constitution's interstate commerce clause no longer was sufficient justification for inserting the federal government into the affairs of states and communities.

Lopez was followed by a series of five-to-four rulings, all made by the same five justices, that displayed a remarkable "determination to reconfigure the balance between state and federal authority in favor of the states [by] thrusting the doctrine of state sovereignty well beyond existing boundaries."[30] The Court did this by holding that the states had "sovereign immunity" (a phrase not to be found in the Constitution), and therefore states could not be sued in federal or state courts when they violated certain federal laws.[31]

From 2003 to 2005, however, there was a movement by the Court to reassert federal power. In two cases, the Court upheld the right, under certain circumstances, of state employees and the disabled to sue state governments, thereby qualifying its earlier rulings that supported the states' "sovereign immunity" from lawsuits. A third case asserted the power of Congress over the states by allowing the federal government to prosecute people who used marijuana for medical purposes, even in states that permitted such purchase.[32]

In 2006, the Court backtracked somewhat, and ruled that Oregon's Death with Dignity Act of 1994, which authorizes physician-assisted suicide,

was legal in that the U.S. attorney general had overstepped his authority in challenging it. The Court drew short of declaring the act unconstitutional.

Even in light of this mixed bag of decisions, it seems that "the Court has moved not so much to grant more power to the states as to prune back the power of Congress."[33]

Ambiguities. These congressional and judicial trends might indicate that the states are resurfacing as important political and fiscal actors in the intergovernmental system. Despite what has been described as Washington's "devolution revolution," however, the federal government continues "to hold much of the power and significance" it has gained over state and local governments since the 1930s.[34] Some have entitled this condition "ambiguous federalism."[35]

In sketching these phases of federalism, we have relied on some hyperbole as a method of getting the main ideas across. However, exaggeration can be misleading, and it is not our intention to promote what one wag has called, "the Henny Penny School of Federalism,"[36] that is, the notion that the sky of the intergovernmental system is falling, either because of too much or too little federal activity.

Fiscal Federalism

The old question in politics of who gets what, when, where, and how is nowhere more evident than in the intergovernmental money game. This game often is called *fiscal federalism*, or the granting of funds by one government to other governments, usually for the purpose of achieving specific policy goals.

A World Turned Upside Down: A Century of Fiscal Change

The relative economic prominence of each level of government underwent some dramatic alterations during the twentieth century. Most notably, local governments' share of the public pie spiraled downward as Washington's share and, to a lesser extent, the states' portion, expanded sharply.

At the beginning of the twentieth century, local governments dominated public finance, accounting for 58 percent of all government expenditures. Washington spent 34 percent of all public outlays, and the states a nominal 8 percent.[37]

Then, in 1913, the Sixteenth Amendment to the Constitution was enacted, and intergovernmental finance would never be the same. As we observed in Chapter 8, the Sixteenth Amendment permitted the federal government to collect taxes on incomes, and Washington began doing so with relish. Today, Washington spends half of all governments' expenditures. The fifty states spend 26 percent, and the nation's 87,849 local governments account for 24 percent, of all government outlays.[38] It is a world turned upside down.

The Grant-in-Aid: Foundation of Fiscal Federalism

The cornerstone of fiscal federalism is the *grant-in-aid*, or a transfer of funds from one government to one or more other governments.

The Purposes of Federal Grants. Close to half, 48 percent, of all federal grant dollars sent to state and local governments is for health programs; more than four-fifths of this growing area is devoted to Medicaid grants, a health program for the poor, the costs of which are shared between Washington and the states. Over a fifth of federal assistance, 21 percent, is devoted to income security—in other words, welfare, or grants for needy families, child nutrition, and food stamps. Nearly 14 percent of federal grants pertains to education, training, employment, and social services, a fourth of which is earmarked for education programs for the disadvantaged. A tenth of federal aid supports transportation projects, more than 70 percent of which is funneled to highways, and less than 4 percent is used for community and regional development.[39]

Washington uses two major types of grants to pass money to state and local governments: categorical grants and block grants.

Categorical Grants. The main type of federal assistance is in the form of *categorical grants* or grants-in-aid that address narrow policy issues, and which rigidly stipulate precisely how federal money is to be expended. Categorical grants account for more than four-fifths of the money that the state and local governments receive from the federal government.[40]

There are three kinds of categorical grants. *Formula grants* are grants distributed by an administratively or legislatively prescribed formula, and the federal government pays without limit (unless one is contained in the formula) according to the formula. *Project grants*, or *discretionary grants*, are distributed to state or local governments at the discretion of federal administrators. More than seven out of ten categorical grants are project grants, and they are growing as a proportion of categorical grants. Finally, there are *formula/project grants*, which are grants that are awarded at the discretion of federal administrators, but within the bounds of a formula, such as the amount of dollars that may be awarded to a state.[41]

Block Grants. A *block grant* is a type of formula grant that allows the recipient to exercise more discretion in the way that federal dollars granted to it are expended in comparison to categorical grants. Until 1966, all federal grants were categorical grants; in that year, some categorical grant programs in health were consolidated and constituted the first block grant.

Since their inception, block grants never have accounted for more than a fifth of all federal aid to states and localities, and their funding by Congress tends to decline over time.[42] Block grants generate substantial political heat. At the center of the argument is the level of trust that one has in state and local officials, as opposed to national officials, and the kinds of programs that each level of government would fund with block grant money.

Congress's Categorical Favorite: Fragmentation. Washington clearly favors keeping control over how its grant money is spent. Accordingly, nearly 98 percent of federal grants programs are categorical grants.[43]

But the huge proportion of categorical grants by no means tells the whole story. The real story is the fragmentation of the grants system that has been caused by the proliferation categorical grants.

Seventy-eight percent of all federal grants dollars are spent through 2 percent of federal grants programs. The remaining 22 percent of grants dollars flow through a fine sieve of more than 800 grants programs. Three-fourths of all federal grants programs administer less than 2 percent of all federal grants dollars, and a fifth of all programs are responsible for less than 1 percent of all grants dollars.[44]

This is intergovernmental micromanagement of a rare order. To their credit, federal officials have attempted to address the implications of grants proliferation and fragmentation, but these efforts, extending over half a century, have come to naught, largely because of congressional resistance,[45] a phenomenon that has been aptly described as "creeping categorization."[46]

Washington's micromanagement is not free. In 1911, Congress first required that some of its modest federal grants be matched by state or local contributions.[47] Today, more than half of all federal grants programs and, of greater significance, over three-quarters of federal dollars, involve some form of matching requirements that states or localities must generate to receive federal funds.[48]

A Shaky Helping Hand: The Erratic Federal Role in State and Local Budgets

As Washington gained fiscal preeminence in the federal system, it dawned on policymakers that state and local governments needed help. The federal government elected to help by offering states and their localities money in the form of grants-in-aid.

As we detail later, federal grants change state and local governments. One carefully done analysis found that 2.86 million ostensibly state and local employees,[49] or close to 16 percent of all state and local workers,[50] are working for these governments only because federal grants pay their salaries. These federal "grantee jobs" inserted into subnational governments have grown by more than 18 percent over twelve years.[51]

It is with this impact in mind that we follow the ups and downs of the federal Ferris wheel of fiscal federalism over the course of the last century and into this one.

Down.   Although the federal government has allocated grants to subnational governments since the eighteenth century, they never amounted to much during the nation's first 150 years or so. Even during the opening thirty years of the twentieth century, federal grants programs amounted to less than one-half of 1 percent of the national economy; their modest number ranged from five to twelve;[52] and they accounted for about 3 percent of all federal outlays,[53] one-half of 1 percent of state budgets (that is, total state revenue), and a trace amount of local budgets.[54]

Up.   Franklin Delano Roosevelt was inaugurated as president in 1932 and quickly set about revolutionizing fiscal federalism. Federal assistance shot from a small fraction of 1 percent of the economy in the years preceding Roosevelt's ascension to almost 4 percent in 1934, and never sank below 2 percent for the remainder of the decade.[55] Between 1933 and 1939, the number of federal grants programs more than doubled,[56] and federal funding of grants to states and localities flexed by a phenomenal factor of fifteen.[57] By 1939, federal grants dollars accounted for 39 percent of all federal spending and hit a record $2.9 billion,[58] a sum that would not be surpassed for more than a decade.[59]

The impact of this federal largesse on state and local governments was dramatic, beneficial, and oddly uneven. In the states, the impact was immediate, and by 1934, federal grants had bloomed from a sliver of 1 percent of all the money in state budgets to a remarkable 27 percent.[60] In 1934, Washington directly contributed a modest 1 percent to local budgets, but by the close of the 1930s, direct federal assistance to local governments had more than tripled to almost 4 percent of all local revenue.[61]

Down.   During the 1940s and 1950s, federal grants to states and localities plummeted and rarely exceeded 1 percent of the national economy.[62] Even by the early 1950s, federal grants numbered fewer than forty,[63] and throughout almost all of the fifties, federal grants accounted from 5 percent to 6 percent of federal outlays, and from 10 percent to 12 percent of state and local revenue.[64] Washington provided about 14 percent of total state revenue, and 1 percent of all local revenue that was received as direct federal grants.[65]

Up. Beginning in 1959,[66] federal grants exploded, and this explosion thundered on throughout the next two decades. By almost every measure, and certainly by every significant measure, federal grants-in-aid peaked to an all-time high in 1978. It was a very good year—at least for the finances of state and local governments.

In 1978, federal grants programs accounted for almost 4 percent of the economy,[67] a proportion that had not been seen since 1934, and there were 492 grants programs pouring money into subnational coffers.[68] These programs comprised 17 percent of all federal expenditures, almost 28 percent of total state and local outlays,[69] and an astounding 47 percent of state and local discretionary spending![70]

The federal impact on state and local budgets during this period is difficult to exaggerate. Between 1957 and 1978, the dollars that federal grants contributed to state revenue burgeoned by more than a third, from 14 percent to 22 percent.[71] In 1978, almost three-fourths of all state agencies received federal grants, and these grants made up *at least half* of the budgets in more than a fourth of all state agencies![72]

The finances of local governments, in turn, were the recipients of that odd federal phenomenon known as "direct federalism," which rocketed during this period. *Direct federalism* occurs when Washington bypasses state governments and sends its grants directly to local governments. Between 1960 and 1978, the portion of federal assistance allocated by Washington directly to local governments more than tripled, from 8 percent to 29 percent.[73] Direct federal aid as a portion of total local revenue jumped ninefold, from 1 percent in 1957 to over 9 percent in 1978.[74]

Down. After 1978, federal assistance to states and communities fell—precipitously. Only a decade later, federal grants as a share of gross domestic product had declined by a third to a bit over 2 percent, and other measures had tumbled by two-fifths: Federal grants-in-aid amounted to less than 11 percent of federal outlays, and 19 percent of state and local budgets. Direct

federal grants amounted to 17 percent of total state revenue, and 3 percent of all local revenue.[75]

This decline in federal assistance, particularly in direct federal aid to local governments, signaled the demise of a federal urban policy that has yet to be restored. The beginning of federal attempts to craft a coherent national urban policy can be traced to the 1930s and proceeded fitfully forward through the 1970s. Although, in 1978, President Jimmy Carter tried in good conscience to implement what was "doubtless the most thorough effort at federal urban policy making ever carried out," he failed. The decline of federal urban policy did not occur because the challenges it had sought to address were conquered. Rather, from 1978 onward, urban policy succumbed to opposition from several sources and to dissension within and fragmentation of the arena. . . .

"The era of federal urban policy is, like, way over."[76]

Up, Down, Whatever. After 1990, Washington began to re-infuse states and localities with federal funds. Today, federal grants-in-aid once again account for close to 4 percent of the gross domestic product.[77] Well over 800 grants offered by twenty-nine federal agencies[78] comprise over 17 percent of federal expenditures.[79] Almost nine out of ten federal grant dollars are sent to the states, and the remainder is sent directly to local governments.[80]

Federal assistance to state and local governments accounts for 19 percent of all state and local outlays,[81] and a third of state and local discretionary spending.[82] Federal grants contribute 26 percent of all state revenue, and federal assistance sent directly by Washington to local governments provides about 4 percent of total local revenue.[83] If we were to engage in a necessarily rough calculation of the contribution to local treasuries that Washington furnishes in the forms of direct federal grants and pass-through grants (or those federal grants to the states that are earmarked for local governments) combined, we can estimate that the federal government provides approximately 15 percent of total local revenue.[84]

A Misleading Rebound. Importantly, however, this rebound in federal grants is attributable entirely to an increase in grants for payments to individuals. *Grants for payments to individuals* are federal grants-in-aid to state governments that are earmarked for particular federal programs, typically welfare programs, that channel federal funds through the states to citizens. Grants for payments to individuals have doubled their share of federal grants-in-aid since 1978, when they accounted for less than a third of federal grants dollars,[85] to almost two-thirds today.[86]

Grants for payments to individuals butter no parsnips for state and local governments. Since these grants are merely passed through by state governments to individual citizens, they cannot, obviously, be used to fund state and local government programs. So, from the standpoint of the subnational governments, what appeared to be a dramatic expansion in federal grants during the 1990s, was, in reality, a flat line that continues, flatly, today.

A Real Decline. Even here, however, the news is not as good as it first sounds. The funding in federal grants for all purposes has, with one exception, steadily eroded over the past few years. The exception is Medicaid. Medicaid is a sufficiently large program—it accounts for considerably more than two-fifths of all federal grant dollars to state and local governments—that it has skewed the overall trend in federal grants from one of a decline in dollars to one of steady state.[87]

In recent years, however, federal Medicaid funding also has declined. In 2004, Washington shifted more Medicaid costs to the states. The Deficit Reduction Act of 2006 shifted still more of its costs to pharmacies and poor people who receive Medicaid benefits and allowed the states to scale back or eliminate payments to certain recipients. Eventually, the cuts and cost shifts in Medicaid may result in an overall decline in federal grants to states and localities.

Those Rascally Recipients!

There is a passing strange irony in all this. Despite Washington's best efforts to exercise tight control over the uses of its grant money, state and local governments have proven themselves to be recipients endowed with a rare wile.

These jurisdictions value federal grants in large part because they allow them to reduce their own expenditures in the program that the federal grant supports and then use the freed money for other purposes. In fact, states, which receive about nine out of ten federal grant dollars, withdraw so much of their own money from programs supported by federal grants that, on average, a program actually receives only forty more cents for every federal dollar that it officially receives.[88] In other words, states effectively skim the equivalent of 60 percent of federal aid and use it for purposes other than the feds intended.

Analyses indicate that states and communities favor using money that they gain from federal grants, either directly or indirectly, less for social services and poor people and more for construction projects and keeping a muzzle on taxes.[89] The less specific and condition-heavy the grant, the more likely that it will be used for "luxury" services, such as parks, recreation, and cultural programs, and the less likely that it will be spent for "normal" services, such as public safety.[90] Federal grants clearly meant for antipoverty programs have been used (quite legally) by local governments to subsidize developers in building luxury hotels and up-market department stores.[91]

Money and Mandates: Federal Instruments of Implementation

Over the decades, Washington has experimented with both honey (in the form of federal money) and vinegar (federal mandates) as inducements to state and local governments to assist Washington in the implementation and enforcement of national policies. We consider next how these approaches have worked—or not.

Does National Money Make Subnational Policy? Lessons from the 1960s and 1970s.

Between 1960 and 1978, the high point for federal assistance to state and local governments, federal grants-in-aid, both as a portion of all federal outlays and as a portion of state and local budgets, more than doubled. This huge monetary impact consumed the energies of subnational officials and had a perverse effect on their formulation of state and local policy.

Grants and Governments: The States.   Governors in the 1960s devoted less of their time to state-federal business than did governors in the 1970s, but by the end of the seventies the typical governor spent almost a full working day in a six-day working week on these concerns. Nearly nine out of ten of the governors expressed genuine concern about the intergovernmental system of grants-in-aid, saying that it needed a "major overhaul."[92]

Policy Perversities.   State administrators also believed that state-federal relations were important but went a step farther: They contended that federal governmental programs had distorted policymaking itself in their states. Seventy percent of state administrators in 1978 (up from 52 percent in 1964) felt that they would use federal grants for different purposes if the "strings" attached to those grants were relaxed, indicating the distorting effect that federal aid was having on state priorities, and three-fourths of them thought that federal aid led to inappropriate national interference in state affairs.[93]

Bureaucratic Fiefdoms.   There is a more subtle, but potentially equally harmful, impact of federal assistance on state governments that continues today. Because a proportion of federal aid flows directly to state agency heads, it has been suggested that those state agencies that are heavily funded by Washington are also more autonomous because they are less dependent upon their governors and legislatures for their budgets. Surveys of state administrators taken since 1964 have found that almost half of state administrators admit they are less subject to supervision by their governors and legislatures because of federal aid.[94]

Grants and Governments: The Communities.   The federal government's grants programs had an even greater impact on local governments during this period than on state governments. As with state administrators, local officials during the seventies also felt that federal grants distorted local policy. A survey of local administrators in all cities and counties that had received federal aid found that officials in about two-thirds of the cities, and roughly four-fifths of the counties, stated that they would have made different budgetary allocations had not federal grants been available.[95]

As federal dollars have departed local governments, so, in effect, have federal overseers. A survey taken of mayors and city managers in Colorado found that most reported that their contacts with state and local officials had increased dramatically at the expense of federal administrators as federal grants shrank.[96]

The Flypaper Effect.   One of the more fascinating findings about the impact of intergovernmental grants on public policy is that those grants have a surprisingly intense effect on the policies that they fund. This is known as *the flypaper effect*, since the grant dollars stick where they land. More to the point, grant money has a larger and longer impact on the policy area for which it is spent than does money from other sources, such as tax revenue. Spending for a particular policy continues at significantly higher levels and longer periods when grant money is present, or has been present, than when it is not, or never has been, a factor.[97]

At the state level, an analysis of federal categorical grants and state expenditures in the same policy categories found that these category-specific grants had "a much stronger effect" on state policies than did any other financial variable, such as total federal aid or general state revenues. "Category-specific aid sticks to the [policy] category in which it is granted not only for the year in which it is granted but also for several years to come."[98]

The same is true for state grants to local governments. A study of the impact of state grants on local governments in Wisconsin found a "positive flypaper effect" in eight out of ten policy categories that were analyzed.[99]

Do National Mandates Make Subnational Policy? Lessons from the 1980s and 1990s.

The federal bureaucracy is more involved in state and local affairs than ever. This is because of the proliferation of federal regulations on state and local governments that began in the 1970s and have continued ever since. By 1960, Washington had imposed a grand total of two "major" intergovernmental regulations on state and local governments, and for the remainder of the decade enacted only seven more. In the 1970s, twenty-eight new major intergovernmental regulations were promulgated; in the 1980s, fifty-eight more were added; and by the late-1990s, another thirty-two.[100] One study found that, by the close of the 1970s, long before the increases in federal intergovernmental regulations had hit their stride, the average number of federal regulations affecting state and local jurisdictions was 570 regulations per government![101]

The Federal Mandates Maw.   The great bulk of these regulations deal with what one would expect in the way of assuring fiscal accountability and programmatic propriety in the administration of intergovernmental programs, but not all. Some are highly intrusive federal "mandates" that are designed to make state and local governments extended enforcers of Washington in implementing federal policies within their jurisdictions.[102] Just how many federal mandates there are is unknown, but counts include 36,[103] 63,[104] 185,[105] and 439.[106]

And these counts are of only mandates imposed by Congress, not by the courts! Yet, court-imposed mandates on state and local governments are far more numerous. One study found some 3,500 decisions made by the federal judiciary in a single year, relating to over 100 federal laws, which involved state and local governments.[107]

Despite all this mandating by Congress and the courts, just what a mandate is remains undefined. "There is no universally accepted definition of a federal mandate, and surprisingly little consensus on the matter."[108] Nevertheless, we offer our own definition, A *mandate* is an intergovernmental regulation imposed by one government on another government that requires the receiving government to advance specific social goals or meet certain standards; usually, but not always, these purposes are linked to a grant-in-aid.

Federal mandates have proliferated since 1960, and the tilt from the traditional federal reliance on providing financial subsidies to state

and local governments to regulating them is unambiguous.[109]

Mandates and Management: A Federal Failure. Quite aside from any policy implications, federal mandates can amount to tossing the proverbial monkey wrench into the managerial mechanisms of state and local governments. Close to four-fifths of state agency heads reported in one poll that "federal involvement" in their agencies' "daily administrative operations" was "moderate" or "high," and over half of these administrators contacted federal personnel daily, weekly, or monthly.[110]A survey of local officials found that most thought that federal mandates were "excessively detailed" and "needlessly difficult."[111]

The Paperwork Reduction Act of 1980, the Regulatory Flexibility Act of 1980, and the State and Local Government Cost Estimate Act of 1981 all were designed, at least in part, to provide regulatory relief to subnational governments but have not been noticeably successful. In 1987, President Ronald Reagan issued Executive Order 12612, designed to minimize the adverse impact of federal policies on the grass-roots governments, but it has been followed barely, if at all, by federal agencies. An analysis by the GAO found that, despite Reagan's executive order and legislation requiring federal agencies to assess the effects of new agency rules on states and communities, they have had "little effect on agencies' rulemaking activities."[112]

Mandates and Policy: Turns, Torques, and Twists: The policy effects of federal mandates and regulations have not gone unnoticed by state and local officials.

In the states, nearly nine out of ten governors in one survey said that the federal government had assumed many of the responsibilities that appropriately belonged to the states.[113] More than four out of ten state agency heads think that federal involvement in their agencies' "substantive program policies" is "high," another three out of ten think that it is "moderate," and more than half report that Washington has "skewed" state programs.[114]

A survey of state officials with special responsibilities for federal relations found that large pluralities reported that federal agencies had overridden state decisions at least sometimes "There is a consensus among state officials. . . . that there is too much federal preemption and that the Congress delegates too much authority to federal administrators."[115]

It is at the local level, however, where federal regulations seem most onerous. Perhaps three-quarters of federal intergovernmental mandates apply only to local governments or directly affect local governments through the states.[116] A national survey of cities found that two-fifths of local officeholders believed in most cases that federal regulations on local governments resulted from Washington playing an inappropriate role in urban affairs.[117] A benchmark study of the effects of mandates in ten diverse communities concluded that "there are significant fiscal impacts of mandates on local governments . . . and these impacts have political as well as fiscal importance."[118]

Unfunded Federal Mandates: Arrogant Orders and a Dearth of Dollars. Unfunded federal mandates are the form of federal regulation that is the most irksome to state and local officials. And there seems to be some reason for these officials to be irked.

An *unfunded mandate* is an order issued by a government to another government that occupies a lower level on the federal hierarchy, which passes the cost of implementing that order to the receiving government. The U.S. Advisory Commission on Intergovernmental Relations contended that "the nation's state, local, and tribal governments urgently need relief from the burdens of unfunded federal mandates."[119]

How Much Do Unfunded Federal Mandates Cost? Unfunded federal mandates are costly to state and local governments. Their actual price and that of other federal regulations is not really known, but the indications are that the cost is high. One review of estimates of the expense of federal mandates to state and local governments found that they ranged "from 2 to 3 percent" of their budgets "to 20 percent or more."[120] The Congressional Budget Office states that, since 1986, federally mandated costs to state and local governments have been growing at a pace that exceeds the amount of overall federal aid.[121]

The states are particularly distressed over unfunded federal mandates. The National Conference of State Legislatures contends that "the minimum cumulative gap" between federal mandates and the revenue needed by states to implement them amounts to 7 percent of the states' general funds, a proportion that is rising rapidly.[122]

Local governments, the bottom tier in the intergovernmental hierarchy, appear to bear the brunt of mandates, both federal and state.[123] One review of the research on their effects on local governments concluded that, "from a range of studies, it appears localities dedicate anywhere from 20 percent to 90 percent of their expenditures to implementing federal and state mandates."[124]

The citizenry seems to sense that state and local governments are under duress as a result of federal regulations. One survey found that a majority of Americans believe that the costs of federal mandates should be shared among all governmental levels.[125]

The Unfunded Mandates Reform Act of 1995. In 1995, Congress responded to the grass-roots revulsion over unfunded federal mandates and passed the Unfunded Mandates Reform Act, which discourages the imposition of unfunded mandates by Washington on states, localities, and the private sector. The act does not, we should emphasize, prohibit unfunded mandates. Instead, it does little more than require the Congressional Budget Office to report on any proposed bill that would impose a minimum of $50 million in annual costs on state and local governments. The act's effectiveness is uncertain. On the one hand, it seems to have attuned members of Congress more fully to the destructive implications of unfunded mandates;[126] increased the volume and quality of information provided to Congress about mandates;[127] and "appears to have indirectly . . . limited mandates in some cases."[128] The GAO analyzed all 377 laws enacted by Congress and 122 "major or economically significant final rules" issued by federal agencies over two years that concerned federal mandates, and concluded that no law and only "one final rule . . . contained an intergovernmental mandate" that violated the Unfunded Mandates Reform Act.[129] The Congressional Budget Office contends that only three statutes enacted over ten years following the act's passage violate the act.[130]

Others beg to differ with these relatively roseate reports. Interviews with knowledgeable people representing academia, public-interest advocacy groups, businesses, and the federal, state, and local governments found that most believed that the act's "numerous definitions, exclusions, and exceptions leave out many federal actions that may significantly impact nonfederal entities."[131]

Certainly the cacophonous and continuing outcry from state and local governments about the burden of unfunded federal mandates gives pause to claiming that the issue no longer is with us.

The Meaning of Mandates.   A unique survey of state and local employees provides some convincing data that the federal government not only continues to load state and local governments with heavy fiscal baggage, but that it also has seriously affected the policy directions of these governments.

The survey's researchers found that state and local governments were heavily staffed by employees whom these governments were forced to hire by Washington to implement national programs. The researchers estimated that 4.65 million full-time equivalent positions in state and local governments were the result of unfunded federal mandates. Nearly three out of every ten state and local employees, in other words, owe their jobs to at least one federal mandate, a proportion that is almost twice that of those state and local workers who are funded by federal grants.[132]

There can be little doubt that Washington's mandates to state and local governments are a method of growing importance in the implementation of federal policy.

Victims of Federalism

Federal involvement in state and local affairs runs deeper than even this review of fluctuating funds and multiplying mandates implies. Other factors come into play, too.

For the states, the main ones include not only the episodic ups and downs in federal grants,

federal preemptions of state authority, and unfunded or underfunded mandates, but also the shifting of costs in some programs, such as Medicaid, from the federal government to the states; federal failure to keep up with rising costs of grant administration that is borne by the states; federal tax changes that cause states to lose tax revenue, including a decline in the value of the federal income tax deduction for state and local taxes; and "the failure of the federal government to solve problems in state finances that only it can solve," such as the inability of state and local governments to tax electronic commerce, described in Chapter 8, and international tax shelters.[133]

By the first decade of the twenty-first century, these and other "negative impacts" had reduced the federal government's "positive impacts" on the budgets and finances of state and their local governments by fully one-third, and the pace of these negative impacts were accelerating. It is projected that these federal policies, parsimony, and restrictions will continue to reduce the value of federal assistance programs to states and communities in the future.[134]

Federalism Among Equals: The States

So far we have been discussing federalism largely from the viewpoint of the government in Washington. But the states also have active governments, so we review here the states' relations with each other, which can range from cooperation to conflict.

Interstate Cooperation

The Constitution requires that "full faith and credit shall be given in each state to the public acts, records, and judicial proceedings of every state," and as a partial consequence, four devices of interstate cooperation have emerged over the centuries that are designed to solve their common problems. We consider them in turn.

Regional Cooperation.   A number of interstate associations have cropped up that are designed to advance regional interests. For example, in 1972, the Southern Growth Policies Board was founded, a thirteen-state organization. In 1976, seven states in the Northeast formed a Coalition of Northeastern Governors. In 1977 the thirteen Western states formed the Western Governors' Policy Office.

In Congress, states have banded together in a variety of regional formats, including the New England Congressional Caucus, the Northeast-Midwest Economic Advancement Coalition, the Great Lakes Conference, the Sunbelt Conference, and the Western States Coalition.

Interstate Compacts and Agencies. The grand-daddy of interstate cooperation is the *interstate compact*, which is a formal agreement between two or more states. There are more than 200 interstate compacts in operation, but only 36 compacts were agreed to between 1789 and 1920, so states evidently are finding them increasingly useful.[135] The typical state has entered into twenty-three interstate compacts.[136]

Interstate compacts normally require congressional approval to be set into motion, and many have established ongoing interstate authorities and commissions to monitor and enforce their provisions. There are 116 such agencies dealing with educational concerns, river basin management, transportation, waterfronts, fisheries, and energy, among other issues.[137]

Multistate Legal Action. *Multistate legal action* refers to the willingness of states to enter into lawsuits with other states against a common adversary. These sorts of lawsuits have been facilitated by the National Association of Attorneys General, an organization composed of the chief legal officers of states and territories. A notable example of multistate lawsuits are the state-initiated cases that were brought against the tobacco industry.

On average, each state was a party in twenty-five multistate lawsuits over a period of seven years during the 1990s. States with a higher level of administrative capacity favor using multistate legal action more than do states with a lower level of capacity.[138]

Uniform State Laws. *Uniform state laws* are identical, or virtually identical, statutes that have

been enacted in two or more states. They represent an effort by the states to preempt possible congressional passage of national legislation that could deepen the federal government's involvement in state affairs.

The writing of uniform state laws was formalized with the creation in 1892 of the National Conference of Commissioners on Uniform State Laws, a nonprofit organization funded by state appropriations and staffed largely by legal experts from each state. The commission drafted twenty-two uniform state laws during the decade of the 1990s, of which the states enacted, on average, not quite eight. In contrast to multistate legal action, states that have less capability favor enacting uniform laws more than states with a greater capacity.[139]

Interstate Conflict

Even in light of these manifold levels of interstate cooperation, the states remain competitive, and occasionally conflictual. The most obvious example occurred in 1861 when the nation went to war with itself, an event that in the North is called the Civil War, but in the South is still referred to as the War Between the States.

A more recent example concerns the gradually developing shortage of water in the nation,[140] which is already straining relationships among states. Montana and Idaho threatened to sue the state of Washington if that state seeded clouds over the Pacific Ocean, thereby "stealing" water that might have fallen as rain farther inland. The eight states and two Canadian provinces that surround the Great Lakes—the world's largest reservoir of fresh water—agreed in 1982 to block attempts to divert their water unless all ten governments agreed.

Although water wars long have erupted among the states and will continue to do so as long as water supplies deplete, hydraulic technology innovates, and rivers meander, interstate antagonism is surfacing in other fields as well. Forty states use some sort of *severance tax*—that is, a tariff on natural resources exported to other states—and some states have been using the device, according to some regional analysts, as a weapon against other states to recruit new industry by lowering taxes.

Other statewide "exports" are free of severance taxes, such as pollution spawned in one state, but which ends up in another states. Northeastern states long have argued that they are the primary recipients of Midwestern air pollutants that produce acid rain. Other states export other kinds of undesirable items. Over a five-year period, for example, South Dakota gave ninety-three people charged with burglary, forgery, theft, and other felonies the choice of facing prosecution or moving to California; all ninety-three moved to the Golden State, whose officials promptly dubbed South Dakota's actions as outrageous. Following Congressional devolution of welfare in 1996, Kentucky established a program for moving its most impoverished denizens to wealthier areas—including wealthier states.[141]

All is not happy in the realm of the American states.

Intergovernmental Administration in the States

The states can cooperate with each other as equals, but their relationships with their own local governments are quite different.

The States Tame Their "Creatures"

The phrase, "creatures of the states," describes more than adequately the place of local governments relative to their state governments. It is drawn from a statement made in 1868 by Judge John F. Dillon of the Iowa supreme court that is now known as "Dillon's rule." "Creatures of the state," a concept upheld by the U.S. Supreme Court in 1923, simply means that local governments have no independence beyond what the state grants them. Sometimes this state oversight can be miasmic in detail, and state legislatures have been known to legislate the procedures for paving city sidewalks, the methods for removing local weeds, and the design of county stationery.[142]

Home Rule: The Structure of Local Governments. Slowly but steadily, however, Dillon's rule has been eroded by the rise of "home rule." *Home rule* may be defined as "all forms of local or regional self-determination,"[143] but, as a practical matter, home rule usually refers to *structural home rule*, or the states' empowerment of localities to form their own governments.[144]

Missouri gave home rule political meaning when it adopted a constitution in 1875 that delegated to the people of St. Louis a power that, until that year, had been the exclusive right of the state legislature: "the power to make a charter."

Today, either through their constitutions or general law, forty-eight states grant home rule authority to their municipalities (Alabama and Vermont are the exceptions), and thirty-seven states grant it to their counties, a gift of governing that was granted to counties mostly during the 1970s but has since waned.[145]

Home Rule: The Functions of Local Government. Although the states have been increasingly liberal in giving their local governments structural home rule, they have been increasingly conservative in granting them *functional home rule*, which is the states' empowerment of localities to conduct their affairs as they see fit. States impose laws (there are about 4,300 of them) on their local governments that deal with more than 200 local functions and procedures, and, on the whole, these laws are proliferating. However, the states also remove a significant number of these laws from the books, indicating that the relationship between state governments and their local governments is a sensitive and dynamic one.[146]

States concentrate on five broad areas of functional home rule: human resource management, changing local boundaries, administrative operations, local elections, and financial management. Only in the area of elections have state laws governing localities decreased; the greatest growth in these laws has occurred in human resource management and financial management.[147]

A Slow but Steady Centralization of State Power. Overall, there has been a steady, if slow, centralization of state power at the expense of local governments. In a classic analysis, G. Ross Stephens ranked the local proportions of financial resources, services, and worker availability by state and concluded that larger states tend to be decentralized governmentally, whereas smaller states are more centralized. Nevertheless, there is a remarkably clear trend toward state centralization, and a growing dominance by state governments over their local governments; a third of the states are categorized as "centralized" and none as "decentralized."[148] Other studies by and large confirm Stephens's findings.[149]

State Styles of Intergovernmental Administration

Just as state governments have their own sets of intergovernmental relationships that differ from those at the national level, they often conduct these relationships quite differently from the feds. In fact, there is a difference in philosophy, and control over intergovernmental programs seems, on the whole, tighter at the state level than at the national one.

State government dominance of the statewide intergovernmental assistance system seems to associate with the more populous, urbanized, and wealthy states.[150]

One of the local benefits of the states keeping things simple is that local administrative costs can be held down. An analysis of public school districts across the United States found that, because federal education grants were much more complex, fragmented, and formal than were state fiscal transfers to school districts, those districts that had to rely more on federal funds than they did on state funds generated significantly more administrative positions.[151]

As with the federal government, states also impose mandates, and there is a strong and positive correlation between a state's high affluence, the competitiveness of a state's political parties, and a high quality of state public administration and a state's propensity to mandate local governments.[152] On average, a fifth of the hundreds of measures introduced each year in state legislatures directly affect the authority, procedures, and finances of local governments.[153]

Most controversial, unsurprisingly, are state mandates on local governments that do not provide the money to implement them. As with federal unfunded mandates, we do not know how much state mandates cost their local governments, and one careful review of this issue labeled efforts to estimate the costs of state mandates a "fool's errand."[154]

Ten states, as a result of local political mobilization, have voted in constitutional amendments prohibiting the imposition of unfunded state mandates on local governments.[155] Often, these amendments require the vote by a "supermajority" of legislators, such as two-thirds or three-fifths, to pass an unfunded mandate, and observers agree that requiring super-majority votes is "the best anti-mandates strategy" that has been developed by localities to date, whereas other approaches such as forecasting the fiscal impact of mandates and reimbursing localities, "have been recognized as helpful but not effective."[156]

Fiscal Federalism in the States

If the states occasionally have been high-handed in their dealings with their localities, they also have been stand-up governments in addressing their communities' fiscal needs.

The States' Steady Support. State grants-in-aid have accounted for no less than 30 percent of all local outlays since 1970—a tribute to the states' constancy of purpose.[157] States concentrate their grants to local government in education (62 percent, and well over half of all state grant dollars go to school districts), welfare (12 percent, almost all of which goes to counties), general local government support (8 percent), and highways (at 4 percent), followed by health, transit subsidies, corrections, and housing.[158]

Of course, as we noted earlier, one should keep in mind that the federal government plays a large fiscal role in the states' support of their communities, and perhaps a third of the federal grants that the states receive are pass-through grants earmarked by Washington for the exclusive use of local governments.[159] As a result, possibly two-fifths of all the intergovernmental revenue that localities receive is actually provided by Washington.[160]

Nevertheless, the indications are that, in the longer haul, the states seem to be a steadier

A Load of Local Governments: Definitions, Scope, Services, Revenue Sources, Government, and Forms of Government for Counties, Municipalities, Townships, School Districts, and Special Districts

States establish, either in their constitutions or by general law, five kinds of local governments that are officially recognized by the U.S. Census Bureau, but their distinctions and characteristics often are unclear to most people. Some definitions and clarifications follow.

Counties

Definition.   *Counties* are the administrative arms and territorial subdivisions of the state that provide general government services.

Scope.   First created in 1634 by Virginia, there are now 3,034 counties. Only Connecticut and Rhode Island do not have counties, but they once had them. Only Alaska, Montana, and South Dakota do not have counties covering all of their states' land. Counties in Alaska are called *boroughs*, and in Louisiana they are called *parishes*. Texas, with 254 counties, has the most, and Delaware and Hawaii, with three apiece, the fewest. Counties are handily the most stable type of local government (their number has decreased by only sixteen since 1942), and it has been observed that, "the legislature may create municipalities, but only God can create a county."

Services.   In order of the largest portions of county budgets expended, the main services that counties provide are social services, at over a fourth of all expenditures, including public welfare, health, and hospitals. Social services are followed by education at 14 percent, transportation and corrections at about 6 percent each, parks and recreation, sewerage, and solid waste management. Counties traditionally are responsible for property tax assessment and collection and deed recording as well. More than any other type of local government, county services focus on the elderly, the ill, and the indigent.

Revenue Sources.   The largest source of county income, slightly more than a third, is taxes, especially the property tax, which provides more than two-thirds of county tax revenue, and the sales tax, which accounts for almost all of the remaining tax revenues. A third of county revenue is provided by state governments. Charges constitute over a sixth of revenues, and the principal provider of revenues here, accounting for close to two-fifths of this source, is county hospital charges to patients. Four percent of county revenue is provided by interest earnings, and 3 percent is furnished in the form of direct grants-in-aid by Washington.

Government.   County legislative bodies go by no fewer than seventeen designations, including *levy court, police jury, freeholders, county legislature*, and *borough assembly*, but the more common titles are *board of commissioners* or *supervisors*, or *county council*. More than half, 52 percent, of county legislators serve terms of just one year; 29 percent serve four-year terms, and 15 percent serve terms of two years. County commissions average about six members, three-fourths of whom are elected in *single-member districts* (or electoral wards in which voters may elect only one legislator), and the remainder who are elected *at-large* (that is, all voters in a governmental jurisdiction may vote in each electoral race). Close to two-thirds, 62 percent, of all counties use district elections exclusively (a growing trend); nearly three out of ten, 28 percent, use at-large elections solely; and 11 percent combine the two voting systems (a declining arrangement). Over four-fifths, 82 percent, of counties use *partisan elections* (that is, the party affiliations of candidates are identified on the ballot) to elect legislators and constitutional officers, and the rest use *nonpartisan elections* (the candidates' political party, if any, is not identified on the ballot).

All county legislative bodies have a *presiding officer*, usually called a *board chair, council president*, or *county judge*, among other titles. Sixty-four percent of these officers are selected by their fellow legislators, 23 percent are elected by the voters, and 12 percent rotate in and out of office. Ninety-four percent of all presiding officers also are members of the county commission and have the power to vote on all issues. More than half, 52 percent, have terms of only one year, and 15 percent have terms of two years. A remarkable 95 percent have no veto power. These figures remain quite stable over time.

County voters elect large numbers of *row officers*, so named for the rows and rows of these positions that appear on the ballot, although these officials prefer to be called by the equally accurate title, *constitutional officers*, indicating that their election is required by state constitutions. Counties elect more of these row officers by far—an average of almost fourteen per county, *not* including county legislators—than any other type of local government. Virtually all sheriffs (99 percent), more than nine out of ten prosecutors, close to nine out of ten recorders and treasurers, more than seven out of ten clerks of the court, and significant majorities of clerks of the governing board and tax assessors are elected, followed by large minorities of civil attorneys and controllers, who also are elected.

Increasingly, counties are hiring *chief appointed officers*, such as *county managers, county administrators*, and *county administrative assistants*, to run their governments. Fifty-four percent, up from 38 percent fourteen years earlier, of all counties do so.

Forms of County Government.   There are four forms of county government: the commission, council-administrator, council-manager, and council-elected executive forms.

Historically, the *commission*, or *plural executive*, plan has been the dominant form of government used by counties, although its use clearly is in decline. Commission plans make no distinction between legislative and executive roles; individual county commissioners are responsible for both enacting legislation and directly managing county government. Individual elected commissioners are the chief administrators of each of the departments of the government (hence the term, "plural executive"), such as roads, corrections, and planning; typically, the commissioners decide by consensus who among their number will be responsible for which departments. We reckon that roughly half of counties still use this form, but the data are mixed. (The *Notes* at the end of this box explain the disparate data concerning the use of the commission plan by counties.)

In the *council-administrator* form of government, an administrator is appointed by the county council (and may be fired by it) to run the day-to-day business of the county, recommend policy to the council, and prepare the budget. However, the county administrator may not hire and fire county employees; only the county council may do that. The council-administrator plan is used in slightly more than a third, 34 percent, of counties, and its use is favored in the suburbs.

The *council-manager* form of county government shares all the characteristics of the council-administrator form, with one important exception: the county manager is empowered to hire and fire employees. It used by 22 percent of counties, and is adopted most frequently by large, urban counties.

Earlier surveys of county government did not distinguish between the council-administrator and council-manager forms, but both appear to be growing in popularity.

Finally, the *council-elected executive* plan gives the most authority to the executive branch. In the council-elected executive form, a county executive is elected at-large, is not a member of

(cont.)

A Load of Local Governments: (*Cont.*)

the board, and usually has the power of the veto and significant appointment powers. Twelve percent of counties use it, and its use is in steep decline; fourteen years earlier, 22 percent of responding counties reported that they had a council-elected executive plan in place. It is used most frequently in nonmetropolitan areas and by smaller to medium-sized counties.

Municipalities

Definition.   *Municipalities* are political units incorporated for general purpose, local self-government that provide public services for a specific concentration of population in a defined area.

Scope.   All fifty states have municipalities, and there are 19,431 of them, but the numbers of municipalities vary widely from state to state; Illinois, with 1,291, has the most, and Hawaii the fewest: one. Depending on the rough size of their population, municipalities are called *cities* (or those municipalities with the most people), *towns* (although the Census Bureau classifies "towns" in eight states as townships), *villages*, or *boroughs*.

The criteria that states use to *incorporate* (that is, create, charter, and recognize) municipalities vary, but minimal requirements concerning population density and distance from other municipalities characterize most of them. To be incorporated as a municipality, citizens usually must present a petition to the state requesting incorporation, hold an election that endorses it, and have the secretary of state certify that all requirements have been met.

Services.   Municipalities deliver more services than does any other type of local government. The services provided most frequently by municipalities are, in order of the largest portions of the municipal budgets expended, education services (over a fifth of all expenditures), public safety and corrections (a sixth), transportation (8 percent, almost half of which is for highways), sewerage (5 percent), hospitals and health and parks and recreation (4 percent each), and public welfare and housing and community development (3 percent each).

Revenue Sources.   More than a third of the total revenue of municipalities derives from municipal taxes, the primary one being the property tax, which contributes about half of all tax revenues, followed by sales taxes (a third of the municipal tax base), and income taxes (a tenth). Municipalities garner 18 percent of their revenues from their state governments. Utility revenue accounts for 16 percent of all municipal revenue, and over four-fifths of this revenue derives from payments by customers for water and electricity. Charges amount to 15 percent of total revenue, with charges for sewerage, hospital care, and solid waste management the leaders in this category. Roughly 4 percent of all municipal revenue each comes directly from the federal government and in interest earnings.

Government.   All municipalities are governed by *councils, boards,* or *commissions*. These legislatures average fewer than six members, who are called, among other titles, *council members, aldermen, selectmen, freeholders, trustees,* or *commissioners*. About six out of ten of these legislators serve terms of four years, and most of the remainder serve two-year terms. In contrast to counties, most, 62 percent, municipal council members are elected at-large and the rest, 38 percent, in single-member districts. Almost two-thirds, 64 percent, of all municipalities use at-large elections exclusively (a practice that is growing at the expense of other representation systems), 14 percent use only districts, and over a fifth, 21 percent, use a mix of the two electoral systems. In another stark difference with counties, over three-fourths, 77 percent, of municipal legislators are elected in nonpartisan elections. About three out of ten eligible voters, on average, vote in municipal elections, and voter turnout in these elections has been in decline since the 1930s. The small and sliding voter turnout in these elections may be a factor in the growing perception that many city councils are increasingly micromanaging, provincial, parochial, bloated, bickering, and balkanized bodies that give them "an image of irresponsible flakiness" (Gurwit, p. 21).

The *chief elected officer* of a municipal government is called *mayor, president,* or *board chair,* among other titles. In more than three-fourths, 76 percent, of municipalities, the chief elected officer is chosen by the voters, in 22 percent the mayor is selected from among the council members, and in 2 percent the office rotates among the council members.

Seven out of ten mayors serve as members of their municipal councils. More than nine out of ten mayors, 92 percent, may vote on issues before the council: 55 percent can vote on all issues before the council, and 35 percent are restricted to a tiebreaker role.

Over four-fifths, 84 percent, of mayors are part-timers, and the 16 percent who are full-timers are found in the largest cities. Forty-four percent, a plurality, have terms of four years, a third have terms of two years, 14 percent have terms of a single year, and 6 percent have three-year terms. More than seven out of ten mayors have no veto power. A modest 12 percent of mayors have overall responsibility for developing and recommending a budget to the city council. In just 17 percent of municipalities does the mayor have full authority to appoint department heads, and this power is declining over time.

Unlike states, counties, and townships, municipalities elect few—fewer than two, on average—row officers. Nevertheless, voters in 14 percent of all municipalities elect some or all of their governments' department heads.

Municipalities often are categorized as *weak-mayor governments,* in which the mayor does not have a veto power and lacks a formal role in the government's budgeting and appointment processes, or *strong-mayor governments,* in which the mayor has these powers. The International City/County Management Association (ICMA) classifies 22 percent of all municipalities as having a weak-mayor form of government, and 20 percent as having a strong-mayor form (the remaining 58 percent of municipalities were "not classifiable").

Four-fifths of all municipalities hire a *chief appointed official,* typically called a *manager* or *administrator,* to manage the day-to-day affairs of the government, and this proportion is rising over time. In 68 percent of those municipalities that hire a chief appointed official, he or she is hired solely by the city council, but in 27 percent the selection is a joint project between the mayor and council, and in 5 percent of cities the chief appointed official is appointed exclusively by the chief elected officer.

Forms of Municipal Government.   As with counties, there are four major forms of government in municipalities: the council-manager, mayor-council, town meeting, and commission forms.

Most, 53 percent, of cities and towns use the *council-manager* plan, which continues to expand. In this form, a professional *chief administrative officer,* usually called a *city* or *town manager,* is hired (and may be fired) by the municipal council to manage the government. The manager reports directly to the council and has full authority to administer the city, develop and propose a budget, and hire and fire all personnel. Dayton, Ohio, was the first major city to adopt the plan, in 1914.

Under a *mayor-council* arrangement, a mayor is elected at-large as the chief elected officer and usually is not a member of the city council. Thirty-eight percent of municipalities use a mayor-council plan, which is slowly declining in popularity.

(cont.)

A Load of Local Governments: (*Cont.*)

Seven percent of municipalities, all in New England, use the *town meeting* form of government. The ICMA (the source of our 7 percent figure) categorizes New England towns as municipalities, but the Bureau of the Census classifies New England towns (which, as the Census Bureau readily verifies, are the functional equivalents of municipalities) as townships. We explain the town meeting form of government in the next section, "Townships."

One percent of municipalities use a *commission* form of government, in which commissions of three to five members are elected, usually on a nonpartisan basis, and who both make laws and manage the government's departments directly, much in the same mode that counties with commission plans function. As with counties, the commission plan also is in decline in municipalities.

Townships

Definition. *Townships* are political units that function as local governments, and which provide public services for residents of areas without regard to population concentration.

Scope. Twenty states in the Northeast and Midwest have 16,506 townships, and a fifth of Americans are governed directly by them. In four of the six New England states, New York, and Wisconsin, townships are called *towns*; in Maine they are called *plantations*, and in New Hampshire they are known as *locations*. In Minnesota, the terms *township* and *town* are interchangeable, but both terms refer to township governments. In the remaining eleven states, townships are called *townships* exclusively.

The Census Bureau categorizes most townships in New England, New Jersey, Pennsylvania, and, to a lesser degree, those in Michigan, New York, and Wisconsin, as *strong townships*, and in these eleven states townships function like municipalities. In the remaining nine Midwestern states, most townships are *rural townships*, and these townships have very limited responsibilities; some rural townships are no more than subdivisions of counties, with no powers of their own. Overall, the number of townships has been in slow decline over the past several decades, and most, 58 percent, have no full-time employees of their own.

Services. The services provided most frequently by townships are, in order of the largest portions of township budgets expended, education (at more than half of township dollars), transportation and public safety (at about a seventh each), followed by sewerage, solid waste management, and parks and recreation in that order.

Revenue Sources. Taxes are the main source of township revenues, and six out of ten township dollars derive from taxes; almost all of this source is property taxes. About a fifth of townships' revenue comes from their state governments. Charges for such services as sewerage, recreation, and education amount to 9 percent of all revenue. Bills issued to customers by utilities, especially bills for water, electricity, and gas, account for 5 percent of total township revenue. A pittance, 1 percent, of all revenue comes directly from the federal government.

Government. The governing boards of townships are small, averaging about three elected members. As in municipalities, nonpartisan, at-large elections are favored, and more than seven out of ten township legislators are elected at-large and the remaining 29 percent are elected by district.

Less than half of the chief elected executives in townships are voted into office directly by the voters. Most are selected by fellow members of the town council or are rotated into office. More than nine out of ten chief elected officers are permitted to vote on all issues before the council. Only about a tenth of these officials have overall responsibility for the budget.

As in states and counties, voters in townships elect a large number of row officers, such as treasurers and clerks. Other than legislators, townships elect, on average, close to five constitutional officers per township.

About three-fourths of townships hire a township manager who, in more than four-fifths of townships, is appointed by the council. In over a third of townships, the chief appointed officer has overall control of the budget.

Forms of Township Government. As with counties and municipalities, there are four principal forms of government used by townships. They are the town meeting, mayor-council, council-manager, and commission forms.

The most democratic and interesting form of township government is used by towns in the six New England states: the *town meeting*, a form of government that originated in 1636, when the Pilgrims of Plymouth Colony (now Massachusetts) authorized its use in the town of Scituate. Although, as noted earlier, the town meeting accounts for only 7 percent of all municipal forms of government, it dominates townships; 85 percent of all townships use the town meeting to govern.

In town-meeting governments, all the townspeople who wish to attend annual town meetings enact legislation, write and approve the budget, form town policies, and elect part-time *selectmen* (as their legislators are called) and other town officers to take care of things between town meetings. In the roughly one-fourth of town-meeting governments that do not appoint a town manager, the day-to-day administration of the town usually falls to the popularly elected town clerk.

Most, 84 percent, of New England towns with 2,500 people or more use the *open town meeting*, in which all townspeople may participate, and the remainder use the *representative town meeting*, in which all the town's people may attend, but only 100 to 150 elected townspeople may vote. Anywhere from 1 percent to over two-fifths of townspeople attend open town meetings, on average, and the smaller the town the higher the turnout.

The three remaining forms of township government correspond to their municipal counterparts. Less than 4 percent each of townships use a *mayor-council* or *council-manager* form of government, and less than 3 percent use a *commission* form.

School Districts

Definition. *School districts* are organized local entities providing public elementary, secondary, and/or higher education, which, under state law, have sufficient administrative and fiscal autonomy to qualify as separate governments.

Scope. There are 13,522 independent school districts that qualify as governments, and their number declines with every census of governments. Thirty-one, predominantly western, states use these school districts exclusively.

The states that do not have school districts at all, or do not use them exclusively, employ dependent school systems. *Dependent school systems* are departments of state, county, municipal, or township governments. There are 1,508 of them, and the Census Bureau does not recognize dependent school systems as governments. Alaska, Hawaii, Maryland, North Carolina, and the District of

(*cont.*)

A Load of Local Governments: (*Cont.*)

Columbia rely entirely on dependent school systems and have no independent school districts. Fifteen states use both independent school districts and dependent school systems. In all, nineteen states and Washington, DC, use dependent school systems, either exclusively, mostly, or partially.

Services.   Over six out of ten public schools' expenditures are allocated to instruction. A third of school dollars go to support services, the next highest outlay.

Revenue Sources.   The dominant source of local school district revenue is the states. Almost half, 49 percent, of the revenue of school districts is provided by state governments. When we include federal pass-through grants in the states' funding of local school districts, the states' share of district budgets rises to 57 percent.

No other type of local government acquires anything close to this level of state generosity, which is relatively new. In 1900, states contributed about a sixth of the revenue of local schools, and the remaining funding was provided exclusively by the local school districts. It was only in 1973 that, for the first time, the average share of education budgets furnished by local school districts dipped below 50 percent because of steadily growing contributions from both the state and federal sectors.

Local sources contribute 43 percent of school district revenue, and over two-thirds of this local contribution, and 29 percent of school districts' total revenue, is derived from taxes. The local property tax is virtually the only tax that school districts levy. The general-purpose governments, such as cities and counties, of the local jurisdictions in which school districts reside provide a surprisingly large portion of district revenue—more than a fourth of all revenue derived from local sources, and over 7 percent of total district revenue.

Washington contributes 8 percent of local schools' revenues, over 90 percent of which is passed through state governments to the schools. The remainder is sent directly to school districts and dependent school systems.

Government.   *School boards*, or *boards of educations*, are the local legislatures of independent school districts. They were originated in 1647 by Plymouth Colony, which instructed its towns to select men to manage the "prudential affairs" of their schools.

Over time, school boards have lost much of their policymaking powers to their state governments. All states constrain the independence of their local school boards through *state boards of education* (except Wisconsin, which does not have one) that serve as the main school policymaker in many states; *state departments of education*, which are often the implementation arm of state school policy; and *chief state school officers* (usually called *commissioners of education*, or *superintendents of schools* or *public instruction*, among other titles), who typically head the departments of education.

The average size of independent school boards is approximately six elected members, 60 percent of whom are elected at-large, and 34 percent are elected in districts. Almost all elected board members are elected in nonpartisan elections. Six percent of school board members are appointed by county, municipal, or township governments.

Most school boards appoint professional *superintendents* to manage the schools, although about a fifth of school superintendents are elected independently by district voters, and "report" directly to the electorate instead of to the school board. School districts in at least nine states elect school officials other than board members.

Dependent school systems also engage in electoral politics. The governing boards of dependent school systems average approximately six members, two-thirds of whom are elected rather than appointed. Of those system board members who are elected, more than 70 percent are elected at-large, and the remaining 30 percent are elected by district. Arizona, New York, and Tennessee permit their local governments to elect system officials, such as superintendents of schools, who are not system board members.

Special Districts

Definition. *Special districts* are organized local entities (other than school districts) authorized by state or local law to provide only one or a limited number of designated services with sufficient administrative and fiscal autonomy to qualify as separate governments.

Scope. There are an impressive 35,356 special districts in all the states and the District of Columbia, and they usually are called *districts* or *authorities*. Not all state or local agencies that are entitled districts or authorities qualify as separate governments, and some are so closely related to local governments that the Census Bureau classifies them not as special districts, but as subordinate government agencies.

Special districts are the fastest growing type of local government and have been the most numerous of all five types since 1972. Illinois, with 3,145 special districts, has the most, and Alaska the fewest: fourteen. Two-thirds of special districts overlap the boundaries of two or more *general-purpose governments*—that is, townships, municipalities, counties, and even states. A third of all special districts have boundaries that match the boundaries of a county, municipality, or township.

For a government to create a special district, voters in the affected jurisdictions typically must vote it up or down (with some exceptions—at least a few have been created by legislatures), and anywhere from 5 percent to 50 percent of a jurisdiction's electorate will turn out for these referenda. In the view of some experts, special interests often manipulate these referenda for their own purposes. Real estate interests in particular push for the creation of special districts as a means of lowering their risks and costs by leveraging in public funds for their development projects, and land developers now "dominate the politics of special district formation" (Burns, p. 25).

A large number of special districts in an area can make it difficult for general-purpose governments to plan and set priorities. But the presence of numerous special districts seems to be a consequence of default by general-purpose governments. Stephens and Wikstrom found that the activity level of special districts associates with state centralization and local government activity. In states with centralized governments and with general-purpose local governments that actively provide services, there is a low level of activity by special districts.

Services. Special districts normally specialize in a single function, and often they are services that we associate with general-purpose governments. A fifth of special districts manage some aspect of natural resources, such as flood control, irrigation, or conservation, and the large number of these districts is due in part to federal environmental legislation that began appearing in the 1970s. Sixteen percent of special districts control fires; 10 percent each supply water or are in housing and community development; nearly 6 percent provide sewerage; almost 5 percent preside over cemeteries; and about 4 percent each administer libraries or parks and recreation programs. Two percent or less of special districts are involved with highways, health, hospitals, education, or airports. Only 9 percent of special districts are *multiple-function districts*, which are responsible for more than one governmental program (although more than half of these are nothing more than water *and* sewer districts, thus making them "multiple function").

(cont.)

A Load of Local Governments: (*Cont.*)

Less than half, 46 percent, of special districts use their own employees to provide services directly; most contract out the provision of these services or simply finance them by issuing bonds. Foster's study of 300 metropolises found that services provided by special-purpose governments had a higher cost per capita than did the same services provided by general-purpose governments.

Revenue Sources.   User fees are the major revenue source for special districts, and charges and utility revenue account for more than half, 55 percent, of all revenue dollars.

Special districts collect a surprisingly large chunk of their revenues directly from Washington—13 percent, the largest proportion for any type of local government. Two-thirds of this federal largesse is in the form of housing and community development grants.

Almost half of special districts may collect property taxes, and nearly a fifth may levy other sorts of taxes and assessments. Yet, not much more than a tenth, 12 percent, of the revenues that all special districts derive is from taxes, and about two-thirds of their tax revenues are from property taxes; sales taxes make up the rest.

State governments contribute about 7 percent to the total revenue of special districts. Local governments and interest earnings each account for some 6 percent of district revenue.

Some types of special districts generate disproportionately large shares of all district revenue, and this is especially true for electric power utilities and hospitals. Even though electric utilities account for considerably less than 1 percent of all special districts, they produce an impressive 14 percent of the total revenues of all special districts. Hospital districts account for only 2 percent of all special districts, yet hospitals match electric utilities as an income generator, accounting for another 14 percent of total district revenue. Water districts, which make up a tenth of all special districts, contribute the third largest portion, 7 percent, of all district revenue. Airports and public transit each account for approximately 1 percent of all special districts, but provide about 3 percent each of total district revenue.

Government.   Special districts are governed by boards of five, on average, *directors* or *commissioners*, who have fixed terms and normally are unpaid and part-time. Slightly more than half, 52 percent, of these legislators are elected by district voters. Special districts with the power to tax usually have elected boards. Some districts, notably irrigation districts in the West, retain the atavistic practice of allowing only property owners to vote in board elections.

The appointment, by chief elected executives or legislative bodies, of board members is a rising trend, and their share of board memberships has risen from 40 percent to 48 percent over fifteen years. The larger and more urban the district, the more likely that its board will be appointed, and a large number, 44 percent, of all special districts have no elected officials whatsoever. Passing few voters turn out for elections in those special districts that elect boards of directors, and from 2 percent to 5 percent is considered to be an unusually high turnout.

---

source of local revenue than are the feds. We described earlier the erratic, up-and-down behavior of the federal government over the past 100 years or so in supporting local budgets, but, conversely, another analysis brings home the solid, sober support of the states. This study of 162 large cities found that Washington, over a period of twenty-four years, had steadily withdrawn financial assistance from those cities, but that the states, responsibly and consistently,

Whether a district board is elected or appointed, however, may make little difference in district responsiveness to citizens. Molloy's study of 100 airport and port districts found that elected boards were no more likely to respond to public preferences than were appointed boards, although Bauroth's analysis of all special districts indicated a possible influence by property owners on the tax and revenue policies enacted by elected boards.

Notes: The *Definition* of each type of local government, all the figures on the *Scope* of these governments, and most of the information on their *Services* are calculated from data in the Census Bureau's 2002 census of governments.

Most of the information on *Revenue Sources* is also from this census. *Revenue* refers to *all* revenues, that is, general revenue and other than general revenue. *Other than general revenue* is revenue derived from insurance trusts, current charges for services, and government-owned enterprises, and it may be spent only in those areas. Chapter 8 provides details. Other than general revenue constitutes, on average, 19 percent of the total revenue of county governments; 15 percent of all municipal revenue; 14 percent for townships; 27 percent for special districts; and 4 percent of all school district revenue.

Many of the figures on *Government,* particularly those dealing with elections, legislators, and row officers, are drawn from the 1992 census of governments, which is the latest and most comprehensive source on the topic.

Most of the data on the *Forms of Government* used by counties and municipalities is provided by surveys published by the ICMA in 2004 and 2003, respectively. Most of the data on governmental forms used by townships is provided by the 1992 census of governments, although details about the town meeting form and other governmental characteristics are provided by ICMA polls appearing in 1998 and 2003.

Data on the use by counties of the commission form of government vary widely and warrant some explanation. The census of governments found that 60 percent of counties used the commission plan in 1992, but the ICMA concluded that only 32 percent of counties were using it in 2002. Although the commission form is in clear decline, it seems dubious that the number of counties using the plan plummeted by nearly half in just ten years. At least some of the explanation lies in the response rates to the two studies. The 1992 census had a dramatically higher response rate—all counties responded—than did the 2002 survey, to which only a third of counties responded. Moreover, the commission form is overwhelmingly favored by small rural counties, which were underrepresented in the 2002 poll.

Sources (in alphabetical order by author): Nicholas Bauroth, "The Influence of Elections on Special District Revenue Policies: Special Democracies or Automatons of the State?" *State and Local Government Review* 37 (3, 2005), pp. 193–205; Scott Bollens, "Examining the Link between State Policy and the Creation of Local Special Districts," *State and Local Government Review* 18 (Fall 1986), pp. 117–124; Nancy Burns, *The Formation of American Local Government: Private Values in Public Institutions* (New York: Oxford, 1994); Tim De Young, "Governing Special Districts: The Conflict between Voting Rights and Property Privileges," *Arizona State Law Journal* 2 (Summer 1982), pp. 419–452; Kathryn A. Foster, *The Political Economy of Special Purpose Governments* (Washington, DC: Georgetown University Press, 1997); Rob Gurwit, "Are City Councils a Relic of the Past?" *Governing* (April 2003), pp. 20–24; Nicholas Henry, *Governing at the Grassroots: State and Local Politics,* 3rd ed. (Englewood Cliffs, NJ: Prentice Hall, 1987); Susan A. MacManus and Charles S. Bullock III, "The Form, Structure, and Composition of America's Municipalities in the New Millennium," *Municipal Year Book, 2003* (Washington, DC: International City/County Management Association, 2003), pp. 3–18; Michael A. Molloy, "Local Special Districts and Public Accountability," paper presented at the Annual Meeting of the Midwest Political Science Association, Chicago, 2000; Tanis J. Salant, "Trends in County Government Structure," *Municipal Year Book, 2004* (Washington, DC: International City/County Management Association, 2004), pp. 35–41; G. Ross Stephens, "The Least Glorious, Most Local, Most Trivial, Homely, Provincial, and Most Ignored Form of Local Government," *Urban Affairs Quarterly* 24 (June 1989), pp. 499–506; G. Ross Stephens and Nelson Wikstrom, "Trends in Special Districts," *State and Local Government Review* 30 (Spring 1998), pp. 120–138; U.S. Advisory Commission on Intergovernmental Relations, *State and Local Roles in the Federal System,* A-88 (Washington, DC: U.S. Government Printing Office, 1982); U.S. Bureau of the Census, *Census of Governments, 1992,* Vol. 1, No. 2 (Washington, DC: U.S. Government Printing Office, 1995); U.S. Bureau of the Census, *Census of Governments, 2002,* Vol. 1, No. 1, and Vol. 4, No. 5 (Washington, DC: U.S. Government Printing Office, 2002 and 2004, respectively); U.S. Bureau of the Census, *Statistical Abstract of the United States, 2006,* 125th ed. (Washington, DC: U.S. Government Printing Office, 2006), Table 242; and Joseph F. Zimmerman, "The New England Town Meeting: Lawmaking by Assembled Voters," *Municipal Year Book, 1998* (Washington, DC: International City/County Management Association, 1998), pp. 23–29.

made up for most of the shortfall. Federal aid per capita to these cities dropped by almost three-fifths, but state aid per capita to those cities rose by close to half, with the most significant increases in state aid to urban education.[161]

The States and Urban Stress. As this analysis implies, the states also are increasingly sensitive to the needs of their more distressed cities. This sensitivity is remarkable because, according to one carefully-done study, "At a time when central cities are more dependent on their states than ever, there is considerable evidence that their clout in state legislatures is eroding."[162]

Research indicates that state aid to needy cities is increasingly comparable to federal aid in that it is targeted toward the most distressed areas and poorest people, although federal aid seems to be slightly more focused on meeting the needs of the most distressed inner cities.[163]

Thirteen states have enacted growth management legislation that, among other goals, attempts to improve the quality of urban areas and reduce urban sprawl.[164]

At least some states are preparing for tough economic times in their local governments. This is appropriate, as thirty-six states report that at least one of their local governments had experienced a fiscal crisis in their "recent history."[165] Ten states have formal definitions of "fiscal crisis" for their local governments,[166] and thirteen states have formal procedures for helping local governments in fiscal stress.[167]

The overall scholarly assessment of the states' role in urban affairs is showing indications of positive change. One indication of this change is that all states now have departments of community affairs that are concerned with the health and viability of their local governments.

Creeping Regionalism: The Role of Local Collaboration

An unsurprising development in our era of metropolitan governance is renewed levels of collaboration among local governments. If there is tension among the levels of government, local governments themselves seem to be getting on famously with each other.

For example, just as the states have grouped themselves regionally, local governments have aligned themselves along functional lines for purposes of lobbying Congress and state legislatures for improved policies for communities. Appendices A and D provide details about these national associations of local governments.

Similarly, there are in Congress a Suburban Caucus, a Rural Caucus, and a Metropolitan Area Caucus, which function as local interests' counterpart to the states' regional alliances in Congress but are arrayed along demographic lines.

Regionally, the story in much the same. There are over 500 regional councils of local governments. Most engage in a "dual planning and service role," and the services most favored for implementation by regional councils are economic development, transportation, solid waste, and land use. "Other entities seeking regional authority have emerged" as well, "ranging from private sector associations and foundations to environmental coalitions and citizen groups," that work closely with local governments and regional councils.[168]

Interlocal Service Arrangements

With the encouragement of their state governments (forty-two states have enacted legislation that specifically authorizes their local governments to enter into agreements with each other to deliver services[169]), cities and counties have devised a number of ways of working together in an attempt to provide more, better, and cheaper services to their citizens. This cooperation is done through *interlocal service arrangements*, or agreements entered into by local governments with other local governments to deliver services to their citizens.

There are three major types of such arrangements. We consider them in turn.

Intergovernmental Service Agreements. The *intergovernmental service agreement* occurs when one jurisdiction pays another to deliver certain services to its residents. More than half of cities and counties have entered into intergovernmental service agreements.[170] Less than 17 percent of all services provided by local governments are delivered via these agreements,[171] and their use is rising; twenty years earlier, not quite 13 percent of all local services were provided through this means.[172] Most favored services delivered through intergovernmental service agreements are job training and public health programs.[173]

Studies of intergovernmental service agreements consistently find that their use usually lowers the costs of delivering the service contracted, at least in comparison to contracting out services to for-profit companies. An extensive review of the empirical analyses of "public sector to public sector" service contracting found that average savings amounted to 22 percent, which was over half again as much in savings than "public sector to private sector" contracting.[174]

Joint Service Agreements. Another form of interlocal service arrangement is the *joint service agreement*, or agreements between two or more governments for the joint planning, financing, and delivering of certain services to the residents of all participating jurisdictions. Fifty-five percent of local governments have entered into joint service agreements. Libraries and public safety communication are popular areas.[175]

Intergovernmental Service Transfers. A third type of interlocal service arrangement is the *intergovernmental service transfer*, or the permanent transfer of a responsibility from a jurisdiction to another government, a private corporation, or a nonprofit agency. Transferring a responsibility permanently is a serious matter for any government because it is a sacrifice of authority and power, so it is perhaps surprising that 40 percent of cities and counties executed such transfers over an eight-year period. Favored areas of transfer are public works and utilities, health, and welfare.[176]

Patterns of Interlocalism

Regardless of the type of interlocal arrangement, patterns emerge.

Poor, Burdened, Big, Professional, and Urban. One pattern is that, in contrast to those local governments that contract out a high proportion of their services to the private sector, governments that enter into relatively large numbers of arrangements with other local governments are generally poorer, not wealthier, governments.[177] Cities that are burdened with many service responsibilities and employees are more likely to contract out their services for delivery by other governments than are those cities that have fewer services and employees.[178] Larger jurisdictions are more willing to enter into intergovernmental

arrangements than are smaller ones. Council-manager cities and counties with a county manager or administrator tend to favor them, as do inner cities more than suburbs and metropolitan counties more than rural ones.[179]

The Centralization of Local Services. In national studies conducted over eleven years, it was found that, generally speaking, larger local governments are taking over the responsibilities of smaller ones. Fifty-six percent of the intergovernmental service agreements let by cities, for example, are given to counties. Nearly half, 48 percent, of all joint service agreements are entered into with counties, and counties are the principal service providers for more than half of all services provided through these agreements.[180]

Of greatest significance, however, counties and regional organizations receive most of the intergovernmental service transfers; in other words, the largest units of local government are *permanently* taking over the traditional duties of cities and towns, *and at the request* of those cities and towns. Fifty-four percent of all intergovernmental service transfers go to counties, and 14 percent (the next highest) to regional organizations. Whatever the cause and whatever the outcome, it appears that local governments, like state governments, are centralizing functionally, if not structurally.[181]

Place, People, and Power: The Puzzle of Metropolitan Governance

Almost two-fifths of all local governments are concentrated in *metropolitan areas*, or cities of at least 50,000 people and their suburbs,[182] and it is these local governments that govern the vast majority of Americans: nearly four-fifths of all Americans, are found on the one-fifth of American land that constitutes the nation's 331 metropolitan areas.[183]

One of the most vexing questions facing citizens and their governments in metropolitan areas is that of matching, on the one hand, the people and their public problems with, on the other hand, the appropriate scope, jurisdiction, functions, and even number of governments that would deal most effectively, efficiently, responsively, and justly with those problems. "A great deal of intellectual energy, spanning several decades, has gone into efforts to determine the correct pattern of organization for metropolitan areas."[184]

What is the best way, in other words, of reconciling area with power?

No question is more central—and wholly unique—to public administration than is this one. Only governments, among all organizational forms, must wrestle with the very large and real dilemma of coherently integrating the array and reach of their own powers with the size and complexity of the geographic areas in which they exercise their powers. These are genuinely taxing intellectual issues, but they are not merely academic ones; they are at the core of determining the very capacity of public administrators and public leaders to improve the quality of civic life itself.

Ultralocalism: The Compound Republics of Metropolitan America

Americans have made clear in practice their preference about how metropolitan areas should be paired with public power: that preference is, by and large, the more governments the merrier.

There is an average of 102 local governments per metropolitan area, a figure that has remained remarkably stable for more than a half-century. Nevertheless, the proportion of all local governments found in metropolitan areas has nearly quadrupled since 1942, from 10 percent to 38 percent, even though the number of metropolitan areas in the country only doubled.[185]

Americans not only like a lot of local governments, but they also like them small. More than half, 52 percent, of the 35,935 cities, towns, and townships in the United States govern fewer than 1,000 people per government![186] Not all of these general-purpose, if Lilliputian, local governments are in metro areas, but many are, and there are fewer than 6,000 citizens, on the average, per local government in metro areas.[187]

Americans, in sum, like *ultralocalism*,[188] or the presence of a large number of local governments, often overlapping in authority and jurisdiction,

that are charged with governing in a metropolitan area. Ultralocalism (an admittedly loaded word) is more conventionally called *governmental fragmentation*, or *governmental differentiation*, which is formally defined as "the number of governmental units per 10,000 residents in a metropolitan area."[189] Ultralocalism not only is the most pervasive and popular form of metropolitan governance but also is one that embodies all the values extant in the American tradition of constrained public administration, described at the beginning of this book, that is, checks, balances, divided powers, weak executives, and disjointed, uncoordinated, and often unaccountable governance.

Ultralocalism: The Theory.   Theory has belatedly followed reality. The intellectual roots of a theory of ultralocalism can be traced in particular to James Madison, the primary author of the nation's Constitution. It was Madison who coined the terms "compound republic" and "extended republic" as descriptions of how the new federal structure and its division of powers would work in the nation that he helped devise. Madison, however, was thinking only of the respective roles of the state governments and the national government, and not of local governments in metropolitan areas. Madison's ignorance of metropolitan America was paralleled by that of his colleague Thomas Jefferson, who thought that there should be four centers of republican government in the nation: the "federal republic" (or Washington, DC), the state republics, the county republics, and the "ward republics, for the small, and yet numerous and interesting concerns of the neighborhood."[190]

Our point is that most local governments, much less thickly peopled metropolitan regions, were not a part of the Founders' calculus. And this is understandable, as there were no metropolitan areas in the country when Madison and Jefferson were forming their ideas about the best ways to govern; the largest American city in 1790 was New York, with 33,131 residents, and another 16,000 or so people in what were old New York's equivalent of suburbs. When the Founders contemplated the United States, they contemplated a rural nation of farmers.

Even though the nation's Founders never really thought about the governance of large numbers of people dwelling on small plots of land, ultralocalist analysts who write about these conditions today honor Madison and Jefferson as their intellectual forebears, and Madison's phrase, "compound republic," frequently appears in their essays. Jefferson's, and especially Madison's, progeny are the "public choice" crowd that we reviewed in Chapter 10, and these researchers have applied their theories of political economy to the governments in metropolises. This literature often is called "metropolitan organization," or research on "local public economies," and its writers argue for what they term "polycentric" or "multinucleated political systems" as the most responsive to the citizenry's needs. Their contention is that many units of government, units that often overlap jurisdictionally, will be the most efficient, effective, and responsive to a citizen's demands.

These happy ends are achieved because many governments are competing—and collaborating—to serve the citizens who live in their metropolis, much like private firms compete and collaborate to serve customers in the marketplace. By contrast, a single, metropolitan-wide government would be less efficient, effective, and responsive in serving citizens in its metropolis, just as a corporate monopoly is less likely to give its customers the best goods and services at the best price in a marketplace that it completely controls.[191]

Ideas have power. The political economists' idea that ultralocalist, fragmented, local governance brings about more efficient, effective, and responsive governments took hold in policymaking circles, especially among federal policymakers.[192]

Ultralocalism: The Practice. Public choice theorists[193] have found that small governments can be effective and efficient governments. Analysts have shown, fairly consistently, that smaller police departments (those with fewer than 350 officers) tend to be more responsive providers of police services than larger ones, and often at a lower cost.[194] Once school districts exceed a certain size, according to a study of 144 unified school districts in California, students score lower on standardized tests and, because

teacher turnover was lower in larger districts than in smaller ones (thus raising overall salaries due to seniority), larger districts were less efficient.[195]

Ultralocalism also seems to enhance, or at least not impede, governmental responsiveness, effectiveness, and efficiency. A number of researchers have found that lower levels of expenditure and slower growth of expenditures associate with higher levels of governmental fragmentation,[196] although at least a couple of empirical studies have concluded that high levels of governmental fragmentation can associate with low levels of public satisfaction with governmental service, at least in some functional areas.[197]

In essence, what the students of local public economies have found is that, in comparison to metropolises dominated by a relatively few large governments, large numbers of small governments working in close proximity do not necessarily hinder effectiveness and efficiency, and often enhance them; ultralocalism may render government more responsive; and fragmentation results in citizens having more methods of service delivery from which to choose.[198] To quote one review of this literature: "Generally, this line of research has found *lower* levels of local government expenditures to be associated with *higher* levels of fragmentation and overlap."[199]

Gargantua: The Mincing Movement Toward Metropolitan Government

Even though ultralocalism seems to associate with more efficient metropolitan governance, local public executives nonetheless are, as we observed earlier, making arrangements among themselves that clearly reduce governmental fragmentation. Smaller local governments, quietly but rapidly, are transferring their responsibilities to larger local governments or to regional governments; these transfers are occurring both inside and outside metropolitan areas, but much more frequently, in metropolitan areas than in rural ones.[200]

Why is this? Perhaps local officials believe that, in the longer view, a real metropolitan government "is much better than trying to get multiple local governments to act like a metropolitan government"?[201]

Gargantuan Temptations: Coordination and Accountability.   It is this kind of thinking that underlies a notably stubborn and persistent call for the reform of how metropolitan regions are governed. One political scientist has labeled, memorably, this movement "gargantua."[202] As with ultralocalism, *gargantua* is an admittedly loaded word, and the more common phrases are *regional government, regionalism, metropolitan government*, or *metro government*, all of which refer to the elimination of all or most small governments in metro areas, and their replacement by a single, general purpose, powerful, metropolitan-wide government. Such a system, it is argued, would reduce the buck passing, confusion, and absence of accountability that the reformers believe are endemic to ultralocalist metropolises. Ultralocalism can degenerate into a jurisdictional tragedy of the commons: When everyone is responsible, no one is responsible.

For example,[203] there was the occasion when St. Louis County plainclothes detectives conducting a gambling raid were promptly arrested by police from the town of Wellston, who were staging their own raid. Another example: There was a fire in a house less than three blocks from a fire station in Las Vegas, Nevada, but just beyond the city limits. The Las Vegas fire fighters watched the house burn until county fire engines arrived. The city fire fighters had been instructed by their superior to prevent the fire from reaching city property. Angry neighborhood residents hurled rocks at the immobile city fire engines, causing substantial damage. Yet another: "A woman tourist who stopped overnight at a motel near Miami had to telephone three police departments to report a suspected prowler outside her door."[204] We do not know if any of these departments responded to her call.

The Suburbs: A Great Sucking Sound.   It is these sorts of anecdotes, and the logic that links them, that have helped to maintain the pressures for gargantuan reform. But there is more underlying the reform movement than simply a concern for governmental effectiveness and efficiency. Most Americans regard the desertion of the nation's cities, and the corresponding emergence of the "gated communities" which comprise

Fortress Suburbia, with alarm. And the evidence of this fundamental demographic shift is not anecdotal; it is statistical. Between 1950 and 1990, the population density of the nation's 522 largest central cities plummeted, on the average, by an astounding 50 percent! These central cities lost their citizens almost entirely to their surrounding suburbs, and this loss "happened almost everywhere—in big cities and small."[205]

In 1950, nearly 70 percent of Americans in the major metropolitan areas lived in central cities, but by 1990 this figure had essentially been turned upside down, and more than 60 percent of the metropolitan population lived in suburbs.[206]

This trend continues. In the 1990s, suburbs grew at more than twice the rate of central cities.[207] This is not to say that some central cities did not grow, too.[208] But the underlying reality is that "The only cities in America that swam against the suburban stream were cities swimming with the immigrant stream" after 1950, and, fifty years later, most central cities "were thinly populated areas waiting to become populated."[209]

Destructive developments accompany the population shrinkage of central cities, whether measured relative to their suburbs or simply over time. The metropolitan areas that they anchor bisect along racial and class lines.[210] Central city economies suffer. Most metropolitan jobs in 1950 were found in the central cities; today, most jobs are in the suburbs. Housing, education, and family structure in the central cities slide, while crime climbs.[211]

The Moral Grail of Gargantua.   For these and related reasons, the numerous studies suggesting that fragmented governance is really neat—that is, it delivers metropolitan services better than anyone would have guessed—seem somewhat hollow to the critics of the *status quo.* Fixating on governmental effectiveness and efficiency when so many metro areas are in advanced states of division, decay, and degradation smacks of rearranging the deck chairs on the *Titanic.* A consequence of these discomforts is the call for the gargantuan reform of metropolitan governance and its consolidation into "metro government."[212]

Metro government goes far beyond the core concerns of the ultralocalists. At root, the ultralocalists are concerned with only two values: effectiveness and efficiency in the delivery of government services. So, too, are those who advocate metro government, but they embrace more values than effectiveness and efficiency and are concerned as well with equity and social justice. From the perspective of the advocates of metro government, the grails of a healthier metropolis and a more ennobling civic culture must be central in the debate over how best to govern metropolitan areas.

The proponents of metro government deal with deeper and ultimately more important issues than do the public-choice proponents of "polycentric political systems." In fact, the rational choice theorists, by focusing attention only on the issues of effectiveness and efficiency, may have deflected the nation's confronting and dealing with the larger concerns of social equity and civic health in metropolitan America. If so, then the friends of fragmentation have done the nation a disservice.

In a slim and eloquently written tome, David Rusk suggests that a more rational and authoritative approach to the emplacement of more coherent government is needed if metropolitan governments are to do more in bettering the lives of their citizens. (There are other analysts[213] who, like Rusk, advocate metro government, although we concentrate here on Rusk's research as it is the most comprehensive.) Rusk, a former mayor of Albuquerque, pulls no punches: "What I want to achieve is to help key policy makers and opinion leaders face the fact that racial and economic segregation is the heart of America's 'urban problem.' "[214]

Urban Elasticity

In his unique statistical analysis of all 320 metropolitan areas (as of 1990) and the 522 major cities in them (by contrast, almost all urban analyses dwell on only a small number of the nation's largest central cities), covering the years 1950 through 1990, Rusk concludes that, "In general, the more highly fragmented a metro area is, the more segregated it is racially and economically. . . . Reversing the fragmentation of urban areas is an essential step in ending severe racial and economic segregation."[215]

Noting these trends, Rusk suggests that the key notion in understanding the health of a metropolitan area is that of "elasticity." *Elasticity* refers to a city's ability to grow, either by in-filling vacant urban areas with people, or (more commonly) by expanding its boundaries to include people living in its suburbs, or both. The more elastic a city is, the more likely it is to grow. Inelastic cities, by contrast, have, since 1950, "suffered catastrophic population losses," and the growth in their metropolitan populations occurred entirely in their suburbs.[216]

Rusk and others make a persuasive, and even compelling, case that elastic jurisdictions are better for people than are inelastic ones. In contrast to elastic metropolitan areas, inelastic metro areas are older; are demonstrably more racially segregated (during the 1990s, the fastest growing cities were those that drew new residents from all racial groups[217]); have far wider income gaps between inner city and outer suburb (which is "the single most important indicator of an urban area's social health"[218]); are more governmentally fragmented; are less prudently managed and fiscally viable, at least as measured by municipal bond ratings;[219] are less able to adjust to economic change; are less effective in advancing the prosperity of the entire metropolitan area; and have more concentrated areas of poverty—and, as Rusk notes, "as social tinder, poverty in elastic areas typically lacks the critical mass it has in the highly concentrated ghettos of inelastic cities. . . ."[220]

This final point is of particular note. The three most disastrous urban race riots of the 1960s—in Los Angeles in 1965 and in Newark and Detroit in 1967, in which 100 people died—all occurred in cities with ratings of "zero elasticity" (Newark and Detroit), or "low elasticity" (Los Angeles, which reexploded in 1992 at a cost of fifty-five lives). These are the lowest two rankings of the five possible elasticity rankings. Miami's wrenching race riot in 1980, in which eighteen died, and Cincinnati's three-day riot in 2001 also occurred in cities with zero elasticity. Ultralocalist governance would seem to associate with civic anger.

For a city to gain elasticity, Rusk suggests "metro government." Using Rusk's crisp criteria, a *metro government* is a general-purpose local government with "all of the powers of a munici-pality under state law" (especially "key planning and zoning powers"), which contains within its limits at least 60 percent of the people living in its metropolitan area, and most (but preferably all) of the area's major cities; a metro government "need not be responsible for all local public functions," but "it must exercise exclusive powers within its jurisdiction."[221]

The creation of metro governments has much room for progress. Using Rusk's criteria, only forty-eight (or 15 percent) of metropolitan areas are served by metro governments in twenty-one states, and most of these are medium sized com-munities; only 3 percent of the four-fifths of Americans living in metro areas live in areas served by metro governments.[222]

In Part Four, we have been reviewing the ways that public administrators implement public poli-cies, ways that range from outsourcing service delivery to restructuring metropolises. But imple-mentation rests on decision making, and decision making in the public sector, in turn, is based on underlying moral and ethical assumptions held by individual decision makers about how the world works and what is right or wrong about how the world works. We consider this final, and perhaps most important, aspect of public administration next.

Notes

1. Two good discussion of the definitional differences among the terms used in this paragraph are Deil S. Wright, "Federalism, Intergovernmental Relations, and Relations, and Intergovernmental Management: Historical Reflections and Conceptual Comparisons," *Public Administration Review* 50 (March/April 1990), pp. 168–178; and Vincent L. Marando and Patricia S. Florestano, "Intergovernmental Management: The State of the Discipline," in Naomi B. Lynn and Aaron Wildavsky, eds., *Public Administration: The State of the Discipline* (Chatham, NJ: Chatham House, 1990), pp. 287–317.
2. Henry S. Reuss, *Revenue Sharing: Crutch of Catalyst for State and Local Governments?* (New York: Praeger, 1970), pp. 53–56.
3. This discussion is drawn largely from Kenneth N. Vines, "The Federal Setting of State Politics," in Herbert Jacob and Kenneth N. Vines, eds., *Politics in the American States*, 3rd ed. (Boston: Little, Brown, 1976), p. 4.

4. Alexander Hamilton, John Jay, and James Madison, *The Federalist* (New York: Random House, 1937), p. 347.
5. Unless noted otherwise, the following discussion is drawn from Deil S. Wright, *Understanding Intergovernmental Relations*, 2nd ed. (Monterey, CA: Brooks/Cole, 1982), pp. 43–82; and David B. Walker, *The Rebirth of Federalism: Slouching Toward Washington*, 2nd ed. (New York: Chatham House, 2000).
6. President Franklin Pierce, quoted in Walker, *The Rebirth of Federalism*, p. 69.
7. Ibid., p. 74.
8. Ibid., p. 75.
9. Ibid., p. 92.
10. Norton Long, as cited in William R. Barnes, "Beyond Federal Urban Policy," *Urban Affairs Review* 40 (May 2005), p. 578.
11. John Shannon, "The Return of Fend-for-Yourself Federalism: The Reagan Mark," in U.S. Advisory Commission on Intergovernmental Relations, *Readings in Federalism: Perspectives on a Decade of Change*, SR-11 (Washington, DC: U.S. Government Printing Office, 1989), pp. 119–122; and John Shannon, "Competitive Federalism—Three Driving Forces," *Intergovernmental Perspective* 15 (Fall 1989), pp. 17–18.
12. John Shannon and James Edwin Kee, "The Rise of Competitive Federalism," *Public Budgeting and Finance* 9 (Winter 1989), p. 11.
13. John Kincaid and Richard L. Cole, "Public Opinion on Issues of U.S. Federalism in 2005: End of the Post-2001 Pro-Federal Surge?" *Publius* 35 (Winter 2005), pp. 169–188. Public opinion about the federal, state, and local governments had returned to pre-2001 levels by 2005.
14. U.S. Advisory Commission on Intergovernmental Relations, *Changing Public Attitudes on Government and Taxes, 1992*. S-22 (Washington, DC: U.S. Government Printing Office, 1993), p. 3; and U.S. Bureau of the Census, *Statistical Abstract of the United States, 2001*, 121st ed. (Washington, DC: U.S. Government Printing Office, 2001), Table 398.
15. Kincaid and Cole, "Public Opinion on Issues of U.S. Federalism in 2005," p. 172.
16. Ibid., and U.S. Advisory Commission on Inter-governmental Relations, *Changing Public Attitudes on Government and Taxes*, p. 3.
17. Hart-Teeter Poll, *Finding from a Research Project about Attitudes Toward Government* (Washington, DC: Council for Excellence in Government, 1997), p. 11. Figure is for 1997. In 1995, 60 percent of Americans believed this.
18. U.S. Advisory Commission on Intergovernmental Relations, *Changing Public Attitudes on Government and Taxes, 1992*, p. 3.
19. Ibid.; U.S. Bureau of the Census, *Statistical Abstract of the United States, 2001*, Table 398; and Kincaid and Cole, "Public Opinion on Issues of U.S. Federalism in 2005."
20. Kincaid and Cole, "Public Opinion on Issues of US Federalism in 2005," pp. 172, 178, and 180. Figures are for 2005.

21. Hart-Teeter Poll, *Findings from a Research Project about Attitudes Toward Government*, p. 11. Figures are for 1997. In 1995, 60 percent of Americans believed this.

22. John Bohte and Kenneth J. Meyer, "The Marble Cake: Introducing Federalism to the Government Growth Equation," *Publius* 30 (Summer 2000), p. 44.

23. Cynthia J. Bowling and Deil S. Wright, "Public Administration in the Fifty States: A Half-Century Administration Revolution," *State and Local Government Review* 30 (Winter 1998), pp. 52–64.

24. Ibid., pp. 55–56.

25. As derived from data in Katherine Barrett and Richard Greene, "Grading the States, 2005: A Management Report Card" *Governing* (February 2005), pp. 24–95. In 1999 (the project's first year), the states' average grade was 2.70, and in 2001 and 2005, it was 2.75 on a 4-point scale. It is somewhat misleading to make these comparisons, as the graders changed their criteria for 2005. In 2005, the criteria were money, people, infrastructure, and information; previously, they were: financial management, capital management, human resources, managing for results, and information technology. The grades are provided by the Government Performance Project conducted, in its earlier stages, primarily at Syracuse University, and later primarily at the University of Pennsylvania, in conjunction with *Governing Magazine*. The project is funded by the Pew Charitable Trusts.

26. As derived from data in Katherine Barrett and Richard Greene, "Grading the Cities: A Management Report Card," *Governing* (February 2000), pp. 22–91. In 2000, the thirty-five cities with the largest revenue bases (which also were, for the most part, the most populous) averaged a grade of 2.80 on a 4-point scale. As with the states, the grades are provided by the Government Performance Project, described in the previous note.

27. Peter S. Kilborn, "With Welfare Overhaul Now Law, States Grapple with the Consequences," *New York Times* (August 23, 1996).

28. David B. Walker, "The Advent of an Ambiguous Federalism and the Emergence of New Federalism III," *Public Administration Review* 56 (May/June 1996), p. 272.

29. As derived from data in U.S. Bureau of the Census, "Table 1. Summary of State and Local Government Finances: 2002–03," *Census of Government*, 2002 (Washington, DC: U.S. Government Printing Office, 2005), http://www.census.gov/govs/extimate/03s100us.html. In 2002–2003, 89 percent of federal assistance went directly to the states.

30. Linda Greenhouse, "States Are Given New Legal Shield by Supreme Court," *New York Times* (June 24, 1999).

31. The Court's pro-states' rights cases are *Seminole Tribe* v. *Florida* (decided in 1996; this is the case in which the phrase "sovereign immunity" made its debut); *Printz* v. *United States* (1997; local sheriffs cannot be required to conduct background checks under the Brady gun control law); *Alden* v. *Maine* (1999; state employees cannot sue state governments); *Florida* v. *College Savings*

Bank (1999, patents and universities), *College Savings Bank* v. *Florida* (1999; businesses victimized by states engaging in unfair competition cannot sue), *United States* v. *Morrison* (2000; when the Court struck down the Violence Against Women Act in *Morrison,* the Court also decided that women whose legal rights were violated by state government cannot sue the state government); *University of Alabama* v. *Garrett* (2001; states were given immunity from suits brought by state employees under the Americans with Disabilities Act); *Alexander* v. *Sandoval* (2001); and *Federal Maritime Commission* v. *South Carolina State Ports Authority* (2002). In *Alexander*, the Court held that states receiving federal funds could be sued only for intentional discrimination, and not for policies that merely have a discriminatory impact. In *Federal Maritime Commission*, the Court ruled that South Carolina (and, by inference, all states) was not subject to the authority of the Commission (and, by inference, all federal agencies). The five, unusually well-united justices in each of these decisions were Justices Kennedy, O'Connor, Rehnquist, Scalia, and Thomas. By 2006, when the Court decided in *Gonzalez* v. *Oregon* that the U.S. attorney general had exceeded his authority in challenging Oregon's right-to-die law, the bloc of five justices had split.

32. The Court's pro-federal-power cases are *Nevada* v. *Hibbs* (decided in 2003 by a vote of 6–3; upholds the ability of state employees to sue states under the Family and Medical Leave Act); *Tennessee* v. *Lane* (2004, decided 5–4; upholds the applicability of the Americans with Disabilities Act to ensure accessible state courthouses); and *González* v. *Ralch* (2005, decided 6–3; permits the federal government to prosecute cases involving medical marijuana).

33. Dale Krane and Heidi Koening, "The State of American Federalism, 2004: Is Federalism Still a Core Value?" *Publius* 35 (Winter 2005), p. 1.

34. Sanford F. Schram and Carol S. Weissert, "The State of American Federalism, 1996," *Publius* 27 (Spring 1997), p. 1.

35. Walker, "The Advent of Ambiguous Federalism and the Emergence of New Federalism III," pp. 271–280.

36. Donna Wilson Kirchheimer, "Entrepreneurial Implementation of the U.S. Welfare State," paper presented at the Annual Meeting of the American Political Science Association, Washington, DC, August 28–31, 1986, p. 1.

37. Vines, "The Federal Setting of State Politics," p. 16. When we eliminate defense and foreign affairs from the calculus, local government accounted for an astonishing 73 percent of all domestic spending in 1902!

38. As derived from data in U.S. Bureau of the Census, *Statistical Abstract of the United States, 2006*, 125th ed. (Washington, DC: U.S. Government Printing Office, 2006), Tables 438, 441, 442, and 459. Figures are for 2002. Intergovernmental revenue from the federal government has been subtracted from the states' expenditure and debt redemption so that federal intergovernmental expenditures are not double counted. Direct intergovernmental revenue from the federal and state

governments has been subtracted from local governments' total expenditure so that federal and state intergovernmental expenditures are not double counted.

39. As derived from data in ibid., Table 422. Figures are for 2005.

40. Walker, *The Rebirth of Federalism*, p. 9.

41. U.S. Advisory Commission on Intergovernmental Relations, *Characteristics of Federal Grant-In-Aid Programs to State and Local Governments: Grants Funded, FY 1993*, M-183 (Washington, DC: U.S. Government Printing Office, 1993), p. 1. Figures are for 1993.

42. Kenneth Finegold, Laura Wherry, and Stephanie Schardin, *Block Grants: Historical Overview and Lessons Learned*, No. A-63 in the series, New Federalism: Issues and Options for the States (Washington, DC: Urban Institute, 2004).

43. U.S. Advisory Commission on Intergovernmental Relations, *Federal Grant Profile, 1995: A Report on ACIR's Federal Grant Fragmentation Index*, SR-20 (Washington, DC: U.S. Government Printing Office, 1995), p. 1. Figure is for 1995.

44. As derived from data in U.S. General Accounting Office, *Federal Assistance: Grant System Continues to Be Highly Fragmental*, GAO–03–718T (Washington, DC: U.S. Government Printing Office, 2003), p. 5. Figures are for 2001, when there were 836 federal grants programs expending $331.5 billion. Twenty programs accounted for $258.7 billion.

45. Ibid., p. 15. Washington has been trying to improve the management of its grants system for state and local governments since the 1940s. Examples include the report of the *Commission on Organization of the Executive Branch* (the first Hoover Commission), released in 1949, which noted the lack of coordination among granting agencies and promoted the equivalent of block grants; the report by the *Commission on Intergovernmental Relations* (the Kestenbaum Commission) of 1955, which chastised the first Hoover Commission for its promotion of block grants and urged the use of categorical grants to achieve federal objectives; creation in 1959 of the *U.S. Advisory Commission on Intergovernmental Relations,* which, for almost four decades, provided invaluable data and charted trends in the nation's intergovernmental relations; the *Intergovernmental Cooperation Act of 1968,* which attempted to improve coordination among levels of government; the *Federal Assistance Review,* which was a government-wide effort, conducted from 1969 to 1973, to streamline the flow of federal aid to states and communities; *Federal Management Circular 74–7* of 1974, which standardized administrative provisions across grant programs; the *Joint Funding Simplification Act of 1974*, which assisted grantees in streamlining federal assistance by letting them combine funding from several grants that were administered by one or more federal agencies; and the *Federal Financial Assistance Management Act of 1999*, which simplified application and reporting requirements and facilitates greater coordination. Despite these attempts, problems of grant proliferation and fragmentation have not been measurably relieved. Our sources for most of this review are: ibid., p. 3, and Barbara Floersch, "Federal Grantmaking: The Long View of History," *The Grantsmanship Magazine* (Summer 2001), p. 4.

46. Finegold, Wherry, and Schardin, *Block Grants*, p. 4.

47. Floersch, "Federal Grantmaking," p. 2. The legislation was the Weeks Act of 1911.

48. U.S. Advisory Commission on Intergovernmental Relations, *Federal Grant Profile, 1995*, p. 7. Figures are for 1995.

49. Paul C. Light, *Fact Sheet on the New True Size of Government* (Washington, DC: Center for public Service, Brookings Institution, 2003), p. 4. Figure is for 2002.

50. As derived from data in U.S. Bureau of the Census, *Statistical Abstract of the United States, 2006*, Table 451. Figure is for 2002.

51. As derived from data in Light, *Fact Sheet on the New True Size of Government*, p. 5. Grantee jobs grew by 444,000 between 1990 and 2002.

52. U.S. Advisory Commission on Intergovernmental Relations, *The Federal Role in the Federal System: The Dynamics of Growth, A Crisis of Confidence and Competence*, A-77. (Washington, DC: U.S. Government Printing Office, 1980), pp. 120–121. In 1902, there were five federal grants accounting for 0.01 of GNP; in 1925, there were twelve grants (a number that remained stable through 1932), and in 1927 they accounted for 0.03 of GNP.

53. Floersch, "Federal Grantmaking," p. 3. Figure is for 1929.

54. As derived from data in American Council on Intergovernmental Relations, *Significant Features of Fiscal Federalism, 1995*, Vol. 2 (Washington, DC: Author, 1998), p. 52. When we refer to state or local "budgets," we are referring to total revenue, including other than general revenue derived from special funds as described in Chapter 8. When we refer to "discretionary spending," we are referring only to general expenditures.

55. U.S. Advisory Commission on Intergovernmental Relations, *The Federal Role in the Federal System*, pp. 120–121. In 1934, federal grants accounted for 3.7 percent of GNP.

56. Ibid., p. 121. In 1932 there were twelve federal grants, in 1937 there were twenty-six, and 1946, twenty-eight.

57. Walker, *The Rebirth of Federalism*, p. 99.

58. Floersch, "Federal Grantmaking," pp. 3, 5.

59. U.S. Advisory Commission on Intergovernmental Relations, *The Federal Role in the Federal System*, p. 120. In 1950, federal aid to state and local government hit $3 billion.

60. As derived from data in American Council on Intergovernmental Relations, *Significant Features of Fiscal Federalism, 1995*, Vol. 2, p. 52. Figures are for 1940.

61. As derived from data in ibid. Local revenue increased by 21 percent, 1934–1940.

62. U.S. Advisory Commission on Intergovernmental Relations, *The Federal Role in the Federal System*, p. 120. Figures for GNP cover 1950 and 1952–1958.

63. Ibid, p. 121. In 1952, the federal government offered thirty-eight grants to state and local governments.

64. Ibid, p. 120 and American Council on Intergovernmental Relations, *Significant Features of Fiscal Federalism, 1995*, Vol. 2, p. 38. Figures for federal outlays and state and local budgets cover 1950 and 1955–1958.

65. As derived from data in American Council on Intergovernmental Relations, *Significant Features of Fiscal Federalism, 1995*, Vol. 2, p. 52. Figures are for 1952 and 1957.

66. Ibid, p. 38. In 1959, federal grants hit 1.4 percent of GDP, 7 percent of federal outlays, and exceeded 14 percent of state and local outlays.

67. U.S. Advisory Commission on Intergovernmental Relations, *The Federal Role in the Federal System*, p. 120. In 1978, federal aid accounted for 3.7 percent of GNP.

68. Walker, *The Rebirth of Federalism*, p. 6.

69. American Council on Intergovernmental Relations, *Significant Features of Fiscal Federalism, 1995,* Vol. 2, p. 38.

70. Walker, *The Rebirth of Federalism*, p. 6. The figure refers to only own source outlays, or general expenditures, that are found in the general fund. See Chapter 8 for details.

71. As derived data in American Council on Intergovernmental Relations, *Significant Features of Fiscal Federalism, 1995*, Vol. 2, p. 52.

72. U.S. Commission on Intergovernmental Relations, *The Federal Role in the Federal System*, p. 121. In 1978, 74 percent of all state agencies received federal aid, and in 26 percent of all agencies, federal grants accounted for at least 50 percent of their budgets.

73. Walker, *The Rebirth of Federalism*, p. 7.

74. As derived from data in American Council on Intergovernmental Relations, *Significant Features of Fiscal Federalism, 1995*, Vol. 2 p. 52.

75. Ibid., pp. 38, 52. Data are for 1988, when federal grants accounted for 2.3 percent of GDP. With some exceptions, these benchmarks continued their decline through 1990.

76. Barnes, "Beyond Federal Urban Policy," pp. 576, 582, and 575, respectively.

77. U.S. Bureau of Census, *Statistical Abstract of the United States, 2006*, Table 421. In 2005, federal grants programs accounted for 3.5 percent of GDP.

78. U.S. General Accounting Office, *Electronic Government: Initiatives Sponsored by the Office of Management and Budget Have Made Mixed Progress,* GAO–04–561T (Washington, DC: U.S. Government Printing Office, 2004), p. 7. In 2004, the Grants.gov portal offered "835 grant opportunities at 29 grant-making agencies."

79. U.S. Bureau of the Census, *Statistical Abstract of the United States, 2006*, Table 421. Figure is for 2005.

80. As derived from data in U.S. Bureau of the Census, Table 1. "Summary of State and Local Finances by Level of Government: 2002–03," *Census of Governments, 2002*, http://www.census.gov/govs/estimate.03s100us.html. Figures are for 2002–2003. Eighty-nine percent of federal aid dollars went to the states, and 11 percent to local governments.

81. As derived from data in Ibid. Figures are for 2002–2003.

82. U.S. Bureau of the Census, *Statistical Abstract of the United States, 2006*, Table 421. In 2004, federal grants accounted for not quite 32 percent of state and local own source spending.

83. As derived from data in Ibid. Figures are for 2002–2003.

84. As derived from data in ibid. Figure is for 2002–2003 and assumes that federal pass-through grants account for about one-third of federal grants to the states. The one-third figure is derived from data in Walker, *The Rebirth of Federalism*, p. 227.

85. American Council on Intergovernmental Relations, *Significant Features of Fiscal Federalism, 1995*, Vol. 2, p. 38. In 1978, grants for payments to individuals accounted for less than 32 percent of all federal grants dollars.

86. U.S. Bureau of the Census, *Statistical Abstract of the United States, 2006*, Table 421. In 2004, grants for payments to individuals accounted for less than 64 percent of all federal grants dollars.

87. Iris J. Lav, "Piling on Problems: How Federal Policies Affect State Fiscal Conditions," *National Tax Journal* 56 (September 2003), pp. 535–554. In 2005, Medicaid accounted for 44 percent all federal grant dollars. See U.S. Bureau of the Census, *Statistical Abstract of the United States, 2006*, Table 421.

88. U.S. General Accounting Office, *Federal Grants: Design Improvements Could Help Federal Resources Go Further*, GAO/AIMD–97–7 (Washington, DC: U.S. Government Printing Office, 1996), p. 2. Other analyses find comparable results. See, for example, E. Kathleen Adams and Marcia Wade, "Fiscal Response to Matching Grants: Medicaid Expenditures and Enrollments, 1984–1992," *Public Finance Review* 20 (January 2001), pp. 26–48; and Shama Gamkhar, "Is the Response of State and Local Highway Spending Symmetric to Increases and Decreases in Federal Highway Grants?" *Public Finance Review* 20 (January 2001), pp. 3–25.

89. Paul R. Dommel et al., *Decentralizing Community Development: Second Report of the Brookings Institution Monitoring Study of the Community Development Block Grant Program* (Washington, DC: Brookings, 1978); and Richard P. Nathan et al., *Revenue Sharing: The Second Round* (Washington, DC: Brookings, 1977).

90. Steven C. Deller and Craig S. Maher, "Categorical Municipal Expenditures with a Focus on the Flypaper Effect," *Public Budgeting and Finance* 25 (September 2005), pp. 73–90. This was a study of the effects of Wisconsin's shared revenue program on local governments.

91. Donald F. Kettl, "Boutiques for the Poor," *Governing* (June 1999), p. 14.

92. Dennis O'Grady, "American Governors and State-Federal Relations: Attitudes and Activities, 1960–1980, *State Government* 57 (3, 1984), pp. 110–111.

93. U.S. Advisory Commission on Intergovernmental Relations, *State Administrators' Opinions on Administrative Change, Federal Aid, Federal Relationships*, M-120 (Washington, DC: U.S. Government Printing Office, 1980), pp. 49, 55.

94. Ibid., p. 51. From 44 to 48 percent said so.

95. Albert J. Richter, "Federal Grants Management: The City and County View," *Municipal Year Book, 1977* (Washington, DC: International City Management Association, 1977), pp. 183–184.

96. Robert W. Gage, "Intergovernmental Change: A Denver Area Perspective," *Intergovernmental Perspective* 14 (Summer 1988), p. 15.

97. James R. Hines, Jr. and Richard H. Thaler, "The Flypaper Effect," *Journal of Economic Perspectives* 9 (Winter 1995), pp. 217–226.

98. Therese A. McCarty and Stephen J. Schmidt, "Dynamic Patterns in State Government Finance," *Public Finance Review* 29 (July 2001), p. 220. The authors studied welfare, highways, and education policies.

99. Deller and Maher, "Categorical Municipal Expenditures with a Focus on the Flypaper Effect."

100. As derived from data in Walker, *The Rebirth of Federalism*, p. 7.

101. Catherine H. Lovell et al., *Federal and State Mandating on Local Governments: An Exploration of Issues and Impacts* (Riverside: Graduate School of Administration, University of California, 1979), p. 82. See also Catherine Lovell and Charles Tobin, "The Mandate Issue," *Public Administration Review* 41 (May/June 1981), pp. 218–339.

102. U.S. Advisory Commission on Intergovernmental Relations, *Federal Regulation of State and Local Government: The Mixed Record of the 1980s*, A-126 (Washington, DC: U.S. Government Printing Office, 1993), p. 46.

103. U.S. Advisory Commission on Intergovernmental Relations, *Regulatory Federalism: Policy, Process, Impact, and Reform*, A-95 (Washington, DC: U.S. Government Printing Office, 1984), Appendix I.

104. U.S. Advisory Commission on Intergovernmental Relations, *Federal Regulation of State and Local Government*, p. 46.

105. National Conference of State Legislatures, *Mandate Catalogue* (Washington, DC: Author, 1993).

106. U.S. Advisory Commission on Intergovernmental Relations, *Federal Statutory Preemption of State and Local Authority: History, Inventory, and Issues*, A-121 (Washington, DC: U.S. Government Printing Office, 1992), p. 9. This number refers to explicit federal preemption statutes.

107. U.S. Advisory Commission on Intergovernmental Relations, *Federal Court Rulings Involving State, Local, and Tribal Governments, Calendar Year 1994*, M-196 (Washington, DC: U.S. Government Printing Office, 1995).

108. U.S. Advisory Commission on Intergovernmental Relations, *Federally Induced Costs Affecting State and Local Governments*, M-193 (Washington, DC: U.S. Government Printing Office, 1994), p. 3.

109. U.S. Advisory Commission on Intergovernmental Relations, *Federal Regulation of State and Local Governments*, p. 55.

110. U.S. Advisory Commission on Intergovernmental Relations, *State Administrators' Opinions on Administrative Change, Federal Aid, Federal Relationships*, pp. 52, 45. Twenty-six percent said that federal involvement was moderate, and 11 percent said it was high; 54 percent reported "frequent contact" with federal personnel.

111. U.S. Advisory Commission on Intergovernmental Relations, *Regulatory Federalism*, p. 175. The survey was taken in 1981.

112. U.S. General Accounting Office, *Federalism: Comments on S.1214—The Federalism Accountability Act of 1999*, GAO/T–GGD–99–143. (Washington, DC: U.S. Government Printing Office, 1999), p. 1. Of 11,414 final rules issued by federal agencies between 1996 and 1998, a whopping total of five contained a "federalism assessment" as required by the Unfunded Mandates Reform Act and Executive Order 12612.

113. Grady, "American Governors and State-Federal Relations," p. 107.

114. U.S. Advisory Commission on Intergovernmental Relations, *State Administrators' Opinions on Administrative Change, Federal Aid, Federal Relationships*, pp. 52–53.

115. U.S. Advisory Commission on Intergovernmental Relations, *Federal Statutory Preemption of State and Local Authority*, pp. 34, 36. The survey was taken in 1988 and polled governors, attorneys general, community affairs departments, and state advisory commissions on intergovernmental relations.

116. Lovell, *Federal and State Mandating on Local Governments*, p. 82.

117. National League of Cities, *Municipal Policy and Program Survey* (Washington, DC: Author, 1981), as cited in U.S. Advisory Commission on Intergovernmental Relations, *Regulatory Federalism*, p. 175. But see also Jeffrey L. Pressman, *Federal Programs and City Politics: The Dynamics of the Aid Process in Oakland* (Berkeley: University of California Press, 1975), p. 85.

118. Lovell, *Federal and State Mandating on Local Governments*, p. 194.

119. U.S. Advisory Commission on Intergovernmental Relations, *Federal Mandate Relief for State, Local, and Tribal Governments*, A-129 (Washington, DC: U.S. Government Printing Office, 1995), p. 4.

120. U.S. Advisory Commission on Intergovernmental Relations, *Federally Induced Costs Affecting State and Local Governments*, p. 7.

121. As cited in Conlan and Beam, "Federal Mandates," p. 9. Figures are for 1991.

122. National Conference of State Legislatures, *Mandate Monitor* (Washington, DC: Author, 2005). In 2004, this gap stood at more than $26 billion, and in 2005 at $31 billion.

123. See, for example, Thomas Muller and Michael Fix, "The Impact of Selected Federal Actions on Municipal Outlays," in *Government Regulation: Achieving Social*

and Economic Balance, Vol. 5, of *Special Study on Economic Change*, Joint Economic Committee, U.S. Congress (Washington, DC: U.S. Government Printing Office, 1980), pp. 327, 330, 368; U.S. Conference on Mayors/Price Waterhouse, *Impact of Unfunded Mandates on U.S. Cities: A 314 City Survey* (Washington, DC: U.S. Conference of Mayors, 1993); National Association of Counties/Price Waterhouse, *NACo Unfunded Mandates Survey* (Washington, DC: National Association of Counties, 1993); and U.S. Environmental Protection Agency, *Environmental Investments: The Cost of a Clean Environment* (Washington, DC: U.S. Government Printing Office, 1990), pp. 8-49–8-51.

124. David R. Berman, "State–Local Relations: Authority, Finances, Cooperation," *Municipal Year Book, 2002* (Washington, DC: International City/County Management Association, 2002), pp. 49–50.

125. U.S. Advisory Commission on Intergovernmental Relations, *Changing Public Attitudes on Governments and Taxes, 1991*, S-20 (Washington, DC: U.S. Government Printing Office, 1991), p. 10.

126. Theresa A. Gullo and Janet M. Kelly, "Federal Unfunded Mandate Reform: A First-Year Retrospective," *Public Administration Review* 58 (September/October 1998), pp. 386–387.

127. Theresa Gullo, "History and Evaluation of the Unfunded Mandates Reform Act," *National Tax Journal* 57 (September 2004), pp. 559–570.

128. U.S. Government Accountability Office, *Unfunded Mandates: Views Vary about Reform Act's Strengths, Weaknesses, and Options for Improvement*, GAO–05–454 (Washington, DC: U.S. Government Printing Office, 2005), p. 2.

129. U.S. Government Accountability Office, *Federal Mandates: Identification Process Is Complex and Agency Rules Vary*, GAO–05–401T (Washington, DC: U.S. Government Printing Office, 2005), Highlights page, GAO analyzed 377 statutes and 122 significant rules enacted or issued in 2001 and 2002 and found that five laws and nine rules violated the Unfunded Mandates Reform Act's threshold of $50 million (in 1996 dollars) in costs to recipients. However, all of these five laws and nine regulations, save one regulation, applied only to the private sector.

130. U.S. Congressional Budget Office, as cited in National Conference of State Legislatures, *Mandate Monitor* (2005). All three laws would appear to apply to state and local governments.

131. U.S. Government Accountability Office, *Unfunded Mandates: Views Vary about Reform Act's Strengths, Weaknesses, and Options for Improvement*, Highlights page.

132. As derived from data in Light, *Fact Sheet on the New True Size of Government*, p. 4, and US Bureau of the Census, *Statistical Abstract of the United States, 1999*, 119th ed. (Washington, DC: U.S. Government Printing Office, 1999), Table 534. Figures are for 1996–1997. "State and local mandated employees" accounted for almost 28 percent of all state and local employees.

Fifteen percent of state and local employees were funded by federal grants.

133. Lav, "Piling on Problems," p. 538.

134. Ibid. See also Deborah A. Robert J. Eger III, and Justin Marlowe, "Managing Local Intergovernmental Relations: The Imperative of Diversification," *International Journal of Public Administration* 26 (December 2003), pp. 1495–1519.

135. John J. Mountjoy, "National Center for Interstate Compacts: A New Initiative," *Spectrum* 77 (Fall 2004), p. 8. Figure is for 2004.

136. Ann O'M. Bowman, "Horizontal Federalism: Exploring Interstate Interactions," *Journal of Public Administration Research and Theory* 14 (October 2004), p. 537. Figure is for 1999.

137. William Kevin Voit, *Interstate Compacts and Agencies, 1998* (Lexington, KY: Council of State Governments, 1999).

138. Bowman, "Horizontal Federalism," pp. 538, 540–541, 544. The years were 1992–1999.

139. Ibid., pp. 538, 541–542, 544.

140. Much of the following discussion on interstate conflict is drawn from Joanne Omang, "In This Economic Slump, It's a State-Eat-State Nation," *Washington Post* (June 14, 1982); and Richard Benedetto, "States Skirmish in 'Border War'," *USA Today* (February 24, 1984).

141. Roger Alford, "Kentucky Program Pays Moving Expenses to Relocate Welfare Recipients," *Savannah Morning News* (June 21, 2001). The Kentucky Cabinet for Families and Children gave $1.5 million over three years to some 2,000 families to cover moving expenses, including 389 families who moved to other states.

142. David R. Berman, "State-Local Relations: Authority, Policies, Cooperation," *Municipal Year Book, 1999* (Washington, DC: International City/County Management Association, 1999), p. 50.

143. William B. Munro, "Home Rule," *Encyclopedia of the Social Sciences*, Vol. 4 (New York: Macmillan, 1930), p. 434.

144. U.S. Advisory Commission on Intergovernmental Relations, *Local Government Autonomy: Needs for State Constitutional, Statutory, and Judicial Clarification*, A-127 (Washington, DC: U.S. Government Printing Office, 1993), p. 41.

145. U.S. Advisory Commission on Intergovernmental Relations, *State Laws Governing Local Government and Administration*, M-186 (U.S. Government Printing Office, 1993), p. 20. Figures are for 1990. There is some difference of opinion on just how many states grant their counties "real" home rule, and the number may be as low as twenty-three. These twenty-three states permit *county charter home rule*, which allows counties to not only choose a form of government but also frees them functionally, including the functions of personnel and finance. The remaining fourteen states authorize *optional form county home rule*, which grants counties structural home rule (that is, they can choose their own form of government) but denies counties functional home rule. However, both county charter home rule and optional

form county home rule are types of structural home rule, so we think that our statement in the text—that thirty-seven states grant home rule to their counties—is accurate. See: Lawrence L. Martin and Ronald C. Nyhan, "Determinants of County Charter Home Rule," *International Journal of Public Administration* 17 (May 1994), pp. 955–970.

146. Osbin L. Ervin, "Understanding American Local Government: Recent Census Bureau and ACIR Contributions," *Public Administration Review* 55 (March/April 1995), p. 210. In 1990, there were 4,294 such laws.

147. Ibid. The period of growth is from 1978 (when the first counting of these laws was done) to 1990.

148. G. Ross Stephens, "State Centralization and the Erosion of Local Autonomy," *Journal of Politics* 36 (February 1974), pp. 44–76; and Stephens, "Patterns of State Centralization/Decentralization during the Last Half of the Twentieth Century," paper presented at the annual meeting of the Southwestern Political Science Association, Austin, Texas, March 18–21, 1992. As late as 1932, no states were categorized as "centralized," but by 1992 sixteen were. In 1902, all states were "decentralized," but by 1977 none were.

149. See, for example, U.S. Advisory Commission on Intergovernmental Relations, *State and Local Roles in the Federal System*, A-88 (Washington, DC: U.S. Government Printing Office, 1982), pp. 39, 259–264; U.S. Advisory Commission on Intergovernmental Relations, *The Condition of Contemporary Federalism: Conflicting Theories and Collapsing Constraints*, A-78 (Washington, DC: U.S. Government Printing Office, 1981), pp. 68–70; Jeffrey M. Stonecash, "Fiscal Centralization in the American States: Increasing Similarity and Persisting Diversity,' *Publius* 13 (Fall 1983), pp. 123–137; and Jeffrey M. Stonecash, "Fiscal Centralization in the American States: Findings from Another Perspective," *Public Budgeting and Finance* 8 (Winter 1988), pp. 81–89.

150. U.S. Advisory Commission on Intergovernmental Relations, *State Mandating of Local Expenditures*, A-67 (Washington, DC: U.S. Government Printing Office, 1978).

151. John Meyer, W. Richard Scott, and David Strang, "Centralization, Fragmentation, and School District Complexity," *Administrative Science Quarterly* 32 (June 1987), pp. 188–201.

152. Rodney E. Hero and Jody L. Fitzpatrick, "State Mandating of Local Government Activities: An Exploration," paper presented at the 1989 Annual Meeting of the American Political Science Association, Washington, DC, August 28–31, 1986, p. 18.

153. Berman, "State-Local Relations," p. 49.

154. Janet Kelly, "Unfunded Mandates: The View from the States," *Public Administration Review* 54 (July/August 1994), p. 405. See also U.S. Advisory Commission on Intergovernmental Relations, *Mandates: Cases in State-Local Relations*, M-173 (Washington, DC: U.S. Government Printing Office, 1990).

155. Linda Wagar, "A Declaration of War," *State Government News* (April 1993), p. 18.

156. Kelly, "Lessons from the States on Unfunded Mandates," p. 138.

157. As derived from data in American Council on Intergovernmental Relations, *Significant Features of Fiscal Federalism, 1995*, Vol. 2. p. 52 for 1970–1994 data, and U.S. Bureau of the Census, Table 1, for 2002–2003 data.

158. Walker, *The Rebirth of Federalism*, p. 228. Figures are for 1996.

159. As derived from data in ibid., p. 227.

160. As derived from data in U.S. Bureau of the Census, Table 1. Figure is for 2002–2003. The two-fifths figure (our precise calculation is 44 percent) combines the intergovernmental revenue that localities receive in direct federal grants and as federal pass-through grants to the states. We have computed this rough estimate on the assumption that Washington continues to earmark about one-third of its assistance to the states as pass-through grants. The two-fifths figure refers to all *intergovernmental revenue* received by local governments and should not be confused with *total local revenue*; direct federal aid and federal pass-through grants contribute an estimated 15 percent of total local revenue.

161. Bruce A. Wallin, *Budgeting for Basics: The Changing Landscape of City Finances* (Washington, DC: Brookings, 2005), p. 5. Figures are for 1977–2000. All cities in the study had populations of at least 100,000 in 1977. Per capita federal aid to these cities decreased by 59 percent; state aid increased by 46 percent; and state aid to education increased by 122 percent over the twenty-four years.

162. Hal Wolman, Todd Swanstrom, Margaret Weir, and Nicholas Lyon, *The Calculus of Coalitions: Cities and States and the Metropolitan Agenda* (Washington, DC: Brookings, 2004), p. 20.

163. Fred Teitelbaum, "The Relative Responsiveness of State and Federal Aid to Distressed Cities," *Policy Studies Review* 1 (November 1981), p. 320; David R. Morgan and Mei-Chian Sheh, "Targeting State and Federal Aid to City Needs," *State and Local Government Review* 23 (Spring 1991), pp. 60–68; and John Yinger, "States to the Rescue? Aid to Central Cities Under the New Federalism," *Public Budgeting and Finance* 10 (Summer 1990), p. 31.

164. Jerry Anthony, "Do State Growth Management Regulations Reduce Sprawl?" *Urban Affairs Review* 39 (January 2004), pp. 376–397.

165. Beth Walter Honadle, "The State's Role in US Local Government Fiscal Crises: A Theoretical Model and Results of a National Survey," *International Journal of Public Administration* 26 (January 2003), pp. 1431–1473.

166. Ibid.

167. Anthony G. Cahill and Joseph A. James, "State Response to Local Fiscal Stress," *Municipal Year Book, 1996* (Washington, DC: International City/County Management Association, 1996), pp. 60–70.

168. Sherman W. Wyman, "Profiles and Prospects: Regional Councils and Their Executive Duties," *Municipal Year*

Book, 1994 (Washington, DC: International City/ County Management Association, 1994), pp. 48–57. Data are for 1990.

169. U.S. Advisory Commission on Intergovernmental Relations, *State Laws Governing Local Government Structure and Administration*, p. 9. Figure is for 1990. In 1978, thirty-nine states did so.

170. Lori M. Henderson, "Intergovernmental Service Arrangements and the Transfer of Functions," *Municipal Year Book, 1985* (Washington, DC: International City Management Association, 1985), pp. 196–201. In 1983, 52 percent of all local governments had interlocal agreements.

171. Mildred Warner and Amir Hafetz, "Pragmatism over Politics: Alternative Service Delivery in Local Government, 1992–2002," *Municipal Year Book, 2004* (Washington, DC: International City/County Management Association, 2004), p. 11. Figure is for 2002. Sixty-eight services were surveyed and include public authorities as well as government agencies.

172. As derived from data in Harry P. Hatry and Carl F. Valente, "Alternative Service Delivery Approaches Involving Increased Use of the Private Sector," *Municipal Year Book, 1983* (Washington, DC: International City Management Association, 1983), pp. 216–217. Figure is for 1982. Sixty services were surveyed and include public authorities as well as government agencies. Although intergovernmental agreements of this sort have increased since 1982, their apex was reached in 1992, at 21 percent of all services. See Warner and Hafetz, "Pragmatism over Politics," p. 11.

173. Warner and Hafetz, "Pragmatism over Politics," p. 11. Data are for 2002.

174. Graeme A. Hodge, *Privatization: An International Review of Performance* (Boulder, CO: Westview, 2000), p. 99. This is a review of 129 privatization studies conducted in numerous countries, but mostly of those done in the United States. "Public sector to private sector" contracting averaged 14 percent in savings. Although the author notes that both figures (14 percent and 22 percent) can be questioned statistically, they nonetheless convey by comparisons the finding that the public delivery of public services may be more efficient than private delivery.

 Other reviews of interlocal service arrangements also find that they save money. See, for example, George A. Boyne, "Bureaucratic Theory Meets Reality: Public Choice and Service Contracting in U.S. Local Government," *Public Administration Review* 58 (November/December 1998), pp. 474–484. Five studies of three services (police, street maintenance, and tax assessment) were reviewed.

175. Henderson, "Intergovernmental Service Arrangements and the Transfer of Functions," pp. 197–199. Figures are for 1983.

176. Ibid., pp. 199–200. Figure is for 1976–1983.

177. Pascale Joassart-Marcelli and Juliet Musso, "Municipal Service Provision Choices within a Metropolitan Area," *Urban Affairs Review* 14 (March 2005), p. 516. This research on cities in Southern California found a correlation between poor cities and contracting with other governments. This and two other investigations also found a correlation between rich cities and contracting with the private sector. See Thomas Pallesen, "A Political Perspective on Contracting Out: The Politics of Good Times, Experiences of Danish Local Governments," *Governance* 17 (October 2004), pp. 573–587; and Jeffrey D. Greene, "Cities and Privatization: Examining the Effect of Fiscal Stress, Location, and Wealth in Medium Sized Cities," *Policy Studies Journal* 24 (Spring 1996), pp. 135–144.

178. James C. Clingermayer, Richard C. Feiock, and Christopher Stream, "Governmental Uncertainty and Leadership Turnover: Influences on Contracting and Sector Choices for Local Services," *State and Local Government Review* 35 (Fall 2003), p. 158.

179. Henderson, "Intergovernmental Service Arrangements and the Transfer of Functions," pp. 196–198. Data are for 1983.

180. This and the following paragraph are based on ibid., pp. 194–202. All data are for 1972–1983. See also U.S. Advisory Commission on Intergovernmental Relations, *Intergovernmental Service Arrangements for Delivering Local Public Services: Update 1983*, A-103 (Washington, DC: U.S. Government Printing Office, 1985), which notes that counties and Councils of Governments have been the primary receivers of intergovernmental service transfers for eighteen years, 1965–1983 (p. 97). A later analysis covering 1982–1997 also found that counties were among the main receivers of transfers of functions from cities, although cities also were inclined to "allow special districts to provide services" at a high rate. See Joassart-Marcelli and Musso, "Municipal Service Provision Choices within a Metropolitan Area," p. 516.

181. Ibid. (all citations).

182. U.S. Bureau of the Census, *Statistical Abstract of the United States, 2001*, Table 29. The Office of Management and Budget (OMB) is responsible for defining metropolitan areas, and a host of related terms.

 In 1983, OMB discarded its long-used term, *standard metropolitan statistical area* (SMSA) and replaced it with *metropolitan statistical area* (MSA), defined as "a core area containing a substantial population nucleus, together with adjacent communities having a high degree of economic and social integration with that core . . . Each metropolitan statistical area must have at least 1 urbanized area of 50,000 or more inhabitants." See U.S. Bureau of the Census, *Statistical Abstract of the United States, 2006*, p. 921.

 Also in 1983, OMB introduced the *consolidated metropolitan statistical area* (CMSA), which describes the nation's largest urban regions, and which are comprised of two to three *primary metropolitan statistical areas* (PMSAs), or large cities. So some metropolitan areas (i.e., CSMAs) have more than one *principal city*, or the area's largest city; some have as many as three if certain population and employment criteria are met. The term, *metropolitan area*, adopted in 1990, refers collectively to MSAs, CMSAs, and PMSAs.

 Smaller urban areas are called *micropolitan statistical areas*. Micropolitan statistical areas have all the characteristics found in the definition of metropolitan statistical areas, with the exception that they "must have at least 1 urban cluster of at least 10,000 but less than 50,000 population" (ibid.). In 2000, the term, *core-based statistical area* (CBSA), became the official collective reference to metropolitan and micropolitan statistical areas.

In addition, there is the *New England city and town area* (NECTA), which the OMB created for those metropolitan areas that do not use counties as their primary unit of local government; typically, they rely on township governments. The term covers both metropolitan and micropolitan statistical areas—that is, CBSAs—in the six states of New England.

183. U.S. Bureau of the Census, *Statistical Abstract of the United States, 2001*, Table 29, and U.S. Bureau of the Census, *1992 Census of Governments: Government Organization*, Vol. 1, No. 1 (Washington, DC: U.S. Government Printing Office, 1994), Table 26. In 2000, 226 million people live in metropolises, and in 1992, 38 percent (33,004) of all local governments were in metropolitan areas. The Census Bureau did not provide this latter datum in its 1997 and 2002 censuses of governments.

184. U.S. Advisory Commission on Intergovernmental Relations, *The Organization of Local Public Economies*, A-109 (Washington, DC: U.S. Government Printing Office, 1987), p. 49. For a good review of this literature, see Robert Bish and Elinor Ostrom, *Local Government in the United States* (San Francisco: ICS Press, 1988).

185. U.S. Advisory Commission on Intergovernmental Relations, *Metropolitan Organization: Comparison of the Allegheny and St Louis Case Studies*, SR-15, (Washington, DC: U.S. Government Printing Office, 1993), p. 3. Figures are from 1942 to 1992. The number of metropolitan areas actually more than doubled, but not by much, from 140 to 331, 1942–2000. See U.S. Bureau of the Census, *Statistical Abstract of the United States, 2001*, Table 29.

186. U.S. Bureau of the Census, *1992 Census of Governments*, Table 26, and U.S. Advisory Commission on Intergovernmental Relations, *Metropolitan Organization: Comparison of the Allegheny and St. Louis Case Studies*, p. 3. The figures cover 1942 through 1992. In 1942 and in 1987, there was an average of 113 governments per metro area, the two record highs since the U.S. census of governments began in 1942; 1972 was the low point, with an average of eighty-four governments per metro area. Typically, over the years, the average number is in the nineties.

187. As derived from data in U.S. Bureau of the Census, *Statistical Abstract of the United States, 1994*, 114th ed. (Washington, DC: U.S. Government Printing Office, 1994), Tables 39 and 462, and U.S. Bureau of the Census, *1992 Census of Governments*, Table 26. Figures are for 1992. Half of the nation's 19,279 cities and towns govern fewer than 1,000 souls. Nearly a fifth of the country's 3,043 counties have fewer than 10,000 people.

188. The term is Reuss's, in *Revenue Sharing*, and is both descriptive and memorable.

189. U.S. Advisory Commission on Intergovernmental Relations, *Metropolitan Organization: Comparison of the Allegheny and St. Louis Case Studies*, p. 5.

190. Quoted in Anwar Syed, *The Political Theory of American Local Government* (New York: Random House, 1966), p. 40.

191. Vincent Ostrom, Charles M. Tiebout, and Robert Warren, "The Organization of Government in Metropolitan Areas: Theoretical Inquiry," *American Political Science Review* 55 (December 1961), p. 834.

192. Grigsby, "Regional Governance and Regional Councils," p. 55. See also Florida Advisory Commission on Intergovernmental Relations, *Substate Regional Governance: Evolution and Manifestation Throughout the United States and Florida* (Tallahassee: Author, 1991), p. 28.

193. Public choice theorists analyze metro governance by separating what they call the "production" of governmental services from the "provision" of those services. *Production* is the *delivery* of services, such as police policing and teachers teaching, but a government need not directly deliver these services itself; instead, it may provide the services it produces not only by delivering them directly, but also by making other arrangements to do so, such as by contracting with another government or a company, or organizing volunteers. So *provision* is the *arrangement* for delivering (or "producing") government services. Both production and provision are types of policy implementation, or, more specifically, both are ways of delivering metropolitan services.

The distinctions between "production" and "provision" as used in this literature strike us as unnecessarily arcane. But the terms pop up with sufficient frequency that an explanation of them (which we have tried to keep clear) may be useful, at least as a footnote.

194. See for example, Elinor Ostrom and Gordon P. Whitaker, "Does Local Community Control of Police Make a Difference? Some Preliminary Findings," *American Journal of Political Science* 17 (February 1973), pp. 48–76; Elinor Ostrom and Roger B. Parks, "Suburban Police Departments: Too Many and Too Small?" in Louis H. Masotti and Jeffrey K. Hadden, eds., *Urban Affairs Annual Review: The Urbanization of the Suburbs* 7 (Beverly Hills: Sage, 1973), pp. 303–402; and Elinor Ostrom and Gordon P. Whitaker, "Community Control and Governmental Responsiveness: The Case of Police in Black Neighborhoods," in Terry N. Clark, ed., *Urban Affairs Annual Review: Urban Policy Analysis: Directions for Future Research* 8 (Beverly Hills: Sage, 1974), pp. 303–304. For a good review of this literature, see: Elinor Ostrom, "Size and Performance in a Federal System," *Publius* 6 (Spring 1976), pp. 33–73.

195. William Niskanen and Mickey Levy, "Cities and Schools: A Case for Community Government in California," *Working Paper No. 14* (Berkeley: Graduate School of Public Policy, University of California, 1974).

196. Mark Schneider, "Fragmentation and the Growth of Government," *Public Choice* 48 (1, 1986), pp. 255–263; Jeffrey S. Zax, "The Effects of

Jurisdiction Types and Numbers on Local Public Finance," in Harvey S. Rosen, ed., *Fiscal Federalism: Quantitative Studies* (Chicago: University of Chicago Press, 1988), pp. 79–103; Christopher Bell, "The Assignment of Fiscal Responsibility in a Federal State," *National Tax Journal* 41 (June 1988), pp. 191–207; David L. Chicoine and Norman Walzer, *Governmental Structure and Local Public Finance* (Boston: Oelgeschlager, Gunn, and Hain, 1985); Richard E. Wagner and Warren E. Weber, "Competition, Monopoly, and the Organization of Government in Metropolitan Areas," *Journal of Law and Economics* 18 (December 1975), pp. 661–684; Thomas J. Di Lorenzo, "Economic Competition and Political Competition: An Empirical Note," *Public Choice* 40 (1, 1983), pp. 203–209.

197. James A. Christianson and Carolyn E. Sachs, "The Impact of Government Size and Number of Administrative Units on the Quality of Public Services," *Administrative Science Quarterly* 25 (March 1980), pp. 89–101; and Chicoine and Walzer, *Governmental Structure and Local Public Finance.*

198. U.S. Advisory Commission on Intergovernmental Relations, *Metropolitan Organization: Comparison of the Allegheny and St. Louis Case Studies*, p. 5.

199. U.S. Advisory Commission on Intergovernmental Relations, *The Organization of Local Public Economies*, pp. 27–28. Emphasis is original.

200. U.S. Advisory Commission on Intergovernmental Relations, *Intergovernmental Service Arrangements for Delivering Local Public Services.*

201. David Rusk, *Cities Without Suburbs* (Washington, DC: Woodrow Wilson Center Press, 1993), p. 88.

202. Robert C. Wood, "The New Metropolises: Green Belt, Grass Roots versus Gargantua," *American Political Science Review* 52 (March 1958), pp. 108–122. This reform movement also is called "regionalism," a less loaded title, perhaps, but also a less clear one.

203. The following examples are drawn from Reuss, *Revenue Sharing*, pp. 58, 60.

204. Ibid., p. 59.

205. Rusk, *Cities Without Suburbs*, p. 8.

206. Ibid, p. 5.

207. Bruce Katz and Jennifer Bradley, "Divided We Sprawl," *Atlantic Monthly* 284 (December 1999), pp. 26–34. Between 1990 and 1997, central cities grew by 4.2 percent and suburbs by 9.6 percent.

208. Edward L. Glaeser and Jesse M. Shapiro, *City Growth and the 2000 Census: Which Places Grew, and Why* (Washington, DC: Brookings, 2001), pp. 1–9. In the 1980s, 195 cites with 100,000 people or more grew by 9 percent and in the 1990s by 11.2 percent on average. Typically, cities grow if, in order of importance, they have warm, dry weather; residents who have high levels of education and income; strong service industries (as opposed to manufacturing industries); and are car-dependent, with little mass transit.

It appears that old housing stock in cities may act as a brake against precipitous population decline (the largest decline in the 1990s was St. Louis, at 13 percent); "as long as a city has homes, people will live in them." If they did not, "then large numbers of houses would be vacant, which does not really happen." Ibid., p. 8.

209. Rusk, *Cities Without Suburbs*, pp. 8–9.

210. During the 1990s, 71 of the 100 most populous cities (as of 1990) lost record numbers of white people to their suburbs, and non-Hispanic whites constituted less than half (44 percent) of the residents of these 100 cities in 2000, down from 52 percent in 1990. In 1990, whites were a majority in 70 of these 100 cities; in 2000, they were a majority in 52. Hispanic Americans constituted the largest influxes, while African American and Asian American remained stable. See Brookings Institution Center on Urban and Metropolitan Policy, *Racial Change in the Nation's Largest Cities: Evidence from the 2000 Census* (Washington, DC: Author, 2001).

211. Confirmation of the continuing and worsening deterioration of big American cities is contained in Amy L. Nelson, Kent P. Schwirian, and Patricia M. Schwirian, "Social and Economic Distress in Large Cities, 1970–1990: A Test of the Urban Crisis Thesis," *Social Science Research* 27 (December 1998), pp. 410–431. The authors found that "urban distress" had increased over twenty years in four critical dimensions: crime, housing, educational efficacy, and family structure.

212. For examples of the call for gargantuan reform, see *Governing Magazine's* issue of September 1995, especially Alan Ehrenhalt, "Cooperate or Die," pp. 28–32, and Charles Mahtesian, "The Civic Therapist," pp. 24–27. Ehrenhalt observes, "Just about everybody agrees that governments must begin to consolidate, and just about every place resists the idea" (p. 28).

213. See for example, Henry Cisneros, ed., *Interwoven Destinies: Cities and the Nation* (New York: W. W. Norton, 1993); H. V. Savitch, "Ties that Bind: Central Cities, Suburbs, and the New Metropolitan Region," *Economic Development Quarterly* 7 (November 1993), pp. 341–357; Richard Voith, "City and Suburban Growth: Substitutes or Complements?" *Business Review* (September/October 1992), pp. 21–33; William R. Barnes and Larry C. Ledebur, *Local Economies: The U.S. Common Market of Local Economic Regions* (Washington, DC: National League of Cities, 1994); Henry G. Cisneros, *Regionalism: The New Geography of Opportunity* (Washington, DC: U.S. Department of Housing and Urban Development, 1995); and Oliver E. Byrum, *Old Problems in New Times: Urban Strategies for the 1990s* (Chicago: American Planning Associates, 1992).

214. Rusk, *Cities Without Suburbs*, p. xiii.

215. Ibid., pp. 34, 85.

216. Ibid., pp. 8–9.

217. Brookings Institution Center on Urban and Metropolitan Policy, *Racial Change in the Nation's Largest Cities*, p. 4.

218. Rusk, *Cities Without Suburbs*, p. 31.

219. A study of municipal bond sales by municipalities in Oregon from 1994 to 1997 found some supporting evidence in this regard, concluding that "smaller jurisdictions pay an interest cost penalty in the municipal bond market." See Bill Simonson, Mark D. Robbins, and Lee Helgerson, "The Influence of Jurisdiction Size and Sale Type on Municipal Bond Interest Rates: An Empirical Analysis," *Public Administration Review* 61 (November/December 2001), pp. 709–717. The quotation is on page 709.

220. Rusk, *Cities Without Suburbs*, p. 43.

221. Ibid., p. 89.

222. Ibid., p. 95. We are using Rusk's definition of metro government and a universe of 320 metro areas.

CHAPTER 13

Toward a Bureaucratic Ethic

Public administration has been, in comparison with other professions, slow to recognize its own ethical practices. There were reasons for this lethargy, and the reasons had less to do with a determination among public administrators to permit and condone unethical practices in their field, and more to a common assumption held by society (including public administrators) about what the proper role of public administration and government was. Prior to the abandonment of the politics/administration dichotomy and the principles of administration (recall Chapter 2), the public administrator needed morality no more than a hotel clerk carrying out his or her daily duties. After all, of what use was morality to a person who did no more than execute the will of the state according to certain scientific principles? Provided that public administrators accomplished their given tasks efficiently and economically, they were by definition, moral in the sense that they were responsible. (In fact, the original city managers' and federal codes of ethics placed notable stress on efficiency as an ethical concept—a notion that many ethicists might find puzzling.) Morality, after all, necessitates ethical choice, and, as the literature was wont to stress, ethical choice simply was not a function of the functionaries. As one scholar has observed, with the experiences of France and Germany chiefly in mind, public bureaucrats "have obediently and even subserviently responded to whatever political leaders have gained power."[1]

Codes and Commissions: The Rise of Public Sector Ethics

This perspective began to change in the United States in the early twentieth century, and it was a change that was felt both in governments and in the public professions.

Ethics for Governments

Governments at all levels have been deepening their involvement in ethics since the mid-twentieth century, if with somewhat mixed results.

Federal Ethics. Congress first imposed a general code of ethics on federal administrators in 1958, and twenty years later expanded the code and founded the federal government's Office of Government Ethics as part of the Ethics in Government Act of 1978. In 1992, the Office of Government Ethics released the federal government's first comprehensive set of standards of ethical conduct, consolidating, in the process, a jumble of ethics codes that had been promulgated by federal agencies over the years. Consuming some forty pages in the *Federal Register*, the revised standards cover gifts, conflicts of financial interest, impartiality, misuse of office, seeking outside employment, and outside activities.

Nevertheless, even after this ethical house-cleaning, federal ethics regulations remain complex and confusing. The National Commission on the Public Service contends that, "over the past 40 years, Congress has enacted laws and presidents have issued executive orders that have produced a deeply layered and extraordinarily cumbersome regulatory scheme designed to insure the integrity of federal employees," and has urged that Congress "make federal ethics rules cleaner, simpler, and more directly linked to the goals they are intended to achieve.[2] Although there are varying counts, it appears that there are nearly 9,000 federal employees who work in ethics programs, but that more than half of these workers spend less than 5 percent of their time on ethics.[3]

Ethics in the Grass-Roots Governments. The first general code of state ethics was legislated in 1954 by the New York general assembly, and now at least forty-seven states have some form of written ethics code for their government employees.[4] Most of these codes are pedestrian in language, enumerating conflicts of interest and prohibited practices, rather than promoting integrity and broadly democratic ideals.[5]

Within this context, the stringency of state ethics codes varies widely. One analysis concluded that more than half the states did not address even four out of six basic areas of ethics legislation.[6]

Thirty-six states have established agencies or commissions to oversee ethics issues.[7] How effective these state ethics commissions are is uncertain. Most are "highly legalistic" in their approach,[8] and most are underfunded. One study of "ethics officials and stakeholders" in three states estimated that from only 5 percent to 10 percent of all financial disclosure forms submitted by public officials received a "substantive review," and these low review rates were attributed to a lack of funds. This analysis found that state ethics commissions are not only resource-starved but also are largely toothless, vulnerable, reactive, fragmented, and symbolic.[9]

Almost seven out of ten cities have a code of ethics, and it appears that a third of all cities may have an ethics commission, or at least some one or some body that functions as the equivalent of an ethics commission, as 33 percent of all cities review their employees' ethical conduct on a regular basis. Nearly three out of ten cities require ethical training for all managers, and almost a third "regularly conduct workshops where ethics are discussed."[10]

Ethics for the Public Professions

The adoption by public administrators of the first professional code of ethics precedes by decades the adoption of ethics codes by governments. What is now the International City/County Management Association adopted the first code of ethics for a public profession in 1924. The code reflected the anticorruption and antipolitics values of the municipal reform movement of the period and was not really a statement of professional ethics in the tradition established by the fields of education, engineering, law, and medicine, among other fields. But it was groundbreaking testimony to the importance of public ethics, nonetheless.

It was only in 1984 that the chief association of public administrators at all levels of government, the American Society for Public Administration, saw fit to write and adopt a code of ethics for professionals in the public sector. A decade later, it was reorganized, rewritten, and reduced but still covers the basic points: serve the public interest, respect the Constitution and the law, demonstrate personal integrity, promote ethical organization, and strive for professional excellence.

Today, although some public codes of ethics may fall short of attaining broad sophistication, codes of ethics, ethics boards, and ethics training are now facts of life in the public sector. All the major professional associations of public administrators actively offer workshops and other formats so that public managers may refine their sense of ethical conduct. The National Association of Schools of Public Affairs and Administration requires ethics education if a university wishes to accredit its public administration program, and all introductory public administration textbooks include a discussion of ethics.[11]

Practicing Ethical Public Administration

Writing codes of ethics is one matter. Practicing ethics is quite another, and likely more challenging.

Public Administrators and the Importance of Ethics

Public administrators take ethics seriously—more seriously, perhaps, than do business managers and even the taxpaying public.

An Ethical Commitment.   A survey of 1,000 graduates of the top public administration programs in the United States found that "maintaining ethical standards" was ranked as the single most important "skill" for achieving success out of thirteen possibilities. No other skill even came close, and this was the case irrespective of where the graduates were employed—federal, state, or local government; the private sector; or the nonprofit sector.[12]

National surveys of public administrators at all levels of government in the United States found that well over two-thirds believe that the interest in ethical issues among public administrators seemed to be "steadily growing over time"; and over 90 percent take issue with the statement that there "is no real need for codes of ethics in work organizations."[13]

A Higher Standard.   A review of ethics surveys concluded that public administrators are more critical of the ethics of business than of government, with 85 percent spurning the notion that "government morality in America is lower than business morality." Public employees also seem to have a higher sense of ethical behavior than do employees in the private sector.[14]

More surprising, perhaps, is that public administrators appear to hold themselves to a higher ethical standard than does even the public that pays their salaries. For example, more than 90 percent of public administrators believed that the corruption involved in overcharging the Pentagon by private contractors in 1988 was "a scandal just waiting to happen,"[15] compared to 82 percent of

the general public.[16] Over three-quarters of the public administrators dismiss the notion that the administration of Ronald Reagan "did a good job in enforcing ethical standards,"[17] compared to only 43 percent of the citizenry who reject this statement.[18]

In sum, public administrators seem to believe that ethics in government is extraordinarily important. Compared to business, government appears to be the more ethical institution, and public administrators are more critical of ethical lapses in government than are the taxpayers themselves. These perspectives among public administrators are encouraging ethical auguries.

Public Administrators and the Perception of Unethical Conduct

In light of these findings, it is perhaps not surprising that public administrators are less than tolerant of perceived ethical violations.

It is reasonably heartening to learn that almost seven out of ten federal employees think that their agencies, in general, promote "high standards of integrity, conduct, and concern for the public interest" among their workers, and only two out of ten believe that their agencies' failure to do so is a "major problem."[19] It is even more heartening to learn that 100 percent of high-level municipal officials report that their managers "demonstrate" ethical conduct, 94 percent believe that most city employees are honest, and 92 percent think that their managers "promote" ethical conduct.[20]

Despite these gratifying numbers, however, large portions of public administrators report that they work in an environment that is ethically challenging. Nearly half of public administrators state that "supervisors are under pressure to compromise personal standards," and virtually all public administrators agree that they "encounter ethical dilemmas at work."[21] A national study questioned public financial managers if "people outside ask for special treatment." It found that they do, and ardently so. On a five-point scale, these administrators scored an average of 3.34 in agreeing that outsiders do indeed request special treatment.[22]

A biennial national survey of ethical conduct in all three sectors finds that government employees are more likely to perceive acts that violate the law or their organizations' ethics standards than are workers in the nonprofit and private sectors.[23]

Public administrators' perceptions of ethical failures also may reflect their deepening depression over public corruption. A poll of federal administrators found that over 60 percent of the respondents disagreed with the view that "governmental practices today suffer from a 'moral numbness' following a decade of strife.[24] Fifteen years later, only 28 percent of public administrators disagreed with the statement that "society suffers a 'moral numbness' following a decade of scandals."[25] Although the surveys differ slightly, the trend of professional opinion seems clear: The nation's public administrators are growing increasingly worried about the nation's moral posture.

Whatever their status—career or noncareer, senior or junior, experienced or inexperienced—public administrators are increasingly willing to act on their perceptions of unethical behavior. Fully half of federal employees who observe illegal or wasteful acts in their agencies report them to appropriate authorities. This is "a fairly dramatic increase" from only ten years earlier, when only three out of ten federal workers reported illegality or wastefulness.[26] Public administrators are not only talking the ethical talk, but walking it, too.

Do Morals Matter? Ethics and the Effective Organization

Do ethics matter? Are organizations more effective because they are ethical? Or are ethics a counterproductive impediment to organizational effectiveness?

Ethics and the Effective Corporation

Data from the private sector appear to support the notion that good ethics are good business. In a careful study of twenty retail stores in the United States, researchers found that when nonsupervisory employees "report organizational climates deficient in these so-called 'soft'

areas [of ethical behavior, i.e., trust, truthfulness, integrity and justice], the company can expect to bear significantly higher bottom-line costs in the area of employee sickness and accident compensation costs. The data are strikingly clear: Out in the real world, not just in the college-freshmen psychology experiment, fairness does make a difference."[27]

In another analysis, researchers thoroughly questioned employees in eighteen Midwestern companies that held national reputations for being kinder and gentler workplaces, but that had downsized within the past five years. Their intent was to investigate recently "traumatized" corporations, and to determine what constituted a "virtuous" company, or corporations that placed a high value on integrity, trustworthiness, honesty, courage, openness, and a sense of calling, among other qualities. Further, the researchers wanted to know if these characteristics (that is, virtue) associated with superior or inferior corporate performance.

These analysts found that, in the more virtuous firms, revenue and profits were larger, employees were more productive, morale was higher, and employee turnover lower. Customers were more loyal, too.[28] Virtue pays.

Ethics and the Effective Government

Data from the public sector buttress the conclusion that ethical behavior associates with more effective organizations. Austin, Texas, conducts a periodic "Citywide Ethics Audit," and researchers used this unusual audit to match an agency's "ethical climate" with its "organizational costs." *Ethical climate* was defined as high agreement among departmental employees that their managers set a good ethical example; enforced high ethical standards; advocated frequently reminding employees of ethical considerations related to their work; and the extent of employee awareness of unethical or illegal behavior by city employees.

The investigators found that when a department received a *lower* rating for ethical climate, it was more likely to cause greater damage and injury to Austin residents and businesses, and to receive more complaints from the public. By contrast, departments receiving a *higher* rating for ethical climate had fewer employees who took sick leave, and took less of it; were more likely to think that their departments provided customers with better value for their money; and were more likely to have employees who planned to keep working for the city.[29]

Austin's experience is paralleled nationally. In a large study of the chief administrative officers in all 544 American cities with populations of 50,000 or more, it was found that "responsible risk taking" by these senior managers correlated positively with both a high sense of ethics and better managed cities. That is, the responsible risk takers' cities (which constituted about a third of the sample) had fewer law suits, better bond ratings, and were more likely to implement state-of-the-art productivity improvements than were cities managed by "at-risk entrepreneurs." At-risk entrepreneurs (17 percent of the sample) ranked lower on the researchers' ethics scale than did responsible risk takers; they "pursue innovation but disregard accountability and responsiveness."[30] At-risk entrepreneurs also associated with lower levels of education and professionalism than did responsible risk takers.

Ethics, in brief, are better business and good government.

Deeper Currents: Bureaucracy and the Public Interest

While it is comforting to know that public administrators take ethics and their practice seriously, and that ethical government may equate with more efficient and effective government, we have yet to address some deeper ethical currents that are unique to government. Those currents course around questions of the public interest. What is "the public interest," and how should public administrators make decisions that are in the public interest? "Little of the literature of public administration reflects on the nature of the public interest."[31]

The other branches of democratic government have addressed these questions far more effectively than has the executive branch. In the legislature, the operational concept for deciding the public interest is majority rule—a fundamental precondition of democracy. In the judiciary, the concept is *stare decisis* or judicial precedent, by which the evolutionary development of legal principles is perceived as the basic method for obtaining a system of justice that reflects the public interest. In both of these examples, there are, of course, flaws. The "myths" of majority rule and *stare decisis* may, in the words of one critique, "serve several functions—to meet the psychoemotional needs of the society and to protect and defend both legislators and judges."[32] Nevertheless, the point stands that these concepts do not pretend to be value-neutral, and they do go far toward defining the abstract notion of the public interest in workable terms that meet the needs of the legislative and adjudicative branches of government.

Not so in the executive branch, where there is little operational guidance for public administrators seeking to make decisions—often far-reaching decisions—that are in the public interest.[33]

This is not to say, however, that public administration scholars have not tried to develop such guidance. One major attempt is represented by the large literature on administrative accountability, and another is the thinking on organizational humanism. We review these efforts here.

Bureaucratic Accountability

Bureaucratic accountability, in this context, refers to assuring that public administrators make decisions that are in the public interest. The body of research on bureaucratic accountability does deal with bureaucrats making decisions that are, or are not, in the public interest, and this is useful. Unfortunately, the premise of bureaucratic accountability holds that public administrators in a democracy are safely constrained by a welter of restraints (just what those restraints are depends on the writer) from making decisions and policies that are antidemocratic, unfair, unethical, or illegal; hence, not to worry. Implicitly, this line of logic asserts that using an explicit ethical framework for making bureaucratic decisions is a waste of time.

Checks for Assuring Accountability. For example, some scholars contend that the normal scruples and professional commitments that public administrators glean from being socialized into the public service, along with the "representative elite" nature of their bureaucracies, act as internal constraints against the perpetration of antidemocratic policies,[34] and that the public administrators' "moral foundations" of honor, benevolence, and justice protect the public.[35]

Most public administrationists, however, argue that a plethora of external checks exist as well, and these checks assure executive compliance with the public interest. These external checks include legislative surveillance;[36] citizen participation in bureaucratic decision making;[37] introducing to government an Ombudsman, a figure in Scandinavian governments and elsewhere who has no official power but great personal prestige, which he or she uses to rectify unjust bureaucratic decisions on an individual basis;[38] decentralization of the bureaucracy;[39] publicizing bureaucratic information;[40] judicial review of administrative decisions;[41] and "regime values," or law and legal tradition.[42]

Increasingly, mixes of the two perspectives—that is, both internal *and* external controls—are emerging.[43]

Internal or External Assurances: What Do Public Administrators Use? What checks do practicing public administrators actually use to assure their accountability? Do they rely on internal or external checks?

There is not a lot of research on this question, and what exists is a mixed bag.

Some researchers find that internal checks are more important. A survey of local administrators concluded that internal controls are very salient, and that a "trust and lead" working environment—that is, a workplace in which the values of efficiency, effectiveness, quality, excellence, and teamwork were dominant—correlated with a strong government of high ethical expectations and standards.[44]

Other public administrationists find quite the opposite. One researcher who interviewed forty-two midlevel federal managers found that these administrators relied heavily on an external control, the law itself, which provided the principal guide to these managers when dealing with ethical issues in the workplace; internal controls—personal belief systems and professional values—ran a distant second.[45]

A Missed Point. Regardless of what public administrative philosophers may contend, (and there are more writings on the topic than we have reviewed here[46]), and what public administrators may practice, the arguments over bureaucratic accountability miss the point. The point is that public administrators, unlike legislators and judges, have no systematic, practical framework of values that they can use to guide them in making decisions that are in the public interest. The literature of bureaucratic accountability, while useful, does not do this; rather it merely suggests mechanisms that may inhibit, prevent, correct, or punish public administrators for making decisions that are not in the public interest.

Why not get it right in the first place? Are there no public-interest frameworks for public administrators that are comparable to, and as explicit as, legislators' majority rule or judges' judicial precedent?

Organizational Humanism

Yes, there are. One such framework is called *organizational humanism*, and it has gained academic currency over the years.[47] Unlike the literature of bureaucratic accountability, the organizational humanists do not skirt the issue of values; they state up front what a public administrator should rely on if he or she is to make a decision that is truly in the public's interest. That value is, always treat a person humanely.

The Ultimate Bureaucratic Value. The argument for doing so is practical and even, to some degree, empirical.[48] It states, in essence, that treating members of an organization humanely leads to greater organizational efficiency and effectiveness; treating organizational members humanely promotes organizational change; and treating both a member of an organization and a client of the organization in a humane way is in and of itself a desirable objective.[49] The dignity of the person is "the ultimate value."[50]

Organizational humanism, in its more explicit mode, "forwards the proposition that the ends of man are the ends of man. . . . it is not willing to compromise its human values on any grounds. . . . [and] calls for the ultimate capitulation of operational mechanics and political strategies to a concept of the public interest based on man as the most important concern of bureaucratic power."[51]

The values of organizational humanism are clear, and this is an advantage over the literature of bureaucratic accountability, which concerns itself less with values and more with internal and external mechanisms. The problem with organizational humanism lies in its application. Devils always lurk in the details.

Applying Organizational Humanism: A NonStarter? Consider, for an example, a classic dilemma in the field of public human resource management: hiring members of socially disadvantaged groups. There are two, value-based positions. One is that government should make special efforts, including the reduction of entrance standards, to hire members of those segments of American society who have endured various forms of racial, religious, disability, ethnic, or sexual discrimination. The reasoning is that, because of cultural bias in testing, lack of educational opportunity, and general social prejudice, government owes those people who have suffered these injustices a special chance to get ahead. If this should entail some bending of the civil service regulations (as is done for veterans), then so be it. Such rule bending will, after all, only balance the social equities for those applicants who have had to suffer bigotry in the past, and this is only as it should be since government is the single institution most responsible for assuring equality of opportunity in society.

The other position is that no "lowering of standards" should be considered, regardless of the applicant's past tribulations. The logic for this viewpoint is that government owes the best governance possible to all the governed. To hire applicants who do not score as well on tests as other applicants, or who do not have comparable educational attainments, or who are just less qualified, irrespective of the tough breaks in their backgrounds, is to do a disservice to the populace generally, deprived groups included. Governmental economy, efficiency, effectiveness, and responsiveness will deteriorate to the detriment of us all, unless only the top applicants are hired.

It is reasonably apparent from this example that organizational humanism does not offer much of a guide to the public administrator in formulating a decision in terms of promoting the public interest. Organizational humanism states that treating people humanely should be the ultimate end in bureaucratic decision making, but which option should the public administrator choose in this case? Is humanity best served by hiring or promoting a deprived-group member who may not execute his or her duties especially well, or is humanity best served by not hiring (or by holding back) the same disadvantaged group member, thus never permitting him or her to try realizing his or her full human potential nor aiding the cause of his or her people? This dilemma can be rendered even more exquisite by making the hypothetical deprived-group member in question an applicant to an agency designed to end discrimination against deprived groups, such as the Equal Employment Opportunity Commission; thus, to hire or not to hire him or her implies a lack of sincerity in advancing the cause of disadvantaged groups, depending on one's point of view. In any event, organizational humanism would seem to lack a viable framework of clear-cut referent points for a public administrator in making an ethical choice that is in "the public interest."

Justice-as-Fairness: A View of the Public Interest

What is needed for the public administrator is a simple and operational articulation of the public interest that permits him or her to make a decision in the public interest on the basis of rational thinking. Such a concept may exist in the form of a theory of justice offered by philosopher John Rawls.[52]

Rawls extends the notion of a social contract formulated by John Locke, Jean-Jacques Rousseau, and Thomas Hobbes and contends that the public interest can be discerned in most situations by applying two "principles of justice": (1) "Each person is to have an equal right to the most extensive basic liberty compatible with a similar liberty for others," and (2) that "social and economic inequalities are to be arranged so that they are both (a) reasonably expected to be to everyone's advantage, and (b) attached to positions and offices open to all."[53] Should these principles come into conflict, the second is expected to yield to the first; thus, just as in organizational humanism, the dignity of the individual person is considered to be of paramount importance.

Rawls's theory of justice goes further, however. His principles necessarily lead to the conclusion that inequalities of wealth, authority, and social opportunity "are just only if they result in compensating benefits for everyone, and in particular for the least advantaged members of society. These principles rule out justifying institutions on the grounds that the hardships of some are offset by a greater good in the aggregate. It may be expedient but it is not just that some should have less in order that others may prosper."[54]

In short, as Rawls observes, his principles in essence are a rigorous statement of the traditional Anglo-Saxon concept of fairness. In the context of managing organizations, "fairness" is comprised of trust, consistency, truthfulness, integrity, clearly stated expectations, equitable treatment, a sense of ownership and influence in the organization, impartial decision making, and mutual respect.[55]

Intuitionism, Perfectionism, and Utilitarianism

The usefulness of Rawls's justice-as-fairness philosophy can be elucidated by contrasting it with other philosophies of the public interest.

Morally Muddling Through

One is the intuitionist philosophy, expressed by Aristotle, among others.[56] *Intuitionism* expounds a plurality of first principles, which may conflict when applied to particular situations, but which offer no precise method for choosing the principle that should take precedence in cases of conflict. Such dilemmas are resolved by intuition, by what seems most nearly right. Intuitionist philosophies do not help the conscientious public administrator make a rational decision in light of an explicit theory of the public interest, other than rendering him or her some solace in justifying present practices.

Promoting Perfect People

A second major philosophical school that addresses the public interest is *perfectionism*. The first and sole principle of perfectionism is to promote, via society's institutions, the attainment of excellence in art, science, and culture. Friedrich Nietzsche is exemplary.

In its absolutist form there are no problems of ambiguity: The public administrator should always strive to support the upper intellectual crust of his or her society; any misfortune for society's least fortunate segments that accrues from the necessary allocation of resources and that results from implementing the perfectionist principle is morally justified by the benefits incurred by the best members that the society has. As Nietzsche put it so pithily, the deepest meaning that can be given to the human experience is "your living for the rarest and most valuable specimens."[57] (Nietzsche evidently included himself among those specimens.)

The Most Benefits for the Most People

A third ethical framework for the determination of the public interest is *utilitarianism*, as represented by Adam Smith and John Stuart Mill, among others.[58] Of the philosophies that have had the most influence on public administrators in terms of intellectual rigor and social appropriateness, utilitarianism holds first place in theory, if not in actual practice.

The reasoning of utilitarianism is both democratic in values and systematic in thought. It holds that a public policy will be in the public interest provided the policy increases the net balance of social satisfaction summed over all the individuals belonging to the society. In other words, if a public policy makes everybody slightly better off, even if some individuals are left slightly worse off in other ways as a result of that policy, then the policy is just and the public interest is served. An example of a utilitarian public policy would be one that increased the income of medical doctors by raising everyone's taxes and turning over these new revenues to doctors, thereby increasing everyone's net balance of health by inducing a greater net balance of individuals to enter the medical profession. Even though society's least well-off individuals would lose money under this arrangement, the policy nevertheless would be just and in the public interest under a utilitarian theory because everyone's net balance of health would be increased, including that of the least well-off. The ethical theory of justice-as-fairness, however, would hold that such a public policy was not just and not in the public interest because it reduced the welfare of the least well-off people in society, even if it is for the net benefit of the whole society.

Does Philosophy Affect Policy?

We have reviewed some philosophic criteria for determining the public interest. So what? Does the ivory tower carry any relevance in the corridors of power?

To those who might answer "no" to this question, we remind them that the combination of cynicism and unworldliness is particularly unattractive in people. In reality, public agencies implement each of our philosophies of the public interest. Philosophy, in fact, does affect public policy, and it does so in deep and meaningful ways.

For example, Rawls's theory of justice furnishes the philosophic foundation for every government in the United States that levies a tax on personal income. The income tax structure for all governments that use it is one that is mildly progressive. That is, they tax the rich proportionately more than the poor, rather than regressively

taxing the poor proportionately more than the rich, or even taxing the indigent and the wealthy at the same rate. The income tax structure in the United States is purposely designed not to make the least well-off less well-off, a principle that is central to Rawls's theory of justice.

Aristotle's intuitionism pervades the public sector. Although intuitionism is widely practiced in governments, its popularity is not due to its intellectual force. Rather, intuitionism is singularly easy to choose as a theory of the public interest, in part because most public administrators are unaware that they are choosing it. Most public administrators make decisions and implement public policies on the basis of what seems to them at the time to be the most nearly right decision or policy. This, in essence, is what intuitionism is all about.

Nietzsche's perfectionism has been consciously selected by the National Science Foundation as its operating philosophy of the public interest. Although it is a policy choice that has been slightly ameliorated in recent years, the Foundation's traditional criterion for financing "pure" scientific research (which is, with few exceptions, the only kind of research that the Foundation funds)—that science should be funded for the sake of science—is a clear expression of the perfectionist principle.

Finally, Smith's and Mill's utilitarianism is the premise on which policy choices are made by the U.S. Army Corps of Engineers, and likely by many other agencies, too. The Corps has adopted "benefit/cost analysis" as its method of deciding which engineering projects are in the best interests of the nation. But the assumptions underlying benefit/cost analysis are squarely set in a utilitarian philosophy, and can bring utilitarian consequences.

The Corps defines benefits and costs in terms of dollars preserved or lost. Hence, to entertain projects, such as flood control, that protect trailer parks and poor people rather than McMansions and rich people, would not make the cut because manors have more dollar value than mobile homes. To protect cheaper homes at the expense of costlier homes would violate benefit/cost precepts. As in utilitarianism, the Corps' benefit/cost policy can make the least well-off less well-off.

Applying the Justice-as-Fairness Theory

Intuitionism, perfectionism, and utilitarianism illuminate by contrast the usefulness of justice-as-fairness as an ethical framework for public administrators in making decisions that are in the public interest. But how would justice-as-fairness help the public administrator in deciding our original dilemma, that of hiring "less qualified" applicants from disadvantaged groups in society? It would, by the inevitability of its logic, argue for the hiring of these applicants on these grounds:

- *Not* hiring them would be further depriving society's most deprived groups for the sake of the whole society.
- Hiring them would facilitate the full realization of their "basic liberty" (or personal dignity) without encroaching on the basic liberty of others.
- Hiring them helps assure that all positions and offices are open to all.
- Hiring them helps assure that privileges innate to such offices continue to work toward the advantage of all in a reasonably equal way, because the privileges and positions are being extended to the least well off in society.

The People *versus* Person Problem

Note that, in applying Rawls's principles to affirmative action, we use the terms "groups" and "all," rather than "individual" and "person," and, one could argue, this is a fatal flaw in our argument: After all, individuals, not groups, should be accorded the benefits of affirmative action. The common example given in making this point is that affirmative action should not be used to promote the interests of an educated black woman who is a millionaire at the expense of an impoverished and disadvantaged white man from the Appalachia. Because affirmative action is applied to groups, and not individuals, it can result in possible injustices to disadvantaged people who do not happen to be in the relevant group; hence, affirmative action goes against the grain of the American tradition

of equality of opportunity and is a disservice to society.

There is some merit to this observation, though less than one might think. First, "disadvantaged" as a basis for favoritism wars in no fashion against the American tradition, and the notion of singling out certain groups for favorable treatment is not a public policy relegated solely to affirmative action. For example, need-based scholarships offered by colleges effectively bear witness to the acceptance that deprivation is an acceptable basis for preferred treatment. Veterans preference, the venerable policy of automatically adding points to the civil service examinations taken by veterans, is another. Small business set-asides, enacted by Congress twenty-four years before it enacted minority business set-asides, is yet another.

So the idea that groups and the individuals constituting them can be tapped for special advantages distributed by government is not a notion unique by any means to affirmative action, and using the terms, "black," "brown," "women," "disabled," and "senior" strikes us as a not unreasonable shorthand for not only identifying groups, but for describing "disadvantaged" as well. These conditions of life, in sum, often associate with disadvantages that are not the doing of the individual, and national statistics on education and income indicate that more black and brown people are disadvantaged than are white people, more women than men, and more disabled people than abled people.

Good Is Not Perfect, and Perfect Is Not Possible

Still, our original dilemma persists (if in diminished form), and it remains possible that, even though affirmative action may help far more disadvantaged people than it hurts, advantaged individuals in disadvantaged groups can be accorded advantages unavailable to disadvantaged individuals in advantaged groups. Should this occur, goes the reasoning, it would be an injustice.

We must agree that it would be. The more important concern, however, is that the "cure" would be far less just than the "disease." The contention that, because some undeserving people may benefit from affirmative action, we should close down affirmative action, is a classic expression of the odd rationale that, because a good policy is not perfect, we should discard that policy because it is merely good. It is a case of throwing out babies with bath water.

And the contention also assumes that we have a perfect method for fairly assessing and ranking, by every single individual, relative merit; no society has that ability, and never will. Does anyone seriously believe, for example, that only scores on a test, which enable an applicant to enter medical school, assure that that applicant will be the best of all possible physicians? Written tests, certainly, can measure and rank *some* critical qualifications, such as scientific knowledge, of budding M.D.s., but they cannot measure and rank *all* qualifications, including some important ones, such as empathy and diagnostic insight.

More to the point, perhaps, justice and life cannot be reasonably separated, and the group-*versus*-individual argument contends that they can. "The black person who moves up the line thanks to affirmative action may not logically 'deserve' the place he gets. But, for the same reason, the white person who loses that place doesn't 'deserve' it either . . . The point is that a pure, discrimination-free society is not merely a hopeless ideal; it is a logical mirage."[59]

So Rawls's principles would appear to apply, and usefully so, to a public administrator making a judgment about whether affirmative action is in the public interest.

The Unique Utility of Justice-as-Fairness

Moreover, of the ethical frameworks considered, only justice-as-fairness would by its logic permit the public administrator the decisional choice of making a special effort to hire people from disadvantaged groups. Utilitarianism would demand that the good of the whole be the first priority, regardless of consequences for society's least well-off. Perfectionism, in effect, would say to hell with society's least well-off since they are not considered at all in its value

structure. Intuitionism, which most public administrators practice, permits the choice of hiring members of minority groups, but only as a coincidental happenstance and not by the force of its theory.

Justice-as-fairness offers the public administrator a workable way for determining the public interest. So, for that matter, do utilitarianism and perfectionism, but we are rejecting those frameworks in this book, the former because it logically permits the least advantaged persons in society to be disadvantaged further and thus is "unfair" and not in the public interest in all instances, and the latter because its antidemocratic values are incompatible with the dominant values of American society. The choice in this book of justice-as-fairness as an operating moral logic for the public administrator is, of course, a value choice by the author and should be recognized as such by the reader. But it is believed to be a reasonable one under the circumstances.

Big Bureaucracy, Big Decisions

It is fitting to close this book with a thought about what the public administrator should and should not do as a moral, amoral, or immoral actor in the public bureaucracy. One can learn the techniques of management, the notions of organization theory, and the intricacies of policy formulation and implementation, but ultimately public administration is a field of thought and practice in which personal ethical choices are made. Those who enter the field, either as thinkers or practitioners (and, one hopes, some of both), are, not infrequently, required to make decisions about moral questions that have real consequences.

Public administration is a profession that offers an unusually rich variety of opportunities to make moral or immoral decisions, to make ethical or unethical choices, to do good or evil things to people. We ask that if you enter the field, you remember when making your choices to ask yourself how people will be helped or hurt by your decisions. Few questions are more important in any context, but in the context of the public life of the nation, none is more important.

The Passion of Public Administration

We observed at the beginning of this book that constraint is the dominating characteristic in the culture immersing the American public administrator. Nevertheless, large—sometimes very large—decisions can be and are being made within this context of constrained administrative action. A public administrator needs a personal ethical compass when making professional decisions. It is needed both for the mental health of the public administrator and for the happiness of the public. Consider the life of the late Robert Moses.

Robert Moses was a legendary figure in public administration. The offices that he held were not entitled governor, mayor, or legislator, but chairman, commissioner, and coordinator. Moses never occupied an elected office; he was never, technically, a policymaker, but merely an administrator of policy, holding such modestly titled positions in New York State and New York City as Chairman of the State Council on Parks, Chairman of the Triborough Bridge and Tunnel Authority, President of the Long Island Parkways Commission, Commissioner of the New York City Parks System, City Construction Coordinator, and a member of the boards of directors of the Henry Hudson Parkway Authority, the Marine Parkway Authority, and the New York City Parkway Authority—but the *only* member of those boards! At his peak, Moses headed fourteen state and city agencies at the same time. And he made them powerful agencies.

These positions proved both professionally and personally rewarding to Moses, whose life as a public administrator dashed the stereotype that bureaucrats timidly live low-profile lifestyles in genteel poverty. Though personally "money honest" (to employ a term for a complex reality that only New Yorkers could express so pithily), his jobs brought some legal, but highly enviable, perks, including a yacht, skippered by three captains, for his personal use, and four dining rooms scattered around the city, each with its own full-time staff, who served only Moses and his guests. The secretaries who worked in his bridge and tunnel authorities were not only paid more than New York City's commissioners, but also were given bigger cars, driven by chauffeurs who were on call twenty-four hours a day. His "Moses men," his closest allies and administrators, were made millionaires and multimillionaires by Moses.

Moses held an unbelievable quantum of power in New York State for forty-four years (1924–1968) and in New York City for thirty-four years (1934–1968). It is not hyperbolic to dub him America's greatest builder. He changed the face of New York by raising and spending $27 billion (in 1968 dollars) for public works.

Through shoreline projects, he added 15,000 acres to the city and changed its physical configuration. With one exception (East River Drive), Moses built every major expressway in the metropolitan region. Nine enormous bridges link the island city of New York; Moses built seven of them. Lincoln Center; the New York Coliseum; the campuses of Pratt Institute and Fordham and Long Island universities; the headquarters of the United Nations; 416 miles of landscaped parkways; Jones Beach; more than 1,000 apartment buildings housing more people than lived in Minneapolis; 658 playgrounds; 673 baseball diamonds; 288 tennis courts—all these and more are his. Beyond the city, Moses built huge power dams on the St. Lawrence and at Niagara, Massens, and elsewhere; more parkways, more public beaches, and more parks. Especially parks. By the time Moses had finished, New York owned 45 percent of the nation's acreage devoted to state parks!

Moses was powerful far beyond the boundaries of the country's most important city. He changed the nation, too. In the fields of parks, highways, and urban renewal, Moses was a formative force in the country.

In parks, it was Moses who conceived the notion of state and urban recreational complexes linked by landscaped parkways. Prior to Moses, twenty-nine states did not even have a single park, and six had only one. The parks system he bulldozed in New York was widely copied across the nation.

In highways, Moses had completed half a dozen urban expressways in metropolitan New York before Congress passed the Interstate Highway Act of 1956, which funneled federal money into the construction of urban freeways across the country. Prior to the act—which Moses was instrumental in drafting—metropolitan highways were virtually nonexistent except in New York.

Moses also was critical in drafting the Housing Act of 1949, which inaugurated the nation's controversial Urban Renewal program, and Moses was quick to exploit the federal program that he himself had helped form. Eight years after the passage of the Housing Act, Moses, who controlled all urban renewal projects in New York, had spent more than twice the amount of federal urban renewal dollars than all other American cities combined! His contracts were used as the model for urban renewal administrators across the country.

As the urban scholar Lewis Mumford, one of Moses's most tenacious foes, has written, "In the twentieth century, the influence of Robert Moses on the cities of America was greater than that of any other person."

Moses transmogrified New York. But whether or not he left the city, and much of the state, better than when he found them is an open question—and ultimately a deeply moral one.

To his everlasting credit, Moses rammed through titanic projects that employed thousands, moved hundreds of thousands, and created greenswards enjoyed by millions. These public works had either languished on planners' shelves for decades, or had never been dreamed of by even the most visionary of urban visionaries. "The canvas was gigantic. . . ." And Moses, uniquely, "saw the whole canvas—city, suburbs, slums, beaches, bridges, tunnels, airports, Central Park and vest-pocket parks—as one, a single whole, which he wanted to shape as a whole. . . . [He had] the mind of a sculptor who wanted to sculpt not clay or stone but a whole metropolis; I saw the genius of a city-shaper" (Caro, 1998, p. 47).

There was, however, a dark side to his genius. To build, Moses destroyed. A quarter-million people—the equivalent population of Chattanooga at the time—were dispossessed for his highways. Perhaps another quarter-million saw their homes leveled for other kinds of projects. His apartment buildings, parks, and playgrounds, with few exceptions, were built for the middle class and the wealthy. His expressways slash through a region of fourteen million people, carving the metropolis into separate and often mutually hostile enclaves of rich, poor, white, black, and brown.

To shape his city, Moses ruthlessly razed homes, ruined neighborhoods, and wrecked lives. He was notorious "for the heartbreaking callousness with which he evicted the tens of thousands of poor people in his way, whom, in the words of one official, he 'hounded out like cattle.' " After visiting those who had been hounded from their homes, this same author wrote, "I had never, in my sheltered middle-class life, descended so deeply into the realms of despair" (Caro, 1998, pp. 42, 50).

Did Moses perceive this despair? Or care about it? Apparently not. His chief biographer asked Moses "if he had ever been worried about having to change his route to save their homes. 'Nah,' he said, and I can still hear the scorn in his voice as he said it—scorn for those who had fought him, and scorn for me who had thought it necessary to ask about them" (Caro, 1998, p. 52).

Robert Moses represents the best and worst of public administrators. He began his career as a "Goo-Goo," that dismissive term used by Tammany Hall politicians to describe "good government" reformers. He had confided to friends his grand plans for New York as early as 1914,

(cont.)

The Passion of Public Administration (*Cont.*)

while still in his twenties, and never really deviated from them. He was, by all accounts, a dreamer and idealist.

Over the years, as Moses secured appointments on various commissions and public authorities, he grew obsessed with making real his stunningly transformational dream. His acquaintances described the "savage energy Robert Moses had put behind his dreams, and his fury when they were checked: how, mapping out strategies for overcoming obstacles, he would pace back and forth across his office hour after hour . . . how he would lunge out of his chair and begin, as one aide put it, 'waving his arms, just wild,' pick up the old-fashioned inkwell on his desk and hurl it at aides so that it shattered against a wall; how he would pound his clenched fists into the walls hard enough to scrape the skin off them, in a rage beyond the perception of pain" (Caro, 1998, pp. 48–49).

Ends were important to Moses, but means were incidental. Moses resorted to deception, slander, libel, blackmail, and thinly veiled bribery to achieve his goals. These tactics resulted in "some of the greatest scandals of twentieth century New York, scandals almost incredible . . . for the colossal scale of their corruption" (Caro, 1998, p. 42). Moses boasted (jokingly, one hopes) that "nothing I have ever done has been tinged with legality."

In 1968, Governor Nelson Rockefeller, using some of Moses's own techniques (notably out-and-out lying), effectively isolated and emasculated Moses as a power broker. But Moses never gave up trying to complete his vision. As one labor leader put it, "They want him to get tired and to go away and get lost. But I say, 'Forget it!' This guy don't blow away." Moses died in 1981. He was ninety-two, still a fighter.

Sources: Robert A. Caro, *The Power Broker: Robert Moses and the Fall of New York* (New York: Alfred A. Knopf, 1974) and Robert A. Caro, "The City Shaper," *The New Yorker* (January 5, 1998), pp. 42–53.

Notes

1. Ferrel Heady, *Public Administration: A Comparative Perspective* (Englewood Cliffs, NJ: Prentice Hall, 1966), p. 45.
2. National Commission on the Public Service, *Urgent Business for America: Revitalizing the Federal Government for the 21st Century* (Washington, DC: U.S. Government Printing Office, 2003), pp. 21–22.
3. Robert W. Smith, "Corporate Ethics Officers and Government Ethics Administrators: Comparing Apples with Oranges or a Lesson to Be Learned?" *Administration and Society* 34 (January 2003), p. 639. In 1998, there were 8,735 federal employees working in "the ethics program," 55 percent of whom spent less than 5 percent of their time on ethics. Another source says that in 1993, 320 federal employees were assigned full-time to "ethics duties" in the executive branch, and another 14,000 "dabble" in ethics. See Marilyn W. Thompson, "Federal Ethics: A Long Way to Go," *Washington Post* (October 8, 1994).
4. Beth A. Rosenson, *Shadowlands of Conduct: Ethics and State Politics* (Washington, DC: Georgetown University Press, 2005), pp. 5, 11. Figures are for 1996. The states that have no general ethics codes are North Dakota, Vermont, and Wyoming.
5. Richard Blake, Jill A. Grob et al., "The Nature and Scope of State Government Ethics Codes," *Public Productivity and Management Review* 21 (June 1998), pp. 453–459.
6. Rosenson, *Shadowlands of Conduct*, pp. 10–11. Data are for 1996. The six categories used by Rosenson are whether a state has a basic ethics code; limits on honoraria; limits on gifts from lobbyists; postgovernment employment restrictions; limits on representation of clients before state agencies and; and mandatory financial disclosure. Twenty-six states did not fulfill four of these categories.
7. Fran Burke and George C. S. Benson, "State Ethics Codes, Commissions, and Conflicts," *State Government Review* 10 (May 1989), pp. 195–198.
8. Smith, "Corporate Ethics Officers and Government Ethics Administrators," p. 640.
9. Robert W. Smith, "Enforcement or Ethical Capacity: Considering the Role of State Ethics Commission' at the Millennium," *Public Administration Review* 63 (May/June 2003), pp. 283–295. The quotations are on

pp. 283 and 292. This was a study of sixty officials and others associated with state ethics commissions in Connecticut, Florida, and New York.

10. Mary Ann Feldheim and Xiaohu Wang, "Ethics and Public Trust: Results from a National Survey," *Public Integrity* 6 (Winter 2003–2004), p. 70. This was a national survey of 248 responding city officials conducted in 2000.

11. James S. Bowman, Evan M. Berman, and Jonathan P. West, "The Profession of Public Administration: An Ethics Edge in Introductory Textbooks?" *Public Administration Review* 61 (March/April 2001), pp. 194–205.

12. Paul C. Light, *The New Public Service* (Washington, DC: Brookings, 1999), p. 110. Light questioned graduates of thirteen of the top twenty schools as ranked by *U.S. News & World Report.* Respondents' rankings of the importance of ethics ranged from 75 percent (state employees) to 89 percent (nonprofit sector employees). The next highest score was for "leading others."

13. James S. Bowman and Russell L. Williams, "Ethics in Government: From a Winter of Despair to a Spring of Hope," *Public Administration Review* 57 (November/December 1997), pp. 518, 521. Figures are for 1996. The authors contacted 750 randomly selected members of the American Society for Public Administration.

14. J. Norman Baldwin, "Public Versus Private Employees: Debunking Stereotypes," *Review of Public Personnel Administration* 11 (Fall 1990–Spring 1991), p. 16.

15. James S. Bowman, "Ethics in Government: A National Survey of Public Administrators," *Public Administration Review* 50 (May/June 1990), p. 346. Figure is for 1986.

16. Associated Press, "Poll: Americans Believe Bribery Rampant," *Tallahassee Democrat* (October 4, 1988), as cited in ibid. Figure is for 1988.

17. Bowman, "Ethics in Government," p. 346. Figure is for 1986.

18. Associated Press, "Poll." Figure is for 1988.

19. U.S. Merit Systems Protection Board, *Adherence to the Merit Principles in the Workplace: Federal Employees' Views* (Washington, DC: U.S. Government Printing Office, 1997), p. 12. Figures are for 1996, and include over 9,700 respondents. Forty-three percent saw a "minor or no problem" in this regard, and 25 percent perceived a "moderate problem."

20. Feldheim and Wang, "Ethics and Public Trust," p. 70. Figures are for 2000.

21. Bowman and Williams, "Ethics in Government," p. 518. Figures are for 1996.

22. Gerald J. Miller, Samuel J. Yaeger, W. Bartley Hildreth et al., "How Financial Managers Deal with Ethical Stress," *Public Administration Review* 65 (May/June 2005), p. 306.

23. Ethics Resource Center, *National Business Ethics Survey, 2005* (Washington, DC: Author, 2005). Figures are for 2005. More than 3,000 workers were surveyed.

24. James S. Bowman, "Ethics in the Federal Service: A Post-Watergate View," *Midwest Review of Public Administration* 11 (March 1977), pp. 7–8. Figure is for 1976.

25. Bowman and Williams, "Ethics in Government," pp. 518, 522; and Bowman, "Ethics in Government," p. 346. Figure is for 1990.

26. U.S. Merit Systems Protection Board, *Whistleblowing in the Federal Government: Federal Employee's Views* (Washington, DC: U.S. Government Printing Office, 1997), p. 9. Data are for 1992 and 1983.

27. Marshall Sashkin and Richard L. Williams, "Does Fairness Make a Difference?" *Organizational Dynamics* 18 (August 1990), pp. 66–67. See also David E. Bowen, Stephen W. Gilliland, and Robert Folger, "HRM and Service Fairness: How Being Fair with Employees Spills Over to Customers," *Organizational Dynamics* 27 (Summer 1999), pp. 7–21.

28. Kim S. Cameron, David Brighton, and Arran Casa, "Exploring the Relationships between Organizational Virtuousness and Performance," *American Behavioral Scientist* 47 (February 2004), pp. 808–827.

29. Colleen G. Waring and C'Anne Daugherty, "Auditing Ethics—Make Them an Offer They Can't Refuse," *Journal of Government Financial Management* 53 (Spring 2004), pp. 34–40. Data are for 2002.

30. Evan M. Berman and Jonathan P. West, "Responsible Risk-Taking," *Public Administration Review* 58 (July/August 1998), p. 349. Response rate was 43 percent (or 236 responses).

31. Eugene D. Dvorin and Robert H. Simmons, *From Amoral to Humane Bureaucracy* (San Francisco: Canfield Press, 1972), p. 61.

32. Ibid., p. 60.

33. For an interesting take on this dilemma, see F. Neil Brady, "'Publics' Administration and the Ethics of Particularity," *Public Administration Review* 63 (September/October 2003), pp. 525–534.

34. Carl J. Friedrich and Taylor Cole, *Responsible Bureaucracy* (Cambridge: Harvard University Press, 1949), and Norton Long, *The Polity* (Chicago: Rand-McNally, 1982).

35. Kathryn Denhardt, "Unearthing the Moral Foundations of Public Administration: Honor, Benevolence, and Justice," in James S. Bowman, ed., *Ethical Frontiers in Public Management* (San Francisco: Jossey-Bass, 1991), pp. 256–283.

36. Charles S. Hyneman, *Bureaucracy* (New York: Harper & Row, 1950); and Herbert Finer, "Administrative Responsibility in a Democratic Government," *Public Administration Review* 1 (Summer 1941), pp. 335–350.

37. J. D. Lewis, "Democratic Planning in Agriculture," *American Political Science Review* 35 (April and June 1941), pp. 232–249, 454–469; and L. Von Mises, *Bureaucracy* (New Haven, CT: Yale University Press, 1944).

38. Henry J. Abraham, "A People's Watchdog Against Abuse of Power," *Public Administration Review* 20 (Summer 1960), pp. 152–157.

39. Dwight Waldo, "Development of a Theory of Democratic Administration," *American Political Science Review* 46 (March 1952), pp. 81–103; and John M. Pfiffner and Robert Presthus, *Public Administration,* 5th ed. (New York: Ronald Press, 1967).

40. Gordon Tullock, *The Politics of Bureaucracy* (Washington, DC: Public Affairs Press, 1965); and Harold L. Wilensky, *Organizational Intelligence: Knowledge and Policy in Government and Industry* (New York: Basic Books, 1967).

41. K. C. Davis, *Administrative Law* (St. Paul: West Publishing, 1951).

42. John A. Rohr, *Ethics for Bureaucrats: An Essay on Law and Values*, 2nd ed. (New York: Marcel Dekker, 1989).

43. See, for example, J. Patrick Dobel, "Integrity in the Public Service," *Public Administration Review* 50 (May/June 1990), pp. 356–366; Terry L. Cooper, *The Responsible Administrator* (San Francisco: Jossey-Bass, 1990); and Donald P. Warwick, "The Ethics of Administrative Discretion," in Joel L. Fleishman, Lance Leibman, Mark. H. Moore, eds., *Public Duties: The Moral Obligations of Public Officials* (Cambridge, MA: Harvard University Press, 1981), pp. 157–175.

44. Donald C. Menzel, "The Ethics Factor in Local Government: An Empirical Analysis," in H. George Frederickson, ed., *Ethics and Public Administration* (Armonk, NY: M. E. Sharpe, 1993), pp. 301–311; and Donald C. Menzel, "The Ethical Environment of Local Government Managers," *American Review of Public Administration* 25 (September 1995), pp. 247–261.

45. Harold F. Gortner, *Ethics for Public Managers* (New York: Praeger, 1991).

46. For some comprehensive volumes on ethics in the public sector, see James S. Bowman, ed., *Ethical Frontiers in Public Administration* (San Francisco: Jossey-Bass, 1991); Terry L. Cooper, ed., *Handbook of Administrative Ethics* (New York: Marcel Dekker, 1994); Frederickson, ed., *Ethics and Public Administration*; Michael W. J. Cody and Richardson R. Lynn, *Honest Governance: An Ethics Guide for Public Service* (Westport, CT: Praeger, 1992): Rohr, *Ethics for Bureaucrats;* and Carol W. Lewis, *The Ethics Challenge in Public Service: A Problem-Solving Guide* (San Francisco: Jossey-Bass, 1991). There are, of course, others.

47. See, for example: Robert B. Denhardt, *Theories of Public Organization* (Monterey, CA: Brooks/Cole, 1984), p. 92; Chris Argyris, *Interpersonal Confidence and Organizational Effectiveness* (Homewood, IL: Dorsey Press, 1962); Robert T. Golembiewski, *Men, Management, and Morality* (New York: McGraw-Hill, 1967); David K. Hart, "Social Equity, Justice, and the Equitable Administrator," *Public Administration Review* 34 (January/February 1974), pp. 3–10; Frederick E. Thayer, *An End to Hierarchy! An End to Competition!* (New York, New Viewpoints, 1973); Omar Aktouf, "Management and Theories of Organization in the 1990s: Toward a Critical Radical Humanism?" *Academy of Management Review* 17 (July 1992), pp. 407–431. In some respects, organizational humanism is a resurrection of "the new public administration," discussed Chapter 2.

48. Golembiewski, *Men, Management, and Morality;* Marcus Buckingham and Curt Coffman, *First, Break All the Rules: What Do the World's Greatest Managers Do Differently?* (New York: Simon and Schuster, 1999).

49. Denhardt, *Theories of Public Organization*, pp. 91–92.

50. Dvorin and Simmons, *From Amoral to Humane Bureaucracy*, p. 61.

51. Ibid., pp. 60–61. The authors are explaining "radical humanism," which would appear to be a more plainly spoken version of organizational humanism.

52. We would be remiss if we did not also note that Karl Popper is very much in Rawlsian tradition (or vice versa, as Popper preceded Rawls in time). Popper held that, "Instead of the greatest happiness for the greatest number [as the utilitarians advocated], one should demand, more modestly, the least amount of avoidable suffering for all; and further, that unavoidable suffering . . . should be distributed as equally as possible" (Vol. 1, p. 285). See his *The Open Society and Its Enemies*, Vol. I, *The Spell of Plato*, and Vol. II, *The High Tide of Prophecy: Hegel, Marx and the Aftermath*, 5th ed. (Princeton, NJ: Princeton University Press, 1966). The volumes were first published in 1945.

53. John Rawls, *A Theory of Justice* (Cambridge, MA: Belknap Press of Harvard University Press, 1971), p. 60.

54. Ibid., pp. 14–15.

55. Sashkin and Williams, "Does Fairness Make a Difference?" pp. 56–71.

56. See, for example: Brian Barry, *Political Argument* (London: Routledge and Kegan Paul, 1965); Nicholas Rescher, *Distributive Justice* (New York: Bobbs-Merrill, 1966); and W. D. Ross, *The Right and The Good* (Oxford: Clarendon Press, 1930).

57. Friedrich Nietzsche, as quoted in J. R. Hollingsdale, *Nietzsche: The Man and His Philosophy* (Baton Rouge: Louisiana State University Press, 1965), p. 127.

58. See, for example, Jeremy Bentham, *An Introduction to the Principles of Morals and Legislation*, J. H. Burns and H. L. A. Hart, eds. (London: Athlone, 1970); Adam Smith, *The Wealth of Nations*, Edwin Cannan, ed., (New York: Modern Library, 1937); David Hume, *Theory of Politics*, Frederick Watkins, ed. (Edinburgh: Nelson, 1951); and John Stuart Mill, *Essays on Politics and Culture*, Gertrude Himmelfarb, ed. (New York: Doubleday, 1962).

59. Michael Kinsley, "The Spoils of Victimhood," *The New Yorker* (March 27, 1995), p. 67.

Information Sources, Journals, and Organizations in Public and Nonprofit Administration by Specialization

The following three appendices, Appendices B, C, and D, list those information sources, journals, and organizations pertinent to public and nonprofit administration. This appendix categorizes these three lists by functional specialization. So, if you want to know quickly what resources are available to you in your particular area of interest, then Appendix A is the place to start, and Appendices B, C, and D are the places to follow up.

By no means are all the publications and organizations listed in Appendices B, C, and D included in Appendix A. This is because Appendix A does not address the broader areas of the field, such as organization theory, public policy, and general public administration. Rather, Appendix A identifies only those publications and organizations that deal with quite specific subfields, such as budgeting and finance and human resource management. Appendix A is a recognition of the data deluge in public administration. Without Appendix A, readers might well overlook some of the more obscure (but very useful) publications and organizations available in some specializations.

The fourteen specializations featured in this appendix, in order of appearance, are: Budgeting and Finance; Criminal Justice; Ethics; Federal Government; Human Resource Management; Independent Sector; Information Resource Management; Intergovernmental Administration; Local Government; Minority and Gender Affairs; Planning; Program Evaluation and Performance Measurement; State Government; and Welfare, Health, and Public Safety.

The first heading under each specialization lists pertinent "Information Sources"—that is, abstracts, bibliographies, dictionaries, directories, encyclopedias, and Web sites—that are described in Appendix B. These are listed alphabetically by title.

"Information Sources" is followed by "Journals" that are described in Appendix C. As with information sources, journals and other periodicals are listed alphabetically by title.

Occasionally, a particular specialization has either no information sources or journals associated with it, so we simply begin with the category of publication that pertains.

The third heading under the specialization lists relevant "Organizations" that are described in Appendix D. These are listed alphabetically.

Budgeting and Finance

Information Sources (See Appendix B)

Budget of the United States Government
Census of Governments
Government Assistance Almanac
Statistical Abstract of the United States

Journals (See Appendix C)

Financial Accountability and Management
Government Finance Review
Grantsmanship Center Magazine

*International Journal of Government
    Auditing*
Journal of Accounting and Public Policy
*Journal of Government Financial
    Management*
*Journal of Public Budgeting, Accounting, and
    Financial Management*
Journal of State Taxation
Journal of Taxation
National Public Accountant
National Tax Journal
OECD Journal on Budgeting
Public Budgeting and Finance
Public Finance Review

Organizations (See Appendix D)

Association of Inspectors General
Center on Budget and Policy Priorities
Federation of Tax Administrators
Government Accounting Standards Board
Government Finance Officers Association
Grantsmanship Center
National Association of State Auditors, Controllers,
    and Treasurers
National Association of State Budget
    Officers
National Tax Association
Organisation for Economic Co-operation and
    Development
Tax Foundation

Criminal Justice

Information Sources (See Appendix B)

Book of the States
Sourcebook of Criminal Justice Statistics
Statistical Abstract of the United States

Journals (See Appendix C)

Journal of Criminal Justice

Organizations (See Appendix D)

American Correctional Association
International Association of Chiefs of Police

Ethics

Information Sources (See Appendix B)

Public Integrity Annual

Journals (See Appendix C)

Administrative Theory and Praxis
Citizen Participation
Financial Accountability and Management
Public Integrity

Organizations (See Appendix D)

Association of Inspectors General
Common Cause
Council on Government Ethics Laws
Freedom of Information Center
Transparency International

Federal Government

Information Sources (See Appendix B)

Budget of the United States Government
Congressional Yellow Book
Fact Book
Federal Regional Yellow Book
Federal Yellow Book
FirstGov
Government Affairs Yellow Book
Statistical Abstract of the United States
Students.gov

Journals (See Appendix C)

*Cityscape: A Journal of Policy Development
    and Research*
Federal Assistance Monitor
Federal Computer Week
Federal Labor Relations Reporter
Federal Merit Systems Reporter
Government Executive
Government Computer News
Government Union Review
Issues of Merit
National Journal

Organizations (See Appendix D)

American Society for Public Administration
Center on Budget and Policy Priorities
Executive Women in Government
Federally Employed Women
National Academy of Public Administration
Partnership for Public Service

Human Resource Management

Information Sources (See Appendix B)

Budget of the United States Government
Census of Governments
Fact Book
Statistical Abstract of the United States

Journals (See Appendix C)

Federal Labor Relations Reporter
Federal Merit Systems Reporter
Government Union Review
HR Focus
HR Magazine
Human Resource Development Quarterly
Human Resource Management
Industrial and Labor Relations Review
Issues of Merit
Journal of Collective Negotiations in the Public Sector
Personnel Law Update
Public Personnel Management
Review of Public Personnel Administration
Workforce
WorldatWork Journal

Organizations (See Appendix D)

International Personnel Management Association
Local Government Institute
National Public Employer Labor Relations Association
Partnership for Public Service
Public Employees Roundtable
Public Service Research Foundation
Society for Human Resource Management
WorldatWork

Independent Sector

Information Sources (See Appendix B)

ARNOVA Abstracts
Government Assistance Almanac
Non-profit Organizations: Current Issues and Developments
Nonprofit Sector Yellow Book

Journals (See Appendix C)

Chronicle of Philanthropy
Citizen Participation
Federal Assistance Monitor
Financial Accounting and Management
Grantsmanship Center Magazine
Nonprofit and Voluntary Sector Quarterly
Nonprofit Management and Leadership
Nonprofit Quarterly
Public Choice

Organizations (See Appendix D)

Alliance for Redesigning Government
American Society of Association Executives
Center for Women in Government and Civil Society
Grantsmanship Center
Independent Sector
National Council for Public-Private Partnerships

Information Resource Management

Journals (See Appendix C)

Federal Computer Week
Government Computer News
Government Technology
Journal of Economic and Social Measurement
Journal of E-Government
Journal of Government Information

Organizations (See Appendix D)

Government Management Information Sciences
National Association of State Chief Information Officers

Intergovernmental Administration

Information Sources (See Appendix B)

Book of the States
Government Assistance Almanac
Municipal Year Book
Statistical Abstract of the United States

Journals (See Appendix C)

Federal Assistance Monitor
Grantsmanship Center Magazine
Publius
Regionalist

Organizations (See Appendix D)

Association of Metropolitan Planning
   Organizations
Council of State Community Development Agencies
Grantsmanship Center
National Association of Regional Councils

Local Government

Information Sources (See Appendix B)

Census of Governments
County and City Data Book
Government Affairs Yellow Book
Government Assistance Almanac
Index to Current Urban Documents
Municipal Year Book
Municipal Yellow Book
National City Government Resource Center
State and Local Sourcebook
State and Metropolitan Area Data Book
Statistical Abstract of the United States

Journals (See Appendix C)

American City and County
*Cityscape: A Journal of Policy Development
   and Research*
Federal Assistance Monitor
Governing
Government Computer News
Government Finance Review

Government Technology
Government Union Review
Grantsmanship Center Magazine
IQ Report
National Civic Review
Public Management
State and Local Government Review
Urban Affairs Review

Organizations (See Appendix D)

American Public Transit Association
American Public Works Association
American Society for Public Administration
Association of Inspectors General
Association of Metropolitan Planning
   Organizations
Council of State Community Development
   Agencies
Government Accounting Standards Board
Government Finance Officers Association
Government Management Information Sciences
Grantsmanship Center
International Association of Chiefs of Police
International Association of Fire Chiefs
International City/County Management Association
International Hispanic Network
International Institute of Municipal Clerks
Local Government Institute
National Academy of Public Administration
National Association of Counties
National Association of Housing and Redevelopment
   Officials
National Association of Regional Councils
National Association of Towns and Townships
National Civic League
National Recreation and Park Association
United States Conference of Mayors
Urban Institute

Minority and Gender Affairs

Information Sources (See Appendix B)

State of Black America
Statistical Abstract of the United States

Organizations (See Appendix D)

Center for Women in Government and Civil Society
Conference of Minority Public Administrators

Executive Women in Government
Federally Employed Women
International Hispanic Network
National Forum for Black Public Administrators
Women Executives in State Government

Planning

Journals (See Appendix C)

American City and County
Evaluation and Program Planning
Journal of the American Planning Association
Urban Affairs Review

Organizations (See Appendix D)

American Planning Association
Association of Metropolitan Planning
   Organizations
Local Government Institute
National Association of Regional Councils
National Council for Public-Private Partnerships

Program Evaluation and Performance Measurement

Journals (See Appendix C)

American Journal of Evaluation
Benchmarking
Evaluation and Program Planning
Evaluation Review
Journal of Economic and Social Measurement
New Directions for Evaluation
Public Performance and Management Review
Total Quality Management

Organizations (See Appendix D)

Alliance for Redesigning Government
American Evaluation Association
Association of Inspectors General
Council for Excellence in Government
National Association of State Chief
   Administrators
National Center for Public Productivity
Public Sector Network

State Government

Information Sources (See Appendix B)

Book of the States
FirstGov
Government Affairs Yellow Book
Government Assistance Almanac
State and Local Source Book
State and Metropolitan Area Data Book
State Yellow Book
Statistical Abstract of the United States

Journals (See Appendix C)

Federal Assistance Monitor
Governing
Government Computer News
Government Finance Review
Government Technology
Government Union Review
Grantsmanship Center Magazine
Journal of State Taxation
Solutions
Spectrum: The Journal of State Government
State and Local Government Review
State Government News

Organizations (See Appendix D)

American Correctional Association
American Society for Public Administration
Association of Inspectors General
Center for Women in Government and Civil
   Society
Council of State Community Development
   Agencies
Council of State Governments
Federation of Tax Administrators
Government Accounting Standards Board
Government Finance Officers Association
Government Management Information Sciences
Grantsmanship Center
National Academy of Public Administration
National Association of Housing and Redevelopment
   Officials
National Association of State Auditors, Controllers,
   and Treasurers
National Association of State Budget Officers
National Association of State Chief
   Administrators

National Association of State Chief Information
  Officers
National Conference of State Legislatures
National Emergency Management Association
National Governors Association
National Institute of Governmental Purchasing
National Recreation and Park Association
Women Executives in State Government

Welfare, Health, and Public Safety

Information Sources (See Appendix B)

Sourcebook of Criminal Justice Statistics
Statistical Abstract of the United States

Journals (See Appendix C)

American Journal of Public Health
Journal of Criminal Justice
Policy and Practice of Public Human Services
Public Works Management and Policy Science

Organizations (See Appendix D)

American Public Human Services Association
American Public Works Association
International Association of Chiefs of Police
International Association of Fire Chiefs
National Association of Housing and Redevelopment
  Officials
National Emergency Management Association
National Recreation and Park Association

APPENDIX B

Annotated Information Sources in Public Administration and Related Fields

This appendix annotates major abstract services, bibliographies, dictionaries, directories, encyclopedias, and unusually comprehensive Web sites in public administration and related fields.

Entries are listed alphabetically by title. If a source had a former title, this is also provided.

Numbers appearing in the right-hand margin are the entries' Library of Congress call numbers and should facilitate your locating the work. If a source is available only on the World Wide Web, then its Web address is listed.

Some sources are accessible electronically *without charge*. When this is the case, we note that the source is "fully accessible" and provide its Web address.

Government document numbers are provided for sources published by the U.S. Government. Your librarian will be grateful to have this number if you request assistance.

ARNOVA Abstracts. Weekly. Abstracts deal with nonprofit organizations and voluntarism. Formerly *Citizen Participation and Voluntary Action Abstracts.* HV41

Basic Documents of American Public Administration 1776–1950. Frederick C. Mosher. New York: Holmes and Meier, 1976. Just as the title states, the book covers the basic early American documents of public administration. An excellent compendium. JK411.B3

Basic Documents of American Public Administration Since 1950. Richard J. Stillman II. New York: Holmes and Meier, 1982. Editor's introductions place each topic and document into perspective. The book reveals postwar reforms in organization, personnel, budgeting and accountability. JK411.B32

Biographical Dictionary of Public Administration. Patricia Moses Wigfall and Behrooz Kalantari. Westport, CT: Greenwood Press, 2000. Provides brief, contextual biographies of principal scholars who have contributed to public administration directly, or indirectly via organization

theory, human resource management, budgeting, and related fields. JA61

Book of the States. Lexington, KY: Council of State Governments. Biennial. Features a mass of descriptive and statistical data about state governments, their organization, finances, programs, and intergovernmental relations, among many other topics. Scholarly essays introduce each section. JK2403.B6

Budget of the United States Government. U.S. Office of Management and Budget, Executive Office of the President. Washington, DC: U.S. Government Printing Office. Three volumes. Annual. Government document number Y1.1/7. The president's executive budget, submitted to Congress for its adjustment and approval. It is a trove of federal financial information including data on government-sponsored enterprises, analytical perspectives, and historical tables. Fully accessible at http://www.whitehouse.gov/omb/budget/. HJ2051

Census of Governments. U.S. Bureau of the Census. Washington, DC: U.S. Government Printing Office. Five volumes. Quinquennial. Government document number C3.145. Statistical tabulations for each local government in the United States, including aggregated data on government organization, elected officials, property taxes, public employment, government finances, and employee retirement systems. Fully accessible at http://www.census.gov/prod/www/abs/govern.hmtl/. JK2403.B6

Congressional Yellow Book. Washington, DC: Leadership Directories. Quarterly. Directory of all members of Congress and staff. Names, titles, addresses, telephone numbers, and e-mail addresses are listed. Updated daily at www.leadershipdirectories.com. JK6.F440

County and City Data Book. U.S. Bureau of the Census. Washington, DC: U.S. Government Printing Office. Quinquennial. A convenient format for extracting statistics from the many different Census Bureau series, such as the Census of Governments. Access by county, by metropolitan area, and by city for all places over 25,000 population. Fully accessible at http://www.census. gov/prod/www/cedb.html.   HA202.A36

Dictionary of Public Policy and Administration. Jay M. Shafritz. Boulder, CO: Westview. 2004. A comprehensive lexicon of words and phrases pertinent to public policy and public administration.   H97

Directory of Journals in Public Affairs, Public and Non-Profit Administration and Political Science. Craig Poulenz Gonovan. Burke, VA: Chatelaine Press. 1999. Comprehensive list of periodicals in public administration and nonprofit management.   Z7164.A2

Directory of Organizations and Individuals Professionally Engaged in Governmental Research and Related Activities. Ocean Gate, NJ: Governmental Research Association. Annual. Notes national, state and local agencies concerned with the improvement of governmental organizations, administration and efficiency. Indexed by names of organizations and individuals.   JK3.G627

Federal Regional Yellow Book. Washington, DC: Leadership Directories. Semiannual. Directory of principal federal administrators located outside of Washington, DC. Names, titles, addresses, telephone numbers, and e-mail addresses are listed. Extensive regional maps. Updated daily at www.leadershipdirectories.com.   JK6.F440

Federal Yellow Book. Washington, DC: Leadership Directories. Quarterly. Directory of federal departments and agencies; names, titles, telephone numbers, and e-mail addresses of elected officials, and principal federal administrators in Washington, DC are listed. Updated daily at www.leadershipdirectories.com.   JK6.F440

FirstGov. A public-private partnership administered by the General Services Administration that is "your first click to the U.S. Government" as well as to state governments and related sites.   http://firstgov.gov

Government Affairs Yellow Book. Washington, DC: Leadership Directories. Semiannual. Major lobbyists in Washington, the states, and large local governments are listed, with addresses, telephone numbers, and e-mail addresses. Effectively organized. Updated daily at www.leadershipdirectories.com.   JK6.F440

Government Assistance Almanac. Detroit, MI: Omnigraphics. Annual. A user-friendly guide to all 1,500 federal assistance programs, with contact information.   HC110.P63

Index to Current Urban Documents. Westport, CT: Greenwood. Quarterly. "The only regularly published guide" to reports generated by local government agencies, civic organizations, and regional agencies. Five hundred U.S. and Canadian cities are covered.   Z7165.U5

International Encyclopedia of Public Policy and Administration. Jay M. Shafritz, ed. Four volumes. Boulder, CO: Westview, 1998. A massive compilation of original and definitive articles written by the world's leading scholars of public administration and public policy.   H97.I574 1998

Municipal Year Book. Washington, DC: International City/County Management Association. Annual. Presents detailed data for city and county governments in the United States and Canada. Articles on management trends and issues, intergovernmental relations, and local salaries.

Guide to directories of local government associations and local officials.   JS342.A2152

Municipal Yellow Book. Washington, DC: Leadership Directories. Biannual. Directory of elected officials and principal administrators of U.S. cities, counties, and public authorities. Names, titles, addresses are listed. Updated daily at www.leadershipdirectories.com.   JF6.F440

National City Government Resource Center. An impressive Web site that links sites for cities, functions, regions, capitals, think tanks, jobs, and other categories.   http://www.geocities.com

Non-profit Organizations: Current Issues and Developments. New York: Practicing Law Institute. Annual. Covers legal, taxation, and other issues pertinent to the third sector. Formerly *Non-profit Cultural Organizations.*   KF1388.Z9N67

Nonprofit Sector Yellow Book. Washington, DC: Leadership Directories. Biannual. Directory of principal administrators of U.S. foundations, schools, colleges, universities, museums, performing arts groups, theaters, medical institutions, libraries, and charitable organizations. Names, titles, addresses, telephone numbers, and e-mail addresses are listed. Updated daily at www.leadershipdirectories.com.   JK6.F440

Public Administration: A Bibliographic Guide to the Literature. 2nd ed. Howard E. McCurdy. New York: Marcel Dekker, Inc., 1986. Some 1,200 books and articles are listed and annotated in thirty-three categories, focusing on the 181 most frequently cited books in the field. Essays on the evolution of public administration as both a scholarly field and a profession are included.   JF1351.M23

Public Administration Desk Book. James R. Coleman and Robert E. Dugan. Newton, MA: Government Research Publications, 1990. Bibliographies cover the field and related ones as well.   Z7164.A2C59 1990

Public Administration Dictionary. William Fox and Ivan H. Meyer. New York: Juta, 1995. Slim volume of terminology and bibliographic references.   JAG1.F69 1995

Public Administration Dictionary. 2nd ed. Ralph Chandler and Jack C. Plano. New York: Wiley, 1988. Terms are alphabetized within chapter headings, but the index gives a term's location. The authors include section explaining the "significance" of the term.   JA61.C47

Public Administration Series: Bibliography. Monticello, IL: Vance Bibliographies. Annual. Bibliographies vary in length and cover a wide range of topics related to public affairs, local to international. Treatment may be empirical, theoretical, or practical.   JT1351.A1B38

Public Affairs Service Bulletin. New York: Public Affairs Service. Monthly. This index, with annual cumulations, unifies a wide variety of sources concerned with public affairs. It lists books, pamphlets, periodicals, and government documents. Most articles include brief explanatory items.   Z7163.P9761B

Public Integrity Annual. Washington, DC: Council of State Governments and the American Society for Public Administration. Annual. Focuses on ethical standards in government.   JK2445.E8P97

Sage Public Administration Abstracts. Beverly Hills, CA: Sage. Quarterly. Lists and abstracts more than 1,000 publications in the field annually. Abstracts are indexed by author, title, and subject, and a year-end cumulative index is published.   JA1.S27

Sourcebook of Criminal Justice Statistics. U.S. Department of Justice, Bureau of Justice Statistics. Washington, DC: U.S. Government Printing Office. Annual. Government document number J1.42. Describes the criminal justice systems, traces public attitudes on crime, records crime rates, and analyzes arrestees, defendants, prisoners, and parolees. Fully accessible at http://www.albany.edu/sourcebook/.   HV7245

State and Local Sourcebook. Supplement to *Governing* magazine. Annual. An unusually useful compendium of up-to-date fiscal information for state and local governments, plus names, addresses, telephone numbers, and Web sites of major allocators of state and local funds, national associations, and vendors. Fully accesible at http://governing.com/source.htm.   JK2503.G686

State and Metropolitan Area Data Book. U.S. Bureau of the Census, Washington, DC: U.S. Government Printing Office. Quinquennial. Government document number C3.134. A convenient format for finding statistics from a variety of Census Bureau series. Organized by states and metropolitan areas. Fully accessible at http://www.census.gov/statab/www/smadb.html.   HA202.A36 C3.134/5

State of Black America. Washington, DC: National Urban League. Annual. A particularly authoritative compendium on the yearly status of African Americans.   E185.5.N317

State Yellow Book. Washington, DC: Leadership Directories. Quarterly. Directory of elected officials and principal administrators in the states. Names, titles, addresses, telephone numbers, and e-mail addresses are listed. Updated daily at www.leadershipdirectories.com.   JK6.F440

Statistical Abstract of the United States. U.S. Bureau of the Census. Washington, DC: U.S. Government Printing Office. Annual. Government document number C3.134. Statistical compilations from federal, state, and local governments are presented. Notation of information source leads researchers to additional information. The best single source for national data (and considerable international data) on every topic. Fully accessible at http://www.census.gov/statab/www/.   HA202.A388 C3.134

Students.gov. "The student gateway to the U.S. Government," this Web site offers information on planning and paying for one's education, military service, career development, and community service, among other items.   http://students.gov

APPENDIX C

Selected Annotated Journals Relevant to Public and Nonprofit Administration

This appendix identifies and describes journals, magazines, newsletters, and other periodicals that are particularly germane to public administration. There are a number of new journals bearing on public administration that, while worthwhile, are not well known. These have been included, as have selected foreign journals published in the English language.

Journals are listed alphabetically by title. Their publication schedules and a brief description accompany each title. If a periodical had a former title, or titles, these are also provided.

Library of Congress call numbers appear in the right-hand margins for your convenience. If a journal is available only on the Internet, then its Web address is listed.

Some periodicals are accessible electronically *without charge*. When this is the case, we note that the publication is "fully accessible" and provide its Web address.

Academy of Management Executive. Quarterly. A good journal focused on the needs of top administrators. Emphasis is on the private sector. Formerly *Executive.* HD28

Academy of Management Journal. Bimonthly. A high-quality publication on general management with a mathematical and behavioral orientation. HD28.A24

Academy of Management Review. Quarterly. High-quality, general journal; has a thematically oriented book review section. HD28.A242x

Administration and Society. Bimonthly. A good, unusually thoughtful journal covering the broad spectrum of public administration. JA3.J65

Administrative Change. Biannually. An Indian journal of high quality that focuses on political and administrative development. JA26

Administrative Science Quarterly. Perhaps the foremost journal in administrative theory and in organization theory of special relevance to public administration. HD28.A25

Administrative Theory and Praxis. Quarterly. "A journal of dialogue in public administration theory." Formerly *Dialogue.* JA1.D53

American City and County. Bimonthly. This is among the better periodicals in the field of planning and urban management. Formerly *American City Magazine.* HT101.A5

American Journal of Evaluation. Quarterly. A major journal on public program evaluation. Formerly *Evaluation Practice,* and before that, *Evaluation News.* AZ101.E93x

American Journal of Public Health. Monthly. Concerns policy and administrative aspects of public health in the United States. RA421.A395

American Review of Public Administration. Quarterly. General articles and broad coverage. Formerly *Midwest Review of Public Administration.* JK1.M5

Australian Journal of Public Administration. Quarterly. A fine source for information on some of the field's pioneering developments. Formerly *Public Administration.* JA8.N12

Benchmarking. Quarterly. British journal that emphasizes international experiences in the private sector. Formerly *Benchmarking for Quality Management and Technology.* HD62.15

California Management Review. Quarterly. A high-quality journal in the style of *Harvard Business Review*, but more data-conscious. HD28.C18

Canadian Public Administration. Quarterly. Devoted to Canadian public administration and comparative analysis. JL1.C35

Chronicle of Philanthropy. Biweekly. "The newspaper of the nonprofit world" is a comprehensive treatment of issues, trends, and job listings. HV85

Citizen Participation. Bimonthly. Newspaper on activities involving citizen participation in policy formation at all levels of government. JK1.C58x

Cityscape: A Journal of Policy Development and Research. Triannually. Published by the U.S. Department of Housing and Urban development, it focuses on research funded by the department. Each issue has a theme. Fully accessible at http://www.huduser.org/periodicals/ cityscape.html. HT123.C4994

Current Municipal Problems. Quarterly. Deals with policy and administrative issues at the local level. JS39.C85

Evaluation and Program Planning. Quarterly. General articles of a theoretical and practical perspective for evaluation researchers. Formerly *Journal of Evaluation and Program Planning.* H62.A1E93

Evaluation Review. Bimonthly. A journal on public program evaluation. Formerly *Evaluation Quarterly.* HM1E8

Federal Assistance Monitor. Biweekly. Reports federal and private grant opportunities by category, such as "Community Services." HC110.P63

Federal Computer Week. Weekly. Focuses on developments in federal information technology, security, and management but covers a surprisingly diverse array of other federal initiatives as well. Fully accessible at http:// www.fcw.com/index.asp. JK468.A8

Federal Labor Relations Reporter. Biannually. Follows developments in the public sector labor force, but especially in the federal government. KF5365.A57

Federal Merit Systems Reporter. Monthly. A companion volume to *Federal Labor Relations Reporter*, it concerns developments in federal human resource management. Cumulated annually. KF3365

Financial Accountability and Management. Quarterly. Published in Britain, specializing in the financial management of governments and third-sector organizations. HJ9701.F55x

Governance. Quarterly. An international journal of policy and administration. Published in Britain. Quite good. JA1.A1 G68

Governing. Monthly. Magazine focusing on the management of state and local governments. In 1994, *Governing* absorbed *City and State.* Fully accessible at http:// www.governing.com. JK2503.G686

Government Computer News. Thirty issues per year. Covers information technology issues in the federal, state, and local governments. TK7885.A1

Government Executive. Monthly. Billing itself as "government's business magazine," it focuses on management issues exclusively at the federal level. Fully accessible at http://govexec.com. JK1.G58

Government Finance Review. Bimonthly. Brief articles that emphasize municipal finance. Formerly *Governmental Finance*, and before that, *Municipal Finance.* HJ9103.G68x

Government Technology. Monthly. Details technological solutions to problems of state and local governments. JK2445.A9G68

Government Union Review. Quarterly. Traces labor-management relations in the federal, state, and local governments. HD8008.A1663

Grantsmanship Center Magazine. Quarterly. An excellent compendium of the latest trends and findings concerning grants for nonprofit organizations. Formerly *Grantsmanship Center Whole Nonprofit Catalog.* Fully accessible at http://www.tgci.com/magazine. HG177

Harvard Business Review. Quarterly. Concerns a variety of administrative processes. An outstanding journal of quality, but has a private-sector emphasis. HF5001.H3

Harvard Journal of Law and Public Policy. Triannually. Fast-paced, but thorough articles on current events. K8

HR Focus. Monthly. Business oriented, often devoting an entire issue to a theme dealing with personnel administration. HF5549.A2

HR Magazine. Monthly. Business-oriented articles on personnel administration. Formerly *Personnel Administrator.* HF5549.A2

Human Performance. Quarterly. Good journal that focuses on "performance in the workplace . . . going beyond the study of traditional job behavior." BF636

Human Relations. Monthly. A behavioral journal of excellent quality, often dealing with organization theory. H1.H8

Human Resource Development Quarterly. A behaviorally oriented journal that emphasizes training. HF5549.15.H86

Human Resource Management. Quarterly. A journal on personnel administration that is distinctly oriented toward business and psychology. HF5549.A2

Human Resource Management Review. Quarterly. Covers both the public and private sectors. HF5549.2.U5.H83

Indian Journal of Public Administration. Quarterly. Relates to administration in India, comparative analysis, and development administration. JQ201.155

Industrial and Labor Relations Review. Quarterly. Devoted to labor relations in both public and private sectors. Substantial book review section. HD4802.153

Innovation Journal. Triannually. An online Canadian journal devoted to innovation in the public sector. http://www.innovation.cc/

International Journal of Government Auditing. Quarterly. A journal that covers all aspects of government accounting and auditing. JQ201.155

International Journal of Public Administration. Monthly, except December. Wide coverage, but much that pertains to the United States. HD4802.153

International Review of Administrative Sciences. Quarterly. Devoted entirely to public administration. Published by the International Institute of Administrative Sciences. European emphasis. JA26.158

International Review of Public Administration. Biannually. Journal of the Korean Association for Public Administration. Formerly *Korean Review of Public Administration.* JA26

IQ Report. Monthly. Practitioner-oriented articles for local managers, published by the International City/County Management Association. "IQ" stands for "InQuiry." Formerly *IQ Service Report*, and before that, *MIS Report,* and before that, *Management Information Service Report.* JS39.M28

Issues of Merit. Quarterly. Government document number MS 1.17. Research conducted by the U.S. Merit Systems Protection Board on policies concerning the federal civilian workforce. Fully accessible at http://www.mspb.gov/studies/newsletters. JK765

Journal of Accounting and Public Policy. Bimonthly. Specializes in "the effects of accounting on public policy and vice-versa." Both the private and public sectors are covered. H97.J56

Journal of Applied Behavioral Science. Quarterly. Devoted largely to organization development. H1.J53

Journal of Collective Negotiations in the Public Sector. Quarterly. Designed to help public managers and employees understand each others' perspectives. LB2842.2J68

Journal of Criminal Justice. Quarterly. Focuses on systemic issues of justice. HV7231.J62

Journal of Economic and Social Measurement. Quarterly. Encourages use of public records in analyzing policy at the local, regional, and national levels. Formerly *Review of Public Data Use.* H62.A1 R47

Journal of E-Government. Quarterly. Issues in electronic government, including citizen use and case studies. JF1525.A8

Journal of Government Financial Management. Quarterly. Focuses on problems of public accountancy at all levels of government. Formerly *Government Accountants Journal.* HJ9801.A1F4

Journal of Government Information. Bimonthly. An international journal dealing with government data policy, issues, and resources. Formerly *Government Publications Review.* Z7164.G7

Journal of Management History. Monthly. Much of this periodical focuses on public administration. HD30.5

Journal of Management Science and Policy Studies. Quarterly. Attempts to join the administrative and policymaking wings of public administration. Formerly *Management Science and Policy Analysis.* JA1.J56

Journal of Organizational Behavior Management. Quarterly. Devoted to behavior management in business, government, and service organizations; quantitatively oriented. HD58.7.J68

Journal of Policy Analysis and Management. Quarterly. Articles are heavily substantive, rather than theoretical. Combined the *Journal of Policy Analysis* and *Public Policy* in 1981. H1.J552x

Journal of Public Administration Research and Theory. Quarterly. *J-PART* is dedicated to tying research in the field to theory. Fully accessible at www.ubalt.edu/jpartjparttoc.html. JA1.J65

Journal of Public Budgeting, Accounting, and Financial Management. Quarterly. A precisely titled journal in terms of its coverage. Formerly *Public Budgeting and Financial Management.* HJ101.P78

Journal of State Taxation. Quarterly. Issues of accounting and taxation in the American states. K10

Journal of Taxation. Monthly. Magazine with a news orientation aimed at financial professionals. HJ2360.J6

Journal of the American Planning Association. Quarterly. Publication devoted to land-use planning in the public sector. Formerly *Journal of the American Institute of Planners.* HD87.5.A46a

Management Review. Monthly. One of the oldest management magazines (first published in 1914) and is business-oriented. Includes survey of books for executives. T58.A2.M37

National Civic Review. Quarterly. Provides short but informative articles on a wide variety of urban problems. JS39.N3

National Journal. Weekly. Designed as a monitor of all federal actions, but especially in the executive agencies. JK1.N28

National Public Accountant. Monthly. A broad review of public accountancy. HF5601.N335

National Tax Journal. Quarterly. *NTJ* is the nation's foremost periodical on taxation. HJ2240.N32x

New Directions for Evaluation. Quarterly. Topical journal that features in-depth coverage of evaluation research issues in public policy. Formerly *New Directions for Program Evaluation.* H62.A1 N4

Nonprofit and Voluntary Sector Quarterly. An interdisciplinary journal on issues of volunteers, nonprofit organizations, philanthropies, and citizen participation. Formerly *Journal of Voluntary Action Research.* HV1.J63

Nonprofit Management and Leadership. Quarterly. Devoted to the managing and leading of nongovernmental, not-for-profit organizations. Quite good. HD62.6.N663

Nonprofit Quarterly. Covers broad themes relating to the independent sector. Formerly *New England Nonprofit Quarterly.* HD62.6

OECD Journal on Budgeting. Quarterly. Published by the Organisation for Economic Co-operation and Development, it focuses on public budgeting in many nations, with an emphasis on the developed world. HJ2005

Organizational Behavior and Human Decision Processes. Bimonthly. A high-quality journal focusing on interaction in small groups, conflict resolution, and the social psychology of organizations. Formerly *Organizational Behavior and Human Performance.* BF638.A.107

Organizational Dynamics. Quarterly. Reviews organizational behavior research but tilted pleasantly toward the practitioner. HD28.O76

Personnel Law Update. Monthly. A newsletter about legislation and court rulings affecting personnel managers in the public and private sectors. Formerly *Personnel Managers' Legal Reporter.* KF3302.P47

Philippine Journal of Public Administration. Quarterly. Devoted to Southeast Asia administration, comparative analysis, and development administration. JA26.P5

Philosophy and Public Policy Quarterly. Slim but interesting publication from the School of Public Affairs, University of Maryland. Covers diverse topics, but articles reflect the quarterly's title. H1

Policy and Practice of Public Human Services. Triannually. The leading journal on welfare policy and administration. Formerly *Public Welfare.* HVI.P75

Policy Sciences. Irregularly. Concerns public policy theory and methodology. International orientation. H1.P7

Policy Studies Journal. Quarterly. Has a political science orientation. H1.P72

Policy Studies Review. Quarterly. Articles on policy in many fields. H97.P66

Public Administration. Quarterly. Devoted to British administration and comparative analysis. Lists recent British government publications. JA8.P8

Public Administration. Biannually. Covers developments in one of the globe's more managerially advanced governments, New Zealand. Formerly *New Zealand Journal of Public Administration.* JA8.N42

Public Administration and Development. Quarterly. British journal that deals largely with development administration. Absorbed *Journal of African Administration* and *Journal of Administration Overseas.* JF60.P83

Public Administration and Management. Quarterly. An online, "interactive journal" devoted to the field; U.S. emphasis. http://www.pamj.com.

Public Administration Quarterly. Wide coverage of many topics. Formerly *Southern Review of Public Administration.* JA1.S68

Public Administration Review. Bimonthly. The most significant American journal concerned with public administration. *PAR* articles are of high quality; "review essays" of books are provided. JK1.P85

Public Administration Times. Biweekly. Newsletter of the American Society for Public Administration; lists employment opportunities. Fully accessible at http://www.aspanet.org/publications/patimes. JA1.P975

Public Budgeting and Finance. Quarterly. Journal dealing with questions of public finance and budgeting. Quite good. HJ2052.A2P8

Public Choice. Quarterly. A policy journal with a political economy orientation. H35.P33

Public Finance Review. Bimonthly. A journal emphasizing economic approaches to budgeting in the United States. Formerly *Public Finance Quarterly.* HJ101.P83

Public Integrity. Quarterly. Published by the American Society for Public Administration, the International City/County Management Association, and the Council of State Governments, the journal "seeks to be a touchstone of ethical commentary and research for the public service." JK2445.E8

Public Management. Eleven times per year. *PM* is "the official magazine of the International City/County Management Association," and focuses on local government issues. JS344.C5

Public Management Review. Quarterly. *PuMa* is an internationally oriented British journal with a European emphasis. JS39

Public Manager. Quarterly. Journal with a federal emphasis. Formerly *The Bureaucrat.* JK1.B861

Public Organization Review. Quarterly. A "global journal" focusing exclusively on issues of organization theory in the public and nonprofit sectors. JF1411

Public Performance and Management Review. Quarterly. Combines case studies and articles by academics and practitioners that focus on questions of program evaluation and productivity. Formerly *Public Productivity and Management Review*, and before that, *Public Productivity Review.* JF1411.P8

Public Personnel Management. Quarterly. Directed at human resource administrators in the federal, state, and local governments. JK671.P48x

Public Works Management and Policy. Quarterly. Designed to "bridge the gap" between practitioners and academics involved in water, sewerage, and other public works operations. HD3881.P83

Publius. Quarterly. A journal devoted to intergovernmental relations and federalism. JK1.P88

Regionalist. Quarterly. Published by the National Association of Regional Councils, *The Regionalist* addresses the issues of governance and economic development and tilts editorially against metropolitan fragmentation and toward regional governments. HT392

Review of Public Personnel Administration. Quarterly. Covers all aspects of the field, particularly at the state and local levels of government. JF1601.R4

Science. Weekly. The major science journal of the nation; extremely useful for articles and reports on public science policy. Q1.S35

Solutions. Irregularly. Each issue focuses on specific state policy questions and options, such as lobbying reform. Published by the Council on State Governments. Formerly *State Trends and Forecasts.* JK2403.S766

Spectrum: The Journal of State Government. Quarterly. The nation's premier journal on state government. Formerly *Journal of State Government*, and before that, *State Government.* JF2403.A454

State and Local Government Review. Triannually. A good journal covering a variety of aspects of subnational government with an emphasis on public administration. JK2403.S684

State Government News. Ten issues per year. Published for over six decades by the Council of State Governments, it informs readers of current developments in the states. JK2403.S75

Total Quality Management. Bimonthly. A British publication devoted to this field. TS 156.A1 T67

Urban Affairs Review. Bimonthly. Has an urban planning emphasis. Formerly *Urban Affairs Quarterly.* HT101.U67

Workforce. Monthly. Oriented toward private-sector human resource managers. Formerly *Personnel Journal.* HF5549.A2P5

WorldatWork Journal. Quarterly. Focuses on all aspects of employee compensation. Formerly *ACA Journal.* HF5549.5.C67

APPENDIX D

Selected Academic, Professional, and Public-Interest Organizations with Web Sites and Descriptions

The following national associations all have relevance to public administration. Virtually all of them publish journals, reports, and newsletters on topics of interest; you may wish to contact some of them for their materials.

The organizations are listed alphabetically. If the organization had a former title, that is also noted. Web site addresses and descriptions of what each organization represents are provided.

Alliance for Redesigning Government

http://www.alliance.napawash.org/alliance. Sponsored by the National Academy of Public Administration, the Alliance promotes government innovation and public-private partnerships.

American Association for Budget and Program Analysis

http://www.aabpa.org. Members represent the entire range of financial management at all levels of government. Web site lists employment openings.

American Correctional Association

http://www.corrections.com/aca. The major association of prison officials.

American Evaluation Association

http://www.eval.org. The major association of public program evaluators.

American Planning Association

http://www.planning.org. The major organization of public planning officials. Formerly the American Society of Planning Officials.

American Public Human Services Association

http://www.aphsa.org. The major organization of public welfare officials. Formerly the American Public Welfare Association.

American Public Transit Association

http://www.apta.com. The major association of public officials interested in mass transit.

American Public Works Association

http://www.pubworks.org. The principal association of public works administrators.

American Society for Association Executives

http://www.aseaneta.org. The major organization of chief executive officers of nonprofit organizations. Offers seminars, job listings, and publications.

American Society for Public Administration

http://www.aspanet.org. The major organization of academics and professionals in public administration at all levels of government.

Association of Government Accountants

http://www.rutgers.edu/agacgfm.org. The major American association of government accountants.

Association of Inspectors General

http://www.inspectorsgeneral.org. Founded in 1996, the Association is open to members from all levels of government, but emphasizes state and local I.G.s.

Association of Metropolitan Planning Organizations

http://www.apmo.org. The major association of metropolitan planning councils.

Brookings Institution

http://www.brookings.edu. A major academic think tank with important concerns in domestic public affairs.

Center for Women in Government and Civil Society

http://www.cwig.albany.edu. Provides excellent research on the advancement of women and African Americans and Hispanics in state governments, and the role of nonprofit organizations.

Center on Budget and Policy Priorities

http://www.cpbb.org Conducts timely analyses of national and state budgets and income distribution.

Committee for Economic Development

http://www.ced.org. Studies issues relating to business and public policy.

Common Cause

http://www.commoncause.org. An organization of more than 300,000 members dedicated to political reform.

Conference Board

http://www.conference-board.org. A business group that often addresses public issues.

Conference of Minority Public Administrators

http://www.compa.org. The major national association of minority public administrators.

Council for Excellence in Government

http://www.excelgov.org. A bipartisan organization of leaders in the private sector, who formerly served in government, dedicated to improving government performance. The Public Employees Roundtable is now a part of it.

Council of State Community Development Agencies

http://www.coscda.org. Chief organization of state community affairs officers. Formerly the Council of State Community Affairs Agencies.

Council of State Governments

http://www.csg.org. Primary association of state governments.

Council on Governmental Ethics Laws

http://cogel.org. COGEL, established in 1978, is the association of government ethics officers and publishes a bimonthly newsletter on ethics issues.

Executive Women in Government

www.execwomeningov.org. A nonprofit organization for women executives in the federal government. Applies to Senior Executive Service and GS Grade 15 levels. Promotes more opportunities for women.

Federation of Tax Administrators

http://taxadmin.org. Founded in 1937, FTA's mission is "to improve the quality of state tax administration" in all the states, the District of Columbia, and New York City.

Freedom of Information Center

http://www.missouri.edu/~foiwww. Conducts studies on the public's uses of federal, state, and local Freedom of Information Acts.

Government Accounting Standards Board

http://www.gasb.org. Establishes standards for financial reporting and accounting for state and local governments.

Government Finance Officers Association

http://www.gfoa.org. Major organization of state and local finance officials, with an emphasis on local government. Formerly the Municipal Finance Officers Association.

Government Management Information Sciences

http://www.gmis.org. Association of state and local information resource managers.

Governmental Research Association

http://www.graonline.org. One of the granddaddys of the municipal research bureaus, the GRA was established in 1914 and is a national organization of individuals professionally engaged in governmental research.

Grantsmanship Center

http://www.tgci.com. "Founded in 1972 to offer grantsmanship training and low-cost publications to non-profit organizations and government agencies." Its GrantDomain database is a well-organized presentation of federal, state, foundation, and corporate grant opportunities.

Independent Sector

http://www.IndependentSector.org. A national leadership forum that encourages philanthropy, volunteerism, and citizen action.

Institute of Public Administration

http://www.theipa.org. The Ur public affairs research group. Originally the New York Bureau of Municipal Research, founded in 1906.

International Association of Chiefs of Police

http://www.theiacp.org. The major organization of police chiefs.

International Association of Fire Chiefs

http://www.iafconline.org. The major organization of fire chiefs.

International City/County Management Association

http://www.icma.org. The major organization of city managers and other individuals interested in city and county management. Formerly the International City Management Association.

International Hispanic Network

http://www.internationalhispanicnetwork.org. IHN's mission is "to encourage professional excellence among Hispanic local government managers." It is affiliated with the Congressional Hispanic Caucus.

International Institute of Administrative Sciences

http://www.iiasiisa.be. The major international organization of public administration, founded in 1930. Operates out of Brussels, Belgium.

International Institute of Municipal Clerks

http://www.iimc.com. The major association of municipal clerks, who, in small towns, often function as the town manager.

International Personnel Management Association

http://www.ipma-hr.org. The major organization of public human resources administrators at all levels of government.

Local Government Institute

http://www.lgi.org. A nonprofit organization that provides technical assistance to local governments, particularly in human resources and community development.

National Academy of Public Administration

http://www.napawash.org. The most selective and prestigious organization of professionals and scholars in American public administration. Chartered by Congress.

National Association of Counties

http://www.naco.org. The major organization of county officials and publisher of research on county government.

National Association of Housing and Redevelopment Officials

http://www.nahro.org. The major association of state and local officials concerned with community development.

National Association of Regional Councils

http://www.narc.org. The major organization of Councils of Governments and related organizations.

National Association of Schools of Public Affairs and Administration

http://www.naspaa.org. The U.S. accrediting body for masters degree programs in public administration and public affairs.

National Association of State Auditors, Comptrollers, and Treasurers

http://www.nasact.org. Founded in 1915, NASACT is the chief organization of these officials.

National Association of State Budget Officers

http://www.nasbo.org. The major association of state financial officers.

National Association of State Chief Administrators

http://www.nasdags.org. The major association of these officials, whose principal duty is to "improve government efficiency and effectiveness."

National Association of State Chief Information Officers

http://www.nascio.org. Association of top state information resource administrators. Formerly the National Association of State Information Resource Executives.

National Association of State Procurement Officials

http://www.naspo.org. The major organization of acquisitions specialists in state governments.

National Association of Towns and Townships

http://natat.org. The major organization representing towns and townships.

National Center for Public Productivity

http://newark.rutgers.edu/~ncpp/ncpp.html. The Center gathers and disseminates information about productivity in public service and publishes a catalog of research on productivity improvement in the public sector.

National Civic League

http://www.ncl.org. Promotes community harmony and participation in local governance; sponsors the All-American City Awards.

National Conference of State Legislatures

http://www.ncsl.org. The national association of state legislatures.

National Council for Public-Private Partnerships

http://www.ncppp.org. Dedicated to fostering public-private partnerships at all levels of government.

National Emergency Management Association

http://www.nemaweb.org. The primary association of state emergency managers.

National Forum for Black Public Administrators

http://www.nfbpa.org. Organization devoted to promoting African Americans' advancement in public administration at all governmental levels.

National Governors Association

http://www.nga.org. The organization of American governors.

National Institute of Governmental Purchasing

http://www.nigp.org. Promotes improved procurement practices in federal, state, and local governments.

National League of Cities

http://www.nlc.org. The nation's largest association of urban governments, it coordinates the forty-nine state municipal leagues.

National Public Employer Labor Relations Association

http://www.npelra.org. Promotes better labor relations management at all levels of government.

National Recreation and Park Association

http://www.nrpa.org. The major organization of public parks and recreation professionals.

National Tax Association

http://ntanet.org. Founded in 1907, NTA studies and recommends tax policies. Publishes the prestigious *National Tax Journal.*

Organisation for Economic Co-operation and Development

http://www.oecd.org. Thirty European countries comprise OECD, and its Public Management Service publishes a variety of analyses on taxation, public administration, and governance.

Partnership for Public Service

http://www.ourpublicservice.org. A nonpartisan, nonprofit organization dedicated to revitalizing the federal civil service.

Public Employees Roundtable

http://www.theroundtable.org. A coalition of organizations representing more than one million public employees designed to "better inform citizens about the quality of people in government." It is now a part of the Council for Excellence in Government.

Public Sector Network

http://www.governmentquality.org. A voluntary group of over 1,300 federal, state, and local administrators devoted to applying total quality management to government. Formerly the Public Sector Quality Improvement Network, it is a division of the American Society for Quality.

Public Service Research Foundation

http://www.psrf.org. A nonprofit public education group whose purpose is to increase research and public awareness regarding public-sector employee and employer relations.

Rand Corporation

http://www.rand.org. A major think tank concerned with public problems.

Society for Human Resource Management

http://www.shrm.org. One of the major associations of human resources managers. Emphasis is on the private sector. Formerly the American Society for Personnel Administration.

Society of Government Meeting Professionals

http://www.sgmp.org. Half of the society's members are government meeting planners and half represent hotels and other "suppliers"; it is the only organization dedicated to improving the quality and cost effectiveness of government meetings. Formerly the Society of Government Meeting Planners.

Tax Foundation

http://www.taxfoundation.org. A private association founded in 1937 concerned with tax issues. Sponsors "Tax Freedom Day," a demonstration of the tax burdens of Americans.

Transparency International

http://www.transparency.de. A not-for-profit, nongovernmental organization to counter corruption both in international business transactions and at national levels. Based in Berlin, Germany.

United States Conference of Mayors

http://www.usmayors.org. The major association of American mayors.

Urban Institute

http://www.urban.org. A research organization devoted to urban issues.

Women Executives in State Government

http://www.wesg.org. Provides professional support to women public administrators in state governments.

WorldatWork

http://www.worldatwork.org. "A total rewards organization" that studies compensation patterns in all sectors. Formerly the American Compensation Association.

Becoming a Public or Nonprofit Administrator

Now that you have read about public and nonprofit administration, why not consider working in it, too? Public and nonprofit administrators alike are in some of the world's most rewarding professions, with professionals in both sectors serving the people's interests.

For public administrators, the job security is high, the pay is good, the benefits are excellent, and the field of public administration is fascinating. Administrators in public-serving nonprofit organizations also work in exciting professions. As with public administrators, nonprofit administrators also serve the people's interests, and, although job security may be lower, salaries at the top are often higher.

Careers in Public and Nonprofit Administration: How Many Jobs, How Much Pay?

In this section, we first examine jobs and pay in government and conclude with a similar review of the independent sector.

Employment in the Public Sector

The *Public Administration Career Directory* (Morgan J. Bradley et al., eds., Detroit, MI: Visible Ink, 1994, Library of Congress Call Number JK716.P1815) is a good introduction to the large array of public professions, and there is a relatively high probability that you can get a good job in government.

Employment in the public sector has been going up almost every year for at least the past five decades, and today there are more than twenty-one million civilian public employees, or about one for every six workers. Most are in local government (64 percent); state government accounts for

a quarter of public employment, and the federal government for 13 percent.[1] Salaries in recent years have been increasing by roughly 5 to 7 percent per year at all levels of government, with local governments leading the way.[2]

Federal Public Administration

More than 1.9 million people work in more than 800 different jobs in the federal civilian workforce. (We are excluding from this figure another 786,000 who work in the U.S. Postal Service, and over 1.4 million who are uniformed military personnel.)[3] Nearly six out of ten of these employees have administrative or policy responsibilities.[4]

Federal salaries at the executive levels are good, and average pay in the General Schedule is nearing $60,000.[5] Grade 7, which most new recruits enter, starts at over $30,000; the top grades, Grade 13 through 15, range from about $65,000 to almost $120,000.[6] The 8,000 Senior Executive Service positions top out at over $165,000.[7]

For the absolutely latest information on federal salaries, check the Office of Personnel Management's Web site at http://www.opm.gov/oca/.

State Public Administration

There are more than five million state employees, a figure that includes over 2.4 million state employees in education, the great bulk of whom are in higher education.[8] The Council of State Governments reports that there are over 120 categories of top state officials, ranging from directors of state lotteries to secretaries of education to directors of emergency management.[9]

About $70,000 to more than $110,000 seems to be the salary level for the appointed administrators (excluding higher education, which pays more) in the states. More populous states pay their administrators the most, but even in the least populated states, it is rare to find the top major job salaries at less than $80,000. Southern states tend to pay their public administrators the least, followed by Eastern states; Western states generally have the highest rates of pay, followed by Midwestern states.[10]

It is increasingly common to find top administrators in state government (particularly in higher education) to be paid more than the governor. Finance, social services, environmental protection, and health are among the highest paying fields, and planning, purchasing, solid waste management, tourism, and transportation are among the lowest.[11]

The Council of State Governments publishes the biennial *Book of the States* (see Appendix B), which lists the average salaries for fifty-one state government positions by state and region. It is worth checking.

Local Public Administration

Local governments employ over 13.6 million people, nearly six out of every ten of whom are in education; almost all local workers in education are in the public schools.[12]

City and town managers command an average salary of over $93,000. However, in the very largest cities, city managers typically earn over $200,000. In the smallest, those with fewer than 2,500 people, town manager salaries are still excellent, and average close to $60,000. West Coast governments pay their public administrators the most; Northeastern cities and towns pay the least—often a third less than Western cities.[13]

County salaries usually are larger than city salaries. County managers earn, on average, more than $100,000, and county salaries generally are higher than are municipal pay rates for comparable positions. The very largest counties pay their county managers close to $200,000, on average, and the smallest, those with fewer than 10,000 people, pay about $70,000. North Central counties pay the least, and, as with cities, Western counties pay the most. County pay patterns for specific jobs generally reflect those of cities.[14]

The International City/County Management Association's annual *Municipal Year Book* (see Appendix B) publishes average salaries for twenty-two city and county positions by region, form of government, city type, and population. Perusing it is enlightening.

It seems that the highest salaries, including entry-level salaries, in the public sector (including federal and state, as well as municipal and county salaries) are offered by public authorities and special districts, such as waterworks, transportation districts, and other single-function jurisdictions. These governments appear to pay better, on the average, than any other type of government.[15]

Independent Sector Administration

The 1.2 million or so public-serving nonprofit organizations in the United States employ an estimated 9.5 million people. Member-serving nonprofit organizations amount to another 400,000 associations and 1.4 million employees.[16]

Profiting Nonprofit Executives. *The Chronicle of Philanthropy* (see Appendix C) conducts surveys of the compensation packages (that is, salaries plus benefits) of more than 200 chief executive officers (CEOs) in major public-serving nonprofit organizations of all types. The median compensation (that is, half earned more and half earned less) of these CEOs tops $290,000. From the mid-1990s, CEO salaries in public-serving nonprofit organizations rose rapidly from about 6 percent to 8 percent per year. In the early 2000s, salary growth dipped to around 4 percent per annum.[17]

Within these patterns, variations loom, some of them large. The CEOs of foundations receive median compensations of more than $300,000, with community foundations (such as the Seattle Foundation) pooling in the lower levels, "operating foundations" (such as the Freedom Forum) occupying the middle range, and private foundations (such as the Ford Foundation) paying their CEOs the highest salaries. The chief executive officers of charities command a median compensation of close to $290,000. CEOs of major museums and libraries have compensation packages ranging from well over $200,000 to more than $600,000. The chief executive officers of social-services groups (such as Volunteers of America), youth groups (such as Girl Scouts), and local United Ways have salaries ranging from under $70,000 to over $300,000.[18]

Paying the Nonprofit Hoi Polloi. The American Society for Association Executives (ASAE; see Appendix D) conducts biennial surveys of the compensation rates of nonprofit professionals who work at levels less lofty than that of CEOs. There are as many as thirty of these specialized areas in nonprofit organizations, and major areas include communication, conventions, education, finance, government relations, and marketing.

The ASAE finds that the highest salaries for top association executives are in the member-serving associations, particularly trade associations. The ASAE does not distinguish between public- and member-serving organizations, but "average total compensation" for functional areas in both types of nonprofit organizations range from close to $70,000 (director of meetings) to over $100,000 (director of international activities). Entry-level salaries may range from about $20,000 to $40,000.[19]

Preparing for a Position in Public or Nonprofit Administration

There are many ways to prepare for a management position in the public and independent sectors, and education, résumé writing, networking, and internships number among them. We consider each of these preparations here.

Gaining a Gainful Education: The Master of Public Administration Degree

The single best educational qualification for a management position in the public and nonprofit sectors is the Master of Public Administration (M.P.A.) degree. (We include in this designation masters' degrees in public policy and public affairs.) With growing frequency, M.P.A. curricula include not only specific tracks in governmental specializations, such as finance and human resources, but also tracks in nonprofit management as well. In some instances, these third-sector tracks are quite specialized. Arts administration, youth program management, community development, and health services administration are examples.

The Emergence of the M.P.A.   Beginning in the 1950s, the M.P.A. began displacing other degrees held by top career administrators and now is the dominant degree. City managers, whose historic degree of choice was engineering (a field useful in understanding waterworks, roads, electrical plants, gasworks, and sewerage, which is how city management was defined in its early years), long ago gave way to M.P.A. degrees, and almost half of *all* city managers now hold the M.P.A.[20]

The public administration degree also has displaced the traditionally preferred degrees in public finance. In 1970, degrees in business and accounting were far more common in state budgeting offices than were those in public administration. Three decades later, public administration was the most widely held degree in these circles.[21]

The M.P.A. and Career Advancement.   M.P.A. degree holders believe that the M.P.A. has made them significantly more knowledgeable and confident in entering government service, and four-fifths of them think that the M.P.A. has been more beneficial to them as professionals than any other kind of master's degree.[22]

The same research found that employers seemed to agree. Nearly three-quarters of the supervisors of these graduates stated that the performance of their employees who held M.P.A.s was slightly to "clearly superior" to the performance of holders of other kinds of advanced degrees who also were under their supervision.[23]

The success rate of M.P.A.s in the public bureaucracy validates these views. One study of a large sample of federal employees with graduate degrees found not only that graduate degree holders as a class advanced significantly higher and faster in the federal service than those without such credentials, but also that M.P.A.s held a higher federal rank, on the average, than did the holders of any other kind of advanced degree (with the exception of law degrees); earned larger salaries than most; and were more likely to hold administrative positions of authority.[24]

Learn More.   To learn more about the Master of Public Administration degree, contact your local university or the National Association of Schools of Public Affairs and Administration (NASPAA) and ask for its highly informative pamphlet, *Make Something Happen with an MPA or MPP*; single copies are available free. A detailed *Directory* of about 250 M.P.A. programs is also available. NASPAA's address is National Association of Schools of Public Affairs and Administration, 1120 G Street, NW, Suite 730, Washington, DC 20005. Its telephone number is (202) 628-8965, and its Web site is http://www.naspaa.org.

Scholarships for Public and Nonprofit Administration

Increasingly, universities are offering scholarships in public and, less so, in nonprofit administration, so check with your M.P.A. director, student financial aid office, and university foundation. Some national scholarships are available, too, many by organizations listed in Appendix D, which provides the Web site for each. Here are the main, and one or two obscure, scholarships in public and nonprofit adminstration.

Truman Scholars.   The richest of the national scholarships in pubic administration is the Truman Scholars. This is a highly competitive national scholarship program is geared exclusively to supporting the graduate studies of students planning to enter the public service. They are awarded to about eighty college seniors each year. Stipends are $30,000 per year, and the application deadline is February 1. The Truman Scholarship Foundation's Web site is http://www.truman.gov.

Land Economics.   There is a renewable $3,000 scholarship for a graduate student in the United States, United Kingdom, or Canada in a passel of fields, including urban or environmental "planning . . . government, public administration . . . or urban studies." Check the Lambda Alpha International Land Economics Foundation Scholarship at LAI@lai.org.

American Society for Public Administration. A number of regional and local chapters of the American Society for Public Administration (ASPA) offer scholarships for M.P.A. students. These are usually modest, geared toward local recipients, and ASPA's national headquarters maintains no guide to them. Your best bet is to join ASPA, attend your chapter's meetings, and apply.

Public Service.   The Public Employees Roundtable offers Public Service Scholarships. Applicants must have at least a 3.5 grade point average, and preference is given to those who have worked or volunteered for government. Eight to ten scholarships are awarded annually for both undergraduate and graduate education. Applications may be completed and submitted at http://www.theroundtable.org/23/pssp.html.

Hispanic Students.   The Congressional Hispanic Caucus Institute awards one-time scholarships ranging from $1,000 to $5,000 to Hispanic high school and college students "who have a history of performing public and/or community service activities in their communities and who plan to continue contributing in the future." The deadline is March 1. Applications are available at www.chicyouth.org.

Public Finance.   The Government Finance Officers Association offers five annual scholarships for undergraduate or graduate students interested in various aspects of public finance, including one scholarship that is reserved for students of color. Awards range from $2,500 to $10,000. The Web site is http://www.gfoa.org/services/scholarships.shtml.

Urban and Regional Planning. The American Planning Association (APA) offers a variety of scholarships for students interested in urban and regional planning. Several are targeted at students of color and women, and the deadline for all of them is April 30. In addition, state APA chapters in Arizona, California, Connecticut, Ohio, and Texas offer their own scholarships. Deadlines vary by chapter. Awards for national and state APA scholarships usually are around $2,000 per year. APA's Web site, at http://www.planning.org/institutions/scholarship.htm?project, provides full information on both its national and chapter scholarships, and on related scholarships, too.

Public Works. The regional and state chapters of the American Public Works Association (APWA) offer a spate of scholarships for undergraduate and graduate students in public administration with a public works emphasis. Numbers of scholarships and their accompanying rewards vary vastly by chapter, but there are *a lot* of these scholarships offered. Check APWA's Web site at http://apwa.net, although Googling "APWA scholarships" works just as well, if not better.

Labor Relations. The National Public Employer Labor Relations Association Foundation offers from two to four Anthony C. Russo Scholarships each year for graduate students in public administration, but especially those with an interest in labor and employee relations. The scholarships are valued at about $3,000 and the amount is rising. The deadline is usually September 30, and an application may be completed and submitted online. The Web site is http://www.npelra.org/articles/foundation0605asp.

Writing Your Résumé

Writing a résumé is a daunting prospect for many. Here are some suggestions for making yours effective.

The Consolidated Résumé. Human resource managers have suggested in the past that those who are new or are returning to the job market can be disadvantaged by using the traditional *chronological résumé*, which lists each job that you have held, and have stated that they should use a *functional résumé* that highlights their training, analytic skills, ability to get along with others, knowledge of organizational dynamics, budgeting strategies, management tools, and other skills and experience.

The latest thinking, however, is that one's résumé should combine both chronological and functional résumés, which, by themselves, leave too many questions that need answering in the minds of their readers: the chronological résumé if there are unexplained gaps in one's career history (which can and should be addressed), and the functional résumé if it is left unclear what one's job history precisely is (and job histories are very difficult to make clear in functional résumés). This combination of a chronological résumé and a functional résumé is called a *consolidated résumé*, and an example of one concludes this appendix.

Tell a Story. Perhaps the most important point to keep in mind when writing your résumé is to think like a journalist. What is most significant about your story? What things were you able to accomplish in your job and education? State your case in terms of projects that you have directed, designed, developed, implemented, researched, reported, managed, controlled, planned, organized, written, edited, or built. Using verbs such as these strengthens your case.

K.I.S.S. When it comes to writing your résumé, keep it simple and succinct. For entrants new to the marketplace, most professionals advise that their résumé be limited to a single page, although references (providing not only name, but title, postal address, telephone number, including area code, and e-mail address) may constitute a second page or the reverse side of the résumé. If you include references (it is appropriate to say instead that they are available on request), list at least three; five references, however, seem to be requested with growing frequency by employers.

Don't Get Personal. Some data are yours and yours alone. The résumé reader may be safely assumed to conclude that your health is "excellent" without being told as much, and your age, gender, and marital status are your own business. Listing hobbies and pastimes can be a plus if they can be construed as giving you an edge for a job, but noting that you like "reading" as a hobby probably is a waste of space.

Be sure, however, to list everything that you think may enhance your qualifications for the job. These qualifications can vary with the job in question, so tailor your résumé accordingly.

It is appropriate to include indicators of your high character and sociability, such as being an Eagle Scout or memberships in civic organizations and clubs. Do *not*, however, list a qualification in such a way that you are obviously stretching the category in which it appears (and perhaps stretching the truth along with it). Rather, develop a separate category for the qualification, such as "Early Achievements" or "Leadership" (either one of which might include your being an Eagle Scout); or "Community Service" (e.g., being a Rotarian); or "Team Experience" (which could include any organized sports that you played). Of course, any honors and recognitions should be listed, too, in their own section.

Do Get Physical. It is critical that you design and lay out your résumé with your reader uppermost in your mind. He or she likely will be plowing through a pile of résumés, and your job is to make your résumé easy to understand, absorb, and remember.

Use a standard font of readable size. If you want your résumé to physically stand out from the others, a fancy font is not the way to do it, as it sends a message of idiosyncracy; use instead a heavy, high-quality, cream-colored (*not* a pastel) stationery.

Embrace negative space. It beats a format of squashed paragraphs and microscopic margins every time.

Be consistent in your overall format. Will you indent the opening sentence in each paragraph, or not? Be consistent in your use of HEADS, **Subheads**, and *Sub-Subheads*. Assign a typeface to each one, as we have done here; that is, all capitals, boldface, and italics, respectively. Then stick to it.

"Bullets" also can be clarifying and useful. Justify the right-hand margin; doing so presents a neater appearance.

If your résumé is more than one page, number the pages and write your name, title, and/or organization in bold italics in an upper corner of each page. This keeps your name and identity in front of your reader at all times.

Get Help.   Do not be shy in asking for help in polishing up your résumé. Your campus's career services or placement office can be a genuine asset in developing a presentable résumé.

USA Jobs, the federal job announcement Web site, offers an Online Résumé Builder that focuses on the applicant's abilities for a specific federal job. It may be accessed at http://www.usajobs.opm.gov.

Networking

You have written your résumé, and are completing your M.P.A. Now is the time to network.

Several professional associations are organized as state, regional, or local chapters, and these chapters offer excellent opportunities to develop contacts and establish relationships that could pay off as internships and jobs. All are listed in Appendix D, including their Web sites.

ASPA: The Broadest and Biggest Network.
Perhaps the most promising of these chapter-based associations is the American Society for Public Administration. ASPA has ninety-one regional and local chapters across the country comprised of public administrators from all governmental levels and specializations, and this generalist approach to the field renders ASPA uniquely useful as a network. Typically, ASPA chapters sponsor monthly luncheons and regional conferences where new contacts are easily made. To learn how to join, ask your course instructor, or contact ASPA directly. ASPA's address is American Society for Public Administration, 1120 G Street, NW, Suite 500, Washington, DC 20005. ASPA's telephone number is (202) 393-7878.

More Specialized Networks.
Other associations are more specialized than ASPA, but one that is at least not much more specialized is the National Leagues of Cities, the nation's largest organization of municipal governments (some 15,000 cities are members), and it sponsors state municipal leagues in every state except Hawaii. To find out more, contact the League at (202) 626-3000.

The National Association of Counties has fifty-three state associations of counties in forty-seven states (some states have more than one association), representing more than 2,000 counties in which four-fifths of Americans dwell. These state associations are essentially lobbies that target the state legislatures, but most hold annual meetings that offer opportunities for networking.

Other specialized, chapter-based professional associations include the American Public Works Association and the National Institute of Governmental Purchasing, each with about seventy chapters in the United States and Canada, and

the National Public Employer Labor Relations Association, with chapters in fifteen states and the Rocky Mountain region.

Who Is Whom?   Knowing who is whom is essential to being an effective networker. Appendix B describes those sources that tell you who's who, notably the *Congressional Yellow Book, Federal Yellow Book, Government Affairs Yellow Book, Federal Regional Yellow Book, Municipal Year Book, Nonprofit Sector Yellow Book, State and Local Source Book,* and *State Yellow Book.*

Internships

Networking can lead to gaining an internship. An internship, paid or voluntary, can be an important step toward acquiring relevant work experience for students lacking it, and frequently can lead to a full-time job in the agency in which one interns. Often, schools of public administration or departments of political science work with governmental agencies in developing local internship opportunities, so check with appropriate faculty members and your university's career services office about possibilities.

In the following review, we first classify internship opportunities according to those offered by professional associations that are listed in Appendix D. We then review the two major federal internship programs and describe information sources for locating additional internships in government and nonprofit organizations.

Internships in Professional Associations.
The major professional associations that sponsor particularly solid internship programs include the following. Their Web sites can be found in Appendix D.

The International City/County Management Association's Local Government Management Fellowship Program, launched in 2004, aims to place 100 M.P.A. students in "management-track positions" in local governments each year. Applications are available in late summer.

The Council for Excellence in Government offers semester-long internships that "focus on practical public-sector reform at all levels" for undergraduate and graduate students. Contact the Council at its Web site and click "Employment/Internship Opportunities."

The International Hispanic Network offers twenty Public Policy Fellowships that provide "hands-on" experience in the District of Columbia for Hispanic college graduates and graduate students. Possibilities include Congress, executive agencies, nonprofit organizations, and media. Thirty Congressional Internships are available for Hispanic undergraduate students; summer housing, airfare, and a $2,000 stipend are included.

The National League of Cities offers internships in a wide variety of areas that relate to urban governance. They and other internships are listed under "Job Announcements." Just contact the League if you spot one that is of interest. Its e-mail address is employment@nlc.org.

Federal Internships.
There are two major federal internships.

The most prestigious is the Presidential Management Fellows (PMF), which was known as the Presidential Management Intern Program until 2003, and offers more than 300 fellowships annually. Fellows receive two-year appointments to developmental positions throughout the executive branch. These positions differ from most entry-level positions in terms of pay and their emphasis on career development. Whereas most entry-level positions begin at GS Grade 7, PMFs enter at Grade 9, are promoted to Grade 11 at the end of the first year, and routinely convert to regular civil service appointments upon the successful completion of the internship at the end of the second year at Grade 12.

Senior Presidential Management Fellowships are available for more experienced applicants, who may be hired at grades higher than that of Grade 9.

The PMF's Web site is http://www.pmf.opm.gov/. The deadline for application is generally in October.

A much bigger federal internship is the Federal Career Intern Program (FCIP), which was established in 2000 by Executive Order 13162. The FCIP allows individual agencies to hire applicants at General Schedule Grades 5, 7, and 9, after spending a two-year training internship in the agency. To learn more, access http://opm.gov/careerintern/.

Information Sources on Public and Nonprofit Internships. One of the best general guides to public- and nonprofit-sector internship opportunities is provided by the National Association of Schools of Public Affairs and Administration at its Web site, http://www.naspaa.org. Click "Public Service Career Institutes" on its home page, then "Find an Internship," and, finally, *"our list of internship databases."* Be sure to check this one.

The National Society for Experiential Education notes internship opportunities in a wide variety of fields and emphasizes the public and nonprofit sectors. See its Web site at http://www.nsee.org.

Public Administration Times, published biweekly by the American Society for Public Administration, also advertises internships at all governmental levels. Its Web site is http://www.aspanet.org/publications/patimes. First click "The Recruiter Online," then "Internship Programs."

State, local, and a few other kinds of internship program are listed by the Placement Office of the LBJ School at the University of Texas. This well-done and very useful Web site is found at http://www.utexas.edu/lbj/osap/career/students/links/mip.html.

Some 150 internships and 6,000 volunteering opportunities in the independent sector are listed at Action Without Borders. The list is global, and the Web site is http://idealist.org.

Finding a Position in Public or Nonprofit Administration

Never discount your own campus's resources when job hunting. Often the public administration program has its own contacts with those who hire, and the campus placement office, or career services, also can be very helpful.

A number of professional associations list government and nonprofit jobs, but many, such as the International City/County Management Association, require that one be a member before being permitted access to their listings. The sources that we review here are open, or largely open, to all for free.

Federal Sources

In 1994, the federal Office of Personnel Management introduced its USA Jobs (originally called Career America Connection) as its principal method of connecting applicants with jobs. Those interested in a career with the federal government may use the telephone or the Internet.

By calling (912) 757-3000, one connects with voice mail, which guides the caller through education requirements, location preferences, job types, and other criteria until the caller requests application materials. These materials are mailed to the applicant, who completes a questionnaire, attaches a résumé, and returns it to the Office of Personnel Management, which sends it to the relevant agencies within two weeks, who then may contact the applicant.

Or one may learn of job opportunities and apply over the Internet. The address is http://www.usajobs.opm.gov. This site offers an Online Résumé Builder that focuses on the applicant's abilities for a specific federal job. Touch screen computer kiosks, which also provide these features, are available at many federal buildings across the nation.

Some 7,500 federal (and a number of state and local) positions are listed through USA Jobs, and the list is worldwide and updated daily. USA Jobs's electronic bulletin board may be reached by modem at (912) 757-3100 or Telnet, fjob.opm.gov.

The Presidential Management Fellows and the Federal Career Intern programs, explained earlier under "Federal Internships," are paths to permanent federal employment. The Federal Career Internship Program has waxed into the principal route by which new federal hires are hired, surpassing tests and other methods of screening applicants.

State and Local Sources

Most state and local government job opportunities are announced the old-fashioned way: in local newspaper want ads, and, more recently, on government Web sites and cable television stations. When perusing the job announcements, it is important to know which jobs are appropriate for public administration students. At the state and local levels, a "I" after a title, such as Analyst I, usually indicates an entry-level position. An Analyst II or Analyst III often indicates that more extensive education or experience is required.

New-fangled means of finding state or local government jobs, however, are now on the scene. *Public Administration Times* contains advertisements for positions at all levels of government, plus some for the nonprofit and private sectors, too. Its Web site lists jobs by state, portals, governmental level, and specialization. There is a résumé posting service as well. Access *PA Times* at http://www.aspanet.org/publications/patimes and click "The Recruiter Online," then "Career Links."

Similarly, the LBJ School at the University of Texas, explained in our earlier discussion of internships, also posts permanent positions in the federal, state, and local governments and nonprofit organizations. Check http://www.utexas.edu/lbj/osap/career/students/links/mip.html.

Another excellent general source is the Public Sector Job Bulletin, which lists state and local government jobs by type from "A" (Administration and Management) to "U" (Utilities). Its Web site is: http://govtjobs.com.

The Council of State Governments lists available state government jobs by state. The Web site is http://www.statesnews.org/other_resources/classifieds.html. The Council also lists its own job availabilities in its Washington and four regional offices.

GovtJob.Net, sponsored by the nonprofit Local Government Institute, specializes in state and local job opportunities. Its Web site is http://www.govtjob.net/.

The best single source for local government databases offering employment opportunities is the National City Government Resource Center, which lists about a dozen job databases in the public and nonprofit sectors, with an emphasis on local governments. Another half dozen databases feature private recruiters. Access its Web site at http://www.geocities.com and click "Job Opportunities."

The National League of Cities (see Appendix D) maintains a good "Job Opportunities" page that lists jobs, as well as internships, in the nation's cities. One may send a résumé and cover letter to the League for specific positions listed on the site. The site provides postal and e-mail addresses, and telephone and fax numbers.

The National Association of Counties (see Appendix D) provides job possibilities in county governments on its "JobsOnline."

Independent Sector Sources

Perhaps the best single source for job openings in the nonprofit sector is the Action without Borders' Web site, http://www.idealist.org. This global network not only lists internships, as we have noted, but some 1,500 jobs, too. The site's sponsor also organizes job fairs around the country, provides career information, and offers other resources and services.

The Chronicle of Philanthropy, "the newspaper of the nonprofit world," advertises virtually every job available in philanthropic circles—typically, several hundred openings appear on its Web site. Access all these listings without charge at http://philanthropy.com/jobs/.

The Independent Sector lists job opportunities available in its member nonprofit organizations, and these are numerous. Go to http://www.independentsector/jobs_postings.htm.

The American Society of Association Executives offers a sophisticated job search service that usually lists around 100 openings in the nonprofit sector. Access its Web site at http://www.aseanet.org and click "Career Headquarters." It is not fully accessible to nonmembers but is still informative.

For those interested in doing well while doing good, try CEO Job Opportunities Update, which specializes in nonprofit executive placements that pay a minimum of $50,000. Opportunities are listed in its pricey *CEO Update*, but its Web site is moderately useful, at http://www.associationjobs.com.

The Job Interview

The final step in securing a job is the interview, and it is a critical step. Almost seven out of ten federal supervisors report that they rely to a "great" or "moderate" extent on the interview in making their decision to offer a job to a candidate. With the exception of prior work experience, no other category of information even comes close to the importance of information obtained during an interview in deciding a job candidate's fate.[25]

Preparing for the Interview

Preparing for an interview is straightforward. Here are the basics.

Do Your Homework.   First and foremost, do your homework. Learn all you can about the organization and the person or people who will be interviewing you. The Internet is an invaluable resource for this. And read the materials that they send you. If you have not received a mission statement, strategic plan, financial summary (for nonprofit organizations), or the name(s) and position(s) of your interviewer(s) prior to your interview, request them and any other information that you feel you need.

Practice, Practice, Practice.   The interview is a splendid example of the axiom, practice makes perfect. Tap a close and patient friend to help you formulate answers to specific questions that are almost certain to be asked, and then practice your answers with him or her out loud. Probable questions include: Would you tell us about yourself? Why do want this job? Why do you think that you are qualified for it? What will you bring to the job? What are the most pressing needs that you think confront our agency? What are your greatest strengths and weaknesses as a manager? (Select a "weakness" that is really a strength, such as tending to get ahead of yourself, providing an excess of opportunities for staff, or overenthusiasm for projects.)

Many campus career services offices offer interview practice sessions that sometimes include videotaping so that you can see for yourself your own interviewing persona and improve it. Take full advantage of this service.

Scheduling Your Interview.   Try to schedule your interview with two objectives in mind. One is to avoid the after-lunch time slot. Interviewers can be loggy, groggy, and foggy after a big lunch, and you want them to be alert, interested, and listening.

Your second scheduling goal is to shoot for the first or last interview, and preferably the last one. Those who interview between the first and final interviews tend to blur in the interviewer's mind, and you want to avoid this.

Dress for Success. The interview is not the place to make a fashion statement. Normally, one should wear a dark suit, although in some nonprofit organizations "the suits" and their namesake apparel are not *de rigueur*. Nevertheless, unless you have information to the contrary, wear a suit; it conveys respect for your interviewer. Conservative ties and white long-sleeved shirts should be worn by men. Women can safely add some color. Neither men nor women should wear dangling, distracting jewelry, and everyone should shine their shoes.

Being Interviewed

There are a number of pointers that can help pull off a successful interview. Here are some.

Shake Hands and Smile. This is standard procedure when one is being interviewed by a single person, but many interviews are conducted by panels of multiple participants. Shake hands with all of them, preferably before the interview begins so that you can warm up your crowd. If you have learned who holds what position in the organization, say something like, "Ah, yes, the comptroller," after they have given you their name.

Know Names. Remember your interviewer's, or interviewers', name or names. This is, admittedly, more easily recommended than done when there are many interviewers, but try anyway. Little will get you as far in your career as remembering names.

Be Succinct, Interesting, and Observant. Keep your answers succinct and pointed, but not dry. Use personal examples to illustrate what you are trying to say. As with your résumé, tell a story. After you have answered a question, ask, at least occasionally, if you have answered the question. Under no circumstances, swear or relate an off-color joke; doing so will kill your chances, even if you are being interviewed by sailors.

Be cognizant of your interviewer's, or interviewers', attention. Should you notice eyes glazing over or panelists nodding off, or hear the rustle of cellophane candy wrappers being unwrapped, bring your answer to a quick close. You likely have spoken too long.

Body Language. Maintain eye contact with your questioner. Smile. Sit erectly, tilting slightly forward, with your hands folded on the table or resting on your chair's arms. Men should keep both feet planted firmly on the floor; women may cross their ankles. Use your hands to make a point.

Interview's End. Toward the end of your interview, you will be asked if you have any questions. Have some, preferably questions that demonstrate that you have done your homework about the organization. If, by some fluke, you are not asked if you have questions, politely ask if you may ask a couple.

Do *not* ask about pay and benefits; doing so indicates that you have not done your homework and that you are a money-grubber. These questions should be asked if you receive a job offer. If you have questions about travel reimbursement, ask the interviewer's secretary.

At the close of the interview, thank your interviewer for his or her time. Express your genuine interest in the job. With a single interviewer, shake hands. With a panel of interviewers, shake their hands if you have not already done so; if you shook their hands earlier, play it by ear as to whether you want to initiate a second round. If you can recall the panelists' names, however, it is most impressive to shake hands with each one and thank them by name just before you leave.

After the Interview

Following the interview, you may be asked to join your interviewers or other employees for a drink or dinner. By all means, join them. But watch yourself. Be under no illusions that the interview is over.

As soon as you get home, write a thank-you note to your interviewer, and again express your interest in the job. If you were interviewed by a panel, writing only to the chair of the panel usually is sufficient, but if you developed a rapport with someone, write him or her, too.

If you have legible handwriting, a fountain pen, and good stationery, write a brief note by hand; this conveys your personal interest. If not, type it on good stationery, sign it, and post it; avoid e-mailing it, as it is more satisfying to the recipient to receive a personally signed letter.

Then wait to learn if you have been hired. If you were selected, congratulations, but do not accept the offer until you are comfortable that you fully understand all aspects of the position, such as pay, benefits, travel, and duties. Ask for twenty-four hours to think it over. If you accept, give yourself a party. You deserve it, and people should celebrate their successes more than they do.

If you were not hired, it is not inappropriate to call your interviewer and ask, extremely politely, how you could improve your qualifications and presentation. If you still have an interest in working for the organization, write another note to your interviewer(s) expressing how honored you were to be a finalist, and that your interest in their fine organization remains keen.

Be aware that some organizations and interviewers are insensitive, impolite, and boorish. They may fail to notify you if you were not selected; or they may do so very late; or they may notify you with scant, if any, courtesy. In these cases, count your blessings.

Sample Consolidated Résumé

RÉSUMÉ
JAY BIRD

Postal Address: 1234 East University Drive
Tempe, Arizona 85281-1234
E-Mail Address: jbird@hotmail.edu

*Telephone Numbers: (602) 000-0000 (office)
(602) 000-0000 (residence)*

Objective

To work in an area of public administration related to legislation or public policy. The ideal position would allow me to utilize my skills in research analysis, interpersonal relations, and communication, both oral and written.

Career Chronology

Administrative Intern, Maricopa County Office of Management Analysis, Phoenix, Arizona. 1-03 to present.
Research Assistant, School of Public Affairs, Arizona State University, Tempe, Arizona. 8-07 to present.
Project Nutrition Consultant, Bureau of Nutritional Services, Arizona Department of Health Services, Tempe, Arizona. 10-00 to 8-07.
Nutritionist, Health Division, Lane County Department of Health and Social Services, Eugene, Oregon. 7-95 to 10-00.
Special Vocational Educational Teacher, Springfield School District No. 19, Springfield, Oregon. 9-90 to 6-95.
Trainer/Nutritionist, Community Nutrition Institute, Washington, DC 10-87 to 6-90.

Education

Degrees

Master of Public Administration. Currently enrolled; expected 5-08. Arizona State University, Tempe, Arizona 1-06 to present.
Master of Public Health. University of Michigan, Ann Arbor, Michigan 9–88 to 6–90.
Bachelor of Science in Nutritional Sciences, Minor in Economics. University of California, Berkeley, California 3-85 to 7-88.

Other Training

Administrative dietetic internship focusing on the management of school food service programs. Food Services Division, Milwaukee Public Schools, Milwaukee, Wisconsin. 9-81 to 6-83.

Notes

1. As derived from data in U.S. Bureau of the Census, *Statistical Abstract of the United States, 2006*, 125th ed. (Washington, DC: U.S. Government Printing Office, 2006), Tables 451 and 452. Figures are for 2003.

2. As derived from data in U.S. Office of Personnel Management, "2006 Federal Employees Pay Tables," http://www.opm.gov; U.S. Office of Personnel Management, *The Fact Book, 2004* (Washington, DC: U.S. Government Printing Office, 2005), p. 64; Council of State Governments, *Book of the States,* Vol. 36 (Lexington, KY: Author, 2004); and International City/County Management Association, *Municipal Year Book, 2005* (Washington, DC: Author, 2005), Sections C-1, C-2, and C-3.

3. U.S. Bureau of the Census, *Statistical Abstract of the United States, 2006*, Table 452. Figures are for 2003.

4. U.S. Office of Personnel Management. *The Fact Book, 2004,* p. 16. In 2003, 33 percent of federal civilian employees were "administrative white collar," and 24 percent were "professional white collar."

5. Ibid., p. 19. Figure is for 2003.

6. U.S. Office of Personnel Management, "Salary Table 2006-GS," http://www.opm.gov/oca/06tables/html/gs.asp. Figures are for 2006.

7. U.S. Office of Personnel Management, "Salary Table No. 2006-ES," http://www. opm.gov/oca/06tables/html/es.asp. Figures are for 2006.

8. As derived from data in U.S. Bureau of the Census, *Statistical Abstract of the United States, 2006*, Table 452. Figures are for 2003.

Skills and Experience

Conducted management audits of county departments to investigate efficiency and effectiveness of services provided. Assessed present and future staffing requirements and made recommendations for improving the service delivery system.

Contract Negotiation   Served as the primary contact person from the Bureau of Nutrition for county and tribal health departments, as assigned. In this capacity, monitored local agency programs for compliance to program and contract requirements, provided assistance in program management, and served as an advocate for local projects, participating in negotiations when appropriate.

At the Bureau level, participated in planning, development, and review of policies and procedures and budget allocation process for state-subvened funds. Researched alternative methods of carrying out the program and completed comparative cost studies. Developed and presented final recommendations for improving the program and reducing costs, which was ultimately adopted by the agency.

Assisted in developing a master copier plan for use by the county in the next five years.

Management Analysis and Performance Assessment   Work on research projects has included assisting in computer-based management and analysis of educational enrollment data for the Phoenix Town Hall, citizen surveys for the city of Glendale, and library research on public choice theory.

Recent Professional Activities and Honors:

2007 to present.	Regents Graduate Academic Scholarship, Arizona State University, Tempe, Arizona. Member, American Society for Public Administration, Arizona Chapter
2004–05.	Co-editor, Legislative Newsletter, Arizona Dietitians for Legislative Action
2000–04.	Community Nutrition Section Chairperson and Executive Board. Member, Central Arizona District Dietetic Association
1998–99.	U.S. Public Health Traineeship, University of Michigan, Ann Arbor, Michigan
1997–98.	Member, Task Force on Dental Health, Nutrition, and Health Education, Western Oregon Health Systems Agency. Member, Nutrition Task Force, Oregon Public Health Association

References

Dr. Harold Heirarch,	*The Honorable Bea Foter,*	*Ms. Jane Mouton,*
Professor of Public Administration	*State Representative*	*Vice President for Human*
Georgia Southern University	House of Representatives	*Resource Management*
Statesboro, Georgia 30460	Phoenix, Arizona 85287	Cave Creek Corporation
(912) 681-0000	(602) 961-0000	Scottsdale, Arizona 85283
pomposity@georgiasouthern.edu	voteforme@pricinct1.org	(602) 841-0000
		jmouton@managerialgrid.com

9. Council of State Governments, *State Administrative Officials Classified by Function, 1985–86* (Lexington, KY: Author, 1985).
10. Council of State Governments, *Book of the States*, Vol. 36, Table 4.11. Figures are for 2004.
11. Ibid.
12. As derived from data in U.S. Bureau of the Census, *Statistical Abstract of the United States, 2006*, Table 452. Figures are for 2003.
13. International City/County Management Association, *Municipal Year Book, 2005*, Section C-1. Figures are for 2004.
14. Ibid., Section C-2. Figures are for 2004.
15. International Personnel Management Association, *Pay Rates in the Public Service: Survey of 62 Common Job Classes in the Public Sector* (Washington, DC: Author, 1985).
16. Lester M. Salamon, *America's Nonprofit Sector: A Primer*, 2nd ed. (New York: The Foundation Center, 1999), p. 22. Figures are for 1996.
17. Ben Gose, "Executive Pay Rises Modestly," *Chronicle of Philanthropy* (September 30, 2004), pp. 31–49. Figures are for 2003.
18. Ibid. Figures are for 2003.
19. American Society of Association Executives (ASAE), "Careers in Associations: Salaries," http://www. aseanet. org. Figures are for 2003. The ASAE conducts biennial surveys on association salaries and requires that one join it to have full access to its findings. It does occasionally open skeletal versions of its research to the public. There are a few other surveys of nonprofit salaries, but they are rarely accessed inexpensively.
20. Victor S. DeSantis and Charldean Newell, "Local Government Managers' Career Paths," *Municipal Year*

Book, 1996 (Washington, DC: International City/County Management Association, 1996), p. 4. In 1995, 45 percent of all city managers had M.P.A.s.

21. Robert C. Burns and Robert D. Lee Jr., "The Ups and Downs of State Budget Process Reform: Experience of Three Decades," *Public Budgeting and Finance* 24 (Fall 2004), p. 15. In 1970, 20 percent of state budget officers held the M.P.A. degree; in 2000, 27 percent held it, and the M.P.A. represented a plurality of all degrees in this field.

22. George Grode and Marc Holzer, "The Perceived Utility of MPA Degrees," *Public Administration Review* 35 (July/August, 1975), pp. 403–412.

23. Ibid.

24. Gregory B. Lewis, "How Much Is an MPA Worth? Public Administration Education and Federal Career Success," *International Journal of Public Administration* 9 (April 1987), pp. 397–415.

25. U.S. Merit Systems Protection Board, *The Federal Selection Interview: Unrealized Potential* (Washington, DC: U.S. Government Printing Office, 2003), p. 7. Ten categories were tested. Seventy-one percent of federal supervisors cited prior work experience as the most important factor, followed by 69 percent who said the interview. The third highest ranking was quality of the applicant at a distant 39 percent, and level of education at 38 percent.

Index

Abuse of authority, 157
Access, 36
Accountability, 84, 159, 334, 397
Achievement motivation, 106
Adarand Constructors, Inc. v. *Peña*, 256
Administerability, 189
Administration, 113
Administrative Behavior, 30, 31, 32, 64
Administrative Management, 53
Administrative science, 34
Administrative Science Quarterly, 34
Affirmative action, 254–266
Age Discrimination in Employment Act of 1967, 255, 257
Agency, 36
Agendas, Alternatives, and Public Policies, 288
Albemarle Paper Company v. *Moody*, 260
American Federation of State, County, and Municipal Employees (AFSCME) v. *State of Washington*, 261
American Political Science Association (APSA), 32, 33
American Political Science Review, 32
American Society for Public Administration (ASPA), 29, 394
   code of ethics, 394
Americans with Disabilities Act of 1990, 256
Arbitration, 242
Arenas of power, 287–288
Article IV of U.S. Constitution, 350
Article VI of U.S. Constitution, 350
Articles of Confederation, The, 6–7
At will employment, 253

Balanced Budget Act of 1997, 200
Balanced Budget and Emergency Deficit Control Acts of 1985 and 1987, 199
Beagle fallacy, 295
Behavioral Theory of the Firm, A, 64
Benchmarking, 169
   bidding, 322

Block grants, 355
Board of directors, 113
Bonds, 329–330
   general obligation bonds, 329
   municipal bonds, 329
   revenue bonds, 329
Bounded rationality, 75
Broadbanding, 233
Budget, 204
Budget Enforcement Act of 1990, 199, 201
Budgetary strategies, 202–204
   contingent strategies, 203
   ubiquitous strategies, 202
Budgeting and Accounting Act of 1921, 206
Budgeting and Accounting Procedures Act of 1950, 208
Budgeting for results, 217–218
   and Performance budgeting, 217
Budgeting periods, 202–218
Budgeting-by-objectives, 211–212
   line item budgeting, 204–207
   planning-programming-budgeting, 209–211
   program/performance budgeting, 207–209
   target base budgeting, 213–217
   zero base budgeting, 212–213
Bureau of the Budget (BOB), 208, 209
Bureaucracy
   democracy and, 2, 3
   elected executive and, 17–18
   growth of, 18–20
   knowledge management, 18–20
   legislative branch and, 19
   power of, 15–16
   public administration and, 3
   satisfaction with, 13
Bureaucratic accountability, 397
Bureaucratic accretion, 86
Bureaucratic image, 12–13